American History

A Problems Approach

Volume I

American History
A Problems Approach

Herman L. Crow
William L. Turnbull
Tarrant County Junior College

Holt, Rinehart and Winston, Inc.
New York Chicago San Francisco Atlanta
Dallas Montreal Toronto London Sydney

Cover design suggested by Sally Norris, Renette Felps,
and Deborah Strock,
students at Tarrant County Junior College,
who experienced learning from this text.

Preface

The method of history which this book follows is not unlike that of science, for it is metaphysical as well as empirical. It introduces a problem, the solution of which demands that the student experience the higher adventure of conceptual learning through active participation. Thus, this exercise rests on the premise that the imagination can and should be cultivated through the interpretation of men and events as they relate to a specific problem in history. It is, therefore, creative history.

The student's job in this problem-centered approach, is to learn to ask questions, defend and attack positions, and speculate and solve problems through open dialogue. In short, he must learn to use logic. The principal task of this approach in history is to teach a strategy of coherence that will, in turn, enable the student to interpret past and present events, as well as past and present values, in the light of his own needs and cultural background. As coherence is the test of truth, teaching coherence through the study of history and its structure, as well as its many limitations, can lead to logical truth, and, thus, to rational man. The ultimate synthesis is a person who can use historical logic for the purpose of controlling and using ideas, rather than having ideas control and use him. Moreover, he is a person who has ceased thinking of history as a chain of events or some other person's interpretations that must be memorized in order to pass an examination. He has developed a skeptical attitude toward what others consider to be overt facts and an open mind to other possible answers to the same problem.

In order to achieve these ends in a study of history, a procedure of several dimensions must be pursued. First, the study should be eclectic—drawing from the other disciplines in the social sciences in order to complement the scope of history and add to a broader understanding. Second, it should involve the student in analytical exercises with carefully structured materials designed to give him divergent viewpoints so that he may weigh the issues and decide for himself. Third, it should provide the student with a chronological narrative of history that will offer fundamental constructs and continuity.

The editors have attempted to satisfy some of the needs with this book. In treating the narrative of history, we have tried to minimize judgmental remarks on controversial issues that might otherwise rob the student of the freedom to doubt and to inquire. The selected essays, which appear at the end of each part, were chosen because they offer a sharp contrast in viewpoints on each problem and because they represent sound scholarship. They also illustrate how different hypotheses may be validated by drawing data from the same primary source. These readings should not be viewed as the sole basis for the solution of the problem, but rather as inviting stepping-stones to other sources and other viewpoints, which are offered in the bibliographies of selected essays and monographs.

The questions posed in the introduction to each group of essays have been designed to elicit maximum thought and imagination without leading the student toward preconceived conclusions. Thus, they are broad and open-ended. Finally, they have been devised to tie the past to the present.

Hurst, Texas
January 1971

H. L. C.
W. L. T.

Contents

American History

A Problems Approach

introduction

A Note on the Nature of History

History lays no claim to an esoteric language; it rests its case on logic and consistency. In fact, it has been described by some historians as being close to the ways of ordinary life. Perhaps it is because of this nearness that so many unwary students fall victim to its many limitations.

The road to the mastery of history may be considerably smoother if the student can accept the premise that man is a social animal "committed to the shifting perspectives of an age or class, biased, partisan and subjective."[1] His journey through the pages of history will be less arduous if he can subscribe to the notion that intelligence is mundane and necessarily biased, that a universal truth is beyond the reach of man. His destination will be less obscured if he can accept the belief that objective history is but an illusion, that complete knowledge is but a myth.

The degree of one's objectivity is always contingent upon the tolerance of society, for as Carl Becker has written, "Mr. Everyman has to live in a world of Browns and Smiths; a sad experience, which has taught him the expediency of recalling certain events with much exactness."[2] While man has come to recognize that his advanced society makes efforts to force upon him a growing amount of coherence in argumentation, he must also be reminded that any slighting of this development may cause him to be viewed as immature and irrational.

Still another area of concern in history is the premise or assumption that is frequently passed on as fact. When to treat a premise as fact or as a working hypothesis is a distinction that often perplexes the inexperienced, and the student soon discovers that premises "will betray you if you take them seriously."[3] This dilemma may be resolved to some extent if we heed an earlier caution in this introduction—namely, that intelligence is subjective and that its products, such as "facts," derived from judgment, are necessarily biased.

There is another kind of fact which we may identify as overt. For example, to use an elemental form, John F. Kennedy succeeded Dwight D. Eisenhower as President of the United States. This is a fact, the character of which no equation of bias plus exaggeration can change; but, on the other hand, this construct also represents the lowest form of learning, since it holds no controversy.

Present-mindedness is another kind of limitation that traps the most experienced historian. Its counterpart, which everyone attempts to achieve, is called past-minded-

---

[1] Charles Frankel. *The Case for Modern Man* (Boston: The Beacon Press, 1959), p. 118.

[2] Carl L. Becker. *Everyman His Own Historian* (New York: Appleton-Century-Crofts, 1935), p. 243. See also G. J. Reiner. *History—Its Purpose and Method* (Boston: The Beacon Press, 1950), p. 250.

[3] Henry Steele Commager. *The Nature and the Study of History* (Columbus, Ohio: Charles E. Merrill Books, Inc., 1967), p. 48.

ness, or history-mindedness, and represents a high degree of sophistication. It demands that one discard the trappings of modern standards, or values, and project oneself into the past in order to view the events of a given age as the contemporaries saw it. Some historians believe that it is an impossible task, while others, like Charles Frankel, warn that "if we do succeed in projecting ourselves into the minds of others, . . . we must then also share their self-deceptions."[4] It has also been suggested that past-mindedness may cause the historian to become so enchanted with a given era in the past that he fails to see its faults.

The subject of documents inevitably arises in almost any kind of examination of facts, and the question regarding their objectivity cannot be avoided. If our answer to this question is that documents represent objective facts, then why, asks Commager, have we compiled 375 volumes of Supreme Court reports in order to explain and interpret the Constitution? Nor would we need our Supreme Court, he adds, if the facts in this document spoke for themselves. Part of the answer lies in the belief that the document must be measured by the standards of its own time, by the implicit values and biases of the age, all of which must be viewed from one's own vantage point and not through the eyes of another.

Not only should we view all secondary and primary sources as necessarily subjective, but we should remember that all records are also highly selective. We shall never know what major events historians chose not to write down, nor how many great personalities they inadvertently or by design excluded from the record.

Historians also distort the past and our view by dwelling on the story of kings and queens, victorious armies, and Anglo-Saxon nations at the expense of the common people, the defeated armies, and the non-Western nations of the world. In the past two decades the developing and non-Western nations have received an apologizing page in the text, or an institute on contemporary conditions in their countries, while their rich histories and cultures have gone almost unnoticed. The main problem, according to C. Vann Woodward, continues to be one of concept. We need to reexamine and de-emphasize our European-dominated curriculum with its concomitant assumption that the rest of the world revolves around Europe; "that history of any consequence [is] a commodity stamped 'Made in Europe,' and that those cultures outside this chosen domain are therefore primitive, decadent, and permanently inferior."[5]

It has been suggested that we might set our self-esteem aside long enough to see what influence these non-Western countries have had on Europe; we might also add, what influence Africa, Asia, and South America have had on the United States. Then, too, what of our own red men whose nature and influence on our civilization have been excluded from most of our leading history textbooks? According to Professor Page Smith, the kind of limited and segregated history that we have been writing and teaching is one of the primary reasons for the attractiveness of Marxism to millions outside the Western world.

Nationalism, which may be the most powerful force in history, offers other kinds of limitations, which frequently appear as omissions and oversimplifications. Try as he may, the historian cannot escape the proposition that he is immediately torn between his own national bias and his *élan* for objectivity. This point is graphically illustrated by Ray Allen Billington, *et al.*, in *The Historian's Contribution to Anglo-American Misunderstanding* (New York: Hobbs, Dorman, 1966). The authors assert that national pride, among other things,

[4] Frankel. *The Case for Modern Man,* p. 130.

[5] C. Vann Woodward. *The Age of Reinterpretation* (Washington, D.C.: Service Center, American Historical Association, 1964), p. 16.

has led to gross distortions in the treatment of the American Revolution, the War of 1812, and World War I.

Modern nationalism has for many generations carried the implied belief that it represents a unique form of loyalty, that man is by nature patriotic to his state. Professor David M. Potter believes that the close relationship between nationalism and the political state is responsible for this misconception, when, in actuality, "it is associated with and even derived from other forms of loyalty."[6]

[6] David M. Potter. "The Historian's Use of Nationalism," *The American Historical Review*, 27 (July 1962), 937.

This note has mentioned only a few of the many and overwhelming limitations facing the historian and the student in their pursuit of coherence. If it has hit upon a theme, it would probably be that the real restriction in history is mind not matter.

The student should not become disillusioned if the narrative is not pure and complete, for the total worth of history does not rest in the record. He should despair if he is deprived of the opportunity to doubt and to inquire in developing a love of truth, for these processes have provided the historical foundations for the political, economic, and social progress of the dignity of man.

part 1

The Colonial Experience

chapter 1

The Second Discovery of the New World

Pre-Columbian America

The red men, the first discoverers of the New World, probably migrated from Asia. By the time of Columbus' arrival in the West Indies they had explored and inhabited vast regions of what later became the United States. These "Indians," as they were erroneously labeled by Columbus, numbered about one million, were divided into hundreds of tribes, and had some fifty-nine families of languages. Their cultures, while still in the Stone Age, varied in level of development from region to region and from tribe to tribe. Contrary to the modern notion, their skin color also varied. Some tribes, such as the blonde Mandans and Tuscaroras, were not unlike northern Europeans. Three examples will serve to illustrate the wide cultural variations among Indians east of the Mississippi River.

THE ALGONQUINS

The Algonquins, who lived along the coastal regions of the northeast and in the Great Lakes area, built "wigwams," or huts, by bending poles and stripping the sides of the domelike frame with bark. These unique dwellings were duplicated by some of our first Pilgrim fathers. The Algonquins, because of their seemingly warlike nature, were probably the most misunderstood by the invading Europeans. They used war as a kind of sport in which courage was frequently tested by torturing the prisoner; but they were kind and generous to proven friends, and brave captives were known to be adopted into their tribes. The community meetings, or "pow-wows," were first used by the Algonquins. During these assemblies, called to resolve serious community problems, a lighted pipe would be passed from member to member; powers of deliberation were believed to be heightened by the pipe's magical qualities.

THE IROQUOIS

The Iroquois, who lived south and west of the Algonquins in what is today New York, obtained their livelihood from the land and the forests in much the same fashion as the Algonquins, but they were miles apart in social and political customs. The Iroquois practiced communal living in their long bark houses, where several families dwelt together in harmony. The family, or clan, functioned on a matrilineal basis whereby kinship and wealth were traced through the mother or oldest woman in the clan; considerable disciplinary powers were vested in this person because of the long absences of the male from the household. More serious matters of a political nature were handled by the chiefs, who held all offices. In cases of war and peace, the unique Iroquois Confederacy would be involved. This Confederacy, or league of five nations (Senecas,

Onondagas, Mohawks, Cayugas, and Oneidas), was first organized by Hiawatha and was still respected for its power near the end of the eighteenth century. Because of their close unity and because they were fierce fighters, the Iroquois were feared by their neighboring tribes.

THE MUSKOGEES

The highest Indian cultures, before the white men came, were located in the southeastern region, the southwestern region, and the northwest coast of the continent. Of these, those tribes known as the Muskogees (located in the southeastern region of the country) were perhaps the most culturally advanced. They lived in thatched-roofed houses, farmed, and, like their northern neighbors, were warlike. Anthropologists believe that these tribes once developed a rich trade with the Aztecs and thus borrowed much of their culture. This was particularly true of the Natchez, who worshiped the sun and fashioned huge dirt mounds in the form of Aztec pyramids. Another close parallel with the Indians of Mexico can be seen in the sophisticated class divisions found in the Natchez society, at the top of which were the hereditary "kings" who ruled with the consent of the people. The Muskogean tribes were much more sedentary and agrarian than their northern neighbors: they cultivated Indian corn, sunflowers, tobacco, and melons, while other gifts to the white man's table include hominy, persimmon bread, and corn bread. These tribes showed a remarkable gift for assimilation; and by the time of their removal to Indian Territory in the 1820s, they had a bicameral government, a written constitution, an alphabet, and printing presses that turned out their own newspaper. These Indians also had Negro slaves and had built several schools and churches.

CLASH OF CULTURES

The clash of the red and white cultures is part of the story of our country, and it was largely precipitated by a simple misunderstanding of the different concepts of property ownership. The Indian did not understand the white man's concept of private property in land. He practiced communal ownership, which theoretically meant that land could not be sold for private use, such as farming; nor did the frontiersman have a clear grasp of the Indian land customs. Ironically enough, it was not the Indian's weakness as a warrior that led to his defeat (he was more than a match for the white man in hand-to-hand combat); it was rather his strong self-reliance, which precluded any possibility of an effective Indian alliance or union.

While the Spaniards and Portuguese, by and large, conquered, worked, and assimilated the Indian in South America, the American policy toward the red man vacillated between removal, destruction, and assimilation. We made a fainthearted effort to bring him into our culture with the development of Dartmouth Indian College, but the legacy of hate, misunderstanding, and mistrust handed down from the past, and particularly the Pequot War in New England, King Philip's War, the French and Indian Wars, and finally the colonial's clash with the Indian in the American Revolution, frustrated any attempts of acculturation. Where the memories of these past conflicts faded on the advancing frontier, the Indian was viewed as an obstruction to economic progress.

INDIAN HERITAGE

The white man's past attitudes toward the red man have not only obscured the latter's true nature but have minimized the validity and influence of his culture on the development of America. During the colonial period, the fur economy of the white man rested firmly on the back of the Indian, while the farmer depended on the various varieties of Indian cotton, including the valuable long-staple. The Indian taught the colonial how to dress against the severe winters and how to fight in the wilderness; he even showed him the way to the West. Today, our highways wind over Indian trails, and our mountains, rivers, cities, states, people, and language carry Indian names. The canoe and pottery are commonplace, and lacrosse is played in many of our colleges. The red man has influenced our ways of dress, our food, our literature, our fine arts, and our woodcraft, and has given currency to the "strong, silent type." His apparent impact on international relations is still to be written. Former Secretary of the Interior Stewart L. Udall reminds us that today's conservationists are finally discovering the truths about nature that the Indian has known all along: namely, that men and nature are inseparable and that this higher spiritual harmony must be preserved for the future.

Alvin M. Josephy, Jr., has written in *The Indian Heritage of America* (New York: Alfred A. Knopf, 1968) that modern psychologists have finally turned to the Indian cultures for lessons in child raising, while our own federal officials of poverty programs are discovering considerable substance in the group-directed activities, rather than competition, long so obvious to the Indian.

The European Background to Exploration

FACTORS ENCOURAGING EXPLORATION

The impetus suddenly given to exploration in the second half of the fifteenth century may be attributed to several developments taking place in Europe and Asia during that time. The feudal institutions of the Middle Ages were declining in the face of the advancing merchant class and monarchs, both of whom were thinking now in terms of nations rather than dukedoms. The material and spiritual values of the medieval period were being pushed aside by the emerging

optimism and worldliness of the Renaissance, while the Catholic Church was being asked to reconsider its teachings by such men as John Huss and Martin Luther. Europe was expanding in ideas as well as in deeds.

The Crusaders and Marco Polo cultivated the European appetite for the luxuries of the Orient, while the burgeoning inventions in transportation (improved maps and sailing charts, the compass and the improved astrolabe, and more efficient ships) encouraged consumers and merchants to seek lower prices and fatter profits. Moreover, the leading universities, particularly those in Spain, were teaching that the earth was round, while Prince Henry of Portugal was encouraged to stimulate exploration with a school of navigation. An all-water route to China and India would eliminate the unpopular middlemen in the Moslem-held Near East, as well as the trade monopolies centered in Venice and Genoa. All of these factors, driven by the love of adventure, willingness to experiment, self-reliance, and desire for wealth ushered in by the Renaissance, helped to send the Italian explorer Christopher Columbus on his voyage.

PORTUGUESE NAVIGATORS

By the time Columbus pulled anchor in the small port of Palos, Spain (Seville, the logical point of embarkation, was overrun with Moorish and Jewish refugees), in August 1492, several other navigators had made giant strides in charting new routes to the Orient. With the aid of Prince Henry's school and with the encouragement of a united national state, little Portugal sent her daring explorers around the coast of Africa in search of a new route, and possibly new ports. In 1488 Bartholomew Diaz sailed into what he called the Cape of Storms, but King John II of Portugal saw it as the Cape of Good Hope. Ten years later Vasco da Gama completed the voyage around Africa and reached India. Portugal, whose early growth was unhampered by the many wars that troubled western Europe, took advantage of her early lead in discovery and ultimately planted her flag in India, Africa, China, and the East Indies, as well as South America. The acquisition of Brazil came in 1500, when Pedro Álvares Cabral dropped anchor off the eastern bulge of South America and claimed that vast wilderness for his country. In 1513 Vasco Núñez de Balboa reached the Pacific Ocean. Six years later another Portuguese mariner, Ferdinand Magellan, became the first to circumnavigate the globe. Unfortunately, Portugal lacked the resources in population that were necessary in order to defend her holdings against larger and stronger challengers.

A Spanish Happening

COLUMBUS

In 1492, Spain was successful in driving the Moors and Jews from her land, which helped to complete the unification of the country. Spain then felt herself free to enter the race for Oriental riches by sending Columbus, who had been waiting in the wing for several months, on his historic expedition. Armed with the belief that the world was round and with the knowledge of telltale signs of land to the west (tropical-type reeds, unlike any in Europe, had washed ashore along the coast of Portugal), Columbus set sail with reluctant crews on three small ships (two caravels and a nau). On October 12, 1492, after thirty-three trying days, land was sighted at the island of San Salvador in the West Indies. Thinking that he had discovered part of India, Columbus pressed ever onward on three additional voyages in his futile efforts to reach the Orient.

TREATY OF TORDESILLES

Spain and Portugal were thrown into immediate conflict over property rights in the New World, and the issue was finally resolved by the papal line of demarcation in 1493, which was modified the following year by the Treaty of Tordesilles. The terms of this instrument divided the non-European world between the two rivals, with the lion's share going to Spain, while Portugal received additional territory in the East Indies.

SPANISH NAVIGATORS

Columbus failed to complete his mission, but the Courts of Spain soon overlooked his mistake when they saw the color of his treasures. In 1513 Juan Ponce de León discovered Florida but found death in his search for the legendary Fountain of Youth. Conquistadores, however, dragged their feet in exploiting the New World until they found their most capable exponents in Hernando Cortes, who ravaged the Aztecs in 1519–1521, and Francisco Pizarro, who conquered the empire of the Incas in 1531–1535. Shortly after the conquest of these two wealthy empires, the Spaniards fell victim to the dream of the mythical "El Dorado," which they relentlessly pursued through the southwest region of North America and into the forbidding jungles of the Amazon. In quest of the seven cities of gold, Francisco Vásquez de Coronado explored parts of present-day Arizona, New Mexico, Texas, Oklahoma, and Kansas between 1540 and 1542, while his counterpart, Hernando de Soto, with an expedition of six hundred armor-plated men, chased the gold bug from Florida to present-day Arkansas. De Soto died while on one of his excursions and was buried in the Mississippi River. In 1565 Spain finally decided to plant her flag in Florida and proceeded to establish a settlement at St. Augustine, the first white settlement north of Mexico.

Other Europeans in North America

The Norse seamen, operating out of Iceland and Greenland, about A.D. 1000, happened upon the shores of North America; but, perhaps because their country was disunited and weak, posted no claim to the vast continent. England was still involved with the problem of trying to unite her country and floundered for over a century before finally generating enough power to launch a serious challenge to Spain and Portugal. Henry VII had made a feeble effort by sending the Italian John Cabot to the New World in 1497 and 1498; but this venture was not pursued since most of Europe looked upon the new land mass as a barrier rather than an asset. A few years later, in 1524, France got into the act by sending Italian navigator Giovanni da Verrazano to seek out a passageway through the barrier; when he failed, Jacques Cartier sailed up the St. Lawrence thinking that he had found the elusive water route through the continent.

FRENCH EXPLORERS

The French, the Dutch, and the Swedes adopted a more serious attitude toward colonization in the seventeenth century when they set up fur-trading stations in America. In 1523, Giovanni da Verrazano explored the coastline from New York to Newfoundland, and thus laid claim to the region for France. Samuel de Champlain, after exploring the coasts around New England and the St. Lawrence region, founded Quebec in 1608 as a fortress to protect French interests on the St. Lawrence River. Champlain, however, made the mistake of siding with the Algonquin Indians in their struggle with the fierce Iroquois. France suffered the consequences during her prolonged struggle with England for empires in the New World. The French pursued two active interests in Canada: the fur trade and Indian conversion. The conversion mission, carried out by the tireless Jesuits, was an extension of the Catholic Reformation.

THE DUTCH

The Dutch got into the act when they sent an Englishman, Henry Hudson, into the area of the Delaware and Connecticut rivers in 1609, where he also took time to discover and name a river for himself. In the 1620s and 1630s the Dutch planted trading stations along these rivers. New Amsterdam (later, New York) became their capital, and the beaver became their emblem. The Dutch settlements never prospered, however, mainly because the governors were inept, and partly because more emphasis was placed on fur trading than on farming.

SWEDES

The Swedes made a belated effort at colonizing when they built Fort Christian on the Delaware in 1638. They lost it some seventeen years later when the Dutch charged them with poaching on Dutch territorial rights. The industrious Swedes, however, left the legacy of the log cabin, which was used to great advantage during the severe northeastern winters. The idea soon spread to other colonies.

Select Bibliography

Andrews, Charles M. *The Colonial Period in American History,* Vols. 1–3. New Haven, Conn.: Yale University Press, 1934–1938.

———. *Our Earliest Colonial Settlements: Their Diversities of Origin and Later Characteristics.* New York: New York University Press, 1959.

Brebner, John B. *The Explorers of North America, 1492–1806.* New York: Doubleday & Company, Inc., 1955.

Brown, Ralph H. *Historical Geography of the United States.* New York: Harcourt Brace Jovanovich, Inc., 1948.

Commager, Henry Steele, and Elmo Giordanetti. *Was America a Mistake: An Eighteenth Century Controversy.* New York: Harper & Row, Publishers, 1968.

Driver, Harold E. *Indians of North America.* Chicago: The University of Chicago Press, 1961.

Farb, Peter. *Man's Rise to Civilization as Shown by the Indians of North America from Primeval Times to the Coming of the Industrial State.* New York: E. P. Dutton & Co., Inc., 1968.

Fey, Harold E., and D'Arcy McNickle. *Indians and Other Americans.* New York: Harper & Row, Publishers, 1959.

Gibson, Charles. *Spain in America.* New York: Harper & Row, Publishers, 1966.

Gillespie, James E. *A History of Geographical Discovery, 1400–1800.* New York: Holt, Rinehart and Winston, Inc., 1933.

Hagan, William T. *American Indians.* Chicago: The University of Chicago Press, 1961.

Hexter, Jack H. *Reappraisals in History.* Evanston, Ill.: Northwestern University Press, 1961.

Holand, Hjalmar R. *Norse Discoveries and Explorations in North America: Leif Ericson to Kensington.* New York: Twayne Publishers, Inc., 1968.

Holmes, Vera Brown. *A History of the Americas,* 2 vols. New York: The Ronald Press Company, 1964.

Huddleston, Lee Elridge. *Origins of the American Indians: European Concepts, 1492–1729.* Austin, Texas: University of Texas Press, 1967.

Huntington, Ellsworth. *The Red Man's Continent.* New Haven, Conn.: Yale University Press, 1919.

Hyde, George E. *Indians of the Woodlands: From Prehistoric Times to 1725.* Norman, Okla.: University of Oklahoma Press, 1962.

Jennings, Jesse D. *Prehistory of North America.* New York: McGraw-Hill, Inc., 1968.

Jones, Gwyn. *Norse Atlantic Saga.* New York: Oxford University Press, 1963.

Josephy, Alvin M., ed. *The American Heritage Book of Indians.* New York: Simon & Schuster, Inc., 1961.

Kirkpatrick, Frederick A. *The Spanish Conquistadores,* 2d ed. New York: Barnes & Noble, Inc., 1967.

Landstrom, Bjorn. *Columbus: The Story of Don Cristóbal Colón, Admiral of the Ocean and His Four Voyages Westward.* New York: Crowell Collier and Macmillan, Inc., 1967.

Livermore, Harold V. *New History of Portugal.* Cambridge, Mass.: Harvard University Press, 1966.

McNickle, D'Arcy. *The Indian Tribes of the United States.* New York: Oxford University Press, 1962.

Morison, Samuel E. *Admiral of the Ocean Sea: A Life of Christopher Columbus.* Boston: Little, Brown and Company, 1942.

————, ed. *The Parkman Reader.* Boston: Little, Brown and Company, 1955.

————. *Portuguese Voyages to America in the Fifteenth Century.* New York: Octagon Books, Inc., 1965.

Nettels, Curtis P. *The Roots of American Civilization.* 2d ed. New York: Appleton-Century-Crofts, 1963.

Noon, John A. *Law and Government of the Grand River Iroquois.* New York: Viking Fund Publication in Anthropology, 1949.

Notestein, Wallace. *English People on the Eve of Colonization.* New York: Harper & Row, Publishers, 1954.

Oswalt, Wendell H. *This Land Was Theirs.* New York: John Wiley & Sons, Inc., 1966.

Parry, John. *The Age of Reconnaissance: Discovery, Exploration and Settle-*

ment, 1450–1650. Cleveland: World Publishing Co., 1963.

Pearce, Roy H. *Savages of America: A Study of the Indian and the Idea of Civilization.* Baltimore, Md.: Johns Hopkins University Press, 1953.

Priestly, Herbert I. *France Overseas.* New York: Octagon Books, Inc., 1966.

Sanceau, Elaine. *Henry the Navigator.* Hamden, Conn.: Shoe String Press, Inc., 1969.

Savelle, Max. *The Foundation of the American Civilization.* New York: Holt, Rinehart and Winston, Inc., 1964.

Semple, Ellen C. *The American History and Its Geographic Conditions.* New York: Russell & Russell, Publishers, 1968.

Silverberg, Robert. *Mound Builders of Ancient America: The Archaeology of*

a Myth. Greenwich, N.Y.: New York Graphic Society, 1968.

Underhill, Ruth. *Red Man's America.* Chicago: The University of Chicago Press, 1953.

Washburn, Wilcomb E. *The Indian and the White Man.* New York: Doubleday & Company, Inc., 1964.

Webb, Walter P. *The Great Frontier.* Austin, Texas: University of Texas Press, 1952.

Williamson, James A., ed. *The Age of Drake.* New York: Barnes & Noble, Inc., 1960.

———. *Cabot Voyages and Bristol Discovery under Henry VII.* New York: Cambridge University Press, 1962.

Wissler, Clark. *Indians of the United States: Four Centuries of Their History and Culture.* New York: Doubleday & Company, Inc., 1966.

chapter 2

The English Colonial Experience

The English Try Again

SIR HUMPHREY GILBERT AND SIR WALTER RALEIGH

After the abortive attempts of Sir Humphrey Gilbert and his half brother, Sir Walter Raleigh, to plant colonies in America (1578–1587) (during which time the former lost a ship and the latter a whole colony), it took almost two decades for the British to muster their resources for another attempt. Political, economic, and religious events paved the way to the first successful English colony. It was during the reign of the Stuarts that Englishmen chafed most from political absolutism and religious coercion. The Stuart kings, half of whom were from other countries, attempted to extend a medieval system of government and divine power into an age in which the emerging middle class was still celebrating victories over such concepts. The growing enmity between the monarch and the merchant class gained even wider currency in 1629 (the year John Winthrop and his followers were preparing to move to America) when Charles I decided that he could rule without the bourgeois-dominated House of Commons and abolished Parliament.

FACTORS IN ENGLISH COLONIZATION

English interest in overseas expansion was kept alive during the sixteenth century by the courageous fishermen who frequented the waters of Newfoundland and no less by the daring buccaneers who raided the Spanish treasure ships. However, the most compelling economic push came from the homeland, where the growing national state demanded additional revenues for an expanding civil service, judiciary, and defense budget.

Religious unrest accompanied the political and economic impulses and found its most ardent radicals among the middle classes, who saw in Puritanism a chance for religious, as well as political and economic, freedom. They rejected the Anglican Church with its medieval trappings, its corrupt and intolerant bishops, with all the individualism that Calvinism could muster. Many finally tired of the struggle and moved out of the country with the hope of finding a more promising way of life in another land. In those years, during the reign of Charles I, more than 25,000 Englishmen moved to the colonies of Virginia and Massachusetts. In addition, the gold and silver that was pouring into the coffers of Europe from the Spanish and Portuguese empires caused price inflation, while the growing demand for wool turned many English farms into sheep pastures, which, in turn, caused widespread unemployment.

Fearing the fate of Gilbert and Raleigh, but desiring their share of the wealth in the New World, a group of merchants and noblemen in 1606 organized what became known as the Joint-Stock Company. By

14

having a larger number of people buy shares in the company, the risk was less, but then, so were the profits.

JAMESTOWN

The group finally received a charter from James I under the title of the Virginia Company of London. Their colony, planted at Jamestown, Virginia, in 1607, struggled with indecision, sickness, gold fever, and famine until twenty-seven-year-old John Smith rescued it from disaster. With the help of the Indians and experimental crops (the first crops proved unsuitable to the climate), the fortunes of Jamestown soon began to look brighter. John Rolfe, the husband of Pocahontas, began to experiment with raising and curing native tobacco, and by 1618 it was the leading export of the colony. In later years it would become the money crop of Virginia. In order to attract a higher class of people, the company began to offer colonists land of their own and a voice in the government; and in 1619 the government of the colony was liberalized by the introduction of a representative assembly, the famous House of Burgesses. It was the first legislative body in the New World.

BACON'S REBELLION

All was not well in Virginia, however, for in 1624 the company was bankrupt. James I, distrusting the House of Burgesses, revoked the company charter and made Virginia a royal colony. Just when it appeared that Virginia was on her way to political and economic recovery, sectional tension developed between the aristocracy in the rich tidelands region and the lower classes of the back country, culminating in Bacon's Rebellion in 1676. The backwoodsmen rose in revolt when Governor Berkeley, who is reported to have had a prosperous fur trade with the Indians, refused to discipline the renegade braves. Nathaniel Bacon and his aroused frontiersmen marched into Jamestown, burned the city, and turned on the Indians. Several of Bacon's men were later captured and hanged after their leader's untimely death from a fever. This revolt has gone down as the commoner's first demand for equal protection and rights under the law in the New World.

PLYMOUTH

While Jamestown was struggling for survival, a group of 100 separatists boarded the *Mayflower* in 1620 and set sail for Virginia, where they hoped to set up a plantation for a group of merchants in England. As fortune would have it, they missed their destination and landed instead at Cape Cod, whereupon they explored the land and decided to make nearby Plymouth their home. Low on supplies, but courageous and determined, this brave little band of Pilgrims, under the leadership of John Carver, saw almost half their number perish during the first winter. The survivors, however, under their second governor, William Bradford, proved that man could prosper in the area. Since they were outside the jurisdiction of the Virginia Charter, the Plymouth Pilgrims set up their own form of government, which respected the principle of "majority rule." It became known as the Mayflower Compact since most of the adult males had signed it before leaving the ship. In 1691 Plymouth became a part of the Massachusetts Bay Colony.

MASSACHUSETTS BAY COLONY

The New England Company, which was organized in 1628, numbered among its subscribers a host of Congregational Puritans (a party within the Church of England) who wished to reform the English church. They finally gained full control of the company, changed its name to the Massachusetts Bay Company, and secured a royal charter, which granted them complete authority to govern their colony. In 1630 their newly appointed governor, John Winthrop, assembled 900 passengers on eighteen ships and sailed for Massachusetts. Their first winter was fraught with hardships. Mentally unprepared for the harshness of frontier life and short on provisions, they struggled through the first long year; but the strong leadership of Winthrop assured them of success. The Massachusetts Puritans have been the subject of much speculation by historians. They have stood for Godliness, thrift, liberty, democracy, industry, frugality, temperance, principle, equal rights, and so on, among their defenders; while others have seen in them the embodiment of philistinism, harsh restraint, beauty-hating, hypocrisy, brutal intolerance, religious persecution, ill-temper, stinginess, bigotry, and so on.

While the Massachusetts Puritans appeared to be strict in enforcing moral behavior, all of the colonies in the New World had strict moral codes and most enforced them. The Bay Puritans placed more emphasis on constant self-examination and self-discipline, for their religion taught that man by nature was sinful, but that he should try to do right amid all the worldly temptations of wrong. They subscribed to a form of government that would enforce the commandments of God and help reduce religion to its purest forms. For various reasons, but mainly to protect its own religious purity and unity, the Bay colony discouraged other religious ideas, especially interpretations within the church that ran counter to accepted orthodoxy. Roger Williams and Anne Hutchinson, who both espoused such divergent religious views, are notable examples of those ostracized for such views.

Williams taught that the New Englanders should break completely with the unholy Church of England. Moreover, he believed that the Massachusetts charter had no legal foundation, since the crown of England had not purchased the land from its rightful owners, the natives. He also called for voluntary church support rather than taxation and argued that the state had no right to enforce church rules. In 1635 he was banished and in the follow-ing year sought refuge in Rhode Island, where he established what is considered to be the first Baptist church in the New World. The hallmark of his colony was complete religious freedom, which ultimately attracted outcasts from the whole colonial setting.

Two years later Anne Hutchinson was ostracized for interpreting and elucidating on the sermons of some of the Puritan ministers. She not only implied that some of the ministers were leading the people to hell, but suggested that true religion is founded on personal faith, rather than on a set of doctrines set forth by the clergy. She fled to Providence with a group of her followers and founded Portsmouth.

FUNDAMENTAL ORDERS

Other parts of New England were settled during the great exodus from England. In 1636 the Reverend Thomas Hooker broke with the Massachusetts Bay Colony over religious differences and led his people into the fertile valley of the Connecticut River, where they founded Hartford. It was here that the Fundamental Orders, which called for a democratic form of government, were drafted. Connecticut was awarded a royal charter in 1662 and annexed New Haven in the same year.

TOLERATION ACT

The settlement of Lord Baltimore (Cecilius Calvert) in Maryland was another kind of colonial experiment designed to extract wealth and protect religious refugees. Unlike the commercial company ventures to the north, Lord Baltimore was granted a charter in his own name in 1632 and secured a 10-million-acre tract of land in the Chesapeake Bay region. As proprietor, he had complete administrative authority and beckoned all his persecuted Catholic friends to seek the shelter of his colony. Freedom of worship was announced by the Toleration Act of 1649; but Jews and atheists, and any other groups that denied the Trinity, were discouraged with threats of death. Other proprietary ventures were soon to follow.

CAROLINAS

The restoration of the Stuarts in England in 1660 prompted the creation of additional colonies. As a kind of reward to his friends for their support, Charles II granted vast lands south of Virginia, called Carolina, to eight proprietors, who soon turned the holdings into business ventures. In 1719 the commoners revolted against the rule of the proprietors and called for a royal charter, whereupon the proprietors sold their holdings and paved the way for the new charter, which was issued by the king in 1729. The new charter divided the territory into two colonies.

The colonial government and economy of South Carolina was founded on a system of aristocratic domination under the Fundamental Constitution. The nobility of the upper house reserved the right to make laws, and the landholdings functioned on a quitrent system for the commoners and a hereditary plantation system for the aristocracy. Rice became the staple cash crop and remained so for more than a century. Freedom of religion was offered in both of the colonies.

North Carolina was settled largely by refugees from debts, taxes, and religious persecution, and soon assumed a more democratic atmosphere when large numbers of small farmers staked out land claims over the territory, which, in turn, discouraged aristocrats or landed nobles. In 1729 North Carolina became a royal colony.

GEORGIA

Georgia, the southernmost and last of the original thirteen colonies, was awarded to the humanitarian James Oglethorpe in 1733 as a first line of defense against Spanish Florida and French Louisiana. Oglethorpe, however, viewed his settlement as a haven for debt-ridden outcasts, as well as a military venture, and welcomed all who found his colony. Despite the royal subsidies that were frequently extended, Georgia, like North Carolina, did not prosper. She was often harassed by the Spanish, and her unhealthful climate discouraged ambitious farmers.

NEW YORK

A few months after the Carolina grants were made in 1663, another member of the Court of England was awarded a prize piece of property in America. This time it was the king's brother, the Duke of York, and the land grant extended from Connecticut to Maryland—the heart of the Dutch holdings. Since there was already a commercial war between the two countries, the duke needed no further pretense to enlist the aid of the English fleet and force the surrender of Peter Stuyvesant, the ill-prepared Dutch director-general. New Amsterdam was changed to New York, and the Dutch departed, leaving behind a legacy of names and folkways. The English now controlled the coast between Maine and South Carolina.

PENNSYLVANIA

None of the English colonies enjoyed the success that the personable William Penn realized in Pennsylvania. Having secured a charter by virtue of his father's services to the king, Penn led his persecuted Quakers to the rich lands west of the Delaware in 1681 and built a commonwealth that appealed to democratic ways in government, landholding, and religion. For the first time land was *bought* from the Indians, and his liberal grants to settlers soon mushroomed the population of the colony. The Quakers were probably the first to espouse broad social reforms within established institutions and to speak out against the indignity and inhumanity of Negro slavery. Their peaceful nature made them an anachronism on the violent frontier.

NEW JERSEY

The territories of New Jersey and West New Jersey, purchased by two Carolina proprietors, came under Quaker control when in 1674–1682 they were purchased by Penn and his associates. In 1702 the crown merged the two Jerseys into a royal colony. Delaware, on the other hand, continued under the governorship of Pennsylvania until the time of the American Revolution, even though she had been granted a separate assembly in 1703.

Select Bibliography

Adams, James Truslow. *The Founding of New England*. Boston: Little, Brown and Company, 1963.

Andrews, Charles M. *The Colonial Period of American History*. 3 vols. New Haven, Conn.: Yale University Press, 1934–1938.

Battis, Emery. *Saints and Sectaries: Anne Hutchinson and the Antinomian Controversy in the Massachusetts Bay Colony*. Chapel Hill, N.C.: University of North Carolina Press, 1962.

Bridenbaugh, Carl. *Cities in the Wilderness*. New York: Alfred A. Knopf, 1955.

————. *Vexed and Troubled Englishmen, 1590–1642*. New York: Oxford University Press, 1968.

Brockunier, Samuel. *The Irrepressible Democrat*. New York: The Ronald Press Company, 1940.

Brown, Robert E., and B. Katherine. *Virginia, 1705–1786: Democracy or Aristocracy*. East Lansing, Mich.: Michigan State University Press, 1964.

Chitwood, Oliver P. *A History of Colonial America*, 3d ed. New York: Harper & Row, Publishers, 1961.

Coulter, E. Merton. *George*, 2d ed. Chapel Hill, N.C.: University of North Carolina Press, 1960.

Craven, Wesley Frank. *The Southern Colonies in the Seventeenth Century*. Baton Rouge, La.: Louisiana State University, Press, 1949.

Dunn, Mary M. *William Penn: Politics and Conscience*. Princeton, N.J.: Princeton University Press, 1967.

Dunn, Richard S. *Puritans and Yankee: The Winthrop Dynasty of New England, 1630–1717*. Princeton, N.J.: Princeton University Press, 1962.

Ettinger, Amos A. *James Edward Oglethorpe: Imperial Idealist*. New York: Oxford University Press, 1936.

Gipson, Lawrence Henry, *The British Empire before the American Revolution*. 10 vols. New York: Alfred A. Knopf, 1958–1965.

Greene, Theodore P. *Roger Williams and the Massachusetts Magistrates*. Boston: D. C. Heath and Company, 1964.

Haller, William. *Liberty and Reformation in the Puritan Revolution*. New York: Columbia University Press, 1955.

Hansen, Marcus Lee. *The Atlantic Migration, 1607–1860*. Harper & Row, Publishers, 1960.

Haskins, George L. *Law and Authority in Early Massachusetts: A Study in Tradition and Design*. New York: Crowell Collier and Macmillan, Inc., 1960.

Havighurst, Walter. *Alexander Spotswood: Portrait of a Governor*. New York: Holt, Rinehart and Winston, Inc., 1967.

Hedges, James B. *The Browns of Providence Plantation: Colonial Years*. Providence, R. I.: Brown University Press, 1968.

Hunt, George T. *The Wars of the Iro-*

quois: *A Study in Intertribal Relations*. Madison, Wis.: University of Wisconsin Press, 1960.

Langdom, George. *Pilgrim Colony: A History of New Plymouth, 1620–1691*. New Haven, Conn.: Yale University Press, 1966.

Leach, Douglas E. *Flintlock and Tomahawk*. New York: Crowell Collier and Macmillan, Inc., 1958.

———. *The Northern Colonial Frontier*. New York: Holt, Rinehart and Winston, Inc., 1966.

Miller, Perry. *New England Mind: The Seventeenth Century*. Cambridge, Mass.: Harvard University Press, 1953.

Morgan, Edmund S. *The Puritan Family*, rev. ed. New York: Harper & Row, Publishers, 1966.

———, ed. *Puritan Political Ideas, 1558–1794*. Indianapolis, Ind.: The Bobbs-Merrill Co., Inc., 1965.

———. *Roger Williams: The Church and the State*. New York: Harcourt Brace Jovanovich, Inc., 1967.

———. *Virginians at Home: Family Life in the Eighteenth Century*. Charlottesville, Va.: The University Press of Virginia, 1963.

———. *Visible Saints: The History of Puritan Ideas*. New York: New York University Press, 1963.

Morison, Samuel E. *Builders of the Bay Colony*. Boston: Houghton Mifflin Company, 1963.

———. *The Story of the "Old Colony" of New Plymouth*. New York: Alfred A. Knopf, 1956.

Morton, Richard L. *Colonial Virginia*. 2 vols. Charlottesville, Va.: The University Press of Virginia, 1960.

Pomfret, John E. *The Province of West New Jersey, 1609–1702*. Princeton, N.J.: Princeton University Press, 1962.

Peare, Catherine Owen. *William Penn: A Biography*. Philadelphia: J. P. Lippincott Co., 1957.

Powell, Sumner. *The Puritan Village*. Middletown, Conn.: Wesleyan University Press, 1963.

Rowse, Alfred L. *The Expansion of Elizabethan England*. New York: St. Martin's Press, Inc. 1955.

———. *The England of Elizabeth*. New York: Crowell Collier and Macmillan, Inc., 1961.

Savelle, Max, and Robert Middlekauff. *A History of Colonial America*. New York: Harcourt Brace Jovanovich, Inc., 1964.

Smith, Bradford. *Captain John Smith: His Life and Legend*. Philadelphia: J. P. Lippincott Co., 1953.

Smith, E. Brooks, ed. *Pilgrim Courage: From the Firsthand Account by William Bradford*. Boston: Little, Brown and Company, 1962.

Stone, Lawrence. *The Crisis of Aristocracy, 1558–1641*. New York: Oxford University Press, 1965.

Vaughan, Alden T. *New England Frontier: Indians and Puritans, 1620–1675*. Boston: Little, Brown and Company, 1965.

Waller, G. M., ed. *Puritanism in Early America*. Boston: D. C. Heath & Company, 1950.

Washburn, Wilcomb E. *The Governor and the Rebel: A History of Bacon's Rebellion in Virginia*. Chapel Hill, N.C.: University of North Carolina Press, 1957.

Waters, David W. *The Art of Navigation in England in Elizabethan and Early Stuart Times*. New Haven, Conn.: Yale University Press, 1958.

Wertenbaker, Thomas J. *The Founding of American Civilization*. 3 vols. New

York: Charles Scribner's Sons, 1938–1947.

_____. *The Old South: The Founding of American Civilization*. New York: Charles Scribner's Sons, 1942.

_____. *The Puritan Oligarchy*. New York: Charles Scribner's Sons, 1947.

_____. *The Shaping of Colonial Virginia*. New York: Russell & Russell, Publishers, 1958.

_____. *Torchbearer of the Revolution: The Story of Bacon's Rebellion and Its Leaders*. Princeton, N.J.: Princeton University Press, 1940.

Winslow, Ola E. *Master Roger Williams*. New York: Crowell Collier and Macmillan, Inc., 1957.

Wright, Louis B. *The American Heritage History of the Thirteen Colonies*. New York: American Heritage Publishing Co., Inc., 1967.

_____. *Atlantic Frontier: Colonial American Civilization, 1607–1763*. Ithaca, N.Y.: Cornell University Press, 1963.

_____. *The First Gentlemen of Virginia: Intellectual Qualities of Early Colonial Ruling Class*. Charlottesville, Va.: The University Press of Virginia, 1964.

chapter 3

Roots of Nationalism

Economic Development

MERCANTILISM

The form of economic venture practiced by the British government during the American colonial period was that of *mercantilism*. Designed to bolster the economy and general trade balance of the mother country, mercantilism was a theory which assumed that colonies should always be kept in a subordinate position and provide raw materials for the factories of the controlling power. In return, the mother country would offer manufactured goods to the colony, along with her surplus population, including political and religious outcasts and other undesirables. Political and economic guidance would also be given to the colonies. While England made no capital outlay in the establishment of her colonies in the New World, she nevertheless expected the mercantile system to be enforced, and passed numerous navigation and trade acts designed to encourage compliance. These regulations, however, were not troublesome to the colonials before the period of the Revolution because they were never strictly enforced.

NEW ENGLAND

The American colonies developed their own peculiar economies during their early growth, and these industries played a significant role in their later history. All of the colonies remained agrarian, for the most part, throughout the colonial period; but New England soon learned that there was considerable demand for her beaver and codfish and built a "fin and fur" industry that rivaled the wealth of the richest gold mines in the New World. The hardy New Englanders were also ship-builders.

MIDDLE COLONIES

The Middle Colonies, with their broad stretches of fertile land, developed into the "bread basket" of the colonial world and prospered from the large quantities of wheat, flour, and meat that were shipped to Europe. Unlike the other two groups of colonies, the Middle Colonies were blessed with both industry and agriculture; and while their industrial development may not have matched that of New England, their farm belt was one of the most promising in America. It has been suggested that the abundance of fertile land in these colonies provided an atmosphere for the growth of democracy, and, as long as free land was available, European feudalism would never work. Nevertheless, forms of feudalism appeared in New York (as well as in Maryland, Virginia, and South Carolina), where high rents and feudal obligations were imposed upon the people; but the system soon faded or was modified beyond rec-

21

ognition. It has been said that the rapid success of the Penn experiment was in no small way attributable to a system of free land, which granted fifty acres to the head of the family, with more available at a minimum cost, if desired.

SOUTHERN COLONIES AND SLAVE LABOR

The southern settlements have been called the "plantation colonies," but this name is not appropriate for North Carolina, where small- and medium-sized farms dominated the landscape. Three crops took an early lead in the plantation economy of the South: tobacco, rice, and indigo. Because of the emphasis placed on only one or two crops in a given colony, quantity production and cheap labor were demanded. White indentured servants (people who had sold themselves into labor for a specified number of years, usually five or more, in order to pay off their passage to the colony) served as one form of cheap service, while Negro slaves, common to all the early colonies, provided another. There were two types of white indentured servants, the voluntary and the involuntary. The former consented to the terms of the contract and knew their destination, whereas the latter were often kidnapped, sold to slave traders, and shipped to the New World against their will.

Black slavery, on the other hand, had its beginnings in the new colonies in 1619, when a Dutch captain sold twenty Negroes to the settlers of Jamestown. Negro slavery was unpopular among most colonials, but it gradually won widespread preference over the white indentured servants (mainly because it represented permanent service) and became a "peculiar institution" in the South. Negro slaves became so numerous in South Carolina that by 1670 they outnumbered the white population two to one. This form of labor, because free labor could not compete, inadvertently transformed the people in many of the Southern Colonies into two classes: the slaves and the landlords.

Intellectual Development

Early America represented, for the most part, a vast expanse of ignorance and superstition. It was no place for a philosopher, for the task of making a livelihood required long hours of hard work. Thus, the people in general were quick to let newcomers know that America was more interested in their skills than in their ideas. Even some of the doctors and clergy had to turn to more mundane pursuits, such as farming, in order to make ends meet.

MEDICINE

The medical profession, by and large, was still under the influence of medieval alchemy and the supposed magical powers of herbs, and thus contributed little more than hope to the physical well-being of colonial America. The scientific revolution had not yet arrived, and even when more scientific remedies and cures were discovered in Europe, they were slow in reaching America. For example, the smallpox innoculation was not introduced to the colonies until 1721, almost a decade after its discovery in England. The dearth of knowledge in medicine extended as well to the field of dentistry, where practitioners often doubled as barbers and used extraction as a cure-all.

EDUCATION

The clergy not only provided spiritual guidance and training, but they also taught the early colonials to read and to write. The Bible was the first text, but European texts were soon introduced for the purpose of teaching the classical languages, Latin and Greek, which prepared the student for university training. Girls were excluded from formal education. The most notable gains in education during our early colonial period were made by the Massachusetts Bay Colony, where a famous law, designed to provide public schools for each township, was passed in 1647. This Puritan colony had already founded America's first college, Harvard, in 1636, the main purpose of which was to train the clergy.

It was not until 1751 that Ben Franklin and his associates introduced a college free of church control, where students might pursue a liberal arts education. It later became the University of Pennsylvania. The Southern Colonies were slow to introduce widespread public education, largely because the population was scattered and the middle class was not as pronounced as that in the other colonies. Thus, a system of parochial schools or a tutor prepared the children of the wealthier families for higher education in Europe.

PRINTING PRESS

The first printing press in America was established in Massachusetts in 1639, where crude books were turned out to help stimulate the intellectual side of life; but it was not until 1704 that the first newspaper rolled off the press of the Boston *News-Letter*. In 1719, *The American Weekly Mercury* appeared on the Philadelphia scene, and by the middle of the century every colony had a press turning out papers, books, pamphlets, and almanacs. It was in Philadelphia that the talented Benjamin Franklin acquired a printing press and for twenty-six years edited the famous *Poor Richard's Almanack*. A mixture of Yankee wit and homespun wisdom, it may have done more than all the combined battles of the Revolution to unite the colonials.

Censorship also accompanied intellectual pursuits. In 1733 John Peter Zenger, editor of the *New York Weekly Journal*, was charged with libel and imprisoned for printing stories of the corrupt politics practiced by the governor. Defended by Andrew Hamilton, one of the ablest lawyers of the colonial period, Zenger was freed when Hamilton urged the jury to set aside the antiquated English law, which denied the right of citizens to print the truth, and to rule in favor of liberty. The Zenger case has stood as a landmark against judicial tyranny and arbitrary laws that tend to curb the right of the press to expose corruption in government.

The colonial period may not have produced any literary giants, the efforts of Jonathan Edwards and Benjamin Franklin excepted; but it did educate and give America a unique ability to write documents on the rights of man that remain unsurpassed in coherence and eloquence.

Political Development

COLONIAL GOVERNMENTS

Colonial governments, like other institutions, leaned heavily on British precedents, but as they developed, unique characteristics began to emerge in the form of self-government. The power structure of colonial governments differed from colony to colony, but the overall form was constant. There were three types of governors: (1) royal, where the governor was appointed by the King of England; (2) proprietary, where the governor was appointed by the proprietor of the colony; and (3) the self-governing type, where the governor was elected by the people. The legislative branch also had the same form of a council and a lower house in each of the colonies, but the powers and methods of election varied. The council, or the upper house, was appointed by the king in the royal colonies, while the self-governing colonies elected their own members. The council members in the proprietary governments were appointed by the proprietor, except in Pennsylvania, where they were elected by the people. The lower house was elected by the propertied voters in almost every instance and functioned in much the same manner throughout the colonies, even though it differed in name from the House of Burgesses in Virginia to the House of Representatives in Massachusetts.

POWERS OF GOVERNOR, ASSEMBLY, AND COUNCIL

With the notable exceptions of Connecticut and Rhode Island, where they were elected, the governors were vested with considerable powers in commanding the military garrisons and in enforcing the laws of the land. A few governors were Americans, but most were from the mother country; some were incompetent, but most were able men. Some of the colonial assemblies, through their power to control finances, tried to control the political behavior of the chief executive by withholding funds requested for projects. It is believed that the power of the assembly could be compared favorably with that of the House of Commons in England. The lower house of the colonial governments shared with the council the right to make and pass laws to govern the colony, but reserved for itself the privilege of initiating and passing tax measures. Thus, this practice may have established the conceptual relationship between taxation and representation.

LOCAL GOVERNMENTS

Local administrative units differed widely from Massachusetts to South Carolina. New England's local government was centered around the "town-meeting," which called for open debate and open voting, while that of the Southern Colonies operated on a county-wide basis. The Middle Colonies had features of both.

Some of colonial America's greatest contributions to our way of life stem from her concepts in political science. Stirring proclamations in charters and compacts combined with the emerging power of her representative assemblies to plant the seeds of nationalism, perhaps inadvertently, and thus set her on a collision course with the imperial power of England.

Religious Development

Religious oppression was a major factor in driving the colonials from England and other European countries, but religious toleration gained little currency before Roger Williams promised religious freedom in Rhode Island and Lord Baltimore welcomed most faiths in Maryland. After these milestones toward toleration appeared, other colonies began to open their doors to other faiths, and by 1660 there were few oppressed sects in America. The result was the outcropping of several denominations. By 1775 the Congregationalists had spread throughout New England, the Anglicans had firm control of the Southern Colonies, the Presbyterians were in great numbers on the frontier, and the Dutch Reformed were to be found in New York, New Jersey, and Pennsylvania.

TAX-SUPPORTED FAITHS

Two faiths were tax supported in eight of the colonies by 1775. The Congregational Church taxed its constituents in three of the New England Colonies, while the Anglican Church collected revenue from all five of the Southern settlements.

It has been suggested that not all of the colonials were devout church members, or churchgoers, and that the "blue laws," while every colony had a few, were not rigorously enforced after the seventeenth century. It was during that century that prosperous times and new denominations with more liberal codes of conduct began to make inroads on the stern doctrines of Calvinism. To some conservative Calvinists it appeared that the devil was winning more converts than God. Alarmed by these secular trends, a few church ministers began to travel from town to town where they combined showmanship with spirited sermons in an effort to drive the devil from the doorstep. These mass revivals reached their apex in The Great Awakening, which spread through Europe and America during the 1730s and 1740s.

GREAT AWAKENING

Perhaps the most effective leaders of this movement in America were George Whitefield, an English Methodist revivalist, and Jonathan Edwards, an itinerant Congregationalist minister from Massachusetts, who gave such rousing and eloquent sermons that thousands flocked to their open-field chapels for salvation. Edwards has been described as America's greatest theologian, and his theories on the emotional experience in conversion influenced religious dialogue in Europe as well as in America. The Great Awakening checked only temporarily the liberal movements in religion, and before the century was spent, many more denominations appeared on the scene. It has been reported that in New England congregations moved from one preacher to another, and sometimes from one church to another, searching for an answer to their shifting values.

Social Development

IMMIGRATION
DURING THE COLONIAL PERIOD

The population of the colonies by 1700 had reached a figure of about 300,000, but by 1775 it had mushroomed to almost 3 million. In addition to the large families

of the eighteenth century, mass movements of immigrants contributed to these figures, for it was during that century that the great exodus of people from Germany and Ireland took place. More than 100,000 Germans came to America before the Revolution in order to escape religious oppression, the inequities of feudalism, and the ravages of wars. Their neat homes and efficient farms dotted the landscapes of the Middle and Southern Colonies, particularly the frontier of Pennsylvania, where a vast majority chose to settle.

The Scotch-Irish, whose migration was even larger than that of the Germans, came to America to escape English taxes (collected to support the Church of England) and unfair trade laws. Their patterns of settlement in the New World were much like that of the Germans, with Pennsylvania receiving the greatest concentration. Highly individualistic, many moved out on the cutting edge of the frontier, where they fought Indians and white speculators for what they considered to be natural rights to "God's land." They are numbered among our most durable pioneers. Thus many nationality groups made up the population of colonial America: French, Irish, German, Swiss, Scotch, English (about 80 percent at the time of the Revolution), and, of course, the Afro-American slave, who had the second largest representation (about 20 percent).

SOCIAL CLASSES

The movement of peoples to America has been described as a middle- and lower-class migration, for they came seeking economic and religious freedom, the hope of which had greatly diminished in Europe. It was from these two groups that new class divisions arose in the colonial world; and in a few colonies, like Virginia and New York, some of the people took on the air of a new nobility. Upper society was made up, by and large, of the wealthy merchant class of New England and the Middle Colonies and the landed gentry of the South. New York led the Middle Colonies with her large group of manorial aristocrats handed down from the Dutch, while the plantation colonies in the South maintained a pronounced class of landed aristocrats with the English law of primogeniture. This law permitted the eldest son to claim most of his father's plantation in order to keep the estate intact. Next in line on the class ladder came the small farmers, the skilled artisans, and the shopkeepers, all of whom were well represented in the Middle Colonies, while a smaller number could be found on the frontier regions of the Southern Colonies. This class naturally made up the bulk of the population. Near the bottom of the class scale were the laborers, while the indentured servants and Negro slaves completed the bottom rungs.

Selected Bibliography

Andrews, Charles M. *Colonial Folkways.* New Haven, Conn.: Yale University Press, 1919.

Bailyn, Bernard. *Education in the Forming of American Society.* New York: Random House, 1960.

————. *The New England Merchants in the Seventeenth Century.* Cambridge, Mass.: Harvard University Press, 1955.

Boorstin, Daniel. *Americans: The Colonial Experience.* New York: Random House, Inc., 1958.

Bridenbaugh, Carl. *Cities in Revolt: Urban Life in America, 1743–1776.* New York: Alfred A. Knopf, 1955.

————. *Myths and Realities: Societies of the Colonial South.* New York: Atheneum Publishers, 1963.

Bruce, Philip A. *Social Life in Old Virginia.* New York: G. P. Putnam's Sons, 1965.

Bruchey, Stuart W. *Roots of American Economic Growth, 1607–1861.* New York: Harper & Row, Publishers, 1965.

Crane, Verner W. *Benjamin Franklin and a Rising People.* Boston: Little, Brown and Company, 1955.

Duffy, John. *Epidemics in Colonial America.* Baton Rouge, La.: Louisiana State University Press, 1953.

Ford, Henry J. *The Scotch-Irish in America.* New York: Arno Press, 1966.

Fox, Sanford J. *Science and Justice: The Massachusetts Witchcraft Trials.* Baltimore, Md.: Johns Hopkins Press, 1968.

Franklin, John Hope. *From Slavery to Freedom: A History of American Negroes.* New York: Alfred A. Knopf, 1956.

Gallman, Robert E. *Developing the American Colonies, 1607–1783.* Glenview, Ill.: Scott, Foresman and Company, 1964.

Hindle, Brook. *The Pursuit of Science in Revolutionary America, 1735–1789.* Chapel Hill, N.C.: University of North Carolina Press, 1956.

Kammen, Michael G., ed. *Politics and Society in Colonial America: Democracy or Deference?* New York: Holt, Rinehart and Winston, Inc., 1967.

Labaree, Leonard W. *Conservatism in Early American History.* Ithaca, N.Y.: Cornell University Press, 1959.

————. *Royal Government in America: A Study of the British Colonial System before 1783.* New York: Frederick Ungar Publishing Co., Inc., 1958.

Levy, Leonard W. *Legacy of Suppression: Freedom of Speech and Press in Early America.* Cambridge, Mass.: Belknap

Press of Harvard University Press, 1960.

Middlekauff, Robert. *Ancients and Axioms.* New Haven, Conn.: Yale University Press, 1963.

Miller, Perry. *Errand in the Wilderness.* Cambridge, Mass.: Harvard University Press, 1956.

———. *Jonathan Edwards.* New York: Dell Publishing Co., Inc., 1967.

———. *New England Mind: From Colony to Province.* Cambridge, Mass.: Harvard University Press, 1953.

———. *Orthodoxy in Massachusetts, 1630–1650.* Cambridge, Mass.: Harvard University Press, 1933.

Monroe, Paul. *Cyclopedia of Education.* 5 vols. Detroit, Mich.: Gale Research Company, 1969.

Morgan, Edmund S. *The Puritan Dilemma: The Story of John Winthrop.* Boston: Little, Brown and Company, 1958.

Morison, Samuel E. *Intellectual Life of Colonial New England.* New York: New York University Press, 1956.

———. *Three Centuries of Harvard, 1636–1936.* Cambridge, Mass.: Harvard University Press, 1946.

Mott, Frank L. *American Journalism: A History, 1690–1960.* New York: Crowell Collier and Macmillan, Inc., 1962.

Nettels, Curtis P. *The Money Supply of the American Colonies before 1720.* New York: Augustus M. Kelley, Publishers, 1934.

Parrington, Vernon L. *Main Currents in American Thought: Colonial Mind, 1620–1800.* New York: Harcourt Brace Jovanovich, Inc., 1927.

Quarles, Benjamin. *The Negro in the Making of America.* New York: Crowell Collier and Macmillan, Inc., 1964.

Savelle, Max. *Seeds of Liberty: The Genesis of the American Mind.* Seattle, Wash.: University of Washington Press, 1965.

Shryock, Richard Harrison. *Medicine and Society in America, 1660–1860.* New York: New York University Press, 1960.

Smith, Abbot E. *Colonist in Bondage: White Servitude and Convict Labor in America, 1607–1776.* Gloucester, Mass.: Peter Smith, 1947.

Winslow, Ola. *Meetinghouse Hill, 1630–1783.* New York: Crowell Collier and Macmillan, Inc., 1952.

Wish, Harvey. *Society and Thought in Early America.* New York: David McKay Co., Inc., 1956.

Wittke, Carl. *We Who Built America: The Saga of the Immigrant.* Englewood Cliffs, N.J.: Prentice-Hall, 1939.

Wright, Conrad. *The Beginning of Unitarianism in America.* Boston: The Beacon Press, 1955.

Wright, Louis B. *Culture on the Moving Frontier.* Bloomington, Ind.: Indiana University Press, 1955.

———. *Dream of Prosperity in Colonial America.* New York: New York University Press, 1965.

The Puritans: In Search of Identity

Ever since John Winthrop landed his colony-bound Puritans at Massachusetts Bay in 1630, their nature and influence have been the subject of considerable debate. They were accused of being intolerant by such contemporaries as Thomas Morton and Roger Williams; but in the nineteenth century historians like John G. Palfrey and George E. Ellis defended them as the fathers of our democracy. Other nineteenth-century historians, however, such as Brooks and Charles Francis Adams, saw the Puritans as a tyrannical theocracy, against which the people struggled until they finally overturned it. During the first two decades of the twentieth century, men like James Truslow Adams and Vernon L. Parrington continued the criticism of the earlier Adamses with only minor modifications, while the new defenders grouped themselves around such names as Charles A. Beard, Samuel Eliot Morison, and Perry Miller. These new sympathizers not only upheld the earlier views of Palfrey, but discovered new contributions of the Puritans in literature, science, art, and the spiritual viability of the faith.

The following selected readings will serve to illustrate that the debate goes on and that it embraces other fields of study. As the student reads the essays, the following *general* questions are offered for his consideration; the pursuit of the answers to these questions will demand that the student read several of the essays in the Select Bibliography at the end of each

group of essays in this text. The *basic* questions, on the other hand, are designed for suggested directed study of the essays provided in this unit. Both groups of questions should be viewed only as stepping-stones to further inquiry.

General Questions for Reflection and Discussion

1. What human limitations hide the Puritans and their environment?
2. In what ways were wealth, religion, and political power related in the Massachusetts Bay colony?
3. To what extent were the Puritans faced with dilemmas in their way of life?
4. How does covenant theology explain the Puritan way of life?
5. How did the Puritan belief that authority was handed down from God lead to problems?
6. To what extent was Puritan intolerance typical or atypical of colonial America?
7. How have the Puritans influenced contemporary America? To what extent has this influence been favorable or unfavorable?

Basic Questions for Reflection and Discussion

1. Compare Miller and Wertenbaker in the treatment of the Puritan exodus from England. Why did the Puritans leave?

2. What "myths" about the Puritans does Miller attempt to exploit?

3. What did the Puritans find in the Quaker doctrines that was considered so blasphemous?

4. According to Miller, in what ways were the Puritans Calvinists?

5. How do Miller· and Wertenbaker view Puritan democracy?

6. According to Wertenbaker, how were the Puritans planting seeds of self-destruction?

7. According to Weber, what was the Puritans' version of the ideal man?

8. Why did some Germans view American Puritans as hypocrites?

9. According to Weber, how does Protestantism fit into capitalist ideology?

10. Assuming that there is some substance to what Weber says, to what extent is man today bound to the capitalist system of which he speaks?

11. According to Walzer, why was work considered a virtue by Puritans?

12. How does Walzer's Puritan differ from Weber's?

13. What does Walzer mean when he says that Weber's argument is "founded upon anachronism" and is therefore weak?

14. Compare the various ways in which the authors have framed their theses and have defended them with evidence. To what extent have they achieved coherence —in other words, do their data hold together to prove their points?

Thomas Jefferson Wertenbaker

The Decline and Fall of the Puritan Theocracy

Although the English government in permitting the settlement of New England was actuated by economic considerations, a large proportion of the settlers themselves journeyed into the wilderness chiefly for religion's sake. Not only did they wish to escape persecution in England, but they were determined to establish in America a retreat for all of like faith with themselves, a bulwark against the forces of Antichrist. "All other churches of Europe have been brought under desolations," they said, "and it may be feared that the like judgements are coming upon us; and who knows but God hath provided this place to be a refuge for many, whom he means to save out of the General Destruction." They hoped to better their condition in a new and fertile country, of course, for the decline of industry and the lack of employment made conditions difficult in England. "The whole earth is the Lord's garden, . . . why then should we stand starving here for places of habitation, and in the meantime suffer whole countries . . . to lye waste without any improvement?"

But their minds were fired chiefly with the hope of establishing a Bible commonwealth, sealed against error from without and protected from schism from within. "What can be a better or nobler work, and

From *The First Americans* by Thomas Jefferson Wertenbaker, pp. 87–109. Copyright 1927 by The Macmillan Company, renewed 1955 by Thomas Jefferson Wertenbaker.

more worth of a Christian," they said, "than to erect and support a reformed particular Church in its infancy. . . ." It is incorrect to infer that most of the colonists were not deeply religious merely because it is found that church members were in the minority. Many righteous Puritans were unable to state an overwhelming religious experience which would qualify them for membership, yet they were sympathetic with the church's purpose.

In so large a movement some were unquestionably impelled by one motive, some by another. Of the thousands of men and women who landed on the New England shores in the years from 1629 to 1640, there were many who felt little sympathy with the erection there of a powerful theocracy, some who had come on the representations of the shipping agents as to the opportunities to win a competence in America. But they were forced to conform to the wishes of the leaders, men of the type of John Winthrop, John Cotton, John Norton and John Wilson. This latter group enjoyed a prestige which was born not only of superior education but of an extraordinary talent for leadership. Schooled in the bitter controversies of the day, hardened in the fires of adversity, they were well fitted to play the role of Moses in the removal of this modern host to the promised land. "Though the reformed church, thus fled into the wilderness, enjoyed not the miraculous pillar," Cotton Mather tells us, "we enjoyed many a person, in whom the good spirit of God gave a conduct unto us, and mercifully dispensed those directing, defending, refreshing influences, which were as necessary for us, as any that the celebrated pillar of cloud and fire could have afforded."

These men were intent on establishing a theocracy in which their tenets and their form of worship should be upheld by the hand of the law. They were not Separatists but Church of England men, and what they designed was an established church in New England. At the very outset they made it clear that "they did not separate from the Church of England, nor from the ordinances of God there, but only from the corruptions and disorders of that Church; that they came away from the Common-Prayer and Ceremonies." On another occasion they called the Anglican church "their dear mother, desiring their friends therein to recommend them unto the mercies of God in their constant prayers, as a Church now springing out of their own bowels, nor did they think that it was their mother who turned them out of doors, but some of their angry brethren, abusing the name of their mother."

The migrating preachers had fought in the old country, not only for the right to worship as they chose in their individual churches but also for control of the Anglican establishment. Had they succeeded, they would have forced the church into complete conformity with their views, driving out those who persisted in opposing them. Failing in their efforts, they removed to America where there could be no opposition to their plans. Having set up their reformed church, having transplanted what they believed to be the true Anglican church to their new homes, they intended to protect it from innovation by the authority of civil law. "We came hither because we would have our posterity settled under the pure and full dispensations of the gospel; defended by rulers that should be of ourselves." These words, delivered at one of the notable election sermons, give the keynote of the movement. Their church they intended to buttress by a state especially designed for its protection.

Obviously toleration had no part in such a plan. It is a singular perversion of history which attributes ideals to the prime movers in this great migration that they themselves would have been the first to repudiate. The fact that the Puritans deserted their homes to settle in the wilderness in order to worship God as they chose led even Charles II to suppose that they had openly espoused the principles of toleration. That the same mistake should be so common today, when religious freedom has been widely accepted as a principle essential to the welfare of mankind, is perhaps natural, if not inevitable. "On no subject dealt with among us," says a son of New England in an address before the Massachusetts Historical Society, "in lectures, orations, sermons, poems, historical addresses, and even in our choice school literature, has there been such an amount of crude, sentimental, and wasteful rhetoric, or so much weak and vain pleading, as on this. . . . The root of the whole error, common alike to those who censure and those who defend those ancient Fathers, is the assumption that they came here mainly to seek, establish, and enjoy liberty of conscience."

The sermons and published writings of the founders of Massachusetts make it clear that they never entertained the thought of opening the doors of their new Zion to those who differed from them. So far from being champions of toleration, they opposed it bitterly. "'T is Satan's policy, to plead for an indefinite and boundless toleration," said Thomas Shepard. Urian Oakes denounced religious freedom as the "first born of all Abomination," while Increase Mather sternly rebuked the "hideous clamours for liberty of Conscience." John Norton denounced liberty of worship as liberty "to answer the dictates of the errors of Conscience in walking contrary to Rule. It is a liberty to blaspheme, a liberty to seduce others from the true God. A liberty to tell lies in the name of the Lord." The Puritan community thought that heretics should have only the liberty to leave. As Nathaniel Ward said, "All Familists, Antinomians, Anabaptists, and other Enthusiasts shall have free liberty to keepe away from us." We gain an insight into the depth of this feeling from the dismay of Edward Johnson when he found Massachusetts rent by the Anne Hutchinson heresy. He had fled to what he thought would be a safe retreat from heresy, where his soul could rest in peace free from the dread of error. Now he found controversy raging within the very walls of the new Zion, and he had to choose once more, at the peril of his soul, between truth and falsehood.

We fail to grasp the spirit of these men unless we realize that they considered themselves a chosen people, one to whom God had revealed himself and had led to the promised land far from the sins and corruptions of the Old World. "The ministers and Christians, by whom New England was first planted, were a chosen company of man," says Cotton Mather, "picked out of, perhaps, all the counties of England, and this by no human contrivance, but by a strange work of God upon the spirits of men that were, no ways, acquainted with one another, inspiring them as one man, to secede into a wilderness, they knew not where." William Stoughton expressed the same idea in his famous statement that "God hath sifted a nation, that he might send choice grain into this wilderness." God's concern for his settlement had been lovingly manifested by striking the Indians with a plague a few years before the migration, thus making the waste places safe for his children. Such an attitude does not conduce to toleration. Convinced that he had been selected by God to receive and expound the truth, the Puritan minister could but look upon those who opposed him as minions of Satan. The red men, as has been intimated, were probably of these infernal hosts, and must be ignored or ruthlessly brushed aside; differences in theology as well as in economic circumstances brought about a contrast between the Indian relations of the Puritan and those of the northern Frenchmen on the one hand and the southern Spaniards on the other. John Eliot and the Mayhews, in proportion to their missionary zeal, were exceptions in the priesthood of New England. But to most of the leaders the Indians seemed less dangerous than heretics to their own race and neighborhood.

The Massachusetts leaders were intent upon establishing, not a government representative of the wishes of the people but an oligarchy in which the clergy would have the deciding voice. The civil authorities of the new state were to serve as handmaidens to the church, and the ministers, although themselves not holding public office, were to be the final depository of power in the colony. This power they exercised chiefly through their control of the franchise. No man was to vote who was not a member of the church, and no man could be a member of the church until he had been admitted by the clergy. The clergy, in turn, took care to admit none who were in opposition to the established order. "In as much as very much of an Athenian democracy was in the mould of the government by the royal charter," says Cotton Mather, "Mr. Cotton effectually recommended it unto them, that none should be electors, nor elected therein, except as were visible subjects of our Lord Jesus Christ, personally confederated in our churches. In these, and many other ways, he propounded unto them an endeavour after aristocracy, as near as might be, to that which was the glory of Israel, the peculiar people."

As for democracy, the New England fathers dreaded it as a form of government inconsistent with the rule of the best and most pious men. "Democracy I do not conceive that God did ever ordain as a fit government for either church or commonwealth," says John Cotton. "If the people be governors, who shall be governed? As for monarchy and aristocracy, they are both clearly approved and directed in the Scriptures. . . .

He setteth up theocracy . . . as the best form of government in the commonwealth as in the church." Winthrop agreed heartily, averring that democracy had no warrant in Scripture and that "among nations it has always been accounted the meanest and worst of all forms of government."

Thus the earnest men who led the Puritan exodus planned their new Bible commonwealth and thus they built it. Composed in large measure of persons of like faith, protected from invasion by its very isolation, guided by the clergy and by magistrates in close sympathy with them, this wilderness Zion was the culmination of their fondest hopes. Yet from the first the theocracy found itself faced by a multitude of difficulties, which threatened its supremacy and slowly undermined its strength.

The first of these was that love for self-government so universal among Englishmen. All the reverence, all the love, all the admiration which the people had for their leaders, did not reconcile them to the loss of their liberty. In the early days of the colony the outstanding leader was John Cotton. This remarkable man has been spoken of as "the unmitred pope of a pope-hating people." What he advised from the pulpit was usually enacted into law. The chronicler of Christ's wonders in America says that Cotton was the great director, "the father and glory of Boston." Yet even the influence of John Cotton could not prevent a strong faction of the people from demanding that in their new home they should not be deprived of their rights and liberties. According to the charter all important matters of government were left to the discretion of the stockholders, or freemen, in the general court. Only twelve of these freemen had come to Massachusetts in 1630, and all had been made magistrates. Since they were

in full sympathy with the leading clergymen, and supported them in all their policies for both church and state, the arrangement constituted the government by the best which Winthrop and Cotton so earnestly advocated. Democratic it was not. When the first general court convened in October, 1630, the magistrates had shrunk in number to eight, and this small group were confronted with a demand from one hundred and nine of their fellow settlers to be admitted as freemen. These men . . . could see in their demand for citizenship nothing inconsistent with the dictates of their religion.

The magistrates postponed action on this petition until the spring. In the meanwhile they decreed that the assistants and not the freemen should make laws and elect the governor, and that the assistants should hold office during good behavior. This left the freemen only the right to select new assistants when vacancies occurred. The applicants agreed to this arrangement although it left them only the husks of real citizenship, and for some months more the little body of magistrates continued to tax and legislate. In 1632, however, when the assistants voted a levy for fortifications, the town of Watertown entered a vigorous protest. Under the leadership of their minister the people passed a resolution "that it was not safe to pay moneys after that sort, for fear of bringing themselves and posterity into bondage." Governor Winthrop, greatly disturbed at this show of insubordination, summoned the Watertown men before him, and after they had made their submission, pardoned them. But the other towns were not less concerned at the limitations set upon their liberty. When the general court met in May, the body of the freemen voted that the governor and his assistants must be elected each year, and that every town should elect two delegates to act with them in levying taxes.

Although this was a long step toward representative government, it still left the deputies without a hand in making laws.

In 1634 they assumed this right also. In May two men from each of the eight towns met in Boston and demanded to view the charter of the colony. Winthrop dared not refuse, and they at once called his attention to the fact that the charter gave the making of laws to the whole body of freemen. When the general court met a few days later, three deputies appeared from each town, ready to demand their rightful share in the government. Against this action the magistrates and leading ministers protested. The very foundations of the newly established theocracy seemed to be crumbling. John Cotton threw the full weight of his influence in favor of upholding the established order, pleading that the Bible clearly showed that the magistrates ought to hold office for life. But the freemen, so far from yielding, refused to reelect Winthrop governor, and actually imposed fines upon some of the magistrates for abuse of power. They then decreed that henceforth the general court, consisting of the governor, the assistants and deputies elected by the towns, alone should have the right to tax, make laws and admit freemen.

Thus, four years after the Massachusetts Bay charter was brought to America, the government was changed from a narrow oligarchy to what appeared to be a little republic. Yet, even after the establishment of representative government, very little real liberalism existed, and the theocracy still ruled almost supreme. The freemen were only a small part of the population and the law forbidding the admission of nonchurch-members was rigidly enforced. Moreover, the prestige of the few leading laymen of the colony was such that they were selected as magistrates over and over again. John Cotton insisted "that a magistrate ought not to be turned into the condition of a private man, without just cause, and be publicly convict, no more than the magistrate may not turn a private man out of his freehold, etc., without like public trial." The idea became fixed that every official should be reelected unless convicted of misconduct.

Consequently the governor and his assistants continued to represent only the narrowest aristocratic clique in the colony, and the deputies a comparatively small body of voters, picked by the ministers from church members.

The theocratic form of government not only created internal dissension, but it was a leading cause in weakening Massachusetts by the withdrawal of several congregations to the Connecticut Valley. The liberal views of Thomas Hooker were so greatly at variance with those of Winthrop and Cotton that he could not rest at ease in his Newtown settlement. "There is a great disunion of judgement in matters of religion amongst good ministers and people which caused Mr. Hooker to remove," wrote the Reverend R. Stansby to John Wilson, "and that you are so strict in the admission of members to your church, that more than halfe are out of your church in all your congregations, and that Mr. Hooker before he went away preached against that." Winthrop expostulated with Hooker about the danger of "referring matters of counsel or judicature to the body of the people," arguing that "the best part is always the least, and of that part the wiser part is always the lesser." Hooker replied that to leave all power in the hands of rulers who were not responsible to the people, was to invite tyranny. I "must plainly profess if it was in my liberty, I should choose neither to live nor leave my posterity under such a government. . . . A general councel chosen by all, I conceive under favour most suitable to rule and most safe for the relief of the people."

Although those who favored representative government had won a certain measure of success, schismatics and heretics at first could do nothing. The magistrates and ministers were adamant against attempts to break down the unity of their "City of God on earth." Yet both schism and heresy were prompt in showing themselves. In 1631 the scholarly and liberal Roger Williams arrived, and accepted a pastorate at Salem. An avowed

Separatist, he at once attacked the established order for not renouncing fellowship with the Church of England. Besides inveighing against legal oaths and against the validity of titles to land granted by the general court, he also denounced the union of church and state, declaring from the pulpit that the magistrates had no right to punish Sabbath breaking or other violations of the first four commandments.

This open attack upon the theocracy could not be passed over. The ministers rendered their judgment "that he who should obstinately maintain such opinions, whereby a church might run into heresy, apostasy, or tyranny, and yet the civil magistrate could not intermeddle," was too dangerous to be tolerated. Williams was cited to appear before the authorities, and after a trial was sentenced to banishment. The decree was suspended until spring, on condition that he refrain from attempting to spread his opinions. This he was unable to do, and when the magistrates decided to keep him on shipboard pending the next sailing for England, he escaped through the frozen forests to the Narragansett Bay region. The theocracy had won an easy victory, but one which was costly because achieved by appealing to the civil authorities. Schism for the moment had been blocked, but physical force cannot prevent the growth of divergent opinions, and before long heresy reappeared in a far more dangerous form.

Anne Hutchinson, who had been a parishioner of John Cotton in England, is described by Winthrop as a woman of "ready wit and bold spirit." Several years after her arrival in Boston she began the dangerous practice of holding meetings in her house to rehearse and discuss the sermon of the previous Sunday. From this she passed to comparing the teachings of the clergymen, and then to the evolution of a doctrine of her own. The ministers were expounding a covenant of works, she maintained, whereas the Bible showed that salvation was based on a covenant of

grace. Although Winthrop wrote that "no man could tell (except some few who knew the bottom of the matter) where any difference was," he and the other leaders of the theocracy understood clearly enough that her ideas were inconsistent with the established order. The covenant of grace made religion a matter of direct communication between man and his Maker, while the covenant of works required only obedience to a prescribed code of which the minister was the official interpreter. Should the former doctrine secure wide acceptance, not only would unity be lost, but a stunning blow would be struck at the theocracy.

For a time Boston supported Mrs. Hutchinson with something like unanimity. Even the great John Cotton was inclined to embrace her doctrines. The religion of love which she preached was more in keeping with his naturally kindly nature than the established tenets of law and judgment. But he drew back in time. John Wheelwright, Mrs. Hutchinson's brother-in-law, and young Harry Vane bore the brunt of the battle. The former was summoned before the general court, and although he refused to answer questions because the proceedings were held in secret, was found guilty of sedition and contempt. To weaken the influence of Boston, a resolution was passed transferring the next court of elections to Newtown. When the vote was taken, the orthodox party succeeded in restoring Winthrop to the governorship. Boston, however, sent as its deputies Vane, Coddington and Hoffe, all favorable to Mrs. Hutchinson. The court at first refused to seat them but when Boston held a new election and returned them again, "the Court not finding how they might reject them, they were admitted." In the following summer the clergy met in synod and condemned as erroneous and blasphemous the Hutchinson heresies. At the November court Wheelwright was disfranchised and banished, while other members of the dissenting faction were severely punished. Mrs. Hutchinson was "banished from out this jurisdiction as being a woman not fit for our society."

In this way was the church purged of heresy, and the theocracy saved from what to its leaders seemed the most deadly peril. It is folly to condemn these men for bigotry and intolerance. They had given up their homes and had fled into the wilderness for the purpose of establishing a society free from error. How natural, then, that they should have combated what they considered error, when to their horror they found that it had followed them across the Atlantic. "Two so opposite parties could not contain in the same body without hazard of ruin to the whole," said Winthrop. Conformity was gained, but only at the cost of a bitter struggle which left scars that were slow to heal. Theocracy was so weakened that another great heresy might shatter it.

Though for some time no such heresy arose from within, the ministers soon found themselves confronted with a peril from without. In 1656 Quaker missionaries invaded New England with the avowed purpose of making converts. The democratic leanings of the Quakers, their refusal to accord especial respect to magistrates, their denial of the need of an established clergy, combined to make them obnoxious to the Puritan leaders. When Mary Fisher and Ann Austin arrived in Boston, the colony was stirred to its foundations. "Why was it that the coming of two women so shook ye, as if a formidable army had invaded your borders?" George Bishop inquired of the magistrates. But the magistrates would undoubtedly have been less dismayed at the invasion of an armed host. Powder and shot could only imperil men's lives; the Quakers were assaulting their souls. We gain an insight into the state of mind of these stern Puritans, not so much from their action in arresting these women, denouncing their doctrines and burning their books, as from the care they took

to board up the windows of the cell so that the prisoners could not preach to the people. After five weeks of imprisonment they were shipped back to Barbados whence they had come.[1]

A few days later eight more Quakers arrived from London. Governor Endicott immediately put them in prison and at the first opportunity sent them out of the country. In October the general court fixed the fine of any master who should bring in a Quaker at 100 pounds of sterling, and declared that the Quaker himself should be severely whipped. By a later enactment the offender's tongue was to be bored with a hot iron, his ears cut off, he was to be banished, and if he returned, to be executed. New Haven, Plymouth and Connecticut also passed severe laws against the Quakers, but the death penalty was prescribed by Massachusetts alone. Rhode Island, under the leadership of Roger Williams, would have none of this persecution. A band of Quakers who landed at Newport were received with kindness. But the other colonies, fearing that the missionaries would use Rhode Island as a base of operations, entered a vigorous protest. Pointing out that the "contagion" could easily spread across the borders, they threatened to take strong action "to prevent the aforesaid mischief."

The reply of Williams might well have given pause to the Massachusetts magistrates and ministers. We "finde that in those places where these people, aforesaid, in this colony, are most of all suffered to declare themselves freely, and are opposed by arguments in discourse, there they least of all desire to come . . . surely we find that they delight to be persecuted by civil powers, and where they are soe, they are like to gain more adherents by the conseyte of their patient sufferings." The Rhode Island assembly

---

[1] It must be remembered, however, that the Quakers were rather trying, judged by any standard.

answered in similar vein, reiterating their intention to uphold freedom of conscience which they prized as their greatest happiness.

The Massachusetts magistrates continued their pitiless warfare against the invaders. In September, 1659, Mary Dyer, William Robinson and Marmaduke Stevenson, who had come to Boston courting martyrdom, were all banished. Mrs. Dyer reached Rhode Island, whence she immediately returned, but the two men went only to Salem before facing about. All were sentenced to death. Robinson and Stevenson were hanged, but Mrs. Dyer, after her hands and legs had been bound, her face covered and the rope adjusted about her neck, received word that she had been reprieved. Once more she was sent to Rhode Island, but the efforts of her family to keep her there failed. In the spring she came back to Boston where she too was executed. In November, 1660, another Quaker, William Leddra, suffered the same fate.

Though the theocracy went to those extremes, the battle was going against them. Endicott and Norton had good reason to realize that Roger Williams had been more farseeing than they, for the sufferings of the Quakers won for them the sympathy of thousands who had only contempt for their doctrines. A few days before the execution of Leddra, Wenlock Christison, another Quaker, strode into the courtroom, and looking into the face of Endicott, said to him, "I came here to warn you that you should shed no more innocent blood, for the blood that you have shed already cries to the Lord for vengeance to come upon you." He was seized and brought to trial. The magistrates debated long as to what should be done, for public sentiment was turning rapidly against them; but for Endicott there was no hesitancy. Pounding the table he shouted out, "You that will not consent, record it. I thank God I am not afraid to give judgement." Christison was condemned to death, but the sentence was never carried out. Partly from fear of interference from the crown, partly because of the evident opposition of the people, the persecution had to take a milder form. There were no more executions.

It was a severe defeat for the theocracy. The ideal of a Puritan commonwealth walled in against heresy had broken down. The suffering Quakers had proved that the New World did not offer so safe a refuge from the "poison of error" as the leaders of the exodus had hoped. Moreover it had been made apparent that there were limits beyond which the people of Massachusetts would not follow the magistrates and ministers. The sight of a suffering Quaker, stripped to the waist and tied to a cart's tail, his back clotted with blood from frequent whippings, trudging through snow and ice, could but cause revulsion in men's minds against the system which was responsible for it. The Puritan leader in the days of his exile and his sacrifices was an inspiring figure; the Puritan persecutor seemed in contrast unlovely indeed.

In addition, the conflict brought interference from England, and with it the threat of an early termination of the charter upon which the established order was based. Charles II, displeased at the executions, gave orders that the vein of innocent blood opened in his dominions should be closed. . . .

When they [Charles' advisers] became aware that Massachusetts had made itself almost independent of the crown, that power there had fallen into the hands of a narrow theological group, that the laws of England were disregarded, the oath of allegiance neglected, the Anglican worship forbidden, they at once took steps to reestablish the king's authority in the colony. . . .

With the advent of the second Stuart despotism the situation suddenly changed. The unprincipled but astute Charles II, having freed himself from the domination of Parliament by accepting a pension from Louis XIV, devoted the last years of his life to the task of ending liberty both in England and America. . . .

Had Charles confined his attack to the narrow theocratic group in Massachusetts, he would have found powerful support within the colony itself. But he was bent not only upon overthrowing the established order but upon substituting for it the despotic rule of the crown. The people were not to benefit by this transfer of power and even the forms of representative government which had persisted under the old regime were to be swept away in the new. Edmund Andros, who was made governor-general of all New England despite the guarantees of the Connecticut and Rhode Island charters, trampled ruthlessly upon the rights held most sacred by Englishmen. In conjunction with his council he made laws, gave judicial decisions and ordered the collection of taxes. The Massachusetts general court was abolished, and every freeholder was made uneasy by the threat to revoke existing land grants.

. . . The new charter, which was issued in 1691, instituted a royal government not unlike that of Virginia. There was to be a representative assembly, while the franchise was based, not on church membership, but on property holdings. The crown appointed the governor, who had the power to veto bills of the assembly, appoint judges and other officials, and put the laws into execution. Members of the council were nominated by the legislature and confirmed by the governor. Religious freedom for Protestants was guaranteed. Thus was established a new order distinctly more liberal than that under which Massachusetts had lived during the past six decades. The power of the clergy was not completely crushed; the social and political structure of the colony was not revolutionized. A full century and more was to pass before Massachusetts became in any real sense democratic. But the old buttressed Bible commonwealth, the Zion which had been the dream of Winthrop and Cotton and for which they had made such sacrifices, was gone forever.

Perry Miller

In Defense of the Massachusetts Puritans

Puritanism may perhaps best be described as that point of view, that philosophy of life, that code of values, which was carried to New England by the first settlers

From *The Puritans* by Perry Miller and Thomas H. Johnson (New York: American Book Company, 1938), pp. 1–3, 8–12, 14–19, 55–63.

in the early seventeenth century. Beginning thus, it has become one of the continuous factors in American life and American thought. Any inventory of the elements that have gone into the making of the "American mind" would have to commence with Puritanism. It is, indeed, only one among many: if we should attempt to enumerate these traditions, we should certainly have to mention such philosophies, such "isms," as the rational liberalism of Jeffersonian democracy, the Hamiltonian conception of conservatism and government, the Southern theory of racial aristocracy, the Transcendentalism of nineteenth-century New England, and what is generally spoken of as frontier individualism. Among these factors Puritanism has been perhaps the most conspicuous, the most sustained, and the most fecund. Its role in American thought has been almost the dominant one, for the descendants of Puritans have carried at least some habits of the Puritan mind into a variety of pursuits, have spread across the country, and in many fields of activity have played a leading part. The force of Puritanism, furthermore, has been accentuated because it was the first of these traditions to be fully articulated, and because it has inspired certain traits which have persisted long after the vanishing of the original creed. Without some understanding of Puritanism, it may safely be said, there is no understanding of America.

Yet important as Puritanism has undoubtedly been in shaping the nation, it is more easily described than defined. It figures frequently in controversy of the last decade, very seldom twice with exactly the same connotation. Particularly of recent years has it become a hazardous feat to run down its meaning. In the mood of revolt against the ideals of previous generations which has swept over our period, Puritanism has become a shining target for many sorts of marksmen. Confusion becomes worse confounded if we attempt to correlate modern usages with anything that can be proved pertinent to the original Puritans themselves. To seek no further, it was the habit of proponents for the repeal of the Eighteenth Amendment during the 1920s to dub Prohibitionists "Puritans," and cartoonists made the nation familiar with an image of the Puritan: a gaunt, lank-haired killjoy, wearing a black steeple hat and compounding for sins he was inclined to by damning those to which he had no mind. Yet any acquaintance with the Puritans of the seventeenth century will reveal at once, not only that they did not wear such hats, but also that they attired themselves in all the hues of the rainbow, and furthermore that in their daily life they imbibed what seem to us prodigious quantities of alcoholic beverages, with never the slightest inkling that they were doing anything sinful. True, they opposed drinking to excess, and ministers preached lengthy sermons condemning intoxication, but at such pious ceremonies as the ordination of new ministers the bill for rum, wine, and beer consumed by the congregation was often staggering. Increase Mather himself—who in popular imagination is apt to figure along with his son Cotton as the archembodiment of the Puritan—said in one of his sermons:

> Drink is in itself a good creature of God, and to be received with thankfulness, but the abuse of drink is from Satan; the wine is from God, but the Drunkard is from the Devil.[1]

Or again, the Puritan has acquired the reputation of having been blind to all aesthetic enjoyment and starved of beauty; yet the architecture of the Puritan age grows in the esteem of critics and the household objects of Puritan manufacture, pewter and furniture, achieve prohibitive prices by their appeal to discriminating collectors. Examples of such discrepancies between the modern usage of the word and the historical fact could be multiplied indefinitely.[2] . . .

Just as soon as we endeavor to free ourselves from prevailing conceptions or misconceptions, and to ascertain the historical facts about seventeenth-century New Englanders, we become aware that we face still another difficulty: not

[1] *Wo to Drunkards* (Cambridge, Mass., 1673), p. 4.
[2] Cf. Kenneth B. Murdock, "The Puritan Traditions in American Literature," *The Reinterpretation of American Literature* (New York: 1928), chap. V.

only must we extricate ourselves from interpretations that have been read into Puritanism by the twentieth century, but still more from those that have been attached to it by the eighteenth and nineteenth. The Puritan philosophy, brought to New England highly elaborated and codified, remained a fairly rigid orthodoxy during the seventeenth century. In the next age, however, it proved to be anything but static; by the middle of the eighteenth century there had proceeded from it two distinct schools of thought, almost unalterably opposed to each other. Certain elements were carried into the creeds and practices of the evangelical religious revivals, but others were perpetuated by the rationalists and the forerunners of Unitarianism. Consequently our conception of Puritanism is all too apt to be colored by subsequent happenings; we read ideas into the seventeenth century which belong to the eighteenth, and the real nature of Puritanism can hardly be discovered at all, because Puritanism itself became two distinct and contending things to two sorts of men. The most prevalent error arising from this fact has been the identification of Puritanism with evangelicalism in many accounts, though in histories written by Unitarian scholars the original doctrine has been almost as much distorted in the opposite direction.

. . . In their [the Puritans'] eyes, as in those of Anglicans, the most important issue in the Western world was the struggle between Catholicism and Protestantism. They were not unique or extreme in thinking that religion was the primary and all-engrossing business of man, or that all human thought and action should tend to the glory of God. John Donne, Dean of St. Paul's, preached in London, "all knowledge that begins not, and ends not with his glory, is but a giddy, but a vertiginous circle, but an elaborate and exquisite ignorance"; the content, though not the style, of the passage might just as well come from any Puritan preacher. Both the Anglican and the Puritan were

at one in conceiving of man as sinful, they both beheld him chained and enslaved by evil until liberated by the redeeming grace of Christ. They both believed that the visible universe was under God's direct and continuous guidance, and that though effects seemed to be produced by natural causes—what at that time were called "secondary causes"—the actual government of the minutest event, the rise of the sun, the fall of a stone, the beat of the heart, was under the direct and immediate supervision of God. This conception, a fundamental one in the Puritan view of the world, was no more limited to them than their habits of eating and drinking. . . .

In its major aspects the religious creed of Puritanism was neither peculiar to the Puritans nor different from that of the Anglicans. Both were essentially Protestant; both asserted that men were saved by their faith, not by their deeds. The two sides could agree on the general statement that Christians are bound to believe nothing but what the Gospel teaches, that all traditions of men "contrary to the Word of God" are to be renounced and abhorred. They both believed that the marks of a true church were profession of the creed, use of Christ's sacraments, preaching of the word—Anglican sermons being as long and often as dull as the Puritan—and the union of men in profession and practice under regularly constituted pastors. The Puritans always said that they could subscribe the doctrinal articles of the Church of England; even at the height of the controversy, even after they had left England rather than put up with what they considered its abominations, they always took care to insist that the Church of England was a "true" church, not Anti-Christ as was the Church of Rome, that it contained many saints, and that men might find salvation within it. Throughout the seventeenth century they read Anglican authors, quoted them in their sermons, and even reprinted some of them in Boston.

The vast substratum of agreement

which actually underlay the disagreement between Puritans and Anglicans is explained by the fact that they were both the heirs of the Middle Ages. They still believed that all knowledge was one, that life was unified, that science, economics, political theory, aesthetic standards, rhetoric and art, all were organized in a hierarchical scale of values that tended upward to the end-all and be-all of creation, the glory of God. They both insisted that all human activity be regulated by that purpose. Consequently, even while fighting bitterly against each other, the Puritans and Anglicans stood shoulder to shoulder against what they called "enthusiasm." The leaders of the Puritan movement were trained at the universities, they were men of learning and scholars; no less than the Anglicans did they demand that religion be interpreted by study and logical exposition; they were both resolute against all pretences to immediate revelation, against all ignorant men who claimed to receive personal instructions from God. They agreed on the essential Christian contention that though God may govern the world, He is not the world itself, and that though He instills His grace into men, He does not deify them or unite them to Himself in one personality. He converses with men only through His revealed word, the Bible. His will is to be studied in the operation of His providence as exhibited in the workings of the natural world, but He delivers no new commands or special revelations to the inward consciousness of men. The larger unanimity of the Puritans and the Anglicans reveals itself whenever either of them was called upon to confront enthusiasm. The selections given in this volume include Governor John Winthrop's account of the so-called Antinomian affair, the crisis produced in the little colony by the teachings of Mistress Anne Hutchinson in 1636 and 1637. Beneath the theological jargon in which the opinions of this lady appear we can see the substance of her contention, which was that she was in direct communi-

cation with the Godhead, and that she therefore was prepared to follow the promptings of the voice within against all the precepts of the Bible, the churches, reason, or the government of Massachusetts Bay. Winthrop relates how the magistrates and the ministers defended the community against this perversion of the doctrine of regeneration, but the tenor of his condemnation would have been duplicated practically word for word had Anne Hutchinson broached her theories in an Anglican community. The Anglicans fell in completely with the Puritans when both of them were confronted in the 1650s by the Quakers. All New England leaders saw in the Quaker doctrine of an inner light, accessible to all men and giving a perfect communication from God to their inmost spirits, just another form of Anne Hutchinson's blasphemy. John Norton declared that the "light of nature" itself taught us that "madmen acting according to their frantick passions are to be restrained with chaines, when they can not be restrained otherwise." About the same time George Hickes, Dean of Worcester, was advocating that Quakers be treated likewise in England, and he ended a sermon upon them by calling them "Imposters, or enthusiasts, and Blasphemers of the Holy Ghost." Enthusiasts, whether Antinomian or Quaker, were proposing doctrines that threatened the unity of life by subduing the reason and the intellect to the passions and the emotions. Whatever their differences, Puritans and Anglicans were struggling to maintain a complete harmony of reason and faith, science and religion, earthly dominion and the government of God. When we immerse ourselves in the actual struggle, the difference between the Puritan and the Anglican may seem to us immense; but when we take the vantage point of subsequent history, and survey religious thought as a whole over the last three centuries, the two come very close together on essentials. Against all forms of chaotic emotionalism, against all oversimplifications of theology, learning, philosophy, and science, against all materialism, positivism or mechanism, both were endeavoring to uphold a symmetrical union of heart and head without impairment of either. By the beginning or middle of the next century their successors, both in England and America, found themselves no longer capable of sustaining this unity, and it has yet to be reachieved today, if achieved again it ever can be. The greatness of the Puritans is not so much that they conquered a wilderness, or that they carried a religion into it, but that they carried a religion which, narrow and starved though it may have been in some respects, deficient in sensuous richness or brilliant color, was nevertheless indissolubly bound up with an ideal of culture and learning. In contrast to all other pioneers, they made no concessions to the forest, but in the midst of frontier conditions, in the very throes of clearing the land and erecting shelters, they maintained schools and a college, a standard of scholarship and of competent writing, a class of men devoted entirely to the life of the mind and of the soul. . . .

When we say that the majority of the people in the early seventeenth century still acceded to the dictation of the learned in religion and the superior in society, we must also remark that the Puritan leaders were in grave danger of arousing a revolt against themselves by their very own doctrines. Puritans were attacking the sacerdotal and institutional bias which had survived in the Church of England; they were maintaining a theology that brought every man to a direct experience of the spirit and removed intermediaries between himself and the deity. Yet the authority of the infallible church and the power of the bishops had for centuries served to keep the people docile. Consequently when the Puritan leaders endeavored to remove the bishops and to deny that the Church should stand between God and man, they ran the hazard of starting something among the peo-

ple that might get out of hand. Just as the Puritan doctrine that men were saved by the infusion of God's grace could lead to the Antinomianism of Mrs. Hutchinson, and often did warrant the simple in concluding that if they had God's grace in them they needed to pay no heed to what a minister told them, so the Puritan contention that regenerate men were illuminated with divine truth might lead to the belief that true religion did not need the assistance of learning, books, arguments, logical demonstrations, or classical languages. There was always a possibility that Puritanism would raise up a fanatical anti-intellectualism, and against such a threat the Puritan ministers constantly braced themselves. It was no accident that the followers of Mrs. Hutchinson, who believed that men could receive all the necessary instructions from within, also attacked learning and education, and came near to wrecking not only the colony but the college as well. . . . The true Puritans were forced to resort to repressive measures to save Puritanism itself. Oliver Cromwell was the most liberal of seventeenth-century Puritan leaders; it is his eternal glory that he did not confront with the sword all the zealots who ran riot over the land, but strove to work out a scheme of toleration for as many of them as would behave with civil decency. But even Cromwell had to draw the line somewhere, and he drew it when the upsurge of popular religious frenzies turned against the universities and the learned ministry. His assumption of the dictatorship in 1653, unlike later seizures of arbitrary power, was prompted in great part by his determination to protect a sober and instructed clergy and the universities from an assault by the lunatic fringe in his own party. Cromwell's New England brethren thoroughly sympathized with his efforts, but they thought he had invited the trouble by allowing ignorant men to preach at all; they looked upon his policy of toleration as the sole stain upon the otherwise flawless record of the preeminent warrior saint of the age. They were determined to run no such risks in their communities. They would have the rabble entirely submissive to the intellectual aristocracy, even though many or all of the mass were supposedly saints of God.

. . . In America the character of the people underwent a change; they moved further into the frontier, they became more absorbed in business and profits than in religion and salvation, their memories of English social stratification grew dim. A preacher before the General Court in 1705 bewailed the effects of the frontier in terms that have been echoed by "Easterners" for two hundred years and more; men were no longer living together, he said, in compact communities, under the tutelage of educated clergymen and under the discipline of an ordered society, but were taking themselves into remote corners "for worldly conveniences." "By that means [they] have seemed to bid defiance, not only to Religion, but to Civility itself: and such places thereby have become Nurseries of Ignorance, Prophaneness and Atheism." In America the frontier conspired with the popular disposition to lessen the prestige of the cultured classes and to enhance the social power of those who wanted their religion in a more simple, downright and "democratic" form, who cared nothing for the refinements and subtleties of historic theology. Not until the decade of the Great Awakening did the popular tendency receive distinct articulation through leaders who openly renounced the older conception, but for half a century or more before 1740 its obstinate persistence can be traced in the condemnations of the ministers.

. . . By the beginning of the eighteenth century the task of buttressing the classified society, maintaining the rule of the well-trained and the culturally superior both in church and society seems to have become the predominant concern of the clergy. Sermon after sermon reveals that in their eyes the cause of learning and the cause of a hierarchical, differentiated social order were one and the same. For example, Ebenezer Pemberton, who was a tutor at Harvard College and then colleague minister with Samual Willard at the Old South Church, delivered a funeral sermon upon the death of the Honourable John Walley, member of the council and judge, in 1711. Judge Walley, said Pemberton, rendered his country great service; there are various ways in which the country can be served. One of them is by the promotion of "good literature":

> . . . The more of good literature civil rulers are furnished with, the more capable they are to discharge their trust to the honour and safety of their people. And learning is no less necessary, as an ordinary medium to secure the glory of Christ's visible kingdom. Without a good measure of this the truth can't be explained, asserted and demonstrated; nor errors detected and the heretick baffled. . . .

A second way in which the welfare of the nation is served is by each and every person's keeping to his proper station:

> This intends that we keep within the *line and place,* that providence has set us. . . . We must not without God's call quit our post, thrust ourselves into *anothers province,* with a conceit that *there* we may best serve, and promote the good of the world. . . .

Leadership by the learned and dutiful subordination of the unlearned—as long as the original religious creed retained its hold upon the people these exhortations were heeded; in the eighteenth century, as it ceased to arouse their loyalties, they went seeking after gods that were utterly strange to Puritanism. They demanded fervent rather than learned ministers and asserted the equality of all men.

Thus Puritanism appears, from the social and economic point of view, to have been a philosophy of social stratification, placing the command in the hands of the properly qualified and demanding implicit obedience from the uneducated; from the religious point of view it was the dogged assertion of the unity of intellect and spirit in the face of a rising tide of democratic sentiment suspicious of the intellect and intoxicated with the spirit. It was autocratic, hierarchical, and authoritarian. It held that in the intellectual realm holy writ was to be expounded by right reason, that in the social realm the expounders of holy writ were to be the mentors of farmers and merchants. Yet in so far as Puritanism involved such ideals it was simply adapting to its own purposes the ideals of the age. Catholics in Spain and in Spanish America pursued the same objectives, and the Puritans were no more rigorous in their application of an autocratic standard than King Charles himself endeavored to be—and would have been had he not been balked in the attempt.

The Puritan attitude toward the Bible, to the extent that it was a preservation of intellectual values within the dogmatism, may elicit our hearty approbation. But when we come to the content of the dogma, to what the Puritan insisted the Bible did teach, and to what he expected the regenerate man to find reasonable, in short, when we come to Puritan theology, many persons encounter an insuperable stumbling block to an unqualified approval of Puritan thinking. Not only does the conventional picture of the Puritan creed seem exceedingly unattractive to twentieth-century taste, but the idea of theology in any form is almost equally objectionable. In most secondary accounts Puritans are called Calvinists, and then and there discussion of their intellectual life ceases. Dr. Holmes's "One-Hoss Shay" is deemed a sufficient description.

It is true, the Puritans were Calvinists, if we mean that they more or less agreed with the great theologian of Geneva.

They held, that is, that men had fallen into a state of sin, that in order to be saved they must receive from God a special infusion of grace, that God gives the grace to some and not to others out of his own sovereign pleasure, and that therefore from the beginning of time certain souls were "predestined" to heaven and the others sentenced to damnation. But if the New Englanders were Calvinists, it was because they happened to agree with Calvin; they approved his doctrine not because he taught it, but because it seemed inescapably indicated when they studied scripture or observed the actions of men. The sinfulness of the average man was a fact that could be empirically verified, and in itself demonstrated that he needed divine grace in order to be lifted above himself; the men who did receive what they thought was an influx of grace learned by experience that only in such an ecstasy of illumination did truth become thoroughly evident and completely understandable. Obviously the experience was given to relatively few men; therefore God, who is outside time and who is omniscient, must have known from the beginning of time who would and who would not achieve it. This is the law of life; some men are born rich and some poor, some intelligent and some stupid, some are lucky and others unfortunate, some are happy and some melancholy, some are saved and some are not. There is no reason but that God so ordained it.

The Lord to shew the soveraign freedom of his pleasure, that he may do with his own what he wil, and yet do wrong to none, he denyes pardon and acceptance to those who seek it with some importunity and earnestness ... and yet bestowes mercy and makes known himself unto some *who never sought him.*[3]

[3] Thomas Hooker, *The Application of Redemption,* p. 299.

Puritan theology, therefore, is simply a statement in dogmatic guise of a philosophy of life, wherein it is held on the one hand that men must act by reason and abide by justice, and strive for an inward communication with the force that controls the world, but on the other hand that they must not expect that force always to be cribbed and confined by their conceptions of what is reasonable and just. There is an eternal obligation upon men to be equitable, fair, and good, but who can say that any such morality is also binding on the universe? There are certain amenities which men must observe in their dealings with men, but who can say that they must also be respected by the tiger, by the raging storm, by the lightning, or by the cancer? It is only when the theology of "predestination" is seen in these less technical terms that its vitality as a living faith and its strength as a sustaining philosophy become comprehensible.

But the theology of New England was not simple Calvinism, it was not a mere reduplication of the dogmas of the *Institutes*. What New Englanders believed was an outgrowth, as we have seen, of their background, which was humanistic and English, and it was conditioned by their particular controversy with the Church of England. Simon-pure Calvinism is a much more dogmatic, anti-rational creed than that of the Congregational parsons in Massachusetts. The emigrants went to New England to prove that a state and a church erected on the principles for which they were agitating in England would be blessed by God and prosper. The source of the New England ideology is not Calvin, but England, or more accurately, the Bible as it was read in England, not in Geneva.

Though, of course, the controversy in England was a political, social, and economic one, it was also the intellectual dispute we have outlined. We might summarize it at this point by saying that in order to harmonize reason and scripture, the Anglican endeavored to reduce the

doctrines imposed by scripture to the barest minimum; the Puritan extended scripture to cover the whole of existence and then set himself to prove the content of all scripture essentially reasonable. Only with this definition of origins and tendencies in mind can we read Puritan theology aright. In order to demonstrate that the content of scripture was comprehensible to reason, the Puritan theorists worked out a substantial addition to the theology of Calvinism which in New England was quite as important as the original doctrine. This addition or elaboration of the Calvinist doctrine is generally called the "Covenant Theology," or the "Federal Theology." There is no necessity here for examining it in detail. It was a special way of reading scripture so that the books assembled in the Bible could all be seen to make sense in the same way. The doctrine held that after the fall of man, God voluntarily condescended to treat with man as with an equal and to draw up a covenant or contract with His creature in which He laid down the terms and conditions of salvation, and pledged Himself to abide by them. The covenant did not alter the fact that those only are saved upon whom God sheds His grace, but it made very clear and reasonable how and why certain men are selected, and prescribed the conditions under which they might reach a fair assurance of their own standing. Above all, in the covenant God pledged Himself not to run athwart human conceptions of right and justice; God was represented while entering the compact as agreeing to abide by certain human ideas. Not in all respects, not always, but in the main. I have said that any Puritan would have subscribed to Laud's argument concerning the authority of scripture; it is now necessary to add that if called upon to discuss the question himself, the Puritan would not go about it in the same way. He would not make a distinction between testimonies brought in from another realm of experience besides faith, between rational confirmations and the act of belief, but he would begin with scripture itself, the object of faith and the measure of reason. His principal argument for the satisfaction of the reason would be that once the Bible is believed by faith, it appears wholly and beautifully rational; it contains a consistent doctrine, that of the covenant, which makes it at once the source of belief and the fountain of reason.

To find equivalents in modern terms for the ideas we have been discussing is well-nigh impossible. To translate seventeenth-century issues into twentieth-century phrases, when they cannot possibly mean the same things, is to forego any accurate understanding of them. The results of modern historical investigation and textual criticism have made fantastic, even for those who believe the scripture to be the word of God, acceptance of it in anything like the spirit of the seventeenth century. But if we cannot find a common denominator for equating the ideas of the Puritans with ideas of today, we may possibly get at them by understanding the temperament, the mood, the psychology that underlay the theories. If Puritanism as a creed has crumbled, it can be of only antiquarian significance to us, but if Puritanism is also a state of mind, it may be something closer home.

There is probably no admirer of Puritanism so blindly devoted that he will not find the Anglican apologists in some respects much more attractive. The richness of their culture, the catholicity of their taste, the calmness of their temper, the well-controlled judgment, the mellow piety, and above all the poetry of Richard Hooker and Jeremy Taylor are qualities which unhappily are not too conspicuous in the pages reprinted in this volume. There is an air about these men of breadth and wisdom, they do not labor under terrific and incessant pressure, they are not always taut under the critical scrutiny of an implacable taskmaster. Simple humanity cries at last for some relief from the interminable high seriousness of the

Puritan code, the eternal strenuousness of self-analysis, and the never-ending search of conscience. Though it is a great mistake to think the Puritans could not forget their theology and enjoy themselves, and though Nathaniel Ward proves that they could possess a rollicking sense of humor, the general impression conveyed by Puritan writing is that of men who lived far too uninterruptedly upon the heights of intensity. Perhaps the most damning feature of their intensity was that it could become, over a period of time, as conventional and as stereotyped as worldliness itself. Thomas Shepard, telling the story of his conversion, has a vivid and living sense of the eternal presence of God, but Samuel Sewall, moralizing over God's grace while feeding his chickens, is at best quaintly amusing, and when he bears down with the authority of scripture on the question of wigs he becomes tiresome, as Madam Winthrop undoubtedly felt. There was almost always an element of narrowness, harshness, and literal-mindedness associated with Puritanism, enough to justify some of the criticisms of the bishops and some of the condemnations that have been made on the Puritan spirit in more recent times.

The strength of Puritanism was its realism. If we may borrow William James's frequently misleading division of the human race into the two types of the "tough-minded" and the "tender-minded" and apply it with caution, it may serve our purposes. Though there were undoubtedly men in the Church of England, such as John Donne, whom we would have to describe as "tough," and a number of Puritans who would fit the description of "tender," yet in the main Anglicans such as Hooker and Taylor are quite clearly on the side of the more tender-minded, while the Puritan mind was one of the toughest the world has ever had to deal with. It is impossible to conceive of a disillusioned Puritan; no matter what misfortune befell him, no matter how often or how tragically his fellowmen failed him, he would have been prepared for the worst, and would have expected no better. At the same time, there was nothing of the fatalist about him; as so often happens in the history of thought, the believers in a supreme determining power were the most energetic of soldiers and crusaders. The charge of Cromwell's Ironsides was, on the particular score, proof positive of the superiority of the Puritan over the Anglican, and the Indians of New England learned to their very great sorrow how vehement could be the onset of troops who fought for a predestined victory. There was nothing lukewarm, half-hearted, or flabby about the Puritan; whatever he did, he did with zest and gusto. In that sense we might say that though his life was full of anguish of spirit, he nevertheless enjoyed it hugely. Existence for him was completely dramatic, every minute was charged with meaning. And when we come to an end of this roll call of characteristics, the one which yet remains the most difficult to evoke was his peculiar balance of zeal and enthusiasm with control and wariness. In his inner life he was overwhelmingly preoccupied with achieving a union with the divine; in his external life he was predominantly concerned with self-restraint. . . . He lived in the world according to the principles that must govern this world, with an ever-present sense that they were only for the time being and that his true home was elsewhere. "There is," said John Cotton, "another combination of virtues strangely mixed in every lively holy Christian, and that is, Diligence in worldly businesses, and yet deadnesse to the world; such a mystery as none can read, but they that know it." The Puritan ideal was the man who could take all opportunities, lose no occasions, "and bestir himself for profit," and at the same time "be a man deadhearted to the world." He might wrest New England from the Indians, trade in the seven seas,

and speculate in lands; "yet his heart is not set upon these things, he can tell what to do with his estate when he hath got it."

The most serious of charges laid against the Puritans has been their supposed deficiency in aesthetic perceptions. Because they did not want men to fix their veneration upon worldly things, they had no use for sculpture, distrusted the arts when they were prized merely for their sensuous appeal, were contemptuous of the beautiful ritual and ornamentation of the Church of England. The poet George Herbert, defending the habiliment of his church against what he thought the trappings of the Church of Rome, found the plainness of Puritan worship going much too far in the other direction:

She in the valley is so shie
Of dressing that her hair doth lie
   About her eares;
While she avoids her neighbour's pride,
She wholly goes on th'other side,
   And nothing wears.

The New Model Army has incurred infamy with posterity for hacking to pieces the furnishings of cathedrals. But the asperity of the Puritan discipline and the Puritan distrust of merely sensuous beauty did not mean that the Puritan was without an aesthetic of his own, or that he was hostile to beauty. John Preston defined beauty in characteristic Puritan fashion: "Beauty that consists in a conformity of all the parts"; Thomas Hooker said that sin "defaceth the beautiful frame, and that sweet correspondence and orderly usefulness the Lord first implanted in the order of things." The Puritan conceived of beauty as order, the order of things as they are, not as they appear, as they are in pure and abstract conception, as they are in the mind of God. He spoke of his church polity, his bare, crude churches, without altars or choirs, foursquare and solid, as lovely; they were so to him because they incarnated the beauty of the one polity Christ had ordained. His conception of the beautiful was, like Plato's, the efficient order of things; in that sense, he held indeed that beauty is truth, and truth beauty, though he did not think that was quite all he needed to know in life.

When the historian thus attempts to consider Puritanism in all its ramifications, he finds himself at the end hesitating to deliver judgment upon it, or to be wholly satisfied that it has passed into the limbo of anthologies. Certainly we can look upon the disappearance of some features with no regrets, and only deplore some others where they still survive. We have had enough of the Puritan censoriousness, its tendency to make every man his brother's keeper. When the Puritan habit of probing into the soul has degenerated into the "New England conscience"—where it is apt to remain as a mere feeling that everything enjoyable is sinful—then the ridicule heaped upon Puritan inhibitions becomes a welcome antidote. Certainly many amenities of social life have increased in New England and in America in direct proportion as Puritanism has receded. But while we congratulate ourselves upon these ameliorations, we cannot resist a slight fear that much of what has taken the place of Puritanism in our philosophies is just so much failure of nerve. The successors of Puritanism, both the evangelicals and the rationalists, as we survey them today, seem to have been comparatively sentimental, to have lacked a stomach for reality. The optimism and cheerfulness to which the revolters against Puritanism turned now threaten to become rather a snare and a delusion than a liberation. "Science" tells us of a world of stark determinism, in which heredity and environmental conditioning usurp the function of the Puritan God in predestining men to ineluctable fates. It is, indeed, true that the sense of things being ordered by blind forces presents a different series of problems than does the conception of determination by a divine being; no matter how unintelligible the world might seem to the Puritan, he never lost confidence that ultimately it was directed by an intelligence. Yet even with this momentous difference in our imagination of the controlling power, the human problem today has more in common with the Puritan understanding of it than at any time for two centuries: how can man live by the lights of humanity in a universe that appears indifferent or even hostile to them? We are terribly aware once more, thanks to the revelation of psychologists and the events of recent political history, that men are not perfect or essentially good. The Puritan description of them, we have been reluctantly compelled to admit, is closer to what we have witnessed than the description given in Jeffersonian democracy or in transcendentalism. The Puritan accounted for these qualities by the theory of original sin; he took the story of the fall of man in the Garden of Eden for a scientific, historical explanation of these observable facts. The value of his literature today cannot lie for us in his explanation; if there is any, it must rest in the accuracy of his observations.

Max Weber

The Spirit of Capitalism

In the title of this study is used the somewhat pretentious phrase, the *spirit* of capitalism. What is to be understood by it? The attempt to give anything like a definition of it brings out certain difficulties which are in the very nature of this type of investigation.

If any object can be found to which this term can be applied with any understandable meaning, it can only be an historical individual, i.e. a complex of elements associated in historical reality which we unite into a conceptual whole from the standpoint of their cultural significance. . . .

Remember this saying, *The good paymaster is lord of another man's purse.* He that is known to pay punctually and exactly to the time he promises, may at any time, and on any occasion, raise all the money his friends can spare. This is sometimes of great use. After industry and frugality, nothing contributes more to the raising of a young man in the world than punctuality and justice in all his dealings; therefore never keep borrowed money an hour beyond the time you promised, lest a disappointment shut up your friend's purse for ever.

The most trifling actions that affect a man's credit are to be regarded. The sound of your hammer at five in the morning, or eight at night, heard by a creditor, makes

Reprinted with the permission of Charles Scribner's Sons from *The Protestant Ethic and the Spirit of Capitalism,* ·pp. 47 and 49–56, by Max Weber, translated by Talcott Parsons. Footnotes omitted except where necessary for understanding.

him easy six months longer; but if he sees you at a billiard-table, or hears your voice at a tavern, when you should be at work, he sends for his money the next day; demands it, before he can receive it, in a lump.

It shows, besides, that you are mindful of what you owe; it makes you appear a careful as well as an honest man, and that still increases your credit.

Beware of thinking all your own that you possess, and of living accordingly. It is a mistake that many people who have credit fall into. To prevent this, keep an exact account for some time both of your expenses and your income. If you take the pains at first to mention particulars, it will have this good effect: you will discover how wonderfully small, trifling expenses mount up to large sums, and will discern what might have been, and may for the future be saved, without occasioning any great inconvenience.

For six pounds a year you may have the use of one hundred pounds, provided you are a man of known prudence and honesty.

He that spends a groat a day idly, spends idly above six pounds a year, which is the price for the use of one hundred pounds.

He that wastes idly a groat's worth of his time per day, one day with another, wastes the privilege of using one hundred pounds each day.

He that idly loses five shillings' worth of time, loses five shillings, and might as prudently throw five shillings into the sea.

He that loses five shillings, not only loses that sum, but all the advantage that might be made by turning it in dealing, which by the time that a young man becomes old, will amount to a considerable sum of money.[1]

It is Benjamin Franklin who preaches to us in these sentences, the same which Ferdinand Kürnberger satirizes in his clever and malicious *Picture of American Culture*[2] as the supposed confession of faith of the Yankee. That it is the spirit of capitalism which here speaks in characteristic fashion, no one will doubt, however little we may wish to claim that everything which could be understood as pertaining to that spirit is contained in it. Let us pause a moment to consider this passage, the philosophy of which Kürnberger sums up in the words, "They make tallow out of cattle and money out of men." The peculiarity of this philosophy of avarice appears to be the ideal of the honest man of recognized credit, and above all the idea of a duty of the individual toward the increase of his capital, which is assumed as an end in itself. Truly what is here preached is not simply a means of making one's way in the world, but a peculiar ethic. The infraction of its rules is treated not as foolishness but as forgetfulness of duty. That is the essence of the matter. It is not mere business astuteness, that sort of thing is common enough, it is an ethos. *This* is the quality which interests us.

[1] The final passage is from *Necessary Hints to Those That Would Be Rich*, (written 1736, *Works,* Sparks edition, II, p. 80), the rest from *Advice to a Young Tradesman* [written 1748, Sparks edition, Vol. 2 (1748), pp. 87 ff.]. The italics in the text are Franklin's.

[2] *Der Amerikamüde* (Frankfurt: 1855), well known to be an imaginative paraphrase of Lenau's impressions of America. As a work of art the book would today be somewhat difficult to enjoy, but it is incomparable as a document of the (now long since blurred-over) differences between the German and the American outlook, one may even say of the type of spiritual life which, in spite of everything, has remained common to all Germans, Catholic and Protestant alike, since the German mysticism of the Middle Ages, as against the Puritan capitalistic valuation of action.

When Jacob Fugger, in speaking to a business associate who had retired and who wanted to persuade him to do the same, since he had made enough money and should let others have a chance, rejected that as pusillanimity and answered that "he (Fugger) thought otherwise, he wanted to make money as long as he could,"[3] the spirit of his statement is evidently quite different from that of Franklin. What in the former case was an expression of commercial daring and a personal inclination morally neutral,[4] in the latter takes on the character of an ethically coloured maxim for the conduct of life. The concept spirit of capitalism is here used in this specific sense, it is the spirit of modern capitalism. For that we are here dealing only with Western European and American capitalism is obvious from the way in which the problem was stated. Capitalism existed in China, India, Babylon, in the classic world, and in the Middle Ages. But in all these cases, as we shall see, this particular ethos was lacking.

Now, all Franklin's moral attitudes are coloured with utilitarianism. Honesty is useful, because it assures credit; so are punctuality, industry, frugality, and that is the reason they are virtues. A logical deduction from this would be that where, for instance, the appearance of honesty serves the same purpose, that would suffice, and an unnecessary surplus of this virtue would evidently appear to Franklin's eyes as unproductive waste. And as a matter of fact, the story in his autobiography of his conversion to those virtues, or the discussion of the value of a strict maintenance of the appearance of modesty, the assiduous belittlement of one's own deserts in order to gain general re-

[3] Sombart has used this quotation as a motto for his section dealing with the genesis of capitalism (*Der Moderne Kapitalismus,* first edition, Vol. 1, p. 193. See also p. 390).

[4] Which quite obviously does not mean either that Jacob Fugger was a morally indifferent or an irreligious man, or that Benjamin Franklin's ethic is completely covered by the above quotations.

cognition later, confirms this impression. According to Franklin, those virtues, like all others, are only in so far virtues as they are actually useful to the individual, and the surrogate of mere appearance is always sufficient when it accomplishes the end in view. It is a conclusion which is inevitable for strict utilitarianism. The impression of many Germans that the virtues professed by Americanism are pure hypocrisy seems to have been confirmed by this striking case. But in fact the matter is not by any means so simple. Benjamin Franklin's own character, as it appears in the really unusual candidness of his autobiography, belies that suspicion. The circumstance that he ascribes his recognition of the utility of virtue to a divine revelation which was intended to lead him in the path of righteousness, shows that something more than mere garnishing for purely egocentric motives is involved.

In fact the *summum bonum* of this ethic, the earning of more and more money, combined with the strict avoidance of all spontaneous enjoyment of life, is above all completely devoid of any eudaemonistic, not to say hedonistic, admixture. It is thought of so purely as an end in itself, that from the point of view of the happiness of, or utility to, the single individual, it appears entirely transcendental and absolutely irrational. Man is dominated by the making of money, by acquisition as the ultimate purpose of his life. Economic acquisition is no longer subordinated to man as the means for the satisfaction of his material needs. This reversal of what we should call the natural relationship, so irrational from a naïve point of view, is evidently as definitely a leading principle of capitalism as it is foreign to all peoples not under capitalistic influence. At the same time it expresses a type of feeling which is closely connected with certain religious ideas. If we thus ask, *why* should "money be made out of men," Benjamin Franklin himself, although he was a colourless deist, answers in his autobiography with a quotation from the Bible, which his strict Calvinistic father drummed into him again and again in his youth: "Seest thou a man diligent in his business? He shall stand before kings" (Prov. xxii. 29). The earning of money within the modern economic order is, so long as it is done legally, the result and the expression of virtue and proficiency in a calling; and this virtue and proficiency are, as it is now not difficult to see, the real Alpha and Omega of Franklin's ethic, as expressed in the passages we have quoted, as well as in all his works without exception.

And in truth this peculiar idea, so familiar to us today, but in reality so little a matter of course, of one's duty in a calling, is what is most characteristic of the social ethic of capitalistic culture, and is in a sense the fundamental basis of it. It is an obligation which the individual is supposed to feel and does feel towards the content of his professional activity, no matter in what it consists, in particular no matter whether it appears on the surface as a utilization of his personal powers, or only of his material possessions (as capital).

Of course, this conception has not appeared only under capitalistic conditions. On the contrary, we shall later trace its origins back to a time previous to the advent of capitalism. Still less, naturally, do we maintain that a conscious acceptance of these ethical maxims on the part of the individuals, entrepreneurs or labourers, in modern capitalistic enterprises, is a condition of the further existence of present-day capitalism. The capitalistic economy of the present day is an immense cosmos into which the individual is born, and which presents itself to him, at least as an individual, as an unalterable order of things in which he must live. It forces the individual, in so far as he is involved in the system of market relationships, to conform to capitalistic rules of action. The manufacturer who in the long run acts counter to these norms, will just as inevitably be eliminated from the economic scene as the worker who cannot or will not adapt himself to them will be thrown into the streets without a job.

Thus the capitalism of to-day, which has come to dominate economic life, educates and selects the economic subjects which it needs through a process of economic survival of the fittest. But here one can easily see the limits of the concept of selection as a means of historical explanation. In order that a manner of life so well adapted to the peculiarities of capitalism could be selected at all, i.e. should come to dominate others, it had to originate somewhere, and not in isolated individuals alone, but as a way of life common to whole groups of men. This origin is what really needs explanation. Concerning the doctrine of the more naïve historical materialism, that such ideas originate as a reflection or superstructure of economic situations, we shall speak more in detail below. At this point it will suffice for our purpose to call attention to the fact that without doubt, in the country of Benjamin Franklin's birth (Massachusetts), the spirit of capitalism (in the sense we have attached to it) was present before the capitalistic order. There were complaints of a peculiarly calculating sort of profit-seeking in New England, as distinguished from other parts of America, as early as 1632. It is further undoubted that capitalism remained far less developed in some of the neighbouring colonies, the later Southern States of the United States of America, in spite of the fact that these latter were founded by large capitalists for business motives, while the New England colonies were founded by preachers and seminary graduates with the help of small bourgeois, craftsmen and yoemen, for religious reasons. In this case .the causal relation is certainly the reverse of that suggested by the materialistic standpoint.

Michael Walzer

Puritanism as a Revolutionary Ideology

It was, perhaps, not without a certain malice that the early Puritans were called "disciplinarians." But malice has its in-

From "Puritanism as a Revolutionary Theology," by Michael Walzer, in *History and Theory*, Vol. 3 No. 1, by permission of Wesleyan University Press, publisher. Copyright © 1963 by Wesleyan University.

sights and this one is worth pursuing. The association of the brethren was voluntary indeed, but it gave rise to a collectivist discipline marked above all by a tense mutual "watchfulness." Puritan individualism never led to a respect for privacy. Tender conscience had its rights, but it was protected only against the interference of worldlings and not against "brotherly admonition." And the admonitions of the brethren were anxious, insistent, continuous. They felt themselves to be living in an age of chaos and crime and sought to train conscience to be permanently on guard against sin. The extent to which they would have carried the moral discipline can be seen in the following list of offenses which merited excommunication in one seventeenth-century congregation:

> for unfaithfulness in his master's
> service.
> for admitting cardplaying in his
> house. . .
> for sloth in business.
> for being overtaken in beer.
> for borrowing a pillion and not
> returning it.
> for jumping for wagers. . .
> for dancing and other vanities.

Had the saints been successful in establishing their Holy Commonwealth, the enforcement of this discipline would have constituted the Puritan terror. In the congregation there was already a kind of local terrorism, maintained by the godly elders as the national discipline would have been by an elite of the saints. Thus, Richard Baxter reported that in his Kidderminister parish the enforcement of the new moral order was made possible "by the zeal and diligence of the godly people of the place who thirsted after the salvation of their neighbours and were in private my assistants."

It was for this moral discipline that the saints fought most persistently, and it was over this issue that Baxter and his colleagues left the Established Church in 1662.

The crucial feature of the Puritan discipline was its tendency to transform repression into self-control: worldlings might be forced to be godly, but saints voluntarily gave themselves to godliness. Liberalism also required such voluntary

subjection and self-control but, in sharp contrast to Puritanism, its political and social theory were marked by an extraordinary confidence in the possibility of both a firm sense of human reasonableness and of the ease with which order might be attained. Liberal confidence made repression and the endless struggle against sin unnecessary; it also tended to make self-control invisible, to forget its painful history and naively assume its existence. The result was that liberalism did not create the self-control it required. The Lockeian state was not a disciplinary institution, as was the Calvinist Holy Commonwealth, but rather rested on the assumed political virtue—the "natural political virtue"—of its citizens. It is one of the central arguments of this essay that Puritan repression has its place in the practical history, so to speak, of that strange assumption. . . .

The very existence and spread of Puritanism in the years before the Revolution surely argue the presence in English society of an acute fear of disorder and "wickedness." The anxious tone of Tudor legislation—which Puritan leaders like William Perkins often vigorously seconded—is itself a parallel argument. On the other hand, the triumph of Lockeian ideas suggests the overcoming of that anxiety and fear, the appearance of men for whom sin is no longer a problem. In a sense, it might be said that liberalism is dependent upon the existence of "saints" —that is, of men whose good behavior can be relied upon. At the same time, the secular and genteel character of liberalism is determined by the fact that these are men whose goodness (sociability, self-discipline, moral decency, or mere respectability) is self-assured and relaxed, entirely free from the nervousness and fanaticism of Calvinist godliness.

This, then, is the relationship of Puritanism to the liberal world: it is perhaps one of historical preparation, but not at all of theoretical contribution. Indeed, there was much to be forgotten and much to be surrendered before the saint could become a liberal bourgeois. During the great creative period of English Puritanism, the faith of the saints and the tolerant reasonableness of the liberals had very little in common.

Roughly the same things can be said about the putative connection of Calvinism and capitalism. The moral discipline of the saints can be interpreted as the historical conditioning of the capitalist man; but the discipline was not itself capitalist. It can be argued that the faith of the brethren, with its emphasis upon methodical endeavor and self-control, was an admirable preparation for systematic work in shops, offices and factories. It trained men for the minute-to-minute attentiveness required in a modern economic system; it taught them to forego their afternoon naps—as they had but recently foregone their saints' day holidays—and to devote spare hours to bookkeeping and moral introspection. It somehow made the deprivation and repression inevitable in sustained labor bearable and even desirable for the saints. And by teaching self-control, it provided the basis for impersonal, contractual relationships among men, allowing workmanlike cooperation but not involving any exchange of affection or any of the risks of intimacy. All this, Calvinism did or helped to do. Whether it did so in a creative fashion or as the ideological reflection of new economic processes is not immediately relevant. The saints learned, as Weber has suggested, a kind of rational and worldly asceticism, and this was probably something more than the economic routine required. They sought in work itself what mere work can never give: a sense of vocation and discipline which would free them from sinfulness and the fear of disorder.

But Weber has said more than this; he has argued that systematic acquisition as well as asceticism has a Calvinist origin. The psychological tension induced by the theory of predestination, working itself out in world activity, presumably drove men to seek success as a sign of salvation. The sheer willfulness of an inscrutable God produced in its turn, if Weber is correct, the willfulness of an anxious man, and set off the entrepreneurial pursuit of better business techniques and more and more profit. At this point his argument breaks down. If there is in fact a peculiar and irrational quality to the capitalists' lust for gain, its sources must be sought elsewhere than among the saints. For Puritanism was hardly an ideology which encouraged continuous or unrestrained accumulation. Instead, the saints tended to be narrow and conservative in their economic views, urging men to seek no more than they needed for a modest life, or, alternatively, to use up their surplus in charitable giving. The anxiety of the Puritans led to a fearful demand for economic restriction (and political control) rather than to entrepreneurial activity as Weber had described it. Unremitting and relatively unremunerative work was the greatest help toward saintliness and virtue.

The ideas of Puritan writers are here very close to those of such proto-Jacobins as Mably and Morelli in eighteenth-century France, who also watched the development of capitalist enterprise with unfriendly eyes, dreaming of a Spartan republic where bankers and great merchants would be unwelcome. The collective discipline of the Puritans—their Christian Sparta—was equally incompatible with purely acquisitive activity. Virtue would almost certainly require economic regulation. This would be very different from the regulation of medieval corporatism, and perhaps it was the first sense of that difference which received the name *freedom*. It was accompanied by a keen economic realism: thus the Calvinist acknowledgement of the lawfulness of usury. But Calvinist realism was in the service of effective control and not of free activity or self-expression. Who can doubt that, had the Holy Commonwealth ever been firmly established, godly self-discipline and mutual surveillance would have been far more repressive than the corporate system? Once again, in the absence of a Puritan state the discipline was enforced through the congregation. The minutes of a seventeenth-century consistory provide a routine example: "The church was satisfied with Mrs. Carlton," they read, "as to the weight of her butter." Did Mrs. Carlton tremble, awaiting that verdict? Surely if the brethren were unwilling to grant liberty to the local butter-seller, they would hardly have granted it to the new capitalist. The ministerial literature, at least, is full of denunciations of enclosers, usurers, monopolists, and projectors—and occasionally even of wily merchants. Puritan casuistry, perhaps, left such men sufficient room in which to range, but it hardly offered them what Weber considers so essential—a good conscience. Only a sustained endeavor in hypocrisy, so crude as to astonish even the Marxist epigone, could have earned them that. The final judgment of the saints with regard to the pursuit of money is that of Bunyan's pilgrim, angry and ill-at-ease in the town of Vanity, disdainful of such companions as Mr. Money-love and Mr. Save-all.

The converse is equally true: to the triumphant bourgeois sainthood, with all its attendant enthusiasm and asceticism, would appear atavistic. And this is perhaps the clearest argument of all against the casual acceptance of the Whig or Weberian views of Puritanism. It suggests forcefully that the two views (and the Marxist also, for surprisingly similar reasons) are founded upon anachronism. Even if it is correct to argue that Calvinist faith and discipline played a part in that transformation of character which created the bourgeois—and too little is known about the historical development of character to say this without qualification—the anachronism remains. The historical present is hopelessly distorted unless the tension and repression so essential to the life of the saint are described and accounted for. Even more important,

the effort to establish a holy commonwealth (to universalize the tension and repression) is rendered inexplicable once liberalism and capitalism are, so to speak, read into the Puritan experience. For then Puritanism is turned into a grand paradox: its radical voluntarism culminates in a rigid discipline; its saints watch their neighbors with brotherly love and suspicion; its ethic teaches sustained and systematic work but warns men against the lust for acquisition and gain. In fact, of course, these seeming contrasts are not paradoxical. The saints experienced a unity, common enough among men, of willfulness and repression, of fanatical *self-control.* Latter-day historians do the Puritans little honor when they search among the elements of the Puritan faith for something more liberal in its political implications or more economically rational. Indeed, the methods of that search invite in their turn the most searching criticism.

Select Bibliography for Problem 1

Brown, B. Katherine. "Puritan Democracy: A Case Study," *Mississippi Valley Historical Review,* 50 (December 1963), 377–396.

_____. "Puritan Democracy in Bedham, Massachusetts: Another Case Study," *William and Mary Quarterly,* 24 (July 1967), 378–396.

Burg, B. Richard. "The Ideology of Richard Mather and Its Relationship to English Puritanism Prior to 1660," *Journal of Church and State,* 9 (Autumn 1967), 364–377.

Fine, Sidney, and Gerald S. Brown, eds. *The American Past: Conflicting Interpretations of the Great Issues,* Vol. I. New York: Crowell Collier and Macmillan, Inc., 1965, pp. 2–27.

Grob, Gerald N., and Billias, George A., eds. *Interpretations of American History,* Vol. I. New York: The Free Press, 1967, pp. 71–125.

Hall, David D., ed. *Puritanism in Seventeenth-Century Massachusetts.* American Problem Studies under the editorial direction of Oscar Handlin. New York: Holt, Rinehart and Winston, Inc., 1968.

James, Sidney V., ed. *The New England Puritans.* Interpretations of American History series, edited by John Higham and Bradford Perkins. New York: Harper & Row, Publishers, 1968.

Larson, David L., ed. *The Puritan Ethic in United States Foreign Policy.* New York: Van Nostrand Reinhold Company, 1966.

Mead, Sidney E. *The Lively Experiment: The Shaping of Christianity in America.* New York: Harper & Row, Publishers, 1963.

Polishook, Irwin H. *Roger Williams, John Cotton and Religious Freedom: A Controversy in New and Old England.* Englewood Cliffs, N.J.: Prentice-Hall, 1967.

Quint, Howard H., *et al.,* eds. *Main Problems in American History,* Vol. 1. Homewood, Ill.: Dorsey Press, 1964, pp. 1–24.

Rutman, Darrett B. *Husbandmen of Plymouth: Farms and Villages in the Old Colony, 1620–1692.* Boston: Beacon Press, 1967.

Rosenmeier, Jesper. "The Teacher and the Witness: John Cotton and Roger Williams," *William and Mary Quarterly,* 25 (July 1968), 408–431.

———. *Winthrop's Boston: Portrait of a Puritan Town.* Chapel Hill, N.C.: University of North Carolina Press, 1969.

Simmons, Richard C. "Freemanship in Early Massachusetts: Some Suggestions and a Case Study," *William and Mary Quarterly,* 53 (July 1963), 422–428.

———. "Godliness, Property and the Franchise in Puritan Massachusetts: An Interpretation," *The Journal of American History,* 55 (December 1968), 495–511.

———. "The Massachusetts Revolution of 1689: Three Early American Political Studies," *Journal of American Studies,* 2 (April 1968), 1–12.

Sprunger, Keith L. "Technometria: A Prologue to Puritan Theology," *Journal of the History of Ideas,* 29 (January 1968), 115–122.

Starkey, Marion L. *The Devil in Massachusetts: A Modern Inquiry into the Salem Witch Trials.* New York: Doubleday & Company, Inc., 1949.

Wall, Robert E., Jr. "A New Look at Cambridge," *Journal of American History,* 52 (December 1965), 599–605.

Waller, George M., ed. *Puritanism in Early America.* Problems in American Civilization under the editorial direction of George Rogers Taylor. Boston: D. C. Heath & Company, 1950.

Wolff, Cynthia G. "Literary Reflections of the Puritan Character," *Journal of the History of Ideas,* 29 (January 1968), 13–32.

Woodward, C. Vann. "The Southern Ethics in a Puritan World," *William and Mary Quarterly,* 25 (July 1968), 343–370.

part 2

The Revolutionary Era

chapter 4

Wars for the Continent

Empires Collide

FRENCH EXPANSION

The clashes between England and France in the New World during the seventeenth and eighteenth centuries were merely extensions of their European campaigns for world empire, colonial commerce, and supremacy on the seas. France, one of the latecomers to America, got into the colonial act in 1608 when Champlain established Quebec on the Saint Lawrence River. Subsequent efforts, and particularly those of Louis Jolliet, Sieur de La Salle, Father Marquette, and countless Jesuit missionaries under the direction of their capable governor, Count Frontenac (1672–1682 and 1689–1698), extended the French empire to the southern limits of Louisiana. The gulf port of New Orleans was founded in 1718 with these acquisitions. France thus discouraged any imperial designs Britain may have had on the trans-Appalachia west.

KING WILLIAM'S WAR

France appeared to be living on the laurels of the past hundred years, which had blessed her with capable ministers, international prestige, and prosperity, in spite of mediocre monarchs, when political intrigues in Europe brought on King William's War (1689–1697), known in Europe as the War of the League of Augsburg. In 1688 the reign of the Stuarts in England came to an end with the "Glorious Revolution" and the accession of William and Mary of Orange. Louis XIV, however, chafed at the thought of having an English government headed by an old enemy (who could necessarily lead England into an alliance with Holland) and, therefore, openly supported the return of exiled James II.

During the course of King William's War, the French pursued a "terrorize and hold" strategy along the frontier, while the disorganized and highly individualistic British colonials managed to launch a few concerted attacks against French strongholds. They were particularly interested in demobilizing the head of the war machine in Canada. After failing in their efforts to capture Quebec and Montreal, the British colonials finally subdued Port Royal in 1690. Their glory, however, was short-lived, for when the fighting in Europe reached a stalemate, the English government returned the port to the French in the Treaty of Ryswick (1697). The main provisions of this treaty called for a return to the *status quo*.

RIVALS COMPARED

During this war and the others between England and France that occurred during the eighteenth and nineteenth centuries, England had a marked advantage over her rival in America. In 1688 England boasted of a colonial population in excess of 100,000 as compared to about 12,000 in New France, and by 1750 these figures had jumped to 1.3 million and 80,000 respectively. Moreover, the English military drew from war industries that were better financed than any on the continent, while her naval power went almost unchallenged on the high seas. Her colonial military strength was further buttressed by the powerful Iroquois Confederacy, which commanded a healthy respect throughout the colonial period in America. France, on the other hand, had to rely on superior strategy, all of which was administered by a highly centralized government. She also soon found it to her advantage to fight a defensive war behind her well-built and strategically placed forts and, it might be added, behind the shield of her Indian allies, who outnumbered the Iroquois.

The Advent of World Wars

QUEEN ANNE'S WAR

The peace ushered in by the Treaty of Ryswick was shattered in 1701 when Louis XIV attempted to seat his grandson on the throne of Spain. This precipitated the War of the Spanish Succession (1701–1713), which was known in America as Queen Anne's War. This second war for empire mushroomed into a much broader world conflict than any of the previous when Spain, France, and others united against England and her European allies. The American theater saw a renewal of French and Indian strategy headlined by their successful raid on Deerfield, Massachusetts, while the British colonial marched once again against strategic points in Canada. With luck on their side, the colonials were able to recapture Port Royal—this time for keeps. On the southern front in America the Carolinians deployed the Indians, and particularly the Creek Confederacy, to some advantage

against the Spanish and their Indian allies; but the fighting here soon took on the shades of a war of attrition.

TREATY OF UTRECHT

While France held her own in America, she fared rather badly in Europe; the Treaty of Utrecht (1713) reflects the European complexion of the engagement. France was required to recognize England's claim to the Hudson Bay and to cede Nova Scotia and Newfoundland to the victor. Thus, England got a rather permanent foot in the door of French Canada. From Spain she received the fortress of Gibraltar, the island of Minorca, and slave trade rights that gave her a monopoly of this traffic in the New World.

WAR OF JENKINS' EAR

The War of Jenkins' Ear, named in honor of Captain Robert Jenkins, who lost an ear battling the Spanish coast guards, preceded the larger King George's War by a year and at least prepared the southern colonials for the more serious struggle. The boundary line and charges of smuggling were ever persistent issues between the southern colonials and Spanish authorities, but it appeared that the issues might be resolved when the Convention of Prado was called in 1739. The convention provided that the boundary dispute be handled by a joint commission designed to handle all differences between Georgia and Florida, but the hawks in Parliament, bent on expansion, rejected the plan and war resulted. Governor James Oglethorpe and his Georgia militia were called upon to defend the frontier, which they did in admirable fashion and upon occasion even invaded Spanish territory.

KING GEORGE'S WAR

The War of Jenkins' Ear soon became part and parcel of a troubled Europe and in

1740 the War of the Austrian Succession (1740–1748), known in America as King George's War, erupted. This third world war in the long list of Anglo-French conflicts began when Frederick the Great of Prussia attempted to seize the Austrian province of Silesia on spurious claims. France and Spain and other allies aligned themselves on the side of Prussia, while England and her friends cast their lot with Austria. In America the colonials saw only limited action in this conflict. Nonetheless, a group of New Englanders under the command of William Pepperrell was able to capture Fort Louisbourg, one of France's most vital fortresses; but again their deed was betrayed when England returned the fort to France and restored the *status quo* with the Treaty of Aix-la-Chapelle (1748).

ALBANY CONGRESS

After some sixty-five years and three major wars the two traditional adversaries in the New World had settled none of the major issues—claims to the Ohio Valley were still contested, and the French continued to control the Mississippi River. The year 1754 proved to be an eventful one for both the French and the English colonials. The former built Fort Duquesne (now Pittsburgh), in order to strengthen their Ohio defenses, and the latter summoned their representatives to the Albany Congress, where it was hoped they might realize some plan for cooperation and unity. The most progress, however, that Ben Franklin (the architect of the Albany Plan) could squeeze from the independent-minded colonials was an alliance with the Iroquois Confederacy and a promise for the future. His ideas, nevertheless, were later incorporated in the Continental Congress.

FRENCH AND INDIAN WAR

It was also in 1754 that George Washington, twenty-two-year-old lieutenant colonel, and his Virginia militiamen fired into French troops at Great Meadows and ignited the explosion that became known as the French and Indian War (1754–1763). It was known in Europe as the Seven Years' War (1756–1763).[1] Colonel Washington won this first skirmish but soon tasted defeat when the French surrounded his garrison at Fort Necessity. With the hope of avenging Washington's defeat, the British high command dispatched one of its most experienced warriors, General Edward Braddock, to take Fort Duquesne. The European general, however, unfamiliar with frontier strategy and unwilling to heed advice, led his army into an ambush seven miles short of its destination. When the smoke cleared, Braddock's forces had been routed and the stubborn general lay mortally wounded. Inspired by the victory, France's Indian allies sent most of the Ohio Valley behind barricades with scalping raids. The British meanwhile neutralized Acadia by relocating many of its inhabitants and sent unsuccessful expeditions against the French at Crown Point and Niagara. Forts Edward and William Henry were also hastily erected to secure the Hudson River region, which was threatened by the Canadians.

WILLIAM PITT

In 1756 England made the undeclared war official. The fortunes of the struggle in America, however, continued to smile on France, whose forces under the leadership of General Marquis de Montcalm, reputed to be France's most brilliant military tactician in America, captured both Oswego and Fort William Henry. It was at this time that the British people turned to William Pitt, a man of remarkable ability and self-confidence, for guidance. When Pitt was appointed to the office of

---

[1] England and Prussia against a coalition of France, Austria, Russia, Sweden, several of the German states, and finally, in 1762, Spain.

Secretary of State in 1757, the people rallied behind his command to destroy the French strongholds in Canada and to drive their enemy from the continent. With fresh armies and energetic young officers England took the initiative. The first key fortress marked for conquest was Louisbourg on the St. Lawrence Gulf. It surrendered in 1758. Fort Duquesne fell without a battle, but the third objective, Quebec, proved a worthy foe.

In the summer of 1759, Montcalm was forced to surrender Niagara, Crown Point, and Ticonderoga and to retreat to Quebec, where he awaited the inevitable siege. General James Wolfe, no less a military genius, sent several unsuccessful frontal attacks against the stubborn French. Finally he directed an English force to scale the cliffs above the fort at night, which would put them into position for a surprise assault at dawn. In the battle that followed, perhaps the most significant of the colonial wars, both commanders were killed, but the British held the field and Quebec was theirs. General Amherst took Montreal the following summer to complete the British conquest of Canada.

To many observers it seemed that the long war should have ended with the fall of New France, but the English navy seized the advantage and took Cuba and the Philippines from Spain and the island of Martinique from France. Meanwhile, in the Ohio Valley a final resurgence was staged in 1763 by a pro-French Indian confederacy under the leadership of Pontiac, an Ottawa chieftain. It was not until September of 1764 that they were brought under control.

PEACE OF PARIS

The Peace of Paris, which was finally realized in 1763, marked the end of the French empire in America. The English had won control, not only of Canada, but of all the territory east of the Mississippi River, including Florida, which was ceded by Spain. France, in turn, compensated Spain by signing over the whole of the Louisiana territory. Cuba was returned to Spain, while France was permitted to retain her sugar industry in the West Indies.

The consequences of the French and Indian War are still being measured. It placed England in the favored role as the supreme power on land and sea in both Europe and America. As for the colonials, it has often been suggested that the war served as an initiation rite through which they passed to adulthood and nationalism. As they fought beside the British soldiers, many colonials saw for the first time that they were unlike the Europeans in dress, custom, and, to some extent, language. Perhaps more importantly, the war served to reveal the weaknesses of the British regulars, as evidenced by Braddock's blunders, which the colonials were quick to record. Finally, the removal of the French opened up the Ohio and Mississippi valleys, which, in turn, forced the British to pursue new imperial administrative policies that, for the most part, ran contrary to the independent-minded colonials. Not only did many of the colonials show a reluctance to fight what they considered to be England's war, but they even more adamantly opposed the new taxes levied against them for the purpose of maintaining the peacetime British garrisons.

Select Bibliography

Bakeless, John E. *Daniel Boone, Master of the Wilderness.* Harrisburg, Pa.: Stackpole Books, 1965.

Bird, Harrison. *Battle for a Continent.* New York: Oxford University Press, 1963.

Brebner, John B. *The Explorers of North America, 1492–1806.* New York: Doubleday & Company, Inc., 1955.

Dorn, Walter L. *Competition for Empire,*

1740–1763. New York: Harper & Row, Publishers, 1940.

Eccles, William J. *Canadian Frontier, 1534–1760*. New York: Holt, Rinehart and Winston, Inc., 1969.

Freeman, Douglas S. *George Washington*. 7 vols. New York: Charles Scribner's Sons, 1948–1957.

Hamilton, Charles. *Braddock's Defeat*. Norman, Okla.: University of Oklahoma Press, 1959.

Hamilton, Edward P. *The French and Indian Wars*. New York: Doubleday & Company, Inc., 1962.

Innis, Harold A. *The Fur Trade in Canada*. New Haven, Conn.: Yale University Press, 1956.

Morison, Samuel E. *The Parkman Reader*. Boston: Little, Brown and Company, 1955.

Munro, William B. *Documents Relating to the Seignorial Tenure in Canada*. New York: Greenwood Press, Inc., 1968.

Pares, Richard. *War and Trade in the West Indies, 1739–1763*. New York: Barnes & Noble, Inc., 1963.

_____. *Yankee and Creoles, the Trade between North America and the West Indies before the American Revolution*. Hamden, Conn.: The Shoe String Press, Inc., 1968.

Parkman, Francis. *France and England in North America*. 9 vols. New York: Frederick Ungar Publishing Co., Inc., 1965.

Peckham, Howard H. *The Colonial Wars, 1689–1762*. Chicago: University of Chicago Press, 1964.

_____. *Pontiac and the Indian Uprising*. Chicago: University of Chicago Press, 1947.

Plumb, John H. *Chatham*. Hamden, Conn.: The Shoe String Press, Inc., 1953.

Robertson, Charles G. *Chatham and the British Empire*. New York: Crowell Collier and Macmillan, Inc., 1962.

Savelle, Max. *The Diplomatic History of the Canadian Boundary, 1749–1763*. New York: Russell & Russell, Publishers, 1940.

Sosin, Jack M. *Whitehall and the Wilderness, 1760–1775*. Lincoln, Nebr.: University of Nebraska Press, 1961.

Wrong, George M. *The Rise and Fall of New France*. 2 vols. New York: Crowell Collier and Macmillan, Inc., 1928.

chapter 5

English Policy
and Colonial Unrest

The End of Salutary Neglect

The widespread colonial unrest that arose after the French and Indian War can in part be traced to the revision of English imperial policies in America. The new territorial acquisitions, which more than doubled the British empire in size in North America, presented special problems to the mother country and to the colonials. The English government was faced with the task of devising a plan to administer and control the vast trans-Appalachia region as best it could. It meant an end to the long period of colonial neglect. To further complicate matters, the colonials were growing restless for the Ohio Valley, the right to which they thought they had won by participating in the war. The English, on the other hand, were reluctant to arouse the Indians since the Pontiac uprising had just been quieted; and the fur lobbyists were pressuring Parliament to keep the dirt farmers out of beaver country. Other lobbyists, such as the manufacturers and land speculators who wished to profit from an increased population, opposed the "beaverites" and called for the opening of the Ohio territory to settlement.

PROCLAMATION OF 1763

The English government offered a compromise in the Proclamation of 1763. This instrument not only provided for the governments of newly acquired Quebec, East Florida, and West Florida, but laid down the guidelines with regard to future dealings with the Indians and western land. It was the latter that irritated the colonials and land speculators most, for it closed the area beyond the Appalachia Mountains to settlement. The proclamation line, however, failed to hold the flood of pioneers who viewed the British decision as unfair, and within a few months after its appearance the restraining line was all but forgotten.

External Taxes

NAVIGATION ACTS

Perhaps equally as irritating to the Americans were the new duties and taxes imposed on the colonies, as well as the mother country, for the purpose of paying off the war debt, which was in excess of £130 million, and for the maintenance of garrisons in America, which were believed necessary in order to protect the colonials from themselves and from the dangers of the frontier. The colonials, however, had other ideas. They tolerated the Navigation Acts of 1651–1663, which attempted to give the English shipping companies a monopoly on enumerated items, such as sugar, tobacco, cotton, wool, indigo, and so on, because the acts were never strictly enforced. Smuggling and bribery, therefore, proved effective means of evasion.

MOLASSES, WOOLEN, HAT, AND IRON ACTS

The colonists practically ignored the Molasses Act of 1733, which placed high duties on sugar and molasses from non-British islands, mainly because the British islands could not meet the demand for these items in the colonies. Nevertheless, they did comply, for the most part, with the Woolen, Hat, and Iron Acts (1699–1750), which told the colonials what they could and could not produce in America. Actually, during the course of their business ventures, the colonials frequently found it advantageous to work out special deals with those English officials who were not averse to self-enrichment.

SUGAR ACT

By 1763 Prime Minister Grenville and his cabinet were convinced that the colonials must pay their share of taxes, which would be levied for what they considered to be the defense and economic well-being of all. Accordingly, in March 1764, the American Revenue Act, better known as the Sugar Act, was issued. The provisions of this instrument raised the duties on certain foreign goods imported into the colonies. For example, European wines were to pay ten shillings a ton; the tariff on oriental and European fabrics was increased to two and three shillings per pound respectively, and foreign indigo and coffee imposts were also elevated. Higher duties were placed on other foreign goods that were sent directly to the colonies without stopping in English ports. Sugar, for instance, was raised to twenty-seven shillings per hundredweight—a duty designed to discourage the competition offered by the cheap

sugar supply of the French, Dutch, and Spanish possessions in the West Indies.

The Molasses Act of 1733 was renewed and surprisingly revised downward, which appeared to be a favorable concession to the colonists; but soon thereafter the news broke that all regulations with regard to the collection of duties were to be rigorously enforced. In fact, the old "writs of assistance" were to be used by customs officials, which would permit them to search premises for illegal goods, and all those persons suspected of smuggling were to be tried in royal courts. This was a distressing blow to merchants and smugglers, who had for years appreciated the leniency of the royal coast guards and the sympathy of local jurors.

PARSON'S CAUSE

One of the most sensitive issues of the colonial period arose in 1763 in the so-called Parson's Cause. A controversy developed when the Virginia legislature, hostile to state-supported churches, changed the payment of parsons' salaries from the then high-priced tobacco[1] (in excess of two pence per pound) to money calculated at the rate of two pence per pound of tobacco. The parsons decided to fight for the loss in pay inasmuch as the original law of 1748 had set their salary at 17,280 pounds of tobacco. The church referred their case to the crown, where the Virginia law was disallowed. Out of these suits, however, emerged a brilliant young lawyer, Patrick Henry, from Virginia, who ably defended the case of the colony. He based his argument on a denial of the right of Parliament to revoke or revise a Virginia law that had been signed by the governor, because such an act, as he saw it, violated the compact (or fundamental rights) between the crown and her subjects. Henry's eloquent defense may have

[1] Tobacco was at that time a common medium of exchange.

been instrumental in winning for him a seat in the House of Burgesses.

CURRENCY ACT

The ink had hardly time to dry on the Sugar Act when Parliament passed the Currency Act in the summer of 1764. This measure forbade the colonials to make their paper money legal tender and further strengthened the law by placing a £ 1000 fine on any governor who authorized or signed this sort of medium of exchange. It was at this point that the southern colonists, many of whom relied on paper money, joined the northern dissenters of the Sugar Act in a general protest against what both considered arbitrary acts by the mother country, even though a similar act had been imposed upon some of the colonies in 1751. As a result of this act, colonial debtors experienced mounting despair because paper money had afforded some hope of liberating themselves from indebtedness within a reasonable period of time. Creditors, however, also complained because the value of the paper currency often fluctuated.

Colonial America reacted to the Sugar and Currency Acts by reducing her trade with England and in some instances by boycotting certain British imports. Some colonists, like Samuel Adams, claimed that the Sugar Act represented taxation without proper representation. This bold stand later helped to elect him to the House of Representatives. Perhaps even more significant were the secret societies formed for the express purpose of finding ways to cut what they considered to be the binding strings of mercantilism.

Internal Taxes

STAMP ACT

The Stamp Act of 1765 levied the first direct tax by the English. This measure required certain legal documents to carry a stamp, the cost of which would be determined by the value or nature of the instrument. Hence, commercial and legal contracts demanded the stamp as well as such items as newspapers, pamphlets, advertisements, calendars, almanacs, licenses, and even dice and playing cards. The financial bite ranged from £ 2 to £ 6, all of which, according to the calculations of Grenville, were necessary for the defense and security of the colonies. A few of the unsuspecting colonists, like Benjamin Franklin, thinking that the new tax would be palatable to the Americans, agreed to serve as stamp agents. Much to their embarrassment, however, a major part of the colonial populace rose up in protest. The Stamp Act, unfortunately for Grenville and Parliament, pried into the pocketbooks of those lawyers and publishers who were most eloquent in dissent. In a speech before the Virginia House of Burgesses, Patrick Henry called for the right of self-taxation and an end to British impositions if the colonists were not to be represented in Parliament by Americans. In the meantime, a group of Revolutionists, known as the Sons of Liberty, harassed stamp agents and in 1766 burned the home of Massachusetts' Lieutenant Governor Hutchinson.

STAMP ACT CONGRESS

During the fall of 1765, after heads had cleared, a Stamp Act Congress met in New York to try to resolve some of the problems. Twenty-seven delegates from nine states finally drafted and approved resolutions of rights and grievances and forwarded petitions to King George and Parliament. In these famous papers the colonists formally registered their complaint of taxation without consent, either by the people or their representatives. Finally, the ultimate challenge was made with regard to the right of Parliament to tax any of the colonies.

REPEAL OF STAMP ACT

Faced by this sort of opposition in the colonies and discontent among the English merchants, who were now hard-pressed by the effective boycott, a new government in England, under the leadership of Lord Rockingham, a Whig, repealed the offensive parts of the Stamp Act in March 1766. This action was commended by Benjamin Franklin, William Pitt, and certain members of Parliament whose efforts had not gone unnoticed. In their anxiety to claim victory over the Stamp Act controversy, however, the Americans failed to react to a Declaratory Act passed on the same day. This act was intended to remind the colonists that the principles of mercantilism were still very much in effect (as clearly outlined in colonial charters) and that the mother country, therefore, still retained the final authority to pass and enforce any legislation with regard to the colonies.

QUARTERING ACT

One of the final acts initiated by the Grenville government before leaving office in 1765 provided for a permanent standing army in America. This measure, commonly known as the Quartering Act, called for the billeting of soldiers in private vacant buildings when barracks and hotels proved to be insufficient. Rates for food, lodging, and any necessary transportation were to be set in accordance with local standards. Since more troops were concentrated in New York because of that colony's strategic location, the inhabitants rose up in protest. In fact, many sections of New York refused to abide by certain provisions of the new act, whereupon Parliament voided any impending laws that might be passed by the New York assembly until such time that they experienced a change of heart. The colony finally acquiesced so that legislative functions might resume, but New York's stubbornness caused others to doubt and

to inquire about the constitutionality of such acts.

TOWNSHEND ACTS

Relatively free of the restraints of Prime Minister Pitt, who was at that time ill, and unmindful of the colonial drift toward independence, the new Chancellor of the Exchequer Charles Townshend, in 1767, introduced one of the most ambitious programs of external taxes in the history of the colonies. Townshend, convinced that additional revenues were necessary and that the royal governors and their appointees were in need of emancipation from the colonial assemblies, called for a reorganization of the taxes and their collecting agencies. It was the latter that caused particular concern among the colonists. The revenue would be used not only to defray costs of defense in America, but to pay the salaries of royal civil officials.

BOARD OF CUSTOMS

The Townshend reforms introduced new duties for tea, glass, paper, lead, and paints, and created a Board of Customs (a counterpart of the one in London), which was charged with the responsibility of facilitating tax collecting. In order to deal with those Americans who persisted in trading in the illegal traffic of goods, a system of vice-admiralty courts was established with branches in Boston, Charlestown, Halifax, and Philadelphia. In addition, the Townshend Acts reaffirmed the "writs of assistance" and the right of the admiralty courts to operate without juries in order to expedite the prosecution of lawbreakers.

SECRETARY OF STATE
FOR THE COLONIES

To complement this vast reorganization and to keep the mother country's ear tuned in to the shifting colonial reactions and needs, a position known as the Secretary of State for the Colonies was created. This office was overrun with business when news of the Townshend program spread through the colonies, for the response to the acts was sudden and dramatic. The taxes were rejected by the Americans, and English officials were so harassed that ships and troops had to be summoned to protect them and their families. Bold leadership in opposition to the new program came early from the assemblies of Massachusetts and New York. Samuel Adams, a member of the former, drafted a "circular letter," which called on the other colonies to resist, and New York adopted a nonimportation agreement, despite the fact that she had just been disciplined for resisting the Quartering Act. As a result, the Massachusetts assembly was dissolved and that of New York was suspended.

Protest Turns to Violence

Meanwhile, in June 1772, the British revenue schooner *Gaspee* ran aground off the coast of Providence while attempting to apprehend a suspect, whereupon several merchants led by John Brown boarded the vessel, removed the crew, and put the torch to the schooner. A commission was appointed to investigate the incident, but no convictions were ever realized. In another customs episode, John Hancock's sloop the *Liberty* was seized in the port of Boston for obstructing the collection of duties.

Of the many debates and pamphlets that emerged during this period of colonial unrest, perhaps the best known came from the pen of John Dickinson, a Philadelphia lawyer. Armed with a flair for writing and a zeal for independence, he wrote "Letters from a Farmer" for the *Pennsylvania Chronicle,* in which he attacked the behavior of Parliament for impinging on the liberties of New York and the right of Parliament to levy any kind of taxes against the colonists. He

did, however, recognize the right of the crown to regulate colonial commerce and to collect tariffs that were deemed necessary for that regulation; but duties levied to raise revenue he viewed as another form of taxation and should, therefore, be rejected.

Virginia continued to assert herself as a leader of the rebel colonies by drafting the so-called Virginia Resolves of 1769. Written by George Mason and read by George Washington, these measures restated the popular colonial belief that taxation must carry consent.

Faced again by mounting protests from the colonists and by pleas from hard-pressed English merchants, a new British government under Lord North acquiesced for the second time in less than five years. In 1770 most of the Townshend duties were repealed, except for the time-honored tariffs on tobacco, wine, sugar, and molasses. The new duty on tea, however, was retained, perhaps because England saw a need to keep alive the principle of Parliamentary taxation and perhaps because the crown wished to save some face. In the meantime, the Earl of Hillsborough, Chairman of the Board of Trade, called for a reconciliation between England and the colonies.

"BOSTON MASSACRE"

Encouraged by these victories and cognizant that the main issues with regard to the right of Parliament to tax had not been resolved to the satisfaction of the colonists, the Sons of Liberty, under the leadership of such firebrands as Samuel Adams of Boston and Samuel Chase of Baltimore, continued to harass British officials and garrisons. On March 5, 1770, strained relations between the opposing camps snapped in the altercation that has gone down in history as the "Boston Massacre." In this encounter part of an emotion-packed crowd led by seaman Crispus Attucks, a mestizo, attacked one of the English guards with verbal insults and snowballs, which, in turn, brought out more of the British regulars. During the tension-filled moments of the melee, a rifle was discharged, the source of which remains a moot question, causing a few of the guards to fire into the crowd. When the skirmish ended, five colonists, including Attucks, lay dead.

Samuel Adams and other Sons of Liberty found the Boston incident to be grist for their propaganda mill and soon forced the withdrawal of troops from the city of Boston. Those guards who fired their rifles, six in all, along with the officer in charge, were tried in a local court, and surprisingly enough, all but two were acquitted. Even those two were given light fines on a conviction of manslaughter. Overt provocation was recognized by the court as a prime factor in the case.

"COMMITTEES OF CORRESPONDENCE"

Expressions and acts of discontent continued after the incident at Boston, and Samuel Adams, the "gadfly of the Revolution," stood ever ready to fan the flames of unrest. In 1772 he formed what became known as the "Committees of Correspondence" in Massachusetts. Designed to produce and spread anti-British propaganda through the use of letters and pamphlets, the committee idea soon spread throughout New England, and by 1773 underground cells operated in all of the colonies.

THE TEA ACT OF 1773

By 1773 the mother country and her American colonies had experienced numerous acts of estrangement, but there appeared to be no impending crisis that would cause separation. Some of the British merchants, on the other hand, seemed to move from one financial dilemma to another. In the spring of 1773, the British East India Company was in trouble. Unable to move an enormous supply of its tea because of the efficiency of American smugglers, the company called on the English government for assistance. The crown responded by awarding the company what amounted to a virtual monopoly of the tea trade in America. Bitterness once again spread through the colonies in opposition not only to the tea tax, but to the idea of a monopoly and its concomitant evils. While the giant corporation might make cheaper tea available to some of the pro-British merchants, others, whose radical sentiments were well known, were fearful of this sort of discrimination. They were also aware that precedents might be established.

"BOSTON TEA PARTY"

Merchants and other revolutionaries in the port cities resisted the English imports. Shipments of tea were locked in warehouses and sale was prohibited; some ships were never unloaded, while others were damaged or destroyed by radicals. Out of these tea episodes came another dramatic chapter in the series of revolutionary firsts in Boston. Painted as Indians and under the concealment of darkness, a band of colonists led by the ubiquitous Samuel Adams boarded a vessel in the Boston harbor on December 16, 1773, and dumped 342 chests of tea into the water.

While a considerable number of Bostonians and colonists in other parts saw the "tea party" as a just and deserving reprisal, some of the Patriots, including Benjamin Franklin, as well as conservative property owners, viewed it as wanton destruction of property. Compensation, they felt, should be made immediately.

THE INTOLERABLE ACTS OF 1774

The British government, prodded by arch-conservatives, pushed through a program of harsh punishment, particularly for Massachusetts. These disciplinary measures, sometimes called the Intolerable Acts of 1774, carried four major provisions: the port of Boston was to be closed until compensation for the lost tea was made; royal officials implicated in capital crimes could henceforth be tried in England; royal authority was increased in Massachusetts by providing for royal appointment of executive advisers and judges of the lower courts; and, finally, the Quartering Act of 1765 was revived. In order to reaffirm the seriousness and determination of this program, Lord North replaced Thomas Hutchinson, the governor of Massachusetts, with General Thomas Gage, the commander of royal troops in the colonies.

QUEBEC ACT

It was also at this time that the Quebec Act was passed by Parliament. This act, mistakenly grouped with the Intolerable Acts by the colonists, attempted to resolve several sensitive issues in Canada: the boundaries of the province of Quebec were extended south to the Ohio River; religious freedom was granted to all Catholics; the Canadian courts returned to French principles of law, except in criminal cases;[2] and the government reverted back to the French concept of centralization without a representative assembly. All of the measures were in keeping with the wishes of the French Canadians.

Perhaps for the first time the colonies had some semblance of unity in opposing the regulations of the crown. Support for Massachusetts was not lacking, while veterans (particularly those in Virginia) of the French and Indian War began to wonder if the blood shed for the Ohio Valley had been sacrificed by the Quebec Act. Moreover, Protestants opposed the recognition of Catholicism, which many viewed as a state religion. Equally irritating to the colonists was the suspension of representative government and jury trial. Just how to resolve the new crises facing the Americans now became a common goal for the conservatives and liberals throughout the colonies.

[2] French civil law required no jury.

Select Bibliography

Abernathy, Thomas P. *Western Lands and the American Revolution.* New York: Russell & Russell, Publishers, 1959.

Bailyn, Bernard. *The Ideological Origins of the American Revolution.* Cambridge, Mass.: Belknap Press of Harvard University Press, 1967.

————, ed. *Pamphlets of the American Revolution, 1750–1776.* Cambridge, Mass.: Belknap Press of Harvard University Press, 1965.

Boucher, Jonathan. *A View of the Causes and Consequences of the American Revolution: In Thirteen Discourses.* New York: Russell & Russell, Publishers, 1967.

Bridenbaugh, Carl. *Mitre and Sceptre: Trans-Atlantic Faiths, Ideas, Personalities and Politics, 1689–1775.* New York: Oxford University Press, 1967.

Commager, Henry S., and Richard B. Morris. *The Spirit of Seventy-Six.* 2 vols. Indianapolis, Ind.: The Bobbs-Merrill Co., Inc., 1958.

Dickerson, Oliver M. *The Navigation Acts and the American Revolution.* Philadelphia: The University of Pennsylvania Press, 1951.

Gipson, Lawrence H. *Coming of the Revolution, 1763–1775.* New York: Harper & Row, Publishers, 1954.

Granger, Bruce I. *Benjamin Franklin.* Ithaca, N.Y.: Cornell University Press, 1964.

Greene, Jack P. *The Quest for Power: The Lower Houses of Assembly in the Southern Royal Colonies, 1689–1776.* Chapel Hill, N.C.: University of North Carolina Press, 1963.

Jensen, Merrell, ed. *American Colonial*

Documents to 1776. New York: Oxford University Press, 1955.

Kammen, Michael G. *A Rope of Sand: The Colonial Agents, British Politics, and the American Revolution.* Ithaca, N.Y.: Cornell University Press, 1968.

Knollenberg, Bernhard. *Origin of the American Revolution: 1759–1766.* New York: Crowell Collier and Macmillan, Inc., 1960.

Labaree, Benjamin W. *The Boston Tea Party.* New York: Oxford University Press, 1964.

Main, Jackson T. *The Social Structure of Revolutionary America.* Princeton, N.J.: Princeton University Press, 1965.

Miller, John C. *Origins of the American Revolution.* Stanford, Calif., Stanford University Press, 1959.

Morgan, Edmund S. *The Birth of the Republic, 1763–89.* Chicago: University of Chicago Press, 1956.

Morris, Richard B. *Peacemakers, Great Powers and American Independence.* New York: Harper & Row Publishers, 1965.

Namier, Lewis B. *Charles Townshend.* New York: Cambridge University Press, 1964.

————. *England in the Age of the American Revolution.* New York: St. Martin's Press, Inc., 1961.

Palmer, Robert R. *The Age of Democratic Revolution, 1760–1800.* Princeton, N.J.: Princeton University Press, 1959.

Robson, Eric. *The American Revolution, 1763–1783.* New York: W. W. Norton & Company, Inc., 1966.

Rossiter, Clinton. *Seedtime of the Republic.* New York: Harcourt Brace Jovanovich, Inc., 1953.

Savelle, Max. *Seeds of Liberty: Genesis of the American Mind.* Seattle, Wash.: University of Washington Press, 1965.

Schlesinger, Arthur M. *Colonial Merchants and the American Revolution, 1763–1776.* New York: Frederick Ungar Publishing Co., Inc., 1957.

————. *Prelude to Independence: The Newspaper War on Britain, 1764–1776.* New York: Alfred A. Knopf, 1958.

Stourzh, Gerald. *Benjamin Franklin and American Foreign Policy.* Chicago: University of Chicago Press, 1954.

Sydnor, Charles S. *Gentlemen Freeholders: Political Practices in Washington's Virginia.* Chapel Hill, N.C.: University of North Carolina Press, 1952.

Van Tyne, Claude H. *The Causes of the War of Independence.* Gloucester, Mass.: Peter Smith, 1951.

chapter 6

Protest Turns to Revolution

Imperial Politics

WHIGS AND TORIES

In England King George III (1760–1820) attempted to combine parliamentary government with his own concept of enlightened despotism and thereby won many supporters in the House of Commons. His strongest opposition came from the sometimes disorganized Whigs who numbered among their liberal supporters William Pitt and the Marquess of Rockingham. The Whigs, in general, were suspicious of kings, Catholics, and Frenchmen, and found considerable support among the middle class and merchants of London, particularly the upper aristocracy, who had everything to gain by weakening the power of the king. They called not only for constitutional monarchy, but for parliamentary supremacy, rule of law, and the toleration of dissenting Protestants. American Patriots were also known as Whigs, in keeping with the opposition party in England, but their objectives did not always coincide with those of the English.

The Tories, on the other hand, drew their strength from the lesser aristocracy and gentry—those who were suspicious of the merchants of London—and gave unreserved support to church and king. Their counterparts in the colonies, also known as Loyalists, made up about one-third of the population and claimed a considerable following in the Carolinas, Georgia, Pennsylvania, New York, and New Jersey. American Tory leadership emerged from the ranks of the Anglican Church, British officials, and certain well-to-do conservative families. Their views naturally ran contrary to separation from the mother country and to the Patriots' concepts of democracy. At the time of the American Revolution, however, Parliament was supreme and the Tories had so declined in power that the British government appeared to be primarily composed of Whig factions. Thus the term Tory, as used by Americans, was little more than a propaganda device.

Lord North, the prime minister (1770–1782), was capable but bowed to every wish of the king, however ill-advised; and other ministers passed in and out of office at the whim of the king, thus precluding any chance of responsible and continuous policies. The American revolutionists took advantage of this vacillating conditions in the "royal house" and began to assert their independence, which, in the opinion of some historians, had been growing since the planting of the first colonies.

The Congress: Conservatives versus Radicals

FIRST CONTINENTAL CONGRESS

Meanwhile, the colonists, and the radicals

72

in particular, advocated the traditional boycott of English goods and called for a colonial congress in order to discuss the dilemma of Massachusetts and plan the future of the colonies. The first Continental Congress assembled at Philadelphia (this city was one of the early leaders in the colonial unity movement) on September 5, 1774, with fifty-six delegates representing twelve colonies. Georgia voted against sending delegates. When the Congress finally turned to the crucial issues at hand, it became obvious that both conservative and radical viewpoints were well represented. Conservative leaders included John Dickinson and Joseph Galloway of Pennsylvania, John Rutledge of South Carolina, John Jay and James Duane of New York, and George Read of Delaware. The radicals numbered among their torchbearers John and Samuel Adams of Massachusetts, Richard Henry Lee, Patrick Henry, and Peyton Randolph of Virginia, Roger Sherman of Connecticut, Charles Thomson (nondelegate) of Pennsylvania, and Christopher Gadson of South Carolina. Peyton Randolph was elected chairman and Charles Thomson secretary.

SUFFOLK RESOLVES

The conservatives eloquently defended their belief in the efficacy of law and order and the strength of petitions against oppressive measures. The radicals, on the other hand, while affirming their loyalty to the king, rested their case on the natural rights of men derived from natural law. Moreover, they suggested that the colonies as a whole be treated as a federation of independent states whose external affairs might well be regulated by Parliament, but whose internal affairs were inalienable rights. This philosophy was incorporated in the Suffolk Resolves[1] introduced for consideration by the Con-

[1] These resolutions had been written by a convention at Suffolk County, Massachusetts, and were carried to Philadelphia by Paul Revere.

gress. Accordingly, the resolutions: (1) condemned the Intolerable Acts as unconstitutional; (2) advised the colonies to establish their own militia for defensive purposes; (3) recommended a stringent plan of nonintercourse with the mother country; and (4) encouraged Massachusetts to organize a new government.

GALLOWAY'S PLAN

With the appearance of these revolutionary measures, the conservatives, under the leadership of Joseph Galloway, a noted lawyer of Philadelphia, drafted their own resolutions in an effort to dilute the Suffolk Resolves. Galloway's Plan of Union called for a colonial confederation under a royal executive head, with a legislative council (an American Parliament) elected by the colonial assemblies. This, Galloway believed, would resolve the problem of parliamentary taxation for all parties concerned.

"A DECLARATION OF RIGHTS"

The radicals of the Continental Congress, however, adverse to almost any kind of conciliation to the British, defeated Galloway's Plan by one vote and approved the Suffolk Resolves. In addition, the delegates took time to draft and adopt a list of grievances entitled "A Declaration of Rights" that were designed to reaffirm their loyalty to the king, but also reminded the crown that Parliament intrusions into colonial internal affairs were matters of grave concern.

CONTINENTAL ASSOCIATION

Lest these measures go the way of other resolutions, the Congress put "teeth" into the new boycott by providing for an enforcement arm known as the Continental Association. Trade with the British Empire was to be phased out by September 1775, and those merchants who took the new regulations too lightly were to be blacklisted by the association. Finally, colonial manufacturing was encouraged in order to make the colonies less dependent on England.

With these bold steps taken, the First Continental Congress adjourned on a note of determination to meet again in May should its grievances go unnoticed.

Most of colonial America no doubt endorsed the resolutions adopted by the Congress, in view of the disciplinary measures levied against Massachusetts, while the Whigs in Parliament, much to the chagrin of the king, smiled on the events. English merchants soon extended an appeal to Parliament to soften its stand in order to save their trade. Parliament and King George, however, were not hard-pressed to find support. In fact, the parliamentary elections of October 1774 appeared to be a clear endorsement of the Lord North government and its coercive policy.

Protest Turns to War

Goaded by the ever persistent Samuel Adams' "Committees of Correspondence" and consoled by the penned justifications of James Wilson's *Considerations on the Nature and Extent of the Legislative Authority of the British Parliament* and Thomas Jefferson's *A Summary View of the Rights of British America,* many Americans were pulled along by the radical tide. The arming of the colonials naturally proved to be one of the areas of greatest concern to the English and one that was impossible to control.

LEXINGTON

After several confrontations, General Thomas Gage decided on a show of force before the Hancock-and-Adams-led rebels in Concord during which, if possible, the British would capture rebel arms and munitions. The alert insurgents, however, planned a raid of their own.

William Dawes and Paul Revere warned the countryside of the impending clash, while seventy "minutemen," under the command of Captain John Parker, assembled at Lexington. On April 19, 1775, open rebellion began with an unknown shot at Lexington, and in the running skirmishes and ambushes that took place at Concord and during the British retreat to Boston, the regulars suffered almost 300 casualties while the colonists were reported to have had 93 either killed, wounded, or missing. The revolution was now a reality.

SECOND CONTINENTAL CONGRESS

The Second Continental Congress began to assemble (again without Georgia)[2] in Philadelphia on May 10 as prescribed by the First Congress, and a whole host of new faces appeared on the scene. Benjamin Franklin, John Hancock, James Wilson, and Thomas Jefferson were among the new, and of those not in attendance the conservative Joseph Galloway was perhaps the most notable. The previous presiding officers, Peyton Randolph and Charles Thomson, were again installed. However, Randolph withdrew from the Congress, and John Hancock was elected as the new president. Preparing for any sort of eventuality, but perhaps with the hope that war would not continue, the Congress provided for a Continental Army and appointed George Washington as its commander in chief. With this task out of the way, the delegates wrote a "Declaration of the Causes and Necessity of Taking Up Arms" in order to justify their rebellion. This document traced the long history of "tyranny and oppression" which the English had imposed on their colonies and which had ultimately "driven the subjects to rebellion." It ended by relating the events of General Gage's assault on the colonials at Lexington.

---

[2] Georgia finally sent a team of delegates in September.

"OLIVE BRANCH PETITION"

The door of reconciliation was left open, however, and many of the colonials undoubtedly desired and expected that differences would be resolved once again. Moreover, the "Olive Branch Petition," in which the Congress renewed its expression of loyalty and called on the king to use his influence to curb the arbitrary acts of Parliament against the colonies, was sent to George III. Parliament responded by stepping up British mobilization and by sending more troops to America; the colonials retaliated by harassing British strongholds and overturning royal officials. By the end of 1775 the insurrectionists had staged *coups d'etat* in all of the provincial governments.

BUNKER HILL

While these events were taking place, the young Continental Army was learning the art of war against the British regulars. In May 1775, Benedict Arnold and Ethan Allen captured the lightly garrisoned Forts Ticonderoga, Crown Point, and St. John, while the colonials in Massachusetts placed a virtual siege around General Gage in Boston. It was near Boston that the first major campaign of the young war took place. On June 17, the colonials faced the British regulars on Breed's Hill (erroneously given the name of nearby Bunker Hill). The colonials lost the battle, but the campaign has gone down in history as a moral victory, inasmuch as the British lost almost twice as many men in three frontal attacks, the last of which is reported to have been successful only because the colonials exhausted their ammunition.

"COMMON SENSE"

The opening month of 1776 saw the appearance of the revolution's most eloquent penman. Thomas Paine, a vagabond immigrant, was writing for a publisher in Philadelphia at the turn of the new year when the first of his articles, entitled "Common Sense," was conceived. His pamphlets were an immediate success, for he explained the meaning of the revolutionary movement in the framework of ideals that appealed to the conscience of America. He called for complete separation from England since common sense should reveal the superiority of republicanism over monarchy as the most viable agent for freedom-loving men. Paine thus lifted the debate from the basic issue of taxation to permanent separation.

RESTRAINING ACT

During that same eventful month, the colonists received the response of Lord North and Parliament to the resolutions of the Second Continental Congress. Known as the Restraining Act, it prohibited any further dealings with the American rebels and authorized the seizure or destruction of American vessels.

DECLARATION OF INDEPENDENCE

As the troubled Continental Congress approached the summer of 1776, the aims of the radical element became increasingly clear. On July 2, in spite of conservative resistance from the Middle Colonies, all but New York approved a resolution (introduced by Richard Henry Lee of Virginia a month earlier), which stated that "these United Colonies are, and of right ought to be, free and independent States. . . ."[3] In the meantime, a committee composed of Thomas Jefferson, John Adams, Benjamin Franklin, Roger Sherman, and Robert R. Livingston had been appointed to restate the Virginia Resolution in a more formal declaration of independence. The Congress later entitled it "The unanimous

[3] If we were more history-minded we would honor July 2 instead of July 4.

Declaration of the thirteen united States of America." The burden of the task was carried by Jefferson and the document was passed by the delegates on July 4.[4]

Jefferson, who had now turned revolutionary, used the eloquence of Paine to express the concepts of John Locke and the European Enlightenment on natural law in human rights. He thus identified government as an instrument of and for the people that could be altered or abolished should it fail to serve the needs of the people. In addition, Jefferson set forth a long list of colonial grievances that had accumulated over the years and stood as self-evidence of the harshness of British acts imposed upon the colonials by the king and Parliament.

The Continental Congress Prosecutes a War

STRENGTHS AND WEAKNESSES

The British war machine, if viewed numerically, had a frightening advantage. England boasted a population of about 10 million as compared to only 3 million colonials, 1 million of whom either sympathized with or were outright dyed-in-the-wool Loyalists. The Patriots, representing a minority movement, vied with this group for the support of the million or so who for varying reasons chose to remain neutral. In addition, Great Britain controlled the seas and maintained a vast empire from which to draw financial resources. It is not so surprising, then, that France delayed her support to the Americans.

Great Britain, on the other hand, failed to live up to her potential strength in fighting the American rebels: her army probably never numbered more than 100,-000, even though she enlisted several

[4] Contrary to popular belief, the delegates (Hancock excepted) did not sign the document until August 2, and several signed after that date.

thousand German mercenaries, and her people were reluctant to shoulder additional war taxes with the French and Indian war debt still on the books. Ever alert to avail themselves of this sort of propaganda, the Whig elements in Parliament represented a perpetual thorn in the side of the North government. In addition, the British had to maintain an Atlantic supply line, and her troops had to fight the unpopular war on foreign terrain.

The revolutionary army was "outnumbered, out-supplied, and out-payed," and, therefore, had a marked psychological advantage even though the great number of desertions fail to attest to this. The officer class, extremely capable and highly motivated, tended to offset any desertions by their ability to rally the troops for the crucial battles. Moreover, American weapons made up in quality what they lacked in quantity. For example, the American rifle was considered to be more effective in range and accuracy than the smoothbore British muskets. Their financial backing, however, was probably the worst of any major organized army. Unable to levy taxes, the Continental Congress finally had to turn to France, Holland, and Spain for loans. Actually, since March, the colonists had been receiving gunpowder and other contraband from the French and Spanish through a company bearing a fictitious name. This arrangement was instigated by Caron de Beaumarchais and Silas Deane and provided as much as 90 percent of the gunpowder used by the Americans.

One of the first major campaigns in the Southern Colonies occurred when General Cornwallis decided to attack General Charles Lee and the Charleston defenses on June 28, 1776; much to the former's surprise, the South Carolina fort proved to be much too stubborn and the British naval squadron was turned back with heavy casualties.

BATTLE OF LONG ISLAND

After the evacuation of Boston by the British, General Washington gambled that the next strike would be at New York and moved his troops there in the spring of 1776; whereupon, the brothers, General and Admiral Howe, landed a force of some 32,000 men in August and, in the battle of Long Island, routed the colonials with heavy losses. Thinking that the rebels might be ready to talk, the Howes, appointed as peace commissioners by the king, offered to negotiate with the battle-weary Americans should the latter care to renounce the Declaration of Independence. Since this was unthinkable to the rebels, the conference soon ended and Washington withdrew his forces from the precarious Manhattan Island and retreated to Harlem Heights, where new fortifications were built.

TRENTON AND PRINCETON

General Washington soon found it advisable to retreat to New Jersey and Pennsylvania, but promptly left those colonies for Baltimore because New Jersey was uncomfortably crowded with Loyalists and Pennsylvania was expecting the British. It was at this point in mid-December, with his army dwindling and supplies low, that Washington decided to surprise the lightly garrisoned town of Trenton. On the night of December 26, he led a force of 2400 men across the ice-choked Delaware and captured Trenton with the loss of only five men. Washington next evaded a trap set by Cornwallis and surprised the British garrison at Princeton, after which he retreated to Morristown, where he established winter headquarters.

The British, now bent on teaching the upstart rebels a lesson, began three major offenses. General Burgoyne pushed down from Montreal toward the Hudson River valley, while General Howe moved his army near Philadelphia to engage Washington. A third and smaller force under Colonel St. Leger advanced from Lake Ontario to support General Burgoyne in the Hudson campaign. The forces under General Burgoyne, however, got so bogged down fighting the hit-and-run tactics of the Americans that they were finally forced to surrender at Saratoga on October 17, 1717. Meanwhile, even though Colonel St. Leger was turned back, General Howe did manage to defeat Washington in two separate engagements and secured Philadelphia and the lower Delaware for the British. Before winter set in, Washington made another surprise counterattack against Howe, who had moved to Germantown; but a heavy fog added confusion to the ordeal of battle, and he retreated to Valley Forge after an indecisive engagement. Some tacticians, with the advantage of hindsight, have criticized Howe's move against Philadelpia when a thrust to the north to meet Burgoyne might have proved more profitable.

FRANCO-AMERICAN ALLIANCE

The French, in the meantime, had withheld overt support until such time that the Americans demonstrated their ability on the battlefield. The battle of Saratoga not only warmed the hearts of the French but moved the British to extend a belated and futile offer of colonial self-rule within the empire. Meanwhile, in Paris, the American commission of Silas Deane, Arthur Lee, and Benjamin Franklin, waiting in the wing since the Declaration of Independence, were at last cordially received by the French foreign minister, Vergennes. Two treaties were signed on February 6, 1778: one provided for equal and reciprocal trade between the parties, while the other provided for mutual assistance against the British if and when the French entered the conflict, and guaranteed the independence of the United States. American designs on Canada and

Bermuda would be recognized, while France was given permission to seize the British West Indies. Finally, neither was to sign a peace treaty with Britain without the other's consent. The Continental Congress ratified the treaties on May 4 despite Lord North's offer of reconciliation.

The Revolution Becomes a World War

France was now in the war and it would be only a matter of time before this became formal. One of her countrymen had already entered the conflict on the side of the Americans, namely the Marquis de Lafayette. France sent a war fleet to American waters in April of 1778, and Spain entered the conflict against her traditional rival in June, but without a formal alliance. Holland joined France and Spain in 1780. Poland contributed Count Pulaski and Thaddeus Kosciusko who did yeoman service in training the American soldiers. Unable to engage the British fleet along the New England coast, Count d'Estaing, the French commander, sailed to the West Indies, where he met and defeated a British squadron under the command of Admiral Byron.

The American navy was slow in developing even though the New England clippers had a long illustrious maritime record. Commissioned privateers, sometimes alluded to as legalized pirates, made considerable contributions in keeping the British navy off balance (as many as 115 operated along the American coast during the year 1778), and John Paul Jones, a navy regular, distinguished himself aboard the *Ranger* and later the *Bon Homme Richard* when he carried the war to British waters. In one dramatic engagement he lost his own flagship in the act of capturing the British man-of-war *Serapis*.

SECURING THE OHIO VALLEY

The war in the West went well for the Americans. In the summer of 1778 George Rogers Clark marched a group of frontiersmen into the Ohio Valley and captured Kaskaskia on the upper Mississippi, and on his return trip the following winter he seized Vincennes on the Wabash River. The Northwest was now firmly under American control.

SOUTHERN CAMPAIGNS

The years 1780–1781 saw the British renew their efforts to win the war in the Southern Colonies. They had captured Savannah in 1778, and in the spring of 1780, General Clinton seized Charleston along with four ships and a garrison that numbered in excess of 5000 men—the most damaging defeat of the war for the Americans. With the fall of Camden in August 1780, the British added control of South Carolina to the already secured provinces of New York and Georgia. Their efforts to take North Carolina were aborted by the determined stand of a force of frontiersmen in the battle of King's Mountain. The campaigns of the southern theater finally settled into guerrilla warfare with Patriot and Loyalist giving no quarter, while such commanders as Morgan and Greene distinguished themselves with carefully planned strikes. Morgan finally defeated the British commander Tarleton at Cowpens, and Greene's riflemen so weakened the army of Cornwallis at Guilford Courthouse, North Carolina, that the latter was unable to pursue the costly advantage.

The morale of Washington's troops was boosted and then shaken by two events of 1780. The Americans were elated when some 5000 French troops landed in July to assist Washington in the assault on New York, but many were shocked to learn of the treason of Benedict Arnold. Arnold, a spirited veteran of several campaigns, was reportedly distraught with his assigned role in the war and conspired to turn West Point over to the British. The plot was discovered in September, but Arnold defected to the British before he could be captured, where he was commissioned a brigadier general. He later led several raids against the Americans.

YORKTOWN

Cornwallis, now convinced that the only way to defeat the Southern Colonies was to strike a lethal blow at their source of supplies, Virginia, moved his army to Yorktown, where he strengthened his forces with those of General Arnold, among others. Washington, meanwhile, joined forces with the French commander Rochambeau, and the allied army marched to Yorktown to join Lafayette and Anthony Wayne in the siege. While these events were taking shape, a French naval squadron blockaded the port. The outcome was never in doubt and Cornwallis surrendered his army on October 18, 1781. While Yorktown virtually ended the British threat in America, the war, nevertheless, dragged on for another year, much of it in the form of guerrilla skirmishes between the Patriots and the Loyalists.

TREATY OF PARIS (1783)

Anxious to collect the tribute of the Revolution, the Continental Congress sent Benjamin Franklin, John Adams, and John Jay to Paris with instructions to start peace negotiations within the guidelines established by the treaty of 1778. The French, however, delayed the talks and Jay and Adams became suspicious of possible French and Spanish intrigues at the expense of America and offered to negotiate secretly with the British. A new Whig ministry under Lord Rockingham, hard-pressed by the costly war and anxious to drive a wedge between France and her allies, signed a preliminary treaty of peace with the Americans in November of 1782. It was formalized in the Treaty of Paris in September of 1783. By the terms of the treaty, Britain agreed to recognize the United States and set the boundaries at the Great Lakes in the north, the Missis-

sippi River in the west, and Spanish Florida in the south. Franklin was mildly disappointed that they had failed to acquire Canada, but the Americans were granted liberal fishing rights off Newfoundland.

The Americans, in return, agreed to: (1) prohibit further harassment of the Loyalists; (2) encourage the states to restore lost property to the Loyalists; and (3) encourage the states to permit the English merchants to collect old debts long overdue. These last two provisions were all but ignored by the states and the federal government finally assumed the responsibility of paying off the merchants. The Loyalists had to shift for themselves.

Select Bibliography

Alden, John. *The American Revolution, 1775–1783.* New York: Harper & Row, Publishers, 1954.

―――. *The South in the Revolution, 1763–1789.* Baton Rouge, La.: Louisiana State University Press. 1957.

Becker, Carl L. *The Declaration of Independence.* New York: Alfred A. Knopf, 1942.

Bemis, Samuel F. *The Diplomacy of the American Revolution.* Gloucester, Mass.: Peter Smith, 1958.

Bradley, Arthur G. *The United Empire Loyalist, Founders of British Canada.* London: Butterworth & Co. (Publishers) Ltd., 1932.

Burnett, Edmund C. *The Continental Congress.* New York: W. W. Norton & Co., Inc., 1964.

Chinard, Gilbert. *Honest John Adams.* Gloucester, Mass.: Peter Smith, 1933.

―――. *Thomas Jefferson, The Apostle of Americanism.* Ann Arbor, Mich.: University of Michigan Press, 1957.

Clark, Dora Mae. *British Opinion and the American Revolution*. New York: Russell & Russell, Publishers, 1966.

Einstein, Lewis. *Divided Loyalties.* New York: Russell & Russell, Publishers, 1933.

Engleman, Fred L. *The Peace of Christmas Eve*. New York; Harcourt Brace Jovanovich, Inc., 1962.

Ferguson, E. James. *The Powers of the Purse: A History of American Public Finance, 1776–1790.* Chapel Hill, N.C.: University of North Carolina Press, 1961.

Freeman, Douglas S. *George Washington: A Biography.* 6 vols. New York: Charles Scribner's Sons, 1948–1954.

Granger, Bruce I. *Benjamin Franklin.* Ithaca, N.Y.: Cornell University Press, 1964.

Greene, Evarts B. *The Revolutionary Generation, 1763–1790.* New York: Crowell Collier and Macmillan, Inc., 1943.

Gummere, Richard Mott. *Seven Wise Men of Colonial America.* Cambridge, Mass.: Harvard University Press, 1967.

Guttridge, George Herbert. *English Whiggism and the American Revolution.* Berkeley, Calif.: University of California Press, 1963.

Humphrey, Edward Frank. *Nationalism and Religion in America, 1774–1789.* New York: Russell & Russell, Publishers, 1965.

Lancaster, Bruce. *From Lexington to Liberty: The Story of the American Revolution.* New York: Doubleday & Company, Inc., 1955.

Lutnick, Soloman. *The American Revolution and the British Press, 1775–1783.* Columbia, Mo.: University of Missouri Press, 1967.

McDonald, Forrest. *E Pluribus Unum: The Formation of the American Republic, 1776–1790.* Boston: Houghton Mifflin Company, 1965.

McDowell, Bart. *The Revolutionary War: America's Fight for Freedom.* Washington, D.C.: National Geographic Society, 1967.

Mackesy, Piers. *The War for America, 1775–1783.* Cambridge, Mass.: Harvard University Press, 1964.

Meade, Robert D. *Patrick Henry: Practical Revolutionary.* Philadelphia: J. B. Lippincott Co., 1969.

Miller, John C. *Sam Adams: Pioneer in Propaganda.* Stanford, Calif.: Stanford University Press, 1960.

_____. *Triumph of Freedom, 1775–1783.* Boston: Little, Brown and Company, 1948.

Mitchell, Joseph Brady. *Discipline and Bayonets: The Armies and Leaders in the War of the American Revolution.* New York: G. P. Putman's Sons, 1967.

Montross, Lynn. *The Reluctant Rebels: The Story of the Continental Congress, 1774–1790.* New York: Harper & Row, Publishers, 1950.

Morris, Richard B. *The American Revolution Reconsidered.* New York: Harper & Row, Publishers, 1967.

Nettels, Curtis P. *The Emergence of a National Economy, 1775–1815.* New York: Harper & Row, Publishers, 1950.

_____. *George Washington and American Independence.* Boston: Little, Brown and Company, 1951.

Newmann, George C. *The History of the Weapons of the American Revolution.* New York: Harper & Row, Publishers, 1969.

Patterson, Samuel White. *Horatio Gates, Defender of American Liberty.* New York: AMS Press, 1966.

Quarles, Benjamin. *The Negro in the American Revolution.* Chapel Hill, N.C.: University of North Carolina Press, 1967.

Smith, Page. *John Adams.* 2 vols. New York: Doubleday & Company, Inc., 1962.

Thane, Elswyth. *The Family Quarrel: A Journey through the Years of the Revolution.* London: Robert Hale, 1960.

Van Alstyne, Richard W. *Empire and Independence: The International History of the American Revolution.* New York: John Wiley & Sons, Inc., 1965.

Wallace, Willard M. *Appeal to Arms: A Military History of the American Revolution.* Chicago: Quadrangle Books, Inc., 1964.

Wright, Esmond. *Fabric of Freedom.* New York: Hill and Wang, Inc., 1961.

The American Revolution: In Search of Lost Causes and Meaning

The principal causes of the insurrection that has gone down in history as the American Revolution have preplexed historians since the time of the great event. The eighteenth-century Whig writers such as Thomas Paine and John Adams viewed the causes as largely grounded on ideas of freedom which through reason moved the people to resist the forces of tryanny. This view so dominated the scene in the nineteenth century that it swept men, like George Bancroft, along by the sheer magnitude of its force. Bancroft even traced the struggle for liberty to the infant colonies along the Atlantic seaboard.

Beginning in the 1890s a group of historians headed by Herbert L. Osgood and Charles M. Andrews called for an examination of British imperial administration and society. Much in keeping with the early Tory writers, they found the Revolution to have been a natural culmination of differing concepts of empire that evolved during the colonial period, and not to have been caused by British imperial policies.

After the turn of the century a group of historians under the leadership of Carl Becker, Charles Beard, and Arthur M. Schlesinger embraced the socioeconomic causes of the Revolution. They believed the economic stress between the mother country and her colonies provided the basic cause of the Revolution.

Since World War II a corruption of the old Whig school has been evident in the writings of Daniel J. Boorstin and Benjamin F. Wright, who place more emphasis on the conservative nature of the Revolution. They believed that the insurrection was designed to protect old and traditional rights and liberties as opposed to creating new ones.

The following questions are offered for the student's consideration as he reads the selected essays:

General Questions for Reflection and Discussion

1. To what extent was the American Revolution a political movement?
2. In what ways was the Revolution a class struggle over economic issues?
3. To what extent was the Revolution designed to change a social order?
4. In what ways was the Revolution really revolutionary?

5. In what ways, if any, did the American Constitution alter the goals of the Revolution?

6. To what extent did the Revolution teach America that "liberty requires Constitutional order"?

Basic Questions for Reflection and Discussion

1. How does Schlesinger distinguish between the American Revolution and the American war?

2. According to Schlesinger, why did the farmers revolt?

3. How does Schlesinger explain what he calls a counterrevolution?

4. In what ways was the Boston Tea Party a "turning point in the course of events"?

5. In Brown's essay, to what extent was the Massachusetts Constitution of 1780 representative of the various state constitutions?

6. What evidence does Brown use to demonstrate that democracy had already arrived in Massachusetts before the Revolution? Does it appear to be valid data?

7. How does Hacker explain the alliance within and between the planters and merchants and the more numerous lower middle-class artisans and mechanics and the working class?

8. Why was the Proclamation Line of 1763 and the Quebec Act of 1774 a blow to the southern economy?

9. According to Andrews, in what ways did English societal attitudes cause the Revolution?

10. Why does Andrews call the period from 1850 to the Revolution "epochal years in the history of England's relations with America"?

11. Compare Andrews and Brown with respect to the development of independent colonial governments.

12. Why does Andrews say that "the American Revolution was a political and Constitutional movement and only secondarily one that was either financial, commercial or social"?

Arthur M. Schlesinger

The Revolution as a Radical Movement

Most of our textbooks and popular treatises, ... have continued to perpetuate the obscurantism of the earlier time, and the students in our graduate schools seem to have been the only persons to be admitted within the inner portals where is to be found the shrine of Truth. The coming age promises to be an era in which an international comity will be attained that has never before been approached in the history of the world. This imposes upon those writers who interpret history for the masses the grave responsibility of being as scrupulously fair to other nations as to the United States in dealing with the events of American history; and it is a fact not to be denied that no episode requires re-examination more than the American Revolution. Furthermore, we are living in an epoch of popular revolutions; and every day's reading convinces one that, if it was ever proper to regard the American Revolution as a phenomenon operating in accordance with laws of its own and unlike popular uprisings generally, that time has receded into the dim past.

The term "American Revolution" is itself not without difficulties and its use has led to misconception and confusion. In letter after letter John Adams tried to teach a headstrong generation some degree of exactness in the use of an expression whose meaning they had knowledge

From "The American Revolution Reconsidered" by Arthur M. Schlesinger in *Political Science Quarterly*, Vol. 34, No. 1 (March, 1919), pp. 62–63 and 65–76, omitting footnotes except where necessary for understanding.

of only by report. "A history of the first war of the United States is a very different thing from a history of the American Revolution," he wrote in 1815. " . . . The revolution was in the minds of the people, and in the union of the colonies, both of which were accomplished before hostilities commenced. This revolution and union were gradually forming from the year 1760 to 1776." And to another correspondent he wrote: "But what do we mean by the American Revolution? Do we mean the American war? The Revolution was effected before the war commenced. The Revolution was in the minds and hearts of the people."

This distinction is not only valid in point of fact but it offers a helpful avenue of approach for a consideration of the facts of the nation's birth. If the period from 1760 to 1776 is not viewed merely as the prelude to the American Revolution, the military struggle may frankly be regarded for what it actually was, namely a war for independence, an armed attempt to impose the views of the revolutionists upon the British government and a large section of the colonial population at whatever cost to freedom of opinion or the sanctity of life and property. The major emphasis is thus placed upon the clashing of economic interests and the interplay of mutual prejudices, opposing ideals and personal antagonisms—whether in England or America—which made inevitable in 1776 what was unthinkable in 1760. . . .

With this brief view of affairs in Great

Britain it is now possible to consider the situation in America. Conditions there were both simpler and more complex than the traditional accounts represent. In place of thirteen units of population thinking alike on most public questions, there were in fact two or possibly three major groupings of population, differentiated by physiographical conditions, economic interests and political ideals. The communities on the coastal plain from New Hampshire to Pennsylvania constituted one of these divisions; the settlements of the tidewater regions from Maryland to Georgia formed another; and the third, less clearly outlined geographically, consisted of the western sections of many of the provinces. These three divisions represented modes of living and attitudes of mind much more fundamental than those indicated by arbitrary political boundaries.

The first area may conveniently be called the commercial section because the dominant economic interest of the people was the carrying trade and shipbuilding. Here great mercantile families had grown up, who had gained their wealth through smuggling with the West Indies or else through legitimate trading enterprises that embraced the entire world. The merchants were keenly alive to the golden benefits which membership in the British empire had always yielded; and like the business interests of any generation or clime, they might be expected to combat any effort to tamper with the source of their profits. For the merchants the unfolding of the new imperial program involved a very serious interference with their customary trading operations; and during the decade from 1764 to 1774 their constant aim was to effect a restoration of the commercial conditions of 1763. As a class they entertained neither earlier nor later the idea of independence, for withdrawal from the British empire meant for them the loss of vital business advantages without corresponding benefits in a world organized on a basis of imperial trading systems. They strove to obtain the most favorable terms possible within the empire but not to leave it. Indeed they viewed with no small concern the growth of the republican feeling and leveling sentiment which the controversy occasioned.

The great ports of the north—Boston, New York, Philadelphia, Newport—bore eloquent testimony to the prosperity of the mercantile class; and on the continuance of this prosperity depended the livelihood of the mechanics and petty shopkeepers of the towns and, to a lesser degree, the well-being of the farmers whose cereals and meats were exported to the West Indies. This proletarian element was not inclined by temperament to that self-restraint in movements of popular protest which was ever the *arrière pensée* of the merchant class; and being for the most part unenfranchised, they expressed their sentiments most naturally through boisterous mass meetings and mob demonstrations.

In the southern coastal area colonial capital was invested almost exclusively in plantation production; and commerce was carried on chiefly by British mercantile houses and their American agents, the factors. The only town in the plantation provinces that could compare with the teeming ports of the north was Charleston; and political life was focused in the periodical meetings of the great landed proprietors in the assemblies. Under the wasteful system of marketing, which the apparent plenty of plantation life made possible, the planters found themselves treading a morass of indebtedness to British merchants from which it seemed that nothing less than virtual repudiation could extricate them. In the last twenty-five years of colonial dependence the assemblies passed a succession of lax bankruptcy acts and other legislation prejudicial to nonresident creditors; but these laws nearly always ran afoul the royal veto. This fact, together with the sturdy sense of self-determination which the peculiar social system fostered, made the plantation provinces ready to resent any new exercise of parliamentary authority over the colonies, such as the new imperial policy involved. Georgia, as the youngest colony, not yet self-sustaining, and dependent on the home government for protection against a serious Indian menace, was less a part of this picture than other provinces of the group.

On the western fringe of the coastal communities lay an irregular belt of back-country settlements whose economy and modes of thought were almost as distinctive as those of the two tidewater regions. Certainly the western sections of many of the provinces had grievances in common and resembled each other more than they did the older sections with which they were associated by provincial boundaries. These pioneer settlements extended north and south, up and down the valleys between the fall line of the rivers and mountains, from New England to Georgia. Outside of New England the majority of the settlers were of non-English strains, mostly German and Scotch-Irish; but throughout the long frontier the people cultivated small isolated farms and entertained democratic ideas commensurate with the equalitarian conditions to which their manner of living accustomed them. In many of the provinces they had long been discriminated against by the older settlements in the matter of representation in the assemblies, the administration of justice and the incidence of taxation; and they were thus familiar, of their own experience, with all the arguments which the Revolution was to make popular against non-representative government and unjust taxation. Being self-sustaining communities economically, their zeal for popular rights was in no wise alloyed by the embarrassment of their pocketbooks. Although out of harmony with popular leaders of the seaboard in both the commercial and plantation provinces on many matters of intracolonial policy, they could join forces with them against

the new imperial policy; and they brought to the controversy a moral conviction and bold philosophy which gave great impetus to the agitation for independence.

The history of the American Revolution is the story of the reaction of these three sections to the successive acts of the British government and of their interaction upon each other. The merchants of the commercial colonies were the most seriously affected by the new imperial policy and at the outset assumed the leadership of the colonial movement of protest. They were closely seconded by the planters of the south as soon as enough time had elapsed to make clear to the latter the implications of the issue of home rule for which the merchants stood. The democratic farmers of the interior, more or less out of contact with the political currents of the seaboard, were slower to take part; and it is largely true that their measure of participation varied inversely according to the degree of their isolation. Patrick Henry and his fellow burgesses from western counties of Virginia began to undermine the conservatism of the tidewater statesmen as early as 1765, but the Germans and Scotch-Irish of Pennsylvania did not make their influence fully felt until the critical days of 1774–1775.

The new British policy of imperial control assumed its first form under George Grenville (1764–1765). The numerous regulations of trade, which need not be analyzed here, injured fair traders and smuggling merchants alike and threatened bankruptcy to the great mercantile houses of Boston, New York and Philadelphia. The prohibition of colonial legal tender added to their woes and indeed made the hard-pressed planters of the south sharers in the general distress. The Stamp Act, with its far-reaching taxes burdensome alike to merchant and farmer, sealed the union of commercial and plantation provinces at the same time that it afforded an opportunity for placing the colonial argument on constitutional grounds; and because of the character of the taxation, it rallied to the colonial position the powerful support of the lawyers and newspaper proprietors. The plan of the British to garrison their new acquisitions in America and to station a few detachments of troops in the older colonies was, in the feverish state of the public mind, envisaged as a brazen attempt to intimidate the colonists into submission. The merchants of some of the ports, intent on restoring the conditions of their former prosperity, adopted resolutions of non-importation; and little recking the future, they aroused the populace to a sense of British injustice, even to the extent of countenancing and instigating mob excesses and the destruction of property.

In the end of parliament resolved upon the passage of certain remedial laws (1766), an outcome which, from the standpoint of the more radical colonists, can be regarded as little more than a compromise. The Stamp Act was indeed repealed and important alterations were made in the trade regulations; but the Currency Act, the regulations against smuggling and the provisions for a standing army remained unchanged. In addition the Declaratory Act was passed; and the new molasses duty was an unvarnished application of the principle of "taxation without representation" announced in the Declaratory Act. The rejoicing of the colonist can be explained only on the ground that the merchants of the north dominated colonial opinion; and like practical men of affairs, they were contemptuous, if not fearful, of disputes upon questions of abstract right.

The passage of the Townshend Acts in 1767 was the second attempt of parliament to reconstruct the empire in the spirit of the Grenville experiment. Again the merchants of commercial colonies perceived themselves as the class whose interests were chiefly imperiled; but sobered by the mob outrages of Stamp Act days, they resolved to guide the course of American opposition in orderly and peaceful channels. They, therefore, began an active agitation for corrective legislation through merchants' petitions and legislative memorials to parliament; and after much questioning of each other's sincerity they succeeded in developing an elaborate system of commercial boycott, which united the commercial colonies in an effort to secure the repeal of the objectionable laws. After a year or so this movement in a much modified form spread to the plantation provinces, where, under the leadership of Washington and other planters, it was employed as a means of preventing the landed aristocracy from falling more deeply into the toils of their British creditors.

Meantime the merchants began to see that in organizing their communities for peaceful resistance to Great Britain they were unavoidably releasing disruptive forces which, like Frankenstein, they were finding it impossible to control. The failure of non-importation to effect swift redress compelled the merchant bodies, as the months passed, to depend more and more upon the tumultuous methods of the proletariat in order to keep wavering merchants true to the cause. Increasing friction between smuggling merchants and customs officers also produced outbreaks of mob violence in many provinces, and led by a broad, smooth road to such distressing affairs as the Boston "Massacre" on the one hand and to the destruction of the revenue cutter *Gaspee* on the other. As the political agitators and turbulent elements gained the upper hand, the contest began to assume more clearly the form of a crusade for constitutional and natural rights; and when word arrived in May, 1770, that parliament had repealed all the Townshend duties except the trifling tax on tea, the merchants found it difficult to reassert their earlier control and to stop a movement that had lost all significance for hard-headed men of business. The merchants of New York, under the leadership of their newly formed Chamber of Commerce, were the first who were able to wrench loose from their enforced alliance with the radicals; and the cancellation of their boycott resolution was soon followed by similar action in the ports of Philadelphia and Boston. The plantation provinces were coolly left in the lurch notwithstanding that parliament had not receded from its position of arbitrary taxation, and the movement there soon died of inanition.

The two or three years that followed the partial repeal of the Townshend duties were, for the most part, years of material prosperity and political calm. The merchants had grown to look askance at a doctrine of home rule which left ,it uncertain who was to rule at home. As a class they eagerly agreed with the merchant-politician Thomas Cushing that "high points about the supreme authority of Parliament" should best "fall asleep." And so—John Hancock as well as Isaac Low—they deserted politics for business, even to the extent of importing dutied tea which people imbibed everywhere except at Philadelphia and New York, where local conditions made it possible for merchants to offer the cheaper Dutch tea to consumers. The sun of the radical had suffered an eclipse; and quietly biding their time, they began to apply to their own following the lessons of organization that they had learned from the "mercantile dons." In the commercial colonies Sam Adams—"that Matchiavel of Chaos"—sought, through the establishment of town committees of correspondence, to unite the workingmen of the port towns and the farmers of the rural districts in political action; and the burgesses of Virginia launched their plan of a provincial committee of correspondence that might give uncensored expression to the political grievances of the southern planters.

In May, 1773, a new tea act was passed by parliament, which stampeded the merchants into joining forces once more with the political radicals and irresponsible elements. This new law, if put into operation, would have enabled the great East India Company to monopolize the colonial tea market to the exclusion of both American smugglers and law-abiding tea traders. Alarmed at this prospect and fearful lest further monopoly privileges in trade might follow from the success of the present experiment, the colonial merchant class joined in an active popular agitation for the purpose of preventing the landing of any of the tea importations of the East India Company. Though their efforts for a vigorous but restrained opposition met with substantial success elsewhere, they were over-reached at Boston by the superior management of Sam Adams and the unintelligence of Governor Hutchinson; and the British trading company became the involuntary host to a tea party costing £15,000.

The Boston Tea Party marked a turning point in the course of events both in America and Britain. In both countries it was regarded by the merchants and moderates as a lawless destruction of private property and an act of wanton defiance which no self-respecting government could wisely ignore. Plainly the issue between the colonies and the mother country had ceased to be one of mere trading advantage. Outside of New England, colonial opinion, so far as it expressed itself, greeted the event with a general disapproval and apprehension. In the mother country parliament proceeded to the passage of the severe disciplinary measures of 1774.

The effect of this punitive legislation cannot be overestimated, for it convinced many colonists who had disapproved of the Boston vandalism that the greater guilt now lay on the side of parliament. "They look upon the chastisement of Boston to be purposely rigorous, and held up by way of intimidation to all America . . ." wrote Governor Penn from Philadelphia. "Their delinquency in destroying the East India Company's tea is lost in the attention given to what is here called the too severe punishment of shutting up the port, altering the Constitution, and making an Act, as they term it, screening the officers and soldiers shedding American blood." From this time on there occurred in the several provinces a contest for the control of public policy between the moderates on the one hand and the radicals or extremists on the other, the former receiving aid and comfort from the royal officials and their circle of friends. This line of cleavage is unmistakable in the case of practically every province.

The moderates as a group wanted to pay for the tea destroyed and to propose to parliament an act of union which should automatically dispose of all controversial questions for the future. The radicals were opposed to compromise and as a class desired a comprehensive and drastic boycott of Great Britain with which to exact from parliament recognition of the colonial claim to complete home rule. Both parties were willing to make a trial of strength in an intercolonial congress; and after bitter contests in each province to control the *personnel* of the irregularly elected delegations, the First Continental Congress assembled in Philadelphia in September, 1774. In this notable gathering the moderates discovered to their dismay that they were outnumbered; and, in the disconsolate phrase of a Maryland merchant, "Adams, with his crew, and the haughty Sultans of the South juggled the whole conclave of the Delegates." Indeed this extralegal body, by adopting the Association, decreed that the merchants of America should sacrifice their trade for the benefit of a cause from which they had come to be alienated; and the radicals in congress provided for spreading a network of committees over the continent to insure obedience to their decree.

In the popular conventions called prior to the First Continental Congress and in the provincial meetings that were held to ratify its doings, the people from the back-country counties of many provinces were, for the first time, admitted to that full measure of representation which had long been denied them by the unjust system of apportionment in the colonial assemblies. Deeply stirred by the political slogans of the tidewater radicals, they ranged themselves by their side and lent momentum to an agitation that was hastening toward independence. In closely divided provinces like Pennsylvania and South Carolina their voice was undoubtedly the decisive factor.

The proceedings of the First Continental Congress were viewed with mixed feelings by the colonists. The moderates who had lingered in the popular movement in order to control it began to withdraw, although it required the outbreak of hostilities at Lexington or even the Declaration of Independence to convince some that their efforts could be of no avail. The merchants perforce acquiesced in the regulations of the Association, which, in the early months, were not without profit to them. The radical committees of the coast towns, formerly controlled by the merchants, began to fall into the hands of the democratic mechanic class. In New York, Boston and Philadelphia alike, nobodies, and "unimportant persons" succeeded to power; and even in Savannah, Governor Wright declared that "the Parochial Committee are a Parcel of the Lowest People, Chiefly Carpenters, Shoemakers, Blacksmiths, etc. . . ." Flushed with success, the radical leaders busied themselves with consolidating their following in town and country through the creation of committees of observation and provincial committees and conventions. Little wonder was it that, in this changed aspect of public affairs, a worthy minister of Charleston, S.C., should be dismissed by his congregation "for his audacity in . . . saying that *mechanics* and country *clowns* had no right to dispute about politics, or what kings, lords and commons had done," or that the newspaper account should add: "All such *divines* should be taught to know that mechanics and country clowns (infamously so called) are the real and absolute masters of king, lords, commons and priests. . . ."

Events had reached a stage where the extremists in both countries were in control. What Chatham and Joseph Calloway might have adjusted to their mutual satisfaction could not be rationally discussed by North and Sam Adams. Under the circumstances it was inevitable that the policy of commercial coercion, adopted by the First Continental Congress, should soon be superseded by armed warfare as the weapon of the radicals, and that open rebellion should in turn give way to a struggle for independence. The thronging events of these later months are familiar enough in outline and need not be recounted here. The key to these times is to be found in the fact that the radical elements were a minority of the colonial

population and that only through their effective organization and aggressive tactics could they hope to whip into line the great body of timid and indifferent people who lacked either organization or a definite program. . . .

The real significance of the American Revolution, however, is not to be measured in terms of the conflicting emotions and purposes of those who, wittingly or unwittingly, helped to bring it about. What great issue in history has not been scarred by sordid motives, personal antagonisms and unintelligent decisions? Fundamentally the American Revolution represented the refusal of a self-reliant people to permit their natural and normal energies to be confined against their will, whether by an irresponsible imperial government or by the ruling minorities in their midst. . . .

Robert E. Brown

The Revolution as a Conservative Movement

The Massachusetts Constitution of 1780 is convincing evidence that the people of that state considered the conflict in progress as a War of Independence rather than as an internal revolution. John

Reprinted from Robert E. Brown, *Middle-Class Democracy and the Revolution in Massachusetts, 1691–1780*, pp. 399–408. © 1955 by the American Historical Association. Used by permission of Cornell University Press. Footnotes omitted except where necessary for understanding.

Adams summed it up as follows: "I say again that resistance to innovation and unlimited claims of Parliament, and not any new form of government, was the object of the Revolution." It would have been inconceivable that a convention, elected under manhood suffrage, could have written such a frame of government had there been much internal dissatisfaction with the kind of political system in effect before the Revolution. It would have been even more inconceivable that this constitution could have been ratified under manhood suffrage by such a large majority if there had been much demand for change. The contradictions are resolved if we accept the fact that the people of Massachusetts were trying to keep the type of middle-class democracy that they had.

Thus did events after Lexington and Concord demonstrate the absence of an "internal" revolution to democratize society. There was much continuity in the House and Council (now Senate) as members of long standing took over control of the government. With the exception of a few men who went with the British, the leading men in the towns continued to run town affairs and to organize the "revolutionary" movement. Not until the General Court gave representation to the districts that had been denied representation by the British did the larger towns demand increased membership in the House, and then they failed to take advantage of their increased representation. There were no changes in the franchise or in the position of the churches and schools until the Constitution of 1780, and then the changes were of little significance. The property requirement for the franchise was actually increased about 12 per cent, qualifications for office holding were put into effect, but Catholics were given a greater amount of toleration than prevailed under the charter.

Historians who have stressed the internal revolution as an interpretation have long noted the contradictory fact that the results of the American Revolution were not very revolutionary. The logical explanation for this otherwise seemingly illogical phenomenon is that society in Massachusetts was already democratic and that there was no need for an internal revolution.

In Massachusetts . . . we find one of the unique "revolutions" in world history — a revolution to preserve a social order rather than to change it. It was not, as we have often assumed, a dual revolution in which Americans won their independence from the British on one hand, and in which unenfranchised and underprivileged lower classes wrested democratic rights from a privileged local aristocracy on the other.

To understand what happened, we must first have a clear picture of Massachusetts society. Economically speaking, it was a middle-class society in which property was easily acquired and in which a large portion of the people were property-owning farmers. There was undoubtedly more economic democracy for the common man then than there is now. A large permanent labor class was practically nonexistent; men could either acquire land and become farmers or work for themselves as skilled artisans. If we insist that Americans who came to this country brought their accustomed class or caste lines with them, we must do so in the face of all the evidence to the contrary. If there was anything that observers at the time agreed on, it was that American society was almost the exact opposite of European society. There was nothing approaching the spread between the rich and the poor that Europe had at that time or that we have at present; a much larger proportion of society owned property then than now. Yet today, many people, even including many laborers, look on American society as predominantly middle class though the opportunity for almost universal ownership of property is far less now than it was before the Revolution.

Economic opportunity, or economic democracy, in turn contributed to political democracy. While it is true that property ownership was a prerequisite for province and town voting, it is also true that the amount of property required for the franchise was very small and that the great majority of men could easily meet the requirements. There were probably a few men who could not qualify for voting, but the number could not have been very large. We cannot condone the practice of excluding even those few, but we should try to place the unenfranchised in their proper perspective. It makes a tremendous difference in our understanding of colonial society whether 95 per cent of the men were disfranchised or only 5 per cent. Furthermore, representation was apportioned in such a way that the farmers, not a merchant aristocracy, had complete control of the legislature.

It is not enough to say that the people of Massachusetts perhaps had more democracy than the people of Europe, but that they still did not have what we call democracy today. Neither is it sufficient to say that the germs of democracy were present, or that democracy, as a growing process if not as a reality, could be found in colonial times. When Hutchinson said that anything that looked like a man was a voter and that policy in general was dictated by the lower classes, he was certainly using the term "democracy" as we mean it now. A Hutchinson might deplore the view that government existed for the benefit of the people and that the people were to decide when government had served its proper functions, but this is the democratic idea. He might also deplore the fact that the people not only elected their representatives but also told them how to vote, yet this, too, is democracy.

In many respects, the people of Massachusetts had a government more responsive to the popular will than we have at the present time. There were far more representatives in proportion to population than we now have, and the representatives were more responsible to their constituents for their actions than are legislators at present. If a man votes against his belief to please his constituents, so that he can hold his elected position, we cannot demand much more of democracy.

The number of men who could vote in the colony must not be confused with the number who did vote. These are entirely different problems, for the fact that there was much indifference on election day did not mean that many men could not partic-

ipate. If we are attempting to explain events in terms of class conflict or internal revolution, it is especially important that we do not confuse the unfranchised and the disinterested. It is one thing if a man wants the vote but cannot meet the property requirements; it is another if he has the vote but fails to use it. Neither should we confuse the issue by giving percentages of voters in terms of the entire population, for probably less than 20 per cent of the people in colonial times were adult men.

In addition to economics and politics, there were also other manifestations of democracy in colonial Massachusetts. The system of education was, for its day, undoubtedly the best provided for the common people anywhere, and the correct comparison is with other educational systems at the time, not with our own. Many democratic practices were used in the operation of the Congregational church, and again we should remember that some 98 per cent of the people were Congregationalists. Furthermore, the Congregational church was not established as it was in England. Men who belonged to other churches did not pay taxes to the Congregational church; education and political office were open to those who were not Congregationalists. Perhaps there was not the complete religious freedom—or religious indifference—that we now associate with a liberal society, but there was also little dissatisfaction with religion to contribute to internal conflict. Even the colonial militia was democratic in its organization and in the influence which it exerted on politics.

In brief, Massachusetts did not have a social order before the American Revolution which would breed sharp internal class conflicts. The evidence does not justify an interpretation of the Revolution in Massachusetts as an internal class conflict designed to achieve additional political, economic, and social democracy. Although democracy was important as a factor in the conflict, it was a democracy which had already arrived in the colony long before 1776.

If we turn to British-American relations, however, we do not need to search long to find areas of conflict. The British for many years had developed a mercantilist-imperialist colonial system that had not functioned as expected. The aim of the system as men at the time frankly admitted, was the ultimate benefit of the mother country. They believed that colonies should be regulated, both economically and politically, to further the well-being of the parent state. British officials were fully aware of the shortcomings in colonial administration, but, until 1760, Britain was not in a favorable position to remedy these defects. British officials were also fully aware of the fact that colonial democracy was one of the chief obstacles to effective enforcement of British colonial policy.

These two ingredients—an effective middle-class democracy and British imperial policies which had been thwarted by this democracy—explain what happened in Massachusetts from 1760 to 1776. In order to make their colonial system effective, the British believed that they had to recover authority over colonial officials. This, in turn, called for a colonial revenue which would be administered by Parliament, especially to pay the salaries of colonial officials and thus remove them from under the dominating influence of colonial assemblies. But of course the assembly of Massachusetts was fully aware of the power which control of the purse conferred and was equally determined to retain this power over British officials.

Throughout the story runs another thread—the threat, or at least what the British considered the threat, of colonial independence. This gave an air of urgency to British measures. There was the frequently expressed fear that time was on the side of the colonists. A rapidly growing population, bolstered by a phenomenal birthrate due to economic op-portunity and by immigrants attracted by economic and political democracy, posed the problem to the British of recovering authority before the colonies became too large. When the showdown came with the Tea Act and the Coercive Acts, there was no doubt whatever that the British intended to curtail colonial democracy as a necessary step toward recovery of British authority and the prevention of colonial independence. The result was the very thing the British had tried to prevent— American independence.

Obviously democracy played an important part in the events before 1776, not as a condition to be achieved but as a reality which interfered with British policies. If the British had been successful, there would undoubtedly have been much less democracy in Massachusetts—hence the interpretation that the Revolution was designed to *preserve* a social order rather than to change it. We search in vain for evidence of class conflict that was serious enough to justify revolution; we do not have to look far for copious quantities of proof that colonial society was democratic and that the colonists were attempting to prevent British innovations.

Furthermore, the results of the Revolution more than confirm the interpretation presented here. There is a logic to what happened after the Revolution—or perhaps it would be more accurate to say what did not happen—if we accept the fact that the people of Massachusetts were not conducting an internal revolution. We are not confronted with the contradiction, which most writers fail to resolve, of a social revolution which was presumably successful but which failed to achieve social change. Why would a people, who were supposedly demanding a more democratic government, adopt a constitution which restricted democracy even more than had been restricted in colonial days? On the other hand, the Massachusetts Constitution of 1780 was a logical consequence of a middle-class society which believed in the protection of property because most men were property owners. The almost complete absence of social revolution in Massachusetts should stand as convincing evidence that internal social revolution was not one of the chief aims of the American Revolution as far as the people of Massachusetts were concerned.

It is not necessary to explain whatever conservatism existed in colonial times in terms of a limited electorate. There is implied in this approach an assumption that universal suffrage will result in increased liberalism, but this is not necessarily so. The elections of 1920, 1924, 1928, and even 1952, when women as well as men had the vote, should convince us that "the people" can and do vote for conservatism. If the people of Massachusetts believed that a man should own property to be a voter or that an official should be a Protestant to be elected to office, they might well vote for both propositions and not be out of character. And since most men in Massachusetts were Protestants and property owners, the fact that both property and religious qualifications found their way into the Constitution of 1780 should not be surprising.

We do not need a "conservative counterrevolution" or a thermidorean reaction to explain either the Massachusetts Constitution of 1780 or the adoption of the federal Constitution in 1788. If there was no "social revolution," there could hardly be a "conservative counterrevolution." Both constitutions must be explained in terms of a middle-class society in which most men could vote.

In recent years it has been frequently said that the British did not intend to tyrannize the colonies by the policies which they adopted. Colonists thought otherwise, however, and judging by the material presented in these chapters, one might suspect that many British policies looked like tyranny to them. Perhaps we of today would also consider as tyranny trials without juries, instructions by the king which were supposed to be law, taxa-

tion by a people who were considered foreigners, a declaration by the Parliament of these same "foreign people" that it had the power to legislate in all cases whatsoever, appointed governors who could dissolve assemblies or determine town meetings, and navigation acts regulating colonial trade in British interests. It would be interesting to speculate on the reaction of a modern oleomargarine manufacturer whose suit against the butter interests was to be tried in Wisconsin by a jury of Wisconsin dairy farmers presided over by a judge appointed by the governor of Wisconsin. This hypothetical case might seem exaggerated, but it is not too far removed from the attitude expressed by colonists toward their relations with the British. The fact is that colonists looked on British measures as tyrannical, and if we are going to explain colonial actions, we must consider the colonial point of view.

How should we rate in importance the various factors that entered into this British-American war? That, of course, is difficult to answer, but it is not so difficult to say that many items contributed and that some were probably more important to some individuals than to others.

There is no doubt that economic motives were fundamental. That Americans would oppose a mercantilist system which they considered inimical to their interests should not be surprising. After all, they looked on many British regulations as simply devices by which some segments of the Empire were favored at the expense of other segments. The tax program also had its economic side, for as many men said, a mother country which could collect a stamp tax could also tax a man's land, his cattle, or his home. Undoubtedly, too, the threat of monopoly contained in the Tea Act had its economic influence. In fact, a middle-class society would almost inevitably place great emphasis on property and its economic interests, a fact which is only too apparent in the sources. The importance of economic factors, however, did not lie in their contribution to class conflict as a cause of the American Revolution.

But economic elements were not the only forces making for revolution. Equally significant was the fact that Massachusetts had long been accustomed to democratic government and intended to maintain its accustomed system. Politics inevitably include economics, since economic subjects are some of the most important items in politics, but not all politics is economic. The very fact that people govern their own destinies is important in itself. As one old soldier of the Revolution put it, the British intended to govern the Americans and the Americans did not intend that they should. To a people accustomed to the democracy both of province and town affairs, the danger inherent in British imperial controls was far more than a mere threat. When the common people talked of dying for their liberties or pledging their lives and property for the defense of their liberties, they were not dealing in abstractions; and they would not have talked in this way if their society had been dominated by a merchant aristocracy.

Neither can religious democracy be ignored as a factor in the Revolution. We must remember that the people of Massachusetts were accustomed to a church organization which lived by democratic procedures and opposition to the Church of England. We must not forget, either, that many people at the time considered religion more important than politics. The threat that the British might impose the Church of England on them and enforce conformity was not a threat to be taken lightly. As many of them often said, religious and political freedom were inextricably connected and would rise or fall together. Little wonder, then, that the Congregational clergy supported the Revolution almost to a man.

This study of Massachusetts raises some rather serious questions about our interpretation of colonial society and the Revolution in other colonies. Were the other colonies as undemocratic as we have supposed them to be? Was their economic and social life dominated by a coastal aristocracy of planters in the South and merchants in the North? How was property distributed? Exactly how many men could meet the voting qualifications? Was representation restricted in such a way that conservative areas could dominate the legislature? These are questions for which we need well-documented answers before we interpret the colonial and revolutionary periods with any assurance of accuracy.

Evidence which has turned up in the course of this study suggests that Massachusetts was not fundamentally different from the other colonies and states. If so—and the idea is certainly worth extensive investigation—we might be forced to make some drastic revisions in our interpretation of American history before 1830. Perhaps we will find in America as a whole, as in Massachusetts, that American democracy as we know it goes far deeper than the election of 1828 and that the "common man" in this country had come into his own long before the era of Jacksonian Democracy.

Louis M. Hacker

The American Revolution: Economic Factors

At the outbreak of the American Revolution the great majority of the American population—perhaps nine-tenths of it—was engaged on the land. The owning farmers, whether they were planter lords or modest family farmers, were commercial agriculturists: for either they produced cash crops for sale in a market or they developed subsidiary activities to net them a money return. Self-sufficiency, even on the frontier, is impossible under capitalist organization. Cash is needed everywhere, whether it is to pay taxes or for harvesting the crop or to buy salt, iron and a squirrel gun. Hence, the colonial farmer either produced a cash crop or he tried to find employment among a number of occupations that did not interfere with his agricultural activities. He either trapped or hunted; or worked in logging operations; or shipped with a fishing fleet. Often he really obtained his cash from land speculation; that is to say, as the result of constantly mounting land values, the farmer was in a position to sell his improved land and buy a cheaper farm in the frontier areas. Thus, the American farmer was a dealer in land from the very dawn of settlement until 1920, a period of three centuries. When land values began to decline after 1921, the basis of American agricultural well-being was shaken to its foundations.

From Louis M. Hacker, "Western Land Hunger and the War of 1812," *Mississippi Valley Historical Review*, 10 (March 1924). Reprinted by permission of the publisher.

This need to develop a cash crop made for the production of staples everywhere. By the eighteenth century New England was producing and sending to market beef, cattle and hogs, work animals and corn to be used for stall feeding. The Middle Colonies had become the great granary of the English settlements, and on the big farms of New York and Pennsylvania, where tenants and indentured servants were being employed, wheat was being grown, processed into flour and sold in the towns and the far away West Indies. In the Southern Colonies agriculture was the keystone of the whole economic structure: Virginia and Maryland planters grew tobacco for sale in England; interior farmers grew grains and raised cattle to be used in the West Indian trade; the tidewater planters of the Carolinas and Georgia cultivated and harvested rice, indigo and some cotton. These crops were sent to seaports, put on ships and carried to distant places to furnish those funds which were the basis of the commercial enterprise of the day. . . .

The plantation economy sprang up in colonial Virginia and Maryland, notably, for obvious reasons. The cultivation of a staple like tobacco served excellently the purposes of the Mercantilist System: it did not compete with an important English crop and hence might be grown on a grand scale; it produced a colonial return on the basis of which large English exports might be sent to the Southern Colonies; it furnished opportunities for the investment of English capital—short-term funds for the financing of the crops and long-term funds for the hypothecation of plantation properties; and it created an outlet for England's surplus populations. Thus tobacco cultivation was closely bound to English mercantilist policy. . . .

There was no question that the tobacco market kept on expanding: at the end of the seventeenth century Maryland and Virginia were exporting 35,000,000 pounds to the mother country; by 1763 the quantity had trebled. On the other hand, the industry was at the mercy of the imperial system. Tobacco was on the enumerated list and could be sent, therefore, only to England; high sumptuary taxes were placed on it; prices were controlled in London and tended to drop periodically below the cost of production. In addition, capital costs of plantation operation continued to mount due to the high cost of labor (the price of indentured servants and, more particularly, that of slaves went up while their productivity remained constant), the exhaustion of the soil in the older regions, and the necessity on the part of the planters to buy new lands to which they could be ready to transfer their activities. The other charges against operations—of freight costs, insurance, merchants' commissions and profits, interest on borrowings—hung like millstones about the necks of the encumbered planters.

The plantation system was particularly dependent upon credit. The tobacco grower required credit to assist in the acquisition of the labor force; to market his cash crop; to furnish his equipment; and to finance his purchase of consumers goods. The only source of funds was the English merchant capitalist: and to him the Southern planter was compelled to pay high interest rates, mortgage his land and slaves and turn for the supplying of those necessaries without which his home and plantation could not continue. Constantly weighed down by debt, it was

small wonder that the planters of Colonial America ever sought to expand their activities, by extending their tobacco lands and engaging in the more speculative aspects of land dealing; and that they turned to thoughts of inflation as relief from debt oppression was also to be expected.

Because the wild lands of the frontier areas were so important to the maintenance of the stability of the Southern planting economy, Southern capitalists were constantly preoccupied with them. The West was not opened up by the hardy frontiersman; it was opened up by the land speculator who preceded even the Daniel Boones into the wilderness. But the English (and also the Scotch) had also learned to regard with more than a curious interest these wild lands of the West: they saw in them profits from the fur trade and from the speculative exploitation of the region by their own capitalist enterprise. It was at this point that English and Southern merchant capital came into conflict; and when as a result of the promulgation of the Proclamation Line of 1763 and the Quebec Act of 1774, the Western lands were virtually closed to colonial enterprising, the Southern planting economy began to totter. Without the subsidiary activity of land speculation, planters could not continue solvent; there is no cause for wonder, therefore, that the owners of great plantation properties should be among the first to swell the ranks of the colonial revolutionary host in 1775. . . .

The English Mercantilist System, in its imperial-colonial relations, following the triumph of English merchant capital in the Puritan Revolution, was based on the economic subservience of the colonies. Indeed, every imperial and administrative agency had this end constantly in view: and most significant among these was the Board of Trade. The Board of Trade, in its final form, had been established in 1696, and, among its various instruments for control over the colonies, these three were notable: it had the right to deny charters or patents to English-financed companies seeking to engage in enterprises in the colonies which were inimical to the interests of home merchant capitalists; it had the power to review colonial legislation and recommend to the Privy Council the disallowance of such colonial enactments as ran counter to the welfare of the mother country; and it prepared specific instructions for the deportment of the royal governors in the colonies, in particular indicating where the veto power was to be used to prevent colonial encroachments on the privileges and prerogatives of English citizens.

Ever vigilant, the Board of Trade proceeded against the colonies when they threatened to impinge on the interests of Englishmen: it refused to tolerate colonial interference with the mother country's hold on foreign trade and shipping; it checked colonial attempts to control the traffic in convicts and slaves; it prevented colonies from lowering interest rates, easing the judicial burden on debtors and seeking to monopolize the Indian trade. Most significant were the stern checks imposed on attempts by the colonial assemblies to encourage native manufacturing and to relieve the oppression of debts by the increase of the money supply of the colonies.

Following in the footsteps of the English themselves, colonials looked to public authority to aid in the development of native industries. In the best mercantilist tradition, therefore, colonial statute-books came to be filled with legislation which offered bounties to enterprises, extended public credit to them, exempted them from taxation, gave them easy access to raw materials and in their behalf encouraged the location of new towns.

Against such legislation the Board of Trade regularly moved. On important matters, appeal was had to Parliament and general statutes were passed, notably the Woolen Act of 1699, which barred colonial wool, woolen yarn and woolen manufactures from intercolonial and foreign commerce; the Hat Act of 1732, which prevented the exportation of hats out of the separate colonies and restricted colonial hatmakers to two apprentices; and the Iron Act of 1750. . . .

Also, the royal governors were closely instructed to veto all legislation designed to assist the development of such manufactures as might compete with those of England. . . . The overextension of sugar planting, in the West Indies, and of tobacco planting, in the mainland colonies, undoubtedly was due to this restriction and therefore helped in the shaping of the crisis in the imperial-colonial relations which set in in the 1760s.

Thus, at the very time in England when the domestic system was rapidly being converted into the factory system and great advances were being made in the perfection of machinery exactly because the existence of a growing market was demanding more efficient methods of production, in the colonies methods of production remained at a hopelessly backward level because English and colonial capital could not enter manufacturing. An important outlet for accumulated funds was barred. The colonial capitalist economy, therefore, was narrowly restricted largely to land speculation, the dealing in furs and the carrying trade. When English mercantilism, for the protection of its home merchant capital, began to narrow these spheres then catastrophe threatened. The American Revolution can be understood only in terms of the necessity for colonial merchant capital to escape from the contracting prison walls of the English Mercantilist System.

In an imperial economy the capitalist relationships between mother country and colonies as a rule lead to a colonial unfavorable balance of trade. The colonies buy the goods and services of the mother country and are encouraged to develop those raw materials the home capitalists require. In this they are aided by the investment of the mother country's balances and by new capital. Thus, in the

Southern Colonies, tobacco largely was being produced to furnish returns for the English goods and services the plantation lords required; but, because the exchange left England with a favorable balance, by the 1770s, its capitalists had more than £ 4,000,000 invested in Southern planting operations. To meet the charges on this debt, Southern planters were compelled constantly to expand their agricultural operations and to engage in the subsidiary activities of land speculation and the fur trade.

The Northern Colonies were less fortunately placed. The Northern Colonies directly produced little of those staples necessary to the maintenance of the English economy: the grains, provisions and work animals of New England, New York and Pennsylvania could not be permitted to enter England lest they disorganize the home commercial agricultural industry; and the same was true of the New England fishing catches. The Northern Colonies, of course, were a source for lumber, naval stores, furs, whale products and iron, and these England sorely needed to maintain her independence of European supplies. England sought to encourage these industries by bounties and other favored positions; but in vain. Notably unsuccessful was the effort to divert Northern colonial capital from shipbuilding and shipping into the production of naval stores by the Bounty Act of 1706.

The Northern Colonies, therefore, produced little for direct export to England to permit them to pay their balances, that is to say, for the increasing quantities of English drygoods, hardware and house furnishings they were taking. In view of the fact, too, that the Northern Colonies presented slight opportunities for the investment of English capital, it was incumbent upon the merchants of the region to develop returns elsewhere in order to obtain specie and bills of exchange with which to balance payments in England.

Out of this necessity arose the economic significance of the various triangular trading operations (and the subsidiary industries growing out of trade) the Northern merchants organized. Northern merchants and shipowners opened up regular markets in Newfoundland and Nova Scotia for their fishing tackle, salt provisions and rum; they established an ever-growing commercial intercourse with the wine islands of the Canaries and Madeira, from which they bought wines direct and to which they sold barrel staves, foodstuffs and live animals; they sold fish to Spain, Portugal and Italy; their ports acted as entrepôts for the transshipment of Southern staples to England and Southern Europe.

The trade with the West Indian sugar islands—as well as the traffic in Negro slaves and the manufacture of rum, which grew out of it—became the cornerstone of the Northern colonial capitalist economy. . . .

Such commercial transactions—in addition, of course, to the profits derived from the fisheries, whaling and shipbuilding—furnished the needed sources of return and their conduct the outlets for Northern merchant capitalist accumulations. But they were not enough with which to pay all the English bills and to absorb all the mounting funds of the Amorys, Faneuils, Hancocks and Boylstons of Boston, the Whartons, Willings and Morrises of Philadelphia, the Livingstons, Lows and Crugers of New York, the Wantons and Lopezes of Newport and the Browns of Providence. In three illegal forms of enterprises—in piracy, smuggling generally, and the illicit sugar and molasses trade with the foreign West Indian islands—Northern merchants found opportunities for the necessary expansion. . . .

In this West Indian trade was to be found the strength and the weakness of colonial merchant capital. The English sugar interest was the darling of the Mercantilist System. Sugar, more so even than tobacco, was the great oversea staple of the eighteenth-century world; and not only to it was bound a ramified English commercial industry made up of carriers, commission men, factors, financiers, processors and distributors: but sugar was converted into molasses and in turn distilled into rum to support the unholy slave traffic and the unsavory Indian trade. The sugar cultivation therefore had the constant solicitude of English imperial officialdom and a sugar bloc, made up of absentee landlords, exerted a powerful influence in Parliament. Indeed, so significant a rôle did sugar play in the imperial economy that in the 1770s the capital worth of West Indian sugar properties stood at £ 60,000,000: of which at least one-half was the stake of home English investors. When it is noted that in the whole of the Northern American mainland colonies the English capitalist stake at most was only one-sixth as great, then the reason for the favoring of the sugar colonies as against the Northern commercial colonies, after 1763, is revealed in a single illuminating flash.

The feud had long been smoldering. With the third decade of the eighteenth century, Northern merchants increasingly had taken to buying their sugar and molasses from the foreign sugar islands. Prices were cheaper by from 25 percent to 40 percent: due largely to the fact that the English planters were engaged in a single-crop exploitative agriculture in the interests of an absentee landlordism, while the French, Spanish, Dutch and Danish planters were owners-operators who cultivated directly their small holdings and diversified their crops; too, the foreign sugar was not encumbered by imposts and mercantilist marketing restrictions. In the foreign sugar islands, as well, Northern ship captains and owners found it possible to develop new markets for their flour, provisions, lumber, work animals and fish, thus obtaining another source from which specie and bills of exchange could be derived.

So heavy had this traffic become that the alarmed British sugar interest in Parliament succeeded in having passed the Molasses Act of 1733, which was designed virtually to outlaw the colonial-foreign island trade. But the act did not have the desired effect because it could not be adequately enforced: the British customs machinery in the colonies was weak and venal and the naval patrols that could be allocated to this duty were inadequate because of England's engagement in foreign wars from 1740 almost continuously for twenty years. . . .

It is not to be wondered that British planters, threatened with bankruptcy, kept up a constant clamor for the enforcement of the laws and the total stoppage of the foreign island trade. Beginning with 1760, imperial England began to tighten the screws with the stricter enforcement of the Acts of Trade and Navigation; from thence on, particularly after France had been compelled to sue for peace in 1763, England embarked on a systematic campaign to wipe out the trade between the Northern Colonies and the foreign West Indies. Northern merchant capital, its most important lifeline cut off, was being strangulated; it is not difficult to see why wealthy merchants of Philadelphia, New York, Boston, Newport and Providence should be converted into revolutionists. . . .

Such were the objective economic factors which resulted in making the position of the colonies, within the framework of the imperial-colonial relations, intolerable. The period of 1763–1775 was one of crisis, economically and politically: for in that decade it was demonstrated that English and colonial merchant capital both could not operate within a contracting sphere in which clashes of interest were becoming sharper and sharper. From 1760 on, pushed by those various groups whose well-being had been neglected during the years England was engaged in foreign wars, the rulers of the empire labored mightily to repair the rents that had appeared in the Mercantilist System. . . .

The colonies had enjoyed a period of unprecedented prosperity during the years of the war with France. The expanding market in the West Indies, the great expenditures of the British quartermasters, the illegal and contraband trade with the enemy forces, all had furnished steady employment for workers on the fleets and in the shipyards and ports and lucrative outlets for the produce of small farmers. But with the end of the war and the passage of the restrictive legislation of 1763 and after, depression had set in to last until 1770. Stringency and bankruptcy everywhere confronted the merchants and big

farmers; seamen and laborers were thrown out of work, small tradesmen were compelled to close their shops and small farmers were faced by ruin because of their expanded acreage, a diminished market and heavy fixed charges made particularly onerous as a result of currency contraction. Into the bargain, escape into the frontier zones—always the last refuge of the dispossessed—was shut off as a result of the Proclamation of 1763.

Charles M. Andrews

The Economic Interpretation Rejected

You will not, I trust, take it amiss if, on this the occasion of our annual meeting, I select as my topic the familiar subject of the American Revolution. Quite apart from the pleasure that comes from harping on an old string, there is the conviction, which I hold very strongly, that no matter how familiar a subject may be, it can always be reexamined with profit and viewed not infrequently from such points of vantage as to set the scene in quite a new light. The writing of history is always a progressive process, not merely or mainly because each age must write its own history from its own point of view,

From Charles M. Andrews, "The American Revolution: An Interpretation," *American Historical Review,* 31 (January 1926), pp. 219–232. Reprinted by permission of the *American Historical Review.*

but rather because each generation of scholars is certain to contribute to historical knowledge and so to approach nearer than its predecessor to an understanding of the past. No one can accept as complete or final any rendering of history, no matter how plausible it may be, nor consider any period or phase of the past as closed against further investigation. Our knowledge of history is and always will be in the making, and it has been well said that orthodox history and an orthodox historian involve a contradiction in terms.

The explanations of history have been characterized as a rule by overmuch simplicity. So wrote Maitland of the history of England and so with equal justice might he have written of the history of America. As with natural phenomena in the pre-Copernican days of celestial mechanics, when the world believed that the sun moved and the earth was flat, so it has been at all times with historical phenomena, that what to the superficial observer has appeared to be true has been accepted far too often as containing the whole truth. Among these pre-Copernican convictions, for example, widely held in America today, is the belief that the American Revolution was brought about by British tyranny. Whatever explanation of that great event comes to be accepted by competent historians and their intelligent readers as a near approach to the truth, it is quite certain that it will not be anything as easy and simple as all that. There was nothing simple about the Balance of Power or the Balance of Trade, even when construed in terms of such vulgar commodities as fish, furs, and molasses, and particularly when one must give due consideration to the doctrine, as seriously held in some quarters today as it was in the eighteenth century, that colonial possessions are the natural sources for home industries. Our history before 1783 was a much more complex and cosmopolitan affair than older writers would have us believe, for they have failed to account for many deep-lying and almost invisible factors and forces which influence and often determine human action and are always elusive and difficult to comprehend.

Recent writers have approached the subject with a full recognition of the complexity of the problems involved. They have found many and varied conflicting activities making for disagreement and misunderstanding between the mother country and her offspring, giving rise to impulses and convictions, ideas and practices, that were difficult, if not impossible, of reconciliation. Such scholars have expressed their conclusions in many different forms. Some have seen a struggle between two opposing historical tendencies—one imperialistic and expansive, the other domestic and intensive; others,

a clash of ideas regarding the constitution of the British empire and the place that a colony should occupy in its relations with the mother country. Some have stressed the differences that were bound to arise between an old and settled country and one that was not only dominated by the ideas and habits of the frontier, but was opposed also to the continued supremacy of a governing authority three thousand miles away. Others have explained the situation in terms of an antagonism between the law and institutions of England and those, growing constantly more divergent, of the Puritan and non-Puritan colonies in America. All of these explanations are sound, because they are based on an understanding of the deeper issues involved; and taken together, they are illuminating in that they enable a reader to broaden his point of view, and to break away from the endless controversies over immediate causes and war guilt that have hitherto tended to dominate the American mind.

But elucidating as these explanations are, no one of them seems quite sufficient to resolve so complex a subject as the causes of the American Revolution. Today we conjure with such words as evolution and psychology, and look for explanations of acts on the part of both individuals and groups in states of mind produced by inheritance and environment. Fielding, acknowledged expert in the study of human experience, can say that for a man "to act in direct contradiction to the dictates of his nature is, if not impossible, as improbable as anything which can well be conceived." The philosophers tell us that mind can be more resistant even than matter, and that it is easier to remove mountains than it is to change the ideas of a people. That the impact of convictions is one of the most frequent causes of revolution we must acknowledge; and I believe that we have not considered sufficiently the importance of this fact in determining the relations of England with colonial America.

If I may, by way of illustrating my point, I should like to show that certain differences existing between England and her colonies in mental attitudes and convictions proved in the end more difficult to overcome than the diverging historical tendencies or the bridging the three thousand miles of the Atlantic itself.

The American Revolution marks the close of one great period of our history and the beginning of another of even greater significance. It is the red line across our years, because by it was brought about a fundamental change in the status of the communities on the American seaboard—a change from dependence to independence. We sometimes hear that revolutions are not made but happen. In their immediate causes this is not true— for revolutions do not happen, they are made, in that they are the creatures of propaganda and manipulation. But, in reality, revolutions are not made. They are the detonations of explosive materials, long accumulating and often long dormant. They are the resultants of a vast complex of economic, political, social, and legal forces, which taken collectively are the masters, not the servants, of statesmen and political agitators. They are sudden in their origin, but look back to influences long in the making; and it is the business of the modern student of the subject to discover those remoter causes and to examine thoroughly and with an open mind the history, institutions, and mental past of the parties to the conflict. In pursuit of my purpose let me call to your attention certain aspects of that most important of all periods of our early history, the years from 1713 to 1775.

The middle period of the eighteenth century in England, resembling in some respects the mid-Victorian era of the next century, was intellectually, socially, and institutionally in a state of stable equilibrium. The impulses of the Revolution of 1689 had spent their force. English thought and life was tending to become formal, conventional, and artificial, and the En-glish mind was acquiring the fatal habit of closing against novelty and change. The most enlightened men of the day regarded the existing order as the best that could be conceived, and in the main were content to let well enough alone. Those who held the reins of power were comfortable and irresponsible, steeped in their "old vulgar prejudices," and addicted to habits and modes of living that were approved by age and precedent. The miseries of the poor were accepted as due to inherent viciousness; class distinctions were sharply marked, and social relations were cast in a rigid mould; while, as far as the mass of the poor was concerned, the vagrancy laws and the narrow policy of the corporate towns made free movement in any direction practically impossible. Life at large was characterized by brutality and widespread sense of insecurity. Little thought was given to the education of the poor, the diseases of poverty and dirt, the baneful effects of overcrowding in the towns, or the corrupting influence of life in tenements and cellars. Excessive drinking and habitual resort to violence in human relations prevailed in urban sections; and while it is probably true that in rural districts, where life was simple and medieval, there was greater comfort and peace and less barbarity and coarseness, nevertheless, it is equally true that the scenes of English country life in the eighteenth century, that have come down to us in literature and painting, are more often conventional than real. Vested interests and the rights of property were deemed of greater importance than the rights of humanity, and society clung tenaciously to the old safeguards and defenses that checked the inrush of new ideas. There was a great absence of interest in technical invention and improvement. Because the landed classes were in the ascendant, agriculture was the only national interest receiving attention—drainage, rotation of crops, and the treatment of the soil being the only practical activities that attracted capital. The concerns and welfare of those without the right to vote were largely ignored; and it is no mere coincidence that the waste of human life, which was at its worse in London between 1720 and 1750, with the population of England declining during that period, should not have been checked until after 1780. The age was not one of progress in government, social organization, or humanitarianism; and it is important to note that the reconstruction of English manners and ways of living, and the movement leading to the diminution of crime, to sanitation, the greater abundance of food and amelioration of living conditions—particularly in the towns and among the poorer classes—came after and not before, the American Revolution.

The state of mind, to which were due the conditions thus described, permeated all phases of British life and government, and determined the attitude of the ruling classes toward the political, as well as the social, order. These classes were composed in a preponderant degree of landed proprietors, whose feeling of feudal superiority and tenacious adherence to the ideas and traditions of their class were determining factors in political life both in Parliament and the country. They believed that their institutions provided a sufficient panacea for all constitutional ills and could not imagine wherein these institutions needed serious revision. They were convinced that the existing system preserved men's liberties better than any that had gone before, and they wanted no experiments or dangerous leaps in the dark. They not only held as a tenet of faith that those who owned the land should wield political power, but they were certain that such an arrangement had the sanction of God. They revered the British system of government, its principles and philosophy, as the embodiment of human wisdom, grounded in righteousness and destined by nature to serve the purpose of man. They saw it admired abroad as the most enlightened government possessed by any nation in the world, and so credited it with their unprecedented prosperity and influence as a nation. They likened its critics to Milton's Lucifer, attacking "the sacred and immovable mount of the whole constitution," as a contemporary phrased it, and they guarded it as the Israelites guarded the ark of the convenant. Woe to him who would defile it!

Nor were they any less rigid in their attitude toward the colonies in America. Colonial policy had developed very slowly and did not take on systematic form until well on in the eighteenth century; but when once it became defined, the ruling classes regarded it in certain fundamental aspects—at least in official utterance—as fixed as was the constitution itself. At first England did not take her colonies seriously as assets of commercial importance, but when after 1704 naval stores were added to the tobacco and sugar of Virginia and the West Indies, and it was seen that these commodities enabled England to obtain a favorable balance with European countries, the value of the plantations in British eyes increased enormously. However, it was not until after 1750, when a favorable balance of trade was reached with the colonies themselves, that the mercantilist deemed the situation entirely satisfactory; and from that time on for twenty years—epochal years in the history of England's relations with America—the mercantilist idea of the place that a colony should occupy in the British scheme of things became fixed and unalterable. Though the colonies were growing by leaps and bounds, the authorities in Great Britain retained unchanged the policy which had been adopted more than half a century before. They did not essentially alter the instructions to the Board of Trade in all the eighty-six years of its existence. They created no true colonial secretary, even in 1768, and no department of any kind at any time for the exclusive oversight of American affairs. They saw no necessity for adopting new methods of managing colonial trade, even though the colonial situation was constantly presenting new problems for solution. Manufacturing was undoubtedly more discouraged in 1770 than it had been in 1699, when the first restrictive act was passed; and the idea that the colonies by their very nature were ordained to occupy a position of commercial dependence to the advantage and profit of the mother country was never more firmly fixed in the British mind than just before our Revolution. In fact, that event altered in no essential particular the British conception of the status of a colony, for as late as 1823, Sir Charles Ellis, undoubtedly voicing the opinion of his day, could say in Parliament that the colonial system of England had not been established for the sake of the colonies, but for the encouragement of British trade and manufactures. Thus for more than a century England's idea of what a colony should be underwent no important alteration whatever.

Equally unchangeable was the British idea of how a colony should be governed. In the long list of commissions and instructions drawn up in England for the guidance of the royal governors in America, there is to be found, with one exception only, nothing that indicates any progressive advance in the spirit and method of administration from 1696 to 1782. Year after year, the same arrangements and phraseology appear, conforming to a common type, admitting, it is true, important modifications in matters of detail, but in principle undergoing at no time in eighty-six years serious revision or reconstruction. These documents were drawn up in Whitehall according to a fixed pattern; the governors and councils were allowed no discretion; the popular assemblies were confined within the narrow bounds of inelastic formulae, which repeated, time after time, the same injunctions and the same commands; while the crown reserved to itself the full right of interference in all matters that were con-

strued as coming under its prerogative. These instructions represented the rigid eighteenth-century idea of how a colony should be retained in dependence on the mother country. And what was true of the instructions was true of other documents also that had to do with America. For instance, the lists of queries to the governors, the questionnaires to the commodore-governors of the Newfoundland fishery, and the whole routine business of the fishery itself had become a matter of form and precedent, as conventional and stereotyped as were the polite phrases of eighteenth-century social intercourse. Rarely was any attempt made to adapt these instructions to the needs of growing communities such as the colonies were showing themselves to be; and only with the Quebec instructions of 1775, issued after the passage of the Quebec Act and under the guidance of a colonial governor of unusual common sense, was there any recognition of a new colonial situation. In this document, which appeared at the very end of our colonial period, do we find something of a break from the stiff and legalistic forms that were customary in the earlier royal instructions, some appreciation of the fact that the time was approaching when a colony should be treated with greater liberality and be allowed to have some part in saying how it should be administered.

Without going further with our analysis we can say that during the half-century preceding our Revolution English habits of thought and methods of administration and government, both at home and in the colonies, had reached a state of immobility. To all appearances the current of the national life had settled into a backwater, and as far as home affairs were concerned was seemingly becoming stagnant. At a time when Pitt was breaking France by land and sea, and men on waking were asking what new territories had been added during the night to the British dominions, occurrences at home were barren of adventure, either in society or politics. Ministers were not true states-men; they had no policies, no future hopes, no spirit of advance, no gifts of foresight or prophecy. In all that con-cerned domestic interests, they were imper-vious to suggestions, even when phrased in the eloquence of Pitt and Burke. They wanted no change in existing conditions; their eyes were fixed on traditions and precedents rather than on the obligations and opportunities of the future. Their tenure of office was characterized by inac-tivity, a casual handling of situations they did not understand and could not control, and a willingness to let the ship of state drift for itself. As a modern critic has said, they were always turning in an unending circle, one out, one in, one in, one out, marking time and never going forward.

To a considerable extent the narrow point of view and rigidity of attitude exhibited by the men who held office at Whitehall or sat in Parliament at West-minster can be explained by the fact that at this time officials and members of Par-liament were also territorial magnates, lords of manors, and country squires, who were influenced in their political life by ideas that governed their relations with their tenantry and the management of their landed estates. It is not necessary to think of them as bought by king or mini-sters and so bound and gagged against freedom of parliamentary action. In fact, they were bound and gagged already by devotion to their feudal privileges, their family prerogatives, and their pride of landed proprietorship. They viewed the colonies somewhat in the light of tenan-cies of the crown, and as they themselves lived on the rents from their estates, so they believed that the king and the king-dom should profit from the revenues and returns from America. The point of view was somewhat that of a later Duke of Newcastle, who when reproached for com-pelling his tenants to vote as he pleased said that he had a right to do as he liked with his own. This landed aristocracy re-flected the eighteenth-century spirit. It was sonorous, conventional, and self-satisfied, and shameless of sparkle or humor. It clung to the laws of inheritance and property, fearful of anything that might in any way offend the shades of past generations. In its criticism of the man-ners of others it was insular and arrogant, and was mentally so impenetrable as never to understand why anyone, even in the colonies, should wish things to be other than they were or refuse to accept the station of life to which by Providence he had been called.

A government, representative of a privileged social and political order that took existing conditions as a matter of course, setting nature at defiance and de-pending wholly on art, was bound sooner or later to come into conflict with a peo-ple, whose life in America was in closest touch with nature and characterized by growth and change and constant readjust-ments. In that country were groups of men, women, and children, the greater portion of whom were of English ancestry, numbering at least a few hundreds and eventually more than two millions, who were scattered over many miles of con-tinent and island and were living under various forms of government. These peo-ple, more or less unconsciously, under the influence of new surroundings and imperative needs, were establishing a new order of society and laying the foun-dations of a new political system. The story of how this was done—how that which was English slowly and impercepti-bly merged into that which was American —has never been adequately told; but it is a fascinating phase of history, more interesting and enlightening when studied against the English background than when construed as an American problem only. It is the story of the gradual elimi-nation of those elements, feudal and pro-prietary, that were foreign to the normal life of a frontier land, and of the gradual adjustment of the colonists to the re-straints and restrictions that were imposed upon them by the commercial policy of the mother country. It is the story also of the growth of the colonial assemblies and of the education and experience that the colonists were receiving in the art of political self-government. It is above all—and no phase of colonial history is of greater significance—the story of the gradual transformation of these assemblies from the provincial councils that the home government intended them to be into miniature parliaments. At the end of a long struggle with the prerogative and other forms of outside interference, they emerged powerful legislative bodies, as self-conscious in their way as the House of Commons in England was becoming during the same eventful years.

Here was an *impasse,* for the British view that a colonial assembly partook of the character of a provincial or municipal council was never actually true of any assembly in British America at any time in its history. From the beginning, each of these colonial bodies, in varying ways and under varying circumstances, assumed a position of leadership in its colony, and exercised, in a manner often as bewildering to the student of today as to an eighteenth-century royal governor, a great variety of executive, legislative, and judicial functions. Except in Connecticut and Rhode Island, requests for parliamentary privileges were made very early and were granted year after year by the governors—privileges that were essentially those of the English and Irish Houses of Commons and were consciously modelled after them. At times, the assemblies went beyond Parliament and made claims additional to the usual speaker's requests, claims first asked for as matter of favor but soon demanded as matters of right, as belonging to representative bodies and not acquired by royal gift or favor. One gets the impression that though the assemblies rarely failed to make the formal request, they did so with intention of taking in any case what they asked for and

anything more that they could secure. Gradually, with respect to privileges, they advanced to a position of amazing independence, freeing themselves step by step from the interfering power of the executive, that is, the royal prerogative. They began to talk of these rights as ancient and inherent and necessary to the orderly existence of any representative body, and they became increasingly self-assertive and determined as the years passed.

Nor was this the only change affecting the assemblies to which the eighteenth-century Englishman was asked to adapt himself. The attitude of the assemblies in America found expression in the exercise of powers that had their origin in other sources than that of parliamentary privilege. They adopted rules of their own, that were sometimes even more severe than those of Parliament itself. They regulated membership, conduct, and procedure; ruled against drinking, smoking, and profanity, against unseemly, unnecessary, and tedious debate, against absence, tardiness, and other forms of evasion. They punished with great severity all infringement of rules and acts of contempt, and defended their right to do so against the governor and council on one side and the courts of the colony on the other. Nor did they even pretend to be consistent in their opposition to the royal prerogative, as expressed in the instructions to the royal governors, and in their manoeuvres they did not follow any uniform policy or plan. They conformed to these instructions willingly enough, whenever it was agreeable for them to do so; but if at any time they considered an instruction contrary to the best interest of a particular colony, they did not hesitate to oppose it directly or to nullify it by avoidance. In general, it may be said that they evaded or warded off or deliberately disobeyed such instructions as they did not like. Thus both consciously and unconsciously they were carving out a *lex parliamenti* of their own, which, evolving naturally from the necessity of meeting the demands of self-governing communities, carried them beyond the bounds of their own membership and made them responsible for the welfare of the colony at large.

The important point to remember is that the plan of governmental control as laid down in England was never in accord with the actual situation in America; that the Privy Council, the Secretary of State, and the Board of Trade seem not to have realized that their system of colonial administration was breaking down at every point. Their minds ran in a fixed groove and they could construe the instances of colonial disobedience and aggression, which they often noted, in no other terms than those of persistent dereliction of duty. Either they did not see or else refused to see the wide divergence that was taking place between colonial administration as they planned it and colonial administration as the colonists were working it out. Englishmen saw in the American claims an attack upon an old, established, and approved system. They interpreted the attitude of the colonists as something radical and revolutionary, menacing British prosperity, British political integrity, and the British scheme of colonial government. Opposed by tradition and conviction to new experiments, even at home, they were unable to sympathize with, or even to understand, the great experiment, one of the greatest in the world's history, on trial across the sea. There in America was evolving a new idea of sovereignty, inherent not in crown and Parliament but in the people of a state, based on the principle—self-evident it may be to us today but not to the Englishman of the eighteenth century—that governments derive their just powers from the consent of the governed. There was emerging a new idea of the franchise, as a natural right, under certain conditions, of every adult citizen, an idea which theoretically is not even yet accepted in Great Britain. There was being estab-

lished a new order of society, without caste or privilege, free from economic restrictions and social demarcations between class and class. There was taking shape a new idea of a colony, a self-governing dominion, the members of which were competent to develop along their own lines, while working together with the mother country as part of a common state.

For us today with our perspective it is easy to see the conflict approaching and some of us may think perhaps that the British ministers and members of Parliament ought to have realized that their own ideas and systems were fast outgrowing their usefulness even for Great Britain herself; and that their inflexible views of the colonial relationship were fast leading to disaster. Yet we must keep in mind that it is always extraordinarily difficult for a generation reared in the environment of modern democracy to deal sympathetically with the Englishman's point of view in the eighteenth century, or to understand why the ruling classes of that day so strenuously opposed the advance of liberalism both in England and America. The fact remains, however, that the privileged and governing classes in England saw none of these things. They were too close to events and too much a part of them to judge them dispassionately or to appreciate their real significance. These classes, within which we may well include the Loyalists in America, were possessed of inherited instincts, sentiments, and prejudices which they could no more change than they could have changed the color of their eyes or the texture of their skins. That which existed in government and society was to them a part of the fixed scheme of nature, and no more called for reconsideration than did the rising of the sun or the budding of the trees in spring. If Lord North had granted the claims of the colonists he probably would have been looked on by Parliament as having betrayed the constitution and impaired its stability, just as Peel was pilloried by a similar landowning Parliament in 1845, when he advocated the repeal of the corn laws. One has only to read the later debates on the subject of enclosures and the corn laws to understand the attitude of the British landowners toward the colonies from 1763 to 1776. To them in each instance it seemed as if the foundations of the universe were breaking up and the world in which they lived was sinking beneath their feet.

Primarily, the American Revolution was a political and constitutional movement and only secondarily one that was either financial, commercial, or social. At bottom the fundamental issue was the political independence of the colonies, and in the last analysis the conflict lay between the British Parliament and the colonial assemblies, each of which was probably more sensitive, self-conscious, and self-important than was the voting population that it represented. For many years these assemblies had fought the prerogative successfully and would have continued to do so, eventually reducing it to a minimum, as the later self-governing dominions have done; but in the end it was Parliament, whose powers they disputed, that became the great antagonist. Canning saw the situation clearly when, half a century later, he spoke of the Revolution as having been a test of the equality of strength "between the legislature of this mighty kingdom . . . and the colonial assemblies," adding further that he had no intention of repeating in the case of Jamaica, the colony then under debate, the mistakes that had been made in 1776. Of the mistakes to which he referred the greatest was the employment of the deadly expedient of coercion, and he showed his greater wisdom when he determined, as he said, to keep back "within the penetralia of the constitution the transcendental powers of Parliament over a dependency of the British crown" and not "to produce it upon trifling occasions or in cases of petty refractoriness and tem-

porary misconduct." How he would have met the revolution in America, based as it was on "the fundamental principles of political liberty," we cannot say; but we know that he had no sympathy with any attempt to force opinion back into paths that were outworn. That he would have foreseen the solution of a later date and have granted the colonies absolute and responsible self-government, recognizing the equality of the assemblies in domestic matters and giving them the same control over their home affairs as the people of Great Britain had over theirs, can be conjectured only by inference from his liberal attitude toward the South American republics. He stood half-way between the ministers of the Revolutionary period —blind, sensitive, and mentally unprogressive—and the statesmen of the middle of the nineteenth century, who were willing to follow the lead of those courageous and far-sighted Englishmen who saved the empire from a second catastrophe after 1830 and were the founders of the British colonial policy of today.

The revolt of the colonies from Great Britain began long before the battles of Moore's Creek Bridge and Lexington; before the time of James Otis and the writs of assistance; before the dispute over the appointment of judges in North Carolina and New York; before the eloquence of Patrick Henry was first heard in the land; and even before the quarrel in Virginia over the Dinwiddie pistole fee. These were but the outward and visible signs of an inward and factual divergence. The separation from the mother country began just as soon as the mercantile system of commercial control, the governmental system of colonial administration, and the whole doctrine of the inferior status of a colonial assembly began to give way before the pressure exerted and the disruptive power exercised by these young and growing colonial communities. New soil had produced new wants, new desires, new points of view, and the colonists were demanding the right to live their own lives in their own way. As we see it today the situation was a dramatic one. On one side was the immutable, stereotyped system of the mother country, based on precedent and tradition and designed to keep things comfortably as they were; on the other, a vital, dynamic organism, containing the seed of a great nation, its forces untried, still to be proved. It is inconceivable that a connection should have continued long between two such yokefellows, one static, the other dynamic, separated by an ocean and bound only by the ties of a legal relationship.

If my diagnosis is correct of the British state of mind in the eighteenth century, and the evidence in its favor seems overwhelming, then the colonists were as justified in their movement of revolt as were the Englishmen themselves in their movement for reform in the next century. Yet in reality no great progressive movement needs justification at our hands, for great causes justify themselves and time renders the decision. The revolt in America and the later reforms in Great Britain herself were directed against the same dominant ruling class that in their colonial relations as well as in their social and political arrangements at home preferred that the world in which they lived should remain as it was. Reform or revolt is bound to follow attempts of a privileged class to conduct affairs according to unchanging rules and formulae. The colonies had developed a constitutional organization equally complete with Britain's own and one that in principle was far in advance of the British system, and they were qualified to co-operate with the mother country on terms similar to those of a brotherhood of free nations such as the British world is becoming today. But England was unable to see this fact or unwilling to recognize it, and consequently America became the scene of a political unrest, which might have been controlled by compromise, but was turned to revolt by coercion. The situation is a very interesting one, for England is famous for her ability to compromise at critical moments in her history. For once at least she failed. In 1832 and later years, when she faced other great constitutional crises at home and in her colonies, she saved herself from revolution by understanding the situation and adjusting herself to it. Progress may be stemmed for a time, but it cannot be permanently stopped by force. A novelist has expressed the idea in saying:

> You cannot fight and beat revolutions as you can fight and beat nations. You can kill a man, but you simply can't kill a rebel. For the proper rebel has an ideal of living, while your ideal is to kill him so that you may preserve yourself. And the reason why no revolution or religion has ever been beaten is that rebels die for something worth dying for, the future, but their enemies die only to preserve the past, and makers of history are always stronger than makers of empire.

The American revolutionists had an ideal of living; it can hardly be said that in 1776 the Englishmen of the ruling classes were governed in their colonial relations by any ideals that were destined to be of service to the future of the human race.

Select Bibliography for Problem 2

Barrow, Thomas C. "The American Revolution as a Colonial War for Independence," *William and Mary Quarterly*, 25, 3d series (July 1968), 452–464.

Beyer, Richard L. "American Colonial Commerce and British Protection," *Journal of American History*, 22 (December 1928), 265–269.

Billias, George A., ed. *The American Revolution*. American Problem Studies under the editorial direction of Oscar Handlin. New York: Holt, Rinehart and Winston, Inc., 1965.

Blassingame, John W. "American Nationalism and Other Loyalties in the Southern Colonies, 1763–1775," *The Journal of Southern History*, 34 (February 1968), 50–75.

Bond, Jr., Beverly W. "The Colonial Agent as a Popular Representative," *Political Science Quarterly*, 35 (September 1920), 372–392.

Cecil, Robert. "The Famous Tax Included, Tea Was Still Cheaper Here," *American Heritage*, 12 (April 1961), 8–11.

Clark, Dora M. "The American Board of Customs, 1767–1783," *American Historical Review*, 45 (July 1940), 777–806.

Davis, Allen F., and Harold D. Woodman, eds. *Conflict or Consensus in American History.* Boston: D. C. Health and Company, 1966, pp. 1–67.

Duff, Stella F. "The Case against the King: The Virginia Gazette Indicts George III," *William and Mary Quarterly*, 6, 3d series (July 1949), 383–397.

Ernst, Joseph Albert. "The Currency Act Repeal Movement: A Study of Imperial Politics and Revolution Crisis, 1764–1767," *William and Mary Quarterly*, 25, 3d series (April 1968), 177–211.

Farrand, Max. "The Taxation of Tea, 1767–1773," *American Historical Review*, 3 (January 1898), 266–269.

Fine, Sidney, and Gerald S. Brown, eds. *The American Past: Conflicting Interpretations of the Great Issues*, Vol. 1. New York: Crowell Collier and Macmillan, Inc., 1965, 31–84.

Fingerhut, Eugene R. "Uses and Abuses of the American Loyalists Claims: A Critique of Quantitative Analysis," *William and Mary Quarterly*, 25, 3d series (April 1968), 245–258.

Fleming, Thomas J. "Verdicts of History I: The Boston Massacre," *American Heritage*, 18 (December 1966), 6–10, 102–111.

Gipson, Lawrence H. "The American Revolution as an Aftermath of the Great War for the Empire," *Political Science Quarterly*, 65 (March 1950), 86–104.

Greene, Jack P., ed. *The Ambiguity of the American Revolution.* Interpretations of American History, John Higham and Bradford Perkins, eds. New York: Harper & Row, Publishers, 1968.

Grob, Gerald N. and George A. Billias, eds. *Interpretations of American History*, Vol. 1 New York: The Free Press, 1967, pp. 127–260.

Klein, Milton M. "Prelude to Revolution in New York: Jury Trials and Judicial Tenure," *William and Mary Quarterly*, 17, 3d series (October 1960), 439–462.

Laprode, William T. "The Stamp Act in British Politics," *American Historical Review*, 35 (April 1930), 735–757.

Morgan, Edmund S. "The Puritan Ethic and the American Revolution," *William and Mary Quarterly*, 24, 3d series (January 1967), 3–43.

Morris, Richard B. "Then and There the Child Independence Was Born," *American Heritage*, 13 (February 1962), 36–39, 82–84.

Quint, Howard H., *et al.*, eds. *Main Problems in American History*, Vol. 1, rev. ed. Homewood, Ill.: Dorsey Press, 1968, pp. 84–112.

Savelle, Max. "Nationalism and Other Loyalties in the American Revolution," *American Historical Review*, 67 (July 1962), 901–923.

Schlesinger, Arthur M. "The American Revolution Reconsidered," *Political*

Science Quarterly, 34 (March 1919) 61–78.

Scott, A. P. "The Parson's Cause," *Political Science Quarterly,* 31 (December 1916), 558–577.

Smith, Paul H. "The American Loyalists: Notes on Their Organization and Numerical Strength," *William and Mary Quarterly,* 25, 3d series (April 1968), 259–277.

Wahlke, John C., ed. *The Causes of the American Revolution,* rev. ed. Problems in American Civilization under the editorial direction of Edwin C. Rozwenc. Boston: D. C. Heath and Company, 1962.

Winston, Alexander. "Firebrand of the Revolution," *American Heritage,* 18 (April 1967), 60–64, 105-108.

part 3

Forging
the Nation

chapter 7

From the Articles to the Constitution

The Radicals Form a Government

ARTICLES OF CONFEDERATION

Richard Henry Lee's resolution of independence, which was read before the delegates assembled in Philadelphia in 1776, was accompanied by a plan of confederation. A committee headed by John Dickinson finally consummated Lee's proposal in thirteen articles on July 12 under the auspicious title "Articles of Confederation and Perpetual Union." In spite of this promising start, the articles were not fully implemented until March 1881, when Maryland, after having forced a showdown on the question of western lands, finally ratified them.

The disposition of the vast western lands held by such states as Massachusetts, Connecticut, Virginia, the Carolinas, and Georgia stood as a constant source of concern to the landless states of Maryland, New Jersey, and Pennsylvania, because these lands represented considerable power and revenue. Faced with the dilemma of having to choose between their western lands and ratification of the Articles of Confederation, the states ultimately chose the latter. In the meantime, until 1781, the business of government was conducted by the Second Continental Congress.

Because the confederation was launched as one of the many impulses against the highly centralized powers of the crown, the articles endowed each state with "sovereignty, freedom and independence." Under this new instrument, affairs of government were conducted by a unicameral congress with each state having one vote. Matters of a serious nature needed the approval of nine of the thirteen states, but the *enforcement* of any such legislation required the cooperation of all the states. For instance, Congress could declare war and borrow money, but it could not conscript troops and levy taxes without the approval of the states.

A Policy for Expansion

ORDINANCE OF 1784

Soon after Maryland ratified the articles, the Congress established the conditions under which western lands could be obtained and ultimately turned into new states. The first of the land ordinances was introduced in 1784. Drafted by Jefferson, this document provided that all western lands be divided into states, and that this would become a reality when their free population equaled that of the smallest state in the confederation. One of its more important implications was that the land would be free. This ordinance, however, never really got a chance to prove itself because some of its provisions were attacked in Congress. Easterners viewed with alarm the large number of states planned for the Mississippi Valley at their expense in representation, while westerners frowned on that part of the ordinance which called for rectangular state boundaries rather than natural divisions. These protests proved to be enough to set aside Jefferson's plan for shaping the West.

ORDINANCE OF 1785

As the numbers of settlers increased in the Ohio Valley, Congress was finally forced to come to grips with the problem of organizing a workable plan for the West. Accordingly, another land ordinance was passed in 1785. By the provisions of this ordinance, the Northwest Territory was to be surveyed and divided into townships of 36 square miles, with each mile representing a section and each section 640 acres. The sixteenth section of each township was to be set aside for the development of public schools.

This ordinance might have been a boon to settlers, but land speculators influenced Congress to sell the land by section and at a price of $1 per acre. Unable to buy such large tracts, the settlers were forced to turn to private land companies whose business ethics were not always beyond reproach.

NORTHWEST ORDINANCE OF 1787

The third and most significant of these land ordinances was drafted out of necessity to provide order for the rapidly expanding settlements in the Northwest, and as a compromise between factions who had long debated the issue of how and when self-government should be extended to the wilderness peoples. The Northwest Ordinance of 1787 provided: (1) that between three and five states be formed from the territory; (2) that a territorial governor with three judges, appointed by and responsible to Congress, would rule; (3) that as soon as the territory attained a free male population of 5000,

its propertied electorate might organize a bicameral legislature and send a delegate to Congress, where he could debate but not vote; and (4) that when the territory had a free population of 60,000 it might draft a constitution and apply for equal statehood. In addition to these procedural matters, the ordinance prohibited slavery and guaranteed freedom of worship and other fundamental rights.

Thus the Northwest Ordinance of 1787 provided a viable formula for the settlement and development of not only the trans-Appalachia region but also the trans-Mississippi west.

Finances and Foreign Affairs

The problem of financing the confederated government grew more serious with each passing year. The new government had not only accumulated an enormous war debt, but it had no power to collect taxes or tariffs in order to pay off its indebtedness. The soldiers of the Continental army wanted their promised pay, and public creditors wanted the interest on war loans. Meanwhile, the Continental paper money declined in value, which caused considerable hardship to heavily mortgaged farmers.

SHAYS' REBELLION

In 1786, the nadir of the depression, a group in Massachusetts became so troubled that they rose in rebellion. Under the leadership of an army veteran, Captain Daniel Shays, the insurgents demanded that the creditor-dominated legislature ease the tax load and curb the foreclosures, that paper money be printed, and that prosecution for debt be abolished. Though the rebels lost the battle (at Springfield), they won the war, figuratively speaking, for the unpopular Governor James Bowdoin was defeated in the next election by John Hancock, who immediately drafted reform measures.

To many, and particularly to the conservatives, the Shays uprising pointed up the need for a stronger centralized government in order to control the mobs, whereas others felt that the articles simply needed amending. It has been reported, however, that civil war was the last thing they wanted even if it meant sacrificing the principles of the Shaysites.

The Americans fared no better in foreign affairs. In 1783 England recognized the Treaty of Paris, but there respect for her former colonies ended. England not only refused to establish a legation in the United States,[1] but she continued to maintain her military outposts in the Northwest under the pretext that Americans had broken the Treaty of Paris by obstructing the collection of debts by the Loyalists. The United States protested through John Adams, but to no avail.

John Jay had somewhat better success negotiating with the Spaniards over the troubled Southwest Territory. He secured for the United States practically all that it wanted: boundaries at the Mississippi River in the west and west Florida in the south. Unfortunately, there was one item missing from this package—free navigation of the Mississippi River—and the southern states would not rest until they had secured that "right." Thus, the treaty was rejected by these states.

In the meantime, as the young nation moved from one crisis to another with faltering steps, speculators like James Wilkinson, James Robertson, and John Siever negotiated their own bargains with the Spaniards. Wilkinson was implicated in a deal designed to lead Tennessee into the Spanish empire, but the king reversed Spanish policies at the last minute and chose instead to levy a 15 percent duty on American goods shipped through New Orleans.

Americans were also harassed in other parts of the world. North African pirates began to prey on American shippers in

[1] It was not until 1791 that England finally sent a minister.

the Mediterranean once the latter had cut themselves loose from the protective apron strings of the mother country. Unable to demand respect, the infant navy was forced to pay for protection in the Mediterranean until 1815, at which time she dealt the Barbary pirates a crippling defeat.

Strengthening the Union

The Articles of Confederation, among other things, pointed up the need for a more perfect union. They exposed the glaring weaknesses of the tax structure and the regulation of commerce (some controls were initiated during the period of the confederation), and illustrated the need for an executive branch with the necessary power to enforce decisions for the common welfare and progress of the new nation. The latter, of course, meant a centralized government. In actuality, the young government had been moving in that direction, in spirit, since 1781 when conservative candidates like James Madison, Alexander Hamilton, and Robert Morris began to defeat the followers of Samuel' Adams, Patrick Henry, and Richard Henry Lee. The former group called for law and order, which they felt would come only with a strong federal government. The Federalists, many of whom represented business interests, were particularly concerned about the need for more effective regulation of commerce; and in 1786 Virginia assumed the initiative and summoned delegates from the various states to meet in Annapolis for the express purpose of dealing with this problem. However, when only five delegations, out of the nine states that had previously expressed interest, made an appearance, Alexander Hamilton called for another convention that would meet in Philadelphia in May 1787. The second convention would deal not only with commerce but with the question of revising the Articles of Confederation.

PHILADELPHIA CONVENTION

Accordingly, the more serious consideration of the articles attracted fifty-five delegates (all states except Rhode Island were represented). This second gathering represented men of considerable ability, experience, and wealth. The revolutionaries were conspicuous by their small numbers (some, like Patrick Henry, had refused to attend; Paine, John Adams, and Jefferson were in Europe), while the more conservative forces of the Revolution made up a sizable majority and carried the pennants of the planters, merchants, and land speculators. All, however, had shared in the greater drama of the Revolution and desired a dynamic nation that would match the vigor of the revolt.

VIRGINIA PLAN

After electing George Washington presiding officer, the delegates settled down to the fundamental issue of trying to decide between a confederation of states (states' rights) and a federation of states (centralism). The convention had no sooner convened when the Virginia delegation introduced a plan of government. Written for the most part by James Madison and read before the delegates by Edmund Randolph, the Virginia Plan called for a bicameral national legislature whose membership in the lower house would be calculated on the basis of state population, and whose membership in the upper house would be elected by that of the lower. Secondly, the plan proposed the creation of national executive and judicial branches whose officers would be elected by the legislature. The Virginia Plan obviously favored the larger states, such as Virginia, Massachusetts, and Pennsylvania.

NEW JERSEY PLAN

When opposition arose to the Virginia Plan, the delegation from New Jersey proposed a countermeasure. By the provisions of this plan the unicameral legislature of the confederation was to be retained with each state having one vote. There was to be a plural executive elected by Congress and a judiciary appointed by the executive. Since the New Jersey Plan shifted the political advantage to the small states, the task of the convention was to devise a plan that would pacify both factions.

CONNECTICUT COMPROMISE

Roger Sherman and the other Connecticut delegates assumed the role of arbiter when they introduced a compromise plan. The Connecticut proposal suggested the plan of representation by which our federal government operates today, namely, that the legislature was to be bicameral in structure, and that apportionment in the Senate was to be made on the basis of equal representation, and in the House on the basis of population. Finally, all bills designed to raise revenue were to originate in the lower house. Faced with the possibility of another fruitless convention, the delegates finally accepted the Connecticut Plan, which has gone down in history as the "Great Compromise."

3/5 COMPROMISE

Another compromise was needed on the question of slave representation and taxation. The North wanted to tax the slave as property but to extend no representation, while the South wanted the advantages of full slave representation. The compromise agreement provided that five slaves would equal three freeman for purposes of taxation and representation in Congress. In addition, slave trade was extended to the year 1807.

A System of Checks and Balances

The secret proceedings of the Philadelphia convention revealed early that what the delegations had in mind was not a revision of the articles but the drafting of a new constitution. The final product, a "bundle of compromises," reflected a unique system of checks and balances. A popularly elected lower house would serve as a check against the upper chamber; both would balance their power against that of the chief executive; and the third arm of the system, the judiciary, would serve as a check on the other two. Even though these three separate but equal branches were designed to neutralize any emergent power within the triangle, the new federal government was given awesome power in the minds of many western states' righters. To some, it symbolized a return of the British.

One of the most striking features of the new constitution was the sovereignty it gave the federal government—not only sovereignty, but complete freedom to make laws in order to protect that power. The federal government would exercise its power over the states in foreign policy and national defense; it retained the exclusive right to call on the state militia if needed, to declare war, and to make treaties. In other areas, the federal government reserved the right to coin money, regulate interstate commerce, and uphold contracts.

The President was also awarded certain powers through the use of the veto. In addition, he was to be commander in chief of the armed forces, and was given the prerogative to make treaties and appointments with the consent of the Senate. The most significant power bestowed on the judiciary was that of judicial review, and this was particularly true of the Supreme Court's review in state cases.

The conservatives won consolation victories on other issues, namely, in keeping the election of the President out of the hands of the "mob,"[2] and by making the most conservative officials, the Supreme Court judges, appointees for life.

RATIFICATION

Unanimous ratification of the Constitution by all thirteen states was out of the question, since Rhode Island was hostile to the whole affair. Thus, the delegates provided that when two-thirds of the states approved the Constitution through special state conventions, the document would then be considered ratified. Delaware, New Jersey, and Georgia (small states that were pleased with the compromise over representation) approved almost immediately, but others were more cautious. Debates in other states, the larger ones in particular, raged between the Federalists and Antifederalists. Somewhat ambivalent about the power of the government, the Massachusetts convention ratified by a narrow margin, while Virginia and New York experienced long and frustrating debates. In Virginia Patrick Henry and James Monroe staged brilliant debates with Madison and Washington; but the latter, with the governor's support, finally garnered enough votes to gain ratification. New York, meanwhile, argued the issue until July, when Hamilton, with the aid of the *Federalist* papers,[3] secured ratification by three votes. North Carolina, on the other hand, steadfastly refused to ratify until a bill of rights was included. North Carolina and Rhode Island finally decided to join the federal union in September 1789 and May 1790, respectively.

With the official ratification of the Constitution on March 4, 1789, the Americans had completed a cycle of conservative-to-radical-to-conservative coups. The radical Patriots had replaced the conservative and centralist-minded crown with the Articles of Confederation, only to find their government pushed aside by the federal Constitution, which had been framed by another conservative and centralist-minded group. The magic of compromise, however, had held the nation together during the transitional period

---

[2] The electoral college represented another compromise.

[3] Madison and Jay collaborated with Hamilton in writing the *Federalist* papers.

from the articles to the Constitution; future unity would demand the energies of super statesmen.

Select Bibliography

Beard, Charles A. *An Economic Interpretation of the Constitution*, rev. ed. New York: Crowell Collier and Macmillan, Inc., 1935.

Bowers, Claude. *The Young Jefferson, 1743–1789.* Boston: Houghton Mifflin Company, 1969.

Brant, Irving. *James Madison: Father of the Constitution, 1787–1800.* Indianapolis, Ind.: The Bobbs-Merrill Co., Inc., 1950.

———. *James Madison: The Nationalist, 1780–1787.* Indianapolis, Ind.: The Bobbs-Merrill Co., Inc., 1948.

Brown, Robert E. *Charles Beard and the Constitution.* Princeton, N.J.: Princeton University Press, 1956.

Burns, Edward M. *James Madison, Philosopher of the Constitution.* New York: Octagon Books, Inc., 1968.

Chinard, Gilbert. *Honest John Adams.* Gloucester, Mass.: Peter Smith, 1933.

———. *Thomas Jefferson: Apostle of Americanism.* Ann Arbor, Mich.: University of Michigan Press, 1957.

Cooke, Jacob E. *Alexander Hamilton: A Profile.* New York: Hill and Wang, Inc., 1967.

Corwin, Edward S. *The Constitution and What It Means Today.* Princeton, N.J.: Princeton University Press, 1958.

Craven, Wesley F. *The Legend of the Founding Fathers.* Ithaca, N.Y.: Cornell University Press, 1965.

Farrand, Max. *The Framing of the Constitution.* New Haven, Conn.: Yale University Press, 1913.

Hibbard, Benjamin H. *A History of the Public Land Policies.* Madison, Wis.: University of Wisconsin Press, 1963.

Jensen, Merrill. *The Articles of Confederation: An Interpretation of the Social-Constitutional History of the American Revolution, 1774–1781.* Madison, Wis.: University of Wisconsin Press, 1959.

———. *The Making of the American Constitution.* New York: Van Nostrand Reinhold Company, 1964.

———. *The New Nation: A History of the United States During the Confederation, 1781–1789.* New York: Alfred A. Knopf, 1950.

Kelly, Alfred H., and Winifred A. Harbison. *The American Constitution: Its Origins and Development*, rev. ed. New York: W. W. Norton & Company, Inc., 1955.

Koch, Adrienne. *Power, Morals, and the Founding Fathers.* Ithaca, N.Y.: Cornell University Press, 1961.

McDonald, Forrest. *We the People: The Economic Origins of the Constitution.* Chicago: University of Chicago Press, 1958.

Main, Jackson T. *The Anti-Federalists: Critics of the Constitution, 1781–1788.* Chapel Hill, N.C.: University of North Carolina Press, 1961.

Mitchell, Broadus, and Louise Pearson. *A Biography of the Constitution of the United States: Its Origin, Formation, Adoption, Interpretation.* New York: Oxford University Press, 1964.

Nagel, Paul C. *One Nation Indivisible: The Union in American Thought, 1776–1861.* New York: Oxford University Press, 1964.

Nettels, Curtis P. *The Emergence of a National Economy, 1775–1815.* New York: Harper & Row, Publishers, 1969.

Nevins, Allen. *The American States During and After the Revolution, 1775–1789.* New York: Crowell Collier and Macmillan, Inc., 1924.

Ringold, May Spencer. *The Role of the State Legislatures in the Confederacy.* Athens, Ga.: University of Georgia Press, 1966.

Rossiter, Clinton. *Alexander Hamilton and the Constitution.* New York: Harcourt Brace Jovanovich, Inc., 1964.

———. *Seedtime of the Republic.* New York: Harcourt Brace Jovanovich, Inc., 1953.

———. *1787: The Grand Convention.* New York: Crowell Collier and Macmillan, Inc., 1966.

Rutland, Robert A. *The Birth of the Bill of Rights, 1776–1791.* Chapel Hill, N.C.: University of North Carolina Press, 1955.

———. *George Mason: Reluctant Statesman.* Holt, Rinehart and Winston, Inc., 1961.

———. *The Ordeal of the Constitution: The Anti-Federalists and the Ratification Struggle of 1787–1788.* Norman, Okla.: University of Oklahoma Press, 1966.

Schachner, Nathan. *The Founding Fathers.* New York: G. P. Putnam's Sons, 1954.

Turner, Frederick J. *The Significance of Sections in American History.* Gloucester, Mass.: Peter Smith, 1932.

Van Every, Dale. *Ark of Empire: The American Frontier, 1784–1803.* New York: William Morrow & Co., Inc., 1963.

Wright, Benjamin F. *Consensus and Continuity, 1776–1787.* New York: W. W. Norton & Company, Inc., 1967.

Zahniser, Marvin R. *Charles Cotesworth Pinckney: Founding Father.* Chapel Hill, N.C.: University of North Carolina Press, 1967.

chapter 8

Super Statesmen
and the Infant State

Washington
and the New Government

The unfinished business of staffing and starting the machinery of the new government began in the spring of 1789 when the founding fathers established temporary headquarters in New York. The newly elected Congress chose Frederick A. Muhlenburg of Pennsylvania as its Speaker, while the Senate selected John Langdon of New Hampshire as its temporary presiding officer. It was the task of the Senate to count the ballots that had been cast by the presidential electors in February of that year. There was really no contest for the presidency what with General Washington's war record still fresh in the minds of the people. The popular Virginian was drafted and inaugurated on April 30 on a note of confidence in the republican form of government. The runner-up, John Adams of Massachusetts, became the Vice-President. In accordance with the provisions of the Constitution, executive departments were created by Congress and an impressive array of talent was assembled to fill these posts. Thomas Jefferson was made Secretary of State, Alexander Hamilton became Secretary of the Treasury, and Henry Knox was appointed Secretary of War.

One of the major weaknesses of the Articles of Confederation was corrected when the Judiciary Act of 1789 created a Supreme Court, which included a chief

122

justice[1] and five associate justices, circuit courts, and district courts. This act also established the executive office of Attorney General, which was filled by the appointment of Edmund Randolph.

BILL OF RIGHTS

The question of the Bill of Rights also represented unfinished business from the framing of the Constitution. Accordingly, in the summer of 1791, Madison introduced a set of proposals that were considered along with others from certain states. Seventeen amendments were finally approved by the House and sent to the Senate, where, with the help of a special committee, they were reduced to twelve. Two of these were dropped when the list was referred to the states, and the final ten were ratified by three-fourths of the states and became part of the Constitution in December 1791.[2]

The most pressing problem of the young government was that of finance, and the new Secretary of the Treasury approached this task with vigor. Drawing from his keen financial insight, Hamilton urged that the foreign debt, in excess of $11 million, the domestic debt, over $42 million, and the state debts, about $25 million, be refunded at par.

[1] The first Chief Justice was John Jay.
[2] Full ratification was completed on December 15, 1791. For content see the Constitution at the end of this volume.

The state debts were to be assumed by the federal government. Hamilton's program was designed to meet two needs: to stabilize the economy of the country, and thus strengthen its credit image at home and abroad; and to tie the business community to the central government. This marriage, in addition to marshaling the business dollar behind the federal government, would also complement the political thrusts for national unity.

Hamilton's plan for dissolving the foreign debt passed almost unopposed, but the domestic debt and state debts proposals ran into immediate trouble. After heated debates with speculators, who had been buying cheap and selling high,[3] Hamilton finally got the domestic debt funding approved. The state debts issue was still another matter. States with small indebtedness opposed the plan submitted because they held certain reservations about being taxed in order to pay off larger debts of other states. Pointing up the gravity of the matter, and befriending Jefferson and other Virginians by offering that state the new national capital, Hamilton "traded" for enough votes to get the plan approved.

Another part of Hamilton's program called for the creation of a national bank with multiple functions: to provide banking facilities for the business community, to serve as a depository for federal funds, and to issue needed paper notes (currency).[4] In actuality, it would be a joint endeavor, with private business furnishing about four-fifths of the capital.

Opposed to any further political and economic centralization and alarmed by the increasing power of business interests in the federal government, Jefferson and his followers fought Hamilton's bank right down to the wire. Jefferson's argument was grounded in a "strict construction" interpretation of the Constitution—

namely, that Hamilton had gone beyond the "boundaries" of the implied powers granted by the Constitution in proposing his bank plan. The Hamilton forces, on the other hand, argued that the purpose of their bank was designed for the general welfare of the union—in fact, to save it. Since his action was not explicitly prohibited by the Constitution, it must therefore be legal. This "loose construction" interpretation impressed President Washington, and Hamilton's Bank of the United States was chartered in February 1791.

Encouragement for manufacturers was also proposed by Hamilton. His final report called for a high protective tariff to stimulate American manufacturing and less reliance on European goods.[5] Subsidies for agriculture and other federally supported internal improvements were also proposed, but the most powerful merchants were averse to reducing foreign trade, and this part of the financial program was set aside.

The Emergence of Political Parties

The political and economic controversies of the 1790s provided the seeds for the growth of a strange sort of dichotomy that has become known as the American political parties. Hamilton provided the ammunition for the Federalists, and Jefferson, and to some extent Madison, contributed the ideology for the Republicans.[6] The voice of the latter was ably editorialized by Philip Freneau's *National Gazette*.

The differences between the two parties ran much deeper than the battle over the bank. The Republicans, or Antifederalists, were opposed to a strong central government at the expense of states' rights, they fought the power of the mon-

[3] Speculators held most of the domestic debt.
[4] The Treasury was not authorized to perform this service.

[5] The kind of protective tariff suggested by Hamilton was not realized until after the War of 1812.
[6] Their opponents sometimes referred to them as Democratic-Republicans, but Democratic soon lost its appeal as a derogatory label. They should not be confused with the Republicans of today.

eyed interests of eastern cities, and they abhorred the thought of monarchy, aristocracy, or any other political or economic theory that suggested privileged groups. They also championed rural sectors over the cities, and called for more democratic approaches to the solution of problems on local and national levels. The Republicans considered themselves the *real* defenders of the ideals of the Revolution. They believed the Federalists harbored all of these "anti-Republican tendencies."

The Hamiltonians, or Federalists, believed that the masses were unfit to govern themselves without certain controls and guidance from the stronger central government, and that this direction should come from the educated and enlightened class—in brief, moneyed aristocrats. The two groups were not without common interests, however, for they both believed in restraints on the masses (they differed in the amount), the efficacy of the republican form of government, popular elections, sound money, and sound credit.

In 1791 political officials on both the local and national levels began to identify with one or the other of the factions, thus completing the evolution of the American political party system. It has been suggested that Washington tried to hold himself aloof from the political infighting, but his position caused him to be necessarily involved. He was the natural choice of the Federalists for a second term in 1794.

The Taming of the Frontier

Increased settlement of the western frontier brought the young republic again into conflict with the Indians, the French, and ultimately the British. Treaties, such as Fort Stanwix (1784), had proved to be only truces between the Indians and the Americans. Encouraged by the British and Spanish, the Indians sent raiding parties against settlements all along the frontier. In some cases the settlers invited Indian

reprisals by squatting on the redman's land. In 1790 General Josiah Harmar led a contingent of regulars and state militia into the Ohio territory only to be trapped and defeated with heavy losses. The following year General Arthur St. Clair, Governor of the Northwest Territory, assembled an army and marched into the Northwest. He was no more successful than his predecessor. Surprised by a dawn attack, St. Clair's army was cut to pieces and sustained a loss of almost 700 men— half of his army.

BATTLE OF FALLEN TIMBERS

The American government seemed perplexed by the western problem and vacillated between promises and complete silence from 1791 until 1793, when General "Mad Anthony" Wayne was assigned to the troublesome Northwest Territory. Encouraged by a full command of regulars, Wayne marched to Fallen Timbers, where he rendered a crushing defeat on the enemy. This battle prompted the "hostiles" to light up their peace pipes, and at Fort Greenville a treaty was signed that ceded most of the Ohio territory and much of southeastern Indiana. Thus, the heroics of General Anthony Wayne paved the way to the settlement of the Northwest, and within eight years, Ohio became a state.

WHISKEY REBELLION

Hamilton's excise tax on whiskey was not well received in the West and South, for it had hit hard their popular medium of exchange.[7] In 1794 a group in western Pennsylvania not only refused to pay the tax, but harassed the collectors so unmercifully that the militia had to be called out. Because of a strong show of force under the command of Henry Lee,

---

[7] In many frontier settlements whiskey was used in lieu of money, just as tobacco was used in many southern states.

the rebels decided against valor and the crisis ended without bloodshed. The federal government had proved one significant point—that the strong arm of the central government could enforce the law of the land.

Neutrality on Trial

NEUTRALITY PROCLAMATION

The French Revolution brought the first real strain on Washington's foreign policy. The French had aided the Americans during their struggle for independence, and had every right to expect assistance in their fight for liberty. The pro-English forces, however, wanted to see the United States restore friendship with Great Britain in order to renew prosperous trade ties and credit. On the other hand, the pro-French faction, headed by Jefferson, urged the United States to live up to the 1778 Treaty of Alliance[8] and aid the French revolutionaries. The Federalists, under the guidance of Hamilton, countered that the alliance had expired with the death of the king, and that a common heritage bound the Americans to support the English. President Washington surveyed the situation and then with a cool resolve announced his Proclamation of ("friendly and impartial") Neutrality.

CITIZEN GENÊT

In March 1793 Edmond Charles Genêt, the first minister of the newly created French Republic, arrived in the United States. Armed with a plan to turn American ports into a refuge for freebooters, Genêt ignored American neutrality and began recruiting privateers to attack British ships. In the West, he encouraged disgruntled settlers to fight the Spanish

in Florida and Louisiana.[9] Citizen Genêt remained undaunted by warnings from Washington and even tried to go over the head of the President with an appeal to the American people for support. This proved to be his undoing, for Washington promptly demanded his recall. Realizing that a return to France during the "reign of terror" might mean death, Genêt asked for and was granted political asylum in the United States.

ORDERS IN COUNCIL

Great Britain made two disturbing moves in 1793, which prompted the United States to dispatch John Jay to London. The first of these came in the form of a series of Orders in Council, the main purpose of which was to check "illegal" trade between the French West Indies and "neutral" America.[10] Second, she decided against the removal of British troops stationed in the American Northwest Territory.[11]

Jay arrived in London armed with a long list of demands, the main substance of which would benefit merchant America. Trade with the West Indies was desired, and the rights of neutrals on the open seas (particularly the impressment of American sailors) demanded a hearing. Other issues included the British posts in the Northwest, and American debts owed to British Tories.

JAY'S TREATY

The agreements that came out of these negotiations, the Treaty of London, 1794 (better known as Jay's Treaty), have been

---

[8] The French never really put in a formal request for aid of any sort from the United States. This made Washington's task much easier.

[9] It has been suggested that these activities were not unlike those carried out by Benjamin Franklin and Silas Deane in France during the American Revolution.

[10] These Orders in Council were based on a Rule of War of 1756, which said that trade forbidden to a nation in time of peace could not be opened to that nation in time of war.

[11] The British had agreed to evacuate her posts in the Northwest Territory back in 1783.

the subject of much speculation in American history. The short of it was that Jay returned with a British promise to evacuate her troops, but not fur traders, from the Northwest by 1796, and a "most-favored nation" trade agreement with the British East Indies. The sacrificed list included neutral rights, the question of impressment, and trade with the West Indies. Moreover, the question of debts, ship damage adjustments, and the Maine boundary issue were postponed for future arbitration.

The Federalists were not altogether elated, but supported it, while the Republicans called Jay a traitor. Whether or not he could have negotiated a better deal if he had been somewhat more stubborn will never be determined. Nevertheless, there are those who believe that he could have. It has been suggested that Jay would have been in a much stronger position to negotiate if Hamilton had not informed the British that the United States had no intention of joining the Scandinavian Armed Neutrality against Great Britain. The defenders of Jay, on the other hand, remind us that the treaty gave young America valuable time to grow, which she needed in order to strengthen herself for the greater challenges that lay ahead.

The problems in the Southwest, and particularly the question of free navigation on the Mississippi River, caused the young republic considerable anxiety. Western trappers and farmers were also alarmed by fees charged for deposit at the port of New Orleans and by Indian raids. Since peace and prosperity in the West were part and parcel of a united and expanding republic, the State Department approached Spain for a settlement. The latter, hoping that she might court the United States away from an alliance with England, gave in to every major American demand.[12]

TREATY OF SAN LORENZO

The Treaty of San Lorenzo was negotiated by Thomas Pinckney and was signed in 1795. It provided that the United States be given free navigation of the Mississippi River; the "right of deposit" (permission to transfer goods from river boats to ocean vessels free of charge) for a period of three years; and that the boundary between American and Spanish territory would be fixed at the 31st parallel, in accordance with the Treaty of Paris, 1783. The Spanish even agreed to quiet the Indians in the Southwest.

WASHINGTON BIDS FAREWELL

On September 17, 1796, Washington gave his farewell address. Written in simple terms, the message was directed to all the people, and warned them of political factions and their baneful effects. It also advised them to steer clear of Europe's quarrels, for American interests, he believed, could best be served by pursuing a policy of neutrality free of any permanent alliances.

ELECTION OF 1796

As the presidential election of 1796 approached it became increasingly clear that it would be a close race. The main issue was Jay's Treaty. John Adams and Thomas Pinckney were picked by the once powerful Federalists, while Thomas Jefferson and Aaron Burr were selected by the Republicans. After considerable infighting, Adams, despite Hamilton's efforts to derail him,[13] emerged from the electoral college with three more votes than Jefferson—71 to 68. Jefferson thus became the Vice-President.

Adams tried to practice the sage advice of his predecessor in the conduct of for-

---

[12] For a treatment of the belief that European distresses have made for most of America's successes in foreign affairs, see Thomas A. Bailey's *A Diplomatic History of the American People* (New York: Appleton-Century-Crofts, 1964).

[13] Hamilton was the intellectual leader of his party, but carried a lasting enmity for Adams whose tendencies toward a more popular form of government placed him on the fence between Federalism and Republicanism. This made Adams more popular with the people.

eign affairs, but war-torn Europe challenged his patience. The French Directory was convinced that the commercial provisions of the Jay Treaty violated the Franco-American agreement of 1778, and therefore accelerated their strategy of "seize and search" on the high seas. After several American vessels had been captured and impounded in French ports for carrying "contraband" to England, President Adams sent a three-man team of ministers to Paris to replace James Monroe, who had had considerable difficulty in trying to negotiate a treaty of commerce and friendship.

XYZ AFFAIR

When Elbridge Gerry, a Republican, and John Marshall and Charles C. Pinckney, both Federalists, arrived in Paris, they also got a cool reception. In fact, the Americans were practically ignored by Tallyrand, the French foreign minister, who appointed three agents, later to become known as X, Y, and Z,[14] to negotiate with the Americans on an informal, or preliminary, basis. Upon learning that the French not only desired a loan, but requested a "bribe" in the amount of $240,000 before the door to serious negotiations could be opened, Marshall and Pinckney left Paris. America as a whole was furious, and only the strong resolve of President Adams to avert war kept the "hawks" under control. By 1799, Napoleon had become First Consul, and the Americans were extended an apology and invited back. This time the long commercial "marriage" (treaties of 1778) between France and the United States was dissolved and the decision to respect the rights of neutrals on the high seas was established.

ALIEN AND SEDITION ACTS

The Federalists, meanwhile, had taken dead aim at the pro-French Republicans

by passing the Alien and Sedition Acts in 1798. Designed to restore life to the fading strength of the Federalists, the acts were directed at French agents operating in the United States, and at Republican propagandists who were somewhat uninhibited in their attacks on the Federalists. President Adams seldom, if ever, used the Alien Act, but ten Republican editors and printers were convicted and imprisoned under the Sedition Act. These cases accordingly provoked leading Republicans to denounce the acts as a violation of the Constitution, and the first article of the Bill of Rights in particular. Using the "compact theory," namely, that the union was made up of equal and sovereign states that had a right to determine when and where the central government had overstepped its limits of power, the legislatures of Kentucky and Virginia, under the direction of Jefferson and Madison, respectively, drew up resolutions calling for complete nullification of the acts. The Alien and Sedition Acts were not voided, but the fight provided the Republicans with a platform for the approaching election.

Select Bibliography

Baldwin, Leland D. *Whisky Rebels: The Story of a Frontier Uprising.* Pittsburgh, Pa.: University of Pittsburgh Press, 1939.

Beard, Charles A. *Economic Origins of Jeffersonian Democracy.* New York: Crowell Collier and Macmillan, Inc., 1935.

Bemis, Samuel F. *Jay's Treaty.* New Haven, Conn.: Yale University Press, 1962.

Bowers, Claude G. *Jefferson and Hamilton.* Boston: Houghton Mifflin Company, 1925.

Caldwell, Lynton K. *The Administrative Theories of Hamilton and Jefferson.* New York: Russell & Russell, Publishers, 1944.

[14] The French agents were given these designations by the American ministers in their reports.

Chambers, William N., and Walter D. Burnham, eds. *American Party Systems: Stages of Political Development.* New York: Oxford University Press, 1967.

Charles, Joseph. *The Origins of the American Party System.* New York: Harper & Row, Publishers, 1956.

Cunningham, Jr., Noble E., ed. *The Making of the American Party System, 1789 to 1809.* Englewood Cliffs, N.J.: Prentice-Hall, Inc., 1965.

DeConde, Alexander. *Entangling Alliance: Politics and Diplomacy Under George Washington.* Durham, N.C.: Duke University Press, 1958.

Ernst, Robert, *Rufus King: American Federalist.* Chapel Hill, N.C.: University of North Carolina Press, 1968.

Fitzpatrick, John C., ed. *The Writings of George Washington from the Original Manuscript Source, 1745–1799.* New York: Reprint House International, 1940.

Gilbert, Felix. *To the Farewell Address, Ideas of Early American Foreign Policy.* Princeton, N.J.: Princeton University Press, 1961.

Goodman, Paul, *The Federalists vs. the Jeffersonian Republicans.* New York: Holt, Rinehart and Winston, Inc., 1967.

Hammond, Bray. *Banks and Politics in America, from the Revolution to the Civil War.* Princeton, N.J.: Princeton University Press, 1957.

Hyneman, Charles S., ed. *A Second Federalist: Congress Creates a Government.* New York: Appleton-Century-Crofts, 1967.

Koch, Adrienne. *The Philosophy of Thomas Jefferson.* Gloucester, Mass.: Peter Smith, 1943.

Kurtz, Stephen G. *The Presidency of John Adams: The Collapse of Federalism, 1795–1800.* Philadelphia: University of Pennsylvania Press, 1958.

Levy, Leonard W. *Legacy of Suppression: Freedom of Speech and Press in Early American History.* Cambridge, Mass.: Belknap Press of Harvard University Press, 1960.

Link, Eugene P. *Democratic-Republicans Societies, 1790–1800.* New York: Octagon Books, Inc., 1965.

Mayo, Bernard. *Myths and Men: Patrick Henry, George Washington, Thomas Jefferson.* Athens, Ga.: University of Georgia Press, 1959.

Miller, John C. *Alexander Hamilton: Portrait in Paradox.* New York: Harper & Row, Publishers, 1959.

————. *Crises in Freedom: The Alien and Sedition Acts.* Boston: Little, Brown and Company, 1951.

————. *The Federalist Era, 1789–1801.* New York: Harper & Row, Publishers, 1960.

Morris, Richard B., ed. *Basic Ideas of Alexander Hamilton.* New York: Washington Square Press, 1957.

Philbrick, Francis S. *The Rise of the West, 1754–1830.* New York: Harper & Row, Publishers, 1965.

Prucha, Francis P. *American Indian Policy in the Formative Years: The Indian Trade and Intercourse Acts, 1780–1834.* Cambridge, Mass.: Harvard University Press, 1962.

Rossiter, Clinton. *Alexander Hamilton and the Constitution.* New York: Harcourt Brace Jovanovich, Inc., 1964.

Sears, Louis M. *George Washington and the French Revolution.* Detroit, Mich.: Wayne State University Press, 1960.

Taylor, George R., ed. *Hamilton and the National Debt.* Boston: D. C. Heath & Company, 1950.

White, Leonard D. *The Federalists: A Study in Administrative History.* New York: Crowell Collier and Macmillan, Inc., 1948.

chapter 9

Social, Cultural, and Economic Trends

Society in Transition

There was no great upheaval or radical change in American society (as in France) after the Revolution; but social change, long evident in practically all states, was accentuated and accelerated by the revolutionary experience. Change touched the relations of social classes to each other, the system of landholding, the institution of slavery, business practices, forms of education, and the direction of religion. All such reforms, experienced by the people, acted as agents in leveling democracy.

SUFFRAGE

Although suffrage was commonplace during the colonial period, it was noticeably broadened by the Revolution. For example, in keeping with the past experience of rewarding property owners, four new state constitutions expanded the privileges of voting, while two other states extended the ballot to *personal* property holders. Two states granted suffrage to *all* taxpayers.

SLAVERY

The institution of slavery did not go unnoticed during the period of the Revolution. Antislavery societies began to take shape in 1775 and by 1790 sixteen were in existence in predominantly slave states. The determined voice of these groups helped to keep alive the obvious inconsistency between the ideals of the Revolution and reality, and to raise strong objection to the importation of slaves. A nonimportation agreement had been initiated by the First Continental Congress in 1774, and by 1786 five states had arrived at similar agreements; most slave states, however, refused to act on the question. North Carolina apologetically raised the duty on imported Negro slaves.

The next obvious step was the complete abolition of slavery. Pennsylvania provided guidance in this area in 1780 when she passed laws that called for gradual abolition. Massachusetts followed suit in the same year, and Connecticut and Rhode Island took similar action in 1784. Of particular significance was an act passed by Virginia, the oldest slave state, which provided that an owner might free all his slaves if he followed legal procedures and assured them of a means of support.

Liberating the community and the individual both helped to make for a natural leveling of the classes through the extension of previously forbidden privileges. For instance, vast properties of the crown and Tory estates fell to the states and ultimately to the people (although slow and indirect, in some cases) since land speculators moved in with ready cash. A new American aristocracy may have emerged in some states to take the place of the old (Tory), but it was, in most cases, a genteel upper class. Meanwhile,

129

the Proclamation of 1763 and the Quebec Act of 1774 proved to be other social levelers by removing the barriers to the rich western lands. Quitrents, a form of feudal land fee paid by the colonists to the crown or to a landlord, were also forbidden in the new state constitutions, along with the ancient European laws of entail and primogeniture.[1]

In order to insulate the new "democratic society" from other past evils, the remaining vestiges of feudalism such as titles of nobility and hereditary royal privilege were explicitly forbidden in the republic. Thus, the new order liberated itself, in part, from the past and turned to the European Enlightenment with its promise of the progress of man through reason. Armed with this new rationale, man was now in charge of his own destiny —free to reshape the institutions to satisfy his own needs. One of the serious impediments to the growth of this philosophy in America, however, was its concomitant belief that only the elite, or select few, were capable of being "enlightened."

Culture during the Revolutionary Period

ROMANTICISM

Literary styles and models during this period continued to be fashioned after those of Europe. Movements, such as eighteenth-century Romanticism, found their way to America during the decades following the Revolution. Opposed to all rules and accepted authority, the Romantics rejected the self-discipline, self-restraint, and conformity of the Rationalists and their Enlightenment. They had witnessed and become disillusioned with the supposed rationality of man and his society governed within lawful neatly defined rules of conduct. The Romantics looked instead to the efficacy of individual judgment and diversity in opinion and cul-

ture. They sought the lessons of nature, instinct, and emotion, the blessings of the simple and the ordinary. Thus freed from the belief that one must become rational in order to be an effective citizen, the American style of Romanticism announced that the ordinary man could attain perfection through instinct and through the natural processes of involvement. This new creed on the essence of human quality helped to level the classes of society, and produced, among other things, folk heroes, mountain men, eccentrics, and rebels.

LITERATURE

Early Romantics of letters found their greatest solace in the writings of William Hill Brown and Charles Brockden Brown who demonstrated that Americans could write, despite the prevailing belief in England that America was void of culture. William Brown produced what has been called America's first novel when he penned *The Power of Sympathy* in 1789.

The poets of the period were duly impressed by the works of a young Negro girl. Phyllis Wheatley rose above slavery and helped to dispel the belief that intelligence was determined by the color of the skin when she published a book of poetry in 1773 entitled *Poems on Various Subjects, Religious and Moral.* Her work was held in high esteem in both Europe and America. Benjamin Banneker was another Afro-American of particular literary significance. A mathematician and astronomer, Banneker published an almanac during the 1790s that was widely read in the states of Pennsylvania, Delaware, Maryland, and Virginia. He also served on the President's Commission, which drew up the plans for the national capital.

Noteworthy among other American writers were the "Hartford Wits."[2] This

---

[1] A practice designed to keep large estates intact by awarding all, or most, of the land to the eldest son.

[2] The "wits" claimed such names as Joel Barlow, Timothy Dwight, and John Trumbull, but Barlow later deserted their company and went over to the Republicans.

unique group combined eighteenth-century federalism and Yankee humor in compiling epic poems and essays that were designed to defend their philosophy. Their best known counterpart among the Republican writers was Philip Freneau, considered by many to be America's first poet. Freneau was later joined by Francis Hopkinson in writing biting satires on the Federalists.

In the field of political theory, Thomas Jefferson, John Adams, and Thomas Paine had no equals in America. Borrowing the applicable theories of Locke and Rousseau, they reinterpreted the Enlightenment for America; and, in the process, provided a rationale for the Revolution and a formula for responsible government.

The first American play was Thomas Godfrey's "The Prince of Parthia," which was produced in 1767. Two other playwrights bear mentioning, Royal Tyler and William Dunlap, but English companies performing Shakespearean plays continued to dominate the American theater.

ARCHITECTURE

Three men who made significant contributions to the architecture of the period were Charles Bulfinch, Thomas Jefferson, and Benjamin Henry Latrobe. The first is best remembered for his work in modified Georgian style (American Federal); the second, for his revival of classic Roman lines; and the third, for classic Greek orders. In addition to working on the capitol at Washington, Bulfinch designed the capitols in Boston and Augusta, Maine. Jefferson, on the other hand, drew up the plans for the state capitol in Richmond, the University of Virginia, and his classic home at Monticello, while Latrobe applied the Greek influence to the Capitol building at Washington. Actually, William Thornton, working under Major Pierre Charles L'Enfant, the designer of the city of Washington, drafted the first plans for the Capitol

building in 1793, but these plans were later modified by Latrobe, whose own work on the structure was interrupted when the British burned the building during the War of 1812. It was finally completed by Bulfinch.

ART AND MUSIC

Portrait painting continued to be the most popular form of art, but its quality suffered from a lack of talent in the new nation. Notable among those who rose above mediocrity were Charles Willson Peale and Gilbert Charles Stuart, both remembered for their portraits of Washington, and John Trumbull, who turned to themes of the Revolution.

American contributions to music were also dwarfed by the availability of European talent and by the time-consuming work of building a nation. Francis Hopkinson was a jack-of-all-trades type who wrote music and poems, painted, and even designed an American flag, but his talents were but a ripple on the vast sea of cultureless America.

EDUCATION

Despite the numerous declarations of liberty and equality during the post-Revolutionary period, education continued to be "select for the select few." Girls were still forbidden to even think about an education, and boys continued to be narrowly trained in the three R's. The concept of free public education was still confined to Massachusetts and Connecticut, and it would require several decades for the movement to break through the conservative barricades of other states.

The most distinguished innovator in education was the Connecticut lexicographer Noah Webster. Imbued with nationalism and believing in the uniqueness of the American language, Webster broke with British standards and forms and produced the *Elementary Spelling Book* and a dictionary that captured the imagination of America.

The growth of new colleges experienced a boom after the Revolution. In fact, the nine schools of the colonial period had multiplied to twenty-four by 1800. Most, however, were of the small liberal arts type that rested on shaky financial foundations and concomitant low standards. Their curriculum continued to be dominated by the classics. The long overdue state-supported college made its debut in 1795, when the University of North Carolina opened its doors, and soon thereafter, Thomas Jefferson designed a similar institution for Virginia.

LEGAL AND MEDICAL PROFESSIONS

The reputations of the legal and medical professions continued to suffer in post-Revolutionary America. Lawyers were all too frequently linked to questionable land deals, while physicians continued to be equated with "horse doctors" whose chief talents were limited to bleeding the patient and offering an all-purpose pill. Despite the appearance of medical schools in Philadelphia[3] in 1765 and in New York, in 1767, doctors continued to perpetuate their mediocrity by pursuing the medieval guild practice of training the apprentice in the shop of the "master." The training of lawyers followed a similar type of tradition.

NEWSPAPERS

Newspapers began to appear in greater number during this period, and, it has been reported, reached a figure exceeding 350 by 1800. As many as thirty of these were dailies. Perhaps the best known were the propaganda sheets of the *New York Evening Post,* founded by Hamilton, and *The National Gazette* at Philadelphia, edited by Freneau for Jefferson. Dominated by stale news items, the typical newspapers were often dull, but they continued to be in great demand among the news-starved citizens. Magazines were not unknown, but the few that appeared devoted much of their space to the learned sciences and fine arts and thereby limited their appeal.

Technology

FACTORY SYSTEM

The first impulses of the European Industrial Revolution were felt in America before the time of the American Revolution, but the young republic remained outside the mainstream of that economic transformation until she raised her tariffs during the second decade of the nineteenth century. Nevertheless, the first trappings of the factory system were transported to America from England during the three decades following the break with Great Britain, and the passage of a Patent Act in 1790 gave an impetus to experimentation and invention. These two events sent the infant nation on the road to economic independence. Manufacturing in the Middle Colonies began to move from the home to the factory as early as 1782, when Oliver Evans of Philadelphia invented a sophisticated mechanized flour mill. The textile manufacturers rejoiced when, in 1790, Samuel Slater, a mechanic, constructed a spinning machine (the Arkwright water frame) at Pawtucket, Rhode Island. So significant was this feat to the factory system that Slater has been called the "father of American manufacturers." Three years later Eli Whitney revolutionized the cotton industry by inventing the cotton gin and a system of interchangeable parts. In the same year John and Arthur Schofield built the first American factory for the manufacture of woolens. The first power loom made its appearance in 1812 through the efforts of Francis Cabot Lowell, while the Boston Manufacturing Company prepared for the opening of a factory with

---

[3] Philadelphia had also built the first hospital in America in 1752.

power-driven machinery and concomitant mass production, all under one roof.

The states of the northeast seaboard had all of the essential ingredients for the early growth of industry. Commerce enabled the merchants to accumulate profits and to establish banks so necessary for industrial development. In addition, the heavy concentration of people in the area provided a ready market for factory wares, while the new canals and turnpikes not only brought in natural resources from the west but carried manufactured goods to the frontier.

TRANSPORTATION

Robert Fulton, meanwhile, had caused a furor in the world of transportation by inventing a steam-powered engine that pushed a boat up the Hudson River in 1807. By 1830, more than 200 steamboats were moving up and down America's major rivers, linking the west to the east.

The development of two turnpikes during the post-Revolutionary period are of particular significance—the Pennsylvania, completed in 1794, and the Cumberland, opened in 1818. Covered with a hard surface, the Pennsylvania accelerated the flow of goods between Philadelphia and Lancaster, Pennsylvania, while the Cumberland (first National Road) linked Cumberland, Maryland, with Wheeling, Virginia.

From these early growing pains of the republic emerged a stronger commitment to nationalism and a firmer foundation, both social and economic, for an expanding country. Americanism had come of age and many citizens believed that Thomas Jefferson was the greatest embodiment of that spirit.

Select Bibliography

Bond, Jr., Beverly W. *The Civilization of the Old Northwest: A Study of Political, Social and Economic Development, 1788–1812*. New York: Reprint House International, 1934.

Brawley, Benjamin. *Negro Builders and Heroes*. Chapel Hill, N.C.: University of North Carolina Press, 1937.

Butts, Robert F. *The American Tradition in Religion and Education*. Boston: Beacon Press, 1950.

Channing, Edward. *History of the United States*. 6 vols. New York: Crowell Collier and Macmillan, Inc., 1905–1925.

Clark, Victor S. *History of Manufacturers in the United States*. 3 vols. Gloucester, Mass: Peter Smith, 1916–1928.

Cunliffe, Marcus. *The Nation Takes Shape: 1789–1837*. Chicago: University of Chicago Press, 1959.

Dexter, Franklin B., ed. *The Literary Diary of Ezra Stiles*. 3 vols. New York: Garrett Press, Inc., 1969.

Dorfman, Joseph. *The Economic Mind in American Civilization*. 5 vols. New York: Augustus M. Kelley, Publishers, 1946–1959.

Flexner, James T. *That Wilder Image: The Paintings of America's Native School from Thomas Cole to Winslow Homer*. Boston: Little, Brown and Company, 1962.

Green, Constance M. *Eli Whitney and the Birth of American Technology*. Boston: Little, Brown and Company, 1956.

Greene, E. B. *The Revolutionary Generation, 1763–1790*. New York: Crowell Collier and Macmillan, Inc., 1943.

Hulbert, Archer B. *Paths of Inland Commerce: A Chronicle of Trail, Road, and Waterway*. New York: United States Publishers Association, Inc., 1920.

Jordan, Winthrop D. *White over Black: American Attitudes toward the Negro, 1550–1812*. Chapel Hill, N.C.: University of North Carolina Press, 1968.

Kirkland, Edward C. *A History of American Economic Life.* New York: Appleton-Century-Crofts, 1969.

Koch, Gustav A. *Republican Religions: The American Revolution and the Cult of Reasons.* Gloucester, Mass.: Peter Smith, 1964.

Krout, John A., and Dixon R. Fox. *Completion of Independence.* New York: Crowell Collier and Macmillan, Inc., 1944.

Litwack, Leon F. *North of Slavery: The Negro in the Free States, 1790–1800.* Chicago: University of Chicago Press, 1961.

McMaster, John B. *The Acquisition of Political, Social and Industrial Rights of Man in America.* New York: Frederick Ungar Publishing Co., Inc., 1903.

Mirsky, Jeannette, and Nevins, Allan. *The World of Eli Whitney.* New York: Crowell Collier and Macmillan, Inc., 1962.

Moses, Montrose J., and John M. Brown, eds. *American Theatre as Seen by Its Critics, 1752–1934.* New York: Cooper Square Publishers, Inc., 1934.

Nettels, Curtis P. *The Emergence of a National Economy, 1775–1815.* New York: Harper & Row, Publishers, 1969.

Nye, Russel B. *The Cultural Life of the New Nation.* New York: Harper & Row, Publishers, 1960.

Olmstead, Clifton E. *Religion in America: Past and Present.* Englewood Cliffs, N.J.: Prentice-Hall, Inc., 1961.

Philbrick, Francis S. *The Rise of the West, 1754–1830.* New York: Harper & Row, Publishers, 1965.

Shoemaker, Ervin C. *Noah Webster.* New York: AMS Press, Inc., 1936.

Shryock, Richard H. *Medicine and Society in America: 1660–1860.* Ithaca, N.Y.: Cornell University Press, 1962.

Smallwood, William M. *Natural History and the American Mind.* New York: AMS Press, Inc., 1941.

Ware, Caroline F. *The Early New England Cotton Manufacture.* New York: Johnson Reprint Corporation, 1931.

Warfel, Harry. *Noah Webster: Schoolmaster to America.* New York: Octagon Books, Inc., 1967.

Williamson, Chilton. *American Suffrage from Property to Democracy, 1760–1860.* Princeton, N.J.: Princeton University Press, 1960.

chapter 10

Jeffersonian Democracy

The Election of 1800

As the presidential election of 1800 approached, the Republicans selected Jefferson and Aaron Burr to carry their banner, while the Federalists turned to Adams and Charles C. Pinckney. The main issues were the Alien and Sedition Acts, the earlier threat of war with France, and the bothersome impressment of American seamen by the British.

Unfortunately for the Federalists, their party split over foreign policy. Incensed over the pacifist nature of Adams, Hamilton openly attacked the President and thus inadvertently helped the cause of the Republicans. The final tabulation of the electoral votes, however, showed Jefferson and Burr tied with 73 ballots each, while Adams and Pinckney pulled 65 and 64, respectively. Under such conditions, with the would-be President and Vice-President tied for the top spot, the Constitution provided that the election be sent to the House of Representatives —in this case, a Federalist-dominated House[1]—where the two leading candidates would vie for the office. After considerable infighting, Hamilton, distrusting Burr, supported what he considered the lesser of the two evils.

Jefferson was sworn in on March 4, 1801, and delivered the new capital's[2] first inaugural. He called his Republican victory the second American revolution, but there was little, if anything, in his inaugural address that smacked of radical departure from the past. In fact, he tried to unite both parties behind broad idealistic goals by reminding the followers of both major factions that they were all "brethren of the same principle." The new President called for a government of limited powers, but for the preservation of the general government, less spending on the national level, respect for the rights of state governments, and safeguards for the democratic process in resolving problems. Jefferson also asked for a strong militia, the advancement of agriculture and commerce, and, finally, the reaffirmation of all civil liberties. In foreign affairs, the policies of Washington and Adams were to be continued, namely, trade ties but with no entangling alliances. Thus, he wished to make America sensitive to the principles of "simplicity, frugality, and reason."

Jefferson's cabinet included some of the best-trained minds available for public office. The position of Secretary of State went to his old comrade and fellow Virginian James Madison, while Swiss-born Albert Gallatin, whose financial genius

---

[1] The Twelfth Amendment, ratified in 1804, provided for a separate electoral vote for President and Vice-President in order to avoid another tie.

[2] The new capital at Washington was completed during the summer of 1800. Congress assumed control of the District of Columbia in February 1801.

135

rivaled that of Hamilton, became his Secretary of the Treasury. For candidates for the offices of Secretary of War, Attorney General, and Postmaster, Jefferson looked to the New England states, where his appeal was strengthened by the appointment of Henry Dearborn (Massachusetts), Levi Lincoln (Massachusetts), and Gideon Granger (Connecticut), respectively.

Internal Affairs

REPEAL OF THE NATURALIZATION AND JUDICIARY ACTS

Of the many problems facing the new administration, none appeared to be more pressing than the Naturalization Act (the Alien and Sedition Acts expired in 1801), which required a fourteen-year waiting period for citizenship, and the Judiciary Act of 1801,[3] which permitted the outgoing President to appoint several "midnight judges" in order to ensure Federalist control of the judicial branch of the government. Moved to action by these abuses, Jefferson restored the five-year waiting period to the Naturalization Act, and restored the Supreme Court to six members by repealing the Judiciary Act.

The Republicans tended to view the Supreme Court hostility as another example of centralism and abuse of judicial power, and with the repeal of the Judiciary Act attempted to oust many last-minute appointees from their offices. Dismayed by these proceedings, William Marbury, the newly appointed justice of the peace in the District of Columbia, appealed to the Supreme Court for original jurisdiction under a provision of the Judiciary Act of 1789 and asked the Court for a *writ of mandamus* that would direct Secretary of State James Madison to deliver his commission. In the famous case

of *Marbury* v. *Madison,* Chief Justice Marshall, a late appointee himself, ruled that the Supreme Court could not issue the writ since Section 13 of the Judiciary Act of 1789, which authorized such an instrument, was in conflict with Article III of the Constitution, which limits the Court's original jurisdiction to two specified situations that did not cover Marbury's predicament. The Court felt it had to prefer the Constitution to the statute. Thus, for the first time the Court overturned an act initiated and passed by Congress. Marshall not only won the respect of the Republicans, but set a precedent of official judicial review that the Supreme Court has long since exercised over the various acts passed by Congress. In addition, the decision helped to elevate the Court above politics.

In 1804 the Republican-dominated Senate was able to impeach a federal district judge in New Hampshire for "high crimes and misdemeanors."[4] Encouraged by this success, the Senate started impeachment proceedings against the politically biased Justice Samuel Chase of the Supreme Court.[5] The prosecution, however, could produce no more than unethical practices against Chase and the case was dismissed. After this abortive attempt, Jefferson and other Republicans had to be content with the conventional process of replacing justices; moreover, they had to recognize that the Supreme Court was growing more independent.

LAND ACT OF 1800

The Land Act of 1800 boosted the population in the West toward the 1 million mark. By reducing the minimum acreage of public land available for purchase from 640 to 320, and by offering a four-year payment plan, many settlers were

---

[3] The Judiciary Act of 1804 reduced the Supreme Court to five justices and created sixteen circuit judgeships.

[4] Actually, the judge, John Pickering, was reported to have been an alcoholic and emotionally unbalanced.

[5] Judge Chase had led the prosecution against several Republican editors during the administration of Adams.

enticed to "sign up." So great was the migration into the Northwest that Ohio qualified for statehood in 1803.

LAND ACT OF 1804

Despite these signs of prosperity and general well-being, all was not well with the farmer. The new land act required a down payment of 25 percent, which many found difficult to save or borrow, and foreclosures were commonplace among those who managed somehow to buy. Another concurrent evil, land speculators, used their wealth advantage to buy up large tracts of choice land. Disturbed by these inequities, Congress passed another land act in 1804 that reduced the minimum purchase to 160 acres, and lowered the price per acre to $1.64. With the passage of these landmark land acts, the plight of the westerner was eased somewhat. At last he had a President in the White House with whom he could identify.

YAZOO LAND COMPANIES

Jefferson's image suffered in 1802 when he gave the Yazoo land companies, which were organized by a group of speculators, tentative approval to use federal funds to settle claims arising from the ceding of western lands to the federal government.[6] Sensing a possible violation of the state sovereignty clause of the Kentucky Resolutions of 1798, John Randolph and other "Quids"[7] successfully blocked the proposal for several years.

BURR INTRIGUES

Jefferson was also plagued by Vice-President Aaron Burr. Burr, it has been suggested, had become disgruntled with his political fortunes, and in 1804 contrived

to make deals with unethical elements of the party out of power.[8] Hamilton finally exposed the plot but lost his life in a duel with the enraged Burr on July 11, 1804, in New Jersey. Hamilton's death was no doubt the greatest single blow to the hopes of the Federalists.

His political career ended, Burr next turned to intrigues with foreign governments and took as an accomplice General James Wilkinson, the American field commander in the Mississippi Valley. In 1806 Burr was prepared to put his plans into action. Some reports have said that he planned to set up an empire that would serve as a buffer state between Louisiana and Mexico, while others have suggested that he offered to split the western half of the United States from the east coast. Whatever his real plans, they must have been contrary to those of Wilkinson, for the latter soon deserted his comrade and reported the affair to Jefferson. Burr was caught in 1807 and tried in the court of Chief Justice Marshall for plotting treason, but was acquitted because of lack of evidence. In order to escape further prosecution, he fled to England.

Foreign Affairs

TRIPOLITAN WAR

During Jefferson's first term as President, the Barbary pirates[9] continued to extract tribute from Mediterranean commerce. In fact, the Pasha of Tripoli declared war on the United States in 1801 in an effort to further enrich his treasury. Breaking with the pacifist tradition handed down by Washington and Adams, Jefferson responded by dispatching four naval squadrons to the Mediterranean Sea. A block-

---

[6] By making questionable deals with certain Georgia legislators, the speculators had obtained a large land grant from the state of Georgia.

[7] Extreme states' righters who opposed Jefferson's Federalist tendencies.

[8] Political rebels in Massachusetts and Connecticut proposed to Burr that a Northern Confederacy be formed out of New England states, along with Burr's home state of New York.

[9] Raiders from the North African states of Algiers, Morocco, Tripoli, and Tunis.

ade of Tripoli soon brought the Pasha to terms, but other corsairs in the area continued to collect American tribute for another decade.

LOUISIANA PURCHASE

The purchase of Louisiana rivals the acquisition of Alaska as America's best *legitimate* land bargain. If calculated on a cost-per-acre basis, the former averages out to slightly less than three cents per acre, while the latter cost about two cents per acre. It has been called Jefferson's greatest achievement as President. The outright purchase of Louisiana at that unbelievably low price was probably not among Jefferson's wildest dreams when he sent James Monroe to assist Robert Livingston, the United States minister to France, in the purchase of the port of New Orleans for about $2 million.[10] Two days before Monroe arrived, however, Tallyrand, the French minister, broke the surprising news that Napoleon was prepared to sell the whole of the Louisiana Territory. The latter was no doubt prompted in his decision by the fall of the French Caribbean colony of Santo Domingo to Pierre Dominique, Toussaint L'Ouverture, and other revolutionaries in 1802, his own need for capital to carry out his grand designs, and his desperate desire to postpone an Anglo-American alliance. Livingston and Monroe accordingly negotiated a price of $15 million for 828,-000 square miles with vaguely defined borders on the west. This purchase was another of those instances where Europe's distress was America's gain.

The Louisiana transaction put Jefferson in something of a quandary in trying to find constitutional authority for the act. Borrowing a page from the old Federalist book, the President justified the purchase under a loose construction of the Constitution; whereupon the Federalists, anticipating a loss in congressional power through the addition of new western states, also did an about-face and argued for strict interpretation of the Constitution. They viewed the territory as a worthless desert and the purchase as unconstitutional.

LEWIS AND CLARK

It has been observed that Jefferson had designs on the resources of the Louisiana Territory long before it was purchased. In fact, fourteen months before the final transfer papers were signed, he had initiated plans for an expedition to map and catalog the flora and fauna in the vast territory. Accordingly, in the spring of 1804, Meriwether Lewis (Jefferson's private secretary) and William Clark assembled a party of forty-three men and set out up the Missouri River toward the Rockies. Assisted by Sacajawea,[11] a talented Shoshoni Indian woman, and her French husband, Charbonneau, who had purchased and married her, the expedition finally reached the mouth of the Columbia River in November 1805. The following year they returned to St. Louis, where their glowing reports of mountains teeming with beaver, of friendly Indians, and of an all-water route up the Missouri, caused traders and trappers to converge on St. Louis in the winter of 1806–1807, in order to start west as soon as spring freed the ice-bound rivers.

ZEBULON PIKE

In 1805, the same year that the Lewis and Clark party was descending the westward slopes of the Rockies, Lieutenant Zebulon Pike was dispatched up the Mississippi River to seek its source; and in 1806 he

---

[10] Louisiana had just been transferred from Spain to France by the Treaty of San Ildefonso (1800), and the United States, wary of Napoleon's designs on America, wanted to secure the strategic port of New Orleans.

[11] Sacajawea's "vast" knowledge of the various Indian languages and geography of the Northwest has been questioned in recent years by students of the subject.

navigated the Arkansas River to its head-waters in the Rockies. It was during this second expedition that he discovered the Colorado peak named in his honor. Further exploration south of the Colorado was discouraged when the Spanish escorted Pike out of New Mexico.

STEPHEN H. LONG

In 1820 Major Stephen H. Long, an explorer and cartographer, led an expedition into the same general area that Pike had covered. His journey would be of little historical significance if he had not mislabeled the great plains the "Great American Desert" on his maps. Discouraged by this great "desert," the American government and settlers looked instead to the far west for land. Thus for almost a generation the false impressions of one man set up a psychological barrier that kept others from discovering his mistake.

American Neutrality Tested

As Jefferson's administration entered its second term with a landslide victory in electoral votes, 162 to 14, it became increasingly clear that the war in Europe would challenge America's policy of neutrality. After Napoleon took charge of the continent with a smashing victory at the battle of Austerlitz in 1805, the British turned to the weapon that seemed most effective—blockade. Napoleon retaliated with the Berlin Decree, which prohibited neutral ships from trading with England. The British retaliated with the Orders in Council, which required all foreign ships bound for French ports to stop first at British inspection ports.

BROKEN VERSUS
CONTINUOUS VOYAGE

To these restraints on American commerce the British added one more when they further discouraged American ships from taking part in the trade between the French West Indies and France. In 1800, the British had permitted this trade if the goods from the West Indies were first landed at a port in the United States. American skippers, however, soon took advantage of this policy by merely calling at an American port without bothering to unload their cargoes. The United States government in turn repaid these skippers from the American duties levied on goods that had been imported from the French islands and were then sent on their way to France. The Americans had thereby transformed the broken voyage into a continuous voyage. In 1805, the British tried to stop this practice by ruling, in the case of the *Essex,* that French West Indian cargoes could not be sent to France by way of an American port unless the owner of the commodities could show that he originally intended to send them to the United States rather than to France. Since this was often a most difficult thing to prove, the British were in a position to close the door to still another profitable source of American trade.

The daring Yankee merchants were prepared to run the double risk for European trade, but they were not prepared to cope with British warships that were waiting just off the American coast. In addition to searching for contraband, they also combed the ship for escaped British sailors[12] and mistakes in identity were inevitably made.

LEOPARD AND CHESAPEAKE

A war-provoking crisis arose in the summer of 1807, when the British frigate *Leopard* hailed the American warship *Chesapeake* off the Virginia coast and demanded permission to board and search. When the *Chesapeake* refused, the *Leopard* fired three broadsides, kill-

---

[12] During this period in history, many British sailors deserted to the American navy for higher pay. The practice of "search and seize" in recovering such deserters was centuries old.

ing three and wounding eighteen. The British then boarded the *Chesapeake* and seized four sailors charged with desertion. Incensed by this "outrageous act," many Americans called for war. Only Jefferson's resolve to explore every avenue of peace, and the fact that Congress was not in session, kept the guns quiet. The British apologized and removed their ships from American waters, but refused to abandon the search and seize practices. Both sides were guilty of misconduct—the Americans in encouraging desertions, the British in ignoring legal certificates of citizenship.

EMBARGO ACT

In order to appease the "war hawks" in Congress, assert American rights as neutrals, and stimulate industry, Jefferson chose what he considered to be the nobler alternative to war—"peaceful coercion," better known as the Embargo Act of 1807.[13] By its provisions no American ships were to enter foreign ports and no goods were to be shipped to Europe on foreign ships. This economic boycott, however, proved ineffective. If our commerce was valuable to England and France, it was just as valuable in profits to New England merchants. Complaining that western Republicans were out to ruin Federalist shippers, New Englanders passed resolutions condemning the embargo and looked for ways to evade its provisions. The latter they soon discovered in illicit trade through Canada and Florida.

FORCE ACT

In the winter of 1808–1809, an economic depression gripped the country, and when farm prices dipped to record lows, even staunch Republicans began to ques-

tion the wisdom of the boycott. Meanwhile, during the interregnum, Congress passed the Force Act of January 1809, which permitted officials to seize, without warrant, any goods destined for foreign ports. On March 1, 1809, President Jefferson, tired and disappointed, signed the act that repealed the embargo.[14]

Concluding Remarks

Jefferson's administration has been remembered as one of the most precedent-setting in history. He was the first to read an inaugural address at the new capital, and the first to break with the "royal protocol" practiced by the Federalists. Instead of addressing Congress, he chose to send the message to avoid the monarchial image. This example was followed by Presidents for over a century. Jefferson not only founded a political party that transcended class or section, but, unlike his predecessors, he dared to intervene in the selection of his successor, a practice that is commonplace today. Fearing dictatorship, he was also the first to speak out against more than two terms for the President, but, perhaps his most noble precedent, it has been written, was to set America on the path that leads to human liberty and the dignity of the common man.

Select Bibliography

Abernethy, Thomas P. *The Burr Conspiracy.* New York: Oxford University Press, 1954.

Adams, Henry. *John Randolph.* Gloucester, Mass.: Peter Smith, 1882.

Allen, Gardner, W. *Our Navy and the Barbary Corsairs.* Hamden, Conn.: Shoe String Press, Inc., 1965.

---

[13] A Nonintercourse Act had been passed in 1806, which provided that certain British goods could not be imported after November of that year.

[14] Some economic historians have argued rather persuasively that the embargo was a sound move and would have brought the English to terms if given more time.

Bakeless, John. *Lewis and Clark: Partners in Discovery.* New York: William Morrow & Co., Inc., 1947.

Billington, Ray Allen. *Westward Expansion: A History of the American Frontier.* New York: Crowell Collier and Macmillan, Inc., 1967.

Bowers, Claude G. *Jefferson in Power.* Boston: Houghton Mifflin Company, 1936.

Brant, Irving. *James Madison.* 6 vols. Indianapolis, Ind.: The Bobbs-Merrill Co., Inc., 1961.

Channing, Edward. *The Jeffersonian System.* New York: Harper & Row, Publishers, 1968.

Chinard, Gilbert. *Thomas Jefferson, The Apostle of Americanism,* 2d ed. Ann Arbor, Mich.: University of Michigan Press, 1960.

Cunningham, Jr., Noble E. *The Jeffersonian Republicans in Power: Party Operations, 1801–1809.* Chapel Hill, N.C.: University of North Carolina Press, 1967.

De Voto, Bernard, ed. *The Journals of Lewis and Clark.* Boston: Houghton Mifflin Company, 1953.

Dillon, Richard. *Meriwether Lewis.* New York: G. P. Putnam's Sons, 1968.

Fischer, David H. *The Revolution of American Conservatism: The Federalist Party in the Era of Jeffersonian Democracy.* New York: Harper & Row, Publishers, 1965.

Goetzmann, William H. *When the Eagle Screamed: The Romantic Horizon in American Diplomacy, 1800–1860.* New York: John Wiley & Sons, Inc., 1966.

Haines, Charles G. *The Role of the Supreme Court in American Government and Politics, 1789–1835.* New York: Russell & Russell, Publishers, 1960.

Hollon, William E. *The Lost Pathfinder: Zebulon Montgomery Pike.* Norman, Okla.: University of Oklahoma Press, 1969.

Horsman, Reginald. *Expansion of American Indian Policy, 1783–1812.* East Lansing, Mich.: Michigan State University Press, 1967.

Irwin, Ray W. *The Diplomatic Relations of the United States and the Barbary Powers, 1776–1816.* New York: Russell & Russell, Publishers, 1969.

Jacobs, James R., and Glen Tucker. *War of 1812: A Compact History.* New York: Hawthorn Books, Inc., 1969.

Kirk, Russell. *Randolph of Roanoke: A Study in Conservative Thought.* Chicago: University of Chicago Press, 1951.

Koch, Adrienne. *Jefferson and Madison: The Great Collaboration.* New York: Oxford University Press, 1964.

Levy, Leonard W. *Jefferson and Civil Liberties: The Darker Side.* Cambridge, Mass.: Harvard University Press, 1963.

Magrath, C. Peter. *Yazoo: Law and Politics in the New Republic: The Case of Fletcher v. Peck.* Providence, R.I.: Brown University Press, 1966.

Malone, Dumas. *Jefferson and the Ordeal of Liberty.* Boston: Little, Brown and Company, 1962.

———. *Jefferson the Virginian.* Boston: Little, Brown and Company, 1948.

Mayo, Bernard, ed. *Jefferson Himself.* Boston: Houghton Mifflin Company, 1942.

Perkins, Bradford. *The First Rapprochement: England and the United States.* Berkeley, Calif.: University of California Press, 1967.

Peterson, Merrill D. *The Jefferson Image*

in the American Mind. New York: Oxford University Press, 1960.

Reed, V. B., and J. D. Williams, eds. *Case of Aaron Burr.* Boston: Houghton Mifflin Company, 1960.

Sears, Louis M. *Jefferson and the Embargo.* Durham, N.C.: Duke University Press, 1927.

Van Every, Dale. *Ark of Empire: The American Frontier, 1784–1803.* New York: William Morrow & Co., Inc., 1963.

Walters, Raymond, Jr. *Albert Gallatin: Jeffersonian Financier and Diplomat.*

Pittsburgh, Pa.: University of Pittsburgh Press, 1969.

Whitaker, Arthur P. *The Mississippi Question, 1795–1803.* Gloucester, Mass.: Peter Smith, 1934.

Wiltse, Charles M. *Jeffersonian Tradition in American Democracy.* Chapel Hill, N.C.: University of North Carolina Press, 1960.

Young, James. *The Washington Community, 1800–1828.* New York: Columbia University Press, 1966.

Zimmerman, James F. *Impressment of American Seamen.* Port Washington, N.Y.: Kennikat Press, Inc., 1925.

problem 3

The Emergence of Political Parties: Origins Disputed

Few historians take issue with the belief that the phenomenon known as the American political party system emerged from the partisan conflicts following the American Revolution. They do, however, disagree on the precise issues that produced the greatest conflict of interest.

Charles A. Beard and his economic determinists pursued the belief that the first serious and most pervasive conflict stemmed from the battle over the bank. It suggested the culmination of past differences between the conservative sectors (merchants, manufacturers, and speculators) on the one hand, and the radical sectors (mechanics, small farmers, and workers), on the other. Beard thus saw the arrival of political parties as a class-conflict movement.

Another group, led by Joseph Charles and Robert R. Palmer, later challenged the Beard thesis by pointing to the divisive nature of foreign affairs during the turbulent years after the Revolution. They found in the pro-English and pro-French factions, and particularly in the controversy over the Jay Treaty, the essential ingredients for lasting partisan politics.

Marcus Cunliffe and Paul Goodman suggested that Beard had oversimplified the case. Goodman found economic groups to be extremely independent with divergent interests and proposed that religious, ethnic, and sectional interests be considered in the evolution of partisan politics. Cunliffe broadened this thesis to include the natural conflicts between nationalism and sectionalism, conservatism and experimentalism, and urbanism and ruralism.

Professor Richard Hofstadter, on the other hand, discovered more consensus than conflict, more compromise than stubborn resolve in the post-Revolutionary political battles. He thus sees a common climate of opinion emerging from the Hamilton-Jefferson differences, which, he asserts, has become the hallmark of the American political tradition.

In his reading of the selected essays, the following questions are offered for the student's consideration:

General Questions for Reflection and Discussion

1. In what ways could the later political parties have been a continuation of the pre-Revolution and Revolution factions?

2. To what extent are political parties used as agents to discourage the centralization of power?

3. To what extent does a political party system encourage democratic responsibility and coherence?

4. To what extent did Jefferson and Hamilton envision the kind of democracy which we have and idealize today?

5. To what extent are the constitutional controversies of that time still alive today?

6. How relevant are political parties to our contemporary political needs?

Basic Questions for Reflection and Discussion

1. What were the arguments for establishing a bank? Against?

2. What controversy over the meaning of the Constitution was ushered in by Hamilton's Bank Bill?

3. How did the Bank Bill treat such subjects as ownership, capitalization, currency issuance, and government funds?

4. What clause in the Constitution was used by Hamilton to justify the bank? How did Jefferson interpret this clause?

5. Compare Jefferson's principle or rule of construction with that of Hamilton.

6. To what extent was the battle over the bank a conflict between capitalists and agrarians?

7. According to Beard, what Federalist measures "divided the country into two powerful parties"?

8. To what extent did the National Bank benefit the mercantile interests only?

9. According to Beard, how did foreign policy further divide the Federalists and Republicans?

10. How does Palmer relate the European war and the French Revolution to the development of political parties in the United States?

11. Why does Palmer consider the year 1792 a turning point in America and in Europe?

12. Why did the Republicans accuse the Federalists of betraying the American Revolution?

Thomas Jefferson

A Challenge
on the Constitutionality
of the Bank
February 15, 1791

The bill for establishing a National Bank undertakes among other things:

1. To form the subscribers into a corporation.
2. To enable them in their corporate capacitites to receive grants of land; and so far is against the laws of *Mortmain.* [1]
3. To make alien subscribers capable of holding land; and so far is against the laws of *Alienage.*
4. To transmit these lands, on the death of a proprietor, to a certain line of successors; and so far changes the course of *Descents.*
5. To put the lands out of the reach of forfeiture or Escheat; and so far is against the laws of *Distribution.*
6. To transmit personal chattels to successors in a certain line; and so far against the laws of *Forfeiture and Escheat.*
7. To give them the sole and exclusive right of banking under the national authority; and so far is against the laws of *Monopoly.*
8. To communicate to them a power to make laws paramount to the laws of the States: for so they must be con-

strued, to protect the institution from the control of the State legislatures; and so, probably, they will be construed.

I consider the foundation of the Constitution as laid on this ground: That "all powers not delegated to the United States, by the Constitution, nor prohibited by it to the States, are reserved to the States or to the people." [XIIth amendment.] To take a single step beyond the boundaries thus specially drawn around the powers of Congress, is to take possession of a boundless field of power, no longer susceptible of any definition.

The incorporation of a bank, and the powers assumed by this bill, have not, in my opinion, been delegated to the United States, by the Constitution.

I. *They are not among the powers specially enumerated: for these are:*

1st. A power to lay taxes for the purpose of paying the debts of the United States; but no debt is paid by this bill, nor any tax laid. Were it a bill to raise money, its origination in the Senate would condemn it by the Constitution.
2d. "To borrow money." But this bill neither borrows money nor ensures the borrowing it. The proprietors of the bank will be just as free as any other money holders, to lend or not to lend their money to the public. The operation proposed in the bill, first, to lend them two millions, and then to borrow them back again, cannot change

---

[1] Though the Constitution controls the laws of Mortmain so far as to permit Congress itself to hold land for certain purposes, yet not so far as to permit them to communicate a similar right to other corporate bodies. — T. J.

Paul Leicester Ford, ed. *The Works of Thomas Jefferson,* Vol. 6 (New York: G. P. Putnam's Sons, 1904). pp. 197–204.

the nature of the latter act, which will still be a payment, and not a loan, call it by what name you please.

3. To "regulate commerce with foreign nations, and among the States, and with the Indian tribes." To erect a bank, and to regulate commerce, are very different acts. He who erects a bank, creates a subject of commerce in its bills; so does he who makes a bushel of wheat, or digs a dollar out of the mines; yet neither of these persons regulates commerce thereby. To make a thing which may be bought and sold, is not to precribe regulations for buying and selling. Besides, if this was an exercise of the power of regulating commerce, it would be void, as extending as much to the internal commerce of every State, as to its external. For the power given to Congress by the Constitution does not extend to the internal regulation of the Commerce of a State, (that is to say of the commerce between citizen and citizen,) which remain exclusively with its own legislature; but to its external commerce only, that is to say, its commerce with another State, or with foreign nations, or with Indian tribes. Accordingly the bill does not propose the measure as a regulation of trade, but as "productive of considerable advantages to trade." Still less are these powers covered by any other of the special enumerations.

II. *Nor are they within either of the general phrases, which are the two following:*
1. To lay taxes to provide for the general welfare of the United States, that is to say, "to lay taxes for *the purpose* of providing for the general welfare." For the laying of taxes is the power, and the general welfare the *purpose* for which the power is to be exercised. They are not to lay taxes *ad libitum for any purpose they please; but only to pay the debts or provide for the welfare of the Union.* In like manner, they are not *to do anything they please* to provide for the general welfare, but only to *lay taxes* for that purpose. To consider the latter phrase, not as describing the purpose of the first, but as giving a distinct and independent power to do any act they please, which might be for the good of the Union, would render all the preceding and subsequent enumerations of power completely useless.

It would reduce the whole instrument to a single phrase, that of instituting a Congress with power to do whatever would be for the good of the United States; and, as they would be the sole judges of the good or evil, it would be also a power to do whatever evil they please.

It is an established rule of construction where a phrase will bear either of two meanings, to give it that which will allow some meaning to the other parts of the instrument, and not that which would render all the others useless. Certainly no such universal power was meant to be given them. It was intended to lace them up straitly within the enumerated powers, and those without which, as means, these powers could not be carried into effect. It is known that the very power now proposed *as a means* was rejected *as an end* by the Convention which formed the Constitution. A proposition was made to them to authorize Congress to open canals, and an amendatory one to empower them to incorporate. But the whole was rejected, and one of the reasons for rejection urged in debate was, that then they would have a power to erect a bank, which would render the great cities, where there were prejudices and jealousies on the subject, adverse to the reception of the Constitution.

2. The second general phrase is, "to make all laws *necessary* and proper for carrying into execution the enumerated powers." But they can all be car-

ried into execution without a bank. A bank therefore is not *necessary,* and consequently not authorized by this phrase.

It has been urged that a bank will give great facility or convenience in the collection of taxes. Suppose this were true: yet the Constitution allows only the means which are *"necessary,"* not those which are merely "convenient" for effecting the enumerated powers. If such a latitude of construction be allowed to this phrase as to give any nonenumerated power, it will go to every one, for there is not one which ingenuity may not torture into a *convenience* in some instance *or other,* to *some one* of so long a list of enumerated powers. It would swallow up all the delegated powers, and reduce the whole to one power, as before observed. Therefore it was that the Constitution restrained them to the *necessary* means, that is to say, to those means without which the grant of power would be nugatory.

But let us examine this convenience and see what it is. The report on this subject, page 3, states the only *general* convenience to be, the preventing the transportation and re-transportation of money between the States and the treasury, (for I pass over the increase of circulating medium, ascribed to it as a want, and which, according to my ideas of paper money, is clearly a demerit.) Every State will have to pay a sum of tax money into the treasury; and the treasury will have to pay, in every State, a part of the interest on the public debt, and salaries to the officers of government resident in that State. In most of the States there will still be a surplus of tax money to come up to the seat of government for the officers residing there. The payments of interest and salary in each State may be made by treasury orders on the State collector. This will take up the greater part of the money he has collected in his State, and consequently prevent the great mass of it from being drawn out of the State. If there

be a balance of commerce in favor of that State against the one in which the government resides, the surplus of taxes will be remitted by the bills of exchange drawn for that commercial balance. And so it must be if there was a bank. But if there be no balance of commerce, either direct or circuitous, all the banks in the world could not bring up the surplus of taxes but in the form of money. Treasury orders then, and bills of exchange may prevent the displacement of the main mass of the money collected, without the aid of any bank; and where these fail, it cannot be prevented even with that aid.

Perhaps, indeed, bank bills may be a more *convenient* vehicle than treasury orders. But a little *difference* in the degree of *convenience,* cannot constitute the necessity which the constitution makes the ground for assuming any non-enumerated power.

Besides; the existing banks will, without a doubt, enter into arrangements for lending their agency, and the more favorable, as there will be a competition among them for it; whereas the bill delivers us up bound to the national bank, who are free to refuse all arrangement, but on their own terms, and the public not free, on such refusal, to employ any other bank. That of Philadelphia, I believe, now does this business, by their post-notes, which, by an arrangement with the treasury, are paid by any State collector to whom they are presented. This expedient alone suffices to prevent the existence of that *necessity* which may justify the assumption of a non-enumerated power as a means for carrying into effect an enumerated one. The thing may be done, and has been done, and well done, without this assumption; therefore, it does not stand on that degree of *necessity* which can honestly justify it.

It may be said that a bank whose bills would have a currency all over the States, would be more convenient than one whose currency is limited to a single State. So it would be still more convenient that there should be a bank, whose bills should have a currency all over the world. But it does not follow from this superior conveniency, that there exists anywhere a power to establish such a bank; or that the world may not go on very well without it.

Can it be thought that the Constitution intended that for a shade or two of *convenience,* more or less, Congress should be authorized to break down the most ancient and fundamental laws of the several States; such as those against Mortmain, the laws of alienage, the rules of descent, the acts of distribution, the laws of escheat and forfeiture, the laws of monopoly? Nothing but a necessity invincible by any other means, can justify such a prostitution of laws, which constitute the pillars of our whole system of jurisprudence. Will Congress be too straight-laced to carry the constitution into honest effect, unless they may pass over the foundation-laws of the State government for the slightest convenience of theirs?

The negative of the President is the shield provided by the constitution to protect against the invasions of the legislature: 1. The right of the Executive. 2. Of the Judiciary. 3. Of the States and State legislatures. The present is the case of a right remaining exclusively with the States, and consequently one of those intended by the Constitution to be placed under its protection.

It must be added, however, that unless the President's mind on a view of everything which is urged for and against this bill, is tolerably clear that it is unauthorised by the Constitution; if the pro and the con hang so even as to balance his judgment, a just respect for the wisdom of the legislature would naturally decide the balance in favor of their opinion. It is chiefly for cases where they are clearly misled by error, ambition, or interest, that the Constitution has placed a check in the negative of the President.

Alexander Hamilton

A Defense on the Constitutionality of the Bank
February 23, 1791

The Secretary of the Treasury having perused with attention the papers containing the opinions of the Secretary of

From Henry Cabot Lodge, *Constitutional Edition: The Works of Alexander Hamilton,* Vol. 3 (New York: G. P. Putnam's Sons), 1904, pp. 445–455, 457–458, 471–472 and 485–486.

State and the Attorney-General, concerning the constitutionality of the bill for establishing a national bank, proceeds, according to the order of the President, to submit the reasons which have induced him to entertain a different opinion.

It will naturally have been anticipated,

that in performing this task he would feel uncommon solicitude. Personal considerations alone, arising from the reflection that the measure originated with him, would be sufficient to produce it. The sense which he has manifested of the great importance of such an institution to the successful administration of the department under his particular care, and an expectation of serious ill consequences to result from a failure of the measure, do not permit him to be without anxiety on public accounts. But the chief solicitude arises from a firm persuasion, that principles of construction like those espoused by the Secretary of State and the Attorney-General would be fatal to the just and indispensable authority of the United States.

In entering upon the argument, it ought to be premised that the objections of the Secretary of State and the Attorney-General are founded on a general denial of the authority of the United States to erect corporations. The latter, indeed, expressly admits, that if there be anything in the bill which is not warranted by the Constitution, it is the clause of incorporation.

Now it appears to the Secretary of the Treasury that this *general principle* is *inherent* in the very *definition* of government, and *essential* to every step of the progress to be made by that of the United States, namely: That every power vested in a government is in its nature *sovereign,* and includes, by *force* of the *term,* a right to employ all the *means* requisite and fairly applicable to the attainment of the *ends* of such power, and which are not precluded by restrictions and exceptions specified in the Constitution, or not immoral, or not contrary to the *essential ends* of political society.[1]

This principle, in its application to government in general, would be admitted as an axiom; and it will be incum-

bent upon those who may incline to deny it, to prove a distinction, and to show that a rule which, in the general system of things, is essential to the preservation of the social order, is inapplicable to the United States.

The circumstance that the powers of sovereignty are in this country divided between the National and State governments, does not afford the distinction required. It does not follow from this, that each of the portion of *powers* delegated to the one or to the other, is not sovereign with *regard to its proper objects.* It will only *follow* from it, that each has sovereign power as to *certain things,* and not as to *other things.* To deny that the Government of the United States has sovereign power, as to its declared purposes and trusts, because its power does not extend to all cases, would be equally to deny that the State governments have sovereign power in any case, because their power does not extend to every case. The tenth section of the first article of the Constitution exhibits a long list of very important things which they may not do. And thus the United States would furnish the singular spectacle of a *political society* without *sovereignty,* or of a *people governed,* without *government.*

If it would be necessary to bring proof to a proposition so clear, as that which affirms that the powers of the Federal Government, as to *its objects,* were sovereign, there is a clause of its Constitution which would be decisive. It is that which declares that the Constitution, and the laws of the United States made in pursuance of it, and all treaties made, ... under their authority, shall be the *supreme law of the land.* The power which can create the *supreme law of the land* in *any case,* is doubtless *sovereign* as to such case.

This general and indisputable principle puts at once an end to the *abstract* question, whether the United States have power to erect a *corporation;* that is to say, to give a *legal* or *artificial capacity* to one or more persons, distinct from the *nat-*

[1] This is the beginning of the argument in favor of the implied powers of the Constitution which Hamilton was the first to evoke.

ural. For it is unquestionably incident to *sovereign power* to erect corporations, and consequently to *that* of the United States, in *relation* to the *objects* intrusted to the management of the government. The difference is this: where the authority of the government is general, it can create corporations in *all cases;* where it is confined to certain branches of legislation, it can create corporations *only* in those cases. . . .

It is not denied that there are *implied,* as well as *express powers,* and that the *former* are as effectually delegated as the *latter.* And for the sake of accuracy it shall be mentioned that there is another class of powers, which may be properly denominated *resulting powers.* It will not be doubted that if the United States should make a conquest of any of the territories of its neighbors, they would possess sovereign jurisdiction over the conquered territory. This would be rather a result from the whole mass of the powers of the government, and from the nature of political society, than a consequence of either of the powers specially enumerated.

But be this as it may, it furnishes a striking illustration of the general doctrine contended for; it shows an extensive case, in which a power of erecting corporations is either implied in, or would result from, some or all of the powers vested in the National Government. The jurisdiction acquired over such conquered country would certainly be competent to any species of legislation.

To return: It is conceded that *implied powers* are to be considered as delegated equally with *express ones.* Then it follows, that as a power of erecting a corporation may as well be *implied* as any other thing, it may be well be employed as an *instrument* or *means* of carrying into execution any of the specified powers, as any other *instrument* or *means* whatever. The only question must be in this, as in every other case, whether the means to be employed, or, in this instance, the corporation to be erected, has a natural relation to any of

the acknowledged objects or lawful ends of the government. Thus a corporation may not be erected by Congress for superintending the police of the city of Philadelphia, because they are not authorized to *regulate* the *police* of that city. But one may be erected in relation to the collection of taxes, or to the trade with foreign countries, or to the trade between the States, or with the Indian tribes; because it is the province of the Federal Government to *regulate* those objects, and because it is incident to a general *sovereign* or *legislative* power to *regulate* a thing, to employ all the means which relate to its regulation to the best and greatest advantage. . . .

Through this mode of reasoning respecting the right of employing all the means requisite to the execution of the specified powers of the government, it is to be objected, that none but necessary and proper means are to be employed; and the Secretary of State maintains, that no means are to be considered *necessary* but those without which the grant of the power would be *nugatory.* . . .

It is essential to the being of the national government, that so erroneous a conception of the meaning of the word *necessary* should be exploded.

It is certain that neither the grammatical nor popular sense of the term requires that construction. According to both, *necessary* often means no more than *needful, requisite, incidental, useful,* or *conducive to.* It is a common mode of expression to say, that it is *necessary* for a government or a person to do this or that thing, when nothing more is intended or understood, than that the interests of the government or person require, or will be promoted by, the doing of this or that thing. The imagination can be at no loss for exemplifications of the use of the word in this sense. And it is the true one in which it is to be understood as used in the Constitution. The whole turn of the clause containing it indicates, that it was the intent of the Convention, by that clause, to give a liberal latitude to the exercise of the specified powers. The expressions have peculiar comprehensiveness. They are, "to make all *laws* necessary and proper for *carrying into execution* the *foregoing powers,* and *all other powers* vested by the Constitution in the *Government* of the United States, or in any *department* or *officer* thereof."

To understand the word as the Secretary of State does, would be to depart from its obvious and popular sense, and to give it a restrictive operation, an idea never before entertained. It would be to give it the same force as if the word *absolutely* or *indispensably* had been prefixed to it. . . .

The *degree* in which a measure is necessary can never be a *test* of the legal right to adopt it; that must be a matter of opinion, and can only be a *test* of expediency. The *relation* between the *measure* and the *end;* between the *nature* of the *means* employed towards the execution of a power, and the object of that power, must be the criterion of constitutionality, not the more or less of *necessity* or *utility.*

The practice of the government is against the rule of construction advocated by the Secretary of State. Of this, the act concerning light-houses, beacons, buoys, and public piers is a decisive example. This, doubtless, must be referred to the powers of regulating trade, and is fairly relative to it. But it cannot be affirmed that the exercise of that power in this instance was strictly *necessary,* or that the power itself would be *nugatory,* without that of regulating establishments of this nature.

This restrictive interpretation of the word *necessary* is also contrary to this sound maxim of construction; namely, that the powers contained in a constitution of government, especially those which concern the general administration of the affairs of a country, its finances, trade, defence, etc., ought to be construed liberally in advancement of the public good. This rule does not depend on the particular form of a government, or on the particular demarcation of the boundaries of its powers, but on the nature and objects of government itself. The means by which national exigencies are to be provided for, national inconveniences obviated, national prosperity promoted, are of such infinite variety, extent, and complexity, that there must of necessity be great latitude of discretion in the selection and application of those means. Hence, consequently, the necessity and propriety of exercising the authorities intrusted to a government on principles of liberal construction. . . .

But the doctrine which is contended for is not chargeable with the consequences imputed to it. It does not affirm that the National Government is sovereign in all respects, but that it is sovereign to a certain extent—that is, to the extent of the objects of its specified powers.

It leaves, therefore, a criterion of what is constitutional, and of what is not so. This criterion is the *end,* to which the measure relates as a *means.* If the *end* be clearly comprehended within any of the specified powers, and if the measure have an obvious relation to that *end,* and is not forbidden by any particular provision of the Constitution, it may safely be deemed to come within the compass of the national authority. There is also this further criterion, which may materially assist the decision: Does the proposed measure abridge a pre-existing right of any State or of any individual? If it does not, there is a strong presumption in favor of its constitutionality, and slighter relations to any declared object of the Constitution may be permitted to turn the scale. . . .

It is presumed to have been satisfactorily shown in the course of the preceding observations:

1. That the power of the government, as to the objects intrusted to its management, is, in its nature, sovereign.
2. That the right of erecting corporations is one inherent in, and insepara-

ble from, the idea of sovereign power.

3. That the position, that the government of the United States can exercise no power but such as is delegated to it by its Constitution, does not militate against this principle.

4. That the word *necessary,* in the general clause, can have no *restrictive* operation derogating from the force of this principle; indeed, that the degree in which a measure is or is not *necessary,* cannot be a *test* of *constitutional right,* but of *expediency only.*

5. That the power to erect corporations is not to be considered as an *independent* or *substantive* power, but as an *incidental* and *auxiliary* one, and was therefore more properly left to implication, than expressly granted.

6. That the principle in question does not extend the power of the government beyond the prescribed limits, because it only affirms a power to *incorporate* for purposes *within the sphere* of the *specified powers.*

And lastly, that the right to exercise such a power in certain cases is unequivocally granted in the most *positive* and comprehensive terms. To all which it only remains to be added, that such a power has actually been exercised in two very eminent instances: namely, in the erec-

tion of two governments; one northwest of the river Ohio, and the other southwest — the last independent of any antecedent compact. And these result in a full and complete demonstration, that the Secretary of State and the Attorney-General are mistaken when they deny generally the power of the National Government to erect corporations. . . .

A hope is entertained that it has, by this time, been made to appear, to the satisfaction of the President, that a bank has a natural relation to the power of collecting taxes—to that of regulating trade—to that of providing for the common defence—and that, as the bill under consideration contemplates the government in the light of a joint proprietor of the stock of the bank, it brings the case within the provision of the clause of the Constitution which immediately respects the property of the United States.

Under a conviction that such a relation subsists, the Secretary of the Treasury, with all deference, conceives that it will result as a necessary consequence from the position, that all the specified powers of government are sovereign, as to the proper objects; that the incorporation of a bank is a constitutional measure; and that the objections taken to the bill, in this respect, are ill-founded.

Charles A. Beard

The Origins of American Political Parties: An Economic Interpretation

It is customary to separate American political history into three periods, using changes in party names as the basis of the division. According to this scheme, there have been three great party alignments since the formation of the Constitution: Federalists against Republicans (1789–1816), Whigs against Democrats (1830–1856), and Republicans against Democrats (1856 to the present time). Although the dates are merely approximate, they furnish useful chronological clues.

But this division is arbitrary and only for convenience. In fact, there has been no sharp break in the sources of party strength, in policy, or in opinion. On the contrary, these three alignments have been merely phases of one unbroken conflict originating in the age of George Washington and continuing without interruption to our own time. . . .

The first of these alignments—Federalists against Republicans—was connected more or less directly with the contest over the framing and adoption of the federal Constitution.

Authorities are generally agreed that the main support for the Constitution came from merchants, manufacturers, government bondholders, and other people of substantial property interests "along the line of the seaboard towns and

From *The Economic Basis of Politics and Related Writings,* by Charles A. Beard. Copyright 1922, 1934, 1945 by Alfred A. Knopf, Inc., and renewed 1950, 1962, by William Beard and Miriam B. Vagts. Reprinted by permission of the publisher.

populous regions." They are likewise agreed that the opposition came mainly from the inland farmers, debtors, and from those in less prosperous sections of the country.

The feelings aroused by the contest over the Constitution had not disappeared when the first administration was organized in 1789 with Washington as President and friends of the new system installed in all branches of the government—executive, legislative and judicial. With Alexander Hamilton, first Secretary of the Treasury, in the lead, the advocates of the new order, soon to be known as Federalists, carried through a series of economic measures which in time divided the country into two powerful parties. In summary form, these measures were as follows:

1. *The funding of the national debt.* . . .

2. *The assumption of the revolutionary debts of the states.* . . .

These two operations, funding and assumption, deeply affected the purses of classes and masses. . . . To raise the money to pay the interest on the debt, the federal government had to lay heavy taxes on the people, most of whom were farmers, not bondholders. . . .

3. *Protective tariff.* The third measure on the Federalist program was the protection of American industries

153

by the imposition of customs duties on imports coming into competition with American products. Hamilton openly favored an elaborate system of protection. . . .

4. *The United States Bank.* Under Hamilton's leadership, Congress chartered a banking corporation, authorized it to raise a large capital composed, three-fourths, of new federal bonds, and enpowered it to issue currency and do a general banking business.

5. *A sound national currency.* Under the new Constitution, the states had to stop issuing paper money. The gold and silver coin of the United States now provided by law became the money of the country, with the notes of the United States Bank circulating on a parity.

6. *Discrimination in favor of American shipping.* To encourage the construction of an American merchant marine, Congress provided that the tonnage duties on foreign-built and foreign-owned ships should be five times as high as the duties on American ships. . . .

7. *National defense.* In creating a navy and a standing army, Congress had more in mind than the mere defense of the country against foreign foes. The navy was useful in protecting commerce on the high seas and the army in suppressing uprisings such as had occurred in Massachusetts in 1786. In other words, economic factors as well as patriotism were involved in the process.

8. *Foreign affairs.* When the wars of the French Revolution broke out in Europe, the Washington administration, largely inspired by Hamilton, frankly sympathized with England as against France and looked on the contest in the Old World as a conflict between property and order on the one side and democracy and anarchy on the other—akin in fact to the political dispute at home.

Now these measures were not excursions in theory. They were acts of power involving the pocketbooks of groups, affecting the distribution of wealth and the weight of classes in politics. Certainly the first six of them bore directly upon the economic interests of the citizens.

Under these laws, large sums of money were paid to the holders of government bonds who had been receiving little or nothing; people who were moderately well off one day found themselves rich the next. Under these laws, stockholders in the United States Bank earned handsome profits on their investment, protected manufacturers entered upon a period of prosperity and merchants and money lenders were enabled, by the sound currency system and adequate judicial assistance, to carry on their operations safely in all parts of the country. Under these laws, heavy taxes were collected to pay the interest on the bonds and to maintain the new government.

Were these things done for beneficiaries at the expense of other classes, notably the farmers, or did the increased production caused by the operations more than cover the cost? On this point economists disagree and the historian cannot answer the question mathematically.

At all events, however, a considerable portion of the American people came to the conclusion that the Federalist measures and policies above enumerated in fact transferred money to investors, merchants, manufacturers, and the capitalistic interests in general, at the expense of the masses—a majority of whom were farmers and planters. "This plan of a National Bank is calculated to benefit a small part of the United States, the mercantile interest only; the farmers, the yeomanry, will derive no advantage from it," complained a member of Congress from Georgia. The protective tariff on steel will operate "as an oppressive, though indirect, tax upon agriculture," lamented a Congressman from Virginia. "The funding system was intended to effect what the Bank was contrived to accelerate: 1. Accumulation of great wealth in a few hands. 2. A political moneyed engine," protested another Virginia statesman.

In time, the citizens who took this view of the Hamiltonian program were marshalled, first as Anti-Federalists and later as Republicans, under the leadership of Thomas Jefferson, who was by occupation and opinion well fitted for his mission. A planter, Jefferson was acquainted with the interests of agriculture. Moreover, he believed and said openly that "cultivators of the earth are the most valuable citizens. They are the most vigorous, the most independent, the most virtuous, and they are tied to their country and wedded to its liberty and interests by the most lasting bonds." In logical relation, he had a low opinion of commerce and industry, which created urban masses. "The mobs of great cities," he asserted, "add just so much to the support of pure government as sores do to the strength of the human body."

Holding such opinions, Jefferson set out to enlist a large following in this struggle against the capitalistic measures of Hamilton. He made his strongest appeal directly to the agriculturalists of the country. And when his party was fully organized he took pride in saying that "the whole landed interest is republican," that is, lined up on his side of the contest.

Speaking of the Federalists arrayed against him on the other side, Jefferson said that they included all the federal officeholders, "all who want to be officers, all timid men who prefer the calm of despotism to the boisterous sea of liberty, British merchants and Americans trading on British capitals, speculators and holders in the banks and public funds, a contrivance invented for the purposes of corruption."

Appealing to the farmers and the masses in general against the larger capitalistic interests, Jefferson's party inevitably took a popular, that is, a democratic turn. This was in keeping with his theories, for he thought that kings, clergy, nobles, and other ruling classes of Europe had filled their countries with poverty and misery and kept the world in turmoil with useless wars. The common people, he reasoned, if given liberty and let alone, would be happier under their own government than under any ruling class.

To their economic arguments, the Jeffersonians added a constitutional theory. They declared that the Constitution did not give Congress the power to charter a bank, provide protection for manufacturers, and pass certain other measures sponsored by the Federalists. This was a "strict construction" of the Constitution; that is, the powers of Congress were to be interpreted narrowly and the rights of the states liberally. Although the Federalists included in their ranks most of the leading men who had made the Constitution, they were thus accused of violating the very fundamental law which they had conceived and adopted. In this way, arose the wordy battle over the "true meaning" of the Constitution and the "rights of states" which occupies such a large place in the history of American political loquacity.

To the disputes over domestic questions were added differences of opinion about foreign policies. . . .

The more radical elements of the population, fresh from their own triumph over George III, remembered with satisfaction the execution of Charles I by their ancestors, and took advantage of the occasion to rejoice in the death of another ruler—the French monarch. A climax came in 1793, when France called on the United States to fulfill the terms of the treaty of 1778, in return for the assistance which had been given to the Americans in their struggle with England. The radicals wanted to aid France, either openly or secretly, in her war on England, but Washington and his conservative supporters refused to be drawn into the European controversy. So the Americans were divided into contending groups over foreign policy, and the division ran in the main along the line already cut by the

Federalist-Republican contest over domestic questions.

As the critics of the administration, known at first as Anti-Federalists, slowly changed from a mere opposition group into a regular party and took on the name Republican, the friends of the administration with Hamilton, John Jay, and John Adams in the lead, began to organize for political warfare under the banner of Federalism. In the third presidential election, the party alignment was complete. Jefferson, the leader of the Republicans, was roundly denounced as an atheist and leveler; while Adams, the Federalist candidate was condemned by his opponents as "the monarchist." So sharply drawn was the contest that Adams was chosen by the narrow margin of three electoral votes. . . .

It has been the fashion to ascribe to the Federalists a political philosophy born of innate ill-will for the people. "Your people, sir," Hamilton is supposed to have said, "is a great beast"—as if in a burst of petulance.

Now this imputation is not entirely just. No doubt some of the emotions to which Federalists gave free vent were the feelings common to persons of large property —feelings of superiority and virtue. But there were practical grounds for distrusting "the people." Throughout the Revolution "the lower orders" had given trouble to the right wing of patriotism, threatening to upset the new ship of state before it was launched. Indeed, some blood has been shed in conflicts among the Patriots themselves before independence was won.

To the Tories who remained in America and rallied to the Federalist cause, the masses were, of course, contemptible in opinion and conduct. In the eyes of the Patriots of the right, the new democracy was responsible for the failure to pay the interest on the national and state debts between 1783 and 1789, for the refusal to grant aid and protection to American industry, for the uprising against the "rich and well-born" in Massachusetts in 1786, and for sundry other disturbances in the body politic. When, therefore, Federalists cursed the people—as they did in gross and in detail—they were not merely expressing a conservative temper. Rather were they reasoning, so they thought, from experience, bitter realistic experience at that.

For twenty-eight years, from 1801 to 1829, Presidents calling themselves Republican occupied the White House— Jefferson, Madison, Monroe, and John Quincy Adams—and except for a short time at the beginning they were well supported in Congress by party members of their own persuasion. During this period, the Federalist party, as a national organization, died a lingering death. It continued to put up candidates until 1816, but after that failure it disappeared from the national theater. Deprived of a shelter all their own, active Federalists then went into the Republican organization and did what they could to bend it in their direction, while the intransigents of the old generation often sulked in their tents, lamenting the evil days upon which they had fallen.

Although they possessed the power of government, the Republicans, it must be said, did not have a perfectly free hand in carrying their policies into effect. For more than half of this period, the nations of Europe were engaged in the devastating Napoleonic wars which interfered with the shipment of American agricultural produce to Europe, and for a brief time the United States was at war with Great Britain. Owing to foreign events beyond their control, the Republicans were compelled to adopt many devices not to their liking, or at least contrary to their professions.

Robert R. Palmer

The Origins
of American Political Parties:
The French Revolution

It was the Americans who had first given the example of rebellion, proclaimed the rights of man and the sovereignty of the people, and established a new public authority in their state constitutions by recognizing a constituent power in bodies called conventions. They had attracted the lively notice and admiration of dissatisfied persons in many parts of Europe. A mere fifteen years later the American image had already faded in a more blinding light on the screen of the world's opinion, and the mild accents of the heralds of liberty had been succeeded by a more ringing and compelling voice. If an influence had passed from America to Europe before 1789, after that year the direction was reversed. If, as Barruel said, the "sect" had first shown itself in America, within two decades the United States was in the worthy position of a kind of Israel, and the ecumenical church, as embodied in the New Republican Order, had its center —complete with power, doctrines, and abuses—in Paris.

Like other countries, the United States felt the strong impact of the French Revolution. As elsewhere, the development was twofold. On the one hand, there was an acceleration of indigenous movements.

From R. R. Palmer, *The Age of Democratic Revolution: A Political History of Europe and America, 1760–1800.* Vol. 2, *The Struggle,* chapter 16. Copyright © 1964 by Princeton University Press. Reprinted by permission of Princeton University Press.

On the other, there was an influence that was unquestionably foreign. The latter presented itself especially with the war that began in Europe in 1792, and with the clash of armed ideologies that the war brought with it. The warring powers in Europe, which for Americans meant the governments of France and Great Britain, attempted to make use of the United States for their own advantage. Different groups of Americans, for their own domestic purposes, were likewise eager to exploit the power and prestige of either England or France. Some Americans saw the future of the United States best secured by a victory of the French Republic; others saw no hope for their own country except in a triumph by Great Britain. Political thought was also sharpened, heated emotionally, and broadened to the all-embracing dimensions that the word "ideology" suggests. American democracy, as expressed in the new Republican party, was shaped in part by the revolution in Europe; and American conservatism, as it came to be expressed by High Federalists, shared in some of the ideas of the European counter-revolution, especially as transmitted in books imported from England. The indigenous and the foreign became indistinguishable. In the way in which internal dissension passed into favoritism for foreign powers, the United States did not differ from the countries described from Ireland to Poland and from Scotland to Naples. . . .

It is widely agreed . . . that the two American parties, and hence the beginnings of a two-party system, were produced in the United States by reactions to the European war and the French Revolution. The paradox, therefore, is that the ideological differences aroused in the United States, which became very heated, and the actual dangers of subservience to foreign powers, which were very real, may have contributed, by creating national parties to debate national issues and elect candidates to national office in the atmosphere of public involvement, to the solidarity of the union, the maintenance of the constitution, and the survival of the republic.

There was, to be sure, something peculiar in the entire phenomenon. Hamilton, who loathed the French Revolution, was more of a revolutionary than Jefferson both in temperament and in the policies that he espoused. He was more impatient of the compromises on which the federal constitution rested, he wanted to make over the country, and he would have liked, if he could, to abolish the states (especially Virginia) and replace them with small *departments* created by a national government, as in the French and other revolutionary republics in Europe. Jefferson, who sympathized with the French Revolution, was actually a good deal of a moderate, both in personality and in his ideas of what should be done. He spoke for a kind of liberty and equality that had long existed in America, and did not have to be fought for as in Europe, a liberty that meant freedom from government, and an equality of the kind that obtained among yeoman farmers—a way of life that had been threatened by British policy before 1775, and was threatened by Hamiltonian policy after 1790, in each case with the support of American "aristocrats" or persons aspiring to become such. Because of their different views on the need for change, it was Hamilton who was

the "unitarist," and Jefferson the "federalist," in the sense then current in Europe, where, as has been seen, the radical democrats were unitarists, and the moderates inclined to the decentralization of power. The unitarist and "revolutionary" Hamilton was certainly no Jacobin, but he was the nearest that the United States ever produced to a Bonaparte.

On a more general plane, also, the kinds of people who in the United States favored the French Revolution were not the same as in Europe. Nor were conservatives in America socially akin to those of Europe. There was a curious reversal or transposition. In Europe, on the whole, those who favored the French Revolution were middle-class people living in towns, including a good many bankers and businessmen, especially those interested in the newer forms of economic enterprise and development. Among the rural population, on the Continent, it was the landowners and property-owning farmers living nearest to the cities, most involved in a market economy, and enjoying the best communications with the outside world who were most receptive to the Revolutionary ideas. In America the opposite was more nearly true. The business and mercantile community, and the farmers who lived nearest to the towns, or along the rivers and arteries of traffic and communication, were generally Federalist, and they became anti-French and anti-Republican. The same inversion holds for the counter-revolution, which in Europe was essentially agrarian. It drew its strength from the landed aristocracy, and from peasants who were politically apathetic, or looked upon cities as the abodes of their enemies. In the United States the Virginia gentry, and the farmers farthest from towns, along the frontier from Vermont through western Pennsylvania into Kentucky, were strongly Jeffersonian, Republican, anti-British and partisan to the French Revolution. To this broad generalization various exceptions must be recognized, since in America (as in Europe) many urban "mechanics" and many of the professional classes, notably doctors, favored the newly forming republicanism; but the cities in America were still small compared with those of Europe in any case; and the broad features of the transposition would appear to be valid.

This reversal of roles can best be explained by the differences between the United States and Europe, differences which Louis Hartz has summed up as the lack of the "feudal factor" in America. It was due also to a certain failure on the part of Americans, because of these very differences, to understand the Revolution beyond the Atlantic. In Europe the revolutionary movement, though it carried aristocratic liberalism and Babouvist communism at its fringes, was most especially a middle-class or "bourgeois" affair, aimed at the reconstruction of an old order, and at the overthrow of aristocracies, nobilities, patriciates, and other privileged classes. It is hard to see how Jefferson, who so much disliked cities with their moneyed men and their mobs, could have been so sympathetic to the French Revolution had he seen it in an altogether realistic light. The same is true of American democrats generally. But Hamilton and the Federalists were if anything even more mistaken. They imagined that men like themselves, in Europe, were as hostile to the Revolution as they were. Or rather, in their own self-definition, they failed to identify with the European urban middle classes, which they really resembled, and preferred to associate themselves with the British and European aristocracies, which they hardly resembled at all. Hamilton was a self-made man, a parvenu; even George Cabot, who became a very "high" Federalist, and whose family later became prominent, was the author of his own fortune, largely made in privateering during the War of Independence. These men could not see, and probably did not even know, that many men of business in Europe—

the Watts and Boultons, Walker and Wilkinson, Gogel, Sieveking and the Bohemian banker, J. F. Opiz, were willing enough to sympathize with the ideas of the French Revolution in principle. . . .

The point is, of course, that both parties in America, far from being interested in an exact understanding of events, were using the current ideological arguments for their own purposes. Nor, for all the reversed of roles, were those arguments irrelevant to American issues. The bankers, merchants and shipping magnates who supported the Federalist party would not have been considered really high-class in Europe. In the class structure of America, however, they were upper crust; and the fact that there was no higher or older aristocracy for them to rebel against is what made it possible for them to be so conservative. The High Federalists seem to have thought (John Adams and merely moderate Federalists were not so sure) that the upper classes of the United States and Great Britain had a great deal in common. Aspiring to be aristocrats, they made themselves into legitimate targets for democrats. Appropriating the language of the European counter-revolution, they naturally found "republicans" arrayed against them. The great dispute in America was no mere comedy of errors, nor incongruous shadow-boxing; it was, as in Europe, a contest between different views on right and justice, on the form of the good society, and on the direction in which the world in general, and the new United States in particular, ought to move. . . .

To the constitution itself there was no basic opposition. Those who had argued against it in 1787, while the argument was open, accepted it in good faith after its ratification, and after adoption of the first ten amendments to protect individual and state rights. Here again the difference from France and its sister-republics was pronounced. The divisions that formed in the 1790s did not prolong earlier differences over the constitution itself. That the anti-Federalists were unfriendly to the new constitution was an empty accusation; the chief founder of the Republican party, James Madison, was himself one of the authors of the new federal document, and co-author with Hamilton of the *Federalist* papers. If Madison and Jefferson, in 1798, toyed with ideas of "nullification," it was Hamilton and the High Federalists who, under pressure were tempted by the thought of scrapping the constitution altogether. As the constitution itself was not a party issue, neither was "democracy" in the mere sense of the extent of the suffrage. The issue, as it developed, was the activation of voters whose right to the suffrage was not in question. As the decade passed, more men already qualified to vote actually voted.

At first, in 1790 and 1791, there was only Hamilton's program, and the opposition to it. Or rather, there were Hamilton's various measures, and sporadic critiques in which different individuals, in the new Congress and outside it, objected to some of these measures while accepting others. Hamilton, supported by Washington, took the view that the opposition was opposition to the government itself. Since no parties of modern kind yet existed, nor was the idea or need of them even recognized, the issues soon took on larger dimensions, becoming a question of the propriety of opposition itself, or the right of citizens to disagree with, criticize, and work against public officials. In addition, Hamilton's plans required good relations with England. It may be that at this time, in the aftermath of the American Revolution, a dislike of England, or rather of its government and social institutions, was a more positive and more popular sentiment in America than was affection for France. With France the alliance of 1778 was still in effect, and there were memories of French aid in the late war with England; but what aroused fellow-feeling in America was the French Revolution, since the French declaration

of rights, the new constitution, and the vocabulary of debate, vindicating liberty against tyrants, and equally against privilege, echoed what had been heard in America for some time. When Adams and Hamilton spoke out against the French Revolution, they aroused others all the more fiercely to its defense. A feeling spread that the French Revolution was a continuation of the American, and that the American Revolution itself was endangered, or unfinished.

In America, as in England and Europe, the year 1792 was a turning point. The war was seen by some as an outburst of militant destructive revolutionary crusading, and by others, probably far more numerous, as a defense against a brutal intervention in French affairs by a league of aristocrats and despots. The proclamation of the French Republic was seen by some as a piece of madness and violence, and by others, far more numerous, as the dawn in Europe of a light first seen in America. The French victories at Valmy and Jemappes were enthusiastically hailed. On February 1, 1793, the French declared war against England; they were now fighting that old bugbear of Americans, King George III. News of this development came almost simultaneously with the arrival of the first minister of the French Republic, Edmond Genêt, who disembarked at Charleston, South Carolina, on April 8, 1793. . . .

During the months of Genêt's ministry new political clubs began to form, the democratic or republican societies. While active Federalists had met in each other's living rooms, or the public rooms of the better hotels, people of a plainer sort now began to meet in more modest quarters, in taverns or country stores. Over forty such clubs are known to have existed, beginning in March 1793, chiefly in the seaboard towns and along the frontier. According to Oliver Wolcott they were composed of "the lowest order of mechanics, laborers and draymen"; and Timothy Dwight, perhaps recalling a famous remark of Burke's, thought that democracy, like the devil, was entering into "a herd of swine." It is true that the societies had numerous members of inferior station, but about half the membership was middle-class, consisting of merchants, lawyers, larger landowners, and a good many doctors. They somewhat resembled the Sons of Liberty of the 1760s, or the radical clubs that sprang up in England and Scotland in 1792, or similar groups in Holland, or the provincial Jacobin clubs of France. They hardly resembled the Paris Jacobin club, which, especially in 1793, was full of men active in the government. Men in the American government of republican opinions, such as Madison and Jefferson, did not belong to these clubs, which were of local, spontaneous, and popular origin. They were not yet a political party but only a step in that direction; most of them disappeared within two or three years, as a more organized Republican party came into being. Some of the clubs did take part locally in elections, and it was these clubs, apparently, that inspired the older Tammany societies with political interests. Their attitude was one of suspicion of government and of officeholders, an anti-élitism, a class consciousness of a general sort pitting the "many" against the "few." The tone was suggested by the Ulster Democratic Club in the Catskills of New York which stood "on guard against designing men in office and affluent circumstances, who are forever combining against the rights of all but themselves." The clubs were opposed to Hamilton's policies, to British influence, and to fine gentlemen who used hairpowder or wore silk stockings. At a time when the newspapers carried more foreign than local news, they were fascinated by the great spectacle of the war in Europe. They were unanimously and excitedly pro-French. On the success of the French Revolution against its armed enemies, according to the prospectus of the Massachusetts Constitutional Society,

in January 1794, depended the happiness of *"the whole world of Mankind."*

To men who still conceived themselves as the proper guardians of society, suited by wisdom, experience, and position to form a governing class—that is, to most of the more articulate Federalists—this sprouting up of popular clubs, whose stock in trade was the criticism of government, seemed novel and alarming, if not revolutionary. When the farmers of Western Pennsylvania demonstrated against the new federal tax on spirits (in the so-called Whiskey Rebellion of 1794), it was charged that the clubs promoted insurrection, which was not true; but it was true that both the formation of clubs and the resistance to taxes expressed an antipathy to Hamilton's program, and indeed to government itself. President Washington called the clubs "self-created." He meant that they were extra-legal, and that only duly constituted bodies and duly elected representatives should deliberate or exert pressure on public issues; the phrase recalled what the British authorities had said of American correspondence committees twenty years before, and were saying of the London Corresponding Society at precisely this moment. So far as the Federalists found themselves denying the legitimacy of any opposition to government arising outside government circles, the emerging Republicans could rightly accuse them of betraying the American Revolution. . . .

The American popular democrats, though not Jefferson and the Republican leaders might if left to themselves have welcomed, or even forced, another war with England (as in 1812), especially in view of the uncompromising demands of the British, which at times filled even Hamilton with dismay. John Jay went to England to negotiate a treaty. At the same time James Monroe went as minister to Paris, to maintain good relations with France while Jay tried to deal with England. Monroe, an enthusiastic republican, arriving just after the death of Robespierre, was very partial to the French Convention and to the Directory after it. Well disposed to democrats everywhere, he befriended Thomas Paine and Wolfe Tone in Paris. He was so eager to please the French that he sometimes failed to put the policies of his own government in their proper light. He believed that Jay in London was betraying him; he was so opposed to an American rapprochement with England that the French thought he must be deceiving them; and he seems not to have known, or to have been unconcerned, about French designs on the region west of the Alleghenies. Washington finally recalled him, and the ensuing uproar formed another stage in the differentiation of Federalists and Republicans. Meanwhile Jay negotiated his famous treaty, with Alexander Hamilton secretly working, through the British minister in Philadelphia, to satisfy the British in a way that even Jay thought too extreme. The British conceded practically nothing except evacuation of the Northwest Territory. They refused to moderate their position on the impressment of sailors, or on matters of contraband, search, and seizure at sea in wartime; they refused to pay for American slaves taken off during the War of Independence (a sensitive matter to southern Republicans); and they refused to open their West Indian islands in a useful way to American commerce. The best that could be said in America for the treaty was that it prevented war with England. Undoubtedly such a war at this time would have been ruinous to the new republic, both from the impact of British power, and the effects of internal dispute and break-up within the United States. Politically, however, the argument was not a strong one; it sounded too much like appeasement.

It was in the controversy over the Jay treaty that the democratic movement grew into a Republican party, and that the Federalists closed ranks to obtain the goodwill of Britain, which was necessary both to their practical program and to

their view of life and society. When Washington and the Senate ratified the treaty, debate raged in the House on measures for putting it into effect. The treaty became a question between government and opposition, or Federalists and Republicans. It raised also, above the prosaic problems of debt and taxation, and above localized grievances such as the excise on spirits, a question on which people of all kinds, throughout the country, could form an opinion and become emotionally aroused. The question was seen, and strongly felt, as a choice between England and France, between . . . the old forces and the new in a contest without geographical boundaries, between monarchy and republicanism, Anglomen and Gallomen, men of substance and Jacobins—and between those who wished to move forward with a continuing American Revolution, and those who wished to restrain or qualify the implications of that event. On this basis the treaty was attacked and defended in the newspapers. Political leaders had an issue on which they could ignite public opinion, form connections with interested local groups, bring out the vote, and offer candidates for election on a basis of continuing principle, not merely of momentary issues or personal or passing factional groupings. The decisive bill to implement the treaty passed the House in April 1796 by a narrow margin, 51 to 48, on a clear party division. The two parties, Federalist and Republican, then girded for the presidential election of that year, which, with the retirement of Washington, was the first contested presidential election.

Both contenders for the office of President of the United States, in 1796, were denounced as the tools of foreign ideologies and foreign powers. Both parties presented themselves, their candidates, their opponents, and the issues in terms of the struggle raging in Europe. For Federalists, Jefferson was a Jacobin, an atheist, a libertine, a leveller, and almost a Frenchman. Adams was the friend of order, talent, and rational liberty. For the Republicans, Adams was a monocrat and an aristocrat who longed to mix with English lords and ladies; and Jefferson the upholder of republican principles. An electoral circular put out by the Republican Committee of Pennsylvania explained the choice. It was "between the uniform advocate of equal rights among citizens, or the champion of rank, titles and hereditary distinctions; . . . the steady supporter of our present republican constitution; or the warm panegyrist of the British Monarchical form of Government." That the bland Virginian was a Jacobin, or the irritable Boston lawyer an Anglomaniac, were about equally fantastic; but such was the atmosphere of debate. . . .

Select Bibliography for Problem 3

Ammon, Harry. "Genêt Mission and the Development of American Political Parties," *Journal of American History*, 52 (March 1966), 725–741.

Bailey, Thomas A. *The American Spirit.* Boston: D. C. Heath and Company, 1967, pp. 141–147.

Barber, William D. "Among the Most Techy Articles of Civil Police: Federal Taxation and the Adoption of the Whiskey Excise," *William and Mary Quarterly*, 25, 3d series (January 1968), 58–84.

Bowman, Albert H. "Jefferson, Hamilton and American Foreign Policy," *Political Science Quarterly*, 71 (March 1956), 18–41.

Brooks, Robin. "Alexander Hamilton, Melancton Smith, and the Ratification of the Constitution in New York," *William and Mary Quarterly*, 24, 3d series (July 1967), 339–358.

Charles, Joseph. "Adams and Jefferson: The Origins of the American Party System," *William and Mary Quarterly*, 12, 3d series (July 1955), 410–446.

————. "Hamilton and Washington: The Origins of the American Party System," *William and Mary Quarterly*, 12, 3d series (July 1955), 410–446.

————. "The Jay Treaty: The Origins of the American Party System," *William and Mary Quarterly*, 12, 3d series (October 1955), 581–630.

————, ed. *The Origins of the American Party System.* New York: Harper & Row, Publishers, 1956.

Davis, Jim E. "Alexander Hamilton: His Politics and Policies," *Southwestern Social Science Quarterly*, 42 (December 1961), 233–239.

DeConde, Alexander. "Washington's Farewell, the French Alliance, the Election of 1796," *Mississippi Valley Historical Review*, 43 (March 1957), 641–658.

Diamond, Martin. "Democracy and the Federalist: A Reconsideration of the Framers' Intent," *American Political Science Review*, 53 (March 1959) 52–68.

Dixon, Lawrence W. "Attitude of Thomas Jefferson toward the Judiciary," *Southwestern Social Science Quarterly*, 28 (June, 1947), 13–19.

Fine, Sidney, and Gerald S. Brown. *The American Past*, 2d ed., Vol. 1. New York: Crowell Collier and Macmillan, Inc., 1956, pp. 87–116.

Garraty, "Marbury v. Madison: The Case of the 'Missing' Commissions," *American Heritage*, 14 (June 1963), 6–9, 84–89.

Goodman, Paul, ed. *The Federalists vs. the Jeffersonian Republicans.* American Problem Studies under the editorial direction of Oscar Handlin. New York: Holt, Rinehart and Winston, Inc., 1967.

Hoey, Edwin A. "A New and Strange Order [of the Cincinnati] of Men," *American Heritage*, 19 (August 1968), 44–49, 72–80.

Howe, Jr., John R. "Republican Thought and the Political Violence of the 1790s," *American Quarterly*, 19 (Summer 1967), 147–165.

Kenyon, Cecelia M. "Alexander Hamilton: Rousseau of the Right," *Political Science Quarterly*, 73, 2 (June 1958), 161–178.

_____. "Men of Little Faith: The Anti-Federalists on the Nature of Representative Government," *William and Mary Quarterly*, 12, 3d series (January 1955), 3–43.

Koch, Adrienne. "Hamilton and Power," *Yale Review*, 47, 4 (June 1958), pp. 537–551.

Kurtz, Stephen G. "French Mission of 1799–1800: Concluding Chapter in the Statecraft of John Adams," *Political Science Quarterly*, 80 (December, 1965), 543–557.

Leopold, Richard W., Arthur Link, and Stanley Coben, eds. *Problems in American History*, Vol. 1. Englewood Cliffs, N.J.: Prentice-Hall, Inc., 1966, pp. 152–192 and 193–203.

Lippmann, Walter. "Living Past: Jeffersonian and Hamiltonian Traditions in American History," *State Government*, 16 (June 1943), 139.

Rouche, John P. "The Founding Fathers: A Reform Caucus in Action," *American Political Science Review*, 55 (December 1961), 799–816.

Schachner, Nathan. "The Legacy of Hamilton," *William and Mary Quarterly*, 3, 3d series (December 1946), 720–725.

Smelser, Marshal. "Federalist Period or an Age of Passion," *American Quarterly*, 10 (Winter 1958), 391–419.

_____. "George Washington and the Alien and Sedition Acts," *American Historical Review*, 59 (January 1964), 322–334.

Sterling, David L. "A Federalist Opposes the Jay Treaty: The Letters of Samuel Bayard," *William and Mary Quarterly*, 18, 3d series (July 1961), 408–424.

Swindler, William F. "The Letters of Publius," *American Heritage*, 12 (June 1961), 4–7, 92–97.

Turner, Kathryn. "Federalist Policy and the Judiciary Act of 1801," *William and Mary Quarterly*, 22, 3d series (January 1965), 3–32.

part 4

Democracy for the Masses

chapter 11

The War of 1812

The Election of 1808

Even though the Republican party was weakened by the embargo controversy, it managed to muster enough strength to elect Jefferson's Secretary of State, James Madison, President in 1808. Madison garnered 122 electoral votes, while Charles C. Pinckney, the Federalist candidate, received 47. George Clinton, the governor of New York, was elected Vice-President. It was not a total loss for the Federalists, however, for they gained congressmen in both houses and were once again in control of New England, Vermont excepted.

MILITARY PREPAREDNESS

As the new President assumed his duties in 1809, America was ill-prepared to deal with the problems of French seizures and British impressments. Jefferson's embargo had failed, and other economic sanctions appeared to have had questionable value. As for military preparedness, the United States was still a second-rate power. Following Washington's advice, Jefferson had relied chiefly on non-involvement. The regulars, including the militia, numbered no more than 7000, and even those were led by retirement-age officers, many of whom had never seen combat. Furthermore, Jefferson had, with the exception of three frigates, reduced the navy to a fleet of small boats designed to guard the coastlines. Mobili-

zation was further handicapped because the Republicans had decided against rechartering the Bank of the United States, which was to expire in 1811. Worse still, at least for preparedness, war was unwanted in many sectors.

The British, though superior in numbers and resources, were not in an enviable position. Preoccupied with the Napoleonic wars in Europe, their commitment to the American theater was limited, whereas Canada, underpopulated and undefended by natural barriers, appeared to be a "sitting duck."

MACON'S BILL NO. 2

In May 1810, when the nonintercourse measure failed, Congress removed all restrictions on imports with the passage of Macon's Bill No. 2, in the hope that England and France would reciprocate. If either country repealed its offensive measures, the Nonintercourse Act would be renewed against the other nation. England was not overly impressed, although it has been suggested that Parliament was moving toward concessions.

The Emergence of the War Hawks

ELECTIONS OF 1810

The elections of 1810 sent to Congress a group of young westerners who had built a career on enmity toward England.

Among them were John C. Calhoun of South Carolina, Henry Clay of Kentucky, William Crawford of Georgia, Peter Porter of New York, and Felix Grundy of Tennessee. Convinced that the Canadian-based Englishmen were inciting the western Indians, that British maritime policy was damaging agrarian prosperity, and anxious to avenge any damage to national honor on the high seas, these "war hawks" called for immediate action against the British, particularly those in Canada.

TECUMSEH AND THE PROPHET

While Congress debated a course of action, events in the west moved in favor of the "war hawks." President Madison responded to petitions from settlers in West Florida by annexing that territory, and, in June 1811, the Shawnee Chief, Tecumseh, and his brother, the Prophet, responded to new white settlements on Indian lands by attempting to organize tribes in the northwest and south into an Indian Confederacy.[1] The plan was foiled when General William Henry Harrison was surprised by the Prophet's warriors[2] at Tippecanoe, but managed to turn defeat into victory.

On June 1, 1812, President Madison[3] asked for a declaration of war, and a divided Congress responded on June 18 with votes of 19 for and 13 against in the Senate, and 74 for and 49 against in the House.[4] Most of the votes for war came from the West, the South, Pennsylvania,

[1] The British were believed to be in support of the plan when English rifles were found in the hands of Indians.

[2] Tecumseh was in the south trying to win the support of the Creeks.

[3] Madison had won his second term in November of 1811 by a whopping 128 to 89 electoral count over De Witt Clinton. Madison had carried the pro-war South and West, while Clinton had taken New England and most of the mid-Atlantic states.

[4] Parliament voted to revoke her orders restricting American trade with France on June 16. This, of course, was unknown to Congress because of the slowness with which news traveled. The United States further added to the confusion by not having a minister in England.

and Vermont. The New England states, New Jersey, and New York, on the other hand, opposed the war for several reasons. These states, by and large, had long been friends to England, and they were not interested in Canada, which would only add congressional strength to the western states. They preferred instead to negotiate with the British in the hope of restoring the prosperous trade both countries once enjoyed.

The Land and Sea Engagements (1812–1813)

The United States prepared for the impending military action by deploying three volunteer armies under four generals. General William Hull advanced against Detroit in the west, while two commanders, Generals Stephen Van Rensselaer and Alexander Smyth prepared to assault Fort Niagara. Finally, General Henry Dearborn was to mastermind an invasion of Canada via Lake Champlain.

DETROIT AND FORT NIAGARA

The results of these first fall offensives were not impressive from the American point of view. On August 16, after occupying Detroit, General Hull overestimated the strength of the enemy and surrendered the fort along with his army to General Brock, the British commander, and Tecumseh, after a short bombardment. In October and November Generals Van Rensselaer and Smyth attacked the British at Fort Niagara. During a crucial battle, however, the militia under Van Rensselaer refused to cross into Canada, even to rescue an American army under heavy attack, and the drive failed.

MONTREAL

The last fall offensive fared no better. General Dearborn's bid to capture Montreal was frustrated when the New York militia in his command refused to leave the confines of their state. Fortunately for the Americans, the British were not yet prepared to launch an effective counter-attack, but they did manage to capture, in addition to Detroit, Fort Michilimackinac in Michigan and Fort Dearborn in Illinois.

CONSTITUTION AND UNITED STATES

The navy was the only bright spot in America's arsenal in 1812. The frigates *Constitution* and the *United States* distinguished themselves by destroying three British warships, the last battle of which won for the *Constitution* the name "Old Ironsides."

CHESAPEAKE

The first campaign of 1813 appeared to signal another series of disasters for the United States when General Harrison suffered a costly defeat at Frenchtown; and, in June of that same year, Captain James Lawrence lost his frigate, the *Chesapeake*,[5] in a duel with the *Shannon*. In September, however, Commodore Oliver Perry helped to turn the fortunes of battle when he met and defeated six enemy ships on Lake Erie. A week later General Harrison, with a new army, marched on Detroit only to find it deserted; whereupon, he pushed north toward Canada and met and defeated the British and their Indian allies at the Thames River. This crucial battle secured the Northwest for the United States. The remainder of the year was marked by desultory skirmishes, the final of which saw the British burn Buffalo on December 30.

CHIPPEWA PLAINS AND LUNDY'S LANE

Despite America's successes in 1813, Canada was still under British control, and, much to the distress of Washington, the English had defeated Napoleon. Now she would be ready for a full-scale invasion of the United States. The British plans called for a blockade of America's eastern and southern coasts, and for three major offensives: one at Niagara, a second along Lake Champlain, and a third at New Orleans. American Generals John Brown and Winfield Scott met the first Niagara expedition at Chippewa Plains and Lundy's Lane. The Americans, now under a new corps of young and energetic generals, stopped the first British invasion by winning the first battle and fighting to a standstill in the second. The second British expedition at Lake Champlain received a crippling blow on September 11 when Commodore Thomas Macdonough, with a squadron of fourteen ships, met and defeated a British naval squadron. The battle, one of the most significant of the war, secured the lake for the United States and helped to save the American position at Plattsburg. A week later the English bombarded Fort McHenry at Baltimore, but did little more than provide Francis Scott Key with a setting for a famous poem.

BATTLE OF NEW ORLEANS

The third British invasion of the United States was launched at New Orleans against the fully prepared defenses of Andrew Jackson. Jackson repulsed more than 7000 invaders in the battle of New Orleans (January 8, 1815), during which 2000 Englishmen were killed, including their commander, General Edward Pakenham. The Americans lost fewer than 100 men. The battle was obviously of no strategic importance,[6] but the victory made Jackson a national hero and set the stage for his advent into politics.

HARTFORD CONVENTION

As the last battle of the war raged, many of the New England Federalists remained

---

[5] It was during this battle that Lawrence coined the navy battle cry, "Don't give up the ship!"

[6] The Battle of New Orleans was fought about two weeks after the Peace of Ghent was signed.

faithfully defiant to the end. In fact, one group assembled at Hartford[7] (in secrecy) in December of 1814 to write a list of "grievances" and demands to be presented to the federal government. Anxious to regain the leadership of the nation, the Hartfordites called for constitutional amendments that would recognize states' rights: a two-thirds vote would be required of Congress to declare war,[8] impose an embargo on the country, and admit a new state; the President would be limited to one term; and slaves would not be counted in apportionment. It has been reported that some of the more radical elements of the convention even advocated secession and a separate peace with England.

Their hopes for success, however, were short-lived. The Hartford proposals arrived in Washington concurrently with the news of victory at New Orleans, and were soon lost in wild celebrations. It was the beginning of the end for the Federalist party.

TREATY OF GHENT

Meanwhile, the peace treaty had been signed on December 24, 1814. Negotiated at Ghent, Belgium, the Peace of Ghent simply terminated hostilities and provided for a commission to arbitrate the northeast boundary between the United States and Canada. The United States failed in her bid to get the neutral rights issue resolved, and England lost in her bids for the creation of an independent Indian state in the northeast and control of the Great Lakes. In short, the *status quo* was restored. If the worth of a treaty can be measured in its ability to salve over the ills of the day and otherwise placate both sides, the Peace of Ghent was highly successful. There was no victory, thus no reparations.

[7] A group of twenty-six, primarily from Connecticut, Massachusetts, and Rhode Island.

[8] These Federalists believed that the war was unconstitutional since a simple majority in Congress had carried the nation into the conflict.

If the war failed in its immediate objectives, it inadvertently helped America in the long run. The crisis provided President Madison with an occasion (with the aid of a plebiscite) to annex Spanish property in the south, and it forced American industry to go it alone since hostilities had cut off the usual imports from Great Britain. Much to the benefit of the common man, the war produced another western-oriented President whose influence on democracy is still being measured.

Select Bibliography

Adams, Henry. *History of the United States during the Administrations of Jefferson and Madison.* Ernest Samuels, ed. Chicago: University of Chicago Press, 1967.

Bemis, Samuel F. *John Quincy Adams and the Foundation of American Foreign Policy.* New York: Alfred A. Knopf, 1949.

Borden, Morton. *Parties and Politics in the Early Republic, 1789–1815.* New York: Thomas Y. Crowell Company, 1967.

Brant, Irving. *James Madison and American Nationalism.* New York: Van Nostrand Reinhold Company, 1968.

———. *James Madison: Commander in Chief, 1812–1836.* Indianapolis, Ind.: The Bobbs-Merrill Co., Inc., 1961.

———. *James Madison: President.* Indianapolis, Ind.: The Bobbs-Merrill Co., Inc., 1956.

Brown, Robert H. *The Republic in Peril: 1812.* New York: Columbia University Press, 1964.

Burt, Alfred L. *The United States, Great Britain, and British North America from the Revolution to the Peace after the War of 1812.* New York: Russell & Russell, Publishers, 1961.

Coles, Harry L. *The War of 1812.* Chicago: University of Chicago Press, 1965.

Current, Richard N. *Daniel Webster and the Rise of National Conservatism.* Boston: Little, Brown and Company, 1955.

Eaton, Clement. *Henry Clay and the Art of American Politics.* Boston: Little, Brown and Company, 1957.

Engelmann, Fred L. *The Peace of Christmas Eve.* New York: Harcourt Brace Jovanovich, Inc., 1962.

Forester, Cecil S. *The Age of Fighting Sail.* New York: Doubleday & Company, Inc., 1956.

Hitsman, J. Macksay. *The Incredible War of 1812.* Toronto, Canada: University of Toronto Press, 1965.

Horsman, Reginald. *The Causes of the War of 1812.* Philadelphia: University of Pennsylvania Press, 1962.

James, Marquis. *Andrew Jackson: The Border Captain.* Indianapolis, Ind.: The Bobbs-Merrill Co., Inc., 1933.

Labaree, Benjamin W. *Patriots and Partisans: The Merchants of Newburyport, 1764–1815.* Cambridge, Mass.: Harvard University Press, 1962.

Mahan, Alfred T. *Sea Power in Its Relation to the War of 1812.* 2 vols. London: S. Low, Marston & Co., Ltd., 1905.

Mayo, Bernard. *Henry Clay: Spokesman of the New West.* Boston: Houghton Mifflin Company, 1937.

Nettels, Curtis P. *The Emergence of a National Economy, 1775–1815.* New York: Harper & Row, Publishers, 1969.

Perkins, Bradford. *Castlereagh and Adams: England and the United States, 1812–1823.* Berkeley, Calif.: University of California Press, 1964.

————, ed. *The Causes of the War of 1812.* New York: Holt, Rinehart and Winston, Inc., 1962.

————. *Prologue to War: England and the United States, 1805–1812.* Berkeley, Calif.: University of California Press, 1961.

Pratt, Julius W. *Expansionists of 1812.* Gloucester, Mass.: Peter Smith, 1957.

Sears, Louis M. *Jefferson and the Embargo.* Durham, N.C.: Duke University Press, 1927.

Taylor, George R., ed. *The War of 1812: Past Justification and Present Interpretation.* Boston: D. C. Heath & Company, 1963.

Tucker, Glenn. *Poltroons and Patriots.* 2 vols. Indianapolis, Ind.: The Bobbs-Merrill Co., Inc., 1954.

Weigley, Russell F. *History of the United States Army.* New York: Crowell Collier and Macmillan, Inc., 1967.

White, Patrick T. *A Nation on Trial: America and the War of 1812.* New York: John Wiley & Sons, Inc., 1965.

Wiltse, Charles M. *John C. Calhoun.* New York: Russell & Russell, Publishers, 1968.

Wood, William. *The War with the United States.* Toronto, Canada: Glasgow, Brook & Co., 1922.

chapter 12

Isolationism
and Nationalism

Recovery

America was ready for the blessings of peace in 1815. Although she had gained little from the Treaty of Ghent, she had given up nothing, and many people therefore assumed that the United States had won the war. Thus it was believed that the young giant could rest in splendid isolation and prosperity now that she had proved herself a world power. Accordingly, President Madison tried to deliver both, even if it meant departing from traditional Jeffersonian principles.

AMERICAN SYSTEM

Grounded to internal improvements, and with Henry Clay as the chief architect, the new plan, or American System, asked for a stronger defense, tariff protection for new manufacturers, and improved transportation through the construction of new roads and canals. It also urged the creation of a new national bank, which was believed necessary in order to restore faith in the dollar and check inflation.

TARIFF OF 1816

Foremost among these priority items was the protective tariff for infant businesses. Although they had been spared by the war and had prospered while it lasted, many found themselves hard pressed to compete in the open market after the peace treaty ended the conflict, and parti-

cularly with the British, who had flooded the market with inexpensive goods. They therefore called for an upward revision of the tariff, and Congress responded in 1816 by passing a tariff that placed 25 percent duties on woolen and cotton goods, while the tariff on iron products was elevated to 30 percent. The new duties were designed to protect home manufacturing, and they did just that—industry soon showed signs of recovery. Thus the War of 1812 taught the young republic the value of economic independence.

In the meantime, the question of the bank came before Congress, and in 1816, with the endorsement of Clay and Calhoun (note that Clay had reversed his position on the bank since 1811), it was given a twenty-year charter.

BONUS BILL

The transportation bill, better known as the "Bonus bill,"[1] hit a snag. After finally winning the approval of Congress over the opposition of New England, where it was viewed as politically dangerous to their power in Congress since it would inevitably usher in new western states, the measure was vetoed by Madison. The President said he doubted its constitutionality. Consequently the problem of transportation was turned back to the various states, many of which lacked the

---

[1] An annual bonus paid by the national bank to the Treasury.

will and resources to handle it; a few like New York, on the other hand, demonstrated remarkable ability and willingness in accepting the challenge. The Erie Canal, completed in 1825, linked Albany and Buffalo, and over the years stood as a constant reminder of the progress that might come to a state through local initiative.

New Nationalism

JOHN MARSHALL

The nationalist upsurge after the war found its most ardent champion in Chief Justice John Marshall. Dominating the judicial branch of government, this astute Virginian handed down nationalistic measures for thirty-four years. He was a Federalist by appointment and by persuasion, and remained true to his colors while others deserted to the Republican camp.

JUDICIAL REVIEW

Soon after taking office Marshall established the doctrine of judicial supremacy over the other branches of government by declaring an act of Congress unconstitutional in *Marbury* v. *Madison* (1803). He also emphasized the supremacy of the federal government over the states by voiding a measure passed by the Georgia legislature. In the case of *Fletcher* v. *Peck* (1810) he reminded Georgia that contracts were "sacred and inviolable" when he refused to let that state break a contract with the Yazoo land companies. This lesson was repeated in 1819, when in *Dartmouth College* v. *Woodward* Marshall refused to sanction any altering of the college charter in order to put the institution under state control.

JUDICIAL REVIEW
OVER STATE COURTS

Finally, three notable cases helped Marshall establish the supremacy of the Supreme Court over state courts. In *Martin* v. *Hunter's Lessee* (1816) he upheld the Judiciary Act of 1789, which granted the Supreme Court the right to overrule state courts, and in *McCulloch* v. *Maryland* (1819) he denied the right of Maryland to tax the Bank of the United States, reserving this power for the federal Congress under the "implied powers" doctrine. The third case involved an attempted steamboat monopoly on the Hudson River. When the practice was challenged, Marshall ruled in *Gibbons* v. *Ogden* (1824) that the regulation of interstate commerce was reserved for Congress under the "commerce clause" of the Constitution. Thus while relying upon the loose construction doctrine in interpreting the Constitution, he had strengthened the old Federalist doctrine of centralism, which, we might add parenthetically, was now also embraced by Republican supporters of the American System.

Marshall's Court decisions, including the lesser and unpopular ones, had far-reaching implications in the history of American constitutional law. If he appeared to be preoccupied with property rights and federal supremacy, it has been suggested that the young and vigorous nation, with a property-minded citizenry, needed both.

Enter Another Virginian

ELECTION OF 1816

The third Virginian in succession entered the White House in 1816 when James Monroe defeated the Federalist candidate, Senator Rufus King of New York. Handpicked by Madison and a close friend of Jefferson, Monroe won decisively with an electoral margin of 183 to 34.[2] By the time he reached the presidency, Monroe's distinguished career had been highlighted by service with the Virginia assembly, the Confederation Congress, and the United States Senate;

---

[2] Daniel D. Tompkins became the Vice-President

he had served as both Secretary of State and Secretary of War.

Monroe's cabinet was headed by the capable John Quincy Adams (son of the former President), for geographical reasons, while William H. Crawford and John C. Calhoun assumed the offices of Secretary of the Treasury and Secretary of War, respectively. For Attorney General he picked William Wirt. It has been described as the most impressive assemblage of talent since Washington's cabinet.

PANIC OF 1819

Mainly because of the absence of an opposition party, Monroe's tenure of office has been called the "era of good feeling." The hard times, however, belie the label. The Panic of 1819 was one of the most serious internal crises the young republic had faced. As a result of overspeculation in western lands, among other things, banks were forced to close, while debtors' prisons were hard pressed to handle the crowds. Particularly hard hit were the easy credit "wildcat" banks of the West, when the Second Bank of the United States suddenly demanded that these state banks pay off their notes in specie. The concomitant evils of mortgage foreclosures sent the westerners into a rage over the "arbitrary" actions of the money lenders of the East; demands were made for federal action against the hated bank of the East and for an immediate solution of the land problem. Once again sectionalism had raised its ugly head.

LAND ACT OF 1820

The western complaints were responsible, in part, for the reorganization of the bank, and for the initiation of a new land act. This Land Act of 1820 reduced the purchasable plots to 80 acres and set the minimum price at $1.25 per acre in cash.[3]

The extent to which the country was divided was further illustrated when the Northeast attempted to get an upward revision of the tariff laws in order to protect its manufacturers. The West and South would have no part of it.

The Missouri Compromise

Sectional tensions reached a new high when Missouri applied for statehood in 1819. Having secured the necessary population to qualify for statehood, a group of Missouri settlers petitioned to join the Union along with Alabama. No serious obstacles were anticipated until Representative James Tallmadge (N.Y.) requested that the bill be amended to close Missouri's borders to slave traffic and to free all those born into bondage in the state just as soon as they reached their twenty-first birthday.

The southern states viewed this move as another attempt of the northern states to dominate Congress and to ultimately destroy the institution of slavery in the South. If passed, the bill, they felt, might very well be used against other slaveholding states. The compromise bill that finally appeased both warring factions permitted Missouri to enter as a slave state, but Maine was also admitted, as a free state, in order to maintain the balance in the Senate.[4] The decision, however favorable it may have looked to either side, was only a reprieve, as Jefferson described it, from more portentous things to come.

Monroe Doctrine

The era's most significant statement in foreign affairs came on December 2, 1823, when President Monroe[5] issued his fa-

[4] There were at the time eleven free states and eleven slave states.

[5] Monroe had run unopposed in the 1820 election. Tompkins was also retained as the Vice-President.

[3] The Land Act of 1804 called for 160 acres at $2 per acre.

mous Monroe Doctrine. Couched in shades of isolationism and nationalism, it reminded Great Britain and the other European powers that (1) "the American continents . . . are not to be considered as subjects for future colonization by any European powers . . . We should consider any attempt on their part to extend their system to any portion of this hemisphere as dangerous to our peace and safety. With existing colonies . . . we . . . shall not interfere. (2) In the wars of the European powers in matters relating to themselves . . . it does not comport with our policy [to interfere]."

RUSH-BAGOT AGREEMENT

A long series of disputes and arrangements, some of which were amicably resolved between Great Britain and the United States, led to the final pronouncement by Monroe. It was not until 1817, for example, that the Rush-Bagot Agreement finally settled the question of warships on the Great Lakes. By its terms neither the United States nor Great Britain could maintain war frigates on those waters.

ANGLO-AMERICAN
CONVENTION OF 1818

During the ensuing year the Anglo-American Convention fixed the long-disputed northern boundary[6] at the 49th parallel that was to extend to the Rocky Mountains but no farther. Beyond lay the valuable Oregon country, which, according to the signatories, was to be jointly occupied by the two powers for a period of ten years.

FLORIDA CRISIS

In the meantime, American interest in the acquisition of Florida continued to mount. It was the only southern territory

[6] The Maine boundary continued to be disputed until 1842.

east of the Mississippi River not in United States possession. Accordingly, expansionists were pleased in 1817 when a crisis arose over the control of hostile Florida-based Indians who had been raiding American settlements across the border. Empowered with secret orders to pursue the Seminoles into Florida, and with tacit approval to conquer all of the peninsula if the opportunity presented itself, General Andrew Jackson marched his volunteers across the border, seized two Spanish posts, and executed two Britons who were suspected of being Indian agitators; whereupon Spain terminated preliminary negotiations for the sale of Florida and asked that Jackson be punished.

In the heated cabinet debates that followed, Secretary of War Calhoun led the opposition, while Secretary of State Adams supported the general. The cabinet finally reached a compromise that returned the posts of Pensacola and St. Marks to Spain, but Adams warned that further irritations from Florida could produce more invasions unless Spain sold the territory to the United States. The compromise proved to be unpopular with the American public, mainly because Jackson was still remembered as the hero of the War of 1812.

ADAMS-ONÍS TREATY

Faced with mounting hostility in the United States, Spain decided to sell while she was still in a position to negotiate. The Adams-Onís Treaty was signed in 1819 and was finally ratified in 1821. By its terms, Spain agreed to sell the whole of Florida to the United States for $5 million, the total of which was then paid to United States citizens who had damage claims against the Spanish government. The United States in return renounced all claims to Texas, and a boundary line was fixed between the two powers that extended to the Pacific.

Before the Monroe Doctrine was announced, the United States had also observed Russia's growing interest in the Oregon Territory. The czar had not only planted a colony in Alaska, but announced in 1821 that Russia's claims extended to the 51st parallel in the northwest, and that she intended to protect it. Secretary of State Adams was more alarmed than the President and, in the same year, announced his first noncolonization declaration. It later became part of the Monroe Doctrine.

At its early inception, the spirit of the Monroe Doctrine was to be included in a joint resolution between Great Britain and the United States (it was initiated by British Foreign Secretary George Canning) but Adams, distrusting the British, pursued a course contrary to that of his President and most of his advisers and rejected the offer. It has been suggested by scholars in diplomatic history that Canning wanted to commit the United States to a nonaggression policy in the New World in order to protect British interests. Moreover, it has also been observed that the Americans needed no alliance with Great Britain since the British fleet was already committed to the defense of the New World in the act of defending her own Caribbean possessions. Clinging stubbornly to this brand of shrewd statesmanship, Adams convinced the President of its soundness, and the Monroe Doctrine was drafted on only one side of the Atlantic.

WORLD REACTION
TO THE MONROE DOCTRINE

The monarchs of Europe raised eyebrows at so bold a declaration by the young upstart republic, while Canning was deeply distressed, knowing well that the doctrine was also directed at expansionist-minded Great Britain.

Governments in Latin America gave the pronouncement a cool reception. Realizing that Great Britain had more to offer them, economically speaking, than

did the United States, and that their real safety, in the final analysis, rested with the British imperial navy, they decided to court the lesser of the two evils. Besides, many Latin American republics were governed by military dictators who felt no close affinity to American democracy.

Select Bibliography

Bemis, Samuel F. *John Quincy Adams and the Union.* New York: Alfred A. Knopf, 1956.

Billington, Ray A. *America's Frontier Heritage.* New York: Holt, Rinehart and Winston, Inc., 1966.

_____. *The Protestant Crusade, 1800–1860.* Chicago: Quadrangle Books, Inc., 1964.

_____. *A Study of the Origins of American Nativism.* New York: Holt, Rinehart and Winston, Inc., 1952.

_____. *Westward Expansion,* rev. ed. New York: Crowell Collier and Macmillan, Inc., 1967.

Carpenter, Jesse. *The South as a Conscious Minority, 1789–1861.* Gloucester, Mass.: Peter Smith, 1930.

Corwin, Edward S. *John Marshall and the Constitution.* New York: United States Publishers Association, Inc., 1919.

Cresson, William P. *James Monroe.* Chapel Hill, N.C.: University of North Carolina Press, 1946.

Dangerfield, George. *The Awakening of American Nationalism, 1815–1828.* New York: Harper & Row, Publishers, 1965.

Hacker, Louis M. *The Triumph of American Capitalism.* New York: McGraw-Hill Book Company, 1940.

Haines, Charles G. *The Role of the Supreme Court in American Govern-*

ment and Politics, 1789–1835. New York: Russell & Russell, Publishers, 1960.

Hammond, Bray. Banks and Politics in America from the Revolution to the Civil War. Princeton, N.J.: Princeton University Press, 1957.

Hibbard, B. H. A History of the Public Land Policies. Gloucester, Mass.: Peter Smith, 1924.

Hill, Charles E. Leading American Treaties. New York: AMS Press, Inc., 1969.

Hunter, Louis C. Steamboats on the Western Rivers. New York: Octagon Books, Inc., 1949.

Moore, Glover. The Missouri Controversy. Gloucester, Mass.: Peter Smith, 1953.

Morgan, Donald G. Justice William Johnson, the First Dissenter: The Career and Constitutional History of a Jeffersonian Judge. Columbia, S.C.: University of South Carolina Press, 1969.

Morison, Samuel E. Harrison Gray Otis, 1765–1848. Boston: Houghton Mifflin Company, 1969.

Nagel, Paul C. One Nation Indivisible: The American Thought, 1776–1861. New York: Oxford University Press, 1964.

Perkins, Bradford. Castlereagh and Adams: England and the United States, 1812–1823. Berkeley, Calif.: University of California Press, 1964.

Perkins, Dexter. A History of the Monroe Doctrine, 2d ed. Boston: Little, Brown and Company, 1955.

Rappaport, Armin. A History of the Monroe Doctrine. New York: Holt, Rinehart and Winston, Inc., 1964.

Risjord, Norman K. The Old Republicans: Southern Conservatism in the Age of Jefferson. New York: Columbia University Press, 1965.

Robbins, Roy M. Our Landed Heritage: The Public Domain, 1776–1936. Gloucester, Mass.: Peter Smith, 1942.

Rothbard, Murray N. The Panic of 1819, Reactions and Policies. New York: AMS Press, Inc., 1962.

Sakolski, Aaron M. The Great American Land Bubble: The Amazing Story of Land-Grabbing, Speculations, and Booms from Colonial Days to the Present Time. New York: Johnson Reprint Corporation, 1932.

Somkin, Fred. Unquiet Eagle: Memory and Desire in the Idea of American Freedom, 1815–1860. Ithaca, N.Y.: Cornell University Press, 1967.

Tatum, Jr., Edward H. The United States and Europe, 1815–1823: A Study in the Background of the Monroe Doctrine. New York: Russell & Russell, Publishers, 1967.

Turner, Frederick J. The Frontier in American History. Gloucester, Mass.: Peter Smith, 1920.

———. The Rise of the New West, 1819–1829. New York: Crowell Collier and Macmillan, Inc., 1962.

Van Deusen, Glyndon G. The Life of Henry Clay. Boston: Little, Brown & Company, 1937.

Whitaker, Arthur P. The United States and the Independence of Latin America, 1800–1830. New York: W. W. Norton & Company, 1964.

Wright, Benjamin F. The Contract Clause of the Constitution. Cambridge, Mass.: Harvard University Press, 1938.

chapter 13

The Emergence of Jacksonian Democracy

The Adams Interlude

ELECTION OF 1824

The political campaigns of 1824 proved to be another of those crowded affairs with five capable candidates in the offering. Political parties, as such, were not as significant in this presidential foray as they had been in the past—the Federalist party had succumbed to a natural death at the Hartford Convention, and when the Democratic-Republican party was unable to decide on a successor to Monroe, all five of the candidates in 1824 unfurled the Democratic-Republican banner.

Secretary of the Treasury William Crawford of Georgia was recommended by President Monroe, while Andrew Jackson was selected as Tennessee's favorite son. Kentucky, meanwhile, honored Henry Clay with an endorsement, South Carolina did the same for John Calhoun, and New England advanced John Q. Adams. Since political platforms were just as perplexing to the voting public (all of the candidates subscribed to nationalism, some perhaps more than others, and all stood on common ground with regard to tariff issues and other domestic reforms), it appeared that Crawford might be considered the favorite. A stroke, however, removed him from the race early in the campaign. Thus, the remaining four had little more than their records and personal attraction to win votes, and the

results offer proof that none were overwhelmingly popular. Jackson collected 99 electoral votes, Adams 84, Crawford 41, and Clay 37. Calhoun withdrew from the race in order to concentrate on the vice-presidency, which he won with 182 electoral ballots. Since no candidate had received a clear majority, the Constitution provided for settlement in the House of Representatives, where the states would choose from among the top three.

The powerful House Speaker Henry Clay now held the election of the next President firmly in his hands; and since Adams appeared to be closer to his philosophy as expressed in his "American System," the result was never in doubt. Clay was promptly named Secretary of State, which brought forth the charge of "corrupt bargain" from the camp of Jackson. Politically shaken, but not beyond recovery, the Jacksonians were to keep this issue alive for the election of 1828.

ADAMS' PROBLEMS

President Adams began his office with a great deal of experience but not much capability. The son of a former President, a diplomat, and a Secretary of State, his record promised great success—at least in foreign affairs. However well meaning to all sections of the country Adams may have been, several factors tended to doom his programs from the start. In the first place, he was highly independent and, it has been reported, aloof and tactless—

hardly traits for the chief executive; but, at the same time, he also manifested a deep concern for the rights of conscience and championed the abolitionist movement.

Second, he was a minority President who was, in the eyes of the opposition, indebted to Clay; and during his four years in office, Adams continued to support Clay's national program for internal reforms, such as road and canal construction and exploration of the interior. He even advocated, among other things, a national university and the advancement of the arts, sciences, and literature, the first of which aroused the enmity of states' righters.

Third, his western land and Indian policies further alienated the frontiersmen when he attempted to curb land speculators, who were opening up the West, and when he tried to give the Five Civilized Tribes a fair deal. In the latter case, congressional pressure finally forced him to agree to Indian removal, but not until he revoked the scandalous Treaty of Indian Springs (which was signed with only a faction of the tribe and provided that the Creeks cede all of their lands and leave for the Far West by September 1, 1826). The new treaty promised greater rewards, and the departure date was moved to January 1827.

Fourth, the President, unlike his predecessors, scoffed at the practice of patronage and insisted on competence as a prerequisite for office seekers.[1] This philosophy, unfortunately for Adams, was not in keeping with party rules, and the new President had the unenviable task of working with an unsympathetic Congress.

TARIFF OF ABOMINATIONS

Adams, it seemed, could do little that was right in domestic affairs. In 1828 the passage of a high tariff sent his image to an all-time low. A measure in 1824 had raised the duties on such items as iron, lead, hemp, wool, and textiles, much to the pleasure of the East and the West; but when the Jacksonians attempted to pass another tariff that was unacceptable to New England by tacking on amendments, and in the process to discredit the President, the middle states joined unexpected support from the West in securing its passage.

Known as the Tariff of Abominations, the measure pleased few in the final analysis and brought cries of protest from the South. Southerners resented the predicament in which they were placed. They had the choice of buying imported goods from Europe at inflated prices (because of the tariff), or they could pay a few cents less and purchase northern manufactured wares. Thus, many southerners felt that New England manufacturers were forcing the South to support their system, which all too frequently turned out wares inferior to those of Europe.

So strong was the resentment in some quarters that the South Carolina legislature, viewing the tariff as an impingement on states' rights, called for states to denounce the measure as unconstitutional and therefore null and void in their ports.

It has been observed that the election of Carolina-born Andrew Jackson[2] as President in 1828 soothed the wounds of South Carolinians and possibly saved the Union from a more serious crisis.

Foreign Affairs

The United States was offered an opportunity to extend a hand of friendship and cooperation to the republics of Latin America in 1826, but Congress again obstructed the will of the President by refusing to send delegates to the Panamanian Conference until procedural matters had been agreed upon.[3] By that time,

---

[1] Adams retained much of Monroe's cabinet, removing only twelve men from federal offices during his tenure.

[2] Vice-President Calhoun was also a South Carolinian.

[3] Adams had acted without consulting the Senate.

they were too late to be effective. Adams had no better luck in attempting to renew trade ties with the British West Indies, but he did manage to negotiate several other instruments of commerce.

ELECTION OF 1828

Adams' bid for a second term produced one of the most heated presidential contests in the nineteenth century. The Jacksonians were well prepared. Shifting their political machine into high gear, they reminded the country of the "corrupt bargain," which they had never let rest since the 1824 election. The Adamsites (National Republicans),[4] on the other hand, and without the President's consent, charged Jackson with adultery.[5] To many westerners and southerners, however, it was a contest between the moneyed interests and machine politics of the Northeast on the one hand and the farmers and states' righters on the other.

It has been reported that all of the mudslinging probably had little effect on the outcome of the election. Jackson won with an electoral vote of 178 to 83 for Adams, while the popular vote was considerably closer at 647,286 to 508,064. Records of the election show that support for "Old Hickory" came from all the main sections of the country except New England, and even there he pulled a considerable number of votes from the dock and factory workers in the seaboard states.

Up from Modest Beginnings

Andrew Jackson was born in South Carolina in 1767 to a Scotch-Irish family of

modest means. When he was twenty-one he moved to Nashville, Tennessee, where he speculated in land and studied law and became that state's first representative in Congress when it was admitted to the Union. He later became a senator, only to leave that position after a short stay in order to pursue a law practice and a quiet life on his plantation, The Hermitage. The War of 1812, with his victory at New Orleans, thrust Jackson back into the limelight. A subsequent invasion of Florida helped to mark him as a daring hero destined for high public office.

It has been written that Jackson could be as harsh and boisterous as the frontier from which he came, or that he could reveal a warm heart and a charisma that won for him the love of many. He was quick-tempered and obedient to the code of honor so common on the frontier, and a few paid the supreme price in testing that code.

The Significance of the Election of 1828

THE POSITIVE LEGACY

The election of Andrew Jackson was in many ways a victory for the broadening base of democracy in the United States. To many, he was the very embodiment of the spirit of the American Revolution— "the people's right to govern themselves." Some students of the period have even suggested that it was a class victory and a second revolution of opportunity. Thus, Jackson was not a founder but a representative, a student of the new democratic enlightenment, and, in part, a protégé of Jefferson.

Jackson interpreted, with surprising accuracy, the democratic trend that had been manifesting itself during the first three decades of the nineteenth century, and particularly its impulse in the 1820s. Realizing that the people were dissatisfied with the National Republicans' policies with regard to western land, banks, and tariffs, he offered the western farmers

---

[4] The Republicans had split into two camps during the presidency of Adams. The National Republicans supported Adams and Clay, while the Democratic-Republicans cast their lot with Jackson, Calhoun, and Crawford. The National Republicans became the Whigs during the 1830s.

[5] Jackson and Rachael Robards, thinking that her divorce from a previous husband had been granted, were married in 1791.

and the eastern factory laborers an opportunity to elect one of their own kind—he offered them a government by and for the "common man," with the chief executive as their direct representative. Many responded as evinced by the increase in the number of voters from 1824 to 1828: 355,000 went to the polls in the former and 1,155,000 in the latter. This increasing awareness of mass participation in the political process also helped to terminate the old method of nominating the candidates by a congressional caucus and ushered in the first national nominating convention in 1831.

THE NEGATIVE LEGACY

On the negative side, whereas Jackson was the first to be elected from the new West and the first self-made President, many people began to feel that little, if any, training was necessary in order to enter politics as long as the candidate served their interests.

Jackson disagreed with Jefferson on several significant points. He called for immediate change, while Jefferson subscribed to gradual change through the political and legal processes. The latter was also aristocratic in many respects and weighed the ability of the common man in the light of his education.

To some, the election of Jackson signaled the triumph of "King Mob," and they warned that he had opened the door for the admission of the worst elements of the people, the rule of an ignorant and incapable democracy. They thought republican institutions were threatened with the very gravest danger and would not have been surprised to see them completely subverted.

Select Bibliography

Abernethy, Thomas P. *From Frontier to Plantation in Tennessee.* University, Ala.: University of Alabama Press, 1967.

Bemis, Samuel F. *John Quincy Adams and the Union.* New York: Alfred A. Knopf, 1949.

Capers, Gerald M. *John C. Calhoun, Opportunist.* Gainesville, Fla.: University of Florida Press, 1960.

Dangerfield, George. *The Era of Good Feelings.* New York: Harcourt Brace Jovanovich, Inc., 1952.

Freehling, William W. *Prelude to Civil War: The Nullification Controversy in South Carolina, 1816–1836.* New York: Harper & Row, Publishers, 1966.

Fuess, Claude M. *Daniel Webster.* 2 vols. New York: Plenum Publishing Corporation, 1968.

Lipsky, George A. *John Quincy Adams, His Theory and Ideas.* New York: Apollo Editions, Inc., 1950.

Livermore, Jr., Shaw. *The Twilight of Federalism: The Disintegration of the Federalist Party, 1815–1830.* Princeton, N.J.: Princeton University Press, 1962.

McCormick, Richard P. *The Second American Party System: Party Formation in the Jacksonian Era.* Chapel Hill, N.C.: University of North Carolina Press, 1966.

Marquis, James. *Andrew Jackson.* 2 vols. Indianapolis, Ind.: The Bobbs-Merrill Co., Inc., 1938.

Nevins, Allan, ed. *The Diary of John Quincy Adams.* New York: Frederick Ungar Publishing Co., Inc., 1969.

Remini, Robert V. *Martin Van Buren and the Making of the Democratic Party.* New York: Columbia University Press, 1959.

Syndor, Charles S. *The Development of Southern Sectionalism, 1819–1848.* Baton Rouge, La.: Louisiana State University Press, 1948.

Van Deusen, Glyndon G. *Life of Henry Clay.* Boston: Little, Brown and Company, 1937.

Williamson, Chilton. *American Suffrage, from Property to Democracy, 1760–1860*. Princeton, N.J.: Princeton University Press, 1960.

Wiltse, Charles M. *John C. Calhoun*. 3 vols. Indianapolis, Ind.: The Bobbs-Merrill Co., Inc., 1944–1951.

chapter 14

Jacksonian Democracy at High Tide

Jackson's First Administration

SPOILS SYSTEM

After a rousing and sometimes rowdy[1] inaugural, Jackson began cleaning out the cabinet in order to make room for his own "Jackson men." Adams had discharged only two, and the practice had been to remove officeholders only for incompetence, but the new President looked upon the task as part and parcel of the reforms needed to cleanse the government of all the old "corrupt" officials who had not been elected or appointed, either directly or indirectly, by the people. To Jackson's way of thinking, all of those appointed by the "illegitimate" Adams administration were subject to dismissal; and before he was through, about nine hundred federal officeholders were turned out, and by 1831 all of the cabinet was replaced by loyal partisans, sometimes irrespective of competence. Attracting the label of "spoils system," this practice, though new to the President's office, was not unknown on local levels. In fact, some state governors had used it with considerable regularity.

[1] It has been reported that people rushed to the White House, upset tubs of punch, and stood with muddy boots on fine furniture. They were finally diverted to the lawns when the punch was moved outside.

KITCHEN CABINET

The most notable among Jackson's new cabinet members were Martin Van Buren of New York, who became Secretary of State, Samuel D. Ingham of Pennsylvania, who was picked to be Secretary of the Treasury, and John H. Eaton of Tennessee, who was appointed Secretary of War. Despite its acclaimed capabilities, the cabinet was destined to play a minor role in advising the President on really important issues. Jackson preferred to look instead to a small group of close friends in and around Washington with whom he felt he had more in common. Dubbed the "Kitchen Cabinet," because of their relatively low stations, this quasi-official group was led by Van Buren and included, among others, Major William B. Lewis of Tennessee, Amos Kendall, fourth auditor of the Treasury, Francis P. Blair, Sr., editor of the *Washington Globe,* and Duff Green, editor of the Jacksonian paper, the *Telegraph.*

PEGGY O'NEALE AFFAIR

A full-scale purge of Calhoun's friends in the cabinet occurred in 1831 when the Peggy O'Neale affair divided Jackson's advisers. Secretary of War John Eaton had married Peggy after her first husband died, but because of her popularity with the men around the social circles, Mrs.

Calhoun and several cabinet members refused her company. Jackson, whose own marriage had not gone untouched by scandalous rumors and snobbery, joined Van Buren in an effort to force the social acceptance of Mrs. Eaton. So bitter were the feelings over the affair that Van Buren and Eaton finally resigned, and the President dismissed the remainder of the cabinet early in 1831.

JACKSON-CALHOUN FEUD

Jackson and Calhoun parted company in 1832 after the Vice-President had crystallized his doctrine of state sovereignty in the Webster-Hayne debates and had taken an active stand against the new tariff bill of that year. Perhaps the South's most astute political thinker, Calhoun opposed any force that might destroy the Union, but he also believed that a state had the right to temporarily obstruct the enforcement of a federal law if that law appeared to be unjust to the state. He announced that each state was wholly sovereign, and that the Constitution was merely an agreement among sovereign states; that each state of the Union was not subject to the Constitution as a superior law, but retained the right to govern itself as it so preferred. It naturally followed that if a state had all of these powers of sovereignty, it might also have the right to withdraw from the Union if and when it felt the Constitution had been violated or had been misinterpreted.[2]

WEBSTER-HAYNE DEBATES

In the 1830s Senator Robert Y. Hayne of South Carolina forcefully defended Calhoun's doctrine in the Senate; he was ably challenged by Daniel Webster, who used the substance of Chief Justice Marshall's tract on the nature of the Union. One of the most eloquent speakers ever to stand before the Senate, Webster maintained that the Constitution was a law and not a mere agreement; that it had the force of law, and was binding on each and every member state; and that each state could not at will interpret the Constitution to suit its interests and needs. Nullification, he said, is nothing but interstate anarchy.

TARIFF OF 1832

The Tariff of 1832 provided Calhoun with the opportunity for the supreme test of his doctrine. Even though the tariff was more moderate than the one of 1828, South Carolina felt offended and prepared for a protest. Under the direction of Calhoun, who had resigned as Vice-President to accept the Senate seat vacated by Hayne,[3] a convention was called in November at which the tariff was declared null and void within the state.

Jackson, visibly upset, replied on December 10 with his stern Nullification Proclamation: "I consider . . . the power to annul a law of the United States, assumed by one State, . . . inconsistent with every principle on which it [the Union] was founded. . . ."

FORCE ACT

During the month of February 1833, the Senate passed the Force Act, which gave the President[4] power to use the army and navy should South Carolina resist federal authority. Meanwhile, as this bill was

---

[2] It should be noted that Calhoun was an ardent nationalist before the 1820s, but as the economic fortunes of the South declined he became more and more a states' rights champion.

[3] Senator Hayne gave up his Senate seat in order to become governor of South Carolina.

[4] The presidential election of 1832 had given Jackson a landslide victory over Clay in the electoral college (219 to 49). Van Buren became the new Vice-President. More innovative than most, the election had also produced the country's first third party, the Anti-Masons, which in turn had introduced the first national nominating convention in September 1831.

being debated, Henry Clay called for a compromise tariff that would provide for a gradual lowering of the offensive duties to a minimum of 20 percent by 1842. Finding the compromise at least tolerable, South Carolina accepted the bill the following month, but got in the last word by declaring the Force Act null and void.

The Question
of Indians and Land

INDIAN REMOVAL

Expansion was in full blossom when Jackson became President, and the West felt that he was just the man to put the "red savage" in his place—his place being somewhere west of the Mississippi River. Although the policy of peaceful persuasion had been used by Adams, the discovery of gold in Cherokee holdings meant an early removal of that tribe by any expedient means. By passing legislation that provided that all state laws applied to Indians (at the same time they were denied the right to be a court witness where a white man was involved), Georgia was able to all but destroy the tribal government on which the Cherokee depended. In this fashion the door was thrown open for the wholesale exploitation of the red man. The Cherokee nation promptly appealed to Washington, and Congress replied with a Removal Bill, passed in May of 1830, that empowered the President to remove any tribe by any means necessary.

CHEROKEE NATION v. GEORGIA

Pressed to the wall, the Cherokees carried their complaints to the Supreme Court, where in the case of the *Cherokee Nation* v. *Georgia*, the Court denied their earlier status of a nation within a nation, and thus refused to hear their case.

WORCESTER v. GEORGIA

A final gesture to spare the red man some quarter was made by Chief Justice John Marshall in the case of *Worcester* v. *Georgia*, when he declared the Cherokees a "domestic dependent nation" with a natural right to federal protection. Accordingly, Georgia had no jurisdiction over the tribe and therefore no right to their lands. When word of this ruling reached the desk of the President, Jackson is reported to have said, "John Marshall has made his decision; now let him enforce it."

TREATY OF NEW ECHOTA

In December 1835 the infamous Treaty of New Echota was signed with a faction of Cherokees led by Chief Major Ridge. It ceded all Cherokee lands east of the Mississippi River to the United States in return for $5 million plus reimbursement for their improvements, and free transportation to their new homes in the West. Distraught with the fraudulent treaty, many Cherokees resisted for almost three years before they were finally driven over the "trail of tears," on which almost a quarter of the tribe perished.

The Creeks experienced a similar fate in 1833, but the pesky Sauk and Fox of Illinois, under the leadership of Chief Black Hawk, resorted to violence in a determined resistance. The Seminoles under Osceola held out until 1842, at which time part of the tribe was removed to the West, but a considerable number fled into the Florida Everglades, where they chose a form of asylum in preference to removal.

Although the eastern tribes were discriminated against, cheated out of their land, and finally driven to Indian territory (now Oklahoma) in the West, many concerned whites, as well as some Indians, felt that in the long run the tribes would be better off separated from the diseases and the oppressive ways of the Anglo-Americans.

GRADUATION
AND PREEMPTION BILLS

The frontiersmen also felt that "Old Hickory" would do well by them in the question of western lands. In an effort to fulfill this expectation, Jackson joined Thomas Hart Benton in calling for a liberal land program that would offer the settlers poor land on a graduated price scale from $1.25 to $.50, and for even less if it failed to attract a buyer. Still another plan, the Preemption Act, would permit "squatters" to purchase 160 acres at the minimum price of $1.25 per acre. Even though the President championed both bills, neither gained approval from a Congress with a strong eastern bloc that viewed western expansion as a threat to both its political and economic interests. Expansion not only meant more congressional representation for new western states, but it also pulled workers off the labor-starved New England assembly lines. Eastern land speculators also helped defeat the two land measures because the old land bills placed them in a most favorable position to buy large acreages cheap and sell high —a practice that helped to bring on the inflationary crisis of 1835–1836. This problem of settling the western lands continued to plague the President throughout his tenure in office.

MAYSVILLE VETO

Although an ardent nationalist and forceful executive on the question of federal authority, Jackson was also capable of asserting the belief that the various states should assume certain responsibilities with regard to internal improvements. Accordingly, when a bill designed to finance federally the construction of a road linking Maysville to Lexington, Kentucky, reached his desk, he promptly vetoed it as unconstitutional. Not even this action damaged "Old Hickory's" popularity in the West. In fact, some westerners praised the veto.

The Question
of the United States Bank

FIGHTING BIDDLE'S BANK

Jackson's most formidable battle was with the United States Bank. Believing that the bank was unconstitutional and insensitive to the needs of the West, the President charted a course of action designed to either reform or destroy it. His most capable adversary in this long struggle was the talented Philadelphia financier and president of the bank, Nicholas Biddle. Biddle not only used verbal skills in defending the bank, but, on occasion, employed dollars through loans to win influential support. He was charged at one time with attempts to bribe certain congressmen.

In July 1832 Jackson vetoed a bill designed to grant a new charter to the bank (the charter on which it was operating did not expire until 1836) on the grounds that it was in danger of foreign control. It has been suggested that the President may have been off base in making this charge.

ELECTION OF 1832

As the election of 1832 approached, Jackson's challengers found in Henry Clay, the father of the "American System," a staunch supporter of the bank. He proved to be no match for the President, however, as Jackson support mounted with each growing financial crisis in the South and the West. Accordingly, in the summer of 1833, the President called upon the new Secretary of the Treasury, William J. Duane, to change the part of the bank charter that required federal deposits. When Duane procrastinated in performing this task, Jackson replaced him with Roger B. Taney, who promptly obliged the President. Government deposits thereafter were placed in state banks, where they were heartily welcomed, and soon provided a boon to the growth of such banks.

LOCOFOCOS

Jackson's stand against the bank had multiple supporters. He not only had friends among the various "pet," or state, banks, but he also counted among his backers the Locofocos,[5] a group of radical New York Democrats who championed hard money and liberal business opportunities. The bank, they reasoned, stood in the way of these goals.

President Biddle retaliated by calling in notes, which in turn, he hoped, would start a crippling business recession. If events went according to his calculations, public pressure would force Congress to reconsider the bank charter.

CENSURE OF JACKSON

The Clay-led Congress, in the meantime, was preparing a resolution to censure Jackson for assuming power not conferred by the Constitution, and it was approved on March 28, 1833. So enraged were the Jacksonians that Senator Benton vowed that he would introduce a resolution in each session thereafter to erase the iniquitous censure from the Senate records. His determined efforts finally expunged the censure in 1838.

As another panic approached in 1836, it became increasingly evident that Biddle's plan was not working. In fact, it backfired when the public and the business community revolted and finally forced him to relent on his credit policies. It spelled the doom of the bank.

WHIGS

Jackson and the Democrats had won a battle, but they had created a new and greater enemy in the process. The anti-Jacksonians, under the leadership of Clay and Webster, assumed the name of Whigs

(to show their contempt of "King Andrew") and came back to capture two of the next five presidential elections.

SPECIE CIRCULAR

During his last year as President, Jackson was persuaded to issue the "specie circular," in the hope of preventing another depression. Directing that only gold and silver could be received in payment for lands, the circular not only discouraged further land sales, but it also caused many to seek out and hoard the precious coins, thus contributing to the Panic of 1837.

Jacksonian Diplomacy

As a new student of international affairs, Jackson surprised even his best friends with his high marks of success. Among his accomplishments were the renewal of American trade with the British West Indies, and the collection for damages[6] to American shipping caused by the French during the Napoleonic wars. The latter, however, came with less grace and harmony. Perhaps falling victim to one of his occasional outbursts of anger, Jackson demanded that the French pay up or lose what property they held in the United States. The French were offended, and, for a moment, war hysteria was in the air. It soon passed, however, when the British, hoping to avoid another continental crisis, mediated to the satisfaction of both parties.

TEXAS QUESTION

The Texas issue proved to be more of a challenge, for Europe's distresses could not, in this case, make for America's success in diplomacy as it had in collecting the French debt. If the President recognized the newly formed Texas republic, it

---

[5] Name derived from the new friction matches used by the group to light candles when the regular Democrats of New York City tried to discourage their meetings by turning off the lights.

[6] A debt of over $30 million had gone uncollected by Adams and earlier presidents.

would mean violating the declared neutrality of the United States and would therefore offend Mexico and possibly some European powers. It he annexed Texas, which the South and many Texans desired, the North would object and Mexico might declare war in accordance with an earlier warning. Finally, any one of the above alternatives could easily cast the Democratic party in a most unfavorable light for the 1836 presidential election. Jackson, therefore, waited until his last few days in office to extend recognition to the new republic—he gave his successors the honor of resolving the issue of annexation.

Select Bibliography

Aronson, Sidney H. *Status and Kinship in the Higher Civil Service.* Cambridge, Mass.: Harvard University Press, 1964.

Barker, Eugene C. *The Life of Stephen F. Austin, Founder of Texas, 1793–1836.* New York: AMS Press, Inc., 1925.

Bugg, James L., ed. *Jacksonian Democracy: Myth or Reality.* New York: Holt, Rinehart and Winston, Inc., 1966.

Catterall, Ralph C. H. *Second Bank of the United States.* Chicago: University of Chicago Press, 1960.

Debo, Angie. *The Road to Disappearance.* Norman, Okla.: University of Oklahoma Press, 1967.

De Tocqueville, Alexis. *Democracy in America.* New York: Doubleday & Company, Inc., 1969.

Eaton, Clement. *Henry Clay and the Art of American Politics.* Boston: Little, Brown and Company, 1957.

Filler, Louis, and Allen Guttmann, eds. *The Removal of the Cherokee Nation: Manifest Destiny or National Dis-*

honor? Boston: D. C. Heath & Company, 1962.

Foreman, Grant. *The Five Civilized Tribes.* Norman, Okla.: University of Oklahoma Press, 1966.

Hammond, Bray. *Banks and Politics in America: From the Revolution to the Civil War.* Princeton, N.J.: Princeton University Press, 1957.

Harmon, G. D. *Sixty Years of Indian Affairs.* New York: Kraus Reprint Co., 1941.

Hugins, Walter. *Jacksonian Democracy and the Working Class: A Study of the New York Workingmen's Movement, 1829–1837.* Stanford, Calif.: Stanford University Press, 1967.

Meyers, Marvin. *The Jacksonian Persuasion: Politics and Belief.* Stanford, Calif.: Stanford University Press, 1957.

Miller, Douglas T. *Jacksonian Aristocracy: Class and Democracy in New York, 1830–1860.* New York: Oxford University Press, 1967.

Nichols, Roy R. *The Invention of the American Political Parties.* New York: Crowell Collier and Macmillan, Inc., 1967.

Ogg, Frederick A. *The Reign of Andrew Jackson: A Chronicle of the Frontier in Politics.* New Haven, Conn.: Yale University Press, 1919.

Pessen, Edward. *Most Uncommon Jacksonians: The Radical Leaders of the Early Labor Movement.* Albany, N.Y.: State University of New York Press, 1967.

Ratner, Lorman. *Powder Keg: Northern Opposition to the Antislavery Movement, 1831–1840.* New York: Basic Books, Inc., 1968.

Rayback, Joseph G. *History of American Labor.* New York: The Free Press, 1966.

Remini, Robert V. *Andrew Jackson and the Bank War: A Study in the Growth of Presidential Power.* New York: W. W. Norton & Company, Inc., 1968.

_____. *Martin Van Buren and the Making of the Democratic Party.* New York: Columbia University Press, 1959.

Riegel, Robert E. *Young America, 1830-1840.* Norman, Okla.: University of Oklahoma Press, 1949.

Robbins, Roy M. *Our Landed Heritage, the Public Domain, 1776–1936.* Lincoln, Nebr.: University of Nebraska Press, 1962.

Schlesinger, Jr., Arthur M. *The Age of Jackson.* Boston: Little, Brown and Company, 1945.

Sellers, Jr., Charles. *James K. Polk, Jacksonian.* 2 vols. Princeton, N.J.: Princeton University Press, 1957.

Spain, August O. *The Political Theory of John C. Calhoun.* New York: Octagon Books, Inc., 1968.

Spencer, Ivor D. *The Victory and the Spoils: A Life of William L. Marcy.* Providence, R.I.: Brown University Press, 1959.

Swisher, Carl B. *Roger B. Taney.* Hamden, Conn.: Shoe String Press, Inc., 1936.

Sydnor, Charles S. *The Development of Southern Sectionalism, 1819–1848.* Baton Rouge, La.: Louisiana State University Press, 1948.

Taylor, George R., ed. *Jackson Versus Biddle: Struggle over the Second Bank of the U.S.* Boston: D. C. Heath & Company, 1949.

Ward, John W. *Andrew Jackson: Symbol for an Age.* New York: Oxford University Press, 1955.

White, Leonard D. *The Jacksonians: A Study in Administrative History, 1829–1861.* New York: Crowell Collier and Macmillan, Inc., 1954.

Wiltse, Charles M. *Expansion and Reform, 1815–1850.* New York: The Free Press, 1967.

_____. *John C. Calhoun: Nullifer, 1829–1839.* Indianapolis, Ind.: The Bobbs-Merrill Co., Inc., 1949.

Zetterbaum, Marvin. *Tocqueville and the Problem of Democracy.* Stanford, Calif.: Stanford University Press, 1967.

problem 4

Jacksonian Democracy: In Pursuit of Identity and Meaning

Few Presidents have been the subject of as much prolonged controversy as Andrew Jackson. Until recent years, historians either reviled him as a Caesarean tyrant or championed him as the father of modern democracy. During the second half of the nineteenth century a group of historians, including James Parton, saw in Jacksonian democracy the origin of all the malpractices and corruption in public office. Soon thereafter, however, a new group of twentieth-century historians, headed by Frederick Jackson Turner, Charles A. Beard, and Vernon L. Parrington, came to the rescue of "Old Hickory." Western in origin, this school viewed the Jacksonian movement as the emergence of the common man through egalitarian reforms.

More recently, Arthur M. Schlesinger, Jr., drawing from the works of Beard and Parrington, has observed a class conflict between the Jacksonian laborers and the capitalists in a prolonged struggle for power. Bray Hammond and other members of what has become known as the entrepreneurial school, on the other hand, prefer to think of this conflict not as a class war but as a struggle between the old capitalists and the new Jacksonian entrepreneurs.

General Questions for Reflection and Discussion

1. How is it possible to evaluate the real Jackson? His democracy? What standards should be used?
2. To what extent have the students of Jacksonian democracy added new and significant interpretations that the President did not spell out in his speeches?
3. Why do you suppose that Jackson is often alluded to as the first modern President?
4. To what extent was Jackson the embodiment of the ideals of the eighteenth-century Enlightenment?
5. To what extent has the role of the President changed since Jackson's time? Has it changed for better or worse?
6. In what ways is Jacksonian democracy significant today?

Basic Questions for Reflection and Discussion

1. In his Farewell Address, how does Jackson view the role of the Constitution with respect to the Union?
2. In the same address, what did Jack-

190

son identify as the greatest evils to democracy?

3.   How does Jackson explain his stand against the bank (admittedly no monopoly) in view of his philosophy of economic freedom?

4.   On what grounds did Jackson denounce the bank? To what extent was the destruction of the bank helpful? Harmful?

5.   What arguments were used by Webster to defend the bank?

6.   How does Webster answer Jackson's charges with regard to the bank's harmful effects on the West?

7.   According to Webster, how would the veto weaken the authority of the Supreme Court?

8.   What is the thesis of Schlesinger?

Of Hugins? Where are they found? What kinds of data are used to support these theses? In what ways do their approaches to the problem differ?

9.   What evidence is most useful in helping Schlesinger and Hugins to achieve consistency or coherence.

10.   If Jackson's battles represented a struggle between the working and the privileged classes, where did the small shopowners fit in?

11. In what ways did labor hope to benefit from Jacksonian democracy?

12.   It has been written that Jacksonian economics paved the way to the "Gilded Age." To what extent does Hugins' article support this statement?

Veto
of the Bank Bill
July 10, 1832

The bill "to modify and continue" the act entitled "An act to incorporate the subscribers to the Bank of the United States" was presented to me on the 4th July instant. Having considered it with the solemn regard to the principles of the Constitution which the day was calculated to inspire, and come to the conclusion that it ought not to become a law, I herewith return it to the Senate, in which it originated, with my objections.

A bank of the United States is in many respects convenient for the Government and useful to the people. Entertaining this opinion, and deeply impressed with the belief that some of the powers and privileges possessed by the existing bank are unauthorized by the Constitution, subversive of the rights of the States, and dangerous to the liberties of the people, I felt it my duty at an early period of my Administration to call the attention of Congress to the practicability of organizing an institution combining all its advantages and obviating these objections. I sincerely regret that in the act before me I can perceive none of those modifications of the bank charter which are necessary, in my opinion, to make it compatible with justice, with sound policy, or with the Constitution of our country.

The present corporate body, denominated the president, directors, and company of the Bank of the United States, will have existed at the time this act is intended to take effect twenty years. It enjoys an exclusive privilege of banking under the authority of the General Government, a monopoly of its favor and support, and, as a necessary consequence, almost a monopoly of the foreign and domestic exchange. The powers, privileges, and favors bestowed upon it in the original charter, by increasing the value of the stock far above its par value, operated as a gratuity of many millions to the stockholders.

An apology may be found for the failure to guard against this result in the consideration that the effect of the original act of incorporation could not be certainly foreseen at the time of its passage. The act before me proposes another gratuity to the holders of the same stock, and in many cases to the same men, of at least seven millions more. This donation finds no apology in any uncertainty as to the effect of the act. On all hands it is conceded that its passage will increase at least 20 or 30 per cent more the market price of the stock, subject to the payment of the annuity of $200,000 per year sesured by the act, thus adding in a moment one-fourth to its par value. It is not our own citizens only who are to receive the bounty of our Government. More than eight millions of the stock of this bank

From *A Compilation of the Messages and Papers of the Presidents, 1789–1897*, Vol. 2. Compiled by James D. Richardson. Washington, D.C.: Government Printing Office, 1896, pp. 576–591.

are held by foreigners. By this act the American Republic proposes virtually to make them a present of some millions of dollars. For these gratuities to foreigners and to some of our own opulent citizens the act secures no equivalent whatever. They are the certain gains of the present stockholders under the operation of this act, after making full allowance for the payment of the bonus.

Every monopoly and all exclusive privileges are granted at the expense of the public, which ought to receive a fair equivalent. The many millions which this act proposes to bestow on the stockholders of the existing bank must come directly or indirectly out of the earnings of the American people. It is due to them, therefore, if their Government sell monopolies and exclusive privileges, that they should at least exact for them as much as they are worth in open market. The value of the monopoly in this case may be correctly ascertained. The twenty-eight millions of stock would probably be at an advance of 50 per cent, and command in market at least $42,000,000 subject to the payment of the present bonus. The present value of the monopoly, therefore, is $17,000,000, and this the act proposes to sell for three millions, payable in fifteen annual installments of $200,000 each.

It is not conceivable how the present stockholders can have any claim to the special favor of the Government. The present corporation has enjoyed its monopoly during the period stipulated in the original contract. If we must have such a corporation, why should not the Government sell out the whole stock and thus secure to the people the full market value of the privileges granted? Why should not Congress create and sell twenty-eight millions of stock, incorporating the purchasers with all the powers and privileges secured in this act and putting the premium upon the sales into the Treasury?

But this act does not permit competition in the purchase of this monopoly. It seems to be predicated on the erroneous idea that the present stockholders have a prescriptive right not only to the favor but to the bounty of Government. It appears that more than a fourth part of the stock is held by foreigners and the residue is held by a few hundred of our own citizens, chiefly of the richest class. For their benefit does this act exclude the whole American people from competition in the purchase of this monopoly and dispose of it for many millions less than it is worth. This seems the less excusable because some of our citizens not now stockholders petitioned that the door of competition might be opened, and offered to take a charter on terms much more favorable to the Government and country.

But this proposition, although made by men whose aggregate wealth is believed to be equal to all the private stock in the existing bank, has been set aside, and the bounty of our Government is proposed to be again bestowed on the few who have been fortunate enough to secure the stock and at this moment wield the power of the existing institution. I can not perceive the justice or policy of this course. If our Government must sell monopolies, it would seem to be its duty to take nothing less than their full value, and if gratuities must be made once in fifteen or twenty years let them not be bestowed on the subjects of a foreign government nor upon a designated and favored class of men in our own country. It is but justice and good policy, as far as the nature of the case will admit, to confine our favors to our own fellow-citizens, and let each in his turn enjoy an opportunity to profit by our bounty. In the bearings of the act before me upon these points I find ample reasons why it should not become a law.

It has been urged as an argument in favor of rechartering the present bank that the calling in its loans will produce great embarrassment and distress. The time allowed to close its concerns is ample, and if it has been well managed its pressure will be light, and heavy only in case its management has been bad. If, therefore, it shall produce distress, the fault will be its own, and it would furnish a reason against renewing a power which has been so obviously abused. But will there ever be a time when this reason will be less powerful? To acknowledge its force is to admit that the bank ought to be perpetual, and as a consequence the present stockholders and those inheriting their rights as successors be established a privileged order, clothed both with great political power and enjoying immense pecuniary advantages from their connection with the Government.

The modifications of the existing charter proposed by this act are not such, in my view, as make it consistent with the rights of the States or the liberties of the people. The qualification of the right of the bank to hold real estate, the limitation of its power to establish branches, and the power reserved to Congress to forbid the circulation of small notes are restrictions comparatively of little value or importance. All the objectionable principles of the existing corporation, and most of its odious features, are retained without alleviation.

The fourth section provides "that the notes or bills of the said corporation, although the same be, on the faces thereof, respectively made payable at one place only, shall nevertheless be received by the said corporation at the bank or at any of the offices of discount and deposit thereof if tendered in liquidation or payment of any balance or balances due to said corporation or to such office of discount and deposit from any other incorporated bank." This provision secures to the State banks a legal privilege in the Bank of the United States which is withheld from all private citizens. If a State bank in Philadelphia owe the Bank of the United States and have notes issued by the St. Louis branch, it can pay the debt with those notes, but if a merchant, mechanic, or other private citizen be in like circumstances he can not by law pay his debt with those notes, but must sell them at a

discount or send them to St. Louis to be cashed. This boon conceded to the State banks, though not unjust in itself, is most odious because it does not measure out equal justice to the high and the low, the rich and the poor. To the extent of its practical effect it is a bond of union among the banking establishments of the nation, erecting them into an interest separate from that of the people, and its necessary tendency is to unite the Bank of the United States and the State banks in any measure which may be thought conducive to their common interest.

The ninth section of the act recognizes principles of worse tendency than any provision of the present charter.

It enacts that "the cashier of the bank shall annually report to the Secretary of the Treasury the names of all stockholders who are not resident citizens of the United States, and on the application of the treasurer of any State shall make out and transmit to such treasurer a list of stockholders residing in or citizens of such State, with the amount of stock owned by each." Although this provision, taken in connection with a decision of the Supreme Court, surrenders, by its silence, the right of the States to tax the banking institutions created by this corporation under the name of branches throughout the Union, it is evidently intended to be construed as a concession of their right to tax that portion of the stock which may be held by their own citizens and residents. In this light, if the act becomes a law, it will be understood by the States, who will probably proceed to levy a tax equal to that paid upon the stock of banks incorporated by themselves. In some States that tax is now 1 per cent, either on the capital or on the shares, and that may be assumed as the amount which all citizen or resident stockholders would be taxed under the operation of this act. As it is only the stock *held* in the States and not that *employed* within them which would be subject to taxation, and as the names of foreign stockholders are not to be reported to the treasurers of the States, it is obvious that the stock held by them will be exempt from this burden. Their annual profits will therefore be 1 per cent more than the citizen stockholders, and as the annual dividends of the bank may be safely estimated at 7 per cent, the stock will be worth 10 or 15 per cent more to foreigners than to citizens of the United States. To appreciate the effects which this state of things will produce, we must take a brief review of the operations and present condition of the Bank of the United States.

By documents submitted to Congress at the present session it appears that on the 1st of January, 1832, of the twenty-eight millions of private stock in the corporation, $8,405,500 were held by foreigners, mostly of Great Britain. The amount of stock held in the nine Western and Southwestern States is $140,200, and in the four Southern States is $5,623,100, and in the Middle and Eastern States is about $13,522,000. The profits of the bank in 1831, as shown in a statement to Congress, were about $3,455,598; of this there accrued in the nine Western States about $1,640,048; in the four Southern States about $352,507, and in the Middle and Eastern States about $1,463,041. As little stock is held in the West, it is obvious that the debt of the people in that section to the bank is principally a debt to the Eastern and foreign stockholders; that the interest they pay upon it is carried into the Eastern States and into Europe, and that it is a burden upon their industry and a drain of their currency, which no country can bear without inconvenience and occasional distress. To meet this burden and equalize the exchange operations of the bank, the amount of specie drawn from those States through its branches within the last two years, as shown by its official reports, was about $6,000,000. More than half a million of this amount does not stop in the Eastern States, but passes on to Europe to pay the dividends of the foreign stockholders. In the principle of taxation recognized by this act

the Western States find no adequate compensation for this perpetual burden on their industry and drain of their currency. The branch bank at Mobile made last year $95,140, yet under the provisions of this act the State of Alabama can raise no revenue from these profitable operations, because not a share of the stock is held by any of her citizens. Mississippi and Missouri are in the same condition in relation to the branches at Natchez and St. Louis, and such, in a greater or less degree, is the condition of every Western State. The tendency of the plan of taxation which this act proposes will be to place the whole United States in the same relation to foreign countries which the Western States now bear to the Eastern. When by a tax on resident stockholders the stock of this bank is made worth 10 or 15 per cent more to foreigners than to residents, most of it will inevitably leave the country.

Thus will this provision in its practical effect deprive the Eastern as well as the Southern and Western States of the means of raising a revenue from the extension of business and great profits of this institution. It will make the American people debtors to aliens in nearly the whole amount due to this bank, and send across the Atlantic from two to five millions of specie every year to pay the bank dividends.

In another of its bearings this provision is fraught with danger. Of the twenty-five directors of this bank five are chosen by the Government and twenty by the citizen stockholders. From all voice in these elections the foreign stockholders are excluded by the charter. In proportion, therefore, as the stock is transferred to foreign holders the extent of suffrage in the choice of directors is curtailed. Already is almost a third of the stock in foreign hands and not represented in elections. It is constantly passing out of the country, and this act will accelerate its departure. The entire control of the institution would necessarily fall into the hands of a few citizen stockholders, and the ease with which the object would be accomplished would be a temptation to designing men to secure that control in their own hands by monopolizing the remaining stock. There is danger that a president and directors would then be able to elect themselves from year to year, and without responsibility or control manage the whole concerns of the bank during the existence of its charter. It is easy to conceive that great evils to our country and its institutions might flow from such a concentration of power in the hands of a few men irresponsible to the people.

Is there no danger to our liberty and independence in a bank that in its nature has so little to bind it to our country? The president of the bank has told us that most of the State banks exist by its forbearance. Should its influence become concentered, as it may under the operation of such an act as this, in the hands of a self-elected directory whose interests are identified with those of the foreign stockholders, will there not be cause to tremble for the purity of our elections in peace and for the independence of our country in war? Their power would be great whenever they might choose to exert it; but if this monopoly were regularly renewed every fifteen or twenty years on terms proposed by themselves, they might seldom in peace put forth their strength to influence elections or control the affairs of the nation. But if any private citizen or public functionary should interpose to curtail its powers or prevent a renewal of its privileges, it can not be doubted that he would be made to feel its influence.

Should the stock of the bank principally pass into the hands of the subjects of a foreign country, and we should unfortunately become involved in a war with that country, what would be our condition? Of the course which would be pursued by a bank almost wholly owned by the subjects of a foreign power, and managed by those whose interests, if not affections, would run in the same direction there can be no doubt. All its operations within would be in aid of the hostile fleets and armies without. Controlling our currency, receiving our public moneys, and holding thousands of our citizens in dependence, it would be more formidable and dangerous than the naval and military power of the enemy.

If we must have a bank with private stockholders, every consideration of sound policy and every impulse of American feeling admonishes that it should be *purely American.* Its stockholders should be composed exclusively of our own citizens, who at least ought to be friendly to our Government and willing to support it in times of difficulty and danger. So abundant is domestic capital that competition in subscribing for the stock of local banks has recently led almost to riots. To a bank exclusively of American stockholders, possessing the powers and privileges granted by this act, subscriptions for $200,000,000 could be readily obtained. Instead of sending abroad the stock of the bank in which the Government must deposit its funds and on which it must rely to sustain its credit in times of emergency, it would rather seem to be expedient to prohibit its sale to aliens under penalty of absolute forfeiture.

It is maintained by the advocates of the bank that its constitutionality in all its features ought to be considered as settled by precedent and by the decision of the Supreme Court. To this conclusion I can not assent. Mere precedent is a dangerous source of authority, and should not be regarded as deciding questions of constitutional power except where the acquiescence of the people and the States can be considered as well settled. So far from this being the case on this subject, an argument against the bank might be based on precedent. One Congress, in 1791, decided in favor of a bank; another, in 1811, decided against it. One Congress in 1815, decided against a bank; another, in 1816, decided in its favor. Prior to the present Congress, therefore, the precedents drawn from that source were equal. If we resort to the States, the expressions of legislative, judicial, and executive opinions against the bank have been probably to those in its favor as 4 to 1. There is nothing in precedent, therefore, which, if its authority were admitted, ought to weigh in favor of the act before me.

If the opinion of the Supreme Court covered the whole ground of this act, it ought not to control the coordinate authorities of this Government. The Congress, the Executive and the Court must each for itself be guided by its own opinion of the Constitution. Each public officer who takes an oath to support the Constitution swears that he will support it as he understands it, and not as it is understood by others. It is as much the duty of the House of Representatives, of the Senate, and of the President to decide upon the constitutionality of any bill or resolution which may be presented to them for passage or approval as it is of the supreme judges when it may be brought before them for judicial decision. The opinion of of the judges has no more authority over Congress than the opinion of Congress has over the judges, and on that point the President is independent of both. The authority of the Supreme Court must not, therefore, be permitted to control the Congress or the Executive when acting in their legislative capacities, but to have only such influence as the force of their reasoning may deserve.

But in the case relied upon the Supreme Court have not decided that all the features of this corporation are compatible with the Constitution. It is true that the court have said that the law incorporating the bank is a constitutional exercise of power by Congress; but taking into view the whole opinion of the court and the reasoning by which they have come to that conclusion, I understand them to have decided that inasmuch as a bank is an appropriate means for carrying into effect the enumerating powers of the General Government, therefore the law incorporating it is in accordance with that provision of the Constitution which declares that Congress shall have power "to make

all laws which shall be necessary and proper for carrying those powers into execution." Having satisfied themselves that the word *"necessary"* in the Constitution means *"needful," "requisite," "essential," "conducive to,"* and that "a bank" is a convenient, a useful, and essential instrument in the prosecution of the Government's "fiscal operations," they conclude that to "use one must be within the discretion of Congress" and that "the act to incorporate the Bank of the United States is a law made in pursuance of the Constitution;" "but," say they, *"where the law is not prohibited and is really calculated to effect any of the objects intrusted to the Government, to undertake here to inquire into the degree of its necessity would be to pass the line which circumscribes the judicial department and to tread on legislative ground."*

The principle here affirmed is that the "degree of its necessity," involving all the details of a banking institution, is a question exclusively for legislative consideration. A bank is constitutional, but it is the province of the Legislature to determine whether this or that particular power, privilege, or exemption is "necessary and proper" to enable the bank to discharge its duties to the Government, and from their decision there is no appeal to the courts of justice. Under the decision of the Supreme Court, therefore, it is the exclusive province of Congress and the President to decide whether the particular features of this act are *necessary* and *proper* in order to enable the bank to perform conveniently and efficiently the public duties assigned to it as a fiscal agent, and therefore constitutional, or *unnecessary* and *improper,* and therefore unconstitutional.

Without commenting on the general principle affirmed by the Supreme Court, let us examine the details of this act in accordance with the rule of legislative action which they have laid down. It will be found that many of the powers and privileges conferred on it can not be supposed necessary for the purpose for which it is proposed to be created, and are not, therefore, means necessary to attain the end in view, and consequently not justified by the Constitution.

The original act of incorporation, section 21, enacts "that no other bank shall be established by any future law of the United States during the continuance of the corporation hereby created, for which the faith of the United States is hereby pledged: *Provided,* Congress may renew existing charters for banks within the District of Columbia . . ." This provision is continued in force by the act before me fifteen years from the 3d of March, 1836.

If Congress possessed the power to establish one bank, they had power to establish more than one if in their opinion two or more banks had been "necessary" to facilitate the execution of the powers delegated to them in the Constitution. If they possessed the power to establish a second bank, it was a power derived from the Constitution to be exercised from time to time, and at any time when the interests of the country or the emergencies of the Government might make it expedient. It was possessed by one Congress as well as another, and by all Congresses alike, and alike at every session. But the Congress of 1816 have taken it away from their successors for twenty years, and the Congress of 1832 proposes to abolish it for fifteen years more. It can not be "necessary" or *"proper"* for Congress to barter away or divest themselves of any of the powers vested in them by the Constitution to be exercised for the public good. It is not *"necessary"* to the efficiency of the bank, nor is it *"proper"* in relation to themselves and their successors. They may *properly* use the discretion vested in them, but they may not limit the discretion of their successors. This restriction on themselves and grant of a monopoly to the bank is therefore unconstitutional.

In another point of view this provision is a palpable attempt to amend the Constitution by an act of legislation. The Constitution declares that "the Congress shall have power to exercise exclusive legislation in all cases whatsoever" over the District of Columbia. Its constitutional power, therefore, to establish banks in the District of Columbia and increase their capital at will is unlimited and uncontrollable by any other power than that which have authority to the Constitution. Yet this act declares that Congress shall *not* increase the capital of existing banks, nor create other banks with capitals exceeding in the whole $6,000,000. The Constitution declares that Congress *shall* have power to exercise exclusive legislation over this District *"in all cases whatsoever,"* and this act declares they shall not. Which is the supreme law of the land? This provision can not be *"necessary"* or *"proper"* or *constitutional* unless the absurdity be admitted that whenever it be "necessary and proper" in the opinion of Congress they have a right to barter away one portion of the powers vested in them by the Constitution as a means of executing the rest.

On two subjects only does the Constitution recognize in Congress the power to grant exclusive privileges or monopolies. It declares that "Congress shall have power to promote the progress of science and useful arts by securing for limited times to authors and inventors the exclusive right to their respective writings and discoveries." Out of this express delegation of power have grown our laws of patents and copyrights. As the Constitution expressly delegates to Congress the power to grant exclusive privileges in these cases as the means of executing the substantive power "to promote the progress of science and useful arts," it is consistent with the fair rules of construction to conclude that such a power was not intended to be granted as a means of accomplishing any other end. On every other subject which comes within the scope of Congressional power there is an ever-living discretion in the use of proper means, which can not be restricted or abolished without an amendment of the Constitution. Every act of Congress, therefore, which attempts by grants of monopolies or sale of exclusive privileges for a limited time, or a time without limit, to restrict or extinguish its own discretion in the choice of means to execute its delegated powers is equivalent to a legislative amendment of the Constitution, and palpably unconstitutional.

This act authorizes and encourages transfers of its stock to foreigners and grants them an exemption from all State and national taxation. So far from being *"necessary and proper"* that the bank should possess this power to make it a safe and efficient agent of the Government in its fiscal operations, it is calculated to convert the Bank of the United States into a foreign bank, to impoverish our people in time of peace, to disseminate a foreign influence through every section of the Republic, and in war to endanger our independence.

The several States reserved the power at the formation of the Constitution to regulate and control titles and transfers of real property, and most, if not all, of them have laws disqualifying aliens from acquiring or holding lands within their limits. But this act, in disregard of the undoubted right of the States to prescribe such disqualifications, gives to alien stockholders in this bank an interest and title, as members of the corporation, to all the real property it may acquire within any of States of this Union. This privilege granted to aliens is not *"necessary"* to enable the bank to perform its public duties, nor in any sense *"proper,"* because it is vitally subversive of the rights of the States.

The Government of the United States have no constitutional power to purchase lands within the States except "for the erection of forts, magazines, arsenals, dockyards, and other needful buildings," and even for these objects only "by the consent of the legislature of the State in which the same shall be." By making themselves stockholders in the bank and granting to the corporation the power to purchase lands for other purposes they assume a power not granted in the Constitution and grant to others what they do not themselves possess. It is not *"necessary"* to the receiving, safe-keeping, or transmission of the funds of the Government that the bank should possess this power, and it is not *"proper"* that Congress should thus enlarge the powers delegated to them in the Constitution.

The old Bank of the United States possessed a capital of only $11,000,000, which was found fully sufficient to enable it with dispatch and safety to perform all the functions required of it by the Government. The capital of the present bank is $35,000,000 — at least $24,000,000 more than experience has proved to be *necessary* to enable a bank to perform its public functions. The public debt which existed during the period of the old bank and on the establishment of the new has been nearly paid off, and our revenue will soon be reduced. This increase of capital is therefore not for public but for private purposes.

The Government is the only *"proper"* judge where its agents should reside and keep their offices, because it best knows where their presence will be *"necessary."* It can not, therefore, be *"necessary"* or *"proper"* to authorize the bank to locate branches where it pleases to perform the public service, without consulting the Government, and contrary to its will. The principle laid down by the Supreme Court concedes that Congress can not establish a bank for purposes of private speculation and gain, but only as a means of executing the delegated powers of the General Government. By the same principle a branch bank can not constitutionally be established for other than public purposes. The power which this act gives to establish two branches in any State, without the injunction or request of the Government and for other than public purposes, is not *"necessary"* to the due *execution* of the powers delegated to Congress.

The bonus which is exacted from the bank is a confession upon the face of the act that the powers granted by it are greater than are *"necessary"* to its character of a fiscal agent. The government does not tax its officers and agents for the privilege of serving it. The bonus of a million and a half required by the original charter and that of three millions proposed by this act are not exacted for the privilege of giving "the necessary facilities for transferring the public funds from place to place within the United States or the Territories thereof, and for distributing the same in payment of the public creditors without charging commission or claiming allowance on account of the difference of exchange," as required by the act of incorporation, but for something more beneficial to the stockholders. The original act declares that it (the bonus) is granted "in consideration of the exclusive privileges and benefits conferred by this act upon the said bank," and the act before me declares it to be "in consideration of the exclusive benefits and privileges continued by this act to the said corporation for fifteen years, as aforesaid." It is therefore for "exclusive privileges and benefits" conferred for their own use and emolument, and not for the advantage of the Government, that a bonus is exacted. These surplus powers for which the bank is required to pay can not surely be *"necessary"* to make it the fiscal agent of the Treasury. If they were, the exaction of a bonus for them would not be *"proper."*

It is maintained by some that the bank is a means of executing the constitutional power "to coin money and regulate the value thereof." Congress have established a mint to coin money and passed laws to regulate the value thereof. The money so coined, with its value so regulated, and such foreign coins as Congress may adopt are the only currency known to the Constitution. But if they have other power to regulate the currency, it was conferred to be exercised by themselves, and not to be transferred to a corporation. If the bank be established for that purpose, with a charter unalterable without its consent, Congress have parted with their power for a term of years, during which the Constitution is a dead letter. It is neither necessary nor proper to transfer its legislative power to such a bank, and therefore unconstitutional.

By its silence, considered in connection with the decision of the Supreme Court in the case of McCulloch against the State of Maryland, this act takes from the States the power to tax a portion of the banking business carried on within their limits, in subversion of one of the strongest barriers which secured them against Federal encroachments. Banking, like farming, manufacturing, or any other occupation or profession, is *a business*, the right to follow which is not originally derived from the laws. Every citizen and every company of citizens in all of our States possessed the right until the State legislatures deemed it good policy to prohibit private banking by law. If the prohibitory State laws were now repealed, every citizen would again possess the right. The State banks are a qualified restoration of the right which has been taken away by the laws against banking, guarded by such provisions and limitations as in the opinion of the State legislatures the public interest requires. These corporations, unless there be an exemption in their charter, are, like private bankers and banking companies, subject to State taxation. The manner in which these taxes shall be laid depends wholly on legislative discretion. It may be upon the bank, upon the stock, upon the profits, or in any other mode which the sovereign power shall will.

Upon the formation of the Constitution the States guarded their taxing power with peculiar jealousy. They surrendered it only as it regards imports and exports. In relation to every other object within their jurisdiction, whether persons, property, business, or professions, it was se-

cured in as ample a manner as it was before possessed. All persons though United
States officers, are liable to a poll tax by
the States within which they reside. The
lands of the United States are liable to
the usual land tax, except in the new
States, from whom agreements that they
will not tax unsold lands are exacted
when they are admitted into the Union.
Horses, wagons, any beasts or vehicles,
tools, or property belonging to private
citizens, though employed in the service
of the United States, are subject to State
taxation. Every private business, whether
carried on by an officer of the General
Government or not, whether it be mixed
with public concerns or not, even if it be
carried on by the Government of the
United States itself, separately or in part-
nership, falls within the scope of the taxing
power of the state, nothing comes more
fully within it than banks and the business
of banking, by whomsoever instituted
and carried on. Over this whole subject-
matter it is just as absolute, unlimited,
and uncontrollable as if the Constitution
had never been adopted, because in the
formation of that instrument it was reserved without qualification.

The principle is conceded that the
States cannot rightfully tax the operations
of the Government. They cannot tax the
money of the Government deposited in the
State banks, nor the agency remitting it; but
will any man maintain that their mere selection to perform this public service for the
General Government would exempt the
State banks and their ordinary business
from State taxation? Had the United States,
instead of establishing a bank at Philadelphia, employed a private banker to
keep and transmit their funds, would it
have deprived Pennsylvania of the right
to tax his bank and his usual banking
operations? It will not be pretended.
Upon what principle, then, are the banking establishments of the Bank of the
United States and their usual banking
operations to be exempted from taxation?
It is not their public agency or the de-

posits of the Government which the States
claim a right to tax, but their banks and
their banking powers, instituted and
exercised within State jurisdiction for
their private emolument—those powers
and privileges for which they pay a bonus,
and which the States tax in their own
banks. The exercise of these powers within
a State, no matter by whom or under what
authority, whether by private citizens in
their original right, by corporate bodies
created by the States, by foreigners or the
agents of foreign governments located
within their limits, forms a legitimate
object of State taxation. From this and
like sources, from the persons, property,
and business that are found residing,
located, or carried on under their jurisdiction, must the States, since the surrender of their right to raise a revenue
from imports and exports, draw all the
money necessary for the support of their
governments and the maintenance of
their independence. There is no more
appropriate subject of taxation than
banks, banking, and bank stocks, and none
to which the States ought more pertina-
ciously to cling.

It can not be *necessary* to the character
of the bank as a fiscal agent of the Government that its private business should
be exempted from that taxation to which
all the State banks are liable, nor can I
conceive it *"proper"* that the substantive
and most essential powers reserved by the
States shall be thus attacked and annihilated as a means of executing the powers
delegated to the General Government.
It may be safely assumed that none of
those sages who had an agency in forming
or adopting our Constitution ever imagined that any portion of the taxing power
of the States not prohibited to them nor
delegated to Congress was to be swept
away and annihilated as a means of executing certain powers delegated to Congress.

If our power over means is so absolute
that the Supreme Court will not call in
question the constitutionality of an act of

Congress the subject of which "is not prohibited, and is really calculated to effect any of the objects intrusted to the Government," although, as in the case before me, it takes away powers expressly granted to Congress and rights scrupulously reserved to the States, it becomes us to proceed in our legislation with the utmost caution. Though not directly, our own powers and the rights of the States may be indirectly legislated away in the use of means to execute substantive powers. We may not enact that Congress shall not have the power of exclusive legislation over the District of Columbia, but we may pledge the faith of the United States that as a means of executing other powers it shall not be exercised for twenty years or forever. We may not pass an act prohibiting the States to tax the banking business carried on within their limits, but we may, as a means of executing our powers over other objects, place that business in the hands of our agents and then declare it exempt from State taxation in their hands. Thus may our own powers and the rights of the States, which we can not directly curtail or invade, be frittered away and extinguished in the use of means employed by us to execute other powers. That a bank of the United States, competent to all the duties which may be required by the Government, might be so organized as not to infringe on our own delegated powers or the reserved rights of the States I do not entertain a doubt. Had the Executive been called upon to furnish the project of such an institution, the duty would have been cheerfully performed. In the absence of such a call it was obviously proper that he should confine himself to pointing out those prominent features in the act presented which in his opinion make it incompatible with the Constitution and sound policy. A general discussion will now take place, eliciting new light and settling important principles; and a new Congress, elected in the midst of such discussion, and furnishing an equal representation of the people according to the last census, will bear to the Capitol the verdict of public opinion, and, I doubt not, bring this important question to a satisfactory result.

Under such circumstances the bank comes forward and asks a renewal of its charter for a term of fifteen years upon conditions which not only operate as a gratuity to the stockholders of many millions of dollars, but will sanction any abuses and legalize any encroachments.

Suspicions are entertained and charges are made of gross abuse and violation of its charter. An investigation unwillingly conceded and so restricted in time as necessarily to make it incomplete and unsatisfactory discloses enough to excite suspicion and alarm. In the practices of the principal bank partially unveiled, in the absence of important witnesses, and in numerous charges confidently made and as yet wholly uninvestigated there was enough to induce a majority of the committee of investigation—a committee which was selected from the most able and honorable members of the House of Representatives—to recommend a suspension of further action upon the bill and a prosecution of the inquiry. As the charter had yet four years to run, and as a renewal now was not necessary to the successful prosecution of its business, it was to have been expected that the bank itself, conscious of its purity and proud of its character, would have withdrawn its application for the present, and demanded the severest scrutiny into all its transactions. In their declining to do so there seems to be an additional reason why the functionaries of the Government should proceed with less haste and more caution in the renewal of their monopoly.

The bank is professedly established as an agent of the executive branch of the Government, and its constitutionality is maintained on that ground. Neither upon the propriety of present action nor upon the provisions of this act was the Executive consulted. It has had no opportunity to say that it neither needs nor wants an agent clothed with such powers and favored by such exemptions. There is nothing in its legitimate functions which makes it necessary or proper. Whatever interest or influence, whether public or private, has given birth to this act, it can not be found either in the wishes or necessities of the executive department, by which present action is deemed premature, and the powers conferred upon its agent not only unnecessary, but dangerous to the Government and country.

It is to be regretted that the rich and powerful too often bend the acts of government to their selfish purposes. Distinctions in society will always exist under every just government. Equality of talents, of education, or of wealth can not be produced by human institutions. In the full enjoyment of the gifts of Heaven and the fruits of superior industry, economy, and virtue, every man is equally entitled to protection by law; but when the laws undertake to add to these natural and just advantages artificial distinctions, to grant titles, gratuities, and exclusive privileges, to make the rich richer and the potent more powerful, the humble members of society —the farmers, mechanics, and laborers— who have neither the time nor the means of securing like favors to themselves, have a right to complain of the injustice of their Government. There are no necessary evils in government. Its evils exist only in its abuses. If it would confine itself to equal protection, and, as Heaven does its rains, shower its favors alike on the high and the low, the rich and the poor, it would be an unqualified blessing. In the act before me there seems to be a wide and unnecessary departure from these just principles.

Nor is our Government to be maintained or our Union preserved by invasions of the rights and powers of the several States. In thus attempting to make our General Government strong we make it weak. Its true strength consists in leaving individuals and States as much as possible to themselves—making itself felt, not in its power, but in its beneficence; not in its control, but in its protection; not in binding the States more closely to the center, but leaving each to move unobstructed in its proper orbit.

Experience should teach us wisdom. Most of the difficulties our Government now encounters and most of the dangers which impend over our Union have sprung from an abandonment of the legitimate objects of Government by our national legislation, and the adoption of such principles as are embodied in this act. Many of our rich men have not been content with equal protection and equal benefits, but have besought us to make them richer by act of Congress. By attempting to gratify their desires we have in the results of our legislation arrayed section against section, interest against interest, and man against man, in a fearful commotion which threatens to shake the foundations of our Union. It is time to pause in our career to review our principles, and if possible revive that devoted patriotism and spirit of compromise which distinguished the sages of the Revolution and the fathers of our Union. If we can not at once, in justice to interests vested under improvident legislation, make our Government what it ought to be, we can at least take a stand against all new grants of monopolies and exclusive privileges, against any prostitution of our Government to the advancement of the few at the expense of the many, and in favor of compromise and gradual reform in our code of laws and system of political economy.

I have now done my duty to my country. If sustained by my fellow-citizens, I shall be grateful and happy; if not, I shall find in the motives which impel me ample grounds for contentment and peace. In the difficulties which surround us and the dangers which threaten our institutions there is cause for neither dismay nor alarm. For relief and deliverance let us firmly rely on that kind Providence which I am sure watches with peculiar care over the destinies of our Republic, and on the intelligence and wisdom of our countrymen. Through *His* abundant goodness and *their* patriotic devotion our liberty and Union will be preserved.

Daniel Webster

Challenge of Jackson's Veto

Mr. President, no one will deny the high importance of the subject now before us. Congress, after full deliberation and discussion, has passed a bill, by decisive majorities, in both houses, for extending the duration of the Bank of the United States. It has not adopted this measure until its attention had been called to the subject, in three successive annual messages of the President. The bill having been thus passed by both houses, and having been duly presented to the President, instead of signing and approving it, he has returned it with objections. These objections go against the whole substance of the law originally creating the bank. They deny, in effect, that the bank is constitutional; they deny that it is expedient; they deny that it is necessary for the public service.

It is not to be doubted, that the Constitution gives the President the power which he has now exercised; but while the power is admitted, the grounds upon which it has been exerted become fit subjects of examination. The Constitution

From *The Great Speeches and Orations of Daniel Webster* by Edwin P. Whipple (Boston: Little, Brown and Company, 1879) pp. 320–328, 334–335, 337–338.

makes it the duty of Congress, in cases like this, to reconsider the measure which they have passed, to weigh the force of the President's objections to that measure, and to take a new vote upon the question.

Before the Senate proceeds to this second vote, I propose to make some remarks upon those objections. And, in the first place, it is to be observed, that they are such as to extinguish all hope that the present bank, or any bank at all resembling it, or resembling any known similar institution, can ever receive his approbation. He states no terms, no qualifications, no conditions, no modifications, which can reconcile him to the essential provisions of the existing charter. He is against the bank, and against any bank constituted in a manner known either to this or any other country. One advantage, therefore, is certainly obtained by presenting him the bill. It has caused the President's sentiments to be made known. There is no longer any mystery, no longer a contest between hope and fear, or between those prophets who predicted a *veto* and those who foretold an approval. The bill is negatived; the President has assumed the responsibility of putting an end to the bank; and the country must prepare itself to meet that change in its concerns which the expiration of the charter will produce. Mr. President, I will not conceal my opinion that the affairs of the country are approaching an important and dangerous crisis. At the very moment of almost unparalleled general prosperity, there appears an unaccountable disposition to destroy the most useful and most approved institutions of the government. Indeed, it seems to be in the midst of all this national happiness that some are found openly to question the advantages of the Constitution itself, and many more ready to embarrass the exercise of its just power, weaken its authority, and undermine its foundations. How far these notions may be carried, it is impossible yet to say. We have before us the practical result of one of them. The bank has fallen, or is to fall.

It is now certain, that, without a change in our public counsels, this bank will not be continued, nor will any other be established, which, according to the general sense and language of mankind, can be entitled to the name. Within three years and nine months from the present moment, the charter of the bank expires; within that period, therefore, it must wind up its concerns. It must call in its debts, withdraw its bills from circulation, and cease from all its ordinary operations. All this is to be done in three years and nine months; because, although there is a provision in the charter rendering it lawful to use the corporate name for two years after the expiration of the charter, yet this is allowed only for the purpose of suits and for . . . no other purpose whatever. The whole active business of the bank, its custody of public deposits, its transfer of public moneys, its dealing in exchange, all its loans and discounts, and all its issues of bills for circulation, must cease and determine on or before the third day of March, 1836; and within the same period its debts must be collected, as no new contract can be made with it, as a corporation, for the renewal of loans,

or discount of notes or bills, after that time.

The President is of opinion, that this time is long enough to close the concerns of the institution without inconvenience. His language is, "The time allowed the bank to close its concerns is ample, and if it has been well managed, its pressure will be light, and heavy only in case its management has been bad. If, therefore, it shall produce distress, the fault will be its own." Sir, this is all no more than general statement, without fact or argument to support it. We know what the management of the bank has been, and we know the present state of its affairs. We can judge, therefore, whether it be probable that its capital can be all called in, and the circulation of its bills withdrawn, in three years and nine months, by any discretion or prudence in management, without producing distress. The bank has discounted liberally, in compliance with the wants of the community. The amount due to it on loans and discounts, in certain large divisions of the country, is great; so great, that I do not perceive how any man can believe that it can be paid, within the time now limited, without distress. Let us look at known facts. Thirty millions of the capital of the bank are now out, on loans and discounts, in the States on the Mississippi and its waters; ten millions of which are loaned on the discount of bills of exchange, foreign and domestic, and twenty millions on promissory notes. Now, Sir, how is it possible that this vast amount can be collected in so short a period without suffering, by any management whatever? We are to remember, that, when the collection of this debt begins, at that same time, the existing medium of payment, that is, the circulation of the bills of the bank, will begin also to be restrained and withdrawn; and thus the means of payment must be limited just when the necessity of making payment becomes pressing. The whole debt is to be paid, and within the same time the whole circulation withdrawn.

The local banks, where there are such, will be able to afford little assistance; because they themselves will feel a full share of the pressure. They will not be in a condition to extend their discounts, but, in all probability, obliged to curtail them. Whence, then, are the means to come for paying this debt? and in what medium is payment to be made? If all this may be done with but slight pressure on the community, what course of conduct is to accomplish it? How is it to be done? What other thirty millions are to supply the place of these thirty millions now to be called in? What other circulation or medium of payment is to be adopted in the place of the bills of the bank? The message, following a singular train of argument, which had been used in this house, has a loud lamentation upon the suffering of the Western States on account of their being obliged to pay even interest on this debt. This payment of interest is itself represented as exhausting their means and ruinous to their prosperity. But if the interest cannot be paid without pressure, can both interest and principle be paid in four years without pressure? The truth is, the interest has been paid, is paid, and may continue to be paid, without any pressure at all; because the money borrowed is profitably employed by those who borrow it, and the rate of interest which they pay is at least two per cent lower than the actual value of money in that part of the country. But to pay the whole principal in less than four years, losing, at the same time, the existing and accustomed means and facilities of payment created by the bank itself, and to do this without extreme embarrassment, without absolute distress, is, in my judgment, impossible. I hesitate not to say, that, as this *veto* travels to the West, it will depreciate the value of the every man's property from the Atlantic States to the capital of Missouri. Its effect will be felt in the price of lands, the great and leading article of Western property, in the price of crops, in the products of labor,

in the repression of enterprise, and in embarrassment to every kind of business and occupation. I state this opinion strongly, because I have no doubt of its truth, and am willing its correctness should be judged by the event. Without personal acquaintance with the Western States, I know enough of their condition to be satisfied that what I have predicted must happen. The people of the West are rich but their riches consist in their immense quantities of excellent land, in the products of these lands, and in their spirit of enterprise. The actual value of money, or rate of interest, with them is high, because their pecuniary capital bears little proportion to their landed interest. At an average rate, money is not worth less than eight per cent per annum throughout the whole Western country, notwithstanding that it has now a loan or an advance from the bank of thirty millions, at six per cent. To call in this loan, at the rate of eight millions a year, in addition to the interest on the whole, and to take away, at the same time, that circulation which constitutes so great a portion of the medium of payment throughout that whole region, is an operation, which however wisely conducted, cannot but inflict a blow on the community of tremendous force and frightful consequences. The thing cannot be done without distress, bankruptcy, and ruin, to many. If the President had seen any practical manner in which this change might be effected without producing these consequences, he would have rendered infinite service to the community by pointing it out. But he has pointed out nothing, he has suggested nothing; he contents himself with saying, without giving any reason, that, if the pressure be heavy, the fault will be the bank's. I hope this is not merely an attempt to forestall opinion, and to throw on the bank the responsibility of those evils which threaten the country, for the sake of removing it from himself.

The responsibility justly lies with him, and there it ought to remain. A great majority of the people are satisfied with the bank as it is, and desirous that it should be continued. They wished no change. The strength of this public sentiment has carried the bill through Congress, against all the influence of the administration, and all the power of organized party. But the President has undertaken, on his own responsibility, to arrest the measure, by refusing his assent to the bill. He is answerable for the consequences, therefore, which necessarily follow the change which the expiration of the bank charter may produce; and if these consequences shall prove disastrous, they can fairly be ascribed to his policy only, and the policy of his administration.

Although, Sir, I have spoken of the effects of this veto in the Western country, it has not been because I considered that part of the United States exclusively affected by it. Some of the Atlantic States may feel its consequences, perhaps, as sensibly as those of the West, though not for the same reasons. The concern manifested by Pennsylvania for the renewal of the charter shows her sense of the importance of the bank to her own interest, and that of the nation. That great and enterprising State has entered into an extensive system of internal improvements, which necessarily makes heavy demands on her credit and her resources; and by the sound and acceptable currency which the bank affords, by the stability which it gives to private credit, and by occasional advances, made in anticipation of her revenues, and in aid of her great objects, she has found herself benefited, doubtless, in no inconsiderable degree. Her legislature has instructed her Senators here to advocate the renewal of the charter at this session. They have obeyed her voice, and yet they have the misfortune to find that, in the judgment of the President, *the measure is unconstitutional, unnecessary, dangerous to liberty, and is, moreover, ill-timed.*

But, Mr. President, it is not the local interest of the West, nor the particular interest of Pennsylvania, or any other State, which has influenced Congress in passing this bill. It has been governed by a wise foresight, and by a desire to avoid embarrassment in the pecuniary concerns of the country, to secure the safe collection and convenient transmission of public moneys, to maintain the circulation of the country, sound and safe as it now happily is, against the possible effects of a wild spirit of speculation. Finding the bank highly useful, Congress has thought fit to provide for its continuance.

As to the *time* of passing this bill, it would seem to be the last thing to be thought of, as a ground of objection, by the President; since, from the date of his first message to the present time, he has never failed to call our attention to the subject with all possible apparent earnestness. So early as December, 1829, in his message to the two houses, he declares, that he "cannot, in justice to the parties interested, too soon present the subject to the deliberate consideration of the legislature, in order to avoid the evils resulting from precipitancy, in a measure involving such important principles and such deep pecuniary interests." Aware of this early invitation given to Congress to take up the subject, by the President himself, the writer of the message seems to vary the ground of objection, and, instead of complaining that the time of bringing forward this measure was premature, to insist, rather, that, after the report of the committee of the other house, the bank should have withdrawn its application for the present! But that report offers no just ground, surely, for such withdrawal. The subject was before Congress; it was for Congress to decide upon it, with all the light shed by the report; and the question of postponement, having been made in both houses, was lost, by clear majorities, in each. Under such circumstances, it would have been somewhat singular, to say the least, if the bank itself had withdrawn its application.

It is indeed known to everybody, that neither the report of the committee nor any thing contained in that report, was relied on by the opposers of the renewal. If it has been discovered elsewhere, that that report contained matter important in itself, or which should have led to further inquiry, this may be proof of superior sagacity; for certainly no such thing was discerned by either House of Congress.

But, Sir, do we not now see that it was time, and high time, to press this bill, and to send it to the President? Does not the event teach us, that the measure was not brought forward one moment too early? The time had come when the people wished to know the decision of the administration on the question of the bank. Why conceal it, or postpone its declaration? Why, as in regard to the tariff, give out one set of opinions for the North, and another for the South?

An important election is at hand, and the renewal of the bank charter is a pending object of great interest, and some excitement. Should not the opinions of men high in office, and candidates for reëlection, be known, on this, as on other important public questions? Certainly, it is to be hoped that the people of the United States are not yet mere man-worshippers, that they do not choose their rulers without some regard to their political principles, or political opinions. Were they to do this, it would be to subject themselves voluntarily to the evils which the hereditary transmission of power, independent of all personal qualifications, inflicts on other nations. They will judge their public servants by their acts, and continue or withhold their confidence, as they shall think it merited, or as they shall think it forfeited. In every point of view, therefore, the moment had arrived, when it became the duty of Congress to come to a result, in regard to this highly important measure. The interest of the government, the interests of the people, the clear and indisputable voice of public opinion, all called upon Congress to act without further loss of time. It has acted, and its act has been negatived by the President; and this result of the proceedings here places the questions, with all its connections and all its incidents, fully before the people.

Before proceeding to the constitutional question, there are some other topics, treated in the message, which ought to be noticed. It commences by an inflamed statement of what it calls the "favor" bestowed upon the original bank by the government, or, indeed, as it is phrased, the "monopoly of its favor and support"; and through the whole message all possible changes are rung on the "gratuity," the "exclusive privileges," and "monopoly," of the bank charter. Now, Sir, the truth is, that the powers conferred on the bank are such, and no others, as are usually conferred on similar institutions. They constitute no monopoly, although some of them are of necessity, and with propriety, exclusive privileges. "The original act," says the message, "operated as a gratuity of many millions to the stockholders." What fair foundation is there for this remark? The stockholders received their charter, not gratuitously, but for a valuable consideration in money, prescribed by Congress, and actually paid. At some times the stock has been above *par*, at other times below *par*, according to prudence in management, or according to commercial occurrences. But if, by a judicious administration of its affairs, it had kept its stock always above *par*, what pretence would there be, nevertheless, for saying that such augmentation of its value was a "gratuity" from government? The message proceeds to declare, that the present act proposes another donation, another gratuity, to the same men, of at least seven millions more. It seems to me that this is an extraordinary statement, and an extraordinary style of argument, for such a subject and on such an occasion. In the first place, the facts are all assumed; they are taken for true without evidence. There are no proofs that any benefit to that amount will accrue to the stockholders nor any experience to justify the expectation of it. It rests on random estimates, or mere conjecture. But suppose the continuance of the charter should prove beneficial to the stockholders: do they not pay for it? They give twice as much for a charter of fifteen years, as was given before for one of twenty. And if the proposed *bonus*, or premium, be not, in the President's judgment, large enough, would he, nevertheless, on such a mere matter of opinion as that, negative the whole bill? May not Congress be trusted to decide even on such a subject as the amount of the money premium to be received by government for a charter of this kind?

But, Sir, there is a larger and a much more just view of this subject. The bill was not passed for the purpose of benefiting the present stockholders. Their benefit, if any, is incidental and collateral. Nor was it passed on any idea that they had a *right* to a renewed charter, although the message argues against such right, as if it had been somewhere set up and asserted. No such right has been asserted by any body. Congress passed the bill, not as a bounty or a favor to the present stockholders, nor to comply with any demand of right on their part; but to promote great public interests, for great public objects. Every bank must have some stockholders, unless it be such a bank as the President has recommended, and in regard to which he seems not likely to find much concurrence of other men's opinions; and if the stockholders, whoever they may be, conduct affairs of the bank prudently, the expectation is always, of course, that they will make it profitable to themselves, as well as useful to the public. If a bank charter is not to be granted, because, to some extent, it may be profitable to the stockholders, no charter can be granted. The objection lies against all banks.

Sir, the object aimed at by such institution is to connect the public safety and convenience with private interests. It has been found by experience, that banks are safest under private management, and that government banks are among the most dangerous of all inventions. Now, Sir, the whole drift of the message, is to reverse the settled judgment of all the civilized world, and to set up government banks, independent of private interest or private control. For this purpose the message labors, even beyond the measure of all its other labors, to create jealousies and prejudices, on the ground of the alleged benefit which individuals will derive from the renewal of this charter. Much less effort is made to show that government, or the public, will be injured by the bill, than that individuals will profit by it. Following up the impulses of the same spirit, the message goes on gravely to allege, that the act, as passed by Congress, proposes to make a *present* of some millions of dollars to foreigners, because a portion of the stock is held by foreigners. Sir, how would this sort of argument apply to other cases? The President has shown himself not only willing, but anxious, to pay off the three per cent stock of the United States at *par*, notwithstanding that it is notorious that foreigners are owners of the greater part of it. Why should he not call that a donation to foreigners of many millions?

I will not dwell particularly on this part of the message. Its tone and its arguments are all in the same strain. It speaks of the certain gain of the present stockholders, of the value of the monopoly; it says that all monopolies are granted at the expense of the public; that the many millions which this bill bestows on the stockholders come out of the earnings of the people; that, if government sells monopolies, it ought to sell them in open market; that it is an erroneous idea, that the present stockholders have a prescriptive right either to the favor or the bounty of government; that the stock is in the hands of a few, and that the whole American people are excluded from competition in the purchase of the monopoly. To all this I say, again, that much of it is assumption without proof; much of it is an argument against that which nobody has maintained or asserted; and the rest of it would be equally strong against any charter, at any time. These objections existed in their full strength, whatever that was, against the first bank. They existed, in like manner, against the present bank at its creation, and will always exist against all banks, indeed, all the fault found with the bill now before us is, that it proposes to continue the bank substantially as it now exists. "All the objectionable principles of the existing corporation," says the message, "and most of its odious features, are retained without alleviation"; so that the message is aimed against the bank, as it has existed from the first, and against any and all others resembling it in its general features.

Allow me, now, Sir, to take notice of an argument founded on the practical operation of the bank. That argument is this. Little of the stock of the bank is held in the West, the capital being chiefly owned by citizens of the Southern and Eastern States, and by foreigners. But the Western and Southwestern States owe the bank a heavy debt, so heavy that the interest amounts to a million six hundred thousound a year. This interest is carried to the Eastern States, or to Europe, annually, and its payment is a burden on the people of the West, and a drain of their currency, which no country can bear without inconvenience and distress. The true character and the whole value of this argument are manifest by the mere statement of it. The people of the West are, from their situation, necessarily large borrowers. They need money, capital, and they borrow it, because they can derive a benefit from its use, much beyond the interest which they pay. They borrow at six per cent of the bank, although the value of money with them is at least as high as eight. Nevertheless, although they borrow at this low rate of

interest, and although they use all they borrow thus profitably, yet they cannot pay the interest without "inconvenience and distress"; and then, Sir, follows the logical conclusion, that, although they cannot pay even the interest without inconvenience and distress, yet less than four years is ample time for the bank to call in the whole, both principal and interest, without causing more than a light pressure. This is the argument.

Then follows another, which may be thus stated. It is competent to the States to tax the property of their citizens vested in the stock of this bank; but the power is denied of taxing the stock of foreigners; therefore the stock will be worth ten or fifteen per cent more to foreigners than to residents, and will of course inevitably leave the country, and make the American people debtors to aliens in nearly the whole amount due the bank, and send across the Atlantic from two to five millions of specie every year, to pay the bank dividends.

Mr. President, arguments like these might be more readily disposed of, were it not that the high and official source from which they proceed imposes the necessity of treating them with respect. In the first place, it may safely be denied that the stock of the bank is any more valuable to foreigners than to our own citizens, or an object of greater desire to them, except in so far as capital may be more abundant in the foreign country, and therefore its owners more in want of opportunity of investment. The foreign stockholder enjoys no exemption from taxation. He is, of course, taxed by his own government for his incomes, derived from this as well as other property; and this is a full answer to the whole statement. But it may be added, in the second place, that it is not the practice of civilized states to tax the property of foreigners under such circumstances. Do we tax, or did we ever tax, the foreign holders of our public debt? Does Pennsylvania, New York, or Ohio tax the foreign holders of stock in the loans contracted by either of these States? Certainly not. Sir, I must confess I had little expected to see, on such an occasion as the present, a labored and repeated attempt to produce an impression on the public opinion unfavorable to the bank, from the circumstance that foreigners are among its stockholders. I have no hesitation in saying, that I deem such a train of remark as the message contains on this point, coming from the President of the United States, to be injurious to the credit and character of the country abroad; because it manifests a jealousy, a lurking disposition not to respect the property, of foreigners invited hither by our own laws. And, Sir, what is its tendency but to excite this jealousy, and create groundless prejudices?

From the commencement of the government, it has been thought desirable to invite, rather than to repel, the introduction of foreign capital. Our stocks have all been open to foreign subscriptions; and the State banks, in like manner are free to foreign ownership. Whatever State has created a debt has been willing that foreigners should become purchasers, and desirous of it. How long is it, Sir, since Congress itself passed a law vesting new powers in the President of the United States over the cities in this District, for the very purpose of increasing their credit abroad, the better to enable them to borrow money to pay their subscriptions to the Chesapeake and Ohio Canal? It is easy to say that there is danger to liberty, danger to independence, in a bank open to foreign stockholders, because it is easy to say anything. But neither reason nor experience proves any such danger. The foreign stockholder cannot be a director. He has no voice even in the choice of directors. His money is placed entirely in the management of the directors appointed by the President and Senate and by the American stockholders. So far as there is dependence or influence either way, it is to the disadvantage of the foreign stockholder. He has parted with the

control over his own property, instead of exercising control over the property or over the actions of others. And, Sir, let it now be added, in further answer to this class of objections, that experience has abundantly confuted them all. This government has existed forty-three years, and has maintained, in full being and operation, a bank, such as is now proposed to be renewed, for thirty-six years out of the forty-three. We have never for a moment had a bank not subject to every one of these objections. Always, foreigners might be stockholders; always, foreign stock has been exempt from State taxation, as much as at present; always, the same power and privileges; always all that which is now called a "monopoly," a "gratuity," a "present," has been possessed by the bank. And yet there has been found no danger to liberty, no introduction of foreign influence, and no accumulation of irresponsible power in a few hands. I cannot but hope, therefore, that the people of the United States will not now yield up their judgment to those notions which would reverse all our best experience, and persuade us to discontinue a useful institution from the influence of vague and unfounded declamation against its danger to the public liberties. Our liberties, indeed, must stand upon very frail foundations if the government cannot, without endangering them, avail itself of those common facilities, in the collection of its revenues and the management of its finances, which all other governments, in commercial countries, find useful and necessary.

In order to justify its alarm for the security of our independence, the message supposes a case. It supposes that the bank should pass principally into the hands of the subjects of a foreign country, and that we should be involved in war with that country, and then it exclaims, "What would be our condition?" Why, Sir, it is plain that all the advantages would be on our side. The bank would still be our institution, subject to our own laws, and all its directors elected by ourselves; and our means would be enhanced, not by the confiscation and plunder, but by the proper use, of the foreign capital in our hands. And, Sir, it is singular enough, that this very state of war, from which this argument against a bank is drawn, is the very thing which, more than all others, convinced the country and the government of the necessity of a national bank. So much was the want of such an institution felt in the late war, that the subject engaged the attention of Congress, constantly, from the declaration of that war down to the time when the existing bank was actually established; so that in this respect, as well as in others, the argument of the message is directly opposed to the whole experience of the government, and to the general and long-settled convictions of the country.

I now proceed, Sir, to a few remarks upon the President's constitutional objections to the bank; and I cannot forbear to say, in regard to them, that he appears to me to have assumed very extraordinary grounds of reasoning. He denies that the constitutionality of the bank is a settled question. If it be not, will it ever become so, or what disputed question ever can be settled? I have already observed, that for thirty-six years out of the forty-three during which the government has been in being, a bank has existed, such as is now proposed to be continued.

As early as 1791, after great deliberation, the first bank charter was passed by Congress, and approved by President Washington. It established an institution, resembling, in all things now objected to, the present bank. That bank, like this, could take lands in payment of its debts; that charter, like the present, gave the States no power of taxation; it allowed foreigners to hold stock; it restrained Congress from creating other banks. It gave also exclusive privileges, and in all particulars it was, according to the doctrine of the message, as objectionable as that now existing. That bank continued

twenty years. In 1816, the present institution was established, and has been ever since in full operation. Now, Sir, the question of the power of Congress to create such institutions has been contested in every manner known to our Constitution and laws. The forms of the government furnish no new mode in which to try this question. It has been discussed over and over again, in Congress; it has been argued and solemnly adjudged in the Supreme Court; every President, except the present, has considered it a settled question; many of the State legislatures have instructed their Senators to vote for the bank; the tribunals of the States, in every instance, have supported its constitutionality; and, beyond all doubt and dispute, the general public opinion of the country has at all times given and does now give, its full sanction and approbation to the exercise of this power, as being a constitutional power. There has been no opinion questioning the power expressed or intimated, at any time, by either house of Congress by any President, or by any respectable judicial tribunal. Now, Sir, if this practice of near forty years, if these repeated exercises of the power, in this solemn adjudication of the Supreme Court, with the concurrence and approbation of public opinion, do not settle the question, how is any question ever to be settled, about which any one may choose to raise a doubt? . . .

Mr. President, I have understood the true and well-established doctrine to be, that, after it has been decided that it is competent for Congress to establish a bank, then it follows that it may create such a bank as it judges, in its discretion, to be best, and invest it with all such power as it may deem fit and suitable; with this limitation, always, that all is to be done in the *bona fide* execution of the power to create a bank. If the granted powers are appropriate to the professed end, so that the granting of them cannot be regarded as usurpation of authority by

Congress, or an evasion of constitutional restrictions, under color of establishing a bank, then the charter is constitutional, whether these powers be thought indispensable by others or not, or whether they . . . are more or less appropriate to their end. It is enough that they are suited to produce the effects designed; and no comparison is to be instituted, in order to try their constitutionality, between them and others which may be suggested. A case analogous to the present is found in the constitutional power of Congress over the mail. The Constitution says no more than that "Congress shall have power to establish post-offices and post-roads"; and, in the general clause, "all powers necessary and proper" to give effect to this. In the execution of this power, Congress has protected the mail, by providing that robbery of it shall be punished with death. Is this infliction of capital punishment constitutional? Certainly it is not, unless it be both "proper and necessary." The President may not think it necessary or proper; the law, then, according to the system of reasoning enforced by the message, is of no binding force, and the President may disobey it, and refuse to see it executed.

The truth is, Mr. President, that if the general object, the subject-matter, properly belongs to Congress, all its incidents belong to Congress also. If Congress is to establish post-offices and post-roads, it may for that end, adopt one set of regulations or another; and either would be constitutional. So the details of one bank are as constitutional as those of another, if they are confined fairly and honestly to the purpose of organizing the institution, and rendering it useful. One *bank* is as constitutional as another *bank*. If Congress possesses the power to make a bank, it possesses the power to make it efficient, and competent to produce the good expected from it. It may clothe it with all such power and privileges, not otherwise inconsistent with the Constitution, as may be necessary, in its own judgment, to make it what government deems it should be. It may confer on it such immunities as may induce individuals to become stockholders, and to furnish the capital; and since the extent of these immunities and privileges is a matter of discretion, and matter of opinion, Congress only can decide it, because Congress alone can frame or grant the charter. A charter, thus granted to individuals, becomes a contract with them, upon their compliance with its terms. The bank becomes an agent, bound to perform certain duties, and entitled to certain stipulated rights and privileges, in compensation for the proper discharge of these duties; and all these stipulations, so long as they are appropriate to the object professed, and not repugnant to any other constitutional injunction, are entirely within the competency of Congress. And yet, Sir, the message of the President toils through all the commonplace topics of monopoly, the right of taxation, the suffering of the poor, and the arrogance of the rich, with as much painful effort, as if one, or another, or all of them, had something to do with the constitutional question. . . .

I beg leave to repeat, Mr. President, that what I have now been considering are the President's objections, not to the policy or expediency, but to the constitutionality, of the bank; and not to the constitutionality of any new or proposed bank, but of the bank as it now is, and as it has long existed. If the President had declined to approve this bill because he thought the original charter unwisely granted, and the bank, in point of policy and expediency, objectionable or mischievous, and in that view only had suggested the reasons now urged by him, his argument, however inconclusive, would have been intelligible, and not, in its whole frame and scope, inconsistent with all well-established first principles. His rejection of the bill, in that case, would have been, no doubt, an extraordinary exercise of power; but it would have been, nevertheless, the exercise of a power belonging to his office, and trusted by the Constitution to his discretion. But when he puts forth an array of arguments such as the message employs, not against the expediency of the bank, but against its constitutional existence, he confounds all distinctions, mixes questions of policy and questions of right together, and turns all constitutional restraints into mere matters of opinion. As far as its power extends, either in its direct effects or as a precedent, the message not only unsettles every thing which has been settled under the Constitution, but would show, also, that the Constitution itself is utterly incapable of any fixed construction or definite interpretation, and that there is no possibility of establishing, by its authority, any practical limitations on the powers of the respective branches of the government.

When the message denies, as it does the authority of the Supreme Court to decide on constitutional questions, it effects, so far as the opinion of the President and his authority can effect it, a complete change in our government. It does two things: first, it converts constitutional limitations of power into mere matters of opinion, and then it strikes the judicial department, as an efficient department, out of our system. But the message by no means stops even at this point. Having denied to Congress the authority of judging what powers may be constitutionally conferred on a bank, and having erected the judgment of the President himself into a standard by which to try the constitutional character of such powers, and having denounced the authority of the Supreme Court to decide finally on constitutional questions, the message proceeds to claim for the President, not the power of approval, but the primary power, the power of originating laws. The President informs Congress, that *he* would have sent them such a charter, if it had been properly asked for, as they ought to confer. He very plainly intimates, that, in his opinion, the establish-

ment of all laws, of this nature at least, belongs to the functions of the executive government; and that Congress ought to have waited for the manifestation of the executive will, before it presumed to touch the subject. Such, Mr. President, stripped of their disguises, are the real pretenses set up in behalf of the executive power in this most extraordinary paper.

Mr. President, we have arrived at a new epoch. We are entering on experiments, with the government and the Constitution of the country, hitherto untried, and of fearful and appalling aspect. This message calls us to the contemplation of a future which little resembles the past. Its principles are at war with all that public opinion has sustained, and all which the experience of the government has sanctioned. It denies first principles; it contradicts truths, heretofore received as indisputable. It denies to the judiciary the interpretation of law, and claims to divide with Congress the power of originating statutes. It extends the grasp of executive pretension over every power of the government. But this is not all. It presents the chief magistrate of the Union in the attitude of arguing away the powers of that government over which he has been chosen to preside; and adopting for this purpose modes of reasoning which, even under the influence of all proper feeling towards high official station, it is difficult to regard as respectable. It appeals to every prejudice which may betray men into a mistaken view of their own interests, and to every passion which may lead them to disobey the impulses of their understanding. It urges all the specious topics of State rights and national encroachment against that which a great majority of the States have affirmed to be rightful, and in which all of them have acquiesced. It sows, in an unsparing manner, the seeds of jealousy and ill-will against that government of which its author is the official head. It raises a cry, that liberty is in danger, at the very moment when it puts forth claims to powers heretofore unknown and unheard of. It affects alarm for the public freedom . . . so much as its own unparalleled pretences. This, even, is not all. It manifestly seeks to inflame the poor against the rich; it wantonly attacks whole classes of the people, for the purpose of turning against them the prejudices and the resentments of other classes. It is a state paper which finds no topic too exciting for its use, no passion too inflammable for its address and its solicitation.

Such is this message. It remains now for the people of the United States to choose between the principles here avowed and their government. These cannot subsist together. The one or the other must be rejected. If the sentiments of the message shall receive general approbation, the Constitution will have perished even earlier than the moment which its enemies originally allowed for the termination of its existence. It will not have survived to its fiftieth year.

Arthur M. Schlesinger, Jr.

Class Conflict in Jacksonian Democracy

The Jacksonian revolution rested on premises which the struggles of the thirties hammered together into a kind of practical social philosophy. The outline of this way of thinking about society was clear. It was stated and restated, as we have seen, on every level of political discourse from presidential messages to stump speeches, from newspaper editorials to private letters. It provided the intellectual background without which the party battles of the day cannot be understood.

The Jacksonians believed that there was a deep-rooted conflict in the society between the "producing" and "nonproducing" classes—the farmers and laborers, on the one hand, and the business community on the other. The business community was considered to hold high cards in this conflict through its network of banks and corporations, its control of education and the press, above all, its power over the state: it was therefore able to strip the working classes of the fruits of their labor. "Those who produce all wealth," said Amos Kendall,[1] "are

From Arthur M. Schlesinger, Jr. *The Age of Jackson*, pp. 306–321. By permission of Little, Brown and Company. Copyright 1945 by Arthur M. Schlesinger, Jr.

[1] Ed. note: *Amos Kendall* (1789–1869), a Kentucky journalist and postmaster, rose to the position of Auditor of the Treasury and was also a member of Jackson's Kitchen Cabinet. Later he edited the *Weekly Union Democrat.*

themselves left poor. They see principalities extending and palaces built around them, without being aware that the entire expense is a tax upon themselves."

If they wished to preserve their liberty, the producing classes would have to unite against the movement "to make the rich richer and the potent more powerful." Constitutional prescriptions and political promises afforded no sure protection. "We have heretofore been too disregardful of the fact," observed William M. Gouge,[2] "that social order is quite as dependent on the laws which regulate the distribution of wealth, as on political organization." The program now was to resist every attempt to concentrate wealth and power further in a single class. Since free elections do not annihilate the opposition, the fight would be unceasing. "The struggle for power," said C. C. Cambreleng,[3] "is as eternal as the division of society. A defeat cannot destroy the boundary which perpetually separates the democracy from the aristocracy."

The specific problem was to control the power of the capitalistic groups, mainly Eastern, for the benefit of the noncapitalist groups, farmers and laboring men, East, West and South. The basic Jacksonian ideas came naturally enough from the East, which best understood the nature of business power and reacted most sharply against it. The legend that Jacksonian democracy was the explosion of the frontier, lifting into the government some violent men filled with rustic prejudices against big business, does not explain the facts, which were somewhat more complex. Jacksonian democracy was rather a second American phase of that endur-

ing struggle between the business community and the rest of society which is the guarantee of freedom in a liberal capitalist state.[4]

Like any social philosophy, Jacksonian democracy drew on several intellectual traditions. Basically, it was a revival of Jeffersonianism, but the Jeffersonian inheritance was strengthened by the infusion of fresh influences; notably the antimonopolistic tradition, formulated primarily by Adam Smith and expounded in Amer-

---

[2] Jacksonian editor, economist, and hard money advocate.

[3] Ed. note: *Churchill C. Cambreleng* (1786–1862) of New York was a Democrat in the House of Representatives and later served as Minister to Russia.

[4] It may be well to observe contemporary apprehensions long enough to discuss the relationship of the Jacksonian analysis to Marxism. Clarification would be useful, both for conservatives who declare that any talk of class conflict is Communistic, and for Communists who claim promiscuously any kind of economic insight as the exclusive result of their infallible method. In truth, the Jacksonian analysis, far from being Marxist, is the very core of our radical democratic tradition. The fact that the *Communist Manifesto* was not written until 1848 would seem conclusive on this point; and Marx and Lenin, unlike their disciples, made no irresponsible pretense to the invention of the theory of class conflict. Marx wrote to Weydemeyer, March 5, 1852: "As far as I am concerned, the honour does not belong to me for having discovered the existence either of classes in modern society or of the struggle between the classes. Bourgeois historians a long time before me expounded the historical development of this class struggle, and bourgeois economists, the economic anatomy of classes. What was new on my part, was to prove the following: (1) that the existence of classes is connected only with certain historical struggles which arise out of the development of production; (2) that class struggle necessarily leads to the dictatorship of the proletariat; (3) that this dictatorship is itself only a transition to the abolition of all classes and to a classless society."

Lenin is, if possible, more explicit. "The theory of the class struggle was *not* created by Marx, but by the bourgeoisie *before* Marx and is, generally speaking, *acceptable* to the bourgeoisie. He who recognizes *only* the class struggle is not yet a Marxist; he may be found not to have gone beyond the boundaries of bourgeois reasoning and politics. To limit Marxism to the teaching of the class struggle means to curtail Marxism—to distort it, to reduce it to something which is acceptable to the bourgeoisie. A Marxist is one who *extends* the acceptance of the class struggle to the acceptance of the *dictatorship of the proletariat.*"

ica by Gouge, Leggett,[5] Sedgwick,[6] Cambreleng; and the pro-labor tradition, formulated primarily by William Cobbett[7] and expounded by G. H. Evans,[8] Ely Moore, John Ferral.

The inspiration of Jeffersonianism was so all-pervading and fundamental for its every aspect that Jacksonian democracy can be properly regarded as a somewhat more hard-headed and determined version of Jeffersonian democracy. But it is easy to understate the differences. Jefferson himself, though widely revered and quoted, had no personal influence on any of the leading Jacksonians save perhaps Van Buren. Madison and Monroe were accorded still more vague and perfunctory homage. The radical Jeffersonians, Taylor, Randolph and Macon, who had regarded the reign of Virginia as almost an era of betrayal, were much more vivid in the minds of the Jacksonians. . . .

The period of conservative supremacy from 1816 to 1828 had irrevocably destroyed the agricultural paradise, and the Jacksonians were accommodating the insights of Jefferson to the new concrete situations. This process of readjustment involved a moderately thorough overhauling of favorite Jeffersonian doctrines.

The central Jefferson hope had been a nation of small freeholders, each acquiring thereby so much moral probity, economic security and political independence as to render unnecessary any invasion of the rights or liberties of others. The basis of such a society, as Jefferson clearly recognized, was agriculture and handicraft. What was the status of the Jeffersonian hope now that it was clear that, at best, agriculture must share the future with industry and finance?

Orestes A. Brownson[9] exhausted one possibility in his essay on "The Laboring Classes." He reaffirmed the Jeffersonian demand: "We ask that every man become an independent proprietor, possessing enough of the goods of this world, to be able by his own moderate industry to provide for the wants of his body." But what, in practice, would this mean? As Brownson acknowledged years later, his plan would have "broken up the whole modern commercial system, prostrated the great industries, . . . and thrown the mass of the people back on the land to get their living by agricultural and mechanical pursuits." Merely to state its consequences was to prove its futility. The dominion of the small freeholder was at an end.

The new industrialism had to be accepted: banks, mills, factories, industrial capital, industrial labor. These were all distasteful realities for orthodox Jeffersonians, and, not least, the propertyless workers. "The mobs of great cities," Jefferson had said, "add just so much to the support of pure government, as sores do to the strength of the human body." The very ferocity of his images expressed the violence of his feelings. "When we get piled upon one another in large cities, as in Europe," he told Madison, "we shall become corrupt as in Europe, and go to eating one another as they do there." It

---

[5] Ed. note: *William Leggett* (1801–1839) was a liberal editor who served the Democrat party with his stinging editorials. Appointed to a diplomatic post in Guatemala, he died while preparing for the trip to that Central American republic.

[6] Ed. note: *Theodore Sedgwick, Jr.* (1811–1859) was a New York lawyer and prolific writer on law and Constitutional reform.

[7] Ed. Note: *William Cobbett* (1763–1835), a Federalist journalist was the founder of party journalism in the United States.

[8] Ed. Note: *George H. Evans* (1805–1856), an editor and reformer, helped to form workingmen's parties. During the 1840s he published *A History of the Origin and Progress of the Working Man's Party.*

[9] Ed. note: *Orestes A. Brownson* (1803–1876) was a Universalist minister and a distinguished liberal editor for several magazines, the most noted of which was the *Brownson's Quarterly Review.* He also authored several books, among them his autobiography, *The Spirit Rapper.*

was a universal sentiment among his followers. "No man should live," Nathaniel Macon used to say, "where he can hear his neighbour's dog bark."

Yet the plain political necessity of winning the labor vote obliged a change of mood. Slowly, with some embarrassment, the Jeffersonian preferences for the common man were enlarged to take in the city workers. In 1833 the *New York Evening Post,* declaring that, if anywhere, a large city of mixed population would display the evils of universal suffrage, asked if this had been the case in New York and answered: No. Amasa Walker[10] set out the same year to prove that "great cities are not *necessarily,* as the proverb says, 'great sores,'" and looked forward cheerily to the day when they would be "great fountains of healthful moral influence, sending forth streams that shall fertilize and bless the land." The elder Theodore Sedgwick added that the cause of the bad reputation of cities was economic: "it is the sleeping in garrets and cellars; the living in holes and dens; in dirty, unpaved, unlighted streets, without the accommodations of wells, cisterns, baths, and other means of cleanliness and health"—clear up this situation, and cities will be all right.

Jackson himself never betrayed any of Jefferson's revulsion to industrialism. He was, for example, deeply interested by the mills of Lowell in 1833, and his inquiries respecting hours, wages and production showed, observers reported, "that the subject of domestic manufactures had previously engaged his attentive observation." His presidential allusions to the "producing classes" always included the workingmen of the cities.

The acceptance of the propertyless laboring classes involved a retreat from one of the strongest Jeffersonian positions. John Taylor's distinction between "natural" and "artificial" property had enabled the Jeffersonians to enlist the moral and emotional resources contained in the notion of property. They could claim to be the protectors of property rights, while the business community, by despoiling the producers of the fruits of their labor, were the enemies of property. Yet, this distinction, if it were to have other than a metaphorical existence, had to rest on the dominance of agriculture and small handicraft. The proceeds of the labor of a farmer, or a blacksmith, could be measured with some exactness; but who could say what the "just" fruits of labor were for a girl whose labor consisted in one small operation in the total process of manufacturing cotton cloth? In what sense could propertyless people be deprived of their property?

Taylor had repeatedly warned that "fictitious" property would seek to win over "real" property by posing as the champion of all property against the mob. Now that the Democrats were the party, not only of small holders, but of propertyless workers, the conservative pose seemed more plausible. The Whigs diligently set forth to make every attack on "fictitious" capital an attack on all property rights. "The philosophy that denounces accumulation," said Edward Everett,[11] "is the philosophy of barbarism." The outcry over monopoly, added Henry Clay, is "but a new form of attacking the rights of property. A man may not use his property in what form he pleases, even if sanctioned by the laws of the community in which he lives, without being denounced as a monopolist."

The Whigs slowly won the battle. The discovery of the courts that a corporation was really a person completed their victory. By 1843 William S. Wait could strike the Jeffersonian flag: "'Security to

---

[10] Ed. note: *Amasa Walker* (1799–1853), a Republican congressman and political economist, lectured and wrote articles for the *Boston Daily Patriot.*

[11] Ed. note: *Edward Everett* (1794–1865) of Massachusetts was best known for his essays and orations, but he also served as Secretary of State in the Fillmore administration. He later helped organize the Union party, a branch of the Whig organization.

property' no longer means security to the citizen in the possession of his moderate competency, but security to him who monopolizes thousands—security to a few, who may live in luxury and ease upon the blood and sweat of many."

Jacksonians now tended to exalt human rights as a counterweight to property rights. The Whigs, charged Frank Blair, were seeking such an extension of "the rights of property as to swallow up and annihilate those of persons"; the Democratic party would "do all in its power to preserve and defend them". "We believe property should be held subordinate to man, and not man to property," said Orestes A. Brownson; "and therefore that it is always lawful to make such modifications of its constitution as the good of Humanity requires." The early decisions of Roger B. Taney's court helped establish the priority of the public welfare. But the Democrats had surrendered an important ideological bastion. The right to property provided a sturdy foundation for liberalism, while talk of human rights too often might end up in sentimentality or blood.

In several respects, then, the Jacksonians revised the Jeffersonian faith for America. They moderated that side of Jeffersonianism which talked of agricultural virtue, independent proprietors, "natural" property, abolition of industrialism, and expanded immensely that side which talked of economic equality, the laboring classes, human rights, and the control of industrialism. This readjustment enabled the Jacksonians to attack economic problems which had baffled and defeated the Jeffersonians. It made for a greater realism, and was accompanied by a general toughening of the basic Jeffersonian conceptions. While the loss of "property" was serious, both symbolically and intellectually, this notion had been for most Jeffersonians somewhat submerged next to the romantic image of the free and virtuous cultivator; and the Jacksonians grew much more

insistent about theories of capitalist alienation. Where, for the Jeffersonians, the tensions of class conflict tended to dissolve in vague generalizations about the democracy and the aristocracy, many Jacksonians would have agreed with A. H. Wood's remark, "It is in vain to talk of Aristocracy and Democracy—these terms are too variable and indeterminate to convey adequate ideas of the present opposing interests; the division is between the rich and the poor—the warfare is between them."

This greater realism was due, in the main, to the passage of time. The fears of Jefferson were now actualities. One handled fears by exorcism, but actualities by adjustment. For Jeffersonians mistrust of banks and corporations was chiefly a matter of theory; for the Jacksonians it was a matter of experience. The contrast between the scintillating metaphors of John Taylor[12] and the sober detail of William M. Gouge expressed the difference. Jefferson rejected the Industrial Revolution and sought to perpetuate the smiling society which preceded it (at least, so the philosopher; facts compelled the President toward a different policy), while Jackson, accepting industrialism as an ineradicable and even useful part of the economic landscape, sought rather to control it. Jeffersonian democracy looked wistfully back toward a past slipping further every minute into the mists of memory, while Jacksonian democracy came straightforwardly to grips with a rough and unlovely present.

The interlude saw also the gradual unfolding of certain consequences of the democratic dogma which had not been so clear to the previous generation. Though theoretically aware of the relation between political and economic power, the

---

[12] Ed. note: *John Taylor* (1753–1824) of Virginia was a defender of Jeffersonianism and an astute political thinker and writer. His *An Inquiry into the Principles and Policy of the Government of the United States* has been acclaimed as one of the great historic contributions to political science.

Jeffersonians had been occupied, chiefly, with establishing political equality. This was their mission, and they had little time to grapple with the economic questions.

But the very assertion of political equality raised inevitably the whole range of problems involved in property and class conflict. How could political equality mean anything without relative economic equality among the classes of the country? This question engaged the Jacksonians. As Orestes A. Brownson said, "A Locofoco is a Jeffersonian Democrat, who having realized political equality, passed through one phase of the revolution, now passes on to another, and attempts the realization of social equality, so that the actual condition of men in society shall be in harmony with their acknowledged rights as citizens." This gap between Jeffersonian and Jacksonian democracy enabled men like John Quincy Adams, Henry Clay, Joseph Story and many others, who had been honest Jeffersonians, to balk at the economic extremities to which Jackson proposed to lead them.

The Jacksonians thus opened irrevocably the economic question, which the Jeffersonians had only touched halfheartedly. Yet while they clarified these economic implications of democracy, the Jacksonians were no more successful than their predecessors in resolving certain political ambiguities. Of these, two were outstanding—the problem of the virtue of majorities, and the problem of the evil of government. Since the Jacksonians made useful explorations of these issues after 1840, they will be reserved for later discussion.

A second source of inspiration for the Jacksonians was the libertarian economic thought stirred up by Adam Smith and *The Wealth of Nations*. Believers in the myth of Adam Smith, as expounded by present-day publicists both of the right and of the left, may find this singular; but the real Adam Smith was rich in ammunition for the Jacksonians, as for any foe of business manipulation of the state.

The Wealth of Nations quietly, precisely and implacably attacked the alliance of government and business, showing how monopoly retarded the economic growth of nations, and promoted the exploitation of the people. It was, in effect, a criticism of the kind of mercantilist policy which, in modified form, Hamilton had instituted in the Federalist program of the seventeen-nineties. Smith's classic argument against monopoly appealed strongly to the Jacksonians, and his distinction between productive and unproductive labor converged with the Jacksonian distinction between the producers and the nonproducers. They adopted his labor theory of value, in preference to the physiocratic doctrine which argued that value originated exclusively in land, and toward which Jefferson leaned. Smith's currency views were on the moderate hard-money line, favoring the suppression of notes under five pounds. And, contrary to the Adam Smith of folklore, the real Smith had no objection to government intervention which would protect, not exploit, the nation. "Those exertions of the natural liberty of a few individuals," he wrote, discussing the question of banking control, "which might endanger the security of the whole society, are, and ought to be, restrained by the laws of all governments; of the most free, as well as of the most despotical." His advocacy of education and his general hope for the well-being of the farming and laboring classes further recommended him to the Jacksonians.

In many respects, Adam Smith formulated on the economic level the same sentiments which Jefferson put into glowing moral and political language. Jefferson himself thought *The Wealth of Nations* "the best book extant" on economic questions. The translation of J. B. Say's popularization of Smith increased the currency of laissez faire doctrine. The little village of Stockbridge in Massachusetts was a particular center of free-trade thought. When Theodore Sedgwick observed of Adam Smith in 1838, "His voice has been ringing in the world's ears for sixty years, but it is only now in the United States that he is listened to, reverenced, and followed," the credit for this awakening went in great part to himself. His missionary efforts converted William Cullen Bryant, David Dudley Field and Theodore Sedgwick, Jr., and it was doubtless from Bryant[13] that the previously nonpolitical Leggett got his introduction to *The Wealth of Nations.* . . .

The basic economic conception, which Adam Smith shared with Jefferson, was of a "natural order of things," that, once cleared of monopolistic clogs, would function to the greatest good of the greatest number. This conception, for all its apparent clarity, soon turned out to be packed with ambiguities. Free enterprise might mean, as with Leggett, a fighting belief in the virtue of competition, or it might mean, as with present-day conservatives, a fighting belief in the evil of government intervention. The battles of the Jackson era showed how these two interpretations of *laissez faire* were to come into increasing conflict.

The Jacksonians, vigorously in the first camp, had no hesitation in advocating government intervention in order to restore competition. In any case, their conception of the "natural order"—the region in which government was obligated not to interfere—included the right of the workingman to the full proceeds of his labor. Government, said Van Buren, should always be administered so as to insure to the laboring classes "a full enjoyment of the fruits of their industry."

Left to itself, and free from the blighting influence of partial legislation, monopolies, congregated wealth, and interested combinations, the compensation of labor will

always preserve this salutary relation. It is only when the natural order of society is disturbed by one or other of these causes, that the wages of labor become inadequate.

The prescription of free enterprise thus became government action to destroy the "blighting influence of partial legislation, monopolies, congregated wealth, and interested combinations" in the interests of the "natural order of society."

But the language of Adam Smith, as a result of its origin in a critique of mercantilism as government policy, lent itself also to attacks on government intervention. The presidency of Jackson had begun to reduce the conservative enthusiasm, in the manner of Hamilton, for state interference, and the business community commenced now to purloin the phrases of *laissez faire.* By 1888 E. M. Shepard, a Grover Cleveland Democrat, could dedicate a biography of Van Buren to the thesis that Van Buren was a thoroughgoing foe of government intervention—a thesis which required the total omission of such measures as the order establishing the ten-hour day.

In the end, business altogether captured the phrases of *laissez faire* and used them more or less ruthlessly in defense of monopoly, even coupling them with arguments for the protective tariff, a juxtaposition which would at least have given earlier conservatives a decent sense of embarrassment. Adam Smith himself doubted whether large businessmen really believed in free competition. The sequel confirmed his doubts. The irony was that the slogans of free trade, which he developed in order to destroy monopoly, should end up as its bulwark.

A third important stimulus to the Jacksonians was the foaming tide of social revolt in Britain, reaching them primarily through the writings of William Cobbett. As the "Peter Porcupine" of Federalist journalism, Cobbett had been an early object of Jeffersonian wrath. But, on returning to Britain after some years in

[13] Ed. note: *William C. Bryant* (1794–1878), a practicing lawyer, became best known for his poetry. He also edited the *New York Evening Post* and published a book on his travels.

America, Cobbett discovered that the conservative values he had been so stalwartly defending were rapidly disappearing before the smokey ravages of industrialism. He gave splendid and angry expression to the hatred of independent workingmen for the impending degradation, and his fluent, robust, abusive prose created a new political consciousness among the common people of Britain.

A vehement advocate of the rights of workers to the full fruits of their industry, and a savage enemy of the new financial aristocracy, he found a rapt audience in America, especially in the labor movement. *Paper against Gold,* reprinted in New York in 1834, helped the hard-money campaign. William H. Hale of New York, the author of *Useful Knowledge for the Producers of Wealth,* and Thomas Brothers, the editor of the *Radical Reformer* of Philadelphia, were perhaps his leading disciples, but his unquenchable vitality inspired the whole radical wing.

Cobbett on his part watched events across the Atlantic with immense enthusiasm. Jackson's fight against the Bank stirred him to the inordinate conclusion that Jackson was "the bravest and greatest man now living in this world, or that ever has lived in this world, as far as my knowledge extends." He wrote a life of Jackson (or rather interpolated characteristic comments into a reprint of Eaton's book) and even issued an abridged version of Gouge's *Paper Money,* under the title of *The Curse of Paper-Money and Banking.* He addressed superb open letters to the American President, and his admiration for "the greatest soldier and the greatest statesman whose name has ever yet appeared upon the records of valour and of wisdom" never faltered.

Yet, with all his passion for social justice, Cobbett talked very little about democracy. He seemed almost to feel—and his American followers had similar overtones —that, if the speculators, rag barons and capitalists were thrown out, and the lower classes instituted in power, the main problems of society would be solved. His gusty idealization of the British yeoman, redolent of beef and beer, led him away from theories of class balance into implications of class infallibility, almost at times leaning from democracy toward socialism. These were but shadings, and in his American disciples shades of shadings. Yet George H. Evans, John Commerford, John Ferral and the early labor leaders seemed to regard democracy as more protective doctrine than good in itself. In power they might have acted little differently—if toward different ends—from Daniel Webster and Nicholas Biddle.

The radical democrats had a definite conception of their relation to history. From the Jeffersonian analysis, fortified by the insights of Adam Smith and Cobbett, they sketched out an interpretation of modern times which gave meaning and status to the Jacksonian struggles.

Power, said the Jacksonians, goes with property. In the Middle Ages the feudal nobility held power in society through its monopoly of land under feudal tenure. The overthrow of feudalism, with the rise of new forms of property, marked the first step in the long march toward freedom. The struggle was carried on by the rising business community—"commercial, or business capital, against landed capital; merchants, traders, manufacturers, artizans, against the owners of the soil, the great landed nobility." It lasted from the close of the twelfth century to the Whig Revolution of 1688 in Britain.

The aristocracy of capital thus destroyed the aristocracy of land. The business classes here performed their vital role in the drama of liberty. The victory over feudalism, as the *Democratic Review,* put it, "opened the way for the entrance of democratic principle into the Government." But the business community gained from this exploit an undeserved reputation as the champion of liberty. Its real motive had been to establish itself in power, not to free mankind; to found government on property, not on the equal rights of the people. "I know perfectly well what I am saying," cried George Bancroft,[14] "and I assert expressly, and challenge contradiction, that in all the history of the world there is not to be found an instance of a commercial community establishing rules for self-government upon democratic principles." "It is a mistake to suppose commerce favorable to liberty," added Fenimore Cooper. "Its tendency is to a monied aristocracy." "Instead of setting man free," said Amos Kendall, it has "only increased the number of his masters."

The next great blow for liberty was the American Revolution, "effected not in

favor of men in classes; . . . but in favor of men." But the work of Hamilton halted the march of democracy. "He established the money power," wrote Van Buren, "upon precisely the same foundations upon which it had been raised in England." The subsequent history of the United States was the struggle to overthrow the Hamiltonian policy and fulfill the ideals of the Revolution.

What of the future? The Jacksonians were sublimely confident: history was on their side. "It is now for the yeomanry and mechanics to march at the head of civilization," said Bancroft. "The merchants and the lawyers, that is, the moneyed interest broke up feudalism. The day for the multitide has now dawned." "All classes, each in turn, have possessed the government," exclaimed Brownson; "and the time has come for all predominance of class to end; for Man, the People to rule."

[14] Ed. note: *George Bancroft* (1800–1891) of Massachusetts achieved fame principally as a historian, but he also distinguished himself as Secretary of the Navy and as American minister to Great Britain and later to Germany. He authored several books on the history of the United States.

Walter E. Hugins

Ely Moore:
Entrepreneur and Politician

The thesis that the Eastern laboring class formed one of the major components of Jacksonian Democracy and furnished many local leaders of that movement has

been accepted by so many historians that it has become almost axiomatic.[1] Arthur M. Schlesinger, Jr., gives the clearest statement of this interpretation in recent

From Walter E. Hugins, "Ely Moore: The Case History of a Jacksonian Labor Leader." Reprinted with permission from the *Political Science Quarterly*, 65 (March 1950), 105–108 and 115–125.

[1] Vernon L. Parrington and the Beards may be cited as examples. The former referred to "the will to destroy the aristocratic principle in government" which united the "city proletariat" and "coonskin

years,[2] but its genesis can be found in pioneer studies of American labor history by John R. Commons and his associates more than forty years ago. Without detracting from the permanent contributions to historical knowledge which resulted from their research, it must be realized that in seeking the origins of the American trade-union movement the Commons school often took at face value both the assertions and the terminology employed in the journalistic invective of the Jacksonian period. An example of this is the identification of the words "mechanic" and "workingman" with "wage earner" or laborer,"[3] a practice which has been carried to even greater lengths by other writers. As Joseph Dorfman has recently emphasized, these terms had a much broader meaning: "only your political opponents and the terrible aristocrats and the lazy idlers were clearly not honest 'workingmen.'"

Although these historians have referred

to the political activities of "workingmen" in all the important urban centers of the East, their major attention has been devoted to New York City where the Workingmen's party and later the Locofocos have been cited as examples of anticapitalist labor movements on the radical fringe of Jacksonian Democracy. It has been offered as further evidence of labor's influence in the party of Jackson and Van Buren that some labor leaders were associated directly with that party, and the career of Ely Moore, "labor's first Congressman," has been taken as perhaps the signal illustration of that influence. His election to Congress on the Democratic ticket in 1834, shortly after his elevation to the presidency of the National Trades' Union, was adduced by Commons as proof both that "Tammany catered to the workingmen" and that "the workingmen of New York supported the Bank policy of Jackson's administration."

The former assertion can be easily demonstrated; in fact, attempts to capture the "labor vote" were continually made by all political parties. But the unswerving allegiance of labor to the Democracy during the Jacksonian period is less certain. Recent studies of Philadelphia and Boston have shown, for example, that Jackson and the Democrats did not receive consistent support from working-class wards. While no attempt will be made here to evaluate fully the Commons thesis, the career of Ely Moore seems to demonstrate that the conception of the labor movement as the mainspring of Jacksonian Democracy ignores the predominantly middle-class basis of that political and economic revolution. As Bray Hammond has emphasized, the permanent contribution of the Jacksonians was the "democratization of business." Moore's success story tells, not of a worker's rise to a position of leadership through trade-union activity, but rather of an ambitious middle-class politician who, by capitalizing upon a brief early history as a journeyman printer, endeav-

---

voter" behind Andrew Jackson; *Main Currents in American Thought*, Vol. 2 (New York, 1927), pp. 145–146. The Beards labeled the Democracy of this period "a triumphant farmer-labor party," and interpreted the fight against the Bank of the United States as a manifestation of the struggle between "farmers, mechanics, and laborers in general" and "lawyers, merchants, manufacturers, businessmen of the higher ranges, and college professors." Charles A. and Mary R. Beard, *Rise of American Civilization* (New York, 1934), pp. 1, 142, 573, 580. See also Edward C. Kirkland, *History of American Economic Life* (New York, 1939), p. 352.

[2] *The Age of Jackson* (Boston, 1945), pp. 143, 205–209, 306–307, 344. Since, Schlesinger asserts, Jacksonian Democracy was an "American phase of that enduring struggle between the business community and the rest of society," and since "the best way of elevating labor was to enact the economic program of the radical Democracy," during Jackson's administrations "laboring men began slowly to turn to Jackson as their leader, and his party as their party."

[3] The Commons school, however, did recognize one fact which has been frequently overlooked by some more recent writers; that is, that master mechanics and small tradesmen often allied themselves with journeymen on many issues. *The Age of Jackson*, pp. 17–18, 459.

ored to advance his own and his party's political fortunes.

I. Like other urban leaders of the early nineteenth century, Ely Moore came from a rural environment, for he was born July 4, 1798, on a farm near the village of Belvidere in western New Jersey. He left the farm at the age of fourteen, shortly after the death of his father, when he was apprenticed to a printer in the near-by town of Newton, and after earning his journeyman's papers he went to New York to practice his trade. For a period of approximately five years after his arrival no information as to his activities has been discovered. With his marriage to a daughter of Gilbert Coutant, a well-to-do grocer and lumber merchant, however, his career becomes less obscure. This alliance opened up more exciting opportunities to the young journeyman than the print shop could promise him. Coutant had been speculating in Manhattan real estate for several years, and, of greater significance for Moore's future career, he had also been active in Tammany politics since 1806, his services being rewarded in 1828 by his selection as a Jacksonian elector.

Moore took advantage of this fortunate connection, and abandoned his original vocation for the more promising spheres of speculation and politics. In fact, no evidence has been found that he practiced the printing trade at any time after his marriage until 1850, when he purchased a New Jersey newspaper. Throughout the course of his active life his interests centered in oratory and politics. . . .

In the spring of 1833 the journeyman carpenters struck for higher wages, and the support of other trades enabled them to win their demands after a month's turnout. This success encouraged discussion of making the alliance permanent, and a circular was issued by the Typographical Association calling for a convention of trades, which resulted in the establishment of the General Trades' Union of New York. It was at this time

that Moore's name first appears as a trade-union member, for two days before the meeting was to take place he was named as a delegate from the Association to this preliminary convention, and was subsequently elected first president of the General Trades' Union. These circumstances seem to validate later charges that he "was smuggled into the Trades' Union as one of the Delegates from a trade at which he had entirely ceased to work many years before," and that "numerous meetings were held, and several societies had agreed to organize themselves into a General Society, before Ely Moore made his appearance among them."

According to its constitution, the Union was established "to maintain the present scale of prices [that is, wages] . . . and to alleviate the distresses of those suffering from want of employment." A spirit of moderation was enunciated by the provision that "no Trade or Art shall strike for higher wages . . . without the sanction of the Convention." This same spirit was emphasized in an address by its president later in the year, after a public procession of some four thousand members of the twenty-one trades affiliated with the new organization. Moore declared that the Union, instead of encouraging strikes, would try to "allay the jealousies and abate the asperities which now unhappily exist between employers and employed," . . . But he defended the right of journeymen to form combinations to enable "the producer to enjoy the full benefit of his productions," affirming that they have "the same right to ask their own price for their own property or services that . . . merchants, physicians, and lawyers have." This view was at variance with a doctrine often promulgated in editorial columns of the time which maintained that all such combinations to regulate prices, whether formed by journeymen, merchants or professional men, were "at war with the order of things which the Creator has established for the general good, and therefore wicked."

II. Moore, meanwhile, had become more active in political affairs during the months when Tammany, led by many officers of chartered banks, vigorously supported Jackson's war against the Bank of the United States.[4] This became the chief issue in the campaign preceding the spring elections of mayor and aldermen, the first time that the former was to be elected popularly. While "workingmen" affiliated with both the Democratic and the newly christened Whig parties held rallies and passed resolutions on the Bank question, the closely fought and often violent election saw the triumph of the Democratic candidate. At the same time a Democratic Workingmen's Committee was organized with the announced objective of convincing Tammany "to nominate only anti-bank men," opposed to "*all* banking monopolies," and Moore became a member of this group.

During the spring campaign Moore associated himself with another popular issue, opposition to the contract-labor system in the state prisons, which had long been an object of attack by "honest mechanics," both masters and journeymen. Meetings of the aggrieved mechanics were held and a memorial was submitted to the legislature calling for the abolition of the system. Moore, who had taken no part in the earlier agitation, now went to Albany to lobby for a bill which had been introduced calling for the appointment of three commissioners to investigate prison conditions. After the passage of the bill Moore was appointed to this commission by Governor Marcy. But this appointment met with opposition from some of the mechanics who felt that the bill had been weakened through Moore's connivance with a Democratic

machine hesitant to change a system in which it had a vested interest.[5]

Although hearings were conducted by the commissioners throughout most of the summer, Moore found time to head the New York delegation to the convention which organized the National Trades' Union, a federation of the city central unions of Boston, Philadelphia, Newark and New York. His election as head of this national organization and his subsequent reëlection as president of the New York Trades' Union for another year were evidences that he had maintained his prestige among the organized workers despite the opposition to him over the prison-labor question. But as the November election approached it was inevitable that differences of opinion should appear within the Union, for several officers and prominent members had already aligned themselves with the Whig party. That internal friction in this organization arose from criticism of Moore for using his position as a means to political advancement is evident from his speech at the first anniversary celebration in September. His address the year before, in fact, had contained a brief warning against the "wiles and perfidy" of men who "attempt to excite your jealousy against certain individuals, who, peradventure, may stand somewhat conspicuous among you," by insinuating that "political ambition lies at the root of the whole matter." In 1834 he devoted nearly

---

[4] Moore served as chairman of an anti-Bank of the United States meeting in the Fifteenth Ward and was appointed to a delegation sent by Tammany to Washington to assure the President of its wholehearted support. *Evening Star,* February 5, 1834; *Evening Post,* February 3, 4, 1834.

[5] The New York "mechanics' committee" which had recommended Moore's appointment attempted to withdraw the recommendation when it was learned that an article allowing the governor to prohibit any convict labor found to be in "injurious competition" with any trade had been deleted from the bill on the floor at Moore's suggestion. Moore's defense was that Marcy's unwillingness to take such responsibility, especially since the prison-labor system had been established by the Democrats, would endanger the passage of the entire bill, but the "mechanics" maintained that the revised bill would accomplish nothing "but the appointing and paying of three Commissioners." Letter from a "Mechanic" in the *Evening Star,* November 2, 1838.

half the speech to a similar denunciation of the "grovelling and debasing spirit" of jealousy which had become apparent in the movement. Obviously thinking of the coming election, he reminded them that

> neither in Europe or America, have the producing classes . . . put forward and sustained an individual of their own body, that was capable of taking even a respectable stand in the councils of the nation. . . . The very instant that one of their number rises to a little distinction, some individuals become envious, and instead of aiding and encouraging him, set about detracting from his merits.

He attributed this jealousy to their deficiency in "correct habits of thinking," recommending a process of self-improvement rather than formal instruction as the remedy. He concluded by emphasizing that "the general dissemination of intelligence, and especially of political intelligence," would lead "workingmen" to "choose men for their legislators whose sympathies and interests harmonize with . . . [their] own."

The election campaign began officially four days after this appeal. Moore appeared frequently both at Tammany Hall and before meetings of the Democratic Workingmen's Committee, and his speeches were praised in the journals of both wings of the party. As a result his name was submitted to the nominating committee, and he was one of the four men chosen by the Democrats to represent New York County in Congress. With the other candidates, he promised to oppose recharter of the Bank of the United States and other "exclusive privileges," this adoption of the pledge system being saluted by the *Man* and the *Evening Post*, organs of the party's left-wing faction, as evidence of the triumph within the party of the principles of "equal rights." After three quiet days of balloting the entire Tammany ticket was elected by a sizable majority,

and, although Moore trailed the rest of his party by almost five hundred votes, he enjoyed a comfortable lead over his closest opponent.

A year passed before Moore was sworn in as a member of the House of Representatives, and in the interim his reputation as spokesman of the "mechanics and workingmen" became somewhat tarnished. The instrument of his fall from grace was the report on state prisons which was published early in 1835. Although the three commissioners admitted that "in some articles, and to some extent," the complaints of the mechanics should be relieved, they concluded that the amount of competition from convict labor had been exaggerated. The reaction was immediate and extremely vitriolic. When they saw Moore's signature on the report, the editors of the *Man* and the *Evening Post* denounced as "a barefaced piece of treachery" the action of a man who had "won the suffrages of the mechanics by the incessant and superior loudness of his vociferations against the employment of convict labor." Moore was also under fire in the Trades' Union, his resignation being called for and a committee being chosen to draft a resolution on the prison-labor question. The storm finally subsided when the committee was discharged without being able to agree on a report. His term as president came to an end a few months later, when a resolution was passed in praise of the "able and impartial manner" in which he had presided. Moore, after warning the delegates to "beware of their enemies in disguise, who endeavor to sow the seeds of discord among them," expressed his gratitude for the "many kindnesses" he had received. This was virtually his last contact with the labor movement, as he prepared to leave for Washington and his Congressional career.

III. When he arrived in the national capital, Moore was thirty-seven years old. Those expecting to see a burly, horny-handed laborer, roughly dressed and uncouth in his speech, were disappointed; he was a slender, handsome man almost six feet tall with delicate, almost feminine, features, and long curly hair which he brushed back from his forehead. Always well dressed and usually carrying a heavy ivory-headed cane, he was courteous and reserved, not given to discussing his views in social gatherings. Because of the illness which had afflicted him intermittently throughout his life, he had a pale, unhealthy complexion, and was occasionally subject to fainting spells, but when he rose to speak in public his enunciation was distinct and his voice strong and clear.

His oratorical powers were demonstrated by his first Congressional speech, delivered in answer to the remarks of Waddy Thompson, a South Carolina Whig, warning Northern industrialists that they were "in quite as much danger of insurrection as we are." Moore, who was ill and had recently been bled, was leaning on his cane when he began speaking, but his voice soon penetrated to the farthest corner of the packed galleries. Such an attack as Thompson's, he declared, should help the people to discriminate between the two great political parties, "the Democracy and the aristocracy," the one advocating a government founded on "persons" and "equal rights," the other on "property" and "exclusive privileges." Defending labor combinations against the charge that they promote "agrarianism . . . sedition and revolution," he characterized them as legal measures of "self-defense and self-preservation," necessary to prevent "capital . . . from unjustly appropriating to itself the avails of labor." This outburst was an exception to Moore's normal conduct during his four years in the House, for he seldom participated in debates and almost never crossed party lines when the vote was taken. As a member of the Committee on Naval Affairs, he attempted to raise seamen's pay to fifteen dollars a month, and advocated increasing the salary of warrant officers,

but neither measure was approved. In 1836 he presented a memorial from the National Trades' Union, calling for a ten-hour day on all public works, but it was similarly dismissed by the House, members of both parties maintaining that Congress had no power to "interfere" between workers and their employers.

When Moore returned to New York in 1836 to stand for re-election, the Tammany organization, which had won such an overwhelming victory two years before, was split by dissension over the Bank question. In 1835 the group which adhered to the principles preached by William Leggett in the *Evening Post* and George Henry Evans in the *Man* had formed the Locofoco, or more properly the Equal Rights, party, which was gradually gaining the balance of power in New York politics. Most of its candidates in 1836 were men with long records of opposition to Tammany, many of whom were also nominated by the Whigs. Moore was the only nominee to receive both Democratic and Locofoco endorsement, and as a result he was re-elected while Tammany went down to defeat.

Shortly after moving into the White House, Van Buren called a special session of Congress to deal with the problems created by the panic of 1837. When he asked for the creation of an independent treasury system as the answer to the national financial difficulties, the Locofocos, who earlier had been decidedly cool toward him, now saluted the President for adopting their principles and soon rejoined the "purified" Tammany Wigwam. But in Congress conservative Democrats united with the Whigs to table the Van Buren plan, and an offensive was begun to recharter the old Bank of the United States or a similar institution. Moore delivered his second major Congressional speech during this session, defending the proposed independent treasury which he declared was favored by "ninety-nine out of every hundred workingmen." The Congressional campaign of 1838 in New York was fought almost wholly on this issue, and Moore became the special target of the Whig press. The rumor that he would be the Tammany candidate for governor was broadcast to alarm conservatives, while the prison-labor controversy was disinterred to arouse the "workingmen" against him. A letter in the *Evening Star,* signed "Five Thousand Workingmen," declared that for many years Moore's eloquence had been "transforming our little means and our bread into windy promises," and demanded: "Away with the trumpet tones and the magical intellect of idle demagogues who call themselves workingmen, but never lifted a hammer or made a shoe string." The election was a blow to the Democracy as the Whigs swept New York, Moore running almost four hundred votes behind his ticket.

A Democrat was still ensconced in the White House, however, and Moore returned to New York when the final session of the Twenty-fifth Congress adjourned, with Van Buren's promise of a position in the Customs House as Surveyor of the Port. In spite of protests by conservatives of both parties, the incumbent, described as a "quiet, steady man of business," was persuaded to resign, and Moore, the "noisy politician," took his place until after the Democratic defeat in 1840. Moore remained active in New York politics for ten years after this, but continually failed in his pursuit of elective office. In 1842, after participating in the verbal agitation in support of the Dorrite movement of Rhode Island, his attempt to secure the Tammany nomination for Congress was thwarted by Fernando Wood, who represented the Calhoun partisans in New York, and a compromise candidate was nominated. Early in 1844 Moore began to campaign for the mayoralty, appearing as the principal speaker at a meeting on municipal reform, but again was unsuccessful in his quest of the nomination. In November of that same year, however, he was nominated for Congress, but failed of election, losing by one hundred votes to the American party candidate. Early in 1845 President Polk appointed him United States Marshal for the Southern District of New York, a position he held until his removal by President Taylor four years later. He then returned to his birthplace in New Jersey where he purchased a weekly newspaper and began to participate in politics in that state. When Pierce became President in 1853, Moore was appointed special agent to the Indian tribes in Kansas, and after the passage of the Kansas-Nebraska Act he became the first register of the land office in Lecompton. Although he took little part in the political controversies of that stormy period, he was occasionally mentioned by moderate Democrats as a possible candidate for territorial delegate to Congress. After two years of intermittent illness, he died January 27, 1860, at his farm near Lecompton.

IV. The same relationship between labor leadership and politics which was exemplified by Moore's life existed in other cases, several leaders of the trade-union movement in New York devoting as much or more time to political activities as to the immediate demands of their followers. As has been indicated, some of these men were extremely active in the Whig party. Robert Townsend, a representative of the Journeyman Carpenters in the General Trades' Union, had a long record of opposition to the domination of Van Buren's Regency in Albany and the Tammany Society in New York. In 1830 he was a leader of the faction in the Workingmen's party which formed an alliance with the Clay Republicans and the Anti-Masons, and two years later he was vice chairman of the latter party's state-wide convention. After joining the Whigs in 1834, he moved on to the Locofocos, who were as vehement in their opposition to Tammany as in their avowal of Jacksonian principles. In 1836 he was elected to the Assembly by the combined support of Whigs and Locofocos. After a brief affiliation with the "purified Wigwam" during Van Buren's Administration, he again joined the Whigs and was appointed to a position in the Customs House by President Tyler. Other "workingmen" had similar careers, the main difference being that some followed Moore into the Democratic party while others joined Townsend in opposition.

Although this was the pattern, the labor movement undoubtedly contained unheralded leaders less concerned with politics than with the immediate improvement of working conditions. Seth Luther, the New England reformer and labor leader, was one of these. Working first as a carpenter and then in the textile mills, he became familiar with the lot of both skilled and unskilled labor, and tried unsuccessfully to awaken them to the need for united action. He wrote and spoke throughout the East, emphasizing the evils of the factory and calling for a ten-hour day for all occupations, but had little liking for practical politics and did not affiliate himself publicly with either party. His panacea was the establishment of manual labor schools, not the abolition of the banking system or the election of self-styled spokesmen of the "workingmen."

Moore, on the other hand, viewed political action as the chief road to the salvation of labor, an attitude which was revealed as clearly by his numerous speeches and writings as by his overt activities. While defending the right, and even the necessity, for workers to combine as a protection against associations of employers, he continually impressed upon his hearers that such organizations were only a temporary expedient, worthless without "the acquisition of knowledge and correct habits of thinking." Without "severe mental discipline," he emphasized journeymen "may complain in vain—in vain organize—in vain form Unions and associations," but knowledge would enable them to "elevate men

whose interests . . . feelings and sympathies are identified with . . . [their] own." As he was consistent in his exposition of the twin Democratic doctrines of strict construction and laissez faire, he neither expected nor demanded that such men should advocate ameliorative legislation in behalf of labor. Although he apparently disregarded his own injunction in presenting the ten-hour petition of the National Trades' Union to Congress, his support of this proposal was far from enthusiastic, and he failed to recommend such legislation in any of his discussions of the workingman's problems. His view of the rôle of government was that it should "preserve as perfect an equality of rights as possible" among the members of society, and this objective could be accomplished only by enacting laws "general in their scope and application, and in their operation equal and impartial to all." Despite his demand for the elimination of all special charters and "exclusive privileges," he gave no open support to political parties, like the Locofocos, which were dedicated to that end, preferring instead to battle for his program within the Democratic organization. An avowed exponent of party "discipline" throughout his life, he summarized his practical political philosophy when he wrote that "the key to party success," and hence the eventual defeat of the "aristocracy," is to "forego our own private feelings and predilections and to support the candidate of whom a majority of our party friends shall have made the choice."

While Seth Luther attacked the new capitalism for its social abuses, Moore, like other purveyors of the "equal rights" doctrine, demanded that the fruits of this capitalism be made more accessible to all, a goal which he felt could be realized only through the continued power of the Democratic party. At the same time Moore ignored, while Luther emphasized, the plight of the unskilled; for the labor movement in New York, and generally throughout the nation, was an instrument of the elite of the working class designed to prevent the worsening of its own social position. Many of these artisans, however, were more concerned with rising in the world than with merely holding their own, so they took the offensive to open the avenues of enterprise. Merchant capitalists, because of their easier access to credit, were rapidly coming to dominate the various trades, so ambitious journeymen who hoped to establish their own businesses joined with master craftsmen who wished to expand theirs in denouncing the chartered banks for a discriminatory loan policy which, they insisted, by restricting competition failed to utilize the nation's potential wealth.[6] Moore in his attacks upon the "banking aristocracy" was the spokesman, not of the "laboring class" alone, but of the "enterprising," whether journeyman or master, manufacturer or merchant—all those who were struggling against an aristocratic system which would deny to all but a few the opportunity to share in the future of the new nation.[7] America's chief heritage from Jacksonian Democracy was not the growth of a militant labor movement, but the economic exploitation of a continent.[8]

---

[6] William Gouge, one of the most popular and influential Jacksonian pamphleteers, condemned the banks for refusing to make loans to "thrifty young mechanics," many of them "embryo Doctor Franklins," while at the same time giving credit to those "to whom no man ought to lend"; businesses thus established often fail, "and the wealth of the community is diminished in proportion." *Short History of Money and Banking in the United States* (Philadelphia, 1833), Part 1, pp. 35–37. Locofoco leaders declared that "the banks have been a clog upon the industry of this country," because of their discriminatory loan policy, and advocated free banking under a general law so that "an unprecedented activity on equitable principles would . . . pervade all occupations, and . . . the advances of society would be comparatively uniform and in mass."

[7] This view of Jacksonian Democracy is developed more broadly by Richard Hofstadter in *The American Political Tradition and the Men Who Made It* (New York, 1948), pp. 44–46.

[8] The highest percentage of the business elite in American history with lower-class origins is to be found among those who were born between 1820 and

Select Bibliography for Problem 4

Abernethy, Thomas P. "Andrew Jackson and the Rise of Southwestern Democracy," *American Historical Review,* 33 (October 1927), 64–67.

Bailey, Thomas A., ed. *The American Spirit: United States History as Seen by Contemporaries,* 2d ed. Boston: D. C. Heath & Company, 1967, 230–267.

Baldwin, Leland D., ed. *Ideas in Action: Documentary and Interpretive Readings in American History,* Vol. 1: To 1877. New York: American Book Company, 1968, pp. 308–325.

Bugg, Jr., James L., ed. *Jacksonian Democracy: Myth or Reality?* American Problem Studies under the editorial direction of Oscar Handlin. New York: Holt, Rinehart and Winston, Inc., 1966.

Darling, Arthur B. "Jacksonian Democracy in Massachusetts," *American Historical Review,* 30 (January 1924), 271–287.

_____. "The Workingmen's Party in Massachusetts," *American Historical Review,* 29 (October 1923), 81–86.

Dorfman, Joseph. "The Jackson Wage-Earner Thesis," *American Historical Review,* 54 (January 1949), 296–306.

Eriksson, Erik M. "The Federal Civil Service and President Jackson," *Mississippi Valley Historical Review,* 13 (March 1927), 527–529.

Glad, Paul, Allen Weinstein, *et al.,* eds. *The Process of American History: Early America.* Vol. 1. Englewood Cliffs, N.J.: Prentice-Hall, Inc., 1969, pp. 352–416.

1850, the men who fought the Civil War and led the United States into the industrial expansion of the Gilded Age. C. Wright Mills, "The American Business Elite: A Collective Portrait," *Journal of Economic History,* 5 (December 1945), 20–44.

Hammond, Bray. "Banking in the Early West," *The Journal of Economic History*, 8 (May 1948), 1–25.

———. "Jackson, Biddle, and the Bank of the United States," *The Journal of Economic History*, 7 (May 1947), 1–23.

Hofstadter, Richard. "William Leggett, Spokesman of Jacksonian Democracy," *Political Science Quarterly*, 58 (December 1943), 581–594.

Leopold, Richard W., Arthur S. Link, and Stanley Coben, eds. *Problems in American History: Through Reconstruction*. Vol. 1. Englewood Cliffs, N.J.: Prentice-Hall, Inc., 1966, pp. 229–262.

Longaker, Richard P. "Was Jackson's Kitchen Cabinet a Cabinet?" *Mississippi Valley Historical Review*, 44 (June 1957), 94–108.

Merriman, Jacob. "Climax of the Bank War: Biddle's Contraction of 1833–34," *Journal of Political Economy*, 71 (August 1963), 378–388.

Meyers, Marvin. "The Jacksonian Persuasian," *American Quarterly* (Spring 1953), 3–15.

Mills, C. Wright. "The American Business Elite: A Collective Portrait," *Journal of Economic History*, 5 (December 1945), 20–44.

Morris, Richard B. "Andrew Jackson, Strikebreaker," *American Historical Review*, 55 (October 1949), 54–68.

———. "Measure of Bondage in the Slave States," *Mississippi Valley Historical Review*, 41 (September 1954), 219–240.

Pessen, Edward. "Did Labor Support Jackson? The Boston Story," *Political Science Quarterly*, 64 (June 1949), 262–274.

———. "The Workingmen's Movement in the Jackson Era," *Mississippi Val-*

ley Historical Review, 43 (December 1956), 428–443.

Plous, H. J. "Jackson, the Bank War and Liberalism," *Southwest Social Science Quarterly*, 38 (September 1957), 99–116.

Quint, Howard H., Dean Albertson, and Milton Cantor, eds. *Main Problems in American History*, rev. ed., Vol. 1. Homewood, Ill.: Dorsey Press, 1968, pp. 296–320.

Randall, Edwin T. "Imprisonment for Debt in America: Fact and Fiction," *Mississippi Valley Historical Review*, 39 (June 1952), 89–102.

Rozwenc, Edwin C., ed. *The Meaning of Jacksonian Democracy*. Problems in American Civilization under the editorial direction of Edwin C. Rozwenc. Boston: D. C. Heath & Company, 1968.

Scheiber, Harry. "Pet Banks in Jacksonian Politics and Finance," *Journal of Economic History*, 23 (June 1963), 196–214.

Sellers, Charles G. "Andrew Jackson Versus the Historians," *Mississippi Valley Historical Review*, 44 (March 1958), 615–648.

Somit, Albert. "Andrew Jackson as Administrator," *Public Administration Review*, 8, 3 (1948), 188–196.

———. "New Papers: Some Sidelights upon Jacksonian Administration," *Mississippi Valley Historical Review*, 35 (June 1948), 91–98.

Sullivan, William A. "Did Labor Support Andrew Jackson?" *Political Science Quarterly*, 56 (December 1947), 569–580.

Trimble, William. "Diverging Tendencies in New York Democracy in the Period of the Locofocos," *American Historical Review*, 24 (April 1919), 396–421.

part 5

Economic and Geographic Expansion

chapter 15

From Van Buren
to Tyler

Political Trends

ELECTION OF 1836

Realizing that the bank and tariff issues were all but settled and that it would be political suicide to revive them, the newly organized Whig coalition turned, for lack of a better issue, to one of the images that Americans hated most—kingship. Jackson's handpicked successor, Martin Van Buren, was likened to an heir apparent to the throne, whose continued tyranny in office was sure to complete the ruin of the country. The Whigs, on the other hand, were unable to unite behind a single candidate and so picked several contenders with strong sectional followings in the hope of depriving Van Buren of a clear majority. This would again throw the election of the President into the House of Representatives, where they hoped to see the performance of 1824 repeated.

Most notable among the Whig standard-bearers were Daniel Webster of Massachusetts, Hugh L. White of Tennessee, and General William H. Harrison of Ohio. Even though he campaigned without a formal platform, except for a promise to promote the best of Jackson, Van Buren captured the election with an electoral vote of 170 to 124 for the Whigs. Richard M. Johnson was elected Vice-President by the Senate, where the contest was decided for the first time after the election had failed to produce a majority winner.

PANIC OF 1837

Despite Van Buren's impressive political career, during which he had been senator from New York, Vice-President of the United States, and had won the title of the "Little Magician" as a result of his clever political maneuvers, he failed to generate the necessary magic to stem the tide of the crippling financial crisis of 1837. The optimism occasioned by Jackson's performance soon turned to despair as prices soared and the value of paper money declined; European financiers demanded payment on their investments in America, while speculators searched in vain for markets for their western lands.

DIVORCE BILL

Regardless of the cause, whether Jackson's handling of financial affairs or unchecked speculation, the country now demanded that the administration in power restore prosperity. Van Buren, however, refused to act in accordance with demands from the various states. Trusting instead in Jackson's formula that called for separation of federal and private banking, and believing that he had a sound program for resolving the financial problem, the President proposed to Congress a plan for an independent treasury system. The

235

plan brought an end to the government's reliance on state banks as federal depositories, nor did it encourage the revival of another national bank, but called instead for the federal government to collect and keep federal moneys safe from speculative abuse by storing them in its own strongboxes. This Divorce Bill, as it was called, was approved over Whig protests in 1840, but it was repealed the following year by the next administration.

ELECTION OF 1840

The election of 1840 emerged with issues still somewhat obscure, save for the Panic of 1837; and candidates searched almost in vain for some promising deed with which they might appeal to the electorate. Van Buren chose to stand on his record, whereas the Whigs, enjoying a semblance of unity for the first time, nominated General William H. Harrison of Ohio,[1] the victor at Tippecanoe over Tecumseh, and John Tyler of Virginia. Emotionalism soon carried the day. Taking a cue from what was intended as a derogatory news item that characterized Harrison as the log cabin, cider-drinking type, the Whigs paraded their affluent candidate across the country under the guise of a "most common man" to the tune of "Tippecanoe and Tyler too." Van Buren, on the other hand, was depicted as an aristocrat living in the kind of luxury that only taxes could buy and ignoring the cries of the suffering people. The campaigns set a new mark in electioneering sloganism and frivolity.

The general captured the election for the jubilant Whigs, pulling 234 electoral votes to 60 for Van Buren. The Whig victory was even sweeter when they learned that the electorate had also given them a majority in Congress.

TYLER BECOMES PRESIDENT

The sixty-eight-year-old general, however, had overestimated his physical capacity during the strenuous campaign; after but one month in office he died of complications caused by pneumonia.[2] The Whig joy suddenly turned to remorse when the independent-minded Tyler, the first Vice-President to succeed to Chief Executive, became President. He retained Harrison's cabinet, momentarily at least, which included Secretary of State Daniel Webster, Secretary of the Treasury Thomas Ewing, and Secretary of War John Bell. A strong states' righter and opposed to protective tariffs and national banks, Tyler immediately found himself at odds with the Clay-led cabinet.[3]

TYLER AND THE WHIGS

Clay had for years been recognized as the titular head of his party and had been the power behind the Harrison administration. He felt that this role had not changed under Tyler. The schism came when Clay proposed resolutions that called for repeal of the Independent Treasury Act, establishment of a new national bank, higher tariffs, and the distribution of funds derived from the sale of public lands among the various states for internal improvements. These proposals represented the essential elements of Clay's long-sought-after American System. The Independent Treasury Act was repealed in August, but Tyler was in no compromising mood with regard to the other items; he not only vetoed two national bank bills, but killed two

---

[1] Harrison's appeal, it is said, was further heightened by the fact that he was a native-born Virginian — the state so prolific in producing Presidents.

[2] It has been written that Harrison's doctors, after blistering and "cupping" him, administered violent emetics and cathartics, then switched to opium, camphor, and brandy. Finally, in desperation, they administered Indian medicine men's remedies such as crude petroleum and snakeweed.

[3] Once a Democrat, Tyler had bolted the party after a nullification fight with Jackson.

tariff measures as well.[4] His determination to prevent the distribution of proceeds from the sale of land was just as effective.

Within six months all of the cabinet members, Webster excepted, had resigned, affording the President the opportunity to appoint "Tyler men." The new cabinet reflected Tyler's close affinity with the South—four of the six members came from that region.

TANEY COURT

The philosophy of the judiciary changed significantly after the death of Chief Justice John Marshall in 1835. Adhering strongly to states' rights, the new chief justice, Roger B. Taney, handed down decisions that tended to protect the rights of the state over those of the federal government, and the rights of the popular majority over those of property. For example, in *Charles River Bridge* v. *Warren Bridge* (1837) in the state of Massachusetts, he ruled that the state had a right to issue a charter to the Warren Company to build a second toll bridge that would compete with that of the Charles Company, if it served the best interests of the community. The conservatives viewed Taney's decision as a breach of the sanctity of contracts.

Foreign Affairs

CAROLINE AFFAIR

President Tyler had more success dealing with foreign powers than with the factions of his own government. Relations between the United States and England had been strained for several years over the *Caroline* affair. The United States had lost a vessel, the *Caroline,* while running supplies to insurrectionists in

Canada during Van Buren's administration. One American was killed when the Canadian militia crossed the river to the American side in order to capture the vessel. A Canadian was arrested in New York three years later (1840) and charged with the death of the American, but the awkward affair was soon set aside when the Canadian was acquitted.[5]

NORTHWEST BOUNDARY DISPUTE

Another serious dispute had emerged over the west boundary between Maine and Canada (disputed since the Peace of Paris, 1783). Both parties had laid claim to a large territory, each insisting that her claims were in accordance with the terms of a legal treaty. Maine, moreover, asserted her argument by sending troops into the disputed territory; but the war that almost happened, sometimes called the Aroostook War, was avoided when General Winfield Scott arranged for a truce and the two powers referred the problem to a commission.

WEBSTER-ASHBURTON TREATY

The Webster-Ashburton Treaty (1842) settled the issue. By the terms of this treaty, the boundary was fixed at a point just north of the 45th parallel, which gave the United States a fort on Lake Champlain and about 7000 of the 12,000 disputed square miles, and extended as far west as the Lake of the Woods. Maine and Massachusetts were appeased with a cash payment from the United States of $150,000.

TREATY OF WANGHIA

Two years later, President Tyler dispatched Caleb Cushing to the Orient,

---

[4] A revised tariff bill was finally passed in 1842 which raised duties back to the 1832 level.

[5] Webster secured the passage of a bill in 1841 that provided that a foreign subject on trial in a state court could be transferred to a federal court on a writ of *habeas corpus.*

where he signed the Treaty of Wanghia (1844), which secured for the United States the status of "most-favored-nation" in her trade with China. In addition, it opened the door to foreign residence in China by making Americans immune to Chinese laws.[6]

POINSETT IN MEXICO

The policy of the United States toward Latin America from 1823 (the date of the Monroe Doctrine) to 1845 vacillated between indifference and innocent bunglings in trade negotiations. It appeared to many Latins that the United States all but ignored the important Panama Conference in 1826 when her ministers were embarrassingly tardy in arriving. Soon thereafter, Joel R. Poinsett was appointed head of a mission to negotiate trade agreements between the United States and Mexico. Poinsett, however, was soon recalled for meddling in Mexican politics and the subsequent ill will caused the commercial treaty to be delayed for another two years.

The British and French, in the meantime, had secured commercial agreements with Mexico, and were well ahead of the United States in signing trade instruments. Although these agreements pointed to improved international cooperation and friendship, European and Latin-American relations were not always amicable. The British harassed Argentina in 1833 by seizing the Falkland Islands, and in 1838 the French, seeking redress for supposed wrongs against French nationals, occupied Veracruz but were soon forced to leave. Finally, these two powers joined forces in 1845 and blockaded the Rio de la Plata, for reasons similar to those in the Veracruz incident, with nothing more than a weak protest from the United States. Latin Americans soon began to question the efficacy and sincerity of the Monroe Doctrine.

[6] Americans were to be tried in American courts irrespective of the crime.

Some historians feel that the young republic to the north was in no position to help Latin America during the crises in question because of a preoccupation with its own problems; namely, with settling its western domain, fixing boundaries (particularly those with Mexico), and refereeing the sectional battles between East and West, North and South. Thus, for a time, America's distresses made for Europe's successes.

Select Bibliography

Alexander, Holmes. *The American Talleyrand: Martin Van Buren.* New York: Russell & Russell, Publishers, 1968.

Bailey, Thomas A. *A Diplomatic History of the American People.* New York: Appleton-Century-Crofts, 1969.

Bemis, Samuel F. *Diplomatic History of the United States.* New York: Holt, Rinehart and Winston, Inc., 1965.

Cleaves, Freeman. *Old Tippecanoe: William Henry Harrison.* Ft. Washington, N.Y.: Kennikat Press, Inc., 1969.

Cole, Arthur C. *The Whig Party in the South.* Gloucester, Mass.: Peter Smith, 1959.

Current, Richard N. *John C. Calhoun.* New York: Washington Square Press, 1966.

De Tocqueville, Alexis C. *Democracy in America.* New York: Harper & Row, Publishers, 1965.

Gunderson, Robert G. *The Log-Cabin Campaign.* Lexington, Ky.: The University Press of Kentucky, 1957.

Hofstadter, Richard. *The American Political Tradition.* New York: Alfred A. Knopf, 1948.

Morgan, Robert J. *A Whig Embattled.* Lincoln, Nebr.: University of Nebraska Press, 1954.

Poage, George R. *Clay and the Whig Party*. Gloucester, Mass.: Peter Smith, 1965.

Schlesinger, Jr., Arthur M. *The Age of Jackson*. Boston: Little, Brown and Company, 1945.

Seager, Robert. *And Tyler Too! A Biography of John and Julia Gardiner Tyler*. New York: McGraw-Hill Book Company, 1963.

Turner, Frederick J. *The United States, 1830–1850*. New York: W. W. Norton & Company, Inc., 1965.

Van Deusen, Glyndon G. *Henry Clay*. Boston: Little, Brown and Company, Inc., 1937.

chapter 16

The March of Industry, 1830–1860

Industrial Expansion

The years before 1850 marked the era of the home shop in manufacturing; but by that date improved steam power had transferred American manufacturing to the factory system, a transition that had taken place in England half a century earlier. It might have come earlier to America if she had had the surplus capital, the necessary transportation and communication facilities, and an abundance of cheap labor; but agriculture was the American way of life—a kind of self-sufficient agriculture that was perpetuated by the seemingly boundless areas of inexpensive land. Manufacturing, nevertheless, forged ahead; and when masses of unskilled immigrants began to appear on the east coast during the 1830s and 1840s, and gold was discovered in the California Sierras, the problem of factory labor and capital was solved.

LIGHT INDUSTRY

Textile manufacturing was the first to make strides toward mass power production during the early stages of the Industrial Revolution, and it continued to lead all other industries after 1830. One of its most notable discoveries came in 1846. Answering the demand for more versatile sewing machines, Elias Howe patented machines for cobblers as well as tailors; and five years later Isaac Singer improved the models for mass production.

HEAVY INDUSTRY

Heavy industry, such as iron, was slow in arriving, but achievements during the 1840s provided a strong impetus. Manufacturers, for example, began using coal and coke in order to attain higher temperatures, and soon thereafter rolling mills appeared to make mass production in the iron industry a reality. By 1854 the iron industry was producing wrought-iron buildings, iron locomotives, and iron-plated ships. Its potential seemed limitless.

Steel made its debut during the period from 1851 to 1856, when Henry Bessemer of England and William Kelly of the United States made similar but independent discoveries of a process of making steel by forcing a blast of cold air through molten iron to clean it of impurities. Their subsequent patent controversy was finally resolved by compromise in 1866.

Agricultural inventions and implements, nonetheless, continued to dominate the showcases of America as machinery and gadgets designed to ease the "hard life" of the farmer poured off the assembly lines. For example, Cyrus McCormick's reaper appeared in 1831, the steel-blade plowshare revolutionized ground breaking in 1833, and four years later Hiram and John Pitts introduced the thresher. Among other useful items to appear during the patent-minded 1830s and 1840s were Samuel Colt's revolver, Charles Thurber's typewriter, and Walter Hunt's safety pin.

The new mechanized agriculture had far-reaching implications. While it enabled the farmer to increase his total production of farm goals, it also encouraged him to specialize in one crop. Thus, he became dependent on the crop and on a favorable market; but his crop often stimulated the growth of manufacturing, which, in turn, provided him with more markets.

Despite the rapid expansion in manufactured goods from 1830 to 1860, America's foreign trade continued to be, for the most part, an exchange of raw materials for manufactured goods. Cotton was king among the more valuable exports, followed by tobacco, which was a distant second, and grain crops, such as wheat and corn.

ORIENTAL TRADE

The riches of the Orient were particularly attractive to American merchants. Finding Europeans firmly entrenched in China, the United States turned to Japan, where in 1854 Commodore Matthew Perry, commanding an impressive fleet, persuaded the Japanese to sign a commercial agreement. The Treaty of Kanagawa opened two Japanese ports to foreign trade and secured an agreement to extend a helping hand to American shipwrecked seamen.

Transportation and Communication

The transportation and communication frontiers played vital roles in the greater drama of the Industrial Revolution. In fact, industrial growth could not have taken place without them. The iron horse carried men to the frontier and raw materials to the factories; and when settlements appeared in the wilderness, it brought manufactured goods. The locomotive carried ideas as well as wares and in the final analysis helped to unite the country.

The potential of the steam locomotive was first realized in 1825, when George Stephenson successfully tested his steam-powered "Locomotion" in England. Within a short period of time it was being tested in the United States, the most celebrated demonstration being that of the DeWitt Clinton run from Albany to Schenectady in 1831. These experiments were extremely significant to an age of slow travelers, for they proved that steam could power people and goods safely at high speeds (35 miles per hour).

The first railroads laid in the United States were mere trunk lines designed to feed the steamboats on major rivers and the larger cities, such as New York, Boston, Philadelphia, and New Orleans. Then, as the railroad system branched out across the continent, it began to compete with the steamboat and the overland stagecoach. The result of the contests was never in doubt, however, for the locomotive's greater speed, ability to cover great distances, and relatively inexpensive road construction soon demonstrated its superiority. By 1860 transcontinental lines were on the drawing boards.

RAILROAD LAND GRANTS

Most of the rails laid after 1850 were west of the Alleghenies and, unlike earlier ones in New England, were financed by the federal government through land grants, by private eastern capital, and by foreign capital. Private investors were promised substantial returns. One of the first land grants went to the Illinois Central Railroad at the tune of 2,500,000 acres, thereby establishing a trend that was to make railroad companies America's largest real estate dealers. By using this land as collateral for loans, the Illinois Central was able to defray most of the cost of building its own railroad.

The importance of these land grants becomes clearer when viewed in terms of the location of the land with respect to the railroads. The legislation, for example, provided the companies with a 200-foot-wide right-of-way for the road-bed, while the remainder of the grant was awarded in even-numbered sections (640 acres) not to exceed six miles in depth on either side of the tracks. Thus, a chec-ered pattern of land ownership developed as the railroads advanced westward.

THE CORPORATION

The emergence of industry, and the rail-road in particular, stimulated the growth of corporations. The Constitution pro-vided that corporation charters be granted by the various states, and the prevailing philosophy during the Industrial Revolu-tion was that state corporations brought economic growth and well-being to the states that attracted them. If corporations would build turnpikes, canals, and rail-roads, why should the state appropriate funds for such projects? Accordingly, states began to extend unrestrained privi-leges of monopoly to corporations, and soon states began to compete for favored corporations, which placed the large trusts in a most enviable bargaining posi-tion for additional legal protection. Thus, laissez faire was not only in vogue, but its very interpretation was written by the corporation.

On the other hand, the general incor-poration laws of the 1840s and 1850s enabled a greater number of people, including the common man, to start corporations at a minimum risk since individuals could not be held responsible for debts incurred by the company in which they had invested. Thus, owners could come into the company or leave it at will. These circumstances gave rise to the New York stock market, which by 1850 had become the nation's headquarters for securities.

As corporations grew and as investors multiplied, it became increasingly clear that the management of the large con-glomerate business demanded the ser-vices of a person outside the circle of actual owners. The answer was the cor-porate manager, who evolved as a key officer in a high position that demanded unquestioned loyalty and integrity. Not all managers, however, could be trusted, and scandals soon became fashionable during the post-Civil War era.

STEAMBOATS

The river and ocean steamboats made their appearance long before the railroad, and for many years the side-wheelers were the chief source of transportation and communication on the Ohio and Mississippi rivers. In addition to pas-sengers, manufactured goods and mail moved down the rivers to the south, and on the return trip cotton, rice, and sugar were shipped upstream to the northern states.

The long epic of the sail had its last fling during the 1840s and early 1850s when the "clipper" ships captured the imagination of seamen with their tremen-dous speed and beauty. The slender clip-per, however, had to sacrifice space for speed and soon lost out to the ocean steamer in world commerce. The steam-boat preceded even the stagecoach in the West, for as soon as major rivers were discovered, steamboats began to appear. By 1832 a steamboat had reached the mouth of the Yellowstone River; in 1849 several flat-bottomed side-wheelers made their initial appearance on the San Fran-cisco Bay, and the following year brought two steamboats to the Columbia River in the Northwest.[1]

[1] A British steamship, the *S. S. Beaver*, served the lower Columbia as early as 1843.

TRANSCONTINENTAL MAIL

Besides witnessing the California gold rush, 1849 was also the year of the first regular mail service between New York and San Francisco. Negotiating the Isthmus of Panama with pack mules, the postmen then loaded the mail onto another steamer and sent it on its way to complete the second leg of the trip. One-way delivery required thirty days at a cost of about forty cents per half ounce.[2] The rate, however, was gradually reduced until it was fixed at three cents per half ounce in 1863.

The towns of the interior were served by stagecoach lines, railroad trunks, and for a brief period by the Pony Express. Linking St. Joseph, Missouri, with Sacramento, California, the Pony Express began in 1860 and lasted until the telegraph made it obsolete in 1861. As a private business venture, it has been described as a "miserable failure," even though early charges for first-class mail ran as high as $5 per half ounce.

No less significant to the march of industry and the conquest of the West were the inventions in communication. Perhaps the most amazing discovery came in 1844, when Samuel F. B. Morse, with the aid of a $30,000 government grant, developed the telegraph. His first message, "What hath God wrought?" covered a distance of forty miles between Washington and Baltimore.

The South and King Cotton

Perhaps never in history has a people been more dependent on a single crop than were large areas of the South during the antebellum period. It became a way of life. Consumed by the insatiable appetite of the Industrial Revolution, cotton could not be planted and harvested fast enough to meet the demands of the market. Plantations began to multiply with the expansion of industry after the War of 1812, the value of slaves doubled over a ten-year period, and the price of cotton advanced 40 percent during the same period.

The implications of all these circumstances were far-reaching in the South. It has been written that the cotton culture revived slavery in the South after it was all but dead following the Revolution, and that it widened the gap between the small planter aristocracy and the common folk. Some historians feel that the frantic search for cotton lands caused the forests to be destroyed and in time ruined the soil; and that the pursuit of cotton discouraged industry and in the process made the South dependent on the manufactured goods of the North.[3] It has also been suggested that the overemphasis on an agrarian economy caused the South to become conservatively Whiggish in its politics, at least among the planters who were, after all, the officeholders and the counselors to the common folk. This same culture encouraged the planter class to view physical labor with disdain (as the task of slaves), which in turn caused people among the middle and lower classes to assume the same posture. The cotton culture also kept the small farmers poor by forcing them to compete with the larger planters on the latter's terms; and because there were few demands for white laborers, it drove immigrants into the arms of the northern factory owners.

[2] Before the Civil War, passenger fare for the New York to San Francisco steamer ranged from $100 to $200, depending on the accommodations, while those for the overland stagecoach from St. Louis to San Francisco ran as high as $225.

[3] The South was not without industry, however, for there were iron and coal mines in such states as Virginia, Kentucky, and Tennessee, and foundries were located nearby; elsewhere cotton textile mills were in evidence, while in Virginia the famous tobacco industry continued to flourish.

Select Bibliography

Chandler, Jr., Alfred D., ed. *The Railroads: The Nation's First Big Business.* New York: Harcourt Brace Jovanovich, Inc., 1965.

Clark, Arthur H. *The Clipper Ship Era, 1843–1869.* Riverside, Conn.: 7 C's Press, 1969.

Cochran, Thomas C. *Railroad Leaders, 1845–1890: The Business Mind in Action.* New York: Russell & Russell, Publishers, 1966.

——— and William Miller. *The Age of Enterprise: A Social History of Industrial Enterprise,* 2d ed. New York: Harper & Row, Publishers, 1961.

Eaton, Clement. *The Growth of Southern Civilization, 1790–1860.* New York: Harper & Row, Publishers, 1961.

Fisher, Marvin. *Workshop in the Wilderness: The European Response to American Industrialization, 1830–1860.* New York: Oxford University Press, 1967.

Gates, Paul W. *The Farmer's Age: Agriculture, 1815–1860.* New York: Holt, Rinehart and Winston, Inc., 1960.

Goodrich, Carter. *Government Promotion of American Canals and Railroads, 1800–1890.* New York: Columbia University Press, 1960.

Gray, Lewis C. *History of Agriculture in the Southern United States to 1860.* 2 vols. New York: Augustus M. Kelley, Publishers, 1969.

Gregg, Josiah. *Commerce of the Prairies.* Philadelphia: J. B. Lippincott Co., 1962.

Hafen, Leroy R. *The Overland Mail, 1849–1869.* New York: AMS Press, Inc., 1969.

Hunter, Louis C. *Steamboats on the Western Rivers.* New York: Octagon Books, Inc., 1969.

Josephson, Hanna. *The Golden Threads: New England's Mill Girls and Magnates.* New York: Russell & Russell, Publishers, 1967.

Kouwenhoven, John A. *Arts in Modern American Civilization.* New York: W. W. Norton & Co., Inc., 1967.

Mabee, Carleton. *The American Leonardo: A Life of Samuel F. B. Morse.* New York: Octagon Books, Inc., 1969.

Owsley, Frank L. *Plain Folk of the Old South.* Gloucester, Mass.: Peter Smith, 1949.

Smith, Walter B., and Arthur H. Cole. *Fluctuations in American Business, 1790–1860.* Cambridge, Mass.: Harvard University Press, 1935.

Stover, John F. *American Railroads.* Chicago: University of Chicago Press, 1961.

Sydnor, Charles S. *The Development of Southern Sectionalism, 1819–1848.* Baton Rouge, La.: Louisiana State University Press, 1968.

Taylor, George R. *The Transportation Revolution, 1815–1860.* New York: Holt, Rinehart and Winston, Inc., 1951.

Winther, Oscar O. *Via Western Express and Stagecoach: California's Transportation Links with the Nation.* Lincoln, Nebr.: University of Nebraska Press, 1968.

chapter 17

Westward Expansion and Manifest Destiny

Trans-Mississippi West

After Lewis and Clark made their historic journey to the mouth of the Columbia River, a swarm of trappers and traders converged on the Louisiana Territory. Much to their surprise, their greatest rival in the ill-defined territory was not the Indian, but rather British subjects (in the Southwest and Far West expeditions had similar confrontations with mercantile-minded Spaniards). Thus, the settlement of the trans-Mississippi West is, for the most part, the story of the various clashes between these interest groups; it has been described as a narrative of intimidation, infiltration, and intrigue.

THE ERA OF THE MOUNTAIN MEN

One of the most significant western expeditions attempted after Lewis and Clark was that of Manuel Lisa, who in 1807 led a party of some forty-two trappers to the Big Horn River in the Rocky Mountains. The experience soon convinced Lisa that fur trade in the distant Rockies would be financially impossible for small companies, whereupon he returned to St. Louis and in 1808 organized the Missouri Fur Company. Stimulated by the success of this company, others began to organize fur enterprises, and before another decade had passed, the

West was teeming with young and ambitious fur organizations. One such organization was founded by the visionary John Jacob Astor, a German immigrant, who had become America's leading fur merchant. Planting a small settlement at the mouth of the Columbia River, which he called Astoria, Astor began to build the giant American Fur Company, which he hoped would eventually drive the British Canadians and their hated Hudson's Bay Company from the scene. The War of 1812, however, aborted his strategy.

Perhaps the most colorful trio of Mountain Men to appear in the fur frontier was that of Major Andrew Henry, William Henry Ashley and America's most celebrated explorer, Jedediah Smith. Their organizational skills produced the famous "rendezvous system,"[1] which soon made them the most successful fur traders in the Rockies, and subsequently made fortunes for others before larger operations, like the Rocky Mountain Fur Company, bought them out in the 1830s. By 1840 the era of the Mountain Men was over; the powerful Hudson's Bay Company had purchased Fort Hall and operated a virtual fur monopoly in the Rocky Mountains.

[1] A system whereby trappers were sent out in various directions to make their catch, after which they were to assemble at an appointed place in the mountains to deliver pelts and replenish supplies.

THE SOUTHWEST
AND THE SANTA FE TRAIL

Meanwhile, the southwestern frontier[2] had undergone a similar and eventful chapter in American history. By 1820 the Mexicans had liberated themselves from Spanish commercial restrictions and had sent word to their neighbors that the trade lanes were open to all. William Becknell needed no further inducement. Lashing his pack train over the southern Rockies, he carried St. Louis manufactured goods to Santa Fe, where he exchanged them for furs, silver, and mules. Two years later he blazed a shorter trail across the Cimarron Desert in charting what was to become known as the Santa Fe Trail.

SIGNIFICANCE
OF THE MOUNTAIN MEN

The contributions of the Mountain Men to American history have all too often

[2] It has been written that the American "frontier" cannot be defined, that it can only be discussed. It has often been equated with the trans-Mississippi West, but in actuality it started at the Atlantic coast with the planting of the colonies and moved slowly across the continent. It manifested itself in such traits and characteristics as rugged individualism, self-reliance, freedom, coarseness, strength, ingeniousness, materialism, laxness of business morals, and wastefulness. It revolved around an elemental society with impulses of direct democracy and quick justice. After 1790 the Census Bureau identified it as an area containing not less than two nor more than six inhabitants to the square mile. Thus, its attractiveness was the abundance of cheap virgin land. For the convenience of study, students of the subject have identified the different kinds of frontiers in order of their appearance. For example, the trapper and trader frontiers usually emerged first, then the cattle and mining frontiers, followed by the pioneer farmers. Subsequent frontier groups have been identified, but the real frontier ended with the pioneer farmer. The significance of the frontier in American history was best expressed by Frederick Jackson Turner in his famous frontier hypothesis. He advanced the belief that the unique features of American democracy were produced by the existence of an area of free land, its continuous recession, and the advance of American settlement westward. The serious student of history should look further into the pros and cons of this topic.

been neglected. As the cutting edge of the frontier, they pointed the way to the West; they taught settlers how best to negotiate the deserts and during what seasons to challenge the mountains. South Pass and Chimney Peak and countless other landmark discoveries were their gifts to the emigrants. They not only mapped the West for the settlers, but they later became the dependable wagon masters who led countless wagon trains to the Willamette and the Sacramento valleys.

THE INDIAN FRONTIER

The encounters between the white and red cultures east of the Mississippi River eventually caused the latter to be removed to new homes in the trans-Mississippi West. What happened to them after their arrival in the West is but another of a long series of sad chapters in the history of aboriginal Americans. Accustomed to a sedentary and agrarian life in the East, many of the Indians were confused and frightened by the Great Plains, where short grass and tough sod forced them into a nomadic existence of herding and hunting. Moreover, these problems were compounded by the hostile nature of the Plains Indians, who felt that the removals were an imposition on their traditional hunting grounds, and by the shameful character of Indian agents appointed by the "Great White Father."

In 1834 the federal government apologetically created the Bureau of Indian Affairs and passed the Indian Intercourse Act, both of which were designed to aid and protect the red man. The former established seminary schools, and the latter permitted only licensed traders to enter the reservations (the schools were often slow in coming, and illegal liquor peddlers soon outnumbered the authorized traders).

The removal policy had solved the Indian problem for the whites, at least temporarily, and in the process established a permanent Indian frontier, which was marked by the eastern borders of Indian Territory and Kansas; from that point northward it followed an irregular course to the Great Lakes.

THE MILITARY IN THE WEST

In order to enforce the continued separation of white and red men, a string of forts was established along the permanent frontier during the period from 1825 to 1845. Enforced separation, however, never worked. The forts were too far apart and the army was too small. Often working without uniforms and adequate provisions, a makeshift army of misfits and immigrants patrolled the middle border for almost two decades. Their mission, however, became increasingly difficult after the whites learned that fertile land awaited them in the trans-Mississippi West. By 1850 the "permanent Indian barrier" had all but disappeared.

Elsewhere in the West the military played a more conspicuous role—it protected settlers and trade caravans, punished renegades, and, whenever it appeared expedient, broke treaties. In a more positive light the military helped to explore and map the West, and in some cases the corps of officers played a vital role in carrying a spark of culture to the moving frontier.

Diplomacy and Manifest Destiny

Manifest Destiny[3] reached full blossom when James K. Polk became President in 1844. A real dark-horse candidate at the Democratic convention, Polk was ex-pected to run well behind Van Buren, but expansionists pushed him over on the ninth ballot. As November approached, the Democrats were chanting their expansionist slogans louder than ever and their most popular refrain, "Texas and fifty-four forty or fight," reportedly played a significant role in powering the Polk machine over the ever-popular Whig candidate Henry Clay. The electoral vote was 170 to 105.

Polk was not as unknown as the opposition suggested. He had been Governor of Tennessee, had served in that state's legislature, and had been a powerful Speaker of the House in Washington, D.C. A true Jacksonian, he called upon the combined power of a Democratic House and Democratic Senate to reject another attempt at reinstating the Bank of the United States; and soon thereafter he returned the country to the Independent Treasury System, whereby the federal government maintained its own deposit and withdrawal facilities. Polk further pleased the West and the South when he secured the passage of a low revenue tariff in 1846.

The Pacific Northwest offered one of the most enduring problems of the era in the Oregon dispute.[4] Of the original four nations that once laid claim to the vast territory, only Great Britain and the United States remained; and as the 1840s approached, the main question was not who had what rights, but how long it would take to drive the British out. Both countries based their claims on discovery, exploration, and occupation, with the United States holding a distinct advantage in the last category—at least by 1840.

OREGON TREATY

That Oregon had no formal government between 1818 and 1845 should cause little

[3] The term "Manifest Destiny" was first used by John L. O'Sullivan in 1845 while he was editor of the expansionist periodical *U.S. Magazine and Democratic Review*. The phrase took on a multiplicity of vague expansionist ideas but generally implied that the United States was destined to expand to the four corners of the North American continent. It frequently gained expression under various motives, such as geographic destiny, Anglo-Saxon superiority, and Divine Will.

[4] Oregon at that time included the present states of Oregon, Washington, Idaho, and small parts of Montana and Wyoming west of the Continental Divide.

wonderment inasmuch as the Convention of 1818 provided for joint occupation for a period of ten years; and when the agreement expired in 1827, it was renewed for an indefinite period. The rush of emigrants to the fertile valleys of the Oregon country during the early 1840s, however, caused the long-standing agreement to waver. Desiring law and order, and particularly legal service for land purchases, northwestern pioneers soon began to call for some form of government. England saw that the Americans were determined to control the Northwest when in 1843 the Oregonians formed their own provisional government. Soon thereafter President Polk pleased the northwesterners by announcing that the United States would terminate the joint occupation agreement after the required one-year's notice. In 1846 Great Britain agreed to a settlement. The provisions of the Treaty of Oregon fixed the northern Oregon boundary at the 49th parallel,[5] instead of at the Columbia River, which the British had long demanded.

Other extenuating circumstances that helped usher the British to the conference table were the fact that the valuable beaver had been trapped out of the region, the headquarters of the Hudson's Bay Company had been moved to the safety of Fort Victoria on Vancouver Island and Great Britain desired reciprocal trade agreements with the United States.

CALIFORNIA

The acquisition of California and Texas came in a more dramatic fashion. During the early 1840s, when the wagon trains were wending their way to Oregon, California was experiencing the twilight of the mission era; her land had passed from the Spaniards to the Mexicans and was being rapidly transferred to private land speculators. During the same period of time,

---

[5] President Polk had waged a determined fight for the 54° 40'; nevertheless, he submitted the treaty to the Senate, where it was ratified.

the coast and central valley were dotted with ambitious emigrants and soldiers of fortune who looked forward to the day when California would be claimed by the United States. Among them were Thomas O. Larkin and Captain John A. Sutter, who would figure prominently in securing the Pacific ports for the United States.

Adding to the urgency of the acquisition of California was the prevailing belief that the British were interested in the natural harbors and would soon take possession. Therefore, in November 1845 Polk dispatched John Slidell to Mexico with an offer to buy New Mexico and California outright. Mexico, however, refused to receive the minister because of problems arising over the Texas boundary; and Polk was forced to seek other means of acquiring the territory.

THE "BEAR FLAG" REVOLT

Some scholars have detected a note of intrigue in the President's messages to Tom Larkin and John C. Frémont, which reportedly urged them to elicit the support of Californians in starting an annexation movement. Larkin favored peaceful acquisition, but as events raced toward a confrontation, it appeared that violence was inevitable. Accordingly, on June 14, 1846, a group of settlers near Sonoma, possibly encouraged by Frémont, seized General Mariano G. Vallejo (northern California's most prominent citizen)—in spite of his support for the Larkin plan of nonviolence—and raised a quickly improvised "bear flag" on the Sonoma Plaza. Thus, independence was declared and a "bear flag" republic was announced on July 5, 1846.

TEXAS INDEPENDENCE

Meanwhile, events in Texas had turned from border confrontations to full-scale war. It was the culmination of several years of bitter strife that found its most profound impulses in Manifest Destiny on the one hand and the emotional nationalism of Santa Anna on the other. Santa Anna had emerged as a champion of "civil liberty" and the most popular leader in Mexico after a brief civil war in 1832; but the watchwords lost their meaning when Santa Anna refused to entertain administrative reforms advanced by Stephen F. Austin and his Texas pioneers. Frustrated and angered, the Texans soon began to speak of separate statehood and eventually entertained thoughts of complete independence.

Open hostilities between Mexico and Texas began at Gonzales on October 2, 1835, when a Mexican colonel demanded the surrender of a cannon. The conflict ended with the battle of San Jacinto—Sam Houston not only won the battle, but captured Santa Anna as well. Significant as these battles were, they have long since been overshadowed by the battle of the Alamo, during which Colonel William B. Travis and his brave little band of 186 men held off impossible odds for a period of twelve days. The spirit of their sacrifice helped to carry Texas to independence.

Colonel Stephen W. Kearny, meanwhile, was playing a significant role in the history of California. Supported by Commodore Robert Stockton, Kearny soon discouraged the Mexican general José Castro—it might be added, without firing a shot—and by July 10, 1856, northern California was secure in rebel hands; southern California fell two months later.

As soon as the armed forces had provided Polk's administration with bargaining strength, Nicholas P. Trist, chief clerk of the State Department, with considerable knowledge of the Spanish language, began negotiating a treaty that would fix the southwestern boundary at the Rio Grande River. In addition, his explicit instructions were to secure the purchase of New Mexico and California for $15 million and to offer to assume all claims by United States citizens against Mexico, which amounted to an additional $3,250,000.

These provisions, which were drawn up under extremely unorthodox circumstances (not the least of which was Trist's recall by the President before negotiations were finalized, but which he nevertheless ignored), are better known under the treaty title of Guadalupe Hidalgo. It was signed on February 2, 1848, thus ending an uneasy truce that had been in effect since October 1847.

Select Bibliography

Barker, Eugene C. *Mexico and Texas, 1821–1835.* New York: Russell & Russell, Publishers, 1965.

Billington, Ray A. *The Far Western Frontier, 1830–1860.* New York: Harper & Row, Publishers, 1956.

————. *Westward Expansion: History of the American Frontier,* New York: Crowell Collier and Macmillan, Inc., 1967.

Castaneda, Carlos E., ed. *The Mexican Side of the Texas Revolution.* Dallas, Tex.: P. L. Turner Co., 1928.

Caughey, John W. *California,* 2d ed. Englewood Cliffs, N.J.: Prentice-Hall, Inc., 1953.

De Voto, Bernard. *The Year of Decision: 1846.* Boston: Houghton Mifflin Company, 1961.

Graebner, Norman A. *Empire on the Pacific.* New York: The Ronald Press Company, 1955.

Hines, Robert V. *Bartlett's West: Drawing the Mexican Boundary.* New Haven, Conn.: Yale University Press, 1968.

Lavender, David. *Westward Vision: The Story of the Oregon Trail.* New York: McGraw-Hill Book Company, 1963.

Merk, Frederick. *Manifest Destiny and Mission in American History: A Re-*

interpretation. New York: Alfred A. Knopf, 1963.

Nevins, Allan. *Frémont: Pathmarker of the West.* New York: Frederick Ungar Publishing Co., 1961.

_____. *The Ordeal of the Union.* 2 vols. New York: Charles Scribner's Sons, 1947.

_____, ed. *Polk: The Diary of a President, 1845–1849.* New York: G. P. Putnam's Sons, 1968.

Nichols, Roy R. *The Democratic Machine, 1850–1854.* New York: AMS Press, Inc., 1923.

Oliva, Leo E. *Soldiers on the Santa Fe Trail.* Norman, Okla.: University of Oklahoma Press, 1967.

Parkman, Francis. *The Oregon Trail.* New York: The New American Library, Inc., 1950.

Paul, James C. *Rift in the Democracy.* Cranbury, N.J.: A. S. Barnes & Co., Inc., 1961.

Price, Glenn W. *Origins of the War with Mexico: The Polk–Stockton Intrigue.* Austin, Tex.: University of Texas Press, 1967.

Roe, Frank G. *The Indian on the Horse.* Norman, Okla.: University of Oklahoma Press, 1962.

Russell, Carl P. *Firearms, Traps, and Tools of the Mountain Men.* New York: Alfred A. Knopf, 1967.

Singletary, Otis A. *The Mexican War.* Chicago: University of Chicago Press, 1960.

Smith, Justin H. *The War with Mexico.* 2 vols. New York: Crowell Collier and Macmillan, Inc., 1919.

Still, Bayrd, ed. *The West: Contemporary Records of America's Expansion across the Continent, 1607–1890.* Gloucester, Mass.: Peter Smith, 1961.

Utley, R. M. *Frontiersmen in Blue: The United States Army and the Indian, 1848–1865.* New York: Crowell Collier and Macmillan, Inc., 1967.

Van Deusen, Glyndon G. *The Life of Henry Clay.* Boston: Little, Brown and Company, 1937.

Weinberg, Albert K. *Manifest Destiny: A Study of Nationalist Expansion in American History.* Baltimore, Md.: The Johns Hopkins Press, 1935.

problem 5

The Mexican War: In Search of a Motive

Interpretations of the causes of the Mexican War are numerous and complex. Some blame Mexico, whereas others blame the Polk administration; some accuse the slave interests in the South, and still others point to the various forces of Manifest Destiny.

Those historians of the first school find fault with Mexico's handling of the Slidell mission and mistreatment of Texans. If the Mexican government had received the American envoy and been more equitable with Americans living in Texas, they believe that the war could have been averted.

The second school bases its case on the premise that men make decisions and decisions make wars. In this case they feel that Polk made the decisions that ultimately provoked the Mexican government.

The third group claims to have discovered considerable evidence that shows southern involvement—that there was a southern conspiracy that started the conflict with Mexico in order to grab more land, which, in turn, could be divided into additional slave states.

Manifest Destiny deserves center stage according to the fourth group. Reportedly embraced in varying degrees by every expansionist, this strange philosophy not only called for ocean-to-ocean expansion, but was founded on the assumption that Anglo-Saxon Protestants were willed by God to extend their "su-perior" race, culture, and democratic institutions into the "backward" lands of their neighbors.

General Questions for Reflection and Discussion

1. To what extent did possible American gains justify a war with Mexico?
2. What role, if any, did slavery play in the causes of the Mexican War?
3. To what extent was Manifest Destiny official policy? Public opinion?
4. Why were treaty negotiations not used in the annexation of Texas?
5. What effects do you suppose the Mexican War has had on hemispheric relations during the twentieth century?
6. To what extent was Polk a disciple of Jackson in his views toward expansion?
7. Polk was considered a most successful President by virtue of his foreign policy. Would similar policies make a President great today?

Basic Questions for Reflection and Discussion

1. Compare Polk's treatment of the Slidell episode with that of Sierra.
2. Compare the views of Polk with those of Lincoln with regard to the controversial boundary dispute.
3. To what extent do Polk and Lincoln

251

achieve coherence? What data or words help to establish coherence in each.

4. What is the thesis statement of Smith? of Sierra? Compare the uses made of evidence by each author.

5. Compare the partiality of Smith with that of Sierra. What instances do you find?

6. According to Smith and Sierra, how did centralism and political instability of the Mexican government contribute to the tendency toward war?

7. What events during the 1830s and early 1840s contributed to the conflict?

8. According to Smith, what conditions caused Mexicans to view their side as superior to that of America?

9. What, according to Sierra, thwarted the adjustments of diplomacy?

10. What mistakes on the part of both countries does Sierra find with regard to the annexation of Texas?

11. According to Smith, why did the Mexicans think that war was inevitable after the Shannon declaration of October 1844?

12. What forces inside the United States, according to Sierra, helped to bring on the war?

James K. Polk

The President Calls for a Declaration of War

The existing state of the relations between the United States and Mexico renders it proper that I should bring the subject to the consideration of Congress. In my message at the commencement of your present session, the state of these relations, the causes which led to the suspension of diplomatic intercourse between the two countries in March, 1845, and the long-continued and unredressed wrongs and injuries committed by the Mexican government on citizens of the United States, in their persons and property, were briefly set forth.

As the facts and opinions which were then laid before you were carefully considered, I cannot better express my present convictions of the condition of affairs up to that time, than by referring you to that communication.

The strong desire to establish peace with Mexico on liberal and honorable terms, and the readiness of this government to regulate and adjust our boundary, and other causes of difference with that power, on such fair and equitable principles as would lead to permanent relations of the most friendly nature, induced me in September last to seek the reopening of diplomatic relations between the two countries. Every measure adopted on our part had for its object the furtherance of these desired results.

From *A Compilation of the Messages and Papers of the Presidents, 1789–1897* edited by James D. Richardson (Washington: Government Printing Office, 1896–1899) Vol. 4, pp. 437–443.

In communicating to Congress a succinct statement of the injuries which we had suffered from Mexico, and which have been accumulating during a period of more than twenty years, every expression that could tend to inflame the people of Mexico, or defeat or delay a pacific result, was carefully avoided. An envoy of the United States repaired to Mexico, with full powers to adjust every existing difference. But though present on the Mexican soil, by agreement between the two governments, invested with full powers, and bearing evidence of the most friendly dispositions, his mission has been unavailing. The Mexican government not only refused to receive him, or listen to his propositions, but, after a long continued series of menaces, have at last invaded our territory, and shed the blood of our fellow-citizens on our own soil.

It now becomes my duty to state more in detail the origin, progress, and failure of that mission. In pursuance of the instructions given in September last, an inquiry was made, on the thirteenth of October, 1845, in the most friendly terms, through our consul in Mexico, of the minister for foreign affairs, whether the Mexican government "would receive an envoy from the United States intrusted with full powers to adjust all the questions in dispute between the two governments"; with the assurance that "should the answer be in the affirmative, such an envoy would be immediately dispatched to Mexico." The Mexican minister, on the fifteenth of October, gave an affirmative answer to this inquiry, requesting, at the same time, that our naval force at Vera Cruz might be withdrawn, lest its continued presence might assume the appearance of menace and coercion pending the negotiations. This force was immediately withdrawn. On the 10th of November, 1845, Mr. John Slidell, of Louisiana, was commissioned by me as envoy extraordinary and minister plenipotentiary of the United States to Mexico, and was entrusted with full powers to adjust both the questions of the Texas boundary and of indemnification to our citizens. The redress of the wrongs of our citizens naturally and inseparably blended itself with the question of boundary. The settlement of the one question, in any correct view of the subject, involves that of the other. I could not, for a moment, entertain the idea that the claims of our much injured and long suffering citizens, many of which had existed for more than twenty years, should be postponed, or separated from the settlement of the boundary question.

Mr. Slidell arrived at Vera Cruz on the 30th of November, and was courteously received by the authorities of that city. But the government of General Herrera was then tottering to its fall. The revolutionary party had seized upon the Texas question to effect or hasten its overthrow. Its determination to restore friendly relations with the United States, and to receive our minister, to negotiate for the settlement of this question, was violently assailed, and was made the great theme of denunciation against it. The government of General Herrera, there is good reason to believe, was sincerely desirous to receive our minister; but it yielded to the storm raised by its enemies, and on the 21st of December refused to accredit Mr. Slidell upon the most frivolous pretexts. These are so fully and ably exposed in the note of Mr. Slidell, of the 24th of December last, to the Mexican minister of foreign relations, herewith transmitted, that I deem it unnecessary to enter into further detail on this portion of the subject.

Five days after the date of Mr. Slidell's note, General Herrera yielded the government to General Paredes, without a struggle, and on the 30th of December resigned the presidency. This revolution was accomplished solely by the army, the people having taken little part in the contest; and thus the supreme power in Mexico passed into the hands of a military leader.

Determined to leave no effort untried to effect an amicable adjustment with Mexico, I directed Mr. Slidell to present his credentials to the government of General Paredes, and ask to be officially received by him. There would have been less ground for taking this step had General Paredes come into power by a regular constitutional succession. In that event his administration would have been considered but a mere constitutional continuance of the government of General Herrera, and the refusal of the latter to receive our minister would have been deemed conclusive, unless an intimation had been given by General Paredes of his desire to reverse the decision of his predecessor. But the government of General Paredes owes its existence to a military revolution, by which the subsisting constitutional authorities had been subverted. The form of government was entirely changed, as well as all the high functionaries by whom it was administered.

Under these circumstances, Mr. Slidell, in obedience to my direction, addressed a note to the Mexican minister of foreign relations, under date of the 1st of March last, asking to be received by that government in the diplomatic character to which he had been appointed. This minister, in his reply under date of the 12th of March, reiterated the arguments of his predecessor, and, in terms that may be considered as giving just grounds of offence to the government and people of the United States, denied the application of Mr. Slidell. Nothing, therefore, remained for our envoy but to demand his passports, and return to his own country.

Thus the government of Mexico, though

solemnly pledged by official acts in October last to receive and accredit an American envoy, violated their plighted faith, and refused the offer of a peaceful adjustment of our difficulties. Not only was the offer rejected, but the indignity of its rejection was enhanced by the manifest breach of faith in refusing to admit the envoy, who came because they had bound themselves to receive him. Nor can it be said that the offer was fruitless from the want of opportunity of discussing it; our envoy was present on their own soil. Nor can it be ascribed to a want of sufficient powers; our envoy had full powers to adjust every question of difference. Nor was there room for complaint that our propositions for settlement were unreasonable; permission was not even given our envoy to make any proposition whatever. Nor can it be objected that we, on our part, would not listen to any reasonable terms of their suggestion; the Mexican government refused all negotiation, and have made no proposition of any kind.

In my message at the commencement of the present session, I informed you that, upon the earnest appeal both of the Congress and convention of Texas, I had ordered an efficient military force to take a position "between the Nueces and the Del Norte." This had become necessary, to meet a threatened invasion of Texas by the Mexican forces, for which extensive military preparations had been made. The invasion was threatened solely because Texas had determined, in accordance with a solemn resolution of the Congress of the United States, to annex herself to our Union; and, under these circumstances, it was plainly our duty to extend our protection over her citizens and soil.

This force was concentrated at Corpus Christi, and remained there until after I had received such information from Mexico as rendered it probable, if not certain, that the Mexican government would refuse to receive our envoy.

Meantime Texas, by the final action of our Congress, had become an integral part of our Union. The Congress of Texas, by its act of December 19, 1836, had declared the Rio del Norte to be the boundary of that republic. Its jurisdiction had been extended and exercised beyond the Nueces. The country between that river and the Del Norte had been represented in the Congress and in the convention of Texas; had thus taken part in the act of annexation itself; and is now included within one of our congressional districts. Our own Congress had, moreover, with great unanimity, by the act approved December 31, 1845, recognised the country beyond the Nueces as a part of our territory, by including it within our own revenue system; and a revenue officer, to reside within that district, has been appointed, by and with the advice and consent of the Senate. It became, therefore, of urgent necessity to provide for the defence of that portion of our country. Accordingly, on the 13th of January last, instructions were issued to the general in command of these troops to occupy the left bank of the Del Norte. This river, which is the southwestern boundary of the State of Texas, is an exposed frontier; from this quarter invasion was threatened; upon it, and in its immediate vicinity, in the judgment of high military experience, are the proper stations for the protecting forces of the government. In addition to this important consideration, several others occurred to induce this movement. Among these are the facilities afforded by the ports at Brazos Santiago and the mouth of the Del Norte, for the reception of supplies by sea; the stronger and more healthful military positions; the convenience for obtaining a ready and a more abundant supply of provisions, water, fuel, and forage; and the advantages which are afforded by the Del Norte in forwarding supplies to such posts as may be established in the interior and upon the Indian frontier.

The movement of the troops to the Del Norte was made by the commanding general, under positive instructions to abstain from all aggressive acts towards Mexico or Mexican citizens, and to regard the relations between that republic and the United States as peaceful, unless she would declare war, or commit acts of hostility indicative of a state of war. He was specially directed to protect private property, and respect personal rights.

The army moved from Corpus Christi on the eleventh of March, and on the twenty-eighth of that month arrived on the left bank of the Del Norte, opposite to Matamoras, where it encamped on a commanding position, which has since been strengthened by the erection of field works. A depot has also been established at Point Isabel, near the Brazos Santiago, thirty miles in the rear of the encampment. The selection of his position was necessarily confided to the judgment of the general in command.

The Mexican forces at Matamoras assumed a belligerent attitude, and, on the twelfth of April, General Ampudia, then in command, notified General Taylor to break up his camp within twenty-four hours, and to retire beyond the Nueces River, and, in the event of his failure to comply with these demands, announced that arms, and arms alone, must decide the question. But no open act of hostility was committed until the twenty-fourth of April. On that day, General Arista, who had succeeded to the command of the Mexican forces, communicated to General Taylor that "he considered hostilities commenced, and should prosecute them." A party of dragoons, of sixty-three men and officers, were on the same day dispatched from the American camp up the Rio del Norte, on its left bank, to ascertain whether the Mexican troops had crossed, or were preparing to cross, the river, "became engaged with a large body of these troops, and, after a short affair, in which some sixteen were killed and wounded, appear to have been surrounded and compelled to surrender."

The grievous wrongs perpetrated by Mexico upon our citizens throughout a long period of years remain unredressed; and solemn treaties, pledging her public faith for this redress, have been disregarded. A government either unable or unwilling to enforce the execution of such treaties, fails to perform one of its plainest duties.

Our commerce with Mexico has been almost annihilated. It was formerly highly beneficial to both nations; but our merchants have been deterred from prosecuting it by the system of outrage and extortion which the Mexican authorities have pursued against them, whilst their appeals through their own government for indemnity have been made in vain. Our forbearance has gone to such an extreme as to be mistaken in its character. Had we acted with vigor in repelling the insults and redressing the injuries inflicted by Mexico at the commencement, we should doubtless have escaped all the difficulties in which we are now involved.

Instead of this, however, we have been exerting our best efforts to propitiate her good-will. Upon the pretext that Texas, a nation as independent as herself, thought proper to unite its destinies with our own, she has affected to believe that we have severed her rightful territory, and in official proclamations and manifestoes has repeatedly threatened to make war upon us, for the purpose of reconquering Texas. In the meantime, we have tried every effort at reconciliation. The cup of forbearance had been exhausted, even before the recent information from the frontier of the Del Norte. But now, after reiterated menaces, Mexico has passed the boundary of the United States, has invaded our territory, and shed American blood upon the American soil. She has proclaimed that hostilities have commenced, and that the two nations are now at war.

As war exists, and, notwithstanding all our efforts to avoid it, exists by the act of Mexico herself, we are called upon by every consideration of duty and patriotism to vindicate with decision the honor, the rights, and the interests of our country.

Anticipating the possibility of a crisis like that which has arrived, instructions were given in August last, "as a precautionary measure" against invasion, or threatened invasion, authorizing General Taylor, if the emergency required, to accept volunteers, not from Texas only, but from the States of Louisiana, Alabama, Mississippi, Tennessee, and Kentucky; and corresponding letters were addressed to the respective governors of those States. These instructions were repeated; and, in January last, soon after the incorporation of "Texas into our union of States," General Taylor was further "authorized by the President to make a requisition upon the executive of that State for such of its militia force as may be needed to repel invasion, or to secure the country against apprehended invasion." On the second day of March he was again reminded, "in the event of the approach of any considerable Mexican force, promptly and efficiently to use the authority with which he was clothed to call to him such auxiliary force as he might need." War actually existing, and our territory having been invaded, General Taylor, pursuant to authority vested in him by my direction, has called on the governor of Texas for four regiments of State troops—two to be mounted, and two to serve on foot; and on the governor of Louisiana for four regiments of infantry, to be sent to him as soon as practicable.

In further vindication of our rights, and defence of our territory, I invoke the prompt action of Congress to recognise the existence of the war, and to place at the disposition of the Executive the means of prosecuting the war with vigor, and thus hastening the restoration of peace. To this end I recommend that authority should be given to call into the public service a large body of volunteers, to serve for not less than six or twelve months, unless sooner discharged. A volunteer force is beyond question more efficient than any other description of citizen soldiers; and it is not to be doubted that a number far beyond that required would readily rush to the field upon the call of their country. I further recommend that a liberal provision be made for sustaining our entire military force and furnishing it with supplies and munitions of war.

The most energetic and prompt measures, and the immediate appearance in arms of a large and overpowering force, are recommended to Congress as the most certain and efficient means of bringing the existing collision with Mexico to a speedy and successful termination.

In making these recommendations, I deem it proper to declare that it is my anxious desire not only to terminate hostilities speedily, but to bring all matters in dispute between this government and Mexico to an early and amicable adjustment; and, in this view, I shall be prepared to renew negotiations, whenever Mexico shall be ready to receive propositions, or to make propositions of her own.

I transmit herewith a copy of the correspondence between our envoy to Mexico and the Mexican minister for foreign affairs; and so much of the correspondence between that envoy and the Secretary of State, and between the Secretary of War and the general in command on the Del Norte, as is necessary to a full understanding of the subject.

Abraham Lincoln

Lincoln Challenges Polk's Decision January 12, 1848

Mr. Chairman:

Some, if not all the gentlemen on, the other side of the House, who have addressed the committee within the last two days, have spoken rather complainingly, if I have rightly understood them, of the vote given a week or ten days ago, declaring that the war with Mexico was unnecessarily and unconstitutionally commenced by the President.[1] I admit that such a vote should not be given, in mere party wantonness, and that the one given, is justly censurable, if it have no other, or better foundation. I am one of those who joined in that vote; and I did so under my best impression of the *truth* of the case. How I got this impression, and how it may possibly be removed, I will now try to show. When the war began, it was my opinion that all those who, because of knowing too *little*, or because of knowing too *much*, could not conscientiously approve the conduct of the President, in the beginning of it, should, nevertheless, as good citizens and patriots, remain silent on that point, at least till the war should be ended. Some leading democrats, including Ex-President Van Buren, have taken this same view, as I understand them; and I adhered to it, and acted upon it, until since I took my seat here; and I think I

From *The Collected Works of Abraham Lincoln,* Vol. 1, Roy P. Basler, ed. (New Brunswick, N.J.: Rutgers University Press, 1953), omitting footnotes except where necessary for understanding with permission of the publisher, pp. 431–442.

[1] James K. Polk.

should still adhere to it, were it not that the President and his friends will not allow it to be so. Besides the continual effort of the President to argue every silent vote given for supplies, into an endorsement of the justice and wisdom of his conduct—besides that singularly candid paragraph, in his late message in which he tells us that Congress, with great unanimity, only two in the Senate and fourteen in the House dissenting, had declared that, "by the act of the Republic of Mexico, a state of war exists between that Government and the United States," when the same journals that informed him of this, also informed him, that when that declaration stood disconnected from the question of supplies, sixty-seven in the House, and not fourteen merely voted against it—besides this open attempt to prove, by telling the *truth,* what he could not prove by telling the *whole truth*—demanding of all who will not submit to be misrepresented in justice to themselves to speak out—besides all this, one of my colleagues (Mr. Richardson) at a very early day in the session brought in a set of resolutions, expressly endorsing the original justice of the war on the part of the President. Upon these resolutions, when they shall be put on their passage I shall be *compelled* to vote; so that I can not be silent, if I would. Seeing this, I went about preparing myself to give the vote understandingly when it should come. I carefully examined the President's messages, to ascertain what he himself had said and proved upon the point. The result of this examination was to make the impression, that taking for true, all the President states as facts, he falls far short of proving his justification; and that the President would have gone farther with his proof, if it had not been for the small matter, that the *truth* would not permit him. Under the impression thus made, I gave the vote before mentioned. I propose now to give, concisely, the process of the examination I made, and how I reached the conclusion I did. The President, in his first war message of May 1846, declares that the soil was *ours* on which hostilities were commenced by Mexico; and he repeats that declaration, almost in the same language, in each successive annual message, thus showing that he esteems that point, a highly essential one. In the importance of that point, I entirely agree with the President. To my judgment, it is the *very point,* upon which he should be justified, or condemned. In his message of December 1846, it seems to have occurred to him, as is certainly true, that title—ownership—to soil, or any thing else, is not a simple fact; but is a conclusion following one or more simple facts; and that it was incumbent upon him, to present the facts, from which he concluded, the soil was ours, on which the first blood of the war was shed.

Accordingly a little below the middle of page twelve in the message last referred to, he enters upon that task; forming an issue, and introducing testimony, extending the whole, to a little below the middle of page fourteen. Now I propose to try to show, that the whole of this—issue and evidence—is, from beginning to end, the sheerest deception. The issue, as he presents it, is in these words "but there are those who, conceding all this to be true, assume the ground that the true western boundary of Texas is the Nueces, instead of the Rio Grande; and that, therefore, in marching our army to the east bank of the latter river, we passed the Texan line, and invaded the territory of Mexico." Now this issue, is made up of

two affirmatives and no negative. The main deception of it is, that it assumes as true, that *one* river or the *other* is necessarily the boundary; and cheats the superficial thinker entirely out of the idea, that *possibly* the boundary is somewhere *between* the two, and not actually at either. A further deception is, that it will let in *evidence,* which a true issue would exclude. A true issue, made by the President, would be about as follows "I say, the soil *was ours,* on which the first blood was shed; there are those who say it was not."

I now proceed to examine the President's evidence, as applicable to such an issue. When that evidence is analyzed, it is all included in the following propositions:

1. That the Rio Grande was the Western boundary of Louisiana as we purchased it of France in 1803.
2. That the Republic of Texas always *claimed* the Rio Grande, as her Western boundary.
3. That by various acts, she had claimed it *on paper.*
4. That Santa Anna, in his treaty with Texas, recognised the Rio Grande, as her boundary.
5. That Texas *before,* and the U.S. *after,* annexation had *exercised* jurisdiction *beyond* the Nueces—*between* the two rivers.
6. That our Congress, *understood* the boundary of Texas to extend beyond the Nueces.

Now for each of these in its turn.

His first item is, that the Rio Grande was the Western boundary of Louisiana, as we purchased it of France in 1803; and seeming to expect this to be disputed, he argues over the amount of nearly a page, to prove it true; at the end of which he lets us know, that by the treaty of 1819, we sold to Spain the whole country from the Rio Grande eastward, to the Sabine. Now, admitting for the present, that the Rio Grande, was the boundary of Louisiana, what, under heaven, had that to do with the *present* boundary between us and Mexico? How, Mr. Chairman, the line, that once divided your land from mine, can *still* be the boundary between us, *after* I have sold my land to you, is, to me, beyond all comprehension. And how any man, with an honest purpose only, of proving the truth, could ever have *thought* of introducing such a fact to prove such an issue, is equally incomprehensible. His next piece of evidence is that "The Republic of Texas always *claimed* this river (Rio Grande) as her western boundary[.]" That is not true, in fact. Texas *has* claimed it, but she has not *always* claimed it. There is, at least, one distinguished exception. Her state constitution—the republic's most solemn, and well considered act—that which may, without impropriety, be called her last will and testament revoking all others— makes no such claim. But suppose she had always claimed it. Had not Mexico always claimed the contrary? so that there is but *claim* against *claim*, leaving nothing proved, until we get back of the claims, and find which has the better *foundation*. Though not in the order in which the President presents his evidence, I now consider that class of his statements, which are, in substance, nothing more than that Texas has, by various acts of her convention and congress, claimed the Rio Grande, as her boundary, on *paper*. I mean here what he says about the fixing of the Rio Grande as her boundary in her constitution (not her state constitution) about forming congressional districts, counties &c &c. Now all of this is but naked *claim;* and what I have already said about claims is strictly applicable to this. If I should claim your land, by word of mouth, that certainly would not make it mine; and if I were to claim it by a deed which I had made myself, and with which, you had had nothing to do, the claim would be quite the same, in substance— or rather, in utter nothingness. I next

consider the President's statement that Santa Anna in his treaty[2] with Texas, recognised the Rio Grande, as the western boundary of Texas. Besides the position, so often taken that Santa Anna, while a prisoner of war—a captive—*could* not bind Mexico by a treaty, which I deem conclusive—besides this, I wish to say something in relation to this treaty, so called by the President, with Santa Anna. If any man would like to be amused by a sight of that *little* thing, which the Presi-

[2] The text of the so-called "treaty," printed following Lincoln's speech in the *Congressional Globe Appendix* is as follows:

Articles of an agreement entered into between his Excellency David G. Burnet, President of the Republic of Texas, of the one part, and his Excellency General Santa Anna, President-General-in-Chief of the Mexican army, of the other part.

Article 1. General Antonio Lopez de Santa Anna agrees that he will not take up arms, nor will he exercise his influence to cause them to be taken up, against the people of Texas, during the present war of independence.

Article 2. All hostilities between the Mexican and Texan troops will cease immediately, both by land and water.

Article 3. The Mexican troops will evacuate the territory of Texas, passing to the other side of the Rio Grande Del Norte.

Article 4. The Mexican army, in its retreat, shall not take the property of any person without his consent and just indemnification, using only such articles as may be necessary for its subsistence, in cases when the owner may not be present, and remitting to the commander of the army of Texas, or to the Commissioners to be appointed for the adjustment of such matters, an account of the value of the property consumed, the place where taken, and the name of the owner, if it can be ascertained.

Article 5. That all private property, including cattle, horses, negro slaves, or indentured persons, of whatever denomination, that may have been captured by any portion of the Mexican army, or may have taken refuge in the said army, since the commencement of the late invasion, shall be restored to the commander of the Texan army, or to such other persons as may be appointed by the Government of Texas to receive them.

Article 6. The troops of both armies will refrain

dent calls by that *big* name, he can have it, by turning to Niles' Register volume 50, page 336. And if any one should suppose that Niles' Register is a curious repository of so mighty a document, as a solemn treaty between nations, I can only say that I learned, to a tolerable degree (of) certainty, by enquiry at the State Department, that the President himself, never saw it any where else. By the way, I believe I should not err, if I were to declare, that during the first ten years of

the existence of that document, it was never, by any body, *called* a treaty—that it was never so called, till the President, in his extremity, attempted, by so calling it, to wring something from it in justification of himself in connection with the Mexican war. It has none of the distinguishing features of a treaty. It does not call itself a treaty. Santa Anna does not therein, assume to bind Mexico; he assumes only to act as the President-Commander-in-chief of the Mexican Army and Navy; stipulates that the then present hostilities should cease, and that he would not *himself* take up arms, nor *influence* the Mexican people to take up arms, against Texas during the existence of the war of independence[.] He did not recognise the independence of Texas; he did not assume to put an end to the war; but clearly indicated his expection of its continuance; he did not say one word about boundary, and, most probably, never thought of it. It *is* stipulated therein that the Mexican forces should evacuate the territory of Texas, *passing to the other side of the Rio Grande;* and in another article, it is stipulated that, to prevent collisions between the armies, the Texan army should not approach nearer than within five leagues—of *what* is not said—but clearly, from the object stated it is—of the Rio Grande. Now, if this is a treaty, recognising the Rio Grande, as the boundary of Texas, it contains the singular feature, of stipulating, that Texas shall not go within five leagues of *her own* boundary.

Next comes the evidence of Texas before annexation, and the United States, afterwards, *exercising* jurisdiction *beyond* the Nueces, and *between* the two rivers. This actual *exercise* of jurisdiction, is the very class or quality of evidence we want. It is excellent so far as it goes; but does it go far enough? He tells us it went *beyond* the Nueces; but he does not tell us it went *to* the Rio Grande. He tells us, jurisdiction was exercised *between* the

---

from coming into contact with each other; and to this end, the commander of the army of Texas will be careful not to approach within a shorter distance than five leagues.

Article 7. The Mexican army shall not make any other delay, on its march, than that which is necessary to take up their hospitals, baggage, &c., and to cross the rivers; any delay not necessary to these purposes to be considered an infraction of this agreement.

Article 8. By an express to be immediately despatched, this agreement shall be sent to General Vincente Filisola, and to General T. J. Rusk, commander of the Texan army, in order that they may be apprized of its stipulations; and to this end, they will exchange engagements to comply with the same.

Article 9. That all Texan prisoners now in the possession of the Mexican army, or its authorities, be forthwith released, and furnished with free passports to return to their homes; in consideration of which, a corresponding number of Mexican prisoners, rank and file, now in possession of the Government of Texas, shall be immediately released—the remainder of the Mexican prisoners that continue in the possession of the Government of Texas to be treated with due humanity; any extraordinary comforts that may be furnished them to be at the charge of the Government of Mexico.

Article 10. General Antonio Lopez de Santa Anna will be sent to Vera Cruz as soon as it shall be deemed proper.

The contracting parties sign this instrument for the above mentioned purposes, in duplicate, at the port of Velasco, this 14th day of May, 1836.

David G. Burnet, President
Jas. Collingsworth, Secretary of State
Antonio Lopez de Santa Anna
B. Hardiman, Secretary of the Treasury
P. W. Grayson, Attorney-General

two rivers, but he does not tell us it was exercised over *all* the territory between them. Some simple minded people, think it is *possible*, to cross one river and go *beyond* it without going *all the way* to the next—that jurisdiction may be exercised *between* two rivers without covering *all* the country between them. I know a man, not very unlike myself, who exercises jurisdiction over a piece of land between the Wabash and the Mississippi; and yet so far is this from being *all* there is between those rivers, that it is just one hundred and fifty-two feet long by fifty wide, and no part of it much within a hundred miles of either. He has a neighbor between him and the Mississippi—that is, just across the street, in that direction— whom, I am sure, he could neither *persuade* nor *force* to give up his habitation; but which nevertheless, he could certainly annex, if it were to be done, by merely standing on his own side of the street and *claiming* it, or even, sitting down, and writing a *deed* for it.

But next the President tells us, the Congress of the United States *understood* the State of Texas they admitted into the union, to extend *beyond* the Nueces. Well, I suppose they did. *I* certainly so understood it. But how *far* beyond? That Congress did *not* understand it to extend clear to the Rio Grande, is quite certain by the fact of their joint resolutions, for admission, expressly leaving all questions of boundary to future adjustment. And it may be added, that Texas herself, is proved to have had the same understanding of it, that our Congress had, by the fact of the exact conformity of her new constitution, to those resolutions.

I am now through the whole of the President's evidence; and it is a singular fact, that if any one should declare the President sent the army into the midst of a settlement of Mexican people, who had never submitted, by consent or by force, to the authority of Texas or of the United States, and that *there,* and *thereby,* the first blood of the war was shed, there is not one word in all the President has said, which would either admit or deny the declaration. This strange omission, it does seem to me, could not have occurred but by design. My way of living leads me to be about the courts of justice; and there, I have sometimes seen a good lawyer, struggling for his client's neck in a desperate case, employing every artifice to work around, befog, and cover up, with many words, some point arising in the case, which he *dared* not admit, and yet *could* not deny. Party bias may help to make it appear so; but with all the allowance I can make for such bias, it still does appear to me, that just such, and from just such necessity, is the President's struggle in this case.

Some time after my colleague (Mr. Richardson) introduced the resolutions I have mentioned, I introduced a preamble, resolution, and interrogatories, intended to draw the President out, if possible, on this hitherto untrodden ground. To show their relevancy, I propose to state my understanding of the true rule for ascertaining the boundary between Texas and Mexico. It is, that *wherever* Texas was *exercising* jurisdiction, was hers; and *wherever Mexico* was exercising jurisdiction, was hers; and that *whatever* separated the actual exercise of jurisdiction of the one, from that of the other, was the true boundary between them. If, as is probably true, Texas was exercising jurisdiction along the western bank of the Nueces, and Mexico was exercising it along the eastern bank of the Rio Grande, then *neither* river was the boundary, but the uninhabited country between the two, was. The extent of our territory in that region depended, not on any *treaty-fixed* boundary (for no treaty had attempted it) but on revolution. Any people anywhere, being inclined and having the power, have the *right* to rise up, and shake off the existing government, and form a new one that suits them better. This is a most valuable—a most sacred right—a right, which we hope and believe, is to liberate the world. Nor is this right confined to cases in which the whole people of an existing government, may choose to exercise it. Any portion of such people that *can, may* revolutionize, and make their *own,* of so much of the territory as they inhabit. More than this, a *majority* of any portion of such people may revolutionize, putting down a *minority,* intermingled with, or near about them, who may oppose their movement. Such minority, was precisely the case, of the tories of our own revolution. It is a quality of revolutions not to go by *old* lines, or *old* laws; but to break up both, and make new ones. As to the country now in question, we bought it of France in 1803, and sold it to Spain in 1819, according to the President's statements. After this, all Mexico, including Texas, revolutionized against Spain; and still later, Texas revolutionized against Mexico. In my view, just so far as she carried her revolution, by obtaining the *actual,* willing or unwilling, submission of the people, *so far,* the country was hers, and no farther. Now sir, for the purpose of obtaining the very best evidence, as to whether Texas had actually carried her revolution, to the place where the hostilities of the present war commenced, let the President answer the interrogatories, I proposed, as before mentioned, or some other similar ones. Let him answer, fully, fairly, and candidly. Let him answer with *facts,* and not with arguments. Let him answer, as Washington would answer. As a nation *should* not, and the Almighty *will* not, be evaded, so let him attempt no evasion—no equivocation. And if, so answering, he can show that the soil was ours, where the first blood of the war was shed—that it was not within an inhabited country, or, if within such, that the inhabitants had submitted themselves to the civil authority of Texas, or of the United States, and that the same is true of the site of Fort Brown, then I am with him for his justification. In that case I, shall be most happy to reverse the vote I gave the other day.

I have a selfish motive for desiring that the President may do this. I expect to give some votes, in connection with the war, which, without his so doing, will be of doubtful propriety in my own judgment, but which will be free from the doubt if he does so. But if he *can* not, or *will* not do this—if on any pretence, or no pretence, he shall refuse or omit it, then I shall be fully convinced, of what I more than suspect already, that he is deeply conscious of being in the wrong—that he feels the blood of this war, like the blood of Abel, is crying to Heaven against him. That originally having some strong motive— what, I will not stop now to give my opinion concerning—to involve the two countries in a war, and trusting to escape scrutiny, by fixing the public gaze upon the exceeding brightness of military glory— that attractive rainbow, that rises in showers of blood—that serpent's eye, that charms to destroy—he plunged into it, and has swept, *on* and *on,* till, disappointed in his calculation of the ease with which Mexico might be subdued, he now finds himself, he knows not where. How like the half insane mumbling of a fever-dream, is the whole war part of his late message! At one time telling us that Mexico has nothing whatever, that we can get, but territory; at another, showing us how we can support the war, by levying contributions on Mexico. At one time, urging the national honor, the security of the future, the prevention of foreign interference, and even, the good of Mexico herself, as among the objects of the war; at another, telling us, that "to reject indemnity, by refusing to accept a cession of territory, would be to abandon all our just demands, and to wage the war, bearing all its expenses, *without a purpose or definite object*[.]" So then, the national honor, security of the future, and everything but territorial indemnity, may be considered the *no-purposes,* and *indefinite,* objects of the war! But, having it now settled that territorial indemnity is the only object, we are urged to seize, by legislation here, all that he was content to take, a few months ago, and the whole province of lower California to boot, and to still carry on the war—to take *all* we are fighting for, and *still* fight on. Again, the President is resolved, under all circumstances, to have full territorial indemnity for the expenses of the war; but he forgets to tell us how we are to get the *excess,* after those expenses shall have surpassed the value of the *whole* of the Mexican territory. So again, he insists that the separate national existence of Mexico, shall be maintained; but he does not tell us *how* this can be done, after we shall have taken *all* her territory. Lest the questions, I here suggest, be considered speculative merely, let me be indulged a moment in trying [to] show they are not. The war has gone on some twenty months; for the expenses of which, together with an inconsiderable old score, the President now claims about one half of the Mexican territory; and that, by far the better half, so far as concerns our ability to make any thing out of it. *It* is comparatively uninhabited; so that we could establish land offices in it, and raise some money in that way. But the other half is already inhabited, as I understand it, tolerably densely for the nature of the country; and all its lands, or all that are valuable, already appropriated as private property. How then are we to make any thing out of these lands with this incumbrance on them? or how, remove the incumbrance? I suppose no one will say we should kill the people, or drive them out, or make slaves of them, or even confiscate their property. How then can we make much out of this part of the territory? If the prosecution of the war has, in expenses, already equalled the *better* half of the country, how long its future prosecution, will be in equalling, the less valuable half, is not a *speculative,* but a *practical* question, pressing closely upon us. And yet it is a question which the President seems to never have thought of. As to the mode of terminating the war, and securing peace, the President is

equally wandering and indefinite. First, it is to be done by a more vigorous prosecution of the war in the vital parts of the enemies country; and, after apparently, talking himself tired, on this point, the President drops down into a half despairing tone, and tells us that "with a people distracted and divided by contending factions, and a government subject to constant changes, by successive revolutions, *the continued success of our arms may fail to secure a satisfactory peace*[.]" Then he suggests the propriety of wheedling the Mexican people to desert the counsels of their own leaders, and trusting in our protection, to set up a government from which we can secure a satisfactory peace; telling us, that *"this may become the only mode of obtaining such a peace."* But soon he falls into doubt of this too; and then drops back on to the already half abandoned ground of "more vigorous prosecution." All this shows that the President is, in no wise, satisfied with his own positions. First he takes up one, and in attempting to argue us *into* it, he argues himself *out* of it; then seizes another, and goes through the same process; and then, confused at being able to think of nothing new, he snatches up the old one again, which he has some time before cast off. His mind, tasked beyond its power, is running hither and thither, like some tortured creature, on a burning surface, finding no position, on which it can settle down, and be at ease.

Again, it is a singular omission in this message, that it, no where intimates *when* the President expects the war to terminate. At its beginning, General Scott was, by this same President, driven into disfavor, if not disgrace, for intimating that peace could not be conquered in less than three or four months. But now, at the end of about twenty months, during which time our arms have given us the most splendid successes—every department, and every part, land and water, officers and privates, regulars and volunteers, doing all that men *could* do, and hundreds of things which it had ever before been thought man could *not* do—after all this, this same President gives us a long message, without showing us, that, *as to the end,* he himself, has, even an imaginary conception. As I have before said, he knows not where he is. He is a bewildered, confounded, and miserably perplexed man. God grant he may be able to show, there is not something about his conscience, more painful than all his mental perplexity!

Justin H. Smith

The Mexican War: An American View

In tracing the mutual relations of the United States and Mexico, we have often had occasion to note how each nation felt about the other and about a possible conflict; but it is very desirable now to understand as completely as possible what those feelings were at about the beginning of 1846, and this will require the consideration of many additional facts.

Already there were influential and wealthy Mexicans, particularly in the north, who wished or half-wished that the United States would subjugate their country, so that order and prosperity might come; and others reflected that at least our assistance might be desired, should Paredes undertake to set up a European monarchy. But these were selfish calculations. They seldom implied good-will. Friends we have none at the

From "The Mexican Attitude on the Eve of War" by Justin H. Smith in *The War with Mexico*, Vol. 1. (New York: Crowell Collier and Macmillan Company, 1919), 102–116.

capital, Slidell reported; and our consul at the northern city of Tampico, even though but a faint loyalty to the central government prevailed in that section, wrote in September, 1845: "The most stubborn and malignant feeling seems to exist in the mind of every Mexican against the United States."

The principal cause of this feeling—the supposed misconduct of our government in the settlement, revolution and successful resistance of Texas, and in the recognition and annexation of that republic—has already been explained; but other strong reasons coöperated. All understood that intense dissatisfaction existed in the northern departments. Now that our frontier had been advanced so far south, further peaceful agression seemed easy; and it was believed that we intended to pursue the Texas method progressively, until all of Mexico should little by little become ours. "This first invasion is the threat of many more," said the official journal. It was alleged that we, fearing the competition of that country in the markets of the world, did all we could to hinder its agricultural, industrial and commercial development, and excited the revolutions that paralyzed it; and it was even believed that we incited the Indians to ravage the northern frontiers, and so create discontent against the central government. The privileged classes dreaded the influence of our democratic ideas. The clergy were afraid that Protestantism, or at least free thought, might cross the border, and that so far as Mexican territory should fall under our sway, secular education, the confiscation of their property, and the other anticlerical plans of the Federalists, who appeared to draw their inspiration and their arguments largely from this country, might be put into force. The numerous misunderstandings and clashes with the United States that we have noted had produced an enduring resentment, and in particular our claims and our efforts to have them settled were commonly deemed artificial and unjust.

Behind all these facts lay the general anti-foreign prejudice; and this, we should now observe, was in our case more than a prejudice. Even in the eyes of the intelligent *El Siglo XIX,* an American was "a being detestable to the nation on account of the little accord between [him and] the religion, the language, and the gentle, affable, frank, and generous character of the Mexican." Our directness of thought, speech and action, and the brusqueness of manner that naturally accompanied it appeared inconsiderate and haughty; and no doubt, in dealing with people who seemed to us deceitful, unreliable and unfriendly, our citizens often emphasized these characteristics. In habits and customs there was indeed a profound unlikeness, and below this lay a still more profound racial antagonism. Finally the politicians of all parties, fearing to be outdone in the display of patriotism, encouraged the anti-American feeling. The sharp and rancorous Tornel used every opportunity to speak against

us; and Santa Anna, whose prestige was immense—it must not be forgotten—as late as 1844, both fearing the influence of our freedom and wishing his fellow-citizens to consider him essential, represented the United States as a Minotaur eager to devour them. Few were enlightened enough to correct the misconceptions regarding us; no one had the power, courage or wish to do so; and in the end, very naturally, these dominated the public mind—or, to be more precise, created and kept alive a general impression. Americans "scarcely have the look of men," it was gravely asserted.

In regard to an immediate conflict in arms with us, Mexico by no means felt like the dove threatened by a hawk, as people in this country have generally supposed. To be sure, the national existence was often said to be in danger, but such talk was largely for effect. Castillo asserted that Slidell had been sent in order to obtain a pretext for war; but this was in all probability a bid for Mexican and European support, since he knew that we already had grounds enough, and the council of state evidently believed we did not seek a conflict. Paredes whispered to the British minister at a banquet, "I hope your government does not mean to let us be eaten up"; but this was a plea for English assistance. As we have just said, not American arms but American settlers were the chief danger, in the opinion of Mexico. The very men who clamored that the national existence was threatened by the United States were the ones who called most loudly for war. A circular to the local authorities issued by the central government in December, 1845, invited attention to the prevailing opinion that armed resistance could prevent further usurpations like that of Texas; and another such paper, issued in November of the following year, dwelt strongly upon this point. From military force also there was danger, to be sure. Our superiority in numbers and resources was admitted. But there were many offsets to that superiority, and the Mexicans closely studied and shrewdly counted upon them.

Let us review those offsets. In the first place, while the government of the United States deemed its course honorable and considerate, in the eyes of many, if not all, Mexicans we had been abject as well as knavish, stealing her territory and then trying to buy off her anger, submitting to be gulled, flouted and lashed, and each time going back for more of the same treatment; and it seemed hardly possible that we should suddenly adopt a bold, positive, unflinching course. It was even believed that we dreaded to enter the lists. Almonte, for example, in reporting that his protest against annexation had caused a heavy fall on the stock exchange, observed, "The fears of a war with Mexico are great"; and it was notorious that his departure from the United States created almost a panic in our money market.

Besides, it was assumed that party feeling would go to about the same lengths here as in Mexico, and that our differences over the slavery question and the tariff would probably make it impossible for us to conduct a war vigorously—perhaps impossible to wage it at all. "The northern states, I again repeat to you, will not aid those of the south in case of war with Mexico," wrote Almonte while minister at Washington in June, 1844. European journals like *Le Constitutionnel* of Paris confirmed this opinion;[1] and the London *Times* remarked, It would be a war, not of the United States, but of a party that has only a bare majority, and "odious" to a "large and enlightened minority in the best States." Moreover, argued the official journal of Mexico,

the injustice of the war would of itself excite American opposition.

From a military as well as a political point of view this country seemed feeble. Our regular army was understood to be numerically insignificant and fully occupied with frontier and garrison duties; our artillery appeared weak in quality as well as in numbers; and our cavalry was deemed little more than a cipher. As for volunteers, our citizen-soldiers were represented in Mexico not merely as unwarlike, but as "totally unfit to operate beyond their frontiers." Indeed, as competent a judge as Captain Elliot, British minister in Texas—who knew the United States well, and in the spring of 1845 was in close touch with Mexican leaders at their capital—said that the greater their number, the greater would be the difficulty of invading Mexico. "They could not resist artillery and cavalry in a Country suited to those arms," he believed; "they are not amenable to discipline, they plunder the peasantry, they are without steadiness under reverses, they cannot march on foot." Nor did there exist in this country, added Elliot, either aptitude or adequate means for a regular military invasion.

"America, as an aggressive power is one of the weakest in the world . . . fit for nothing but to fight Indians," declared *Britannia*, an important English weekly; and apparently the war of 1812, to which the Mexicans referred with peculiar satisfaction, had proved even more than this. The military operations in a war between Mexico and the United States would be "contemptible and indecisive," said the London *Times*. As for our navy, it was undoubtedly small; the Mexican consul at New Orleans reported that it lacked the discipline commonly attributed to it; and, however efficient it might really be, Mexico had no commerce to attack.

The Mexicans, on the other hand, were deemed by many observers decidedly formidable. "There are no better troops in the world, nor better drilled and

---

[1] To precisely what extent European journals were read in Mexico cannot be determined; but it seems probable that few important expressions escaped notice there, and certainly the leading journals were quoted freely.

armed, than the Mexicans," asserted Calderón de la Barca, the Spanish minister at Washington; and some of the generals were thought, even by foreigners, equal to the most renowned in Europe. The Americans would be at a vast disadvantage, was Captain Elliot's opinion, "in rapidity of movement" and ability to endure "continued fatigue on the hardest food." The soldiers of the tri-color "are superior to those of the United States," declared the Mexico correspondent of the London *Times* flatly in 1845.[2]

If the military power of Mexico was rated in this way by outside observers of such competence, one can imagine how it was rated at home. The Mexicans regarded themselves as martial by instinct, and viewed their troops, inured to war by an almost unceasing course of revolutions, as remarkably good. Santa Anna once boasted that, if necessary, he would plant his flag upon the capitol at Washington; and the results of the wars with Spain and France had tended powerfully to encourage the self-confidence of his fellow-citizens. "We have numerous and veteran forces burning with a desire to gain immortal renown," said the *Boletín Oficial* of San Luis Potosí. "Not to speak of our approved infantry," it was argued, "our artillery is excellent, and our cavalry so superior in men and horses that it would be an injustice not to recognize the fact"; besides which "our army can be rapidly augmented." Indeed an officer of reputation told Waddy Thompson that the cavalry could break infantry squares with the lasso. In November, 1845, the Mexican minister of war solemnly predicted that his countrymen would gain the victory, even if one third less numerous than their American adversaries. To clinch this matter, the feeling of superior power, which it was known that we entertained, was regarded as an ignorant

over-confidence that would ensure our defeat. In short, "We have more than enough strength to make war," cried the editors of *La Voz del Pueblo;* "Let us make it, then, and victory will perch upon our banners."

The clash, it seemed probable, would come first in Texas, far from our centres of strength. On that field Tornel, the keenest public man in the country, insisted that Mexico could triumph over any force we could bring to bear, and Almonte offered some reasons for entertaining such an opinion. The Texan troops, he said, would exhaust their supplies before the campaign would really begin; and consequently, since there would be no way to subsist a large American force in that extensive, poor and sparsely settled region, the greater the number coming, the greater would be their sufferings. Even the cultivated districts, wrote Elliot, could support only a trifling addition, if any, to the resident population. Moreover, even should an American army be able to exist there, a few light troops placed along the frontier would keep it busy on the defensive, said Pakenham; while it was urged by Mexicans that, should our line break, their invading host would soon find itself among the opulent cities of the southern states, where perhaps it could not only exact money, but free two million slaves, obtain their grateful and enthusiastic assistance, enroll the Indians of the southwest, who detested the United States, and draw aid as well as encouragement from the abolitionists of the north. Almonte himself assured his government that the blacks, the savages and the antislavery extremists could be reckoned on.

Possibly, of course, their line instead of ours might be the one to give way; but in that case the Americans, instead of meeting with conditions like these, would be confronted by immense distances, great deserts, furious rains, long droughts, and barren, easily defended mountains. "If the war should be protracted and

[2] Napoleon said, "The first quality of a soldier is constancy in enduring fatigue and hardship." In this quality the Mexicans excelled.

carried beyond the Rio Grande," said Captain Elliot, "I believe that it would require very little skill and scarcely any exposure of the defending force to draw the invading columns well forward beyond all means of support from their own bases and depots into situations of almost inextricable difficulty"; and a correspondent of Calhoun, referring to such natural obstacles, wrote, "nothing is more certain than your statement that [the] war will have to become defensive [on our part]."

Moreover, it was argued, said the Mexican minister of relations in 1849, that the invaders would be unable to obtain resources of any description from the country about them, would be masters of nothing but the ground actually occupied, and would find the difficuty of maintaining themselves, at such a distance from their base, "invincible." On the other hand should invasion by sea be attempted, the Americans would have to struggle with tempestuous waters, a coast guarded by reefs and currents, lowlands protected by "a terrible and faithful ally" —as Cuevas described the yellow fever, more than one tremendous wall of mountains, and bad roads that could easily be closed; and they would find no vital point of attack within practicable reach. The United States cannot hope to conquer Mexico, was the conclusion of the London *Morning Herald,* commonly regarded as a ministerial organ; while the Paris *Globe,* reputed to be Guizot's personal voice, went farther, and predicted that undertaking to do it would be "ruinous, fatal" to us.

Should we, however, care to make the attempt, Mexico—it was pointed out— would not only fight on the defensive, and enjoy all the advantages of knowing the ground, moving on inside lines, and using fortifications, but would also be able to strike. Nothing would be paid on our claims, either principal or interest. There was considerable American property in the country; and while the means

of her citizens were being spent in righteous self-defence, that property could hardly expect exemption. Above all, one "terrible weapon," as the Mexican consul at New Orleans termed it, could be wielded night and day, near and far, without expense and without risk. This was the issuance of commissions to privateers, for the "nefarious" conduct of the United States in using this weapon, said the London *Times,* authorized Mexico to do the same. The pursuit of slavers had been so close of late that many fine Baltimore clippers, able to outsail anything but a steamer and to go where a steamer could not, were lying idle in Cuban ports, ready to scour the Gulf and the Atlantic.

No less vulnerable seemed the United States in the Pacific Ocean, where—according to the New York *Herald*—American property worth fifteen or twenty millions was afloat. Should letters of marque be "actively and prudently distributed on the coasts of the Pacific," wrote consul Arrangóiz to his government, "the Americans would receive a fatal blow in the captures [of whalers and merchantmen] that would immediately be made in the seas of Asia, where the naval forces of the United States are insignificant and could not promptly be increased"; and he reported in July, 1845, that owing to the prospect of hostilities the insurance companies at New Orleans were refusing to take war risks. Tornel and the other Mexican leaders counted heavily on the value of this weapon. Our own journals were full of the subject, and could find no remedy. American commerce was defenceless against such an attack, the London *Times* cheerfully admitted.

Under these conditions it was most natural to believe that Mexico could make the war "obstinate and tedious," as the London *Standard* said, and therefore extremely expensive for the United States. She could "with trifling inconvenience to Herself," Pakenham told Calhoun, "impose upon this Country the necessity of employing as large a Naval and Military force as if the War was with a far more powerful enemy." Obviously a great number of warships would be needed to blockade seven hundred leagues of coast and patrol two oceans, and the cost of soldiers could be figured thus, it was thought: During the war of independence in Mexico eighty thousand royal troops and sixty thousand insurgents were supported by that country; its population and resources had since increased; the United States would therefore have to send probably two hundred and fifty thousand men; and the American soldier was very expensive.

The people of this nation were looked upon as worshippers of the dollar, and it was believed that war taxes would not be endured here long. Consequently, since the United States had no credit— said European journals—the conflict would soon have to end. "The invasion and conquest of a vast region by a state which is without an army and without credit is a novelty in the history of nations," remarked the London *Times* in 1845. The war losses were expected to reinforce the effect of war taxes. "War with the United States would not last long," wrote Arrangóiz, "because the [American] commerce finding itself attacked on all seas would beg for peace." When the Mexican corsairs have captured a few American ships and the Americans have thrown a few bombs into Vera Cruz, matters will be arranged, predicted *Le Constitutionnel* of Paris.

Evidently, then, Mexico was not likely to suffer disastrously, and certain benefits of great value could be anticipated. The act of crossing swords with us would fulfil a patriotic duty and vindicate the national honor. Glory and the satisfaction of injuring a perfidious and grasping enemy would more than compensate for the cost. A conflict would prevent this greedy neighbor, as the London *Times* argued, from imagining that Mexico dared not resist spoliation. The American

settlers, whom every effort had been made for many years to keep out of the country, would be driven away, and the danger of American ideas averted. Even if the frontier could not be forced back to the Sabine, a long period of hostilities would render it impossible to practice near the border our arts of political seduction, and merely a short contest would tend to re-Mexicanize thoroughly the northern departments. Indeed the whole country would be re-Mexicanized, for the first effect of the war would be to cure disunion and baptize the nation anew in the fires of patriotism. The necessity of meeting a foreign foe would vitalize the courage of the army, which had grown somewhat lax in battling with fellow-citizens, restore discipline, and perfect the officers in their difficult but noble profession. A blockade, many believed with Almonte and Santa Anna, preventing the exportation of silver and the squandering of good money on foreign luxuries, would be "the best possible thing" for the country. Stimulated by exemption from ruinous foreign competition, the industries would at length flourish, and the boundless natural resources of the country become fountains of wealth.

War is no doubt a great evil, argued the editors of *La Voz del Pueblo*, "but we recall what Polybius said, to wit: 'If many empires have been destroyed by war, by war also have many risen from nothing.'" Prussia owes her greatness to the Seven Years War, pointed out *El Siglo XIX*. The conquest of the Moors cost Spain a struggle of centuries, but what Spaniard would undo it? asked others. "Nations determine their history only in the most dangerous crises," urged an anonymous but able pamphlet; "and such a crisis, in which posterity will admire us, has arrived."

So the matter presented itself to many when studied as an exclusively Mexican affair. But could it be regarded as exclusively Mexican? In Central and South America there were countries that naturally entertained a racial prejudice against the "Anglo-Saxon." They were fully capable of discovering the claim to monopoly suggested by the name United States of "America," by our considering none except ourselves "Americans," and by our "Monroe Doctrine"; and moreover our press clamored for the entire continent. Mexico had her eye upon them, and she counted on drawing support from that quarter.

As early as 1836 Cuevas, then minister at Paris, after pointing out to his government how strongly the country was protected by nature against the United States, remarked: "Add to this the interest of the republics of the South to defend Mexico against an always threatening enemy, which with its ever monstrous greed seems a volcano ready to burst upon them." The next year a Mexican agent at Lima reported that the alleged unlawful interference of this country in Texas was the subject of general conversation and of just alarm in the Spanish-American states. In 1842 Dorsey, bearer of despatches from our legation at Mexico, stated at Savannah that Santa Anna had sent envoys to all the South American republics with this message: "Unless you enable us to resist such aggression as will be perpetrated by the United States, she will proceed to embrace in her mighty grasp the whole of the southern continent"; and Dorsey added that Colombia had already promised financial aid and two thousand men. At the close of that year, as a letter from Caracas mentioned, steps were said to have been taken toward forming a league to support Mexico against American encroachments. In 1843 Almonte made up a pamphlet of extracts from John Quincy Adams's brilliant though unfounded speech at Braintree, in which he accused our government of greed and unrighteousness in the Texas business; and this telling document was distributed in the principal cities of South America. During the following years the menace of our ambition to all of the Spanish race in this hemisphere continued to be discussed in the Mexican

press. "Republics of South America," cried *La Aurora de la Libertad,* for example, "your existence also is in danger; prepare for the combat"; and it was easy to believe that official appeals for assistance, in the event of actual invasion, would not fall upon deaf ears.

And there were still better grounds, it was reckoned, for expecting aid from abroad. In the first place, holding more or less honestly that we had trampled on the law of nations, the Mexicans persuaded themselves that every civilized country would feel an interest in their cause. The justice of our case against the United States, declared the official *Diario,* will be recognized at once by all governments to which "public faith and honor are not an empty name." This view was encouraged in Europe. The cause of Mexico, said the Liverpool *Mail,* is that of all just and honest governments. The Mexicans have good ground to complain, proclaimed the sympathetic *Journal des Débats,* for "they have been tricked and robbed."

Covered with so noble a sentiment as devotion to the cause of justice, more practical considerations could be expected to exert their full influence. In Mexico as well as in the United States, the monarchies of Europe were believed to view with jealousy the success of our republican institutions. Our policy of "America for the Americans," which the British minister, Ward, had turned against Poinsett at Mexico, was contrary to the interest of every commercial nation beyond the Atlantic. The United States, exclaimed *Le Correspondant* of Paris,— assumes to exclude Europe from the affairs of that continent—as if Europe had not had rights and possessions there before the United States began to be! as if the United States did not owe its existence to Europe! as if the ocean could change the law of nations; and leading journals in London expressed similar indignation.

As the whole world understood, great Britain had not yet forgiven us for becoming independent, and viewed with great repugnance our extensions of territory, our commercial development and our control over raw cotton; and it was obvious that she would be glad to stop our growth. Sooner or later, warned the British press, the course of this monster will have to be checked. Guizot, the premier of France, regarded the United States as a "young Colossus," and earnestly desired to apply in this hemisphere the principle of the balance of power. Polk was by no means popular at the Tuilleries, and the *Journal des Débats,* commonly regarded as the mouthpiece of the government, courteously described his Message of December, 1845, as bellicose, passionate, full of vain and ludicrous bravado, arrogant, detestably hypocritical, brutally selfish and brutally dishonest.

The plan to annex Texas had greatly disturbed these two governments, and they had not only exerted to the utmost against it their diplomatic strength, both separately and in concert, but, as Mexico knew, had been disposed to take up arms in that cause. Aided by circumstances, the courage and skill of the United States had completely foiled them, but they could not be supposed to view the result with satisfaction; and there was good reason to believe that they contemplated a possible further extension of this country, not only with alarm, but with a strong desire to prevent it. Said the London *Morning Herald* in March, 1845: Mexico will turn to good account the support of her powerful protectors and their intense repugnance to the annexation of Texas; and the London *Times* predicted that our greed in the Texas affair would be punished.

Gifted at vaticination, the *Times* predicted also that our next aim would be the mines of Mexico, and asked the nations of Europe how they would like to find their monetary circulation "dependent on the caprice of the President of the United States." In September, 1845, it printed the assertion of its Mexican correspondent, that England must interfere or be prepared to see not only those mines

but also California in American hands. There is a general feeling, announced the London *Standard,* that only the interposition of England and France can check the United States. The United States will absorb Mexico unless foreign powers avert this, preached the London *Journal of Commerce.* "The conquest of Mexico would create perils for the political balance of the world," said the *Journal des Débats;* and hence "the immense aggrandizements" contemplated by the United States "could not take place without giving umbrage to several nations." Europe would certainly forbid a conquest of Mexico, threatened *Le Constitutionnel.* The Mexicans were fully capable of seeing all this for themselves. The *Monitor Constitucional,* for example, gave currency to the idea that certain powers would prevent the invasion of their country. Indeed they could see even more. "Enlightened nations of Europe," exclaimed *La Aurora de la Libertad,* "a people consumed with ambition and covetousness is already taking up arms to conquer the American continent, lay down the law to your interests and possessions, and some day disturb your peace at home."

Another source of possible trouble for the United States abroad was the idea that territory obtained from Mexico would be given up to slavery. This point came out strongly in the *Journal des Débats,* for example. Considerably more serious was the danger that in coping with Mexican privateers we should offend other nations. In this way, so the British minister warned our secretary of state, the Americans were likely to become involved in "complications of the gravest character"; and it was believed by the Mexicans that a blockade of their coast, in addition to being extremely difficult, was almost or quite certain to have that effect.

To these points they added characteristically that fear of their power, as well as antipathy to us, might lead foreign nations to espouse their side; and all the supporters of the monarchical plans now entertained by the government and the upper classes, felt that if carried out these would pave the way for European assistance. In fact the British minister himself believed that such a change of régime would guarantee Mexico against the United States, and it is reasonable to suppose that in talking with her public men he disclosed this conviction. Being a jealous nation, thoroughly given up to politics, and not industrial or commercial, Mexico could not fail to exaggerate the probable effect of all these influences upon England and France, and to underestimate the factors that were tending to keep them at peace with us.

The strongest basis of hope for effective aid from abroad was, however, none of these considerations, but our dispute with England over Oregon. In January, 1846, Bankhead and Slidell agreed that Mexico's policy toward the United States would depend mainly or wholly upon the outcome of that issue, and to the Mexican eye the outcome was already clear. Each country had rejected the proposition of the other, and Polk's Message of December 2, 1845, committed him afresh to an extreme position. The course of England tended to confirm the natural inference. Her perfectly excusable intention was to hold the Mexicans ready to coöperate with her, should war become her programme, while restraining them from engaging us alone. Bankhead replied with an encouraging vagueness to Mexican hints that British assistance was desired, and Lord Aberdeen talked with the Mexican agent at London of a possible alliance against us. Indeed that agent reported that he believed Aberdeen would like to see Mexico fight the United States and win.[3]

For superficial, touch-and-go people here was enough to build upon, and the long entertained hopes of British aid struck root anew. January 14, 1846, our minister Slidell stated that the idea of an approaching conflict over the Oregon question was assiduously nursed, and seventeen days later the correspondent of the London *Times* reported, that it had become a general conviction. Aberdeen's possible alliance seemed therefore like a certainty, and he himself admitted to our minister at London that Mexico had counted upon a war over Oregon. With France, as we know, Mexico did not stand on the best of terms at this juncture; but in addition to the other reasons for looking to her, Guizot and Louis Philippe were strongly pro-English, and in fact, so Bankhead reported, Paredes hoped for assistance from that country also. From high to low, as we have learned, the Mexicans were inveterate gamblers, passionately fond of calculating probabilities and accepting chances, and a situation like this appealed most fascinatingly to their instincts and their habits. But in the eyes of many—indeed most, it is likely—the outlook seemed more than promising. Vain and superficial, they did not realize their weaknesses. "We could not be in a better state for war," the *Diario* announced in March, 1845. If any one thought of the empty treasury, he assured himself that patriotism and the boundless natural wealth of the country would afford resources. Enthusiasm would supply everything, it was believed. Equally unable were the Mexicans to perceive the frailty of their hopes for European aid. With few exceptions they saw through a veil, darkly. Even Almonte, a military man and better acquainted with the United States than any other prominent citizen, assured his government that in such a conflict the triumph of Mexico would be "certain."[4]

[3] The Mexican thermometer for peace or war is governed by the prospects of war between us and England. The contemptuous and abusive tone of the British journals with reference to the United States encouraged Mexico. Our minister at London reported that the British press as a whole represented that the United States could not wage war sucessfully against Mexico.

[4] Almonte (who, was recent minister to the United States, had great influence on the question of peace and war) held that Mexico ought to fight and protract the war as long as possible in order to make us so tired of it that we should never repeat the experiment.

Here and there one doubted. Some drew back. But the nation as a whole— if Mexico really was a nation—felt convinced that pride and passion could safely be indulged. We shall dictate our own terms, thought many. At any rate, argued others, our honor will be vindicated by a brilliant stroke beyond the Rio Grande; European intervention will then occur; the United States will have to pay a round sum for Texas; and we shall obtain a fixed boundary, guaranteed by the leading powers of Europe, that will serve as an everlasting dike against American aggression. The press clamored for war; the government was deeply committed to that policy; and the great majority of those who counted for anything, panting feverishly, though with occasional shivers, to fight the United States, were passionately determined that no amicable and fair adjustment of the pending difficulties should be made.

"For us [Mexicans]," Roa Bárcena admitted, "the war was a fact after Shannon's declarations of October, 1844, and the fact was confirmed by the admission of Texas to the North-American Union." "Since the usurpation of Texas no arrangement, no friendly settlement has been possible," said *La Reforma*. Besides, a faith in eventual triumph, strong enough to survive a series of disasters, burned in the heart of the nation. The Mexican correspondent of the Prussian minister at Washington— regarded by our secretary of war as entirely trustworthy—reported that the people were bent upon war. But for the procrastination and vanity of Mexico, no conflict would have occurred, said J. F. Ramírez, who stood high among the best public men of that country. "The idea of peace was not popular," states one Mexican historian; the nation was responsible for the war, confess others. *Mexico desired it,* admitted Santa Anna in 1847 and the minister of relations in 1849, both speaking officially.

Justo Sierra

The Mexican War: A Mexican View

The first three decades of our history as a nation were overcast by the menace and fear of a conflict with Spain. But, after the

From *The Political Evolution of the Mexican People* by Justo Sierra, translated by Charles Ramsdell (Austin, Texas: University of Texas Press, 1969), pp. 211–214, 217–219, 230–247, omitting footnotes except where necessary for understanding by permission of the publisher.

death of Ferdinand VII, the rise to power of the reform party in Spain and a terrible civil war changed entirely the situation which had produced the abortive attempts at reconquest. Assaults on the supremacy of the Church and clergy became progressively more drastic and were followed by frightful bloody riots. By comparison, the efforts of our York party to found a lay government in Mexico were mild and innocuous. Any further attempt at reconquest was out of the question. The next step, then, was recognition of the former colonies' independence, and this step was taken by the minister José María Calatrava toward the end of 1836 when solemn diplomatic sanction was accorded to relations between Spain and Mexico. Had this been done ten years earlier, a great deal of grief and woe would have been avoided.

The truth is that federalism and sympathy with the United States to the point of seeking an alliance with them—notions cherished by the founders of our early liberalism—were natural consequences of Spain's attitude. When this began to change, our anxieties turned northward, where the Texas problem loomed on the horizon, scarcely eclipsing, however, the colossus of might and ambition that towered beyond. A war with Texas did not preoccupy the Mexicans; what did overcast the entire period of centralism was the fear of a war with the United States. The fear was well founded: the United States could easily cut off our meager revenues and our communication with the outside world by seizing our unfortified ports, so that we would have to devour ourselves in desperate civil strife. Fortunately for Mexico, the war came as a direct invasion which, while shamefully laying bare some of our intimate weaknesses, stirred our blood, arousing the valor of the most self-abnegating people in the world—for the masses had no positive blessings to defend, nothing but what was abstract or emotional—and the disorganized nation achieved a measure of cohesion at last.

The most redoubtable legacy left to us by Spain was the vast stretch of desert along our northern frontier, beyond the Rio Grande and the Gila, uninhabited and in the main uninhabitable, with extensive belts of fertile land and others hopelessly sterile. The distances separating these regions from our political center and the fact that most of our population was rooted to the soil and the rest sparsely scattered made it impracticable for us to exploit resources which, in any case, were still largely a matter for conjecture. What was certain was that the Anglo-Americans' formidable expansion would sooner or later engulf those regions. The easternmost, Texas, fell so naturally within the scope of that irresistible thrust that our statesmen should have considered only the best way to give away, literally, the land we could never occupy by inviting the whole world to colonize it—the Russians, the French, the English, the Spaniards, the Chinese—thereby erecting a Babel of peoples as a dike to stem the tide of American expansion. But it is easy to prescribe with hindsight; our fathers, prejudiced and necessarily ignorant as they were, could have taken no such step; our knowledge is the consequence of their mistakes.

A thousand little attempts at encroachment made it abundantly clear that the United States coveted Texas, fertile, well-watered, and teeming with cattle, from the day that the expanding nation reached the state's borders. The Spanish government stood staunchly on its rights and was very cautious and parsimonious in granting concessions. The concession that gave rise to the American colonization of Texas was granted to the father of Stephen F. Austin and permitted him to settle three hundred Catholic families in the province. The Mexican government, feeling the need of amity with the United States and lacking the power to assert its rights, confirmed the grant but failed to enforce the restrictions. Texas was soon dotted with small but growing American colonies. Grants made to Mexican citizens, such as those to Zavala and others, were sold to Americans, who promptly settled in the fecund region. The danger was patent and considered so imminent, a law passed in Bustamante's first administration prohibited the acquisition by foreigners of lands within the limits of the frontier states. This law was aimed at the Americans, who nevertheless continued to seep into Texas and to form colonies there, despite the military posts established by General Mier y Terán. The state, then conjoined with Coahuila, first took part in political affairs by siding enthusiastically with the revolution instigated by the smugglers of Vera Cruz against Bustamante's strict administration in 1832 and headed by the inevitable Santa Anna. The following year Texas declared itself, *motu proprio,* separate from Coahuila. Zavala, who owned land in Texas, moved by self-interest, by his Jacobin's venomous hatred for Catholicism (which in that day, to be sure, took on in Mexico the aspect of a vast superstition), and by his congenital affinity, as a Yucatecan, for loose federation, states' rights, and even for local autonomy and secession, carried the grim tidings of centralism's triumph to the Anglo-American colonists. Excited by his eloquence, and by Austin's, and counting on strong support from the United States, the Texans decided to secede from Mexico and declare themselves independent. This was a sad but unavoidable turn of events. Multiple ties bound the Texans to their blood brothers, but no ties at all to the Mexicans. What made our case worse was that the rupture of the federal pact gave a perfectly legal character to the separation—which was sure to occur sooner or later, anyhow. Even if the Constitution of 1824 had been legally reformed, the states of the Federation were clearly under no obligation to remain in the union unless they ratified a new agreement; as parties to a contract, they were at liberty to renew it or not, as they saw fit. Texas seceded without going through the formality of refusing to renew the contract because the Constitution was not reformed—it was abolished. Centralism was proclaimed, and an assembly convoked to stamp a seal of sanction on a *fait accompli.*

If our statesmen had been wise enough to see the matter in this light, if, accepting the secession as legal, they had set about extracting the best possible advantage from a settlement with Texas, the ensuing war, with its aftermath of shame and ruin, could have been averted, and also the conflict with the United States, which was the ineluctable consequence of that war. . . .

The Constitution of the Seven Laws was, at any rate, quite liberal: generous in its bill of rights; hospitable to foreigners, who, as in the American system, were invited to become nationalized and to take up lands; intolerant on religous matters but retaining, in compensation, some of the Patronate's supervision of the Church. Continuing the classic distribution of Powers, it provided for a bicameral Legislature, with a House of Representatives based on a restricted electorate, in recognition of the country's narrowly limited suffrage; an Executive Power composed of a President, whose term was to be eight years, a Cabinet, and Council of Government; an irremovable Judiciary Power; and the division of the country into departments, each with an elected assembly that was to have broad administrative faculties. But the great novelty of the Seven Laws consisted in the compagination of a Conserving Power, intended as a balance wheel between the other Powers. It had the authority to annul the decisions of any one of them and to suspend and restore its functions, but never *motu proprio,* only when instigated by another Power (the aim was to prevent tyranny), and it had the authority to declare, in emergencies, the nation's will —this was to prevent revolutions. The Conserving Power, an extra wheel in the machinery, acted merely as a clog and accomplished nothing. The Power that serves as moderator in a federal constitution is properly the Judiciary, and then only when instigated by private persons.

These good patriots, advocates of a strong but not despotic government, sincere but timid friends of progress, had for their leader General Bustamante, who again became President in April 1837. No one was better fitted to consolidate a centralist regime, as long as war with the United States which now clearly loomed on the horizon, was not yet upon us. His ministers were patriotic and civilized; the country might have enjoyed a breathing spell.

But there was no time for a breathing spell. A humiliation inflicted on our navy, guarding the Texas coast, by the American navy, obliged the government to request authorization to demand satisfaction or to declare war on the United States. In this hour of approaching crisis, all our resources, all our sinews of union and of discipline should have been dedicated to upholding our honor in the world's eyes. At this very moment, however, a pronunciamento in favor of federalism launched a revolt at San Luis Potosí; the real object was to get hold of public funds and promote certain business deals. After a great waste of blood and money, the revolt was crushed, and its leader, the redoubtable General Esteban Moctezuma, killed. The bayonet that should have been pointed, with our ultimatum, at the United States, had been broken off in Mexican breasts.

The federalist revolt at San Luis had repercussions on all sides. Secession in Yucatán, uprising in Sonora, invasion in New Mexico, and insurrection in Michoacán proved the futility of any effort to pacify the country. No sooner would some measure of protection to industry galvanize the social body than the fear and anxiety induced by the desperate struggle for survival would prostrate it again. On top of everything else, we had to face an unjust and absurd war forced on us by the bourgeois government of Louis Philippe, a war which weakened us still further on the eve of the American conflict. This arrogant and shortsighted attempt on the part of the French King's ministers to make us subservient to their industry and trade, this grocer's diplomacy, turned away from France the soul of a new nation which had been powerfully attracted to her and did us even worse harm: it restored the prestige of

General Santa Anna, who, since his return from Texas, had been living, unpunished but in disgrace, at his hacienda in Vera Cruz. . . .

The United States had tried since the birth of the Mexican Republic to acquire the territory between Louisiana and the Rio Grande, from the river's source to its mouth. Poinsett had offered to buy Texas from the Mexican government; the leaders of the Democratic Party, which was strongest in the states of the South, never gave up the idea of acquiring it, either by agreement or by force. Soon they added to this ambition that of acquiring all the Mexican territory on the Pacific north of the tropic of Cancer, to forestall, they said, its acquisition by England or some other nation. In short, their doctrine was that all territory adjoining the United States which Mexico could not effectively govern should belong to the Americans.

Aggression was retarded by treaties and the practices of international equity, by the anxiety of England and France over the Union's expansion, and by the opposition of the Whig Party, led by Henry Clay, great conscience and great orator, to the proslavery, secessionist Democratic Party; but the trend of events made war inevitable.

If the opposing parties in Mexico had not used the Texas question as a political club, each accusing the other of traitorous intentions, catastrophe might have been avoided. The incontrovertible right of Texas to secede once the federal pact was broken should have been recognized to begin with, and the differences between the American political parties should have been exploited.

But no, the constant specter of war with Texas, which seemed certain, and with the United States, which seemed probable, served Santa Anna's purposes. It gave him an excuse to station the ghost of an army, starving and almost unarmed, on the Rio Grande, so that he could incessantly demand funds, which he incessantly frittered away.

In the field of international equity our diplomacy won consistent victories over the Americans. A series of impeccably reasonable notes remonstrated against the unceasing attacks on the dignity of the Mexican Republic which had been countenanced by the government in Washington. Open meetings in some cities of the Union urged war with Mexico and the annexation of Texas, and a sort of armed emigration toward the latter region was organized, a threat which not even Daniel Webster's talents could find excuses for.

But the course of events was inexorable. Over and beyond the issue of illicit aid to Texas (for whether Texas was regarded as a rebel state of Mexico or as an independent nation at war with a friendly nation, the aid was illicit) there arose the issue of annexation. And even if the Texans were within their rights in seeking to join the United States, the Americans had no right to proceed with annexation before arriving at an understanding with regard to mutual responsibilities. President Tyler's Secretary of War, John Calhoun, who would be the Moses of the secession movement, negotiated a treaty of annexation with Texas, which the Senate in Washington refused to approve and which shocked France and England — both had recognized the independence of Texas — into offering us their services as mediators in order to avert further insults. Meanwhile, Santa Anna made preparations to resume the war with Texas as soon as the armistice should expire, and thereby brought down the fulminations of the American plenipotentiary, who candidly bared his government's intentions by warning that any invasion of Texas would mean war with the United States. This was understood by the Mexican government, which had previously warned that the admission of Texas to the Union would be answered with a declaration of war. The whole question hung on the presidential election in the United States. If Polk, candidate of the Democrats and of the South and with a platform calling for annexation, should be elected, conflict was inevitable. If Clay should win, peace was assured. Polk won by fewer than 40,000 votes out of a total of 2,060,000. This spelled disaster for Mexico. One thing was clear, however: the cause of annexation and war in the United States was not a national but a Southern cause.

While the great electoral battle was being waged in the United States, a President was being chosen in Mexico, too. But here the campaign was strictly military: the guns of civil war took the place of ballot boxes. The President, who with all his multifarious powers was bound by law to render an accounting to the constitutional Congress, in which, to the government's chagrin, federalists and reformists predominated, refused to do so. Santa Anna declined to belittle himself by answering to the Congress. Like Scipio, who, when an accounting was demanded of him, invited the populace to a thanksgiving feast in the Capitol, the President, in the same situation reminded the people that he had founded the Republic in Vera Cruz and had saved it at Tampico. There was unanimous protest against his conduct, immense disgust with the hero of usury, of the forced loan, of taxes and impositions without number. From Querétaro, from Guadalajara came the cry that he fulfill his obligation, under the Act of Tacubaya, to render a report to the Congress, which was sparing no effort to curb the dictatorship.

General Paredes y Arrillaga, a man of personal probity but of slippery political expediency and the incarnate hope of the party that wanted to anchor the country to centralism and to the old privileges until such time as an alliance with some European nation should make us more secure from the United States, even at the cost of raising here a throne for a foreign prince — this General Paredes, this always available card in the political deck that was constantly being reshuffled to see who would win honors and emoluments, backed the protest of the Jalisco assembly with a part of the army, while the National Chamber of Deputies openly supported the movement.[1]

Santa Anna, sensing danger, shifted suddenly, as was his wont, from sybaritic languor to feverish activity. He stationed a division or two in the center of the Republic. The task of keeping an eye on the Congress, which insisted that the government should conform to the law, he left to the Vice-President, Canalizo, in whose loyalty, like a faithful canine's, he had confidence. He hastened to the Bajío region, determined to put out the spreading fires of revolt by stratagem or by blood bath.

His outrageous acts at Querétaro[2] provoked indignation among the national deputies, and the entire Chamber, led by the representative Llaca, took a firm stand, realizing that the time had come to bridle the runaway dictatorship. Llaca, in this moment of crisis, was the embodiment of civic honor, denouncing public shame, and the Chamber stood with him. Resorting to force, the government dissolved the assembly, which refused to adjourn.

All society seemed to hold its breath in the presence of this duel between the sword and the word; the outcome was soon decided: Valencia, in La Ciudadela, the capital's barracks, declared for the Paredes plan, and in an overwhelming outburst of enthusiasm the entire city, including every class, the magnate and the worker, the priest and the militiaman, joined in the most spontaneous ovation the capital had ever seen, in honor of the assembly, which serenely resumed the course of debate. The dictator, with an army still intact, headed for the capital,

but fled to Puebla from Paredes' advancing column, while his own evaporated. He became a fugitive, then a prisoner, then an exile. The Presidency was assumed by General José J. Herrera, elected by the Chamber.[3] And thus ended the year 1844.

The Congress turned its attention to the American menace, ever more sinister—like a hand gloved in iron clutching the throat of a frail and bloodless nation, like a brutal knee in its belly, like a mouth avid with the desire to bite, to rip, to devour, while prating of humanity, of justice, of law. The government of the patriotic, honest, and prudent General Herrera did the best it could, and what it achieved was this: one army on the frontier, another on the way to the frontier, an appeal for unity in the cause of a country threatened with death, an admirable and circumspect dignity with regard to the Americans, but no refusal to compromise or to seek an agreement based on the independence of Texas. The underlying reality, however, was this: the minority that could think and read, anxious, febrile, critical, shaken incessantly by spasms of bellicose rage which made the government vacillate, clamored for vengeance, yet balked at any self-sacrifice; money was being hidden away; the military were plotting new revolts; the rural masses were inert, ignorant, without affection for the masters who exploited them, without any common spirit, without feeling for their country.

The Herrera administration had barely commenced to function when the provocation of war which our government had warned against occurred: the Congress and President in Washington enacted and approved the annexation of Texas. Our minister asked for his passport: our relations with the United States were broken off. Since the appetite for territorial ex-

---

[1] On October 29, 1844, the departmental committee of Jalisco petitioned the Congress to review Santa Anna's official acts, in accordance with the Sixth Basis of the Act of Tacubaya. On November 1, General Mariano Paredes y Arrillaga joined in the petition.

[2] He dissolved the departmental committee and imprisoned its members November 27, 1844.

[3] The capital's garrison ousted General Valentín Canalizo December 6, 1844, and General Herrera took charge of the Presidency. The Congress deposed Santa Anna and named Herrera President December 17.

pansion, the primitive form of present-day imperialism, had come to be most voracious in the southern and western states, popular opinion there favored war with Mexico. The Mexican government maneuvered with skill, accepting the good offices of France as mediator with the Texans, who had not as yet taken all the steps required for annexation. But it was too late. A Texas convention ratified the act, United States forces entered Texas and, with flagrant contempt for international law, crossed the Nueces River, boundary of the Union's new state, and invaded the territory of a nation with which they were still at peace, on the pretext that Texas had always claimed the Rio Grande for its boundary. The moment our protests were dispatched to Washington our best troops set out for the frontier. If they could arrive before General Taylor received reinforcements, we might successfully take the offensive.

Our government, while refusing to deal with the American envoy in his official capacity, did not disdain to discuss with him ideas that might serve as a basis for future agreement. It was well understood by now that annexation must be accepted as a historical fact; the important thing was to save, if we could, the rest of our imperiled land. But the pressure of public opinion, violent in its unreasoning emotion, thwarted the delicate adjustments of diplomacy. What was needed in this emergency was not a people sick with distorted imaginings, with hatred and with poverty, but a robust, self-controlled people who would give our ministers leeway to dispel with artful correspondence the formidable danger that loomed over us. One point had already been won: the American plenipotentiary had agreed to have the naval squadron that was threatening Vera Cruz withdrawn; we conceded, in return, official status to our discussions with him.

At this crucial moment, the general[4]

who had been sent with our best soldiers, with our supreme and ultimate recourse for repelling the invasion, made the excuse that Herrera's government was betraying the country, committed the infamy of pointing at the nation's heart the sword that it had confided to him, and with the complicity of Valencia, cleverest of Santa Anna's pupils, who supported the rebellion in the capital, overthrew Herrera in December, 1845. Herrera, that great citizen, departed from power, in defeat, exactly as he had come into it, with his heart full of patriotic concern and unspotted by the least shadow of guilt.

The Washington government, on receiving news of Herrera's fall, reinforced the fleet and ordered Taylor to advance on the Rio Grande, where our forces looking in vain for assistance from Paredes, awaited him. And after one more effort to stave off war with diplomacy, words gave way to force. Meanwhile, the man who had committed the greatest political and military crime of that epoch was trying to organize an administration with a false front, behind which anyone could descry a plot to establish a monarchy. Instead of rushing his army to the Rio Grande, he kept it close at hand where he could rely on it for support.

Paredes had himself appointed President with discretionary powers by an assembly of persons appointed by himself.[5] He then convoked a "constituent" assembly because he found the centralist Constitution "of no use." What was actually of no use was the army, debased into an instrument of cynical ambitions; of no use was the middle class, cowardly, fawning and self-seeking; of no use was the clergy, who considered themselves more important than their country and spent their zeal safeguarding their riches, and, although they could boast men of exemplary Christian virtue, these only served as contrast to the mass of ignorant, superstitious, and corrupt monks. The only

[4] General Mariano Paredes y Arrillaga. The army under his command revolted at San Luis Potosí December 14, 1845.

[5] The committee of representatives of the department named Paredes President January 3, 1846.

element that was of any use was the people, who were ruthlessly exploited by all the others.

A group ostensibly in sympathy with the new President was formed by Alamán and led by him with his habitual skill. These men manifested the tendency of the more aggressive members of the conservative party to take their stand, not around the centralist banner, but around the monarchist one, which they themselves had helped to haul down when Iturbide was killed, which fluttered again in Gutiérrez Estrada's daring pamphlet, and which would prove, fifteen years later, how hopelessly unsuited it was to our country, when the world's first military power would try to impose it.

The menace of the United States sparked the plan for a monarchy with a foreign prince. But if the prince came unprotected, what would happen to the monarchy? If he came with a foreign army, what would happen to our independence? This was, as yet, no more than a dream. One day, translated into action, it would turn into a hideous nightmare.

The order [January 27, 1846] convoking the constituent Congress, a singular document composed by Alamán, divided the voting public, extremely restricted, into classes and allowed each class a fixed proportion of representatives. This was the second time the oligarchy had tried to entrench itself through a constitution. To a majority of the politically conscious part of the nation, whose purely verbal love for democratic ideas revealed the Latin origin of their thought, this was an intolerable outrage: a constitution establishing an aristocracy in anticipation of a monarchy. And that is exactly what it was. The storm of protest was terrific; the press was promptly persecuted, and most of the leading liberals were promptly muzzled, imprisoned, or exiled. But their voices already had been heard, with repercussions echoing in every town of the Republic. The government felt it necessary to reaffirm its allegiance to the republican creed.

Meanwhile, the war had become a fact, although hostilities had not yet commenced. Paredes, anxious to repair his irreparable guilt, was accumulating supplies and slowly sending reinforcements to the frontier. But the Mexican generals were never able to muster a numerical superiority in troops that was sufficient to overbalance the American superiority in armament. At the beginning of May, the Mexican Commander in Chief, General Mariano Arista, resolved to chase the invader from the soil of Tamaulipas, pushing him back across the Nueces River into Texas. He crossed the Rio Grande with an army the same size as the enemy's and was defeated in hot battles on two consecutive days. Forced to retire to Matamoros, he fell back on Linares. This disaster was owing to the incompetence of Arista and his staff and the superiority of the American artillery.

The outcome of these battles inspired President Polk to declare, with a cynicism unexampled in history, that a state of war existed because the Mexicans had invaded Texas and that it must be prosecuted until peace was secured. The Mexican government declared war formally in June, adducing such moderate and sensible reasons, founded on justice, that not a single honest conscience in the United States or Europe could fail to admit that we were in the right.

The country, horrified by our defeats, now burst into flame. Revolution, breaking out at Guadalajara,[6] clamored for Santa Anna, of all men. The minute he got out of sight, the country became obsessed by a vague belief that he could work miracles. He was our man for emergencies, our *deus ex machina*, our savior who never saved anything.[7] What to do? Pare-

[6] The garrison at Guadalajara declared against the government of Paredes May 20, 1846.

[7] The sixth article of the pronunciamento reads as follows: "Whereas, the glory of having founded the Republic belongs to His Excellency, Antonio López de Santa Anna, and whereas he has always been its strongest support, . . . the Jalisco garrison recognizes that distinguished general as its leader in the great enterprise to which this plan is dedicated."

des needed near him a force strong enough to cope with the rebellion, and yet he needed all available forces in the north. He sent some, badly armed, badly supplied, in the direction of San Luis Potosí. One of these brigades, when it was about to march, declared for the Federation and for Santa Anna. The government of Paredes, his Congress, his monarchists, disappeared as if by magic; they never should have appeared in the first place.

The new military revolution took the form of a reaction against monarchism, and while Santa Anna, who had been advised beforehand, was on his way home in the company of General Almonte, for the time being an ardent republican, his allies in the capital convoked a Congress and declared the Constitution of 1824 to be in effect.[8] The departmental committees were accordingly suppressed, and, as a manifestation of the return to pure federalism, Valentín Gómez Farías, leader of the reformist party, was brought in to head the Cabinet.

Santa Anna arrived; the Americans, with the most cunning Machiavellianism, had let him through, as if they were tossing an incendiary bomb into the enemy's camp. The month of August 1846 was coming to an end. What did this man bring to us, he who had so often been vilified by the common people, he whose statues they had dragged in the dust and who was, for all that, persistently regarded by them as a Messiah? What did he bring us, this betrayer of hopes, this champion of any cause that might serve his greed or his ambition, what did he bring to the desperate situation, to that army vanquished before any battle by nakedness and hunger, without confidence in its officers and without faith in victory? He brought but a single purpose: to be, redeeming his sins, a soldier for his country. Alas, this soldier who was not good enough to be a general was going to be Commander in Chief.

Paredes had left more than half a mil-

[8] Decree of August 22, 1846.

lion pesos in the exchequer, and by the time Santa Anna arrived it had all been spent. But he set about concentrating troops in San Luis Potosí for a march on Monterrey. With three thousand men and provisions for eight days he finally started out, he who had been up to now nothing more than a revolutionary chieftain. Meanwhile, Mexico was in the throes of an electoral campaign. The radical element, it appears, with the protection of the authorities, prevented the moderates from voting and *ad terrorem* triumphed at the polls. Even the liberal journals protested. But the hour for men of action had come, and the reform party got set to give the clergy the deathblow.

When Santa Anna had barely started his march he learned that Monterrey had capitulated and that Ampudia's division, with the honors of war, was falling back on Saltillo. In this new and bloody episode of the war our eternal improvidence undid us. The soldiers fought bravely, some of the officers on both sides performed deeds of heroism, but the enemy's superior staff and his superior artillery were effective again and again. And the story would be the same, over and over, to the end.

Santa Anna was a whirlwind of energy at San Luis Potosí. He begged incessantly for money or took it where he found it. His army grew to fifteen or twenty thousand men, what with merciless levies in the surrounding regions and the addition of some state troops and the remnant of the Division of the North. And as the army grew, his demands took on colossal proportions. The situation of the country was this: our ports were blockaded, most of the states paralyzed, the northern ones lost; Yucatán, seceding again, declared itself neutral so as not to fall into the Americans' power; the deficit soared to seven to eight millions; the press clamored against the government; the people of the capital formed battalions of militia, some to support the dominant reformists, others, of the middle class, to prevent any sacrilege against the clergy, who, less from patriotism, perhaps, than from fear, parted, sobbing bitterly, with tiny fractions of their fortune.

The Congress met [December 6, 1846]. The reformists were in majority, and even the opponents of reform were liberals. In the closing days of the year Santa Anna was named President and Gómez Farías Vice-President. Things looked ominous to the clergy and to the great mass of the people who, whether liberal or conservative, regarded the economic power of the Church as an inviolable institution.

Gómez Farías and his advanced thinkers arrived at an agreement with Santa Anna: the property held in mortmain by the clergy was to be taken over and either sold directly until fifteen million pesos had been obtained or sequestered until a loan was elicited. This was a drastic measure, but nobody denied the government's right to decree it. Let us recapitulate briefly. The clergy's possessions were not private, but corporative property; they were, therefore, subject to special restrictions which the State had the right to impose. The clergy's possessions could not, under mortmain, be sold, and so added nothing directly to the circulation of wealth. The government, then, for the common good could change or modify this condition. The clergy's possessions had been acquired through donations, either from the king or with his consent. And these were all definitely revocable. The Spanish kings stood firmly on their prerogatives in this matter. When His Most Catholic Majesty Charles III confiscated the entire property of the Jesuits in his dominions, nobody denied his right to do so. What was criticized was the way he used this right.

The reform party's aims were threefold: political, social, and patriotic. The party considered the clergy's influence to be pernicious, since it was to the Church's advantage to keep the classes in the *status quo,* which meant keeping the lower classes immersed in religious superstition and the upper classes innoculated with the fear of new ideas. The party considered the Church's privileges to be the principal barrier against the advent of a democracy, in which all would be equal, and felt that so long as the clergy remained the dominant financial power in the country they could never be stripped of these special privileges. And the political aim was to do just that. As for the social aim, the same economic problem was involved. Until the vast mass of landed wealth under mortmain could be brought into circulation there could be no general prosperity; governments and private persons alike acted as parasites on the Church. Nor could there be any betterment of class conditions or any social progress. The patriotic aim was to save the very life of the country by securing the financial resources needed to organize an army for defense and to maintain it and move it about. The usurers would lend no money, preferring to wait till the famished Treasury got desperate enough to borrow one peso and pay back one hundred. The clergy would lend scarcely enough to suffice for a day. The recently enacted tax on incomes and rents brought in nothing. It was impossible to collect taxes systematically in the country's disrupted condition. There was but one thing to do: secure enough money to defray expenses for a year. And the only rich treasure belonged to the Church.

The opposition in the Congress consisted of moderate liberals. The majority consisted of radicals known as "reds"— "pure ones," they were called by the people. Both factions agreed on the necessity of stripping the Church of its privileges and landed wealth. But some of the moderates insisted that an indemnity must be paid, and this would mean a compromise with the Church. The pure ones countered that the Church would never consent to anything but an accomplished fact; this had been its invariable policy. The moderates, even those who held no brief for indemnity, were unanimously in favor of postponing the measure. Such a step, they predicted, would be futile or even disastrous at this juncture; there would be no buyers; the reform party was not strong enough to enforce its will, and the consequence would be civil war. But the reform party was confident of its strength because Santa Anna was on its side, confident that buyers would appear because the sequestered properties would be offered at prices so low that the clergy themselves would buy them back. So the law was passed[9] (January 1847). The ministers of the government girded themselves for the struggle with the clergy; protests in the form of pronunciamentos began to erupt here and there; some legislatures approved, and some refused to promulgate the law; the rabble, egged on by monks of the lowest type, swarmed through the streets of the principal cities, crying, "Long live religion, and death to the pure ones!" The whole country was in tumult.

What the government offered was too precarious to provoke any demand; nobody wanted to buy. And Santa Anna never ceased to ask for money. Finally, exasperated by the attacks of the press, which furiously criticized the new law and berated the Commander in Chief for his inactivity, he decided to go out and meet the American army, to cross a fearful desert without tents or adequate supplies, without having given his troops the rudiments of military training. With eighteen thousand men he marched across that interminable stretch of desolation, dust, and thirst, toward Saltillo (February 1847), and by the time he made contact with the enemy he was already beaten. He had lost four thousand men in his battle with the desert. The enemy had chosen an admirable position for defense (La Angostura), and there sustained two tremendous assaults. If the Mexican army had been led by a real general instead of by an officer who, though extremely brave, was vain,

unstable, and ignorant, the assault would have been concerted instead of planless and chaotic, and Taylor would have retreated to Saltillo. The Mexican soldier proved his good qualities in this frightful carnage. He is a soldier who, when hungry and weary, still fights on with courage and ardor. But, subject to sudden fits of despondency, like all the undernourished, and to panic, like all the high-strung, when he loses confidence in his officer or his leader he deserts; remembering that he was carried off by the levy and educated by the rod, he runs away.

Santa Anna was like him; Santa Anna embodied all the defects of the Mexican and one good quality: intrepid disdain for death. A fit of despondency when the battle was at its height moved him to beat a retreat. And he turned back across the desert, where sickness, nakedness, hunger, and desertion made a last assault on that bloodstained, gaunt column straggling under a pitiless sun, in a perpetual cloud of dust that tormented and very nearly devoured it. Santa Anna was fleeing from probable victory, on his way to certain defeat. He was fleeing toward the City of Mexico, where his power was threatened and where he had addressed a bulletin announcing his victory—cream of the jest! True, he had not been vanquished by the enemy: he had been vanquished by himself.

Mexico, at the same time, was likewise vanquishing itself. In the last days of February, while the national army was meeting disaster at La Angostura, a new American army occupied Tampico, previously abandoned, and disembarked on the coast near Vera Cruz. Thus the invasion took a new direction, from the east instead of the north. Vera Cruz was defended by a mere handful of men. It was imperative to contain the enemy till a new army could come to the rescue. The government, still trying to put the law disposing of Church property into effect, lived in a state of constant alarm. Battalions in which men of the upper class predominated were hostile

---

[9] Law of January 11, 1847: "The government is hereby authorized to raise fifteen million pesos by mortgaging or selling the properties under mortmain."

to reform; these, petted by the clergy and promised backing, refused to obey orders to move on Vera Cruz. The mutiny declared itself to be a protest against the continuance in power of Gómez Farías, against the January law, against the Congress. There were incessant skirmishes in the capital, very little bloodshed. The youths from wealthy families who made up these battalions were popularly known as *polkos,* and with this name they pitted themselves against the pure ones. Santa Anna, chosen by the two factions as arbiter, arrived in the City of Mexico, took over the Presidency, and, furious at learning that Vera Cruz had surrendered, left the Presidency *ad interim* in the hands of General Pedro María Anaya, and went forth to cut short the American advance on the capital, beyond Jalapa (his home ground), after abrogating the law which had caused so much unrest.[10]

With his usual access of energy, he soon managed to assemble an army on the rim of the Hot Country. He, and he alone, was in a position to choose the field of battle, among any number of strategic sites along the rugged staircase that climbs to the plateau. He chose the worst and was utterly routed. The same vain pretense, the same petulance, so characteristic of the Veracruzan, that had often defeated him before defeated him again. And still his ardor and activity succeeded in producing a new army out of the very fragments of the old, a feat that amazed General Scott, who advanced on the capital, scattering conciliatory and soothing proclamations to the four winds. He said that he came as a republican, to make war on the monarchist faction, and that no one could have more respect than he for religion and for the Catholic Church. And yet, the monarchist faction, headed by Paredes, had done nothing but sabotage the defense of the frontier. It was the liberal party, aided by some of the military, that

was conducting and organizing the defense of the country; many leading reactionaries cooperated, but not as a party. Scott pretended to be unaware of these facts; in truth, the invaders were disappointed to find themselves face to face with the federalist reformers who shared so many ideas with the people of the United States and who took them for a model.

When the invaders occupied Puebla, the decision was made to defend the capital, and the Federal District was marshaled for the struggle. Among the intellectuals there was little or no faith: "The result is foregone," so their minds ran.

[It is] impossible to vanquish an army that can be reinforced endlessly from the north and from the east. And what if we do lose lands that never belonged to us except in name: Texas, California? Perhaps that would be an advantage; a reduction in size might make for cohesion, concentration, strength.

But the people felt they must beat the Yankees. The people were not afraid; the vague terror that a series of defeats inspires in the masses was not present here.

"The Americans are not really winning; rather the Mexicans are defeating themselves with disunity, disobedience, and mistakes; all that is needed is a unified effort and that handful of intruders will disappear." So thought the people in their hate and contempt for a race incompatible in customs, language, and religion. They failed to recognize what was admirable in that valiant and level-headed handful of intruders who, taking advantage of the superiority of their armament and their cohesion and of the inefficiency of Mexican generals and the damaging dissensions of civil war, had penetrated to the heart of the country, sweeping all before them.

When Scott reached the Valley of Mexico popular excitement rose high. Why should we not be victorious? Here was a veteran's division containing the survivors of La

---

[10] The law of January 11, 1847, was abrogated by decree of March 29, 1847.

Angostura, commanded by General Valencia, who now tried to outrival Santa Anna, and the President made moving speeches to them. Here were the civic militia, the *polkos*, in a picturesque camp, which the flower of high society turned into a continuous gaudy picnic, with the boys receiving, in the presence of their sweethearts and mothers, the eucharistic communion as the supreme viaticum for country and for glory.

The stolid invaders took a position on the lowest spurs of the mountains rimming the Valley on the south, where they could safely pick a time and a route to their liking. The core of the defense was Valencia's division, which took a bad position (Padierna) vulnerable to the invaders. The Commander in Chief ordered him to abandon it; the ambitious subaltern balked. Santa Anna, who probably did not care much what happened to Valencia, failed to enforce his order and watched the first day's battle, but not the second day's disaster. The defeat at Padierna entirely disrupted the defense, and the invaders would have entered the city in pursuit of the fugitives if they had not been exhausted by the heroic stand made against them at the convent and bridge of Churubusco. They were turned back at the southern fortications. The invading army consisted of fewer than ten thousand combatants, and the same number, more or less, were pitted against them during those two terrible August days, when the Mexican army lost five to six thousand men—the best, no doubt. The American officers' superior tactics were demonstrated throughout the Valley campaign, in which they defeated our army piecemeal, always with stronger forces. Curious facts: Scott said in his reports he had captured two ex-Presidents of Mexico (Anaya and Salas); how surprised he would have been if he could have known he had two future Presidents among his officers—Franklin Pierce and Ulysses S. Grant.

Scott asked for an armistice, which was easily arranged. The object was a meeting of an envoy of the United States with Mexican commissioners in order to bring to an end what the American general justly termed "an unnatural war." The envoy, Mr. Trist, demanded a strip of our northern frontier which included New Mexico and the Californias. Our commissioners refused to concede anything except Texas, bounded by the Nueces, and a part of Upper California. The negotiations ended; the armistice expired, and Mexico's fate was decided in the first half of September. Santa Anna's eternal incapacity to concentrate his defense caused him to leave Casa Mata and Molino del Rey weakly guarded; a triumphant defensive fight could not be sustained on the offensive and was turned into rout. The same thing happened a few days later when Chapultepec was taken. The salient episode of these bloody battles was the defense of Chapultepec's summit by the cadets of the Military College; some of them died there. This simple and sublime act was the most glorious of all the brave acts in the entire war, on either side.

On September 15 of this same year of 1847, the victorious army occupied the capital. Scattered attempts at popular resistance were quickly quelled. Santa Anna, in disgrace, resigned as President of the Republic and headed east. A few days later, Manuel Peña y Peña, the Chief Justice, got himself recognized as President by most of the country, assembled some troops, called the governors together, arranged for the Congress to meet, and organized a government that could enter into negotiations with the commander of the invading army. There was a group in the Congress that passionately opposed the idea of peace, the idea that was incarnate in Peña y Peña and in his minister Luis de la Rosa and later in the Provisional President, General Herrera. They and nearly the whole moderate party had desired this peace from the first, foreseeing what was bound to happen. Now they were determined to secure peace in spite of the fulminations of the military and the theatrical eloquence of some deputies. Even before the annexation of Texas, peace was urgent; after that, imperative; after the war, our only salvation. The war had left us without soldiers (9,000 men dispersed about the country), without artillery, without rifles (less than 150 in the armories).

The principle that a country must never cede territory is absurd, and no country, once invaded and conquered, has been able to sustain it. The true principle is quite different: a country in the grip of dire necessity can and should cede a part of its territory in order to conserve the rest.

With these convictions the eminent jurists representing us entered into negotiations with the American envoy Trist, a highly deferent man, and were surprised to learn that the victors had not increased their demands to any extent since their decisive triumphs in the Valley. The discussions produced, one month later, the Treaty of Guadalupe Hidalgo. The Mexicans disputed each demand, yielding only to compulsion. Meanwhile, the national government was in Querétaro, struggling to stay on its feet amidst anarchy and the hostility of the principal states and latent insurrection in others, amidst penury and prostration. If it should fall, the Republic would fall with it. On February 2 the Treaty was signed. We lost what we had already lost in fact: California, New Mexico, Texas, the portion of Tamaulipas beyond the Rio Grande. The rest of the occupied territory was to be delivered to us shortly, together with an indemnification amounting to fifteen million pesos. This was not a price paid for one ceded territory which was already in the Americans' possession (and they delivered to us much that we had thought lost forever)—this was payment for damages caused by the war, and so vital that the government could not have survived without it and the consequences would have been chaos, dismemberment, and annexation. This was a painful treaty but not an ignomin-

ious one. A comparison with the treaty between France and Germany at Frankfurt, and with that between the United States and Spain at Paris, will enable us to judge our forefathers with more fairness. They did what they should have done, and did it well.

Mexico, a weak country because of its scant and sparse population, still partly ignorant of cultured life and of patriotism in its fullest meaning, has been vanquished in all its international wars, though never really conquered. But there is a fatality about the country, a sort of malign influence on its invaders which would seem to have some mysterious relation to justice. French intervention in Mexico led to the Franco-Prussian war; American invasion led to the War Between the States. From the disruption of political parties in the United States there arose the resolutely antislavery Republican Party, which opposed the spread of the black social plague to the newly acquired territories, and against this group the South, feeling itself strong (for to make itself strong it had insisted on the War with Mexico) resorted to arms. The Mexican War was the school for the future generals of the American Civil War.

Select Bibliography
for Problem 5

Bailey, Thomas A., ed. *The American Spirit: United States History as Seen by Contemporaries.* Boston: D. C. Heath & Company, 1963, pp. 274–289.

Baldwin, Leland D., ed. *Ideas in Action: Documentary and Interpretive Readings in American History,* Vol. I–to 1877. New York: Van Nostrand Reinhold Company, 1968, pp. 447–457.

Barker, Eugene G. "The Annexation of Texas," *Southwestern Historical Quarterly,* 50 (July 1946), 49–74.

———. "President Jackson and the Texas

Revolution," *American Historical Review,* 12 (July 1907), 788–809.

Boucher, Chauncey S. *"In Re* That Aggressive Slavocracy," *Mississippi Valley Historical Review,* 8 (June 1921), 13–79.

Bourne, Edward G. "The United States and Mexico, 1847–1848," *American Historical Review,* 5 (April 1900), 491–502.

Chamberlin, Eugene K. "Nicholas Trist and Baja California," *Pacific Historical Review,* 32 (February 1963), 49–63.

De Voto, Bernard. "Manifest Destiny: Understanding the 1840's," *Harper's Magazine,* 182 (April 1941), 557–560.

Ellsworth, Clayton S. "American Churches and the Mexican War," *American Historical Review,* 45 (January 1940), 301–326.

Fine, Sidney, and Gerald S. Brown, eds. *The American Past: Conflicting Interpretations of the Great Issues,* Vol. I. New York: Crowell Collier and Macmillan, Inc., 1965, pp. 455–506.

Franklin, John H. "The Southern Expansionists of 1846," *Journal of Southern History,* 25 (August 1959), 223–238.

Fuller, John D. P. "The Slavery Question and the Movement to Acquire Mexico, 1846–1848," *Mississippi Valley Historical Review,* 21 (June 1934), 31–48.

Gabriel, Ralph H. "American Experience with Military Government," *American Historical Review,* 49 (July 1944), 630–643.

Graebner, Norman A. "Party Politics and the Trist Mission," *Journal of Southern History,* 19 (May 1953), 137–156.

Graf, LeRoy P. "Colonizing Projects in Texas South of the Nueces, 1820–1845," *Southwestern Historical Quarterly,* 50 (April 1947), 431–448.

Hawgood, John A. "The Pattern of Yankee Infiltration in Mexican Alta California, 1821–1846," *Pacific Historical Review,* 27 (February 1958), 27–37.

Mitgang, Herbert. "Mexican War Dove: A. Lincoln," *New Republic,* 156 (February 11, 1967), 23–24.

Quint, Howard H., *et al.* eds. *Main Problems in American History,* Vol. I. Homewood, Ill.: Dorsey Press, 1964, 1968, pp. 341–376.

Rappaport, Armin, ed. *The War with Mexico: Why Did It Happen?* The Berkeley Series in American History. Charles Sellers, ed. Skokie, Ill.: Rand McNally & Co., 1964.

Ruiz, Ramón, ed. *The Mexican War: Was It Manifest Destiny?* American Problem Studies. Oscar Handlin, ed. New York: Holt, Rinehart and Winston, Inc., 1963.

Sears, Louis M. "Nicholas P. Trist, a Diplomat with Ideals," *Mississippi Valley Historical Review,* 11 (June 1924), 85–98.

Spell, Lota M. "Anglo-Saxon Press in Mexico, 1846–1848," *American Historical Review,* 38 (October 1932), 20–31.

Stenberg, Richard R. "The Failure of Polk's War Intrigue of 1845," *Pacific Historical Review,* 4 (March 1935), 39–69.

———. "Intrigue for Annexation," *Southwest Review,* 25 (October 1939), 58–69.

———. "President Polk and the Annexation of Texas," *Southwestern Social Science Quarterly,* 14 (March 1934), 336–356.

Tays, George. "Frémont Had No Secret Instructions," *Pacific Historical Review,* 9 (June 1940), 157–171.

part 6

The Mind
of the Nation

chapter 18

Social Idealism and Reform

The Free Thinkers

UTOPIAN SOCIETIES
AND RELIGIOUS REFORMS

The impulse of democracy influenced every institution in America during the first half of the nineteenth century, and religion was no exception. Skepticism, and to some extent deism, continued to attract followers from among the university communities and the wealthy despite the sometimes hostile opposition of the orthodox clergy. In 1824 Robert Owen, a wealthy Scot, came to America to test an experiment of his own in free thought. Convinced that economic and social happiness could be attained only through a utopian and religious community, he purchased land at New Harmony, Indiana, for his project.[1] There he assembled a group of people whose economic objectives, contrary to capitalist philosophy, called for cooperation for the general welfare of the whole community. The structure of the enterprise soon crumbled, however, when altruism turned to strife.

[1] New Harmony was by no means the first religious society to be organized in America. Several date back to the eighteenth century when the map of Pennsylvania was dotted with such German social experiments as the Dunkers (1732), the Moravians (1740s), and the English Shakers (1776), among others. One group, the German Pietists, were in Pennsylvania as early as 1694.

John Humphrey Noyes, a Yale theology student, tried to establish what he considered to be a utopian socialist society at Oneida, New York, in 1848; but his plan failed when widespread external opposition developed over the community's "perfectionist" philosophy and ideas of free love. Some felt that their doctrines implied that the power of man might become equal to that of God Himself in the pursuit of life, thus making man free of sin.

The revelations of one William Miller in the 1830s were equally sensational. A simple Massachusetts farmer, Miller began preaching the "second coming of Jesus," which was supposed to happen in 1843. By that time it had captured the imagination of almost a million followers, and it was particularly appealing to the victims of the depression of 1837. It would elevate the morale of other panic victims in later years.

MORMON CHURCH

Joseph Smith's revelations made more permanent contributions to America's development. Born in Vermont, young Smith was in upstate New York in 1827 when a vision appeared to him and with its magical powers enabled him to translate a story from hieroglyphics found on two golden plates. The story, according to Smith, was that of a lost tribe—the forefathers of the American Indians. From

291

these fragments came the Book of Mormon and the subsequent Mormon movement.

Unlike many another sect, Mormonism drew a considerable portion of its religious doctrine from the old Puritan virtues of a strict moral code of conduct and set its communal objectives on a "united order" for the economic and social well-being of the whole group.

Despite its appeal for more democracy within the established churches, the free thought movement continued to find closed minds among the clergy. In fact, many clergymen stood closer to the new industrial age than to egalitarian reforms; and their message was one of tolerance toward poverty in this world—a position that was supposed to guarantee a richer reward in the next world. They skirted the issue of slavery as too controversial, but in time a few began to accept the challenge of reform, and the resulting strife caused more churches to divide into slave and nonslave factions.

UNITARIAN CHURCH

An earlier reform movement within the Congregational Church had provided the impetus for a splinter group to form the Unitarian Church.[2] Determined to separate true religion from superstition, its founders rejected the doctrine of the Trinity and the Calvinistic doctrine of the natural depravity of man with the predestination of the few to salvation and the many, on the other hand, to damnation. They looked instead to the positive side of human nature, to salvation as a product derived from character, to freedom of the will rather than autocratic sanction, and to God as a concept of benevolence. Channing believed that man's culture rested not in his calling or station but rather in his nature, and with this in mind he instructed man to achieve self-culture. Self-improvement soon became the gospel of the new movement. Thus Unitarians, along with the other free-will sects such as the Methodists and Baptists, were manifest evidence of the new marriage that had taken place between democracy and religion.

TEMPERANCE MOVEMENT

Other segments of society soon discovered ailments in the American system that needed doctoring. For example, the temperance movement, although active before the 1820s, had its official initiation in 1826 with the founding of the American Society for the Promotion of Temperance.[3] Viewing alcohol as the main cause of crime and hard times, these social reformers called for moderation in drink and a few even demanded total prohibition. Some of the more extreme proposed the formation of a "Cold Water Society," free of the vulgarities of not only liquor but coffee and tea as well, while others got into the act by starting an antitobacco movement. A few states responded by passing temperance laws. Maine, for example, passed a state-wide prohibition bill in 1851; twelve other states followed, but most officials soon realized that it was impossible to legislate what people drink, and by 1865 nine of the states had abandoned the law.

HUMANITARIAN MOVEMENT

Women, such as Dorothea Dix, frequently led the nation in humanitarian reform. Although in poor health herself, Dix carried the fight for hospital and prison reform to the doors of state capitols, where she eventually won land grants to aid state institutions. Between 1841 and 1844

---

[2] The American Unitarian Association was founded in 1825 by William Ellery Channing, but the movement can be traced to the time of the American Revolution when the first Unitarian church was established in Boston in 1785.

[3] More than a thousand such societies were registered between 1830 and 1850.

she visited eighteen state penitentiaries and dozens of county jails and alms-houses collecting evidence which she used to shock legislators by calling their attention to insane persons confined within cages, or locked in closets, cellars, stalls, and pens. Some were chained, beaten with rods, and lashed into obedience. While she brought immediate relief to many such souls, her psychological impact was far more significant in the reform movement; for the first time officials began to view insanity as an illness rather than a hereditary condition.

The humanitarian movement, meanwhile, was making progress in its attempt to abolish capital punishment and imprisonment for debts. Many states reduced the death sentence to crimes such as murder, treason, or arson,[4] and imprisonment for debt was significantly reduced by 1850, and by 1860 was a thing of the past.

WOMEN'S RIGHTS

Few among knowledgeable citizens would deny that women had ample reason for a call to arms, for they were in fact placed in a condition of genteel slavery. Mrs. Amelia Bloomer was one of the pioneers who tried to correct some of the abuses. Vexed by the thought of wearing the traditional but uncomfortable corsets and tight laces, she set them aside and gained considerable notoriety by wearing bloomer trousers underneath her skirt. Others took the cue and began demanding equality in the home, in business affairs, and in employment, and one young lass even had the temerity to ask for the right to vote.

Taking to the public platform traditionally reserved for men, women began to assert themselves. In 1848 Mrs. Lucretia Mott and Mrs. Elizabeth Cady Stanton called a convention at Seneca Falls, New York, and proceeded to adopt a list of grievances that rivaled those of 1776. Meanwhile, independent-minded Lucy Stone refused to assume her husband's name; and other enterprising women like Emma Willard and Catherine Beecher elevated the status of womankind by establishing academies for girls.[5]

Labor Reforms and Immigrants

The emergence of organized labor followed the march of the Industrial Revolution during the first half of the nineteenth century, inasmuch as the latter movement introduced for the first time—at least in agrarian America—an army of landless workers. Toiling under the same roof in the factory system, men soon learned to organize with a common voice in order to secure more benefits from the management—namely, better working conditions and higher wages. In 1827 the Philadelphia Mechanics' Union of Trade Associations was formed, and in 1834 an attempt was made by Ely Moore to form a National Trades Union,[6] but the latter organization was weakened by the Panic of 1837 and after struggling along for several years finally collapsed. Others got the idea, however, and in 1852 the National Typographical Union was organized.

Despite the fact that strikes were illegal from 1835 to 1842 (*People* v. *Fisher*), favorable public pressures (spawned by overproduction of goods and increasing competition from immigrant labor) enabled many eastern labor groups to gain

---

[4] States frequently had a long list of crimes punishable by death—a carryover from the early colonial period.

[5] Mrs. Willard's Middlebury Female Seminary (high school) was established in 1814, and a second was started under her direction at Troy, New York, in 1821. These were followed by Oberlin College (Ohio), which was founded in 1833 as the first coeducational school, and Mount Holyoke (Massachusetts), which was founded in 1836 as the first women's college in the United States.

[6] The first local craft unions were organized in the 1790s in Philadelphia.

quasi-recognition and to extract certain wage and working concessions from industry. For example, the ten-hour workday was common by 1840 (Executive Order by President Van Buren); and labor realized a considerable victory in 1842 when Chief Justice Shaw ruled (*Commonwealth* v. *Hunt*) that trade unions were lawful and that strikes were legal.

Increased participation of labor in politics came with the removal of property qualifications for voting in many states during the 1820s. This action paved the way for the first United States labor party, which was formed in May 1828 in Philadelphia, whereupon other eastern labor organizations followed the example.

IMMIGRATION

Immigration also played a significant role in the development of the United States during the first half of the nineteenth century and continued to do so after the Civil War. (It has been observed that few came to the United States before 1829, except for some political refugees; but in 1846 famine and internal political strife rocked Ireland, and a drought and famine stunned Germany, causing thousands to look elsewhere for a better life.) The more desperate crowded the northern European seaport towns, seeking the twenty or thirty dollars required for passage to America, the land of opportunity.[7]

Students of the subject have reported that this unskilled and penniless mass of humanity provided the sinews with which forests were leveled and buildings were erected; they built roads and dug canals, and when America moved west they built railroads and riverboats. Unable to qualify for skilled factory jobs, many took what was available, and those who felt a

[7] In excess of 50,000 a year arrived during the 1840s, and in the peak year of 1854, as many as 427,000 made their way to the United States.

close affinity to the land went west, where in states like Wisconsin and Minnesota they somehow managed to secure land and became farmers par excellence.

Not all immigrants were without skill, however, as evinced by the world-reowned cabinet- and pianomakers and numerous other small-shop artisans of New York City. Thus, the immigrant could justifiably boast of an America that he had helped to build.

NATIVIST MOVEMENT

Although the immigrants were accepted and appreciated by a sizable majority of Americans, there were those few racists who through ignorance and misinformation viewed them as detrimental to the "American way of life." Out of this discontent emerged the Nativist or antiforeign movement that began in the 1830s and attracted a surprisingly large constituency before the Civil War captured the interest of Americans. Suspicious of the Celts and their possible threat to Anglo-Saxon superiority, the Nativists attacked the clannish ways of the Irish and Germans and spawned the belief that Europe was dumping her "undesirables" on the United States.

Nativism soon turned its "guns" on religious groups, and with the formation of the Sons of '76 and the Order of the Star-Spangled Banner, among other superpatriot groups, a movement was started to keep Catholic-Irish and Germans outside the franchise, thereby neutralizing their potential political power. The final impulse of the Nativists came in 1856, when they organized the Know-Nothing party and nominated Millard Fillmore for President on the American party ticket. Interestingly enough, the American party turned out to be a coalition of Whigs, Democrats, and Nativists—all for different reasons—but the party proved strong enough to elect Fillmore President.

Abolition of Slavery

Of all the reform movements of the era, the most noble was that of the abolition of slavery. Ever mindful of the frustrations of Francis D. Pastorius in the late seventeenth century and of the agonizing efforts of the Quaker-inspired antislavery societies during the Revolutionary period, black and white abolitionists united for the first time in the early nineteenth century in a concerted appeal to the Christian conscience of the slaveholder and to Congress. And, whereas the earlier efforts had convinced seven states to abolish slavery in 1784 and all but Georgia and South Carolina to cease importing slaves,[8] their main objective was the peculiar institution as it existed in the South.

AMERICAN COLONIZATION SOCIETY

In 1815 Paul Cuffe, a prosperous Massachusetts Negro merchant, organized the Sierra Leone Colony in Africa with the expressed purpose of relocating black people who wished to return to that continent; and within two years the American Colonization Society was formed with the support of such men as Henry Clay and John Randolph. Neither organization, however, was successful in getting their movement off the ground because a vast majority of Negroes opposed the idea; and William L. Garrison, a leading white abolitionist who subscribed to the movement at first, later turned against it.

Negroes began to organize in earnest on their own behalf in 1830 when Allen Bishop called a national convention at Bethel Church in Philadelphia for the purpose of resolving Negro problems; a second and similar convention was organized in New York the following year under the leadership of Arthur

[8] A federal law prohibiting the importation of slaves went into effect in 1808.

Tappen. Others heeded these expressions of protest and concern.

LUNDY AND GARRISON

Another kind of impulse against slavery was observed in the press. Notable among the leaders were the Quaker Benjamin Lundy with his abolitionist newspaper, *The Genius of Universal Emancipation,* which began publication in 1821, and the Bostonian William L. Garrison, who for a short time collaborated with Lundy but in 1831 started his own publication, *The Liberator.*

FREDERICK DOUGLASS

Perhaps unsurpassed as a speaker and writer in his time, Frederick Douglass, once a slave, was the recognized leader of the black abolitionists. He not only published a weekly paper called *The North Star,* but he traveled in Europe, where he proclaimed the cause of his race. Oftentimes the main theme of his argument was designed to build pride in his race. He liked to point out, for example, that the seat of Western civilization was held by black people. "The ancient Egyptians were not white," Douglass observed, "but were, undoubtedly, just about as dark in complexion as many in this country who are considered Negroes."

WILLIAM WELLS BROWN

Douglass and other black abolitionists were soon joined in the "noble crusade" by William Wells Brown, who was equally capable of articulating his convictions. Brown, like Douglass, won fame as a speaker and writer and in the course of his illustrious career wrote an account of the rise and fall of Toussaint L'Ouverture and *The Black Man: His Antecedents, His Genius and His Achievements* (1863), among other works. Fighting for the lost dignity of his race, Brown announced in

1862 that "the blacks are the legitimate descendants of the Egyptians." This thesis becomes even more significant, Brown declared, when we remember that the Anglo-Saxon civilizations of northern Europe were still in a state of savagery.

Peaceful at first and posing as the defenders of democracy's time-honored liberties, the abolitionists held frequent meetings to pass resolutions, sign petitions, and organize propaganda campaigns. Tons of informational literature were printed and circulated, and its appeal was heightened by featuring such noted literary figures as John Greenleaf Whittier and Harriet Beecher Stowe.[9]

In the same year that *The Liberator* appeared, Nat Turner took a more violent approach to reform by starting a revolt in Virginia that eventually claimed fifty-five lives. After the Turner incident slave owners began to take the abolitionists more seriously and to insulate their institution against such dangers.

COUNTERABOLITIONIST MOVEMENT

The counterabolitionist movement reached its apex in the writings and speeches of George Fitzhugh, John C. Calhoun, and Thomas R. Dew. In 1854 and 1857 Fitzhugh published *Sociology for the South* and *Cannibals All,* in which he painted a picture of good and benevolent protection for the Negro in the South, as compared to the miserable conditions in the factories of the North, where women and children were exploited and maimed daily. Dew, president of William and Mary, defended slavery on the bases of history, scriptures, and economic necessity.

In 1836 the proslavery majority in Congress struck back at the frequent antislavery petitions appearing in their

chamber by passing the first of the "gag rules," which required that any such petition be tabled without debate. The abolitionist forces amassed an immediate counterattack. Led by ex-President Adams, they finally secured the repeal of these offensive and seemingly unconstitutional measures in 1844.

AMERICAN PEACE MOVEMENT

World peace did not go unnoticed during the period. Reportedly the stepchild of the colonial Quakers, the American Peace Movement organized its first official society in 1828 under the leadership of William Ladd, who proposed a kind of United Nations. The 1830s, however, brought internal dissention and previous gains were soon nullified.

Select Bibliography

Arrington, Leonard J. *The Great Kingdom: An Economic History of Latter-Day Saints, 1830–1900.* Cambridge, Mass.: Harvard University Press, 1958.

Barnes, Gilbert H. *The Anti-Slavery Impulse, 1830–1844.* New York: Harcourt Brace Jovanovich, Inc., 1933.

Beard, Mary R. *A Short History of the American Labor Movement.* New York: Greenwood Press, Inc., 1968.

Billington, Ray A. *The Protestant Crusade, 1800–1860.* Chicago: Quadrangle Books, Inc., 1964.

Brodie, Fawn M. *No Man Knows My History: The Life of Joseph Smith.* New York: Alfred A. Knopf, 1945.

Commager, Henry S. *The Era of Reform, 1830–1860.* New York: Van Nostrand Reinhold Company, 1960.

――――. *Theodore Parker: Yankee Crusader.* Boston: Beacon Press, 1960.

Commons, John R., et al. *History of La-*

[9] Abolitionism was a minority movement and its followers were constantly harassed, their presses were destroyed, Garrison was threatened with hanging, and others were sometimes killed by mobs.

bour in the United States. 4 vols. New York: Augustus M. Kelley, Publishers, 1918–1935.

Crowe, Charles. *George Ripley: Transcendentalist and Utopian Socialist.* Athens, Ga.: University of Georgia Press, 1967.

Curti, Merle. *The American Peace Crusade, 1815–1861.* New York: Octagon Books, Inc., 1965.

Deutsch, Albert. *The Mentally Ill in America.* New York: Columbia University Press, 1949.

Duberman, Martin, ed. *The Anti-Slavery Vanguard: New Essays on Abolitionists.* Princeton, N.J.: Princeton University Press, 1965.

Dulles, Foster R. *Labor in America: A History.* New York: Thomas Y. Crowell Company, 1949.

Dumond, Dwight L. *Antislavery: The Crusade for Freedom in America.* Ann Arbor, Mich.: University of Michigan Press, 1961.

Eaton, Clement. *Freedom of Thought Struggle in the Old South,* 2d ed. Gloucester, Mass.: Peter Smith, 1964.

———. *The Mind of the Old South.* Baton Rouge, La.: Louisiana State University Press, 1967.

Elkins, Stanley M. *Slavery: A Problem in American Institutional and Intellectual Life.* Chicago: University of Chicago Press, 1968.

Filler, Louis. *The Crusade against Slavery, 1830–1860.* New York: Harper & Row, Publishers, 1960.

Fish, Carl R. *The Rise of the Common Man, 1830–1850.* New York: Crowell Collier and Macmillan, Inc., 1927.

Flexner, Eleanor. *Century of Struggle: The Woman's Rights Movement in the U.S.* New York: Atheneum Publishers, 1959.

Foner, Philip S. *Frederick Douglass.* New York: Citadel Press, Inc., 1964.

Franklin, John H. *From Slavery to Freedom,* 2d ed. New York: Alfred A. Knopf, 1956.

Fuller, Margaret. *Memoirs, 1810–1850.* New York: Burt Franklin, 1969.

Handlin, Oscar. *Immigration as a Factor in American History.* Gloucester, Mass.: Peter Smith, 1959.

———. *The Uprooted.* Boston: Little, Brown and Company, 1951.

Hansen, Klaus J. *Quest for Empire: The Political Kingdom of God and the Council of Fifty in Mormon History.* East Lansing, Mich.: Michigan State University Press, 1967.

Higham, John. *Strangers in the Land.* New York: Atheneum Publishers, 1963.

Jones, Maldwyn A. *American Immigration.* Chicago: University of Chicago Press, 1960.

Krout, John A. *The Origins of Prohibition.* New York: Russell & Russell, Publishers, 1967.

Lerner, Gerda. *The Grimke Sisters from South Carolina: Rebels against Slavery.* Boston: Houghton Mifflin Company, 1967.

McKitrick, Eric L., ed. *Slavery Defended: The Views of the Old South.* Gloucester, Mass.: Peter Smith, 1963.

Madison, Charles A. *Critics and Crusaders,* 2d ed. New York: Frederick Ungar Publishing Co., Inc., 1959.

Miller, Perry, ed. *American Transcendentalists: Their Prose and Poetry.* New York: Doubleday & Company, Inc., 1957.

Nevins, Allan. *Ordeal of Union.* 2 vols. New York: Charles Scribner's Sons, 1947.

Nye, Russel B. *Fettered Freedom: Civil Liberties and the Slavery Controversy.* East Lansing, Mich.: Michigan State University Press, 1949.

_____. *William Lloyd Garrison and the Humanitarian Reformers.* Boston: Little, Brown and Company, 1955.

Phillips, Ulrich B. *American Negro Slavery.* Reprint. Baton Rouge, La.: Louisiana State University Press, 1966.

_____. *Life and Labor in the Old South.* Boston: Little, Brown and Company, 1929.

Quarles, Benjamin. *Frederick Douglass.* New York: Atheneum Publishers, 1968.

Ratner, Lorman. *Powder Keg: Northern Opposition to the Anti-Slavery Movement, 1831–1840.* New York: Basic Books, Inc., 1968.

Rusk, R. L. *The Life of Ralph Waldo Emerson.* New York: Columbia University Press, 1949.

Schlesinger, Sr., Arthur M. *The American as Reformer.* New York: Atheneum Publishers, 1968.

Schlesinger, Jr., Arthur M. *Orestes A. Brownson.* Boston: Little, Brown and Company, 1966.

Smith, Timothy L. *Revivalism and Social Reform in Mid-Nineteenth Century America.* Nashville, Tenn., Abingdon Press, 1957.

Stampp, Kenneth M. *The Peculiar Institution.* New York: Random House, Inc., 1956.

Staudenraus, P. J. *The African Colonization Movement, 1816–1865.* New York: Columbia University Press, 1961.

Stephenson, George M. *A History of American Immigration, 1820–1924.* New York: Russell & Russell, Publishers, 1964.

Thomas, John L. *The Liberator.* Boston: Little, Brown and Company, 1963.

_____. *Slavery Attacked: The Abolitionist Crusade.* Englewood Cliffs, N.J.: Prentice-Hall, Inc., 1964.

Tyler, Alice F. *Freedom's Ferment: Phases of American Social History from the Revolution to the Outbreak of the Civil War.* New York: Harper & Row, Publishers, 1944.

Whicher, George F. and Gail Kennedy, eds. *The Transcendentalist Revolt.* Boston: D. C. Heath & Company, 1968.

Wish, Harvey. *Society and Thought in Early America.* New York: David McKay Co., Inc., 1962.

Wittke, Carl F. *We Who Built America: The Saga of the Immigrant.* Cleveland, Ohio: The Press of Case Western Reserve University, 1964.

chapter 19

The Flowering of American Culture

American Letters before 1830

THE EARLY NATIONALISTS

The first three decades of the nineteenth century marked the emergence of a national literature that found a manifest calling in almost every American theme, including reform movements of the era; but to suggest that there was a steady and determined resolve in changing institutions would be a gross oversimplification. Not all great men of letters were nationalists, nor were all dedicated to democratic reforms.

Because America had grown up reading the tales and rhymes of English authors and poets, the break with that habit was not soon realized after the Revolution. In fact, some students of the subject have suggested that the first truly native literature in form and content did not appear until mid-century with Nathaniel Hawthorne's *The Scarlet Letter* (1850); Herman Melville's, *Moby Dick* (1851); and Walt Whitman's, *Leaves of Grass* (1855).

Early impulses of a nationalist leaning, nevertheless, were observed after the War of 1812 in the writings of William Cullen Bryant, Washington Irving, and James Fenimore Cooper. Bryant won a place in history as America's first great poet when at the age of sixteen he produced the remarkable and highly acclaimed poem "Thanatopsis" (1817). Two years later Irving wrote his immensely popular *Sketch Book,* which included "Rip Van Winkle" and "The Legend of Sleepy Hollow," while Cooper was preparing his first big seller, *The Spy* (1821). Cooper later became much better known as the author of *The Last of the Mohicans* (1826) and other Leatherstocking Tales.

Like many another writer in frontier America, Bryant, although still active as a reform writer, gave up producing organic works of literature and accepted the editorship of the *New York Evening Post;* and Irving deserted the American scene for Europe, ultimately turning to a career of diplomacy. Cooper also spent a considerable amount of time in Europe, but, like Bryant, he revealed a growing concern for democratic reforms, as evinced by *Satanstoe, The Chainbearer, The Redskins,* and *The American Democrat.*

All three were influenced in varying degrees by the Romantic movement in Europe, and they continued to borrow rather freely from English forms and themes. Cooper, in fact, achieved his greatest fame by writing American themes into Sir Walter Scott's literary forms, but in the process miseducated two or three generations of Americans with the fictitious deeds of his buckskin heroes.

Literature after 1830

THE GOLDEN AGE

The Golden Age of American Letters, sometimes alluded to as the New England Renaissance, emerged during the 1830s and for almost half a century marked that corner of the United States as the "hub of the Universe." Its brightest star was Ralph Waldo Emerson, and his highest note was struck for creative originality. Disturbed by America's refusal to break from its subservient role to Europe, Emerson asked his New England colleagues to abandon those dead cultures of the past and explore the potentials of America. The response was astounding. Never before or after, it is said, has the United States produced so many penmen in a given era with such sterling quality.

TRANSCENDENTALISM

As for Emerson, he had given up his work as a Unitarian minister in order to devote more time to philosophy and writing; and as a student of Unitarian metaphysics[1] he was soon in the vanguard of a unique school of philosophy that became known as transcendentalism. Its spiritual founders were Jean Jacques Rousseau and Immanuel Kant, among others, and its scriptures could be traced to European Romanticism and Oriental mysticism.

Fostering a cult of self-improvement, transcendentalism marked the beginning of American social philosophy. The short of it is that Emerson believed that man is a free agent who can achieve moral and spiritual progress on his way toward perfection. The new cult soon had a large following among the American common folk, who readily understood and liked its

message of a kind of individualism that seemed to set them free from the insulting restraints of a rigid society. Groups of farmers and laissez-faire businessmen who opposed taxation for the new public schools similarly found a message in the doctrine of self-improvement—if self-education is possible, why have schools?

One of those who answered Emerson's call was the young Henry David Thoreau, who became much more radical than his master. Thoreau attacked civilization, the city in particular, and ultimately turned to isolation and nature. His "eccentric" ways earned for him the disapproval of the whole community of Concord.

THE CONSERVATIVE SCHOOL

Another literary group, which has often been alluded to as the conservative school, eulogized the uniqueness of American democracy exclusive of the controversial themes that many writers of the period found stimulating. Resting their case on style and form, members of this group became some of the most revered figures of the Renaissance. Of those who made up this rival New England school—Henry Wadsworth Longfellow, James Russell Lowell, Oliver Wendell Holmes, John Greenleaf Whittier, Harriet Beecher Stowe, and Nathaniel Hawthorne—only Hawthorne went beyond slavery in posing abstract problems for social thought. His *Scarlet Letter* was a scathing indictment of the rigid Puritan way of life. Lowell distinguished himself as an abolitionist by publishing *The Biglow Papers* in opposition to the slavery issues in the Mexican War, and in 1852 Harriet Beecher Stowe gained almost instant fame by writing the powerful novel *Uncle Tom's Cabin*.

THE MIDDLE STATES

New York dominated the Middle States with the brilliance of Edgar Allan Poe, Herman Melville, and Walt Whitman.

---

[1] The Unitarians of the early nineteenth century generally believed that God is infinite and therefore too great to die on a gallows; that God is love and never predestines men to eternal flames; finally, that man, like God, is good and divine, for the only God is the God whose image dwells in our own souls.

Acclaimed by many students of the subject as America's greatest poet and critic, Poe wrote poems about romantic adventure for the most part, whereas his short stories reveal a preoccupation with the bizarre and mysterious. Melville, on the other hand, deliberated on the forces of good and evil in his celebrated bestseller *Moby Dick,* while Whitman devoted his career to themes of democracy and humanitarian reform.

SOUTHERN LITERATURE

The South produced the most prolific writer of the age in William Gilmore Simms of Charleston, South Carolina. With the charming southern society as his central theme, Simms turned out in excess of eighty works (mostly short novels) to earn the title "the James Fenimore Cooper of the South." Other notable southern writers included Augustus B. Longstreet and Joseph Baldwin, both of whom distinguished themselves by describing the folk life of rural America in the South.

NEGRO LITERATURE

Frederick Douglass and William Wells Brown, both runaway slaves, dominated Negro literature in the antebellum period. Douglass was well established as the leading abolitionist speaker by 1845, but in that year he also won acclaim as a writer by publishing *A Narrative of the Life of Frederick Douglass.* A decade later a second and more refined autobiography appeared under the title *My Bondage and My Freedom.* Brown, perhaps the most prolific Negro writer before the Civil War, was the first black man to produce a novel in the United States *(Clotel, or the President's Daughter,* 1853) and the first to write a play *(The Escape).*

George Moses Horton, the slave poet of North Carolina who bought his freedom in 1791 with money won in a lottery, combined literary insight with humor in producing remarkable poems. Considered one of his best, "The Hope of Liberty" (1829) reveals a remarkable potential that must have been dwarfed by the "peculiar institution." By contrast, James A. Whitfield was more of a reformer than poet, but in 1853 he managed to successfully combine the two interests when he produced *America, and Other Poems.*

HISTORIANS

The events of the period were not without their chroniclers. The new impulse of nationalist history found its clearest expressions in the works of Jared Sparks, whose favorite subject was George Washington, and George Bancroft, who published an ambitious ten-volume *History of the United States.* The latter project required forty years of Bancroft's life. During the 1830s William H. Prescott, though nearly blind, explored the Spanish archives in preparation for his monumental works, *The Conquest of Mexico* (1843) and the *Conquest of Peru* (1847), while Francis Parkman was researching *The Oregon Trail* and French Canada.

The 1840s saw the emergence of Negro chroniclers. James W. C. Pennington and William Cooper Nell probably deserve the title "fathers of American Negro history." Pennington was born a slave, but soon after reaching adulthood ran away and over the years educated himself. Pursuing a life of preaching and teaching, he distinguished himself as a historian in 1841, when he published the first history of the black people in America, which he called *Text Book of the Origin and History of the Colored People.* Nell earned similar acclaim as a chronicler ten years later when he wrote *Services of Colored Americans in the Wars of 1776 and 1812,* reportedly one of the best histories on the Negro to appear during the nineteenth century.

FINE ARTS

The fine arts of the era were dominated by music. Stephen Foster captured the imagination of the country with his Negro folk songs, while Lowell Mason revolutionized church hymns by borrowing from the classics. The latter also established music as a part of the curriculum of the public schools.

The figure of Ira Frederick Aldridge stands out as one of the leading Shakespearean actors of the nineteenth century. He realized early that theater opportunities for a black man would be more promising in Europe; there he came under the influence of Edmund Kean, the famous English actor, and in subsequent years made many sterling performances as Othello.

EDUCATION

Antebellum education continued to be for the select few, mainly private and male-oriented; but schools for the masses were part and parcel of the spirit of democratic reforms and their most able spokesmen were DeWitt Clinton of New York, Henry Barnard of Connecticut and Rhode Island, and Horace Mann of Massachusetts. Observing that progress in a democracy demanded an educated electorate, they set about to campaign for tax-supported public schools and made surprising gains even though private academies were increasing in popularity. As the first secretary of the Board of Education, Mann also directed Massachusetts toward the first state-supported normal school in 1839[2] for the expressed purpose of training teachers. Other states soon adopted the Massachusetts plan.

Higher education before the Civil War showed a history of continued growth,

---

[2] In 1821 Boston established the first public secondary school, which prompted the state to require every town of 500 or more to start a high school by 1827. Five years later New York organized the first public primary school.

but it remained a privilege of the wealthy until the Morrill Act of 1862 accelerated the growth of state colleges and universities. The development of new colleges before 1865, in fact, belie the small numbers of students who were actually in attendance. There is a rational explanation. The number of colleges in the United States before 1865 was in excess of 250, an increase of more than 200 since 1800; but most of the newly created institutions were small private denominational colleges with meager endowments. Thus, the educational level of the average American remained shockingly low. In fact, few could boast of letters beyond the fourth year.

This condition was not viewed with alarm on the frontier, but it shocked European men of letters who visited American shores. It has been observed that Americans were never more anti-intellectual than during the period from Jefferson to Henry James. The factory system was changing America and life was becoming more complex, but the common man simply refused to view education as anything but a waste of time, much less a key to democracy. He preferred instead to rely on experience rather than intelligence; and he approached the classroom only if it held a promise of training or experience for a better-paying job. It would appear that the frontiersman depended on Emerson's self-improvement thesis, but all too frequently he forgot the most important lesson—self-discipline.

NEGRO EDUCATION

The first to accept the responsibility of educating the American Negroes were clergymen. This honorable work received a considerable impetus from the "natural rights" movement that accompanied the American Revolution. Soon after independence the more liberal sects, such as the Quakers, Baptists, Methodists, and Presbyterians, expanded their programs in Negro education. In 1820 Boston opened the first known primary school for blacks, but the Negro, by and large, continued to receive what little education he got from voluntary organizations among whites and free blacks.

Higher education for blacks also emerged slowly before the Civil War. Pennsylvania boasted three Negro colleges: Cheyney State (1837), Avery (1852), and Ashum University (1854), later renamed Lincoln, while Ohio established Wilberforce University in 1856. The District of Columbia got into the act in 1851 when it organized a Negro teachers college.

Where the institutions of formal education failed, the lyceum programs tried to fill in. Beginning in 1826, these cultural oases promoted study and discussion of current events and scheduled well-known lecturers on subjects in the liberal arts. By 1840 lyceums were commonplace.

THE PRESS

Perhaps the most significant inroads against illiteracy were made inadvertently by the press, whose newspapers and journals not only informed but entertained. Their biggest boom came with the successful operation of the "penny press." Competing with the leading dailies, such as the *New York Tribune* and the *New York Evening Post,* the *New York Sun* (1833) and the *New York Morning Herald* (1835) proved that presses could prosper by selling papers for one cent, but more significantly, the penny press established the newspaper as a standard household item. The *Freedom's Journal* (1827) was among the most significant Negro papers, and the first published in the United States, along with *National Watchman* and *North Star.*

Periodicals were led by the *North American Review* (1815), *Harper's Weekly* (1850), and the ultranationalist *U.S. Magazine and Democratic Review* (1837). For a more select clientele, there was *Godey's Ladies' Book* (1830).

Select Bibliography

Adams, Russell L. *Great Negroes: Past and Present.* Chicago: Afro-Am Publishers, 1963.

Arvin, Newton. *Herman Melville: A Critical Biography.* New York: The Viking Press, Inc., 1957.

Bode, Carl. *The American Lyceum: Town Meeting of the Mind.* New York: Oxford University Press, 1956.

————., ed. *The Portable Thoreau.* New York: The Viking Press, Inc., 1947.

Brooks, Van Wyck. *The Flowering of New England.* New York: E. P. Dutton & Co., Inc., 1936.

————. *The World of Washington Irving.* New York: E. P. Dutton & Co., Inc., 1944.

Callow, James T. *Kindred Spirits: Knickerbocker Writers and American Artists, 1807–1855.* Chapel Hill, N.C.: University of North Carolina Press, 1967.

Canby, Henry S. *Thoreau.* Gloucester, Mass.: Peter Smith, 1939.

Commager, Henry S. *The Era of Reform, 1830–1860.* New York: Van Nostrand Reinhold Company, 1960.

Crowe, Charles. *George Ripley: Transcendentalist and Utopian Socialist.* Athens, Ga.: University of Georgia Press, 1967.

Curti, Merle. *The Social Ideas of American Educators.* Totowa, N.J.: Littlefield, Adams & Co., 1959.

Dickson, Harold E. *Arts of the Young Republic: The Age of William Dunlap.* Chapel Hill, N.C.: University of North Carolina Press, 1968.

Drimmer, Melvin, ed. *Black History: A Reappraisal.* New York: Doubleday & Company, Inc., 1969.

Dunlap, William. *History of the Rise and*

Progress of the Arts of Design in the United States. 2 vols. New York: Dover Publications, Inc., 1969.

Elkins, Stanley M. *Slavery: A Problem in American Institutional and Intellectual Life.* Chicago: University of Chicago Press, 1959.

Greenslet, Ferris. *The Lowells and Their Seven Worlds.* Boston: Houghton Mifflin Company, 1946.

Grimsted, David. *Melodrama Unveiled: American Theater and Culture, 1800–1850.* Chicago: University of Chicago Press, 1968.

Hubbell, Jay B. *The South in American Literature, 1607–1900.* Durham, N.C.: Duke University Press, 1954.

Katz, Michael B. *The Irony of Early School Reform: Educational Innovation in Mid-Nineteenth Century Massachusetts.* Cambridge, Mass.: Harvard University Press, 1968.

Larkin, Oliver W. *Art and Life in America.* New York: Holt, Rinehart and Winston, Inc., 1960.

Levin, David. *History as Romantic Art: Bancroft, Prescott, Motley and Parkman.* New York: AMS Press, Inc., 1959.

Litwack, Leon F. *North of Slavery: The Negro in the Free States, 1790–1860.* Chicago: University of Chicago Press, 1961.

Madden, Edward H. *Civil Disobedience and Moral Law in Nineteenth-Century American Philosophy.* Seattle, Wash.: University of Washington Press, 1968.

Marx, Leo, ed. *The Americaness of Walt Whitman.* Boston: D. C. Heath and Company, 1960.

Miller, Perry, ed. *American Transcendentalists: Their Prose and Poetry.* New York: Doubleday & Company, Inc., 1957.

Mott, Frank L. *American Journalism: A History of Newspapers in the United States through 250 Years, 1690 to 1940.* New York: Crowell Collier and Macmillan, Inc., 1947.

Nye, Russel B. *George Bancroft, Brahmin Rebel.* New York: Alfred A. Knopf, 1944.

Somkin, Fred. *Unquiet Eagle: Memory and Desire in the Idea of American Freedom, 1815–1860.* Ithaca, N.Y.: Cornell University Press, 1967.

Stewart, Randall. *Nathaniel Hawthorne.* Hamden, Conn.: The Shoe String Press, Inc., 1970.

Tyack, David B. *George Ticknor and the Boston Brahmins.* Cambridge, Mass.: Harvard University Press, 1967.

Van Deusen, Glyndon G. *Horace Greeley, Nineteenth Century Crusader.* Philadelphia: University of Pennsylvania Press, 1953.

Van Doren, Mark, ed. *The Portable Emerson.* New York: The Viking Press, Inc., 1946.

Whicher, George F., and Gail Kennedy, eds. *The Transcendentalist Revolt.* Boston: D. C. Heath & Company, 1968.

Williams, George W. *History of the Negro Race in America, from 1619 to 1880.* New York: Arno Press, Inc., 1968.

Wish, Harvey. *George Fitzhugh: Propagandist of the Old South.* Gloucester, Mass.: Peter Smith, 1962.

Wood, James P. *Magazines in the United States,* rev. ed. New York: The Ronald Press Company, 1956.

problem 6

Transcendentalism: How Valid as an Instrument of Reform?

Transcendentalism emerged at a time when the United States was experiencing one of its greatest booms in material prosperity. The 1830s and 1840s, with the exception of the late '30s, were years of rapid territorial expansion with concomitant revolutions in communication and transportation; the factory system was turning out an abundance of manufactured goods; and the new affluence even touched the farmer, whose quest for new and fertile lands was checked only by his own ambition.

The transcendentalists, however, were alarmed by society's preoccupation with materialism and apparent neglect of the individual. Disillusioned with the creeping progress of scientific rationalism and "democratic" religion, the transcendentalists introduced a new cult of romantic idealism that had its most profound expression in individualism.

Their goals and methods as reformers were challenged then, and in more recent years they have been questioned by such figures as James Truslow Adams and Heinz Eulau.

As the student studies this problem, the following questions are offered to help further his deliberations:

General Questions for Reflection and Discussion

1. What did the transcendentalists have in mind when they alluded to the "progress of man"?
2. How did the transcendentalists propose to bring about reform? Why do you suppose they shunned group action and legal channels?
3. To what extent would transcendental reform methods work today?
4. To what extent were the transcendentalists in step with the times?
5. To what extent did the transcendentalists' emphasis on intuition of truth and righteousness stimulate reform?
6. Why were the transcendentalists called traitors to the reform movements?
7. How does the individualism of the transcendentalists differ from the individualism of today?

Basic Questions for Reflection and Discussion

1. How does Emerson identify "idealism"? "materialism"?
2. What does Emerson mean when he says "there is no pure Transcendentalist"?

3. According to Emerson, why did the transcendentalists shun society's work?

4. What did Adams see in Emerson's philosophy that was so damaging?

5. To what extent did Emerson's philosophy appeal to the democratic masses?

6. Why does Adams say that Emerson's doctrines are for adolescents?

7. What does Thoreau mean when he says that "government is an expedient"?

8. How does Thoreau distinguish between government by majority and government by justice?

9. To what extent did Thoreau deviate from the "peaceable revolution" doctrines?

10. To what extent was Thoreau representative of the frontier spirit of his time?

11. According to Eulau, why is Thoreau relevant today? Do you agree?

12. What inconsistencies does Eulau find in Thoreau?

On Transcendentalism

The first thing we have to say respecting what are called *new views* here in New England, at the present time, is, that they are not new, but the very oldest of thoughts cast into the mould of these new times. The light is always identical in its composition, but it falls on a great variety of objects, and by so falling is first revealed to us, not in its own form, for it is formless, but in theirs; in like manner, thought only appears in the objects it classifies. What is popularly called Transcendentalism among us, is Idealism; Idealism as it appears in 1842. As thinkers, mankind have ever divided into two sects, Materialists and Idealists; the first class founding on experience, the second on consciousness; the first class beginning to think from the data of the senses, the second class perceive that the senses are not final, and say, The senses give us representations of things, but what are the things themselves, they cannot tell. The materialist insists on facts, on history, on the force of circumstances and the animal wants of man; the idealist on the power of Thought and of Will, on inspiration, on miracle, on individual culture. These two modes of thinking are both natural, but the idealist contends that his way of thinking is in higher nature. He concedes all that the other affirms, admits the impressions of sense, admits their coherency, their use and

beauty, and then asks the materialist for his grounds of assurance that things are as his senses represent them. But I, he says, affirm facts not affected by the illusions of sense, facts which are of the same nature as the faculty which reports them, and not liable to doubt; facts which in their first appearance to us assume a native superiority to material facts, regarding these into a language by which the first are to be spoken; facts which it only needs a retirement from the senses to discern. Every materialist will be an idealist; but an idealist can never go backward to be a materialist.

The idealist, in speaking of events, sees them as spirits. He does not deny the sensuous fact: by no means; but he will not see that alone. He does not deny the presence of this table, this chair, and the walls of this room, but he looks at these things as the reverse side of the tapestry, as the *other end,* each being a sequel or completion of a spiritual fact which nearly concerns him. This manner of looking at things transfers every object in nature from an independent and anomalous position without there, into the consciousness. Even the materialist Condillac, perhaps the most logical expounder of materialism, was constrained to say, "Though we should soar into the heavens, though we should sink into the abyss, we never go out of ourselves; it is always our own thought that we perceive." What more could an idealist say?

The materialist, secure in the certainty of sensation, mocks at fine-spun theories, at star-gazers and dreamers, and believes that his life is solid, that he at least takes

The Complete Works of Ralph Waldo Emerson, Edward W. Emerson, ed. (New York: Sully and Kleinteich, 1883), omitting footnotes except where necessary for understanding with permission of the publisher, pp. 311–339.

nothing for granted, but knows where he stands, and what he does. Yet how easy it is to show him that he also is a phantom walking and working amid phantoms, and that he need only ask a question or two beyond his daily questions to find his solid universe growing dim and impalpable before his sense. The sturdy capitalist, no matter how deep and square on blocks of Quincy granite he lays the foundations of his banking-house or Exchange, must set it, at last, not on a cube corresponding to the angles of his structure, but on a mass of unknown materials and solidity, red-hot or white-hot perhaps at the core, which rounds off to an almost perfect sphericity, and lies floating in soft air, and goes spinning away, dragging bank and banker with it at a rate of thousands of miles the hour, he knows not whither—a bit of bullet, now glimmering, now darkling through a small cubic space on the edge of an unimaginable pit of emptiness. And this wild balloon, in which his whole venture is embarked, is a just symbol of his whole state and faculty. One thing at least, he says, is certain, and does not give me the headache, that figures do not lie; the multiplication table had been hitherto found unimpeachable truth; and, moreover, if I put a gold eagle in my safe, I find it again tomorrow—but for these thoughts, I know not whence they are. They change and pass away. But ask him why he believes that an uniform experience will continue uniform or on what grounds he founds his faith in his figures, and he will perceive that his mental fabric is built up on just as strange and quaking foundations as his proud edifice of stone.

In the order of thought, the materialist takes his departure from the external world, and esteems a man as one product of that. The idealist takes his departure from his consciousness, and reckons the world an appearance. The materialist respects sensible masses, Society, Government, social art and luxury, every establishment, every mass, whether majority of numbers, or extent of space, or amount of objects, every social action. The idealist has another measure, which is metaphysical, namely the *rank* which things themselves take in his consciousness; not at all the size or appearance. Mind is the only reality, of which men and all other natures are better or worse reflectors. Nature, literature, history, are only subjective phenomena. Although in his action overpowered by the laws of action, and so, warmly cooperating with men, even preferring them to himself, yet when he speaks scientifically, or after the order of thought, he is constrained to degrade persons into representatives of truths. He does not respect labor, or the products of labor, namely property, otherwise than as a manifold symbol, illustrating with wonderful fidelity of details the laws of being; he does not respect government, except as far as it reiterates the law of his mind; nor the church, nor charities, nor arts, for themselves; but hears, as at a vast distance, what they say, as if his consciousness would speak to him through a pantomimic scene. His thought—that is the Universe. His experience inclines him to behold the procession of facts you call the world, as flowing perpetually outward from an invisible, unsounded centre in himself, centre alike of him and of them, and necessitating him to regard all things as having a subjective or relative existence, relative to that aforesaid Unknown Centre of him.

From this transfer of the world into the consciousness, this beholding of all things in the mind, follow easily his whole ethics. It is simpler to be self-dependent. The height, the deity of man is to be self-sustained, to need no gift, no foreign force. Society is good when it does not violate me, but best when it is likest to solitude. Everything real is self-existent. Everything divine shares the self-existence of Deity. All that you call the world is the shadow of that substance which you are, the perpetual creation of the powers of thought, of those that are dependent and of those that are independent of your will. Do not cumber yourself with fruitless pains to mend and remedy remote effects; let the soul be erect, and all things will go well. You think me the child of my circumstances: I make my circumstance. Let any thought or motive of mine be different from that they are, the difference will transform my condition and economy. I—this thought which is called I—is the mould into which the world is poured like melted wax. The mould is invisible, but the world betrays the shape of the mould. You call it the power of circumstance, but it is the power of me. Am I in harmony with myself? my position will seem to you just and commanding. Am I vicious and insane? my fortunes will seem to you obscure and descending. As I am, so shall I associate, and so shall I act; Caesar's history will paint out Caesar. Jesus acted so, because he thought so. I do not wish to overlook or to gainsay any reality; I say I make my circumstance; but if you ask me, Whence am I? I feel like other men my relation to that Fact which cannot be spoken, or defined, nor even thought, but which exists, and will exist.

The Transcendentalist adopts the whole connection of spiritual doctrine. He believes in miracle, in the perpetual openness of the human mind to new influx of light and power; he believes in inspiration, and in ecstasy. He wishes that the spiritual principle should be suffered to demonstrate itself to the end, in all possible applications to the state of man, without the admission of anything unspiritual; that is, anything positive, dogmatic, personal. Thus the spiritual measure of inspiration is the depth of the thought, and never, who said it? And so he resists all attempts to palm other rules and measures on the spirit than its own.

In action he easily incurs the charge of antinomianism by his avowal that he, who has the Lawgiver, may with safety not only neglect, but even contravene every written commandment. In the play of

Othello, the expiring Desdemona absolves her husband of the murder, to her attendant Emilia. Afterwards, when Emilia charges him with the crime, Othello exclaims, "You heard her say herself it was not I." Emilia replies, "The more angel she, and thou the blacker devil."

Of this fine incident, Jacobi, the Transcendental moralist, makes use, with other parallel instances, in his reply to Fichte. Jacobi, refusing all measure of right and wrong except the determinations of the private spirit, remarks that there is no crime but has sometimes been a virtue. "I," he says, "am that atheist, that godless person who, in opposition to an imaginary doctrine of calculation, would lie as the dying Desdemona lied; would lie and deceive, as Pylades when he personated Orestes; would assassinate like Timoleon; would perjure myself like Epaminondas and John de Witt; I would resolve on suicide like Cato; I would commit sacrilege with David; yea, and pluck ears of corn on the Sabbath, for no other reason than that I was fainting for lack of food. For I have assurance in myself that in pardoning these faults according to the letter, man exerts the sovereign right which the majesty of his being confers on him; he sets the seal of his divine nature to the grace he accords."

In like manner, if there is anything grand and daring in human thought or virtue, any reliance on the vast, the unknown; any presentiment, any extravagance of faith, the spiritualist adopts it as most in nature. The oriental mind has always tended to this largeness. Buddhism is an expression of it. The Buddhist, who thanks no man, who says "Do not flatter your benefactors," but who, in his conviction that every good deed can by no possibility escape its reward, will not deceive the benefactor by pretending that he has done more than he should, is a Transcendentalist.

You will see by this sketch that there is no such thing as a Transcendental *party;* that there is no pure Transcendentalist;

that we know of none but prophets and heralds of such a philosophy; that all who by strong bias of nature have leaned to the spiritual side in doctrine, have stopped short of their goal. We have had many harbingers and forerunners; but of a purely spiritual life, history has afforded no example. I mean we have yet no man who has leaned entirely on his character, and eaten angels' food; who, trusting to his sentiments, found life made of miracles; who, working for universal aims, found himself fed, he knew not how; clothed, sheltered, and weaponed, he knew not how, and yet it was done by his own hands. Only in the instinct of the lower animals we find the suggestion of the methods of it, and something higher than our understanding. The squirrel hoards nuts and the bee gathers honey, without knowing what they do, and they are thus provided for without selfishness or disgrace.

Shall we say then that Transcendentalism is the Saturnalia or excess of Faith; the presentiment of a faith proper to man in his integrity, excessive only when his imperfect obedience hinders the satisfaction of his wish? Nature is transcendental, exists primarily necessarily, ever works and advances, yet takes no thought for the morrow. Man owns the dignity of the life which throbs around him, in chemistry, and tree, and animal, and in the involuntary functions of his own body; yet he is balked when he tries to fling himself into this enchanted circle, where all is done without degradation. Yet genius and virtue predict in man the same absence of private ends and of condescension to circumstances, united with every trait and talent of beauty and power.

This way of thinking, falling on Roman times, made Stoic philosphers; falling on despotic times, made patriot Catos and Brutuses; falling on superstitious times, made prophets and apostles; on popish times, made protestants and ascetic monks, preachers of Faith against the preachers of Works; on prelatical times, made Puritans and Quakers; and falling on Unitarian and commercial times, makes the peculiar shades of Idealism which we know. . . .

Although, as we have said, there is no pure Transcendentalist, yet the tendency to respect the intuitions and to give them, at least in our creed, all authority over our experience, has deeply colored the conversation and poetry of the present day; and the history of genius and of religion in these times, though impure, and as yet not incarnated in any powerful individual, will be the history of this tendency.

It is a sign of our times, conspicuous to the coarsest observer, that many intelligent and religious persons withdraw themselves from the common labors and competitions of the market and the caucus, and betake themselves to a certain solitary and critical way of living, from which no solid fruit has yet appeared to justify their separation. They hold themselves aloof: they feel the disproportion between their faculties and the work offered them and they prefer to ramble in the country and perish of ennui, to the degradation of such charities and such ambitions as the city can propose to them. They are striking work, and crying out for something worthy to do! What they do is done only because they are overpowered by the humanities that speak on all sides; and they consent to such labor as is open to them though to their lofty dream the writing of Iliads or Hamlets, or the building of cities or empires seems drudgery. . . .

They are lonely; the spirit of their writing and conversation is lonely; they repel influences; they shun general society; they incline to shut themselves in their chamber in the house, to live in the country rather than in the town, and to find their tasks and amusements in solitude. Society, to be sure, does not like this very well; it saith, Whoso goes to walk alone, accuses the whole world; he declares all to be unfit to be his companions; it is very uncivil, nay, insulting; Society will retaliate. Meantime, this retirement does not proceed from any whim on the part of these separators; but if any one will take pains to talk with them, he will find that this part is chosen both from temperament and from principle; with some unwillingness too, and as a choice of the less of two evils; for these persons are not by nature melancholy, sour, and unsocial—they are not stockish or brute—but joyous, susceptible, affectionate; they have even more than others a great wish to be loved. Like the young Mozart, they are rather ready to cry ten times a day, "But are you sure you love me?" Nay, if they tell you their whole thought, they will own that love seems to them the last and highest gift of nature; that there are persons whom in their hearts they daily thank for existing—persons whose faces are perhaps unknown to them, but whose fame and spirit have penetrated their solitude—and for whose sake they wish to exist. To behold the beauty of another character, which inspires a new interest in our own; to behold the beauty lodged in a human being, with such vivacity of apprehension that I am instantly forced home to inquire if I am not deformity itself; to behold in another the expression of a love so high that it assures itself—assures itself also to me against every possible casualty except my unworthiness—these are degrees on the scale of human happiness to which they have ascended; and it is a fidelity to this sentiment which has made common association distasteful to them. They wish a just and even fellowship, or none. They cannot gossip with you, and they do not wish, as they are sincere and religious, to gratify any mere curiosity which you may entertain. Like fairies, they do not wish to be spoken of. Love me, they say, but do not ask who is my cousin and my uncle. If you do not need to hear my thought, because you can read it in my face and behavior, then I will tell it you from sunrise to sunset. If you cannot divine it, you would not understand what I say. I will not molest myself for you. I do not wish to be profaned. . . .

With this passion for what is great and extraordinary, it cannot be wondered at that they are repelled by vulgarity and frivolity in people. They say to themselves, It is better to be alone than in bad company. And it is really a wish to be met—the wish to find society for their hope and religion—which prompts them to shun what is called society. They feel that they are never so fit for friendship as when they have quitted mankind and taken themselves to friend. A picture, a book, a favorite spot in the hills or the woods which they can people with the fair and worthy creation of the fancy, can give them often forms so vivid that these for the time shall seem real, and society the illusion.

But their solitary and fastidious manners not only withdraw them from the conversation, but from the labors of the world; they are not good citizens, not good members of society; unwillingly they bear their part of the public and private burdens; they do not willingly share in the public charities, in the public religious rites, in the enterprises of education, of missions foreign and domestic, in the abolition of the slave-trade, or in the temperance society. They do not even like to vote. The philanthropists inquire whether Transcendentalism does not mean sloth; they had as lief hear that their friend is dead, as that he is a Transcendentalist; for then is he paralyzed, and can never do anything for humanity. What right, cries the good world, has the man of genius to retreat from work, and indulge himself? The popular literary creed seems to be, "I am a sublime genius; I ought not therefore to labor." But genius is the power to labor better and more availably. Deserve thy genius: exalt it. The good, the illuminated, sit apart from the rest, censuring their dulness and vices, as if they thought that by sitting very grand in their chairs, the very brokers, attorneys, and congressmen would see the error of their ways, and flock to them. But the good and wise must learn to act, and carry salvation to the combatants and demagogues in the dusty arena below.

On the part of these children it is replied that life and their faculty seem to them gifts too rich to be squandered on such trifles as you propose to them. What you call your fundamental institutions, your great and holy causes, seem to them great abuses, and, when nearly seen, paltry matters. Each "cause" as it is called— say Abolition, Temperance, say Calvinism, or Unitarianism—becomes speedily a little shop, where the article, let it have been at first never so subtle and ethereal, is now made up into portable and convenient cakes, and retailed in small quantities to suit purchasers. You make very free use of these words "great" and "holy," but few things appear to them such. Few persons have any magnificence of nature to inspire enthusiasm, and the philanthropies and charities have a certain air of quackery. As to the general course of living, and the daily employments of men, they cannot see much virtue in these, since they are parts of this vicious circle; and as no great ends are answered by the men, there is nothing noble in the arts by which they are maintained. Nay, they have made the experiment and found that from the liberal professions to the coarsest manual labor, and from the courtesies of the academy and the college to the conventions of the cotillion-room and the morning call, there is a spirit of cowardly compromise and seeming which intimates a frightful skepticism, a life without love, and an activity without an aim. . . .

New, we confess, and by no means happy, is our condition: if you want the aid of our labor, we ourselves stand in greater want of the labor. We are miserable with inaction. We perish of rest and rust: but we do not like your work.

"Then," says the world, "show me your own."

"We have none."

"What will you do, then?" cries the world.

"We will wait."

"How long?"

"Until the Universe beckons and calls us to work."

"But whilst you wait, you grow old and useless."

"Be it so: I can sit in a corner and *perish* (as you call it), but I will not move until I have the highest command. If no call should come for years, for centuries, then I know that the want of the Universe is the attestation of faith by my abstinence. Your virtuous projects, so called, do not cheer me. I know that which shall come will cheer me. If I cannot work at least I need not lie. All that is clearly due today is not to lie. In other places other men have encountered sharp trials, and have behaved themselves well. The martyrs were sawn asunder, or hung alive on meathooks. Cannot we screw our courage to patience and truth, and without complaints, or even with good-humor, await our turn of action in the Infinite Counsels?"

But to come a little closer to the secret of these persons, we must say that to them it seems a very easy matter to answer the objections of the man of the world, but not so easy to dispose of the doubts and objections that occur to themselves. They are exercised in their own spirit with queries which acquaint them with all adversity, and with the trials of the bravest heroes. When I asked them concerning their private experience, they answered somewhat in this wise: It is not to be denied that there must be some wide difference between my faith and other faith; and mine is a certain brief experience, which surprised me in the highway or in the market, in some place, at some time— whether in the body or out of the body, God knoweth—and made me aware that I had played the fool with fools all this time, but that law existed for me and for all; that to me belonged trust, a child's trust and obedience, and the worship of ideas, and I should never be fool more. Well, in the space of an hour probably, I was let down from this height; I was at my old tricks, the selfish member of a selfish society. My life is superficial, takes no root in the deep world; I ask, When shall I die and be relieved of the responsibility of seeing an Universe which I do not use? I wish to exchange this flash-of-lightning faith for continuous daylight, this fever-glow for a benign climate.

These two states of thought diverge every moment, and stand in wild contrast. To him who looks at his life from these moments of illumination, it will seem that he skulks and plays a mean, shiftless and subaltern part in the world. That is to be done which he has not skill to do, or to be said which others can say better, and he lies by, or occupies his hands with some plaything, until his hour comes again. Much of our reading, much of our labor, seems mere waiting: It was not that we were born for. Any other could do it as well or better. So little skill enters into these works, so little do they mix with the divine life, that it really signifies little what we do, whether we turn a grindstone, or ride, or run, or make fortunes, or govern the state. The worst feature of this double consciousness is, that the two lives, of the understanding and of the soul, which we lead, really show very little relation to each other; never meet and measure each other; one prevails now, all buzz and din; and the other prevails then, all infinitude and paradise; and, with the progress of life, the two discover no greater disposition to reconcile themselves. Yet, what is my faith? What am I? What but a thought of serenity and independence, an abode in the deep blue sky? Presently the clouds shut down again; yet we retain the belief that this petty web we weave will at last be overshot and reticulated with veins of the blue, and that the moments will characterize the days. Patience, then, is for us, is it not? Patience, and still patience. When we pass, as presently we shall, into some new infinitude, out of this Iceland of negations, it will please us to reflect that though we had few virtues or consola-

tions, we bore with our indigence, nor once strove to repair it with hypocrisy or false heat of any kind.

But this class are not sufficiently characterized if we omit to add that they are lovers and worshippers of Beauty. In the eternal trinity of Truth, Goodness, and Beauty, each in its perfection including the three, they prefer to make Beauty the sign and head. Something of the same taste is observable in all the moral movements of the time, in the religious and benevolent enterprises. They have a liberal, even an aesthetic spirit. A reference to Beauty in action sounds to be sure a little hollow and ridiculous in the ears of the old church. In politics, it has often sufficed, when they treated of justice, if they kept the bounds of selfish calculation. If they granted restitution, it was prudence which granted it. But the justice which is now claimed for the black, and the pauper, and the drunkard, is for Beauty—is for a necessity to the soul of the agent, not of the beneficiary. I say this is the tendency, not yet the realization. Our virtue totters and trips, does not yet walk firmly. Its representatives are austere; they preach and denounce; their rectitude is not yet a grace. They are still liable to that slight taint of burlesque which in our strange world attaches to the zealot. A saint should be as dear as the apple of the eye. Yet we are tempted to smile, and we flee from the working to the speculative reformer, to escape that same slight ridicule. Alas for these days of derision and criticism! We call the Beautiful the highest, because it appears to us the golden mean, escaping the dowdiness of the good and the heartlessness of the true. They are lovers of nature also, and find an indemnity in the inviolable order of the world for the violated order and grace of man. . . .

Society also has its duties in reference to this class, and must behold them with what charity it can. Possibly some benefit may yet accrue from them to the state. In our Mechanics' Fair, there must be not only bridges, ploughs, carpenters' planes, and baking troughs, but also some few finer instruments—rain gauges, thermometers, and telescopes; and in society, beside farmers, sailors, and weavers, there must be a few persons of purer fire kept specially as gauges and meters of character; persons of a fine, detecting instinct, who note the smallest accumulations of wit and feeling in the bystander. Perhaps too there might be room for the exciters and monitors; collectors of the heavenly spark, with power to convey the electricity to others. Or, as the storm-tossed vessel at sea speaks the frigate or "line packet" to learn its longitude, so it may not be without its advantage that we should now and then encounter rare and gifted men, to compare the points of our spiritual compass, and verify our bearings from superior chronometers.

Amidst the downward tendency and proneness of things, when every voice is raised for a new road or another statute or a subscription of stock; for an improvement in dress, or in dentistry; for a new house or a larger business; for a political party, or the division of an estate—will you not tolerate one or two solitary voices in the land, speaking for thoughts and principles not marketable or perishable? Soon these improvements and mechanical inventions will be superseded; these modes of living lost out of memory; these cities rotted, ruined by war, by new inventions, by new seats of trade, or the geologic changes—all gone, like the shells which sprinkle the sea-beach with a white colony today, forever renewed to be forever destroyed. But the thoughts which these few hermits strove to proclaim by silence as well as by speech, not only by what they did, but by what they forebore to do, shall abide in beauty and strength, to reorganize themselves in nature, to invest themselves anew in other, perhaps higher endowed and happier mixed clay than ours, in fuller union with the surrounding system.

James Truslow Adams

Emerson Reconsidered

In the past few days I have gone through five volumes of his work and found the task no light one. What, I ask myself, is the trouble? It is obviously not

From "Emerson Reconsidered" by James Truslow Adams in *The Atlantic Monthly,* 146 (Boston: The Atlantic Monthly, October 1930), pp. 484–492. Footnotes omitted except where necessary for understanding by permission of the publisher.

that Emerson is not "modern," for the other evening I read aloud, to the mutual enjoyment of my wife and myself, the *Prometheus Chained* of Aeschylus, which antedates Emerson by some twenty-five hundred years. I turn to Paul More's *Shelburne Essays,* Volume XI, and read the statement that "it becomes more and more apparent that Emerson, judged by an international or even by a true national standard, is the outstanding figure of American letters." . . .

First of all it occurs to me to test him by his own appraisals of others, and I turn to his volume on *Representative Men*. The list of names is itself of considerable significance—Plato, Swedenborg, Montaigne, Shakespeare, Napoleon, Goethe. Four of these are evidently so obvious as to tell us nothing of the mind choosing them. The case is a good deal like that of the Pulitzer Jury in biography, which is forbidden to award prizes for lives of Lincoln or Washington. The essential point is, what has Emerson to say of these men? . . .

When he turns from these names, almost imposed upon him, to another of his independent choosing, it is illuminating that the one he dwells on with greatest admiration is Swedenborg. The fact is significant. For him, the Swedish mystic is "a colossal soul," the "last Father in the Church," "not likely to have a successor," compared with whom Plato is a "gownsman," whereas Lycurgus and Caesar would have to bow before the Swede. Emerson quotes from his as "golden sayings" such sentences as "in heaven the angels are advancing continually to the spring-time of their youth, so that the oldest angel appears the youngest," or "it is never permitted to any one in heaven, to stand behind another and look at the back of his head: for then the influx which is from the Lord is disturbed." Nor should we forget that entry in Emerson's *Journals* in which he noted that "for pure intellect" he had never known the equal of—Bronson Alcott! . . .

His doctrine that art should be extempore stems from his general belief that knowledge comes from intuition rather than from thought, and that wisdom and goodness are implanted in us—a fatally easy philosophy which has always appealed to the democratic masses, and which is highly flattering to their self-esteem. Wordsworth had led the romantic

reaction by making us see the beauty and value in the common things of everyday life, but the philosophy of Emerson has a different ancestry. The two when joined are a perfect soil for democratic belief, and democratic laxity in mind and spirit, far as that might be from Emerson's intention and occasional statements. The more obvious inferences are dangerous, for although a cobbler's flash of insight *may* be as great as the philosopher's lifetime of thought, such is of the rarest occurrence, and preached as a universal doctrine it is a more leveling one by far than universal suffrage.

As the ordinary unimportant man, such as most of us are, reads Emerson, his self-esteem begins to grow and glow. "The sweetest music is not in the oratorio, but in the human voice when it speaks from its instant tones of tenderness, truth, or courage." Culture, with us, he says, "ends in headache." "Do not craze yourself with thinking, but go about your business anywhere. Life is not intellectual or critical, but sturdy." "Why all this deference to Alfred and Scanderbeg and Gustavus? As great a stake depends on your private act today as followed their public and renowned steps." "We are all wise. The difference between persons is not in wisdom but in art." "Our spontaneous action is always the best. You cannot with your best deliberation and heed come so close to any question as your spontaneous glance shall bring you whilst you rise from your bed."

There is a kernel of noble thought in all this, but it is heady doctrine that may easily make men drunk and driveling, and I think we are coming near to the heart of our problem. The preaching that we do not have to think, the doctrine of what I may term, in Emerson's phrase, "the spontaneous glance," is at the bottom of that appalling refusal to criticize, analyze, ponder, which is one of the chief characteristics of the American people today in all its social, political, and international affairs. Many influences have united to bring about the condition, and Emerson cannot escape responsibility for being one of them.

On the other hand, a new nation, a common man with a fleeting vision of the possibility of an uncommon life, above all the youth just starting out with ambition and hope but little knowledge or influence as yet, all need the stimulation of a belief that somehow they *are* important and that not only may their private acts and lives be as high and noble as any, but that the way is open for them to make them so. This is the one fundamental American doctrine. It is the one unique contribution America has made to the common fund of civilization. Our mines and wheat fields do not differ in kind from others. With Yankee ingenuity we have seized on the ideas of others and in many cases improved their practical applications. The ideas, however, have largely come from abroad. The use of coal as fuel, the harnessing of steam and electricity for man's use—the foundations of our era—originated in Europe. Even the invention of the electric light was only in part American. But the doctrine of the importance of the common man is uniquely an American doctrine. It is something different, on the one hand, from the mere awarding to him of legal rights and, on the other, from the mere career open to the talents.

It is a doctrine to which the heart of humanity has responded with religious enthusiasm. It, and not science, has been the real religion of our time, and, essentially, the doctrine is a religious and not a philosophical or scientific one, equally made up as it is of a colossal hope and a colossal illusion. This does not invalidate it. Like all religions it will have its course to run and its part to play in the moulding of man to something finer. It is one more step up, and we need not deny it merely because of the inherent falsity of that gorgeous preamble which proclaims to the world, "All men are created equal." In spite of the self-assertion of the so-called masses, that is a statement which, deep in their hearts, it is as difficult for the inferior as the superior genuinely to believe. It is an ideal, which, like every religious ideal, will be of far-reaching influence, but which must be made believable emotionally. Emerson's greatness lies in his having been the greatest prophet of this new religion, an influence that might well continue to be felt on the two classes that need the doctrine most—the common man striving to rise above the mediocre, and the youth striving to attain a courageous and independent maturity.

Another strain in Emerson, that of the poet and mystic, has also to be reckoned with in making up the man's account. His insistence upon values in life, culminating in the spiritual, is one sorely needed in the America of our day as of his. We are, perhaps, further from the ideal he drew in his "American Scholar" than were the men of his own time. His large hope has not been fulfilled. There is a delicate beauty in his spiritual outlook on life, a beauty akin to that of many an old fresco in Umbria or Tuscany. Unfortunately, there were fundamental flaws in the work of the Italian artists, flaws not of spiritual insight or of artistic craftsmanship, but of wet plaster or of wrong chemical combinations in materials so that little by little their painting has crumbled and faded. If Emerson's mysticism led him too easily toward Swedenborg rather than toward Plato, and if the beauty of his spiritual interpretation of the universe does not carry that conviction or mould his readers as it should, may we not wonder whether there were not some fundamental flaws in the mind of the man that may explain his decreasing influence, just as in examining a wall where a few patches of dim color are all that remain of a Giotto we have to consider, not the artist's love of the Madonna, but his lack of knowledge of the mechanics of his art? Of this we shall speak presently.

The quintessence of Emersonianism is

to be found in the first and second series of *Essays,* and it may be noted that it was these, as my pencilings show, which I myself read most as a boy, and of them, it was such essays as "Self-Reliance," in which the word is found in its purest form, that I read over and over. What do I find marked as I turn the old pages? "Trust thyself: every heart vibrates to that iron string." "Whoso would be a man must be a nonconformist." "Nothing at last is sacred but the integrity of your own mind." "I do not wish to expiate, but to live. My life is not an apology, but a life. It is for itself and not for a spectacle." "What I must do is all that concerns me, not what the people think." "The great man is he who in the crowd keeps with perfect sweetness the independence of solitude." "Always scorn appearances and you always may. The force of character is cumulative." "Life only avails and not the having lived." "Insist on yourself; never imitate." "Nothing can bring you peace but yourself."

This is high and worthy doctrine, the practice of which will tax a man's strength and courage to the utmost, and such sentences as above have proved the strongest influences in the making of literally countless adolescent Americans, stimulating their ambition in the noblest fashion. Unfortunately this part of Emerson's teaching has had less influence than the other. The average American soon slips into preferring "we are all wise" to "scorn appearances." Insisting on being one's self is strenuous and difficult work anywhere, more so in America than any other country I know, thanks to social opinion, mass ideals, and psychologized advertising of national products. Emerson deserves full meed of praise for preaching the value of individualism, but it may be asked, granting that nearly all intelligent, high-minded American youths for nearly a century have, at their most idealistic stage, come under the influence of Emerson's doctrine, why has the effect of his teaching been so slight upon their later manhood? Does the fault lie in them or in the great teacher, for, in such sentences as we have quoted above, I gladly allow that the sage of Concord *was* a great teacher.

The answer, I think, is that the fault lies to a great extent in Emerson himself. His doctrine contains two great flaws, one positive, the other negative, and both as typically American as he himself was in everything. That he had no logically articulated system of thought is not his weakest point. He once said that he could not give an account of himself if challenged. Attempts have been made to prove that his thought was unified and coherent. One may accept these or not. It matters little, for it is not, and never has been, as a consistent philosopher that Emerson has influenced his readers. It has been by his trenchant aphorisms which stir the soul of the young and the not too thoughtful, and set the blood to dancing like sudden strains of martial music. It is in these, and not in any metaphysical system about which philosophers might argue, that we find the fatal flaws and influences I have mentioned.

The first, the positive one, in spite of his high doctrine of self-reliance and individualism, is that Emerson makes life too easy by his insistence on intuition and spontaneity. The style and construction of his writings deliberately emphasize the import of the aphorisms. The occasionally qualifying context sinks into insignificance and out of memory as does the stick of a rocket in the darkness of night. We see and recall only the dazzling shower of stars. If this is now and then unfair to Emerson's thought, he has himself to blame. He took no pains to bind his thought together and loved the brilliancy of his rocket-stars of "sayings." We have already quoted some of these on the point we are now discussing. All teaching is "Intuition." In "Spontaneity or Instinct" he finds "the essence of genius, the essence of virtue, and the essence of life." "It is as easy for the strong man to be strong, as it is for the weak to be weak." "All good conversation, manners, and action, come from a spontaneity which forgets usages, and makes the moment great." "No man need be perplexed by his speculations. . . . These are the soul's mumps and measles and whooping-coughs." "Our moral nature is vitiated by any interference of our will. . . . There is no merit in the matter. Either God is there or he is not there. We love characters in proportion as they are impulsive and spontaneous. The less a man thinks or knows about his virtues the better we like him." A page or two back we noted his theory of spontaneity in art and intellect.

This, as we have said, unless the occasional qualifications are as greatly emphasized as the sayings themselves, is extremely dangerous doctrine. Of all the youths who have read Emerson in the impressionable years, a certain proportion have subsequently retrograded in the spiritual and intellectual scale, and a certain proportion have advanced. Of the difficulty with the master felt by the latter we shall speak presently, but for the first group this doctrine of spontaneity, so emphasized by Emerson, offers all too soft a cushion upon which to recline. Act and do not think. Culture is headache. Perplexities are the soul's mumps and measles. Radiant sentence after sentence, graven with clear precision on the cameo of the mind. It has been said that, of all the sages, Emerson requires the least intellectual preparation to read. He is, indeed, in some respects, and those in which he exerts most influence, fatally easy. Fatally easy and alluring to the busy hundred-per-cent American is this doctrine of intuition and spontaneity. It is a siren voice, a soft Lydian air blown across the blue water of the mind's tropical sea. For a century the American has left the plain hard work of life to his foreign serfs. The backbreaking toil of digging trenches, laying rails, puddling iron in the furnaces, has been delegated

successively to the Irish, the Italians, the Slavs. But thinking is intellectually, willing is spiritually, as backbreaking as these. The ordinary American prefers also to abandon them and to take for himself the easier task of solving the economic problems and puzzles in which he delights. Intuition and spontaneity—fatal words for a civilization which is more and more coming to depend for its very existence on clear, hard, and long-sustained "thinking-through." It is this positive flaw in Emerson's teaching that has made the effect of his really noble doctrines of so little influence upon the boys who have worshiped him this side idolatry at sixteen and then gone into the world and found every invitation to retreat from the high ground rather than to advance.

What now of those others, those who also worshiped Emerson in youth, who have fought the world, and who find him declining in influence over their lives the more they advance? With them we reach Emerson's negative flaw.

What a gulf between the man of fifty and the boy of sixteen! As one has in those intervening years studied the history of the past, watched the daily life of the people of a score of nations, seen wars and famines take their toll of millions, and, nearer one's own heart, watched the physical pain of those closest to one's self, stood at grave after grave found, too, perhaps, that one has wrought evil when most striving to do good, one has come to feel the whole mystery of that problem of Evil—of sin, of suffering, of death. One may yet carry a brave heart and hold one's self erect, but one is no longer content with a philosophy of shallow optimism, a "God's in his heaven—all's right with the world."

I think that here is where Emerson fails us as we grow older and wiser. The trumpet blasts of self-reliance which so thrilled us at sixteen sound a little thin and far-off now. We needed them when they first smote our ear and we are deeply grateful, but we have fought the fight, we have tried to be ourselves, we have tried to live our life for itself and not for a spectacle, and now we are older. We have lived, loved, suffered, enjoyed, fought, and to some extent won. The world has been rich in interest—and in suffering. There are hopeful signs on every side. There is sunlight as well as darkness, but there *is* darkness. One has been close to failure and looked it in the eye. There have been the brows we could not soothe through years of suffering, the waxen faces we kissed for the last time before we laid them away, the mysterious darkness coming toward ourselves like the shadow of a cloud on a summer landscape, but inevitably to overtake us. When we turn again to the great teacher of our youth, what does he say to help or hearten us? Nothing.

Owing largely to material circumstance and a vast and uninhabited continent, the prevailing mood of the American people came to be one of shallow and unlimited optimism the waves of which flowed over even the sectional Calvinism of New England. Nature ceased to be the evil enemy of man's spirit and gave him her fairest gifts, as Mephistopheles bestowed his Helen on the tortured Faust. With material abundance, spiritual evil ceased to appear important and a golden age seemed dawning, as youth came to Faust in that most un-American legend.

For its hundred and fifty years America has been scarcely touched by suffering. Pestilence? None. Think of the Black Death and other great plagues that have swept over Europe. Famine? None. Think of India and China. War? Scarcely more than one. In the Revolution only an infinitesimal part of the population was in the army for any length of time. The War of 1812 was a ripple, almost all at sea, and the deaths were negligible to the population. The Indian Wars? Skirmishes by paid troops. The Mexican War? A junket which never came home to the people. The Civil War? Yes, but even that did not come home to the whole civilian popula-tion, except in the South, as have the wars which have flowed in torrents over Europe. Compare it with the Thirty Years' War, in which, to say nothing of the rest of Europe, the population of Germany, from the ravages of the sword, famine, disease and emigration, sank from 16,-000,000 to 6,000,000, and in which of 35,000 villages in Bohemia less than 6000 were standing at the end, and in which nine-tenths of the entire population of the Palatinate disappeared. The Spanish War was a holiday affair except for a few homes. In the last Great War we lost by death a mere 126,000 as compared with 8,500,000 in the Old World. In civil life our history has been one long business boom, punctuated by an occasional panic, like a fit of indigestion for a man who continually overeats. We have never suffered like the rest of humanity, and have waxed fat without, as yet, having to consider the problems forced upon others, until we have ceased to believe in their reality. The dominant American note has thus been one of a buoyant and unthinking optimism. America is a child who has never gazed on the face of death.

Emerson somewhere speaks of "the nonchalance of boys sure of a dinner." Can any words better express the American attitude toward the universe, and, in spite of his spirituality and the somewhat faded fresco of his mysticism, does Emerson himself really give us anything deeper? Man, according to him, "is born to be rich." Economic evils trouble our sage not at all. The universe, for him, is good through and through, and "success consists in close application to the laws of the world, and, since those laws are intellectual and moral, an intellectual and moral obedience." One thinks of Jay Gould and the career of many a magnate of today! "In a free and just commonwealth, property rushes from the idle and imbecile, to the industrious, brave, and persevering." As I am certainly not idle (I am working on a holiday to write this), and as Americans would not admit that theirs is not a just and free common-wealth, imbecility is the only third horn of the trilemma on which to impale my-self if property has not rushed toward me. "Do not skulk," the sage tells every man in "a world which exists for him." At fifty, we have found, simply, that the world does *not* exist for us. "Love and you shall be loved. All love is mathemati-cally just, as much as the two sides of an algebraic problem." One rubs one's eyes. "There is a soul at the center of nature and over the will of every man, so that none of us can wrong the universe." Man may, he says, "easily dismiss all particu-lar uncertainties and fears, and adjourn to the sure revelation of time the solution of his private riddles. He is sure his wel-fare is dear to the heart of being." Is he so sure? Alas, no longer.

As I think over my most recent visit to Rome, where two thousand years of human history, happiness, and suffering have left their monuments, and Heaven knows how many thousand unmarked before, I contrast it with a visit to Emer-son's house at Concord on an October day many years ago. It is a charming, roomy old house, and in it Emerson was able to live with a large library and three servants on two thousand a year. In the ineffable light of an American autumn, as I saw it, it was a place of infinite peace. Concord in 1840 was an idyllic moment in the history of the race. That moment came and passed, like a baby's smile. Emerson lived in it. "In the morning," he wrote, "I awake, and find the old world, wife, babies, and mother, Concord and Boston, the dear old spiritual world, and even the dear old devil not far off."

It is true that he has very occasional qualms and doubts. He even wonders in one essay whether we must presuppose some "slight treachery and derision" in the universe. As we turn the pages, we ask ourselves with some impatience, "Did this man never really suffer?" and read that "the only thing grief has taught me, is to know how shallow it is. That,

like all the rest, plays about the surface, and never introduces me into the reality, for contact with which we would even pay the costly price of sons and lovers."

One ends. Perhaps Mr. More is right. Perhaps Emerson *is* the outstanding fig-ure in the American letters. Who else has expressed so magnificently the hope, and so tragically illustrated the illusion, of our unique contribution to the world? My own debt to the sage is unpayable. He was one of the great influences in my early life, as, in his highest teaching, he should be in that of every boy. It seems almost the basest of treason to write this essay, and I would still have every youth read his Emerson. But what of America? What of the hope and the illusion? A century has passed. Is no one to arise who will fuse them both in some larger syn-thesis, and who, inspiring youth, will not be a broken reed in maturity? Are our let-ters and philosophy to remain the child until the Gorgon faces of evil, disaster, and death freeze our own unlined ones into eternal stone? Is it well that the out-standing figure in American letters should be one whose influence diminishes in proportion as the minds of his readers grow in strength, breadth, and maturity? And, speaking generally, is this not true of Emerson? Does any man of steadily growing character, wealth of experience, and strength of mind find the significance and influence of Emerson for him grow-ing as the years pass? Does he turn to him more and more for counsel, help, or solace?

There is but one answer, I think, and that is negative. Unlike the truly great, the influence of Emerson shrinks for most of us as we ourselves develop. May the cause not lie in the two flaws I have pointed out, flaws in the man as in his doctrine in spite of the serene nobility of so much of his life? If with all his wide and infinitely varied reading, noted in his *Journals,* we find his culture a bit thin and puerile, is it not because he himself trusted too much to that theory of spontaneity, of the "spontaneous glance," rather than to the harder processes of scholarship and thinking-through coherently; and if we find him lacking in depth and virility, is it not because he allowed himself to become a victim to that vast American optimism with its refusal to recognize and wrestle with the problem of evil? One turns to Aeschylus and reads:

> . . . affliction knows no rest,
> But rolls from breast to breast its vagrant
> tide.

One does not need to be a pessimist, merely human, to find here the deeper and more authentic note.

If Emerson is still the outstanding figure in American letters, is that not the equivalent of saying that America a century after the *Essays* appeared has not yet grown to mental maturity, and that the gospel it preaches is inspiring only for unformed adolescence—of whatever age —without having risen to a comprehension of the problems of maturity? In Europe, the past has bequeathed not only a wealth of art, but a legacy of evil borne and sorrow felt. Perhaps American letters, like American men, will not grow beyond the simple optimism and, in one aspect, the shallow doctrine of Emerson until they too shall have suffered and sorrowed. Emerson, in his weakness as in his strength, is American through and through. He could have been the product, in his entirety, of no other land, and that land will not outgrow him until it has some day passed through the fires of a suffering unfelt by him and as yet escaped by it.

Henry David Thoreau

The Right of Dissent

I heartily accept the motto—"That government is best which governs least"; and I should like to see it acted up to more rapidly and systematically. Carried out, it finally amounts to this, which also I believe—"That government is best which governs not at all"; and when men are prepared for it, that will be the kind of government which they will have.

From *The Works of Thoreau*, Henry S. Canby, ed. (Boston: Houghton Mifflin Company, 1937), omitting footnotes except where necessary for understanding with permission of the publisher, pp. 789–808.

Government is at best but an expedient; but most governments are usually, and all governments are sometimes, inexpedient. The objections which have been brought against a standing army, and they are many and weighty, and deserve to prevail, may also at last be brought against a standing government. The standing army is only an arm of the standing government. The government itself, which is only the mode which the people have chosen to execute their will, is equally liable to be abused and perverted before the people can act through it. Witness the present Mexican war, the work of comparatively a few individuals using the standing government as their tool; for, in the outset, the people would not have consented to this measure.

This American government—what is it but a tradition, though a recent one, endeavoring to transmit itself unimpaired to posterity, but each instant losing some of its integrity? It has not the vitality and force of a single living man; for a single man can bend it to his will. It is a sort of wooden gun to the people themselves. But it is not the less necessary for this; for the people must have some complicated machinery or other, and hear its din, to satisfy that idea of government which they have. Governments show thus how successfully men can be imposed on, even impose on themselves, for their own advantage. It is excellent, we must all allow. Yet this government never of itself furthered any enterprise, but by the alacrity with which it got out of its way. *It* does not keep the country free. *It* does not settle the West. *It* does not educate. The character inherent in the American people has done all that has been accomplished; and it would have done somewhat more, if the government had not sometimes got in its way. For government is an expedient by which men would fain succeed in letting one another alone; and, as has been said, when it is most expedient, the governed are most let alone by it. Trade and commerce, if they were not made of India-rubber, would never manage to bounce over the obstacles which legislators are continually putting in their way; and, if one were to judge these men wholly by the effects of their actions and not partly by their intentions, they would deserve to be classed and punished with those mischievous persons who put obstructions on the railroads.

But, to speak practically and as a citizen, unlike those who call themselves no-government men, I ask for, not at once no government, but *at once* a better government. Let every man make known

what kind of government would command his respect, and that will be one step toward obtaining it.

After all, the practical reason why, when the power is once in the hands of the people, a majority are permitted, and for a long period continue, to rule is not because they are most likely to be in the right, nor because this seems fairest to the minority, but because they are physically the strongest. But a government in which the majority rule in all cases cannot be based on justice, even as far as men understand it. Can there not be a government in which majorities do not virtually decide right and wrong, but conscience?—in which majorities decide only those questions to which the rule of expediency is applicable? Must the citizen ever for a moment, or in the least degree, resign his conscience to the legislator? Why has every man a conscience, then? I think that we should be men first, and subjects afterward. It is not desirable to cultivate a respect for the law, so much as for the right. The only obligation which I have a right to assume is to do at any time what I think right. It is truly enough said, that a corporation has no conscience; but a corporation of conscientious men is a corporation *with* a conscience. Law never made men a whit more just; and, by means of their respect for it, even the well-disposed are daily made the agents of injustice. A common and natural result of an undue respect for law is, that you may see a file of soldiers, colonel, captain, corporal, privates, powder-monkeys, and all, marching in admirable order over hill and dale to the wars, against their wills, ay, against their common sense and consciences, which makes it very steep marching indeed, and produces a palpitation of the heart. They have no doubt that it is a damnable business in which they are concerned; they are all peaceably inclined. Now, what are they? Men at all? or small movable forts and magazines, at the service of some unscrupulous man in power?

Visit the Navy-Yard, and behold a marine, such a man as an American government can make, or such as it can make a man with its black arts—a mere shadow and reminiscence of humanity, a man laid out alive and standing, and already, as one may say, buried under arms with funeral accompaniments, though it may be—

> Not a drum was heard, not a funeral note,
> As his corse to the rampart we hurried;
> Not a soldier discharged his farewell shot
> O'er the grave where our hero we
>   buried.

The mass of men serve the state thus, not as men mainly, but as machines, with their bodies. They are the standing army, and the militia, jailers, constables, *posse comitatus,* etc. In most cases there is no free exercise whatever of the judgment or of the moral sense; but they put themselves on a level with wood and earth and stones; and wooden men can perhaps be manufactured that will serve the purpose as well. Such command no more respect than men of straw or a lump of dirt. They have the same sort of worth only as horses and dogs. Yet such as these even are commonly esteemed good citizens. Others—as most legislators, politicians, lawyers, ministers, and officeholders—serve the state chiefly with their heads; and, as they rarely make any moral distinctions, they are as likely to serve the Devil, without *intending* it, as God. A very few, as heroes, patriots, martyrs, reformers in the great sense, and *men,* serve the state with their consciences also, and so necessarily resist it for the most part; and they are commonly treated as enemies by it. A wise man will only be useful as a man, and will not submit to be "clay," and "stop a hole to keep the wind away," but leave that office to his dust at least:

> I am too high-born to be propertied,
> To be a secondary at control,
> Or useful serving-man and instrument
> To any sovereign state throughout the
>   world.

He who gives himself entirely to his fellow-men appears to them useless and selfish; but he who gives himself partially to them is pronounced a benefactor and philanthropist.

How does it become a man to behave toward this American government today? I answer, that he cannot without disgrace be associated with it. I cannot for an instant recognize that political organization as *my* government which is the *slave's* government also.

All men recognize the right of revolution; that is, the right to refuse allegiance to, and to resist, the government, when its tyranny or its inefficiency are great and unendurable. But almost all say that such is not the case now. But such was the case, they think, in the Revolution of '75. If one were to tell me that this was a bad government because it taxed certain foreign commodities brought to its ports, it is most probably that I should not make an ado about it, for I can do without them. All machines have their friction; and possibly this does enough good to counterbalance the evil. At any rate, it is a great evil to make a stir about it. But when the friction comes to have its machine, and oppression and robbery are organized, I say, let us not have such a machine any longer. In other words, when a sixth of the population of a nation which has undertaken to be the refuge of liberty are slaves, and a whole country is unjustly overrun and conquered by a foreign army, and subjected to military law, I think that it is not too soon for honest men to rebel and revolutionize. What makes this duty the more urgent is the fact that the country so overrun is not our own, but ours is the invading army. . . .

Practically speaking, the opponents to a reform in Massachusetts are not a hundred thousand politicians at the South, but a hundred thousand merchants and farmers here, who are more interested in commerce and agriculture than they are in humanity, and are not prepared to do justice to the slave and to Mexico, *cost what it may.* I quarrel not with far-off foes, but with those who, near at home, cooperate with, and do the bidding of, those far away, and without whom the latter would be harmless. We are accustomed to say, that the mass of men are unprepared; but improvement is slow, because the few are not materially wiser or better than the many. It is not so important that many should be as good as you, as that there be some absolute goodness somewhere; for that will leaven the whole lump. There are thousands who are *in opinion* opposed to slavery and to the war, who yet in effect do nothing to put an end to them; who, esteeming themselves children of Washington and Franklin, sit down with the hands in their pockets, and say that they know not what to do, and do nothing; who even postpone the question of freedom to the question of free-trade, and quietly read the prices-current along with the latest advices from Mexico, after dinner, and, it may be, fall asleep over them both. What is the price-current of an honest man and patriot today? They hesitate, and they regret, and sometimes they petition; but they do nothing in earnest and with effect. They will wait, well disposed, for others to remedy the evil, that they may no longer have it to regret. At most, they give only a cheap vote, and a feeble countenance and God-speed to the right, as it goes by them. There are nine hundred and ninety-nine patrons of virtue to one virtuous man. But it is easier to deal with the real possessor of a thing than with the temporary guardian of it.

All voting is a sort of gaming, like checkers or backgammon, with a slight moral tinge to it, a playing with right and wrong, with moral questions; and betting naturally accompanies it. The character of the voters is not staked. I cast my vote, perchance, as I think right; but I am not vitally concerned that that right should prevail. I am willing to leave it to the majority. Its obligation, therefore, never exceeds that of expediency.

Even voting *for the right* is *doing* nothing for it. It is only expressing to men feebly your desire that it should prevail. A wise man will not leave the right to the mercy of chance, nor wish it to prevail through the power of the majority. There is but little virtue in the action of masses of men. When the majority shall at length vote for the abolition of slavery, it will be because they are indifferent to slavery, or because there is but little slavery left to be abolished by their vote. *They* will then be the only slaves. Only *his* vote can hasten the abolition of slavery who asserts his own freedom by his vote.

I hear of a convention to be held at Baltimore, or elsewhere, for the selection of a candidate for the Presidency, made up chiefly of editors, and men who are politicians by profession; but I think, what is it to any independent, intelligent, and respectable man what decision they may come to? Shall we not have the advantage of his wisdom and honesty, nevertheless? Can we not count upon some independent votes? Are there not many individuals in the country who do not attend conventions? But no: I find that the respectable man, so called, has immediately drifted from his position, and despairs of his country, when his country has more reason to despair of him. He forthwith adopts one of the candidates thus selected as the only *available* one, thus proving that he is himself *available* for any purposes of the demagogue. His vote is of no more worth than that of any unprincipled foreigner or hireling native, who may have been bought. O for a man who is a *man,* and, as my neighbor says, has a bone in his back which you cannot pass your hand through! Our statistics are at fault: the population has been returned too large. How many *men* are there to a square thousand miles in this country? Hardly one. Does not America offer any inducement for men to settle here? The American has dwindled into an Odd Fellow—one who may be known by the development of his organ of gregariousness, and a manifest lack of intellect and cheerful self-reliance; whose first and chief concern, on coming into the world, is to see that the Alms-houses are in good repair; and, before yet he has lawfully donned the virile garb, to collect a fund for the support of the widows and orphans that may be; who, in short, ventures to live only by the aid of the Mutual Insurance company, which has promised to bury him decently.

It is not a man's duty, as a matter of course, to devote himself to the eradication of any, even the most enormous wrong; he may still properly have other concerns to engage him; but it is his duty, at least, to wash his hands of it, and, if he gives it no thought longer, not to give it practically his support. If I devote myself to other pursuits and contemplations, I must first see, at least, that I do not pursue them sitting upon another man's shoulders. I must get off him first, that he may pursue his contemplations too. See what gross inconsistency is tolerated. I have heard some of my townsmen say, "I should like to have them order me out to help put down an insurrection of the slaves, or to march to Mexico;—see if I would go;" and yet these very men have each, directly by their allegiance, and so indirectly, at least, by their money, furnished a substitute. The soldier is applauded who refuses to serve in an unjust war by those who do not refuse to sustain the unjust government which makes the war; is applauded by those whose own act and authority he disregards and sets at naught; as if the state were penitent to that degree that it hired one to scourge it while it sinned, but not to that degree that it left off sinning for a moment. Thus, under the name of Order and Civil Government, we are all made at last to pay homage to and support our own meanness. After the first blush of sin comes its indifference; and from immoral it becomes, as it were *un*moral, and not quite unnecessary to that life which we have made.

The broadest and most prevalent error requires the most disinterested virtue to sustain it. The slight reproach to which the virtue of patriotism is commonly liable, the noble are most likely to incur. Those who, while they disapprove of the character and measures of a government, yield to it their allegiance and support are undoubtedly its most conscientious supporters, and so frequently the most serious obstacles to reform. Some are petitioning the State to dissolve the Union, to disregard the requisitions of the President. Why do they not dissolve it themselves—the union between themselves and the State—and refuse to pay their quota into its treasury? Do not they stand in the same relation to the State that the State does to the Union? And have not the same reasons prevented the State from resisting the Union which have prevented them from resisting the State?

How can a man be satisfied to entertain an opinion merely, and enjoy *it?* Is there any enjoyment in it, if his opinion is that he is aggrieved? If you are cheated out of a single dollar by your neighbor, you do not rest satisfied with knowing that you are cheated, or with saying that you are cheated, or even with petitioning him to pay you your due; but you take effectual steps at once to obtain the full amount, and see that you are never cheated again. Action from principle, the perception and the performance of right, changes things and relations; it is essentially revolutionary, and does not consist wholly with anything which was. It not only divides States and churches, it divides families; ay, it divides the *individual,* separating the diabolical in him from the divine.

Unjust laws exist: shall we be content to obey them, or shall we endeavor to amend them, and obey them until we have succeeded, or shall we transgress them at once? Men generally, under such a government as this, think that they ought to wait until they have persuaded the majority to alter them. They think that, if they should resist, the remedy would be worse than the evil. But it is the fault of the government itself that the remedy *is* worse than the evil. *It* makes it worse. Why is it not more apt to anticipate and provide for reform? Why does it not cherish its wise minority? Why does it cry and resist before it is hurt? Why does it not encourage its citizens to be on the alert to point out its faults, and *do* better than it would have them? Why does it always crucify Christ, and excommunicate Copernicus and Luther, and pronounce Washington and Franklin rebels?

One would think, that a deliberate and practical denial of its authority was the only offense never contemplated by government; else, why has it not assigned its definite, its suitable and proportionate penalty? If a man who has no property refuses but once to earn nine shillings for the State, he is put in prison for a period unlimited by any law that I know, and determined only by the discretion of those who placed him there; but if he should steal ninety times nine shillings from the State, he is soon permitted to go at large again.

If the injustice is part of the necessary friction of the machine of government, let it go, let it go: perchance it will wear smooth—certainly the machine will wear out. If the injustice has a spring, or a pulley, or a rope, or a crank, exclusively for itself, then perhaps you may consider whether the remedy will not be worse than the evil; but if it is of such a nature that it requires you to be the agent of injustice to another, then, I say, break the law. Let your life be a counter friction to stop the machine. What I have to do is to see, at any rate, that I do not lend myself to the wrong which I condemn.

As for adopting the ways which the State has provided for remedying the evil, I know not of such ways. They take too much time, and a man's life will be gone. I have other affairs to attend to. I came into this world, not chiefly to make this a good place to live in, but to live in it, be it good or bad. A man has not everything to do, but something; and because he cannot do *everything*, it is not necessary that he should do *something* wrong. It is not my business to be petitioning the Governor or the Legislature any more than it is theirs to petition me; and if they should not hear my petition, what should I do then? But in this case the State has provided no way: its very Constitution is the evil. This may seem to be harsh and stubborn and inconciliatory; but it is to treat with the utmost kindness and consideration the only spirit that can appreciate or deserve it. So is all change for the better, like birth and death, which convulse the body.

I do not hesitate to say, that those who call themselves Abolitionists should at once effectually withdraw their support, both in person and property, from the government of Massachusetts, and not wait till they constitute a majority of one, before they suffer the right to prevail through them. I think that it is enough if they have God on their side, without waiting for that other one. Moreover, any man more right than his neighbors constitutes a majority of one already.

I meet this American government, or its representative the State government, directly, and face to face, once a year—no more—in the person of its taxgatherers; this is the only mode in which a man situated as I am necessarily meets it; and it then says distinctly, Recognize me; and the simplest, the most effectual, and, in the present posture of affairs, the indispensablest mode of treating with it on this head, of expressing your little satisfaction with and love for it, is to deny it then. My civil neighbor, the taxgatherer, is the very man I have to deal with—for it is, after all, with men and not with parchment that I quarrel—and he has voluntarily chosen to be an agent of the government. How shall he ever know well what he is and does as an officer of the government, or as a man, until he is obliged to consider whether he shall treat me, his neighbor, for whom he has respect, as a neighbor and well-disposed man, or as a maniac and disturber of the peace, and see if he can get over this obstruction to his neighborliness without a ruder and more impetuous thought or speech corresponding with his action. I know this well, that if one thousand, if one hundred, if ten men whom I could name—if ten *honest* men only—ay, if *one* HONEST man, in this State of Massachusetts, *ceasing to hold slaves,* were actually to withdraw from this copartnership, and be locked up in the county jail therefor, it would be the abolition of slavery in America. For it matters not how small the beginning may seem to be: what is once well done is done forever. But we love better to talk about it: that we say is our mission. Reform keeps many scores of newspapers in its service, but not one man. If my esteemed neighbor, the State's ambassador, who will devote his days to the settlement of the question of human rights in the Council Chamber, instead of being threatened with the prisons of Carolina, were to sit down the prisoner of Massachusetts, that State which is so anxious to foist the sin of slavery upon her sister—though at present she can discover only an act of inhospitality to be the ground of a quarrel with her—the Legislature would not wholly waive the subject the following winter.

Under a government which imprisons any unjustly, the true place for a just man is also a prison. The proper place today, the only place which Massachusetts has provided for her freer and less desponding spirits, is in her prisons, to be put out and locked out of the State by her own act, as they have already put themselves out by their principles. It is there that the fugitive slave, and the Mexican prisoner on parole, and the Indian come to plead the wrongs of his race should find them; on that separate, but more free and honorable ground, where the State places those who are not *with* her, but *against* her—the only house in a slave State in which a free man can abide with honor. If any think that their influence would be lost there, and their voices no longer afflict the ear of the State, that they would not be as an enemy within its walls, they do not know by how much truth is stronger than error, nor how much more eloquently and effectively he can combat injustice who has experienced a little in his own person. Cast your whole vote, not a strip of paper merely, but your whole influence. A minority is powerless while it conforms to the majority; it is not even a minority then; but it is irresistible when it clogs by its whole weight. If the alternative is to keep all just men in prison or give up war and slavery, the State will not hesitate which to choose. If a thousand men were not to pay their tax-bills this year, that would not be a violent and bloody measure, as it would be to pay them, and enable the State to commit violence and shed innocent blood. This is, in fact, the definition of a peaceable revolution, if any such is possible. If the tax-gatherer or any other public officer, asks me, as one has done, "But what shall I do?" my answer is, "If you really wish to do anything, resign your office." When the subject has refused allegiance, and the officer has resigned his office, then the revolution is accomplished. But even suppose blood should flow. Is there not a sort of blood shed when the conscience is wounded? Through this wound a man's real manhood and immortality flow out, and he bleeds to an everlasting death. I see this blood flowing now.

I have contemplated the imprisonment of the offender, rather than the seizure of his goods—though both will serve the same purpose—because they who assert the purest right, and consequently are most dangerous to a corrupt State, commonly have not spent much time in accumulating property. To such the State renders comparatively small service, and a slight tax is wont to appear exorbitant, particularly if they are obliged to earn it by special labor with their hands. If there were one who lived wholly without the use of money, the State itself would hesitate to demand it of him. But the rich man—not to make any invidious comparison—is always sold to the institution which makes him rich. Absolutely speaking, the more money, the less virtue; for money comes between a man and his objects, and obtains them for him; and it was certainly no great virtue to obtain it. It puts to rest many questions which he would otherwise be taxed to answer; while the only new question which it puts is the hard but superfluous one, how to spend it. Thus his moral ground is taken from under his feet. The opportunities of living are diminished in proportion as what are called the "means" are increased. The best thing a man can do for his culture when he is rich is to endeavor to carry out those schemes which he entertained when he was poor. Christ answered the Herodians according to their condition. "Show me the tribute-money," said he—and one took a penny out of his pocket;—if you use money which has the image of Caesar on it, and which he has made current and valuable, that is, *if you are men of the State,* and gladly enjoy the advantages of Caesar's government, then pay him back some of his own when he demands it. "Render therefore to Caesar that which is Caesar's, and to God those things which are God's"—leaving them no wiser than before as to which was which; for they did not wish to know. . . . Confucius said: "If a state is governed by the principles of reason, poverty and misery are subjects of shame; if a state is not governed by the principles of reason, riches and honors are the subjects of shame." No: until I want the protection of Massachusetts to be extended to me in some distant Southern port, where my liberty is endangered, or until I am bent solely on building up an estate at home by peaceful enterprise, I can afford to refuse allegiance to Mas-

sachusetts, and her right to my property and life. It costs me less in every sense to incur the penalty of disobedience to the State than it would to obey. I should feel as if I were worth less in that case.

Some years ago, the State met me in behalf of the Church, and commanded me to pay a certain sum toward the support of a clergyman whose preaching my father attended, but never I myself. "Pay," it said, "or be locked up in the jail." I declined to pay. But, unfortunately, another man saw fit to pay it. I did not see why the schoolmaster should be taxed to support the priest, and not the priest the schoolmaster; for I was not the State's schoolmaster, but I supported myself by voluntary subscription. I did not see why the lyceum should not present its tax-bill, and have the State to back its demand, as well as the Church. However, at the request of the selectmen, I condescended to make some such statement as this in writing: "Know all men by these presents, that I, Henry Thoreau, do not wish to be regarded as a member of any incorporated society which I have not joined." This I gave to the town clerk; and he has it. The State, having thus learned that I did not wish to be regarded as a member of that church, has never made a like demand on me since; though it said that it must adhere to its original presumption that time. If I had known how to name them, I should then have signed off in detail from all the societies which I never signed onto; but I did not know where to find a complete list.

I have paid no poll-tax for six years. I was put into a jail once on this account, for one night; and, as I stood considering the walls of solid stone, two or three feet thick, the door of wood and iron, a foot thick, and the iron grating which strained the light, I could not help being struck with the foolishness of that institution which treated me as if I were mere flesh and blood and bones, to be locked up. I wondered that it should have concluded at length that this was the best use it could put me to, and had never thought to avail itself of my services in some way. I saw that, if there was a wall of stone between me and my townsmen, there was a still more difficult one to climb or break through before they could get to be as free as I was. I did not for a moment feel confined, and the walls seemed a great waste of stone and mortar. I felt as if I alone of all my townsmen had paid my tax. They plainly did not know how to treat me, but behaved like persons who were underbred. In every threat and in every compliment there was a blunder; for they thought that my chief desire was to stand the other side of that stone wall. I could not but smile to see how industriously they locked the door on my meditations, which followed them out again without let or hindrance, and *they* were really all that was dangerous. As they could not reach me, they had resolved to punish my body; just as boys, if they cannot come at some person against whom they have a spite, will abuse his dog. I saw that the State was half-witted, that it was timid as a lone woman with her silver spoons, and that it did not know its friends from its foes, and I lost all my remaining respect for it, and pitied it.

Thus the State never intentionally confronts a man's sense, intellectual or moral, but only his body, his senses. It is not armed with superior wit or honesty, but with superior strength. I was not born to be forced. I will breathe after my own fashion. Let us see who is the strongest. What force has a multitude? They only can force me who obey a higher law than I. They force me to become like themselves. I do not hear of *men* being *forced* to live this way or that by masses of men. What sort of life were that to live? When I meet a government which says to me, "Your money or your life," why should I be in haste to give it my money? It may be in a great strait, and not know what to do: I cannot help that. It must help itself;

do as I do. It is not worth the while to snivel about it. I am not responsible for the successful working of the machinery of society. I am not the son of the engineer. I perceive that, when an acorn and a chestnut fall side by side, the one does not remain inert to make way for the other, but both obey their own laws, and spring and grow and flourish as best they can, till one, perchance, overshadows and destroys the other. If a plant cannot live according to its nature, it dies; and so a man. . . .

I have never declined paying the highway tax, because I am as desirous of being a good neighbor as I am of being a bad subject; and as for supporting schools, I am doing my part to educate my fellow-countrymen now. It is for no particular item in the tax-bill that I refuse to pay it. I simply wish to refuse allegiance to the State, to withdraw and stand aloof from it effectually. . . . If I could convince myself that I have any right to be satisfied with men as they are, and to treat them accordingly, and not according, in some respects, to my requisitions and expectations of what they and I ought to be, then, like a good Mussulman and fatalists, I should endeavor to be satisfied with things as they are, and say it is the will of God. And, above all, there is this difference between resisting this and a purely brute or natural force, that I can resist this with some effect; but I cannot expect, like Orpheus, to change the nature of the rocks and trees and beasts.

I do not wish to quarrel with any man or nation. I do not wish to split hairs, to make fine distinctions, or set myself up as better than my neighbors. I seek rather, I may say, even an excuse for conforming to the laws of the land. I am but too ready to conform to them. Indeed, I have reason to suspect myself on this head; and each year, as the tax-gatherer comes round, I find myself disposed to review the acts and position of the general and State governments, and the spirit of the people, to discover a pretext for conformity.

> We must affect our country as our par-
> ents,
> And if at any time we alienate
> Our love or industry from doing it honor,
> We must respect effects and teach the soul
> Matter of conscience and religion,
> And not desire of rule or benefit.

I believe that the State will soon be able to take all my work of this sort out of my hands, and then I shall be no better a patriot than my fellow-countrymen. Seen from a lower point of view, the Constitution, with all its faults, is very good; the law and the courts are very respectable; even this State and this American government are, in many respects, very admirable, and rare things, to be thankful for, such as a great many have described them; but seen from a point of view a little higher, they are what I have described them; seen from higher still, and the highest, who shall say what they are, or that they are worth looking at or thinking of at all? . . .

The authority of government, even such as I am willing to submit to—for I will cheerfully obey those who know and can do better than I, and in many things even those who neither know nor can do so well—is still an impure one:

to be strictly just, it must have the sanction and consent of the governed. It can have no pure right over my person and property but what I concede to it. The progress from an absolute to a limited monarchy, from a limited monarchy to a democracy, is a progress toward a true respect for the individual. Even the Chinese philosopher was wise enough to regard the individual as the basis of the empire. Is a democracy, such as we know it, the last improvement possible in government? Is it not possible to take a step further towards recognizing and organizing the rights of man? There will never be a really free and enlightened State until the State comes to recognize the individual as a higher and independent power, from which all its own power and authority are derived, and treats him accordingly. I please myself with imagining a State at last which can afford to be just to all men, and to treat the individual with respect as a neighbor; which even would not think it inconsistent with its own repose if a few were to live aloof from it, not meddling with it, nor embraced by it, who fulfilled all the duties of neighbors and fellow-men. A State which bore this kind of fruit, and suffered it to drop off as fast as it ripened, would prepare the way for a still more perfect and glorious State, which also I have imagined, but not yet anywhere seen.

Heinz Eulau

A Challenge to the Politics of Thoreau

Modern American Liberalism prides itself on being critical in spirit and pragmatic in method. Yet, if it has inherited anything from a less enlightened past, it is an attitude of self-righteous indignation which can see good only as good and bad only as bad. The logic of this morality is simple enough, but its consequences are paradoxical. Instead of fostering its central value, respect for the uniqueness and personality of the individual, liberalism succumbs to an ethical absolutism. Devoid of imaginative sympathy, it cannot understand that other creeds may have values at least comparable to its own. Liberalism then tends to become an affair of mere pronunciamento and simple magic formula. It seeks to counter the truths and perfections of its enemies by furnishing its own set of truths and perfections.

This paradox is due, I believe, to liberalism's failure to come to grips with the distinction between morality and moral realism. Moral realism, as here used, does not mean knowledge of good and bad, but knowledge of the ambiguities and anomalies of living the moral life. In contrast to morality, moral realism is aware of the possibility of good or bad consequences not as polar opposites, but of the possibility of "good-and-bad" consequences as ambivalent unities. Inasmuch as liberalism derives its values from moral realism, it has to accept ambivalence as necessary.

It is symptomatic of this dilemma, if a dilemma it is, that liberalism allows itself to be challenged by the metaphysical notion of individual moral conscience as a valid axiom of democratic politics. It suggests, in part at least, why Henry David Thoreau, though standing pretty much by the wayside of American life, is as germane today as he ever was in the development of political thought. The one hundredth anniversary of his essay, "Civil Disobedience," is therefore only a fortuitous occasion to write about him. More pertinent, it seems, are the critical implications of his political ideas, absurd and inconsistent as they may appear.

It is unfair, perhaps, to judge Thoreau's political philosophy by present-day standards. Yet, it is necessary to do so because some recent interpreters have tried, in vain I think, to make Thoreau palatable to liberalism by reading their own preferences into his writings. But even if they seek to strike a balance, the end effect of their expositions is tortuous. Max Lerner, for instance, writes inaccurately, I believe, that Thoreau's individualism should be seen as part of "a rebellion against the over-socialized New England town, in which the individual was being submerged. . . . He was not so limited as to believe that the individual could by his own action stem the heedless onrush of American life, or succeed wholly in rechanneling it." Similarly, Townsend Scudder states that "though so intense

From "Wayside Challenger: Some Remarks on the Politics of Henry David Thoreau" by Heinz Eulau, *Antioch Review*, 9 (Winter 1949–1950), 509–522.

an individualist, Thoreau favored the ideal of communal living as in keeping with the spirit of America." Significantly, Lerner, Scudder as well as F. O. Mathiessen repeat, by way of evidence, a single passage from Thoreau's *Walden*—"to act collectively is according to the spirit of our institutions." The bulk of proof is, in fact, on the other side. Even Vernon Parrington, whose progressivist bias is rarely concealed, recognized that Thoreau "could not adopt the cooperative solution." Thoreau refused to join Brook Farm because, in his own words, he "would rather keep a bachelor's hall in hell than go to board in heaven."

Thoreau does not give much comfort to those who seek to prove a point. But it should be remembered that *Walden,* his most famous and widely read book, does not alone represent his ideas. For an understanding of his politics, "Civil Disobedience" as well as the less-known and less-read essays, "Slavery in Massachusetts" (1854) and "A Plea for Captain John Brown" (1859), are of at least equal importance. They leave little doubt that Thoreau's whole political philosophy was based on the theoretical premise of individual conscience as the only true criterion of what is politically right and just. It was the very perfection of his belief in the veracity of each man's soul and conscience as harbingers of some truth higher than human fiat that made inconsistency in his theory inevitable. Action from principle, he wrote in a prophetic sentence in "Civil Disobedience," "not only divides states and churches, it divides families; ay, it divides the *individual,* separating the diabolical in him from the divine." Within the short span of ten years, Thoreau, though holding to the same premise, would draw conclusions as opposite as passive resistance and violent action. Obviously, both his personality and ideas were complex. Any attempt to reduce them to simple, and hence simpleton, propositions is futile.

While the subsequent essays are signif-icant bacause they prove, better than critical argument, that "action from principle" is a politically dangerous concept, "Civil Disobedience" is the most complete theoretical statement of Thoreau's basic assumptions. Because it expounded a queer doctrine, unlikely to make much of an impression on his contemporaries, Thoreau apparently elaborated his political premise more fully in "Civil Disobedience" than in the subsequent essays.

His starting point is the half-mocking, half-serious observation that if Jefferson's motto—"that government is best which governs least"—were carried out, it would amount to "that government is best which governs not at all." Does this mean, as has been suggested, that Thoreau brought Jefferson's ideas to their logical conclusion? By no means. In placing the individual "above" the state, Jefferson attacked the autocratic state, not the democratic state which he did so much to bring about. If Thoreau went at all beyond Jefferson, it consisted in his attack on democracy. But, paradoxically, he attacked democracy not because it was strong; on the contrary, because it was weak. The American government, he wrote, "has not the vitality and force of a single living man; for a single man can bend it to his will." He refused to vote because he considered the democratic ballot an ineffective political instrument. His own contact with the government being limited to the annual *tête-à-tête* with the tax collector, his refusal to pay the poll tax loses some of its bravado. He did not really sacrifice much when he declared, somewhat grandiloquently, that he should not like to think he would ever have to rely on the protection of the state. Basically, Thoreau was the very opposite of Jefferson; he was as unpolitical as Jefferson was political. It is simply not conceivable to hear Jefferson say, as Thoreau said, "the government does not concern me much, and I shall bestow the fewest possible thoughts on it."

If Thoreau had let the matter rest at

this point, his position would have been consistent. But as if he needed to test his own propositions, he would suddenly speak "practically and as a citizen, unlike those who call themselves no-government men." And as a citizen Thoreau demanded "Not at once no government, but *at once* better government." Such a government would anticipate and provide for reform, cherish its "wise minority" and encourage its citizens "to be on the alert to point out its faults."

It appears that Thoreau could not fully discern that his metaphysical assumptions had to lead, almost necessarily, to ambiguous consequences when subjected to the test of practical politics. The essential weakness of the metaphysical premise is that it is absolutist as long as it deals with abstractions, just as it is relativistic when applied to unique and observable situations. Like his fellow idealists, Thoreau was incapable of recognizing those distinctions of degree which are politically decisive. He could not recognize them because he fell back, again and again, on the principle of individual conscience as the sole valid guide in political action. He realized only faintly that this principle was inherently deficient for political purposes, as when he said that while "all men recognize the right of revolution . . . , almost all say that such is not the case now." Individual conscience as a political principle was too obviously in conflict with the democratic principle of majority rule, even for Thoreau. But the rather dogmatic assertion, "there is but little virtue in the masses of men," was too hazardous in view of the manifest strength of the democratic faith of most men in his time. Thoreau's only way out was, once more, a paradox: "Any man more right than his neighbors constitutes a majority of one already."

Consequently, Thoreau had to postulate a (by democratic standards) curious distinction between law and right, with the explanation that one has to have faith in man, that each man can determine for himself what is right and just. Hence, no conflict is possible, so the argument goes, because law is law only if identical with right. Thoreau could not demonstrate, however, that there is, in case the majority is wrong, an objective criterion for assaying the correctness of an individual's or a minority's judgment.

He was content, therefore, with declaring war on the state in his own fashion:

> It is not a man's duty as a matter of course, to devote himself to the eradication of any, even the most enormous wrong; he may still properly have other concerns to engage him; but it is his duty, at least, to wash his hands of it, and, if he gives it no thought longer, not to give it practically his support.

Great as his hurry seemed in "Civil Disobedience," Thoreau remained, in fact, unpolitical. Actually, he did not wish to be bothered at all with the obnoxious phenomenon of slavery. He had other affairs to attend to. "I came into this world," he concluded, "not chiefly to make this a good place to live in, but to live in it, be it good or bad." Joseph Wood Krutch has aptly described this kind of reasoning as Thoreau's "sometimes desperate casuistry."

The ideas expressed in "Civil Disobedience" fell into the Walden period (1845–1847) and are, to some extent, an early reaction to Thoreau's own dim sense of failure as a recluse from society. Existence at Walden Pond was an experiment for the purpose of finding reality. But subjectively real as life at Walden may have been, to judge from his famous report, it came to be unreal, apparently, when Thoreau was forced to compare it with the objective reality of the impending Mexican War which he encountered on his almost daily visits to town. There he would see his neighbors getting ready for what seemed to him a hateful and stupid enterprise. Its effect could only be the extension of the unjust institution of slavery and of the slaveholder's power. Thoreau felt a deep personal disgrace in being associated with a government which was the slaves' government also. So deeply did he feel on the issue that he was ready to warn that "this people must cease to hold slaves, and to make war on Mexico, though it cost them their existence as a people." So great seemed the evil that there was no time to change the laws except by breaking them. Refusal to pay taxes was, in Thoreau's mind, "the definition of a peaceful revolution, if any such is possible." Otherwise, he continued, the conscience is wounded: "Through this wound a man's real manhood and immortality flow out, and he bleeds to an everlasting death. I see this blood flowing now."

All his protestations about "signing off" from human institutions to the contrary, "Civil Disobedience," in contrast to *Walden,* was a first indication of Thoreau's theoretical difficulties. It contained the seeds of its own denial, seeds which were fertilized by the untenable metaphysical premise of individual conscience as a criterion of collective action. In the very act of counseling and practicing individual resistance to and renunciation of government was implicit a growing sense of social responsibility which the hermit of Walden Pond could scarcely disclaim.

Thoreau was not, therefore, as *Walden* might suggest and some critics have said, an American exponent of the Rousseauist doctrine of the natural rights of man. His philosophy certainly lacked the liberating drive which Rousseau's individualism had in the eighteenth-century French context. Thoreau's individualism was, most interpreters agree, an inspired protest against the modern cult of progress, materialism and efficiency, with its deteriorating effect on the individual. But it was essentially out of date. Because it renounced industrialism rather than seeking to bring it under social control, Thoreau's individualism could not possibly find practical application. The moral and the morally real were at odds.

"Civil Disobedience" differed from *Walden* in another respect. *Walden* was the report of a highly personalized experience. And in spite of its persuasiveness, its almost egocentric individualism made communication difficult. Only the most liberal imagination can perceive it for what it was: namely, the attempt of a sensitive spirit to discover his own integrity and convey this discovery, not to be imitated literally—a mistake against which Thoreau himself explicitly warned, but to serve as a symbolic expression of man's need for finding his own integrity in whatever fashion seemed best. "I desire," he wrote, "that there be as many different persons in the world as possible; but I would have each one be very careful to find out and pursue *his own* way. . . ." As such, life at Walden Pond was a meaningful experiment, even though it was meaningless as a form of *social* living.

However, Thoreau's individualism was not simply, as Parrington remarked, "transcendental individualism translated into politics." His radicalism differed in more than degree from the innocuous, often opportunistic, politics of most Abolitionists. Their humanitarianism seemed all too sanguine to him. Were they not actually giving aid and comfort to the enemy by refusing to withdraw from political society altogether? In asking this question it must be admitted that Thoreau himself remained on a largely rhetorical level throughout his political life. Certainly, his refusal to pay the poll tax and being jailed for it was a frankly ephemeral episode. But he found it increasingly necessary to communicate his ideas in a manner which would leave no doubt where he stood.

There is no better index of Thoreau's need to express himself unequivocally than the changing tenor of his humor. In "Civil Disobedience" it is of the most elusive variety. It was all too self-conscious and artificial to make it deeply personal and tragic as his human condition might have warranted. He shared his cell, "the whitest, most simply furnished, and probably the neatest apartment in town," with an alleged incendiary, "a first-rate fellow and a clever man." From the cell window, he reported, "I was an involuntary spectator and auditor of whatever was done and said in the kitchen of the adjacent village inn,—a wholly new and rare experience to me. It was a closer view of my native town. I was fairly inside of it." One cannot but feel that the atmosphere of mischief so created is more literary than political.

But the more Thoreau became involved in the slavery question in later years, the more his sense of frustration grew, the more scornful and vitriolic his humor would become. In "Slavery in Massachusetts" he would direct it at his Yankee audience. The soldier who lets himself be trained to return fugitive slaves to their masters "is a fool made conspicuous by a painted coat." Judges upholding the constitutionality of slavery "are merely inspectors of a pick-lock and murderer's tool." When he reads a newspaper defending the Fugitive Slave Law, he does it "with my cuffs turned up," and hears "the gurgling of the sewer through every column." It is a paper "picked out of the public gutters, the groggery, and the brothel, harmonizing with the gospel of the Merchants' Exchange."

Humor would finally give way to blasphemy in "A Plea for Captain John Brown." Though his counsel of passive, peaceful resistance had by then been replaced by the justification of violence, Thoreau's venom was that of a man close to despair. "Away with your broad and flat churches, and your narrow and tall churches," he cried; "take a step forward, and invent a new style of out-houses. Invent a salt that will save you, and defend your nostrils." He would excoriate the politicians as "office-seekers and speech-makers, who do not so much as lay an honest egg, but wear their breasts bare upon an egg of chalk."

Thoreau's desire to be understood by his fellow citizens is equally apparent if the symbols with which he appealed to his readers in "Civil Disobedience" are compared with those in "Slavery in Massachusetts." In the earlier essay he is preoccupied with Right, Truth and Justice. It is never quite clear whether he regarded passive resistance as a virtuous political goal, an end in itself, or whether he thought of it as the most effective means to abolish slavery. If the latter, he obscured his thinking pretty successfully. While a superb exposition of nonviolent resistance as a political instrument, the language used in "Civil Disobedience" does not indicate that Thoreau was particularly anxious to protest against the evil of slavery.

Indeed, it was not till the surrender by Massachusetts of the fugitive Negro Thomas Sims in 1851, an event which struck him as a "moral earthquake," and again of the Negro Anthony Burns in 1854, that Thoreau's anger was sufficiently aroused to make him abandon the convenient obscurantisms of the political idealists. No longer was the slavery issue a remote question which only incidentally annoyed him. His own state, Massachusetts, had violated a sacred trust when it returned these Negroes into slavery. Thoreau would now resort to patriotic sentiments in order to make his plea effective. "Every man in Massachusetts capable of the sentiment of patriotism," he wrote, must have had his own experience of "having suffered a vast and indefinite loss." And what was this loss which yesterday's anarchist felt so surprisingly? "At last it occurred to me that what I had lost was a country. . . . The remembrance of my country spoils my walk. My thoughts are murder to the State, and involuntarily go plotting against her."

This does not mean, of course, that Thoreau had abandoned his deep conviction that individual conscience is the safest guide in human affairs. It only means that, as time went on and the demands of politics required greater sophistication, Thoreau became somewhat more realistic. It was simply a matter of tactics if, as in "Slavery in Massachusetts," he identified individual conscience with the "laws of humanity," or, as in "A Plea for Captain John Brown," with "respect for the Constitution." Here he used catchphrases which could be more easily grasped by the average citizen than metaphysical abstractions. But his attempt to make out of John Brown "a transcendentalist above all, a man of ideas and principles," did not quite come off. It merely showed that Thoreau knew as little about Brown as about slavery, and that he was projecting his metaphysical notions on a situation which hardly called for them.

As has been mentioned, in spite of the apparent urgency of his argument in "Civil Disobedience," Thoreau had experienced the Mexican War and its implications for the slavery question as a fairly remote conflict. But with the passage of the Fugitive Slave Law in 1850 it became evident, even to a political hermit like Thoreau, that continued detachment from affairs of state would not avert the threat to his personal liberty which the law implied. The state, he now discovered, "has fatally interfered with my lawful business." "Slavery in Massachusetts" was, therefore, as outspoken a piece of indignation as "Civil Disobedience" had been casual. He bade farewell to the pipedream of a state which would permit a few people, who so desired, to live aloof from it, "not meddling with it, nor embraced by it." He had never respected the government, he said, but "I had foolishly thought that I might manage to live here, minding my private affairs, and forget it." Thoreau now dropped the role of the bohemian anarchist who could wash his hands of society's "dirty institutions," as he had called them in *Walden*. Before, he admitted, he had dwelt in the

illusion that "my life passed somewhere only *between* heaven and hell, but now I cannot persuade myself that I do not dwell *wholly* within hell."

Moreover, his rebellion was no longer a matter of denials alone. He still fulminated against majority rule, but a new line of thought occupied him. It would be too simple to say that a democratic faith emerged, but Thoreau's attack on existing institutions is certainly not that of the vociferous anti-democrat of "Civil Disobedience." As against judges deciding questions involving slaves, Thoreau would now "much rather trust the sentiment of the people. In their vote you would get something of value, at least, however small." It was no longer the state in the abstract, but the State of Massachusetts in the concrete which he attacked. He would recognize the possibility of a government which is worth fighting for. "Show me a free state, and a court truly of justice, and I will fight for them, if need be . . .," he proclaimed; "it is not an era of repose. We have used up all our inherited freedom. If we would save our lives, we must fight for them."

"Slavery in Massachusetts" was not a theoretical exercise in political philosophy. It concentrated its verbal fire on an evil situation. But it is indicative of Thoreau's political immaturity that he now went so far as to join the militant abolitionists in advocating the secession of Massachusetts from the union with the slave states. He was apparently quite unaware of the possibility that the consequences of such action might accentuate the evil which he sought to remedy. That is, permit slavery to continue unopposed elsewhere. In addition, he still confused what seemed to him the iniquity of law with the legal process itself. And though he spoke of breaking the law, of boycotting proslavery newspapers, of ousting ignorant politicians and seceding from the Union, it remains unclear just what specific political means Thoreau considered appropriate to achieve his objectives. He had almost given up passive resistance, but he had not completely accepted majority rule.

With all its new affirmations, "Slavery in Massachusetts" did not answer the question which is central from the point of view of political theory—whether the practicality of political concepts can be assessed by any kind of objectively rational standard. It seems that Thoreau was neither willing nor able to develop such a criterion. Not even "truth" would serve that purpose. Truth, he wrote in "Civil Disobedience," is always in harmony with herself, and is not concerned chiefly to reveal the justice that may consist with wrong-doing." In other words, the consequences of an act are separable and, indeed, must be separated from its nature. Even truth is thus reduced to being a matter of individual taste. Thoreau admitted the existence of other truths, but being altogether personal and private they did not permit contact or comparison with each other. As so many of his concepts, his truth is paradoxical. His moral absolutism, being so individualized, becomes relativistic. It is not surprising to find, therefore, that Thoreau envisaged various hierarchial levels of political evaluation. "Seen from a lower point of view," he wrote, "the Constitution, with all its faults, is very good; the law and the courts are very respectable; even this State and this American government are, in many respects, very admirable, and rare things, to be thankful for, such as a great many have described them; but seen from a point of view a little higher, they are what I have described them; seen from a higher still, and the highest, who shall say what they are, or that they are worth looking at or thinking of at all?"

Paradox may serve the purpose of literary construction. In political theory it is self-defeating. Inasmuch as Thoreau's anarchism followed from the doctrine of the individual's duty to his conscience alone, it should lead to at least some mutual tolerance as an avenue to human cooperation. But Thoreau would carry the matter to absurdity. In a sentence remindful of the vicarious a-moralism of the later social Darwinians he wrote:

> I am not responsible for the successful working of the machinery of society. . . . I perceive that, when an acorn and a chestnut fall side by side, the one does not remain inert to make way for the other, but both obey their own laws, and spring and grow and flourish as best they can, till one, perchance, overshadows and destroys the other. If a plant cannot live according to its nature, it dies; and so a man.

It is quite clear that Thoreau's mind was totally closed to the democratic conception of politics as a never-ending process of compromise and adjustment. As a matter of fact, if the politics of "action from principle," with its insistence on ends, is shorn of metaphysics, it appears as little more than the old and familiar doctrine that the end justifies the means. Comparison of "Civil Disobedience" and "A Plea for Captain John Brown" underlines the fact that in Thoreau's mind both passive resistance and violent action were *right* if employed toward the accomplishment of ends whose truth is predicated on the complete assumption of responsibility by the individual for his acts.

Just as nonviolent resistance as an instrument of politics is proper if the state interferes with an individual's principles, so violence can be justified. Given Thoreau's moral intransigence, it is not surprising to find that he would round out his basic position by eulogizing an event which only the most rabid Abolitionists supported as politically justifiable. John Brown, Thoreau came to believe, was not only right in holding that a man has "a perfect right to interfere by force with the slaveholder, in order to rescue the slave"; but the doctrine that the end justifies the means was given explicit expression: "I shall not be forward to think him mistaken in his method who quickest succeeds to liberate the slave." The decisive question, Thoreau finally felt, was not "about the weapon, but the spirit in which you use it." And he would write in his *Journals:* "I do not wish to kill nor to be killed, but I can foresee circumstances in which both these things would be by me unavoidable."

Actually, however, "A Plea for Captain John Brown" was concerned with the slavery issue only indirectly. Thoreau undoubtedly felt its iniquity and the urgency of its solution most intensely, but his primary concern was again with justice and injustice, with principle and expediency, with truth and falsehood. "A Plea for Captain John Brown" is therefore more closely related to "Civil Disobedience" than to "Slavery in Massachusetts." It differed, however, from his first political essay in that Thoreau had abandoned his earlier quietist position. Violence was in the air. Almost everywhere in the nation men were girding themselves for the great conflict which would soon disrupt the Union. While it may have been his intention merely to bring his disagreement with the moderate Abolitionists into sharper focus by advocating violence before the peaceful alternatives had been exhausted, the end effect of "A Plea for Captain John Brown" was the admission of an inveterate moralist that violence can only be combatted by violence.

It is symptomatic of his greater sense of realism that the government did not seem weak any longer as it had in "Civil Disobedience" ten years before. "When a government puts forth its strength on the side of injustice, as ours to maintain slavery and kill the liberators of the slave," he wrote, "it reveals itself a merely brute force, or worse, a demoniacal force. It is the head of the Plug-Uglies. It is more manifest than ever that tyranny rules. I see this government to be effectually allied with France and Austria in oppressing mankind." The government, he continued, is "a semi-human tiger or ox stalking over the earth, with its heart taken out and the top of its brain shot away."

Thoreau could no longer subscribe to the quietist doctrine of "Civil Disobedience" with its counsel of escape. He fiercely excoriated all those who adhered to a nonviolent solution of social conflict. "What sort of violence is that," he now asked, "which is encouraged, not by soldiers, but by peaceable citizens, not so much by laymen as by ministers of the Gospel, not so much by the fighting sects as by the Quakers, and not so much by the Quaker men as by the Quaker women?" Here Thoreau squarely faced the question of resistance by force which modern pacifism, confronted with the infamies of totalitarian terror and violence, slave labor and concentration camps, fails to answer. Here, in essence, he returned to the age-old concept of the "just war," which modern quietists refuse to acknowledge. John Brown would "never have anything to do with any war," Thoreau intimated, "unless it were a war for liberty," expressing an opinion since challenged by competent historians.

In John Brown, Thoreau had found the man of principle whom he had anticipated in "Civil Disobedience," the man "who is a *Man,* and, as my neighbor says, has a bone in his back which you cannot pass your hand through!" That this abstract man of principle had changed from the passive resister envisaged in 1849 into the violent and very real actionist of 1859 suggests that Thoreau had become aware of the futility of peaceful disobedience as much as he was oblivious of the dangers inherent in the idea of "action from principle."

Thoreau's conversion to violence as a legitimate means in the social conflict cannot be attributed to a purely rational thought process. The fervor of his eulogy betrays its emotional content. He identified himself with Brown so much that he experienced the latter's ordeal after the disastrous incident at Harpers Ferry as a personal tragedy. "I put a piece of paper and a pencil under my pillow," he wrote, "and when I could not sleep I wrote in the dark." Brown had the stuff heroes are made of. "No doubt," Thoreau postulated, "you can get more in your market for a quart of milk than for a quart of blood, but that is not the market that heroes carry their blood to." As if he felt a sense of personal guilt about his own irresponsibility in days gone by, Thoreau expressed his admiration for Brown because he "did not wait till he was personally interfered with or thwarted in some harmless business before he gave his life to the cause of the oppressed." And it is more than obvious that Thoreau rationalized the a-moral consequences of his new departure when he stated that people at most criticized Brown's tactics and then added: "Though you may not approve of his method or his principles, recognize his magnanimity."

Significantly, too, the eulogy in defense of John Brown was not characterized by so transitory a feeling as that which attended the experience of his own imprisonment. On being released from jail after having refused to pay the poll tax, he had joined a huckleberry party in the highest hills, where "the State was nowhere to be seen." Many weeks after his passionate plea, he noted in his *Journals* that it was hard for him to see the beauty of a remarkable sunset when his mind "was filled with Captain Brown. So great a wrong as his fate implied overshadowed all beauty in the world." Bronson Alcott reported in his *Journals* that Thoreau had called on him because he thought that "someone from the North should see Gov. Wise, or write concerning Capt. Brown's character and motives, to influence the Governor in his favor."

It has not been my intention to disparage Thoreau's reputation as the outstanding American spokesman for those human values which the empty materialism of our culture so readily relegates to the limbo of sanctimonious oratory. Criticism of his political theory cannot possibly deprive Thoreau's words of that immortality with which his moral sincerity, his spiritual courage and his sense of genuine inquiry have endowed it. His ideas are living ideas for the very reason that he lived them, day in and day out. The acidity of his attack and the persistence of his independence are admired and emulated by thousands who grope for a way to withstand the seemingly invincible force of personal and social maladjustments. As his friend and earliest biographer F. H. Sanborn has said, "The haughtiness of his independence kept him from a thousand temptations that beset men of less courage and self-denial."

But I also believe that those who neglect and even deny the ambiguities and paradoxes of Thoreau's moral intransigence misunderstand the real challenge of his politics. They overlook the essential assumptions underlying his advice of civil disobedience. Hence, they are at a loss in explaining his repudiation of his own advice and his justification of violent resistance.

Thoreau's philosophy should warn us of the dilemma into which he fell and from which he could not escape because he returned time and again, to individual conscience as the "ultimate reality." His thought was full of ambiguity and paradox, and he did not realize sufficiently how contradictory and, in fact, dangerous the moral can be. Granted, he had no fear of consequences in disregarding the law. But, as Pascal observed, "he who would act the angel acts the brute." There is no virtue in accepting the consequences of an act because the premise from which they flow might be essentially good. Thoreau's politics suggests that it is a small step, indeed, from insistence on the principle of morality to insistence on the principle of expediency.

Select Bibliography for Problem 6

Bailey, Thomas A., ed. *The American Spirit: United States History as Seen by Contemporaries,* 2d ed. Boston: D. C. Heath & Company, 1963, pp. 344–351.

Baldwin, Leland D., ed. *Ideas in Action: Documentary and Interpretive Readings in American History,* Vol. 1, to 1877. New York: Van Nostrand Reinhold Company, 1968, pp. 326–333.

Baym, Nina. "Thoreau's View of Science," *Journal of the History of Ideas,* 26 (April 1965), 221–234.

Buranelli, Vincent. "Case against Thoreau," *Ethics,* 67 (July 1957), 250–268.

Detweiler, Robert. "Over Rated over Soul," *American Literature,* 36 (March 1964), 65–68.

Glick, Wendell P. "Thoreau and the Herald of Freedom," *New England Quarterly,* 22 (June 1949), 193–204.

Grob, Gerald N., and Robert N. Beck, eds. *American Ideas: Source Readings in the Intellectual History of the United States,* Vol. 1. New York: The Free Press, 1963, pp. 344–373.

Hendrick, George. "The Influence of 'Civil Disobedience' on Ghandi's 'Satyagraha,'" *New England Quarterly,* 29 (December 1956), 462–471.

Hotson, Clarence P. "Christian Critics and Mr. Emerson," *New England Quarterly,* 2 (March 1938), 29–47.

Kazin, Alfred. "Thoreau and American Power," *Atlantic,* 223 (May 1969), 60–64.

Keller, Karl. "From Christianity to Transcendentalism: A Vote on Emerson's Use of Conceit," *American Literature,* 39 (March 1967), 94–98.

Kern, Alexander C. "Emerson and Economics," *New England Quarterly,* 13 (December 1940), 678–696.

Ketcham, Ralph L. "Some Thoughts on Buranelli's Case against Thoreau," *Ethics,* 69 (April 1959), 206–208.

Nichols, Jr., Charles H. "Thoreau on the Citizen and His Government," *Phylon,* 13 (March 1952), 19–24.

Oliver, Egbert S. "Cock-a-doodle-doo! and Transcendental Hocuspocus," *New England Quarterly,* 21 (June 1948), 204–216.

Ostrander, Gilman M. "Emerson, Thoreau and John Brown," *Mississippi Valley Historical Review,* 39 (March 1953), 713–726.

Padover, Saul K. "Ralph Waldo Emerson: The Moral Voice in Politics," *Political Science Quarterly,* 74 (September 1959), 334–350.

Porte, Joel M. "Emerson, Thoreau and the Double Consciousness," *New England Quarterly,* 41 (March 1968), 40–50.

Silver, Mildred. "Emerson and the Idea of Progress," *American Literature,* 12 (March 1940), 1–19.

Whitridge, Arnold. "Emerson: A Prophet Not without Honour," *History Today,* 16 (February 1966), 77–84.

Woodring, Paul. "Was Thoreau a Hippie?" *Saturday Review,* 50 (December 16, 1967), 68.

part 7

The Nation in Crisis

chapter 20

The Revival
of Sectionalism

The Question of Slavery

WILMOT PROVISO

The Mexican War had no sooner opened in 1846 when the question of the extension of slavery into future territorial acquisitions arose on the floors of Congress. Hoping to settle the issue for all time, Representative David Wilmot of Pennsylvania drafted a bill to exclude slavery from any new territory that might be acquired from Mexico, but he soon realized that the opposition was well organized. The Wilmot Proviso finally passed the House but failed in the Senate, where proslavery forces were stronger than ever.

Among those who stepped forward to defend the southern position was the veteran lawmaker John C. Calhoun. Although advanced in years and weakened by consumption, he still possessed some of the spark and eloquence that had placed him in the forefront of southern statesmen. He argued that each of the sovereign states had a claim to the territories, that they were held in common, and that this joint claim, therefore, permitted those citizens who desired to do so to take their slaves to the territory. Because the federal government did not own the territory, but rather played the role of a joint agent entrusted with certain powers, it could not prohibit slavery.

ELECTION OF 1848

The slavery extension question was expected to dominate the presidential election of 1848, but both sides evaded it. The Democrats met at Baltimore and nominated General Lewis Cass of Michigan, a veteran of the War of 1812, while the Whigs assembled at Philadelphia to name a Mexican War hero, Zachary Taylor. At the time Taylor was a plantation and slave owner in Louisiana although he was a Virginian by birth.

The question of slavery, however, would receive due attention as a Free-Soil party—made up for the most part of "Barn-burner"[1] Democrats, the Liberty party, and Whigs—formed in Buffalo. Disgusted with the "party harmony" speeches of the other two parties, the Free-Soilers embraced the Wilmot Proviso and recruited the old political warhorse Martin Van Buren.[2]

With help from Van Buren, who attracted valuable Cass votes in the state of New York, "Old Rough and Ready" Taylor won the election with 163 electoral votes. Cass pulled 127 while Van

---

[1] So named by the opposition, who said that because of their radical ways they would burn the barn to get rid of the rats.

[2] The Free-Soilers selected Charles Francis Adams of Massachusetts for Vice-President; the Whigs, Millard Fillmore of New York; and the Democrats, William O. Butler of Kentucky.

Buren failed to get on the board, despite a stirring slogan of "free soil, free speech, free labor and free men."

COMPROMISE OF 1850

As mid-century approached, feelings and debates over the question of slavery became more intense. Southerners began to view the articles of the Wilmot Proviso as outright aggression, and some saw it as a danger to the very Union itself. At this point the stage was set once again for the appearance of the "Great Compromiser," Henry Clay. Accordingly, in January 1850 he introduced in the Senate a series of resolutions in which he proposed, among other things, that California be admitted to the Union as a free state; that territories be established with no decision on slavery; that a fugitive slave law be passed; that Texas be paid for her claim in New Mexico; and that the federal government admit that it had no authority to abolish slavery in the District of Columbia, but that slave trade should be terminated for all time.

All through the hot summer months of 1850 Clay's resolutions were debated in Congress, and the outcome was in doubt most of the way. Speakers usually aligned themselves with one of the three groups that emerged at the beginning of the great debates. Supporting Clay's resolutions and popular sovereignty in particular were the strong voices of Stephen A. Douglas and Daniel Webster; a second group led by William H. Seward, Salmon P. Chase, and Charles Sumner called for complete prohibition of slavery in new territories. A third group, sometimes alluded to as extremists, were suspicious of the compromise and questioned the power of Congress to bar slavery from federal territories. Its leaders included John C. Calhoun, Jefferson Davis, and Robert B. Rhett.

It has been reported that the debates reached their pinnacle in the speeches of Clay, Calhoun, Webster, and Seward. Too weak to deliver his speech, Calhoun had it read to Congress. It warned of impending dangers to the Union should the balance of power between the North and South not be preserved. Moreover, he called for sectional understanding of differences and interests and, finally, for the national government to protect slavery. Webster answered with his famous "Seventh of March" speech, in which he suggested that no law was necessary to exclude slavery from new territories because it was already prohibited by a law superior to legislative enactment—the law of nature.

Some scholars of the subject claim that Seward made the most coherent and eloquent speech of the debates. Reminding the nation that "there is a higher law than the Constitution which regulates our authority," he called for an end to the extension of slavery. The forces of economy and even the very forces of civilization, he suggested, were fighting the battles of freedom.

Finally, in September, after the death of President Taylor,[3] the last of the resolutions passed through Congress, thus rewarding Clay for his tireless efforts. The provisions were much the same as the originals: they fixed the boundary between Texas and New Mexico and paid the former $10 million, California was admitted as a free state, and New Mexico and Utah were awarded territorial governments with the question of slavery to be tied to "popular sovereignty." An article was also included that provided for the arrest and return of fugitive slaves.

[3] It has been observed that Taylor and Clay frequently disagreed on major issues. Taylor desired the settlement of the California and New Mexico question before considering anything else and, therefore, opposed the compromise. Taylor died on Tuesday, July 9, 1850, of what has been variously reported as typhoid fever, cholera morbus, and/or acute gastroenteritis—the inflammation of the lining membrane of the stomach and intestines. His successor, Millard Fillmore, was somewhat more friendly toward the resolutions.

FUGITIVE SLAVE LAW

Of all the provisions, the one most distasteful to the North was the last—the fugitive slave law. By its provisions a runaway black slave had no right to a trial by jury and could offer no evidence in his own behalf. Worse still he might be tried before a commissioner, instead of a court, who acted as judge and jury. In time this law did more than any other act to intensify northern hatred toward the "peculiar institution" in the South. Admittedly, the number of slaves who made their way to the North was small; and most of these were returned; the South, nevertheless, saw the increasing northern interference with the capture of runaways as a breach of constitutional guarantees. Northern abolitionists not only hid runaway slaves,[4] but they mobbed and frequently prosecuted slaveholders for false arrests or kidnapping. Some attempts at rescuing fugitive slaves led to riots and the loss of life as evinced by the James Hamlet episode in New York City in 1850 and the Shadrach and Thomas Sims riot in Boston in 1851.

The most penetrating and influential book on the subject of runaway slaves appeared in 1851 under the title of *Uncle Tom's Cabin*. Using the news media to full advantage, the authoress Harriet Beecher Stowe serialized much of the book in the leading antislavery newspaper, the *National Era*. Her book became a best seller during the 1850s.

There were no sharp contrasting issues in the presidential election of 1852, but the result was decisive. The Democrats met at Baltimore and nominated Franklin Pierce of New Hampshire and William R. King of Alabama, while the Whigs picked General Winfield Scott of Louisiana and William A. Graham of South Carolina at their convention in the same city. Both parties embraced the Compromise of 1850, but some of the northern Whigs turned against their party when it gave tacit approval of the fugitive slave law, and thus the election went to Pierce and the Democrats by a landslide electoral vote of 254 to 42. It reportedly was the death of the Whig party. The Free-Soilers also nominated candidates on an antislavery ticket, but their showing was insignificant.

KANSAS-NEBRASKA ACT

The last hopes of an amicable settlement of the lingering and painful slavery question began to fade in 1854, when Senator Stephen A. Douglas of Illinois proposed that Congress authorize free territorial governments for Kansas and Nebraska since both lay north of 36° 30' (see Missouri Compromise). It has been suggested that Douglas and his friends had land speculation in mind when he introduced the bill; that considerable profits might be realized when the planned transcontinental railroad passed through the region. The South, however, saw the consequences of the bill with regard to slavery and railroad building and therefore opposed organizing any new territory that might jeopardize their slave power in Congress and their plans for a southern transcontinental route; whereupon Douglas extended a concession to the South by offering to support the repeal of the Missouri Compromise, which had barred slavery from much of the Louisiana Territory, and to help open the door for the principle of nonintervention, or "popular sovereignty."

In May 1856, after long and heated debates, the Kansas-Nebraska Act along with the repeal of the Missouri Com-

---

[4] Runaway slaves were not without help in seeking freedom. As early as 1830 a unique system, which became known as the "Underground Railroad," provided hiding places and carefully charted routes for the fugitive slaves as they negotiated the dangerous journey to the North. Reverend Theodore Parker and Harriet Tubman, a runaway slave, provided much of the leadership for this organization, which between 1830 and 1860 reportedly rescued as many as 50,000 slaves.

promise passed through the last hurdles of Congress. Reaction in the North was immediate and dramatic. Abolitionists bitterly denounced the bill along with northern congressmen who voted for it, while an effigy of Douglas was burned in almost every hamlet.

BIRTH OF THE REPUBLICAN PARTY

Out of this controversy emerged a new political faction in the North. Meeting at a state convention in Michigan in July of 1854, disillusioned antislavery elements, including Free-Soilers and Whigs, united under the name of the Republican party. Antislavery groups in other states soon followed the example set by the Michigan convention, and thus the first national Republican party became a reality.

Kansas, meanwhile, was rushing headlong into open conflict. The proslavery forces had captured the legislature and had sent one of their members to Congress in Washington. The Free-Soilers, however, were not to be quieted. Charging the party in power with fraud and intimidation—with bringing proslavery residents from Missouri across the border to vote—the Free-Soilers refused to recognize the new government. In fact, they decided to form a government of their own at Topeka, where they met and drew up a constitution, elected officers, and applied for admission to the Union. Recognition, however, was not forthcoming for this extralegal body.

ANARCHY IN KANSAS

By 1856 Kansas was in a state of anarchy. Lawrence was burned, and other towns were sacked as one side tried to outdo the other. In thirteen months of unchecked violence, more than 200 people were killed, and property valued at over $2 million was destroyed.

The violence was not confined to Kansas. After delivering a blistering speech on the "Crime against Kansas," which was liberally sprinkled with insults to the South and to South Carolina in particular, Senator Charles Sumner of Massachusetts was surprised in his office by enraged Representative Preston S. Brooks of South Carolina, who beat him unconscious with a walking cane. Both men were returned to Congress by their respective states.

ELECTION OF 1856

The presidential election of 1856 emerged with three parties and an issue that could not be swept under the rug as so often had been done before. The Democrats picked James Buchanan of Pennsylvania, a former Secretary of State under Polk, and John C. Breckinridge of Kentucky; the newly formed Republicans nominated John C. Frémont of California, a popular pathfinder of the West, and William L. Dayton of New Jersey; while the American (Know-Nothing) party tabbed Millard Fillmore of New York and Andrew J. Donelson of Tennessee.

Hoping to attract votes in both the North and the South with a "popular sovereignty" theme, the Democrats upheld the Compromise of 1850 and approved the Kansas-Nebraska Bill. The Republicans, on the other hand, held that Congress was supreme on the question of slavery, whereas the American party split on the issue. Buchanan won the election with an electoral vote of 174 to 114, but the opposition parties by winning the popular vote reminded the nation that the forces against slavery had reached formidable proportions.

DRED SCOTT

While the nation was preoccupied with electing a new President, the Supreme Court was deliberating the Dred Scott case. Scott, a Negro slave, had been taken by his master into the free states of Illinois and Wisconsin but, after several years, had been returned to Missouri, where he was sold. Believing that having lived in a free state made him free, Scott brought suit against his master for denying his freedom. The case eventually ended up in the Supreme Court, and that tribunal in March 1857 ruled that Congress had no authority to bar slavery from the territories, that the Missouri Compromise was unconstitutional, and that on the basis of the Fifth Amendment, no person could be deprived of his property without due process of law. In view of this the Court said that any man born a slave could not legally sue for liberty inasmuch as he was not a citizen.

The Republicans were faced with a dilemma. If congressional actions of the past were mere myths, "popular sovereignty" was dead, and Congress as an instrument of reform was impotent as were territorial governments. If they ignored the issue, slavery would spread.

LECOMPTON CONSTITUTION

By 1857 Kansas was showing signs of rejecting slavery as a transplanted institution. Turning out in force, the Free-Soilers defeated the proslavery party at the polls and proceeded to set up a free-soil government; but the radical elements of the proslavery legislature refused to admit defeat. Instead, they met at Lecompton in the fall of 1857 and formed a state constitution that recognized slavery and then submitted a referendum to the people, which asked them to vote not on the constitution, but on the proposition of slavery. A vote for slavery would be a vote for the constitution, and a vote against it would guarantee the legal status of slaves already in the state. This sort of political chicanery kept many of the Free-Soilers away from the polls and thus gave what the opposition termed a legitimate state victory. However, when the issues were brought into sharper focus, the Lecompton constitution was defeated, and the federal government demanded a popular vote on that document before considering the territory for statehood.

LINCOLN-DOUGLAS DEBATES

The year 1858 is best remembered in American history as the time of the "Great Debate" between Abraham Lincoln and Stephen A. Douglas. As rival candidates for the United States Senate from the state of Illinois, they were called upon to debate the issues of the day—namely, the Panic of 1857 and slavery. Lincoln failed to defeat Douglas in the election, but through eloquence and sound reasoning he established himself as the leading Republican candidate for future political greatness. The high note of Lincoln's argument was his belief that the slavery issue was growing with each advancing year and that "it would not cease until a crisis shall have been reached and passed. 'A house divided against itself cannot stand.'" In the course of the debates, Lincoln put a momentous question to Douglas. If Congress could not legally exclude slavery from a territory prior to its becoming a state (both the Kansas-Nebraska Act and the Supreme Court ruling on the Dred Scott case had made the Missouri Compromise unconstitutional), then how could the people, under popular sovereignty offered by that same impotent Congress, exclude slavery? Douglas' answer was that slavery could not exist if the local government did not legislate laws to protect and police slavery. Thus, according to Douglas, legislation could make slavery possible or by its inaction could keep the territory free. This answer possibly cost Douglas the presidential election of 1860, for the South soon began to view him as a Free-Soiler.

SOUTHERNERS AGAINST SLAVERY

It would be a gross oversimplification to assume that the South was solidly behind the proslavery forces, for many great Virginians reviled slavery as an evil that would be extremely difficult to stamp out. Antislavery newspaper editors, such as W. G. Brownlow, were not uncommon;

and southerners who opposed Calhoun and nullification found capable leaders in James Petigru and Joel Poinsett.

Between 1830 and 1860, according to Professor Carl Degler, a considerable number of middle-class southerners began to doubt the utility, wisdom, and justice of slavery. Some opposed it for reasons of Christian ethics, while others saw its economic and political failures. Among the latter group was Cassius Marcellus Clay, a cousin of Henry. Observing that the unequal competition of unpaid labor depopulated the country and ruined the towns and villages, he advocated a gradual emancipation program whereby the state would compensate the slave owners for their losses. Others blamed slavery for dwarfing the South's progress in manufacturing and commerce.

In 1832, a year after the Nat Turner crisis, more than half of the House of Delegates in Virginia expressed disfavor toward the institution even though as many as three-quarters of them owned slaves. Nevertheless, enough compromisers among them joined the conservatives to defeat a bill of emancipation.

JOHN BROWN

In October of 1859 John Brown, a fanatic abolitionist, sent a shock wave through the South when he and some eighteen others seized the national arsenal at Harpers Ferry, Virginia. A veteran of the bloody struggle in Kansas, Brown was determined to launch a slave insurrection in Virginia, which would ultimately spread throughout the South. Although his group included five black men, other slaves failed to respond to the call to rebel, and the scheme soon led Brown and several of his insurrectionists to the gallows. Although Brown was said to be emotionally unstable, abolitionists in the North went to great lengths to make him appear a martyr. The whole affair was but another step toward civil war.

Foreign Affairs

CUBA

Manifest Destiny had not yet run its first phase when the turbulent decade of the 1850s arrived. The nation had raced to the Pacific, stopping only long enough to pick up Texas, and now expansionists began to cast covetous eyes toward Cuba. Slave owners were particularly interested in the island because its sugar plantations and slaves meant more southern power in Congress when and if it came into the Union. When the Spaniards turned down a handsome purchase offer by the Polk administration, a band of adventurers (some called themselves Cuban patriots) under the leadership of General Narciso López defied American warnings and assaulted Cuba only to be captured and executed.

OSTEND MANIFESTO

The Pierce administration was just as receptive to the notion that Cuba should become a part of the United States. Accordingly, Pierre Soulé, the newly appointed American minister to Spain, armed himself with $130 million and opened purchase negotiations with Spain. Negotiations, however, were cut short in 1854 when Spain seized the *Black Warrior,* a United States steamer operating off the coast of Cuba, for certain technical violations of customs laws. Soulé promptly demanded an apology and $300,000 in damages among other concessions, but Spain chose to ignore what it considered to be brash and ridiculous charges. Because of this, Soulé met with John Y. Mason, minister to France, and James Buchanan, minister to England, at Ostend, Belgium, in the fall of 1854 to work out a plan for the purchase of Cuba, which would be amenable to European powers. It was later reported by northern papers that if Spain refused to sell for

$20 million, the three ministers were prepared to recommend that the United States take the island should it appear to be a threat to American security. So fierce was public pressure on Pierce and the Ostend Manifesto that the administration was soon forced to deny the whole scheme.

In the meantime the Clayton-Bulwer Treaty had been consummated with England, which prepared the groundwork for a Panama canal. By its provisions the canal, if and when built, was to be a joint undertaking—neutral in time of war and open to ships of all nations.

GADSDEN PURCHASE

President Pierce had even more productive negotiations with Mexico. Desiring a southern railroad to the Pacific, he dispatched James Gadsden to Mexico in 1853, where he successfully negotiated a treaty with Santa Anna for the purchase of a strip of land on the border of northern Mexico for $10 million.

WILLIAM WALKER

If the Gadsden purchase pleased Americans, the antics of William Walker in Nicaragua appalled them except for a handful of expansionists and proslaveryites. "Commodore" Cornelius Vanderbilt had taken an interest in the government of the little republic in the early 1850s when unstable political conditions threatened his shipping interests. In order to assure the continued prosperity of his business in competition with the Panama railway, Vanderbilt hired William Walker, a professional soldier of fortune, to set up a stable government in Nicaragua. In 1855 Walker managed to become dictator, but his luck soon ran out; he was overthrown and died before a Honduran firing squad.

Two years earlier Commodore Matthew Perry had opened the doors of Japan to western trade.

Select Bibliography

Alexander, Thomas B. *Sectional Stress and Party Strength: A Computer Analysis of Roll-Call Voting Patterns in the United States House of Representatives, 1836–1860.* Nashville, Tenn.: Vanderbilt University Press, 1967.

Angle, Paul M., ed. *Created Equal? The Complete Lincoln-Douglas Debates of 1858.* Chicago: University of Chicago Press, 1958.

Catton, William, and Bruce. *Two Roads to Sumter.* New York: McGraw-Hill Book Company, 1963.

Coit, Margaret L. *John C. Calhoun, American Portrait.* Boston: Houghton Mifflin Company, 1950.

Cole, Arthur C. *The Irrepressible Conflict, 1850–1865.* New York: Crowell Collier and Macmillan, Inc., 1934.

Crandall, Andrew W. *The Early History of the Republican Party, 1854–1856.* Gloucester, Mass.: Peter Smith, 1930.

Craven, Avery O. *Civil War in the Making, 1815–1860.* Baton Rouge, La.: Louisiana State University Press, 1968.

———. *The Coming of the Civil War,* 2d rev. ed. Chicago: University of Chicago Press, 1957.

Crowe, Charles, ed. *The Age of Civil War and Reconstruction, 1830–1900.* Homewood, Ill.: Dorsey Press, 1966.

Donald, David. *Charles Sumner and the Coming of the Civil War.* New York: Alfred A. Knopf, 1960.

Fehrenbacher, Don E. *Prelude to Greatness: Lincoln in the 1850's.* Stanford, Calif.: Stanford University Press, 1962.

Filler, Louis. *The Crusade against Slavery, 1830–1860.* New York: Harper & Row, Publishers, 1960.

Garfinkle, Norton, ed. *Lincoln and the Coming of the Civil War*. Boston: D. C. Heath & Company, 1959.

Hamilton, Holman. *Prologue to Conflict: The Crisis and Compromise of 1850*. New York: W. W. Norton & Co., Inc., 1966.

Heckman, Richard A. *Lincoln vs. Douglas: The Great Debates Campaign.* Washington, D.C.: Public Affairs Press, 1967.

Helper, Hinton. *The Impending Crisis of the South: How to Meet It.* Cambridge, Mass.: Belknap Press of Harvard University Press, 1968.

Hopkins, Vincent. *Dred Scott's Case.* New York: Atheneum Publishers, 1967.

Johannsen, Robert W., ed. *The Union in Crisis, 1850–1877*. New York: Free Press, 1965.

Klein, Philip S. *President James Buchanan*. University Park, Pa.: Pennsylvania State University Press, 1962.

Knoles, George H., ed. *The Crisis of the Union, 1860–1861*. Baton Rouge, La.: Louisiana State University Press, 1965.

Malin, James C. *The Nebraska Question, 1852–1854*. Gloucester, Mass.: Peter Smith, 1968.

Mayer, George H. *The Republican Party, 1854–1964*. New York: Oxford University Press, 1967.

Morrison, Chaplin W. *Democratic Politics and Sectionalism: The Wilmot Proviso Controversy.* Chapel Hill, N.C.: University of North Carolina Press, 1967.

Nevins, Allan. *Ordeal of the Union*. 2 vols. New York: Charles Scribner's Sons, 1947.

Nichols, Roy F. *The Democratic Machine, 1850–1854.* New York: AMS Press, Inc., 1923.

———. *The Disruption of American Democracy*. New York: Crowell Collier and Macmillan, Inc., 1962.

O'Connor, Thomas H. *Lords of the Loom: The Cotton Whigs and the Coming of the Civil War*. New York: Charles Scribner's Sons, 1968.

Overdyke, W. Darrell. *The Know-Nothing Party in the South*. Baton Rouge, La.: Louisiana State University Press, 1950.

Perkins, Dexter. *The Monroe Doctrine, 1826–1867*. 3 vols. Gloucester, Mass.: Peter Smith, 1927–1937.

Potter, David M. *The South and the Sectional Conflict.* Baton Rouge, La.: Louisiana State University Press, 1968.

Rozwenc, Edwin C., ed. *The Causes of the American Civil War*. Boston: D. C. Heath & Company, 1961.

———. *The Compromise of 1850*. Boston: D. C. Heath & Company, 1957.

Siebert, Wilbur H. *The Underground Railroad from Slavery to Freedom.* New York: Arno Press, 1968.

Silbey, Joel H. *The Shrine of Party: Congressional Voting Behavior, 1841–1852*. Pittsburgh, Pa.: University of Pittsburgh Press, 1967.

Smith, Theodore C. *Parties and Slavery, 1850–1859*. Westport, Conn.: Negro Universities Press, 1906.

Spencer, Ivor D. *The Victor and the Spoils: A Life of William L. Marcy.* Providence, R.I.: Brown University Press, 1959.

Stampp, Kenneth M., *And the War Came: The North and the Secession Crisis.* Baton Rouge, La.: Louisiana State University Press, 1950.

———. ed. *The Causes of the Civil War.* Englewood Cliffs, N.J.: Prentice-Hall, Inc., 1965.

Van Deusen, Glyndon G. *Horace Greeley: Nineteenth Century Crusader.* Philadelphia, Pa.: University of Pennsylvania Press, 1953.

_____. *William Henry Seward.* New York: Oxford University Press, 1967.

Villard, Oswald G. *John Brown, 1800–1859.* Gloucester, Mass.: Peter Smith, 1942.

Wallace, Edward S. *Destiny and Glory.* New York: Coward-McCann, Inc., 1957.

Warren, Robert P. *John Brown: The Making of a Martyr.* New York: Reprint House International, 1929.

Wellman, Paul I. *The House Divides: The Age of Jackson and Lincoln, from the War of 1812 to the Civil War.* Lewis Gannett, ed. New York: Doubleday & Company, Inc., 1966.

chapter 21

The Coming of the Irrepressible Conflict

The Political Arena

ELECTION OF 1860

As the election of 1860 approached, the real issue was not as yet the right of secession, but rather the age-old question of the extension of slavery into new territories. Unable to unite on this issue, the Democratic party split,[1] with the northern elements clinging to popular sovereignty and the southern wing turning to the principle of the Dred Scott case, which demanded that the federal government protect slavery in the territories. The northern Democrats nominated Douglas of Illinois and Herschel V. Johnson of Georgia, while those of the South selected John C. Breckinridge of Kentucky and Joseph Lane of Oregon.

The young Republican party, surprisingly enough, passed up its most determined antislavery champion, William H. Seward of New York, and nominated Abraham Lincoln of Illinois, a moderate who wanted to check slavery but not abolish it. Their choice for Vice-President

was Hannibal Hamlin of Maine. Their platform denied the authority of Congress or a territorial government to establish or protect slavery, courted the West by promising free homesteads and a Pacific railroad, and pleased the industrial East by calling for a protective tariff.

The Whigs were still showing some signs of life and in order to gain strength formed a coalition with the Know-Nothings, which became known as the Constitutional Union party. Hoping to attract votes from all sections of the country, they adopted an innocent platform of Constitution, Union, and law and order. Their candidates were John Bell of Tennessee and Edward Everett of Massachusetts.

As was expected, Lincoln won with an electoral vote of 180 to 72 for Breckinridge; Douglas collected 12 and Bell, 39. The new President, however, carried the stigma of a minority executive, having captured only 40 percent of a popular vote.

CRITTENDEN COMPROMISE

Sensing an impending crisis, Senator John J. Crittenden of Kentucky tried to salvage some semblance of peace on December 18, when he introduced a compromise resolution in the Senate prohibiting slavery north of 36° 30′ while recognizing the institution in the South. His proposal died in the Senate.

---

[1] The Democrats had met earlier in Charleston to draw up a platform; but when the northern faction refused to denounce popular sovereignty and to support slavery in the territories, the southern wing, representing eight states, walked out and organized its own convention in the same city. The Democrats split again at Baltimore in June when the northern wing nominated Douglas, who was considered unfriendly to the South after his Freeport Doctrine.

352

SOUTH CAROLINA SECEDES

Discordant elements in the South had threatened to leave the Union if Lincoln were elected, and now it remained for them to act. South Carolina was the first to respond. Meeting on December 20, 1860, at Charleston, a popular convention passed a "Declaration of Causes" and an ordinance of secession.

In the meantime, President Buchanan's cabinet had begun to resign. The Secretary of State stepped down because he felt that the President was not asserting himself against secession; three other members resigned in order to go with the South, and by the end of January the cabinet was all Union.

THE CONFEDERATE STATES OF AMERICA

During the month of December, South Carolina had demanded that the United States withdraw all troops from Charleston Harbor and soon thereafter seized the federal arsenal. After the turn of the new year, others joined South Carolina as the Confederacy began to emerge. On February 4, 1861, delegates from six[2] southern states assembled at Montgomery, Alabama, where they organized a government under the name of the Confederate States of America. A constitution similar to that of the United States was written, and Jefferson Davis of Mississippi was elected provisional president along with Alexander H. Stephens of Georgia, who became vice-president.

SOUTHERN UNIONISTS

Once again, as in the question of slavery, the South was divided over the issue of

[2] Forty-two delegates from South Carolina, Georgia, Alabama, Mississippi, Louisiana, and Florida attended the convention and elected Howell Cob of Georgia chairman. On February 6, delegates from North Carolina arrived to plead in vain for conciliation. Five other states joined the Confederacy by the end of June, bringing the total number to eleven.

immediate secession. During the state elections of 1851, according to Professor Degler, Unionist Democrats and Whigs combined to turn back the forces of secession throughout the South, and the strong showing of John Bell of Tennessee in the presidential election of 1860 further demonstrates this division. Running on the Constitutional Union ticket, Bell received 40 percent of the southern vote (compared to 45 percent for his Democratic opponent, Breckinridge), and he won three southern states by a clear majority.

In 1861 the Unionist forces were unable to stop the movement toward secession, but in excess of 28,000 voted against it in Georgia while approximately 35,000 voted for it; over 32,000 opposed secession in Virginia while 128,000 voted for it; in excess of 47,000 cast dissenting votes on secession in Tennessee but were defeated by 104,000; and the North Carolina convention voted secession but refused by a two-thirds vote to submit it to the people for ratification. Surprisingly enough, many southern Unionists were wealthy planters.

LINCOLN'S CABINET

Lincoln's leading cabinet members were Secretary of State Seward, Secretary of the Treasury Salmon Chase, and Secretary of War Simon Cameron (replaced in 1862 by Edwin Stanton). All four of these men had been considered for the presidency in 1860 and, therefore, were with the exception of Cameron strong party leaders. In fact, Seward tried at times to assume executive power at the expense of the President, and on one occasion proposed that the United States unite itself by starting a war in Europe. Lincoln, however, rejected this wild scheme and managed thereafter to keep Seward's ambitious energies directed to his office.

Lincoln's first inaugural is considered one of the great speeches in American history. Hoping to maintain the peace and speaking in conciliatory tones, the new President announced that he had no intention of interfering with slavery where it already existed; but he made it clear that the laws of the Union would be upheld in all the states. Thus, he simply asked the Confederate states that had already seceded to consider the consequences of their action.

FORT SUMTER

One of the most pressing issues facing Lincoln was the crisis at Fort Sumter. He delayed action for a month and then decided to send provisions to the stranded federal garrison, which in a sense forced the Confederacy to choose between peace and war. President Davis decided to act before the Union supplies arrived and, accordingly, instructed General Beauregard to call for the surrender of the Union garrison at Sumter. When Commander Major Anderson refused, the Confederate batteries began a bombardment that lasted for thirty-four hours. On April 13, 1861, the Union forces surrendered.

NORTHERN ADVANTAGES

While the people—North and South—braced for the reality of war, Lincoln called for volunteers to meet the new crisis. Both sides were totally unprepared for an all-out engagement, but the South was better prepared for immediate mobilization since many of its farmer-recruits were already good marksmen with the rifle. The North, on the other hand, was slow to mobilize but had an inexhaustible supply of men and practically all of the nation's heavy industry behind them. For example, the population of the North more than doubled that of the eleven Confederate states; and in addition to manufacturing, locomotives and railroads in the North far outnumbered those in the South while other implements of war, such as firearms and powder, suffered in the South by comparison. The northern navy was also much larger than that of the South, and this superiority enabled Lincoln to blockade Confederate ports throughout most of the conflict.

SOUTHERN ADVANTAGES

The South, however, was not without advantages. It had the finest corps of officers in the country, as evinced by the sterling qualities of General Robert E. Lee and General Thomas J. ("Stonewall") Jackson, and it entered the conflict knowing full well that the North would be forced to wage an offensive war in unfamiliar terrain. The Confederacy also had "King Cotton," the influence of which the South hoped would win allies in Europe. Finally, despite the stigma of slavery, the South considered its cause to be more noble; for it was fighting for "self-determination," thus making the North the aggressor.

Concluding Remarks on Causation

The forces that brought on the war were so vast and so complex that historians of the subject have been hard pressed to arrive at anything like a consensus on the main cause. The early nationalist historians of the Civil War era were quick to blame the "peculiar institution" for having started the conflict. Borrowing heavily from the abolitionist writings, this school saw the war as a contest between an immoral and disuniting institution on the one hand and liberty and union on the other.

After the turn of the century a school of economic determinists began to discover capitalistic forces in the causes of the Civil War. They saw alienation and enmity growing out of two different economies—the industrial of the North and the agrarian of the South—for the southern farm had become so subservient to the northern city that it amounted to economic exploitation. Thus, secession marked the coming of a second great

"American revolution," and the spirit of 1776 would throw off another oppressor of state sovereignty and economic progress.

Another group of historians found substance in the belief that the northern capitalist society revolted against political domination by conservative southern agrarian elements in Congress. This struggle manifested itself in the sectional conflicts over protective tariffs, territorial expansion, and the free land system. More than that, the South had dominated the executive department with the "Virginia dynasty," and the judicial system had been under southern influence since the beginning of the republic.

The Union President has also been criticized by scholars. Some historians have questioned his choice of alternatives and have suggested that a compromise on the territorial issue would have averted war. They have also posed other questions; for example, should Lincoln have recognized southern independence? Should the Confederacy have been given a period in which to experiment with the pitfalls of independence? Thus, the central question of this school is this: Did Lincoln use the powers of his office wisely?

The revisionist school in recent years has blamed the political leaders of the period who acted irrationally and without foresight to save the Union and in the process left Lincoln no alternative but to use force. In fact, this group sees the whole prewar generation as political failures — or political blunderers.

Today historians are beginning to examine once again the sensitive issue of slavery as the fundamental cause. In one sense this group has supported the "political failure" thesis by contending that the real tragedy of the era was the failure of responsible men to deal squarely with slavery as a social institution in the South.

In the final analysis of causation, it has been written, one cannot escape the nagging question as to whether or not the political and economic differences between the North and the South would have been as serious if slavery had not been present.

The Early Campaigns

The strategy of Lincoln was to crush the "rebellion" with the most effective forces available; one such instrument was a blockade that would strangle the South's one-crop economy. This so-called anaconda policy also demanded a land invasion of the Confederacy with a western assault designed to split the South by gaining control of the Mississippi River, while forces in the east would advance toward the Confederate capital of Richmond. Southern strategy was simply to hold until the North tired of the conflict.

CAMPAIGNS OF 1861

The first skirmishes centered around attempts by both sides to capture the other's capital; Confederate forces threatened to cross the Potomac while northern strategists pondered the best route to Richmond. It was in this theater that the first major engagement took place when General Irwin McDowell led about 30,000 Union troops across Bull Run Creek near Manassas Junction, Virginia. On July 21, 1861, he was met by P. G. T. Beauregard and Joseph E. Johnston, whose smaller army waged a gallant stand for four hours. Just when it appeared that the Confederate forces were defeated, reinforcements appeared to turn the course of the battle. A counterattack forced the Union troops to retreat, and the battle soon became a rout, but the Confederate elements were so battered they were unable to pursue their advantage. It was in this battle that Thomas J. Jackson won the name "Stonewall" for his heroic stand.

The Battle of Bull Run revealed glaring weaknesses in the training of Union troops, and in rather harsh terms it told Lincoln that the war was destined to be a long one. Believing that a change in command was in order, Lincoln replaced McDowell with George B. McClellan, who had some success in western Virginia. Moreover, before the year was out, Lincoln retired the aged Winfield Scott, who had commanded a "thousand" past campaigns. Instrumental in these actions was the Joint Committee on the Conduct of the War. It was organized primarily to replace inefficient officers, but according to reports, ended up a politically partisan body that specialized in persecuting Democratic generals. At the same time, it sheltered such Republican generals as Benjamin F. Butler, Ambrose E. Burnside, John C. Fremont, and Joseph Hooker. Lincoln also abolished the three-month enlistment, ordered more aggressive strategy in the west, and tightened the blockade.

CAMPAIGNS OF 1862

Early in 1862 McClellan decided to strike at Richmond. Repelling attacks along the way, his army of some 100,000 reached the vicinity of Richmond in June 1862 and prepared for the assault. It was at this point that Robert E. Lee took command of the Army of Northern Virginia and after summoning Jackson's army from the Shenandoah Valley, engaged McClellan's forces in what became known as the Seven Days' Battle. Both sides lost heavily in a virtual draw, but worse yet for Richmond, McClellan still threatened the city. In the meantime, officials in Washington were shaken over the recurring reports of heavy casualties in the battles and therefore decided to act before another series of blood baths took place. McClellan and his army were accordingly recalled, thus ending the peninsula campaign.

Disappointed by McClellan's failure to capture Richmond, the administration replaced him with Henry W. Halleck, who had made a favorable reputation on the western front. Concurrently, John

Pope had been given a command, and the new strategy directed the two armies to make a southward thrust into the Confederacy that would bypass Richmond, sever communication lines, and strike fear in the heart of the South. Thus, the stage was set for the Second Battle of Bull Run, which occurred on August 29–30, 1862. Pope met Lee and Stonewall Jackson on the old Bull Run battlefield, where he was seriously defeated. Pope was relieved of his command, and McClellan was given a second chance with the Army of the Potomac.

By September Lee had come to believe that the time was right for the invasion of Washington, and accordingly crossed the Potomac into Maryland. It was at this point that Lee divided his command, sending Stonewall Jackson to secure Harpers Ferry in northern Virginia while he engaged McClellan. The campaign culminated in the Battle of Antietam, where the two opposing armies lost as many as 23,000 men — 13,000 on the Union side and as many as 10,000 on the Confederate side. It ended in a stalemate, but it was a strategic blow to Lee, and he safely retreated back across the Potomac.[3]

The northern policy of "musical chairs" in changing commands continued as McClellan was removed once again — this time for not pursuing the enemy — and Burnside was given the post. The new commander, determined to succeed where all others had failed, promptly sent his forces up against Lee at Fredericksburg. However, Lee was well fortified, and the agony of defeat with heavy losses was once again felt by the North. Burnside knew what to expect from Washington; he was replaced by Hooker.

[3] Before this battle took place, a copy of Lee's secret orders fell into federal hands, and McClellan was able to checkmate every move of the Confederate forces. Antietam has been considered the most decisive battle of the Civil War, for it gave the Union new hope and discouraged any possible alliance between the Confederacy and European powers, who reportedly had been waiting for a show of force.

The Union forces on the western front had better luck. By 1862 Kentucky had decided to go with the Union, thus removing a giant roadblock to success in that theater; and Ulysses S. Grant was ready to move against Confederate strongholds at Forts Henry and Donelson in northern Tennessee. Both of these outposts commanded important water routes to the South, and victory for Grant would not only break the first Confederate line of defense but would open the door for a Union charge into the heart of the South. With the support of Don C. Buell's army and a flotilla of gunboats, Grant was able to capture both forts and move on to Corinth and Memphis, the hubs of the new line of Confederate defense. The two Union generals collaborated once again at Shiloh, and the result was victory, but not before the federal army was driven from the field by Albert Sidney Johnston. The Confederate general tasted victory momentarily, but his aggressiveness cost him his life.

Corinth fell next before the northern onslaught, but it was a mere skirmish compared to the bloodshed at Shiloh. By April Grant, supported by a segment of the Union navy, had captured New Orleans, thus freeing the Mississippi River of Confederate forts with the exception of Vicksburg and completing the division of the South.

The War at Sea

Fear gripped the North early in 1862, when the Confederacy launched its first iron-plated man of war, the *Virginia* (known as the *Merrimac* in its Union days). In fact, after the *Virginia* destroyed two federal frigates on the James River, the whole Union blockade of the South was in imminent danger. The Union, however, was able to devise a modified iron-plated ship of its own, called the *Monitor,* a platform-type structure with a two-gun revolving turret, which it sent

against the *Virginia*. The rivals met at Hampton Roads on March 9, 1862, and after several hours of desperate combat the two ships were still afloat. Although the engagement was something of a draw, the invulnerability of the *Monitor* ensured the blockade.

During the year of 1862, significant campaigns were fought in both the eastern and western theaters. In the west Grant decided to attack Vicksburg and sent wave after wave of his troops against the mighty fortress, but finally settled for the slow but less painful strategy of siege. On July 4 Vicksburg surrendered, thereby removing the last Confederate stronghold on the Mississippi River.

William Rosecrans, meanwhile, prepared to meet Braxton Bragg near Chattanooga, but the Confederate commander wisely chose to make his stand at Chickamauga, where in September he routed Rosecrans' army, forcing it to retreat back to Chattanooga. By November Grant had replaced Rosecrans and with the support of George St. Thomas, Hooker, and William T. Sherman won the field on November 25.

As midsummer approached on the eastern front, Hooker prepared to invade Virginia once again; but again met with misfortune, this time at Chancellorsville, where Lee's forces convincingly defeated his army. Encouraged by the victory, Lee decided to cross the Potomac for the second time, but this time he would strike through Pennsylvania. At Gettysburg he encountered Union troops under the command of George G. Meade, who had replaced Hooker. For three days a Union force of some 90,000 battled a Confederate army of about 75,000; and when the end came, with the failure of George Pickett's charge up Cemetery Ridge, Lee had suffered his worst defeat.

With the convenience of hindsight, Gettysburg may be considered the turning point of the war. Although the South fought on, its fortunes languished; its cause was doomed. Soon after the battle Lincoln journeyed to Gettysburg to "dedicate a portion of that field" as a national cemetery. Following a lengthy speech by the noted orator Edward Everett, Lincoln offered his brief address, which in time became one of his most famous.

CAMPAIGNS OF 1864

The eastern campaigns of 1864 opened with Grant assuming full command of the United States armies with the rank of lieutenant general. His immediate objective was the elusive city of Richmond; his hope was to defeat Lee. Determined to "fight it out on this line if it takes all summer," Grant hammered Lee's defenses at the Wilderness, then at Spotsylvania Court House, and then at Cold Harbor, sustaining incredible losses with each battle. At last he captured Petersburg, which cut Richmond's communication lines southward, and waited for the capital's surrender.

In the meantime, Philip H. Sheridan led an army into the Shenandoah Valley to challenge Jubal A. Early, whose Confederate forces threatened Washington. In October, Sheridan met Early at Cedar Creek and after a fierce battle, during which his troops were driven from the field, Sheridan grasped victory from what appeared to be certain defeat and, thus, ended the peril of Washington.

The western front was by no means quiet during the summer and fall of 1864. Grant's able assistant and trusted friend Sherman was in command, and his plan was to march through the heart of the deep South all the way to the Atlantic. After spending the summer battering the defenses of Atlanta, Sherman marched an army of some 60,000 across Georgia to attack Savannah, but much to his surprise he found an evacuated city. He then turned north and led his "wrecking crew" through the Carolinas, reportedly taking particular delight in punishing South Carolina, the leader of the secessionists. By the time Sherman reached Savannah

in December, John M. Schofield and Thomas had defeated John B. Hood at Nashville, which all but ended rebel resistance in the west.

While these campaigns were taking place, Grant and Lee still faced each other at Richmond, but time was running out for the ill-provisioned Confederacy. Lee had hoped to break out of the siege and join forces with Johnston, who had harassed Sherman, but such plans could not be realized, so he settled for a midnight escape on April 2–3, 1865. While leading his army westward, however, Lee found the way blocked by Sheridan, and the only sensible recourse left open was to surrender.

On April 9, 1865, Grant and Lee met at Appomattox Court House, Virginia, where Lee accepted Grant's generous terms, which in part permitted all Confederate soldiers to return to their homes as parolees. Other armies continued to surrender throughout the month, and the president of the fallen Confederate states, Jefferson Davis, was taken into custody in Georgia on May 10.

Select Bibliography

Adams, Henry. *Great Secession Winter of 1860–61.* George Hochfield, ed. Cranbury, N.J.: A. S. Barnes and Company, Inc., 1962.

Angle, Paul M., and E. S. Miers. *The Tragic Years, 1860–1865: A Documentary History of the American Civil War.* 2 vols. New York: Simon & Schuster, Inc., 1960.

Aptheker, Herbert. *Documentary History of the Negro People in the United States from the Colonial Times through the Civil War.* New York: Citadel Press, Inc., 1962.

Boatner, III, Mark M. *The Civil War Dictionary.* New York: David McKay Co., Inc., 1959.

Catton, Bruce. *This Hallowed Ground.*

New York: Doubleday & Company, Inc., 1956.

_____. *U. S. Grant and the American Military Tradition.* New York: Grosset & Dunlap, Inc., 1958.

Cole, Arthur C. *The Irrepressible Conflict, 1850–1865.* New York: Crowell Collier and Macmillan Inc., 1934.

Crenshaw, Ollinger. *The Slave States in the Presidential Election of 1860.* Gloucester, Mass.: Peter Smith, 1945.

Current, Richard N., ed. *Sections and Politics: Selected Essays by William B. Hesseltine.* Madison, Wis.: Society Press, 1968.

Donald, David. *Lincoln Reconsidered.* New York: Alfred A. Knopf, 1956.

Dowdey, Clifford. *The Seven Days: The Emergence of Lee.* Boston: Little, Brown and Company, 1964.

Dumond, Dwight L. *Antislavery Origins of the Civil War in the United States.* Ann Arbor, Mich.: University of Michigan Press, 1959.

_____. *The Secession Movement, 1860–1861.* New York: Octagon Books, Inc., 1931.

Eaton, Clement. *A History of the Southern Confederacy.* New York: Crowell Collier and Macmillan, Inc., 1954.

Foner, Philip S. *Business and Slavery: The New York Merchants and the Irrepressible Conflict.* Chapel Hill, N.C.: University of North Carolina Press, 1941.

Foote, Shelby. *The Civil War: A Narrative.* 2 vols. New York: Random House, Inc., 1958.

Freeman, Douglas S. *Lee's Lieutenants.* 3 vols. New York: Charles Scribner's Sons, 1942–1944.

Hendrick, Burton J. *Statesmen of the Lost Cause: Jefferson Davis and His Cabinet.* Little, Brown and Company, 1939.

Henry, Robert S. *The Story of the Confederacy.* Indianapolis, Ind.: The Bobbs-Merrill Co., Inc., 1957.

Hesseltine, William B., ed. *The Tragic Conflict: The Civil War and Reconstruction.* New York: George Braziller, Inc., 1962.

Johannsen, Robert W. *Democracy on Trial, 1845–1877.* New York: McGraw-Hill Book Company, 1966.

_____, ed. *The Union in Crisis, 1850–1877.* New York: The Free Press, 1965.

Jones, Virgil C. *The Civil War at Sea.* 3 vols. New York: Holt, Rinehart and Winston, Inc., 1960–1962,

King, Willard L. *Lincoln's Manager, David Davis.* Cambridge, Mass.: Harvard University Press, 1960.

Leech, Margaret. *Reveille in Washington, 1860–1865.* New York: Grosset & Dunlap, Inc., 1956.

Merrill, James M. *The Rebel Shore: The Story of Union Sea Power in the Civil War.* Boston: Little, Brown and Company, 1957.

Milton, George F. *The Eve of Conflict: Stephen A. Douglas and the Needless War.* Boston: Houghton Mifflin Company, 1934.

Nevins, Allan. *The Emergence of Lincoln.* 2 vols. New York: Charles Scribner's Sonc, 1950.

_____. *Ordeal of the Union.* 2 vols. New York: Charles Scribner's Sons, 1947.

Newman, Ralph and E. B. Long. *The Civil War Digest.* New York: Grosset & Dunlap, Inc., 1960.

Nichols, Roy F. *The Stakes of Power, 1845–1877.* New York: Hill & Wang, Inc., 1961.

Potter, David M. *Lincoln and His Party*

in the Secession Crisis, 2d ed. New Haven, Conn.: Yale University Press, 1962.

_____. The South and the Sectional Conflict. Baton Rouge, La.: Louisiana State University Press, 1968.

Pressly, Thomas J. Americans Interpret Their Civil War. New York: P. F. Collier, Inc., 1962.

Quarles, Benjamin. The Negro in the Civil War. Boston: Little, Brown and Company, 1953.

Rhodes, James F. History of the Civil War, 1861–1865. E. B. Long, ed. New York: Frederick Ungar Publishing Co., Inc., 1961.

Rozwenc, Edwin C. The Causes of the American Civil War. Boston: D. C. Heath & Company, 1961.

_____. Slavery as a Cause of the Civil War, 2d ed. Boston: D. C. Heath & Company, 1963.

Sandburg, Carl. Storm over the Land: A Profile of the Civil War. New York: Harcourt Brace Jovanovich, Inc., 1942.

Smith, George, and Charles Judah. Life in the North during the Civil War. Albuquerque, N.M.: University of New Mexico Press, 1966.

Stampp, Kenneth M. And the War Came: The North and the Secession Crisis, 1860–1861. Baton Rouge, La.: Louisiana State University Press, 1950.

_____, ed. The Causes of the Civil War, 2d ed. Englewood Cliffs, N.J.: Prentice-Hall, Inc., 1965.

_____. The Peculiar Institution. New York: Alfred A. Knopf, 1956.

Stern, Philip Van Doren, ed. Prologue to Sumter. Bloomington, Ind.: Indiana University Press, 1961.

Thomas, Benjamin P. Abraham Lincoln. New York: Alfred A. Knopf, 1952.

Van Deusen, Glyndon G. William Henry Seward. New York: Oxford University Press, 1967.

Whitridge, Arnold. No Compromise! The Story of the Fanatics Who Paved the Way to the Civil War. New York: Farrar, Straus and Giroux, 1960.

Wiley, Bell I. The Life of Johnny Reb. Indianapolis, Ind.: The Bobbs-Merrill Co., Inc., 1943.

_____. Southern Negroes, 1861–1865. New Haven, Conn.: Yale University Press, 1965.

_____, and Hirst D. Milhollen. They Who Fought Here. New York: Crowell Collier and Macmillan, Inc., 1959.

Williams, Kenneth P. Lincoln Finds a General. 5 vols. New York: Crowell Collier and Macmillan, Inc., 1949–1959.

Williams, T. Harry. Lincoln and His Generals. New York: Alfred A. Knopf, 1952.

chapter 22

Behind the Lines: North and South

Political Affairs in the North

EMERGENCY POWERS OF THE PRESIDENT

At the outset of the war a friendly Republican Congress permitted Lincoln to assume unprecedented powers as Chief Executive. He not only established the blockade, ordered the seizure of neutral ships, and set enlistments at three years, but suspended the privilege of the writ of habeas corpus. Moreover, censorship in the press and in the streets was not uncommon, and martial law ordered civilians to be tried in military courts.

In addition to his regular presidential duties, Lincoln served as a kind of general of the military forces until March 1864, when he named Grant general in chief of the Union armies. Though unschooled and inexperienced in military science, "Abe" learned quickly and soon became a recognized expert on the subject.

KENTUCKY, WEST VIRGINIA, AND MISSOURI

Early in the war concern was expressed in Washington over the possible loss of Kentucky, even though officials in that state assured the Union that they planned to remain neutral. Federal troops, nevertheless, entered Kentucky when rebel elements began to appear; and in Oc-

tober of 1862 that state was secured for the North with the defeat of Confederate forces at the battle of Perryville.

Virginia and Missouri were similarly divided over the war. The poorer mountain folk of western Virginia had little in common with the eastern tidewater slaveholders; and when the war came and Virginia seceded, the western mountain counties organized themselves into a state and applied for admission to the Union under the name of West Virginia. It was recognized as a state on June 20, 1863.

Martial law was also necessary in Missouri, where fighting erupted when Governor Claiborne Jackson started a secession movement; but the rebel elements were soon defeated and driven from the state.

THE EMANCIPATION PROCLAMATION

The old abolitionist movement in the North found renewed life with the outbreak of hostilities between North and South, and it gained momentum as the war progressed. Lincoln's office naturally bore the brunt of the pressure for an end to slavery. Finally, in the fall of 1862, after Congress had abolished slavery in the District of Columbia and after the crucial battle at Antietam, the President issued a Preliminary Emancipation Proclamation in which he warned the southern states of his forthcoming action. The official proclamation came on January 1, 1863, and declared that all slaves in areas still in rebellion "shall be then, thenceforward, and forever free." Postured in terms that would not offend the border states, the document was designed to weaken the Confederacy internally and elicit the support of those European powers hostile to the peculiar institution. Thus, the proclamation suggested to the rest of the world that the real struggle was not between states' rights and nationalism, but rather between freedom and slavery.

DRAFT ACT OF 1863

Filling the ranks of the army with able-bodied men was another problem facing the harried President of the North. Enlistments had provided the necessary manpower during the first two years of the war, but early in 1863 it became apparent that a draft act would be needed. Accordingly, Lincoln pushed a Draft Act through Congress that made all capable men between twenty and forty-five subject to induction. In a way, it was designed to supplement the volunteer program inasmuch as the draft was not enforced in those districts where quotas were filled through enlistments. Some draftees were even permitted to furnish a substitute or buy a special exemption for $300, but open opposition among the poorer classes soon curtailed this discriminatory policy. In July 1863 a riot against the draft erupted in New York City, and before it was brought under control, over a thousand people were killed.

ELECTION OF 1864

As the election of 1864 approached, there were rumors that Lincoln's war failures and the controversy that led to the resignation of Secretary of War Chase might prove his undoing should he seek a second term; but by the time the Republican Convention (under the name of the National Union party) met at Baltimore on June 7, the political air had cleared, and Lincoln was nominated on the first ballot. Andrew Johnson of Tennessee, a popular war Democrat, was his running mate. The Republican platform was simple and straightforward: to prosecute vigorously the war and to stamp out slavery on American soil.

The Democrats met two months later at Chicago and nominated General McClellan for President and George H. Pendleton of Ohio for Vice-President. Besides branding Lincoln a failure, his war effort hopeless, and his usurpation of "unlimited" powers unconstitutional, the Democrats called for a *peace* and *union* platform. Many of the citizens across the country were weary of the war and appeared to be deserting the Republican party, but at a most crucial time word arrived of Sherman's victory over Hood at Atlanta and Lincoln won with 212 electoral votes to 21 for his rival.

Economic Conditions in the North

FUNDING THE WAR

Since over two-thirds of the nation's industry was located in the North, the Union had considerably more success in financing the war than the Confederacy. The principal methods, as in most wars, were new taxes, new paper money, and foreign loans. Notable among the money-raising tax programs were the high Morrill Tariff, an unprecedented excise tax on business, and a personal income tax of 3 percent; bonds also played a significant role in financing the war and were floated through agents, such as Jay Cooke, the noted financier of the Civil War and Reconstruction eras.

The federal government finally had to issue paper money, or "greenbacks," in order to meet the needs of the expanding wartime economy. Accordingly, in 1862, $450 million in paper money was issued;

but since the new certificates had no gold or silver backing, they declined rather rapidly in value, and caused staggering wartime inflation.

NATIONAL BANK ACT

In 1863 Congress passed the National Bank Act. Considered the most important financial legislation of the war, the act unified the banking system of the country (previously handled by inefficient state banks) by providing for a network of federal banks; these banks were then required to purchase United States bonds that were to be deposited in the federal treasury. The comptroller would then be authorized to issue national bank notes to the banks up to 90 percent of the market value of the bonds. Thus was established a system of financing in America, which was to remain in effect for half a century.

Foreign Affairs in the North

As soon as hostilities began, England issued a "proclamation of neutrality"; and France and other European powers soon took similar action. This announcement was a severe blow to the South, whose hope for success in the war rested largely on its ability to attract European allies with "King Cotton." The Confederate government, nevertheless, continued to believe that England and hopefully France would eventually support its cause.

TRENT CRISIS

President Davis, therefore, directed Commissioners George Mason and John Slidell to sail for England in the fall of 1861. The voyage was no sooner underway when their ship, the *U.S.S. Trent* (English owned), was intercepted by the *U.S.S. San Jacinto*, whose captain, Charles Wilkes, removed the Confederate diplomats and placed them under arrest.

Angered to the point of mobilizing for war, the British government demanded the immediate release of the two men and an apology; Lincoln, realizing the gravity of the problem, complied.

FLORIDA AND *ALABAMA* CRISIS

The following year hard feelings between England and the United States were renewed when the former allowed two British-built men-of-war, the *Florida* and the *Alabama*, to escape and prey upon northern shipping. The American ambassador to England, Charles Francis Adams, promptly sent a stiff warning to the British in which he charged that government with violating international laws of neutrality by permitting the Confederacy to operate out of British ports. The British foreign minister, Lord John Russell, admitted only to selling ships to the South but, nevertheless, discontinued any acts that appeared to be contrary to law, and in later years the English government made restitution for damages caused by such raiders.

ENGLISH AND FRENCH NEUTRALITY

England had several reasons for shifting to a policy of neutrality. Her surplus cotton stocks were bulging, the linen and woolen industries were once again beginning to challenge cotton, English munitions and steel industries were reaping untold riches from both sides, and finally, Confederate pirates were destroying the New England merchant marine (England's traditional rival in commerce). Thus, economic motives outweighed any political desires England might have harbored to destroy the United States. France offered to mediate, provided England would collaborate with her in the negotiations; but Washington cooled this offer after the Battle of Antietam, and Napoleon III turned to more lucrative ventures. He found one in Mexico. Operating under the pretext that he intended to help Great Britain and Spain collect back debts from Mexico, the ambitious emperor sent not only an army, but a puppet emperor Archduke Maximilian of Austria, who was to rule over a new French colony in America. Secretary of State Seward protested this action as a violation of the Monroe Doctrine, but to no avail; this problem would have to wait until the war's end.

Napoleon refused to commit himself to the support of the South mainly because France feared her old enemies in Europe, and partly because of the possible displeasure of the French citizenry with another war. Also significant was the fact that the French cotton stores were filled in 1861, and besides, after the Emancipation Proclamation was announced, Napoleon had no desire to appear as the enemy of freedom.

Political Affairs in the South

WAR POWERS OF THE PRESIDENT

Jefferson Davis played much the same role as Lincoln as commander in chief; but unlike his northern counterpart, Davis was a West Pointer, a veteran of the Mexican War, and seldom if ever sought advice from others in conducting the war. In fact, it was not until January of 1865 that he finally offered the title general of the armies to Lee. On the other hand it has been reported that Davis possessed considerable ability in statecraft, despite the difficulties he had with his cabinet; but the southern government was not the most desirable instrument for waging a war that required all states to pull together as one team. In some instances states' rights were so strong that state governments vied with the Confederate government for manpower and supplies. This alone was enough to remind southern leaders that a long war was unthinkable.

CONSCRIPTION ACT OF 1862

In April 1862 Davis signed a Conscription Act to bolster sagging enlistments. By its terms all white males between eighteen and thirty-five (later extended to forty-five) were eligible to be drafted for a "hitch" of three years. As in the North, a negative response from the lower classes swept the South because of the large number of exempted occupations, and many of those who could afford the price took advantage of the liberal substitute policy.

The Economy of the South

INDUSTRIAL SHORTAGES

In the final analysis, it was the economic weakness of the South that caused its ultimate collapse. Its shortages in basic industrial goods, such as plows, horseshoes, shoes, and wool and cotton clothing, were staggering, not to mention the heavier industrials, such as the steam engine. Most critical in the last year of the war was the acute shortage of saltpeter, an essential ingredient in the making of gunpowder.

FINANCING THE WAR

There was a complete breakdown in finances. Credit had to be obtained on an uncertain agricultural base (for example, staple crops, such as cotton and tobacco); and even this form of financing, when it could be found, was greatly impaired by the blockade. The South finally resorted to printing Confederate notes, which brought some relief; but since the paper money had no backing in the Treasury, price inflation soon made this system of financing equally uncertain.

TRANSPORTATION WEAKNESSES

The problems of transportation were also enormous in the South. Enough food was produced, but all too often it was not distributed where it was needed. Working to save time, the southern states frequently laid railroads carelessly; and those in existence were mere trunk lines with as many as eleven different gauges, ranging from three feet to five feet, six inches, thus making it impossible for trains of some lines to use the tracks of others. This system of state-operated trunk lines required a kind of large-scale coordination that was never realized, even with Confederate control, since few, if any, railroad officials had been trained for so vast an operation. Thus, the railroad system of the South operated on a trial-and-error basis throughout the war.

It has been written that the South did remarkably well during the war, considering the intricate, complex, and often baffling political and economic problems with which it had to cope. To solve these problems would have required years of reorganizing the whole regional system, and such time the South did not have.

Select Bibliography

Belz, Herman. *Reconstructing the Union: Theory and Policy during the Civil War.* Ithaca, N.Y.: Cornell University Press, 1969.

Black, III, Robert C. *The Railroads of the Confederacy.* Chapel Hill, N.C.: University of North Carolina Press, 1952.

Callahan, James M. *The Diplomatic History of the Southern Confederacy.* Springfield, Mass.: Walden Press, 1957.

Coulter, E. Morton. *The Confederate States of America, 1861–1865.* Baton Rouge, La.: Louisiana State University Press, 1950.

Current, Richard N. *Old Thad Stevens: A Story of Ambition.* Madison, Wis.: The University of Wisconsin Press, 1942.

_____, ed. *The Political Thoughts of Abraham Lincoln.* Indianapolis, Ind.: The Bobbs-Merrill Co., Inc., 1967.

Duberman, Martin B. *Charles Francis Adams, 1807–1886.* Boston: Houghton Mifflin Company, 1960.

Fite, Emerson D. *Social and Industrial Conditions in the North during the Civil War.* New York: Crowell Collier and Macmillan, Inc., 1910.

Franklin, John H. *The Emancipation Proclamation.* New York: Doubleday & Company, Inc., 1963.

Frederickson, George M. *The Inner Civil War: Northern Intellectuals and the Crisis of the Union.* New York: Harper & Row, Publishers, 1968.

Gray, Wood. *The Hidden Civil War: The Story of the Copperheads.* New York: The Viking Press, Inc., 1942.

Hendrick, Burton J. *Lincoln's War Cabinet.* Gloucester, Mass.: Peter Smith, 1946.

McCague, James. *The Second Rebellion: The Story of the New York City Draft Riots of 1863.* New York: Dial Press, Inc., 1968.

McPherson, James M., ed. *The Negro's Civil War.* New York: Pantheon Books, Inc., 1965.

_____. *Struggle for Equality: Abolitionist and the Negro in the Civil War and Reconstruction.* Princeton, N.J.: Princeton University Press, 1964.

Moore, Albert B. *Conscription and Conflict in the Confederacy.* New York: Hillary House Publishers, 1924.

Murdock, Eugene C. *Patriotism Limited, 1862–1865: The Civil War Draft and the Bounty System.* Kent, Ohio: Kent State University Press, 1967.

Nevins, Allan. *Statesmanship of the Civil War.* New York: Crowell Collier and Macmillan, Inc., 1962.

Oberholtzer, Ellis P. *Jay Cooke, Financier of the Civil War.* 2 vols. New York: Burt Franklin, 1969.

Owsley, Frank L. *King Cotton Diplomacy: Foreign Relations of the Confederate States of America,* 2d ed. Chicago: University of Chicago Press, 1959.

Quarles, Benjamin. *Lincoln and the Negro.* New York: Oxford University Press, 1962.

Randall, James G. *Constitutional Problems under Lincoln,* 2d, ed. Urbana, Ill.: University of Illinois Press, 1964.

———, and David Donald. *The Civil War and Reconstruction,* 2d ed. Boston: D. C. Heath & Company, 1961.

Ringold, May. *The Role of the State Legislatures in the Confederacy.* Athens, Ga.: University of Georgia Press, 1966.

Strode, Hudson. *Jefferson Davis.* 4 vols. New York: Harcourt Brace Jovanovich, Inc., 1955–1966.

Trefousse, Hans L. *The Radical Republicans: Lincoln's Vanguard for Racial Justice.* New York: Alfred A. Knopf, 1969.

Van Deusen, Glyndon G. *William Henry Seward.* New York: Oxford University Press, 1967.

Vandiver, Frank E. *Basic History of the Confederacy.* New York: Van Nostrand Reinhold Company, 1962.

Voegeli, V. Jacque. *Free but Not Equal: The Midwest and the Negro during the Civil War.* Chicago: University of Chicago Press, 1967.

Wiley, Bell I. *The Plain People of the Confederacy.* Gloucester, Mass.: Peter Smith, 1943.

Williams, T. Harry. *Lincoln and the Radicals.* Madison, Wis.: University of Wisconsin Press, 1941.

Wood, Forrest G. *Black Scare: The Racist Response of Emancipation and Reconstruction.* Berkeley, Calif.: University of California Press, 1968.

Yearns, Wilfred B. *The Confederate Congress.* Athens, Ga.: University of Georgia Press, 1960.

problem 7

Black Slavery: The Genesis and Nature of Racial Attitudes

Twenty black slaves were sold to Jamestown in 1619. At that time there was no clear distinction in the English language —at least in the United States—between slavery and servitude; but by 1670 Virginia law had fixed the Negro's status in permanent slavery. On the other hand, *when* the black man became permanently enslaved is not so important as *why* —in short, why his race, among all the races of the world, was selected for chattel material. Various explanations have been chronicled, ranging from biblical interpretations, to biological, to internecine wars between the Christians and the Moors, to economic needs, to states' rights.

One of the first reasons cited was that of heathenism; the Negro was not a Christian and, therefore, was fit only for slavery. This explanation was later changed, after the black man embraced Christianity, to mean he did not measure up to proper standards. One group of slavery apologists described the Negro as physically different and innately inferior to the Anglo-Saxon race, whereas others looked to the biblical stories of Cain and Noah. Realizing that only fanciful interpretations could produce this sort of biblical rationale, opponents of this school reminded the apologists that all the descendants of Cain had been destroyed by the flood; and they pointed to the emphasis that Christianity places on the unity of mankind and Paul's message in which he said that God "hath made of one blood all nations in the earth to dwell. . . ."

During the eighteenth and nineteenth centuries many of the ancient myths about the black man began to crumble under the scrutiny of empirical evidence as Negro scientists, such as Benjamin Banneker, and intellectuals, such as Phyllis Wheatley, demonstrated the potential of their race.

Dr. John Bachman challenged the biological differences during the 1830s, but it was Charles Darwin's theory of evolution more than anything else that dispelled doubts and reaffirmed the belief that all human races belong to a single species. With the turn of the twentieth century science began to focus on the controversy. In 1900 a French scientist named Joseph Deniker proved that there is no significant difference in the size of the brain among the races of man, and Johann F. Blumenback gave up on hair classification.

Thus, the evidence slowly began to reveal that none of the systems that pointed to separate origins of the races worked; but still the annoying notion of inherent differences persisted. Finally, during the 1920s Franz Boas, the father of cultural anthropology, tried to resolve the issue by demanding proof that the races are different and that race determines mentality. No sound evidence was forthcoming, and by 1927 most learned psychologists and anthropologists had reached the conclusion that differences in intelligence cannot be established along racial lines.

As the student studies this problem, the following questions are offered to help further his deliberations.

General Questions for Reflection and Discussion

1. To what extent was the stigma of inferiority placed on the black man during the colonial period of American history?

2. Why do you suppose Congress chose to debate the question of slavery in the territories (at least before 1860) rather than the rationale for the existence of slavery?

3. What main currents in American thought continually rejected the "peculiar institution"?

4. To what extent do people conform to the roles that we set for them through our covert and overt actions?

5. To what extent are good feelings and good manners essential to the democratic creed of individual liberty and constitutional laws in our country? When should equality overrule personal liberty?

6. What forces in the progress of mankind helped to break down the myths about the inferiority of the black man?

Basic Questions for Reflection and Discussion

1. To what extent is Jordan suggesting that words condition attitudes?

2. What happened in the seventeenth century to cause writers to make a distinction between Moors and Negroes?

3. Why did the English experience with Africans differ with that of the Spanish and Portuguese?

4. In what ways did the English idea of blackness express values?

5. What does Jordan mean by "external discipline"?

6. To what extent is Bancroft blaming the Moors for the enslavement of the Negro? To what extent is he blaming the Greeks and Romans? To what extent is he blaming the Spanish and Portuguese?

7. According to Bancroft, why were black men considered better slaves than Indians?

8. Compare Bancroft's treatment of English attitudes toward black slavery with that of Jordan.

9. What do you find wrong with Fitzhugh's comparisons of the different forms of slavery?

10. Why is Fitzhugh opposed to "free society"?

11. What does Sumner mean by assumption of fact and assumption of Constitution? Why does he call the assumption with regard to the Constitution absurd?

12. Compare Fitzhugh's treatment of the Bible with regard to slavery with that of Sumner.

13. To what extent are Fitzhugh and Sumner each appealing both to the emotions and to reason?

Winthrop D. Jordan

The Evolution of English Attitudes toward the Black Man

The most arresting characteristic of the newly discovered African was his color. Travelers rarely failed to comment upon it; indeed when describing Negroes they frequently began with complexion and then moved on to dress (or rather lack of it) and manners. At Cape Verde, "These people are all blacke, and are called Negroes, without any apparell, saving before their privities." Robert Baker's narrative poem recounting his two voyages to the West African coast in 1562 and 1563 first introduced the natives with these engaging lines:

> And entering in [a river], we see
> a number of blacke soules,
> Whose likelinesse seem'd to be,
> but all as blacke as coles.
> Their Captaine comes to me
> as naked as my naile,
> Not having witte or honestie
> to cover once his taile.

Even more sympathetic observers seemed to find blackness a most salient quality in Negroes: "Although the people were blacke and naked, yet they were civill."

Englishmen actually described Negroes as *black*—an exaggerated term

Reprinted with permission of the University of North Carolina Press from *White over Black: American Attitudes toward the Negro, 1550–1812*, by Winthrop D. Jordan in *William and Mary Quarterly*, 7 (April 1950), published for the Institute of Early American History and Culture, omitting footnotes except where necessary for understanding by permission of the publisher, pp. 4–11 and 40–43.

which in itself suggests that the Negro's complexion had powerful impact upon their perceptions. Even the peoples of northern Africa seemed so dark that Englishmen tended to call them "black" and let further refinements go by the board. Blackness became so generally associated with Africa that every African seemed a black man. In Shakespeare's day, the Moors, including Othello, were commonly portrayed as pitchy black and the terms *Moor* and *Negro* used almost interchangeably. With curious inconsistency, however, Englishmen recognized that Africans south of the Sahara were not at all the same people as the much more familiar Moors. Sometimes they referred to Negroes as "black Moors" to distinguish them from the peoples of North Africa. During the seventeenth century the distinction became more firmly established and indeed writers came to stress the difference in color, partly because they delighted in correcting their predecessors and partly because Negroes were being taken up as slaves and Moors, increasingly, were not. In the more detailed and accurate reports about West Africa of the seventeenth century, moreover, Negroes in different regions were described as varying considerably in complexion. In England, however, the initial impression of Negroes was not appreciably modified: the firmest fact about the Negro was that he was "black."

The powerful impact which the Negro's color made upon Englishmen must have been partly owing to suddenness of con-

369

tact. Though the Bible as well as the arts and literature of antiquity and the Middle Ages offered some slight introduction to the "Ethiope," England's immediate acquaintance with black-skinned peoples came with relative rapidity. While the virtual monopoly held by Venetian ships in England's foreign trade prior to the sixteenth century meant that people much darker than Englishmen were not entirely unfamiliar, really black men were virtually unknown except as vaguely referred to in the hazy literature about the sub-Sahara which had filtered down from antiquity. Native West Africans probably first appeared in London in 1554; in that year five "Negroes," as the legitimate trader William Towrson reported, were taken to England, "kept till they could speake the language," and then brought back again "to be a helpe to Englishmen" who were engaged in trade with Negroes on the coast. Hakluyt's later discussion of these Negroes, who he said "could wel agree with our meates and drinkes" though "the colde and moyst aire doth somewhat offend them," suggests that these "blacke Moores" were a novelty to Englishmen. In this respect the English experience was markedly different from that of the Spanish and Portuguese who for centuries had been in close contact with North Africa and had actually been invaded and subjected by people both darker and more highly civilized than themselves. The impact of the Negro's color was the more powerful upon the Englishmen, moreover, because England's principal contact with Africans came in West Africa and the Congo where men were not merely dark but almost literally black: one of the fairest-skinned nations suddenly came face to face with one of the darkest peoples on earth.

Viewed from one standpoint, Englishmen were merely participating in Europe's discovery that the strange men who stood revealed by European expansion overseas came in an astounding variety of colors. A Spanish chronicle translated into English in 1555 was filled with wonder at this diversity: "one of the marveylous thynges that god useth in the composition of man, is coloure: whiche doubtlesse can not bee consydered withowte great admiration in beholding one to be white and an other blacke, beinge coloures utterlye contrary. Sum lykewyse to be yelowe whiche is betwene blacke and white: and other of other colours as it were of dyvers liveries." As this passage suggests, the juxtaposition of black and white was the most striking marvel of all. And for Englishmen this juxtaposition was more than a curiosity.

In England perhaps more than in southern Europe, the concept of blackness was loaded with intense meaning. Long before they found that some men were black, Englishmen found in the idea of blackness a way of expressing some of their most ingrained values. No other color except white conveyed so much emotional impact. As described by the *Oxford English Dictionary,* the meaning of *black* before the sixteenth century included, "Deeply stained with dirt; soiled, dirty, foul. . . . Having dark or deadly purposes, malignant; pertaining to or involving death, deadly; baneful, disastrous, sinister. . . . Foul, iniquitous, atrocious, horrible, wicked. . . . Indicating disgrace, censure, liability to punishment, etc." Black was emotionally partisan color, the handmaid and symbol of baseness and evil, a sign of danger and repulsion.

Embedded in the concept of blackness was its direct opposite—whiteness. No other colors so clearly implied opposition, "beinge coloures utterlye contrary"; no others were so frequently used to denote polarization:

> Everye white will have its blacke,
> And everye sweete its sowre.

White and black connoted purity and filthiness, virginity and sin, virtue and baseness, beauty and ugliness, beneficence and evil, God and the devil.

Whiteness, moreover, carried a special

significance for Elizabethan Englishmen: it was, particularly when complemented by red, the color of perfect human beauty, especially *female* beauty. This ideal was already centuries old in Elizabeth's time, and their fair Queen was its very embodiment: her cheeks were "roses in a bed of lillies." (Elizabeth was naturally pale but like many ladies then and since she freshened her "lillies" at the cosmetic table.) An adoring nation knew precisely what a beautiful Queen looked like.

> Her cheeke, her chinne, her neck, her nose,
> This was a lillye, that was a rose;
> Her hande so white as whales bone,
> Her finger tipt with Cassidone;
> Her bosome, sleeke as Paris plaster,
> Held upp twoo bowles of Alabaster.

Shakespeare himself found the lily and the rose a compelling natural coalition.

> 'Tis beauty truly blent, whose red and white
> Nature's own sweet and cunning hand laid on.

By contrast, the Negro was ugly, by reason of his color and also his "horrid Curles" and "disfigured" lips and nose. As Shakespeare wrote apologetically of his black mistress,

> My Mistress' eyes are nothing like the sun;
> Coral is far more red than her lips' red:
> If snow be white, why than her breasts are dun;
> If hairs be wires, black wires grow on her head.
> I have seen roses damask'd, red and white,
> But no such roses see I in her cheeks.

Some Elizabethans found blackness an ugly mask, superficial but always demanding attention.

> Is *Byrrha* browne? Who doth the question aske?

> Her face is pure as Ebonie jeat blacke,
> It's hard to know her face from her faire maske,
> Beautie in her seemes beautie still to lacke.
> Nay, she's snow-white, but for that russet skin,
> Which like a vaile doth keep her whitenes in.

A century later blackness still required apology and mitigation: One of the earliest attempts to delineate the West African Negro as a heroic character, Aphra Behn's popular story *Oroonoko* (1688), presented Negroes as capable of blushing and turning pale. It was important, if incalculably so, that English discovery of black Africans came at a time when the accepted standard of ideal beauty was a fair complexion of rose and white. Negroes not only failed to fit this ideal but seemed the very picture of perverse negation.[1]

From the first, however, many English observers displayed a certain sophistication about the Negro's color. Despite an ethnocentric tendency to find blackness repulsive, many writers were fully aware that Negroes themselves might have different tastes. As early as 1621 one writer told of the "Jetty coloured" Negroes, "Who in their native beauty most delight,/And in contempt doe paint the Divell white"; this assertion became almost a commonplace and even turned up a hundred and fifty years later in Newport, Rhode Island. Many accounts of Africa reported explicitly that the Negro's preference in colors was inverse to the European's, even the Negro's features were conceded to be appealing to Negroes. By the late seventeenth century, in a changing social atmosphere, some observers decided that the Negro's jet blackness was more handsome than the

---

[1] In the Middle Ages a man's "complexion" was conceived as revealing his temperament because it showed his particular blend of humors, each of which was associated with certain colors . . . Yet Englishmen seem not to have made efforts to link the Negro's skin color specifically to his bile or dominant humor and hence to his temperament.

lighter tawny hues; this budding appreciativeness was usually coupled, though, with expressions of distaste for "Large Breasts, thick Lips, and broad Nostrils" which many Negroes "reckon'd the Beauties of the Country." As one traveler admiringly described an African queen, "She was indifferently tall and well shap'd, of a perfect black; had not big Lips nor was she flat Nos'd as most of the Natives are, but well featur'd and very comely." By this time, the development of the slave trade to America was beginning to transform the Negro's color from a marvel into an issue. In what was surely a remarkable complaint for the master of a slaving vessel, Captain Thomas Phillips wrote in 1694 that he could not "imagine why they should be despis'd for their colour, being what they cannot help, and the effect of the climate it has pleas'd God to appoint them. I can't think there is any intrinsick value in one colour more than another, nor that white is better than black, only we think it so because we are so, and are prone to judge favourably in our own case, as well as the blacks, who in odium of the colour, say, the devil is white, and so paint him." During the eighteenth century the Negro's color was to come into service as an argument for "diversitarian" theories of beauty; Europe's discovery of "blacks" and "tawnies" overseas helped nurture a novel relativism. More important so far as the Negro was concerned, his color was to remain for centuries what it had been from the first, a standing problem for natural philosophers. . . .

The Protestant Reformation in England was a complex development, but certainly it may be said that during the century between Henry VIII and Oliver Cromwell the content and tone of English Christianity were altered in the direction of Biblicism, personal piety, individual judgment, and more intense self-scrutiny and internalized control. Many pious Englishmen, not all of them "Puritans," came to approach life as if conducting an examination and to approach Scripture as if peering in a mirror. As a result, their inner energies were brought unusually close to the surface, more frequently into the almost rational world of legend, myth, and literature. The taut Puritan and the bawdy Elizabethan were not enemies but partners in this adventure which we usually think of in terms of great literature — of Milton and Shakespeare — and social conflict — of Saints and Cavaliers. The age was driven by the twin spirits of adventure and control, and while "adventurous Elizabethans" embarked upon voyages of discovery overseas, many others embarked upon inward voyages of discovery. Some men, like William Bradford and John Winthrop, were to do both.

Given this charged atmosphere of (self-) discovery, it is scarcely surprising that Englishmen should have used peoples overseas as social mirrors and that they were especially inclined to discover attributes in savages which they found first but could not speak of in themselves.

Nowhere is the way in which certain of these cultural attributes came to bear upon Negroes more clearly illustrated than in a passage by George Best, an Elizabethan adventurer who sailed with Martin Frobisher in 1577 in search of the Northwest Passage. In his discourse demonstrating the habitability of all parts of the world, Best veered off to the problem of the color of Negroes. The cause of their blackness, he decided, was explained in Scripture. Noah and his sons and their wives were "white" and "by course of nature should have begotten . . . white children. But the envie of our great and continuall enemie the wicked Spirite is such, that as hee coulde not suffer our olde father Adam to live in the felicitie and Angelike state wherein he was first created, . . . so againe, finding at this flood none but a father and three sons living, hee so caused one of them to disobey his fathers commandment, that after him all his posteritie should bee accursed." The "fact" of this "disobedience," Best continued, was this: Noah "commanded" his sons and their wives to behold God "with reverence and feare," and that "while they remained in the Arke, they should use continencie, and abstaine from carnall copulation with their wives: . . . which good instructions and exhortations notwithstanding his wicked sonne Cham disobeyed, and being perswaded that the first childe borne after the flood . . . should inherite . . . all the dominions of the earth, hee . . . used company with his wife, and craftily went about thereby to dis-inherite the offspring of his other two brethren." To punish this "wicked and detestable fact," God willed that "a sonne should bee born whose name was Chus, who not onely it selfe, but all his posteritie after him should bee so blacke and lothsome, that it might remain a spectacle of disobedience to all the worlde. And of this blacke and cursed Chus came all these blacke Moores which are in Africa."

The inner themes running throughout this extraordinary exegesis testify eloquently to the completeness with which English perceptions could integrate sexuality with blackness, the devil, and the judgment of a God who had originally created man not only "Angelike" but "white." These running equations lay embedded at a deep and almost inaccessible level of Elizabethan culture; only occasionally do they appear in complete clarity, as when evil dreams

> . . . hale me from my sleepe like forked Devils,
> Midnight, though Æthiope, Empresse of Black Soules,
> Thou general Bawde to the whole world.

But what is still more arresting about George Best's discourse is the shaft of light it throws upon the dark mood of strain and control in Elizabethan culture. In an important sense, Best's remarks are not about Negroes; rather they play upon a theme of external discipline exercised upon the man who fails to discipline himself. The linkages he established—"disobedience" with "carnall copulation"

with something "black and lothsome"—were not his alone; the term *dirt* first began to acquire its meaning of moral impurity, of smuttiness, at the very end of the sixteenth century. Perhaps the key term, though, is "disobedience"—to God and parents—and perhaps, therefore, the passage echoes one of the central concerns of Englishmen of the sixteenth and early seventeenth centuries. Tudor England was undergoing social ferment, generated by an increasingly commercialized economy and reflected in such legislative monuments as the Statute of Apprentices and the Elizabethan vagrancy and poor laws. Overseas mercantile expansion brought profits and adventure but also a sense, in some men, of disquietude. One commentator declared that the merchants, "whose number is so increased in these our daies," had "in times past traded chiefly with European countries but "now in these daies, as men not contented with these journies, they have sought out the east and west Indies, and made now and then suspicious voiages."[2] Literate Englishmen generally (again not merely the Puritans) were concerned with the apparent disintegration of social and moral controls at home; they fretted endlessly over the "masterless men" who had once had a proper place in the social order but who were now wandering about, begging, robbing, raping. They fretted also about the absence of a spirit of due subordination—of children to parents and servants to masters. They assailed what seemed a burgeoning spirit of avariciousness, a spirit which one social

[2] . . . A similar sense of the necessity of ordering and controlling the spreading migrations of peoples underlay Sir Walter Raleigh's revealing notation that "first, we are to consider that the world after the flood was not planted by imagination, neither had the children of *Noah* wings, to fly from *Shinaar* to the uttermost border of Europe, Africa, and Asia in haste, but that these children were directed by a wise father, who knew those parts of the world before the flood, to which he disposed his children after it, and sent them not as discoverers, or at all adventure, but assigned and allotted to every son, and their proper parts. . . ."

critic described revealingly as "a barbarous or slavish desire to turne the penie."
They decried the laborers who demanded
too high wages, the masters who would
squeeze their servants, and the landed
gentlemen who valued sheep more than
men—in short, the spirit of George Best's
Cham, who aimed to have his son "inherite and possesse all the dominions of
the earth."

It was the case with English confrontation with Negroes, then, that a society in
a state of rapid flux, undergoing important changes in religious values, and com-
prised of men who were energetically on
the make and acutely and often uncomfortably self-conscious of being so, came
upon a people less technologically advanced, markedly different in appearance
and culture. From the first, Englishmen
tended to set Negroes over against them-

selves, to stress what they conceived to be
radically contrasting qualities of color,
religion, and style of life, as well as ani-
mality and a peculiarly potent sexuality.
What Englishmen did not at first fully
realize was that Negroes were potentially
subjects for a special kind of obedience
and subordination which was to arise as
adventurous Englishmen sought to possess for themselves and their children one
of the most bountiful dominions of the
earth. When they came to plant themselves in the New World, they were to
find that they had not entirely left behind the spirit of avarice and insubordination. Nor does it appear, in light of
attitudes which developed during their
first two centuries in America, that they
left behind all the impressions initially
gathered of the *Negro* before he became
pre-eminently the *slave*.

George Bancroft

Black Slavery: The Influence of the Struggle between Christians and Moors

While Virginia, by the concession of a representative government, was constituted

From *History of the United States of America,
from the Discovery of the Continent,* Vol. 1, by
George Bancroft (New York: D. Appleton & Co.,
1834), pp. 119–126, omitting footnotes except where
necessary for understanding. Reprinted by courtesy
of Appleton-Century-Crofts, Educational Division,
Meredith Corporation.

the asylum of liberty, it became the abode
of hereditary bondsmen.

Slavery and the slave-trade are older
than the records of human society; they
are found to have existed wherever the savage hunter began to assume the habits of
pastoral or agricultural life; and, with the
exception of Australasia, they have extended to every portion of the globe. The

oldest monuments of human labor on the Egyptian soil are the results of slave labor. The founder of the Jewish people was a slave-holder and a purchaser of slaves. The Hebrews, when they broke from their own thraldom, planted slavery in the promised land. Tyre, the oldest commercial city of Phoenicia, was like Babylon, a market "for the persons of men."

Old as are the traditions of Greece, slavery is older. The wrath of Achilles grew out of a quarrel for a slave; Grecian dames had servile attendants; the heroes before Troy made excursions into the neighboring villages and towns to enslave the inhabitants. Greek pirates, roving, like the corsairs of Barbary, in quest of men, laid the foundations of Greek commerce; each commercial town was a slave-mart; and every cottage near the sea-side was in danger from the kidnapper. Greeks enslaved each other. The language of Homer was the mother tongue of the Helots; the Grecian city that warred on its neighbor city made of its captives a source of profit; the hero of Macedon sold men of his own kindred and language into hopeless slavery. More than four centuries before the Christian era, Alcidamas, a pupil of Gorgias, has said that "God has sent forth all men free; nature has made no man slave." While one class of Greek authors of that period confounded the authority of master and head of a family, others asserted that the relation of master and slave is conventional; that freedom is the law of nature, which knows no difference between master and slave; that slavery is the child of violence, and inherently unjust. "A man, O my master," so speaks the slave in a comedy of Philemon, "because he is a slave, does not cease to be a man. He is of the same flesh with you. Nature makes no slaves." Aristotle, though he recognises "living chattels" as a part of the complete family, has left on record his most deliberate, judgement, that the prize of freedom should be placed within the reach of every slave. Yet the idea of universal free labor was only a dormant bud, not to be quickened for many centuries.

Slavery hastened the fall of the commonwealth of Rome. The power of the father to sell his children, of the creditor to sell his insolvent debtor, of the warrior to sell his captive, carried it into the bosom of every family, into the conditions of every contract, into the heart of every unhappy land that was invaded by the Roman eagle. The slave-markets of Rome were filled with men of various nations and colors. "Slaves are they!" writes Seneca; "say that they are men." The golden-mouthed orator Dion inveighs against hereditary slavery as at war with right. "By the law of nature, all men are born free," are the words of Ulpian. The Roman digests pronounce slavery "contrary to nature."

In the middle age the pirate and the kidnapper and the conqueror still continued the slave-trade. The Saxon race carried the most repulsive forms of slavery to England, where not half the population could assert a right to freedom, and where the price of a man was but four times the price of an ox. In defiance of severe penalties, the Saxons long continued to sell their own kindred into slavery on the continent. Even after the conquest, slaves were exported from England to Ireland, till, in 1102, a national synod of the Irish, to remove the pretext for an invasion, decreed the emancipation of all their English slaves.

The German nations made the shores of the Baltic the scenes of the same traffic; and the Dnieper formed the highway on which Russian merchants conveyed slaves from the markets of Russia to Constantinople. The wretched often submitted to bondage as the only refuge from want. But it was the long wars between German and Slavonic tribes which imparted to the slave-trade so great activity that in every country of Western Europe the whole class of bondmen took and still retain the name of Slaves.

In Sicily, natives of Asia and Africa

were exposed for sale. From extreme poverty the Arab father would pawn even his children to the Italian merchant. Rome itself long remained a mart where Christian slaves were exposed for sale, to supply the market of Mahometans. The Venetians purchased alike infidels and Christians, and sold them again to the Arabs in Sicily and Spain. Christian and Jewish avarice supplied the slave-market of the Saracens. The trade, though censured by the church and prohibited by the laws of Venice, was not effectually checked till the mere presence in a Venetian ship was made the sufficient evidence of freedom.

In the twelfth century, Pope Alexander III had written that, "nature having made no slaves, all men have an equal right to liberty." Yet, as among Mahometans the captive Christian had no alternative but apostasy or servitude, the captive infidel was treated in Christendom with corresponding intolerance. In the camp of the leader whose pious arms redeemed the sepulchre of Christ from the mixed nations of Asia and Libya, the price of a war-horse was three slaves. The Turks, whose law forbade the enslaving of Mussulmans, continued to sell Christian and other captives; and Smith, the third president of Virginia, relates that he was himself a run-away from Turkish bondage.

All this might have had no influence on the destinies of America but for the long and doubtful struggles between Christians and Moors in the west of Europe, where, for more than seven centuries, the two religions were arrayed against each other, and bondage was the reciprocal doom of the captive. France and Italy were filled with Saracen slaves; the number of them sold into Christian bondage exceeded the number of all the Christians ever sold by the pirates of Barbary. The clergy felt no sympathy for the unbeliever. The final victory of the Spaniards over the Moors of Granada, an event contemporary with the discovery of America, was signalized by a great emigration of the Moors to the coasts of Northern Africa, where each mercantile city became a nest of pirates, and every Christian the wonted booty of the corsair: an indiscriminate and retaliating bigotry gave to all Africans the denomination of Moors, and without scruple reduced them to bondage.

The clergy had broken up the Christian slave-markets at Bristol and at Hamburg, at Lyons and at Rome. In language addressed half to the courts of law and half to the people, Louis X, by the advice of the jurists of France, in July, 1315, published the ordinance that, by the law of nature, every man ought to be born free; that serfs were held in bondage only by a suspension of their early and natural rights; that liberty should be restored to them throughout the kingdom so far as the royal power extended; and every master of slaves was invited to follow his example by bringing them all back to their original state of freedom. Some years later, John de Wycliffe asserted the unchristian character of slavery. At the epoch of the discovery of America the moral opinion of the civilized world had abolished the trade in Christian slaves, and was demanding the emancipation of the serfs; but the infidel was not yet included within the pale of humanity.

Yet negro slavery is not an invention of the white man. As Greeks enslaved Greeks, as Anglo-Saxons dealt in Anglo-Saxons, so the earliest accounts of the land of the black men bear witness that negro masters held men of their own race as slaves, and sold them to others. This the oldest Greek historian commemorates. Negro slaves were seen in classic Greece, and were known at Rome and in the Roman empire. About the year 990, Moorish merchants from the Barbary coast reached the cities of Nigritia, and established an uninterrupted exchange of Saracen and European luxuries for the gold and slaves of Central Africa.

Not long after the conquests of the Portuguese in Barbary, their navy frequented the ports of Western Africa; and the first ships, which, in 1441, sailed so far south as Cape Blanco, returned not with negroes, but with Moors. These were treated as strangers, from whom information respecting their native country was to be derived. Antony Gonzalez, who had brought them to Portugal, was commanded to restore them to their ancient homes. He did so; and the Moors gave him as their ransom not gold only, but "black Moors" with curled hair. Negro slaves immediately became an object of commerce. The historian of the maritime discoveries of Spain even claims that she anticipated the Portuguese. The merchants of Seville imported gold dust and slaves from the western coast of Africa; so that negro slavery was established in Andalusia, and "abounded in the city of Seville," before the first voyage of Columbus.

The adventures of those days by sea, joining the creed of bigots with the designs of pirates and heroes, esteemed as their rightful plunder the wealth of the countries which they might discover, and the inhabitants, if Christians, as their subjects; if infidels, as their slaves. There was hardly a convenient harbor on the Atlantic frontier of the United States which was not entered by slavers. The red men of the wilderness, unlike the Africans, among whom slavery had existed from immemorial time, would never abet the foreign merchant in the nefarious traffic. Fraud and force remained, therefore, the means by which, near Newfoundland or Florida, on the shores of the Atlantic, or among the Indians of the Mississippi valley, Cortereal and Vasquez de Ayllon, Porcallo and Soto, and private adventurers, transported the natives of North America into slavery in Europe and the Spanish West Indies. Columbus, himself, in 1494, enslaving five hundred native Americans, sent them to Spain, that they might be publicly sold at Seville. The generous Isabella, in 1500, commanded the liberation of the Indians held in bondage in her European possessions. Yet her active benevolence extended neither to the Moors nor to the Africans; and even her compassion for the men of the New World was but transient. The commissions for making discoveries, issued a few days before and after her interference to rescue those whom Columbus had enslaved, reserved for herself and Ferdinand a fourth part of the slaves which the new kingdoms might contain. The slavery of Indians was recognised as lawful.

A royal edict of 1501 permitted negro slaves, born in slavery among Christians, to be transported. Within two years there were such numbers of Africans in Hispaniola that Ovando, the governor of the island, entreated that their coming might be restrained. For a short time the Spanish government forbade the introduction of negro slaves who had been bred in Moorish families, and allowed only those who were said to have been instructed in the Christian faith to be transported to the West Indies, under the plea that they might assist in converting infidel nations. But, after the culture of sugar was begun, the system of slavery easily overcame the scruples of men in power. King Ferdinand himself sent from Seville fifty slaves to labor in the mines, and promised to send more; and, because it was said that one negro could do the work of four Indians, the direct transportation of slaves from Guinea to Hispaniola was, in 1511, enjoined by a royal ordinance, and deliberately sanctioned by successive decrees. Was it not natural that Charles V, a youthful monarch, at his accession in 1516, should have readily granted licenses to the Flemings to transport negroes to the colonies? The benevolent Las Casas, who felt for the native inhabitants of the New World all that the purest missionary zeal could inspire, and who had seen them vanish away like dew before the cruelties of the Spaniards while the African thrived under the tropical sun, in 1517 suggested that negroes might still further be employed to perform the severe toils which they alone could endure. The board of trade at Seville was consulted, to learn how many slaves would be required; four for each Spanish emigrant had been proposed; deliberate calculation fixed the number at four thousand a year. In 1518 the monopoly, for eight years, of annually importing four thousand slaves into the West Indies, was granted by Charles V to La Bresa, one of his favorites, and was sold to the Genoese. The buyers of the contract purchased their slaves of the Portuguese, to whom a series of papal bulls had indeed granted the exclusive commerce with Western Africa; but the slave-trade between Africa and America was never expressly sanctioned by the see of Rome. Leo X declared that "not the Christian religion only, but Nature herself, cries out against the state of slavery." Paul III, two years after he had given authority to make slaves of every English person who would not assist in the expulsion of Henry VIII, in two separate briefs imprecated a curse on the Europeans who should enslave Indians, or any other class of men. Ximenes, the stern grand inquisitor, the austere but ambitious Franciscan, refused to sanction the introduction of negroes into Hispaniola, believing that the favorable climate would increase their numbers, and infallibly lead them to a successful revolt. Hayti, the first spot in America that received African slaves, was the first to set the example of African liberty.

The odious distinction of having first interested England in the slave-trade belongs to Sir John Hawkins. In 1562, he transported a large cargo of Africans to Hispaniola; the rich returns of sugar, ginger, and pearls, attracted the notice of Queen Elizabeth; and five years later she took shares in a new expedition, though the commerce, on the part of the English, in Spanish ports, was by the law of Spain illicit, as by the law of morals detestable.

Conditional servitude, under indentures or covenants, had from the first existed in Virginia. Once at least James sent over convicts, and once at least the city of London a hundred homeless children from its streets. The servant stood to his master in the relation of a debtor, bound to discharge by his labor the costs of emigration. White servants came to be a usual article of merchandise. They were sold in England to be transported, and in Virginia were to be purchased on shipboard. Not the Scots only, who were taken in the field of Dunbar, were sold into servitude in New England, but the royalist prisoners of the battle of Worcester. The leaders in the insurrection of Penruddoc, in spite of the remonstrance of Haselrig and Henry Vane, were shipped to America. At the corresponding period, in Ireland, the exportation of Irish Catholics was frequent. In 1672, the average price in the colonies, where five years of service were due, was about ten pounds, while a negro was worth twenty or twenty-five pounds.

The condition of apprenticed servants in Virginia differed from that of slaves chiefly in the duration of their bondage; the laws of the colony favored their early enfranchisement. But this state of labor easily admitted the introduction of perpetual servitude. In the month of August, 1619, five years after the commons of France had petitioned for the emancipation of every serf in every fief, a Dutch man-of-war entered James river and landed twenty negroes for sale. This is the sad epoch of the introduction of negro slavery; but the traffic would have been checked in its infancy had it remained with the Dutch. Thirty years after this first importation of Africans, Virginia to one black contained fifty whites; and, after seventy years of its colonial existence, the number of its negro slaves was proportionably much less than in several northern states at the time of the war of independence. Had no other form of servitude been known in Virginia than of men of the same race, every difficulty would have been promptly obviated. But the Ethiopian and Caucasian races were to meet together in nearly equal numbers beneath a temperate zone. Who could foretell the issue? The negro race, from its introduction, was regarded with disgust, and its union with the whites forbidden under ignominious penalties.

If Wyatt, on his arrival in Virginia in 1621, found the evil of negro slavery engrafted on the social system, he brought with him the memorable ordinance on which the fabric of colonial liberty was to rest, and which was interpreted by his instructions in a manner favorable to the colonists. An amnesty of ancient feuds was proclaimed. In November and December, 1621, the first session of an assembly under the written constitution was held. The production of silk engaged attention; but silk-worms could not be cared for where every comfort of household existence required to be created. As little was the successful culture of the vine possible, although the company had repeatedly sent vine-dressers. In 1621, the seeds of cotton were planted as an experiment; and their "plentiful coming up" was a subject of interest in America and England. From this year, too, dates the sending of beehives to Virginia, and of skilful workmen to extract iron from the ore. At the instance of George Sandys, five-and-twenty shipwrights came over in 1622.

Charles Sumner

Slavery Attacked

Mr. President—undertaking now, after a silence of more than four years, to address the Senate on this important subject, I should suppress the emotions natural to such an occasion, if I did not declare on the threshold my gratitude to that Supreme Being through whose benign care I am enabled, after much suffering and many changes, once again to resume my duties here, and to speak for the cause so near my heart. . . .

This is no time for soft words or excuses. All such are out of place. They may turn away wrath; but what is the wrath of man? This is no time to abandon any advantage in the argument. Senators sometimes announce that they resist Slavery on political grounds only, and remind us that they say nothing of the moral question. This is wrong. Slavery must be resisted not only on political grounds, but on all other grounds, whether social, economical, or moral. Ours is no holiday contest; nor is it any strife of rival factions, of White and Red Roses, of theatric Neri and Bianchi; but it is a solemn battle between Right and Wrong, between Good and Evil. Such a battle cannot be fought with rosewater. There is austere work to be done, and Freedom cannot consent to fling away any of her weapons. . . .

Thus, by various voices, is Slavery defiantly proclaimed a form of Civiliza-

From *Life and Public Services of Charles Sumner* by C. Edwards Lester (New York: United States Publishing Company, 1874), pp. 311, 313–324.

tion—not seeing that its existence is plainly inconsistent with the first principles of anything that can be called civilization, except by that figure of speech in classical literature where a thing takes its name from something which it has not, as the dreadful Fates were called merciful because they were without mercy. Pardon the allusion, if I add, that, listening to these sounding words for Slavery, I am reminded of the kindred extravagance related by that remarkable traveller in China, the late Abbé Huc, where a gloomy hole in which he was lodged, infested by mosquitoes and exhaling noisome vapors, with light and air entering by a single narrow aperture only, was styled by Chinese pride "The Hotel of the Beatitudes." According to a Hindoo proverb, the snail sees nothing but its own shell, and thinks it the grandest palace in the universe. This is another illustration of the delusion which we are called to witness.

It is natural that Senators thus insensible to the true character of Slavery should evince an equal insensibility to the true character of the Constitution. This is shown in the claim now made, and pressed with unprecedented energy, degrading the work of our fathers, that by virtue of the Constitution the pretended property in man is placed beyond the reach of Congressional prohibition even within Congressional jurisdiction, so that the slave-master may at all times enter the broad outlying territories of the Union with the victims of his oppression, and there continue to hold them by lash and chain.

Such are two assumptions, the first of fact, and the second of Constitutional Law, now vaunted without apology or hesitation. I meet them both. To the first I oppose the essential Barbarism of Slavery, in all its influences, whether high or low—as Satan is Satan still, whether towering in the sky or squatting in the toad. To the second I oppose the unanswerable, irresistible truth, that the Constitution of the United States nowhere recognized property in man. These two assumptions naturally go together. They are "twins" suckled by the same wolf. They are the "couple" in the present slave-hunt. And the latter cannot be answered without exposing the former. It is only when Slavery is exhibited in its truly hateful character that we fully appreciate the absurdity of the assumption, which, in defiance of express letter in the Constitution, and without a single sentence, phrase, or word upholding human bondage, yet foists into this blameless text the barbarous idea that man can hold property in man.

On former occasions I have discussed Slavery only incidentally; as, in unfolding the principle that Slavery is Sectional and Freedom National; in exposing the unconstitutionality of the Fugitive Slave Bill; in vindicating the Prohibition of Slavery in the Missouri Territory; in exhibiting the imbecility, throughout the Revolution, of the Slave States, and especially of South Carolina; and, lastly, in unmasking the Crime against Kansas. On all these occasions, where I spoke at length, I said too little of the character of Slavery—partly because other topics were presented, and partly from a prevailing disinclination to press the argument against those whom I knew to have all the sensitiveness of a sick man. But, God be praised, this time has passed, and the debate is now lifted from details to principles. Grander debate has not occurred in our history—rarely in any history; nor can it close or subside, except with the triumph of Freedom.

Of course I begin with the assumption of fact, which must be treated at length.

It was the often-quoted remark of John Wesley, who knew well how to use words, as also how to touch hearts, that Slavery is "the sum of all villainies." The phrase is pungent; but it were rash in any of us to criticise the testimony of that illustrious founder of Methodism, whose ample experience of Slavery in Georgia and the Carolinas seems to have been all condensed in this sententious judgment. Language is feeble to express all the enormity of an institution which is now exalted as in itself a form of civilization, "ennobling" at least to the master, if not to the slave. Look at it as you will, and it is always the scab, the canker, the "barebones," and the shame of the country — wrong, not merely in the abstract, as is often admitted by its apologists, but wrong in the concrete also, and possessing no single element of right. Look at it in the light of principle, and it is nothing less than a huge insurrection against the eternal law of God, involving in its pretensions the denial of all human rights, and also the denial of that Divine Law in which God himself is manifest, thus being practically the grossest lie and the grossest atheism. Founded in violence, sustained only by violence, such a wrong must by sure law of compensation blast master as well as slave — blast the lands on which they live, blast the community of which they are part, blast the government which does not forbid the outrage; and the longer it exists and the more completely it prevails, must its vengeful influences penetrate the whole social system. Barbarous in origin, barbarous in law, barbarous in all its pretensions, barbarous in the instruments it employs, barbarous in consequences, barbarous in spirit, barbarous wherever it shows itself, Slavery must breed Barbarians, while it develops everywhere, alike in the individual and the society to which he belongs, the essential elements of Barbarism. In this character it is conspicuous before the world.

Undertaking now to expose the BARBARISM OF SLAVERY, the whole broad field is open before me. There is nothing in its character, its manifold wrong, its wretched results, and especially in its influence on the class claiming to be "ennobled" by it, that will not fall naturally under consideration.

I know well the difficulty of this discussion, involved in the humiliating truth with which I begin. Senators, on former occasions, revealing their sensitiveness, have even protested against comparison between what were called "two civilizations," — meaning the two social systems produced respectively by Freedom and Slavery. The sensibility and the protest are not unnatural, though mistaken. "Two civilizations!" Sir, in this nineteenth century of Christian light there can be but one Civilization, and this is where Freedom prevails. Between Slavery and Civilization there is essential incompatibility. If you are for the one, you cannot be for the other; and just in proportion to the embrace of Slavery is the divorce from Civilization. As cold is but the absence of heat, and darkness but the absence of light, so is Slavery but the absence of justice and humanity, without which Civilization is impossible. That slave-masters should be disturbed, when this is exposed, might be expected. But the assumptions so boastfully made, while they may not prevent the sensibility, yet surely exclude all ground of protest, when these assumptions are exposed.

Nor is this the only difficulty. Slavery is a bloody Touch-Me-Not, and everywhere in sight now blooms the bloody flower. It is on the wayside as we approach the National Capitol; it is on the marble steps which we mount; it flaunts on this floor. I stand now in the house of its friends. About me, while I speak, are its most jealous guardians, who have shown in the past how much they are ready to do or not to do, where Slavery is in question. Menaces to deter me have not been spared. But I should ill deserve the high post of duty here, with which I am honored by a generous and enlightened people, if I could hesitate. Idolatry has been exposed in the presence of idolaters, and hypocrisy chastised in the presence of Scribes and Pharisees. Such examples may impart encouragement to a Senator undertaking in this presence to expose Slavery; nor can any language, directly responsive to Senatorial assumptions made for this Barbarism, be open to question. Slavery can be painted only in sternest colors; nor can I forget that Nature's sternest painter has been called the best.

The BARBARISM OF SLAVERY appears, *first,* in the *character of Slavery,* and, *secondly,* in the *character of Slave-Masters.*

Under the *first* head we shall properly consider (1) the Law of Slavery with its Origin, and (2) the practical results of Slavery, as shown in comparison between the Free States and the Slave States.

Under the *second* head we shall naturally consider (1) Slave-Masters as shown in the Law of Slavery; (2) Slave-Masters in their relations with slaves, here glancing at their three brutal instruments; (3) Slave-Masters in their relations with each other, with society, and with Government; and (4) Slave-Masters in their unconsciousness.

The way will then be prepared for the consideration of the assumption of Constitutional Law.

In presenting the CHARACTER OF SLAVERY, there is little for me, except to make Slavery paint itself. When this is done, the picture will need no explanatory words.

1. I begin with the *Law of Slavery and its Origin;* and here this Barbarism sketches itself in its own chosen definition. It is simply this: Man, created in the image of God, is divested of the human character, and declared to be a "chattel,"—that is, a beast, a thing, or article of property. . . .

Sir, look at its plain import, and see the relation which it establishes. The slave is held simply for the *use of his master,* to whose behests his life, liberty, and happiness are devoted, and by whom he may be bartered, leased, mortgaged, bequeathed, invoiced, shipped as cargo, stored as goods, sold on execution, knocked off at public auction, and even staked at the gaming-table on the hazard of a card or a die—all according to law. Nor is there anything, within the limit of life, inflicted on a beast, which may not be inflicted on the slave. He may be marked like a hog,

branded like a mule, yoked like an ox, hobbled like a horse, driven like an ass, sheared like a sheep, maimed like a cur, and constantly beaten like a brute—all according to law. And should life itself be taken, what is the remedy? The Law of Slavery, imitating that rule of evidence which in barbarous days and barbarous countries prevented the Christian from testifying against the Mahometan, openly pronounces the incompetency of the whole African race, whether bond or free, to testify against a white man in any case, and thus, after surrendering the slave to all possible outrage, crowns its tyranny by excluding the very testimony through which the bloody cruelty of the Slave-Master might be exposed.

Thus in its Law does Slavery paint itself; but it is only when we look at details, and detect its essential elements, *five in number,* all inspired by *a single motive,* that its character becomes completely manifest.

Foremost, of course, in these elements, is the impossible pretension, where Barbarism is lost in impiety, by which man claims *property in man.* Against such blasphemy the argument is brief. According to the Law of Nature, written by the same hand that placed the planets in their orbits, and, like them, constituting part of the eternal system of the Universe, every human being has complete title to himself direct from the Almighty. Naked he is born; but this birthright is inseparable from the human form. A man may be poor in this world's goods; but he owns himself. No war or robbery, ancient or recent—no capture—no middle passage—no change of clime—no purchase money—no transmission from hand to hand, no matter how many times, and no matter at what price, can defeat this indefeasible, God-given franchise. And a divine mandate, strong as that which guards Life, guards Liberty also. Even at the very morning of Creation, when God said, "Let there be light,"—earlier than the malediction against murder—he set the everlasting difference between man and chattel, giving to man "dominion over the fish of the sea, and over the fowl of the air, and over every living thing that moveth upon the earth."

> That right we hold
> By his donation; but man over men
> He made not lord: such title to himself
> Reserving, human left from human free.

Slavery tyrannically assumes power which Heaven denied—while, under its barbarous necromancy, borrowed from the Source of Evil, a man is changed into a chattel, a person is withered into a thing, a soul is shrunk into merchandise. Say, Sir, in lofty madness, that you own the sun, the stars, the moon; but do not say that you own a man, endowed with soul to live immortal, when sun and moon and stars have passed away.

Secondly. Slavery paints itself again in its complete *abrogation of marriage,* recognized as a sacrament by the Church, and as a contract by the civil power, wherever civilization prevails. Under the Law of Slavery no such sacrament is respected, and no such contract can exist. The ties formed between slaves are all subject to the selfish interests or more selfish lust of the master, whose license knows no check. Natural affections which have come together are rudely torn asunder: nor is this all. Stripped of every defence, the chastity of a whole race is exposed to violence, while the result is recorded in tell-tale faces of children glowing with a master's blood, but doomed for their mother's skin to Slavery through descending generations. . . . By license of Polygamy, one man may have many wives, all bound to him by marriage-tie, and in other respects protected by law. By license of Slavery, a whole race is delivered over to prostitution and concubinage, without the protection of any law. Surely, Sir, is not Slavery barbarous?

Thirdly. Slavery paints itself again in its complete *abrogation of the parental*

relation, provided by God in his benevolence for the nurture and education of the human family, and constituting an essential part of Civilization itself. And yet by the Law of Slavery—happily beginning to be modified in some places—this relation is set at nought, and in its place is substituted the arbitrary control of the master, at whose mere command little children, such as the Saviour called unto him, though clasped by a mother's arms, are swept under the hammer of the auctioneer. I do not dwell on this exhibition. Sir, is not Slavery barbarous?

Fourthly. Slavery paints itself again *in closing the gates of knowledge,* which are also the shining gates of Civilization. Under its plain, unequivocal law, the bondman, at the unrestrained will of his master, is shut out from all instruction; while in many places—incredible to relate—the law itself, by cumulative provisions, positively forbids that he shall be taught to read! Of course the slave cannot be allowed to read: for his soul would then expand in larger air, while he saw the glory of the North Star, and also the helping truth, that God, who made iron, never made a slave; for he would then become familiar with the Scriptures, with the Decalogue still speaking in the thunders of Sinai—with that ancient text, "He that stealeth a man and selleth him, or if he be found in his hand, he shall surely be put to death"—with that other text, "Masters, give unto your servants that which is just and equal"—with that great story of Redemption, when the Lord raised the slave-born Moses to deliver his chosen people from the house of bondage—and with that sublimer story, where the Saviour died a cruel death, that all men, without distinction of race, might be saved, leaving to mankind a commandment which, even without his example, makes Slavery impossible. Thus, in order to fasten your manacles upon the slave, you fasten other manacles upon his soul. The ancients maintained Slavery by chains and death: you maintain it by that infinite despotism and monopoly through which human nature itself is degraded. Sir, is not Slavery barbarous?

Fifthly. Slavery paints itself again *in the appropriation of all the toil* of its victims, excluding them from that property in their own earnings which the Law of Nature allows and Civilization secures. The painful injustice of this pretension is lost in its meanness. It is robbery and petty larceny under garb of law. And even the meanness is lost in the absurdity of its associate pretension, that the African, thus despoiled of all earnings, is saved from poverty, and that for his own good he must work for his master, and not for himself. Alas, by such fallacy is a whole race pauperized! And yet this transaction is not without illustrative example. A sombre poet, whose verse has found wide favor, pictures a creature who

> with one hand put
> A penny in the urn of poverty,
> And with the other took a shilling out.

And a celebrated traveller through Russia, more than a generation ago, describes a kindred spirit, who, while devoutly crossing himself at church with his right hand, with the left deliberately picked the pocket of a fellow-sinner by his side. Not admiring these instances, I cannot cease to deplore a system which has much of both, while, under affectation of charity, it sordidly takes from the slave all the fruits of his bitter sweat, and thus takes from him the main spring to exertion. Tell me, Sir, is not Slavery barbarous?

Such is Slavery in its five special elements of Barbarism, as recognized by law: first, assuming that man can hold property in man; secondly, abrogating the relation of husband and wife; thirdly, abrogating the parental tie; fourthly, closing the gates of knowledge; and, fifthly, appropriating the unpaid labor of another. Take away these elements, sometimes called "abuses," and Slavery will

cease to exist; for it is these very "abuses" which constitute Slavery. Take away any one of them, and the abolition of Slavery begins. And when I present Slavery for judgment, I mean no slight evil, with regard to which there may be reasonable difference of opinion, but I mean this fivefold embodiment of "abuse," this ghastly quincunx of Barbarism, each particular of which, if considered separately, must be denounced at once with all the ardor of an honest soul, while the whole fivefold combination must awake a fivefold denunciation. The historic pirates, once the plague of the Gulf whose waters they plundered, have been praised for the equity with which they adjusted the ratable shares of spoil, and also for generous benefactions to the poor, and even to churches, so that Sir Walter Scott could say—

> Do thou revere
> The statutes of the Buccaneer.

In our Law of Slavery what is there to revere? what is there at which the soul does not rise in abhorrence?

But this fivefold combination becomes yet more hateful when its *single motive* is considered; and here Slavery paints itself finally. . . . It is an outrage, where five different pretensions all concur in one single object, looking only to the profit of the master, and constituting its ever-present motive power, which is simply *to compel the labor of fellow-men without wages.* If I pronounce this object not only barbarous, but brutal, I follow the judgment of Luther's Bible, in the book "Jesus Sirach," known in our translation as Ecclesiasticus, where it is said: "He that giveth not his wages to the laborer, *he is a bloodhound.*"

Slavery is often exposed as degrading Humanity. On this fruitful theme nobody ever expressed himself with the force and beautiful eloquence of our own Channing. His generous soul glowed with indignation at the thought of man, supremest creature of earth, and first of God's works, despoiled of manhood and changed to a thing. But earlier than Channing was Jean Jacques Rousseau, who, with similar eloquence and the same glowing indignation, vindicated Humanity. How grandly he insists that nobody can consent to be a slave, or can be born a slave! Believing Liberty the most noble of human attributes, this wonderful writer will not stop to consider if descent to the condition of beasts be not to degrade human nature, if renunciation of the most precious of all God's gifts be not to offend the Author of our being; but he demands only by what right those who degrade themselves to this depth can subject their posterity to the same ignominy, renouncing for them goods which do not depend upon any ancestors, and without which life itself is to all worthy of it a burden; and he justly concludes, that, as to establish Slavery, it is necessary to violate Nature, so, to perpetuate this claim, it is necessary to change Nature. . . .

If the offense of Slavery were less ex-tended, if it were confined to some narrow region, if it had less of grandeur in its proportions, if its victims were counted by tens and hundreds instead of millions, the five-headed enormity would find little indulgence; all would rise against it, while Religion and Civilization would lavish choicest efforts in the general warfare. But what is wrong when done to one man cannot be right when done to many. If it is wrong thus to degrade a single soul, if it is wrong thus to degrade you, Mr. President, it cannot be right to degrade a whole race! And yet this is denied by the barbarous logic of Slavery, which, taking advantage of its own wrong, claims immunity because its usurpation has assumed a front of audacity that cannot be safely attacked. Unhappily there is Barbarism elsewhere in the world; but American Slavery, as defined by existing law, stands forth as the greatest organized Barbarism on which the sun now looks. It is without a single peer. Its author, after making it, broke the die.

George Fitzhugh

Negro Slavery Defended

We have already stated that we should not attempt to introduce any new theories of government and of society, but merely try

From *Sociology for the South,* or *The Failure of Free Society* by George Fitzhugh (New York: Burt Franklin, 1854), pp. 82–96, footnotes omitted except where necessary for understanding.

to justify old ones, so far as we could deduce such theories from ancient and almost universal practices. Now it has been the practice in all countries and in all ages, in some degree, to accommodate the amount and character of government control to the wants, intelligence, and moral capacities of the nations or individuals to be governed. A highly moral and intellectual people, like the free citizens of ancient Athens, are best governed by a democracy. For a less moral and intellectual one, a limited and constitutional monarchy will answer. For a people either very ignorant or very wicked, nothing short of military despotism will suffice. So among individuals, the most moral and well-informed members of society require no other government than law. They are capable of reading and understanding the law, and have sufficient self-control and virtuous disposition to obey it. Children cannot be governed by mere law; first, because they do not understand it, and secondly, because they are so much under the influence of impulse, passion and appetite, that they want sufficient self-control to be deterred or governed by the distant and doubtful penalties of the law. They must be constantly controlled by parents or guardians, whose will and orders shall stand in the place of law for them. Very wicked men must be put into penitentiaries; lunatics into asylums, and the most wild of them into straight jackets, just as the most wicked of the sane are manacled with irons; and idiots must have committees to govern and take care of them. Now, it is clear the Athenian democracy would not suit a negro nation, nor will the government of mere law suffice for the individual negro. He is but a grown-up child, and must be governed as a child, not as a lunatic or criminal. The master occupies towards him the place of parent or guardian. We shall not dwell on this view, for no one will differ with us who thinks as we do of the negro's capacity, and we might argue till dooms-day, in vain, with those who have a high opinion of the negro's moral and intellectual capacity.

Secondly. The negro is improvident; will not lay up in summer for the wants of winter; will not accumulate in youth for the exigencies of age. He would become an insufferable burden to society. Society has the right to prevent this, and

can only do so by subjecting him to domestic slavery.

In the last place, the negro race is inferior to the white race, and living in their midst, they would be far outstripped or outwitted in the chase of free competition. Gradual but certain extermination would be their fate. We presume the maddest abolitionist does not think the negro's providence of habits and money-making capacity at all to compare to those of the whites. This defect of character would alone justify enslaving him, if he is to remain here. In Africa or the West Indies, he would become idolatrous, savage and cannibal, or be devoured by savages and cannibals. At the North he would freeze or starve.

We would remind those who deprecate and sympathize with negro slavery, that his slavery here relieves him from a far more cruel slavery in Africa, or from idolatry and cannibalism, and every brutal vice and crime that can disgrace humanity; and that it christianizes, protects, supports and civilizes him; that it governs him far better than free laborers at the North are governed. There, wife-murder has become a mere holiday pastime; and where so many wives are murdered, almost all must be brutally treated. Nay, more: men who kill their wives or treat them brutally, must be ready for all kinds of crime, and the calendar of crime at the North proves the inference to be correct. Negroes never kill their wives. If it be objected that legally they have no wives, then we reply, that in an experience of more than forty years, we never yet heard of a negro man killing a negro woman. Our negroes are not only better off as to physical comfort than free laborers, but their moral condition is better.

But abolish negro slavery, and how much of slavery still remains. Soldiers and sailors in Europe enlist for life; here, for five years. Are they not slaves who have not only sold their liberties, but their lives also? And they are worse treated than domestic slaves. No domestic affection and self-interest extend their aegis over them. No kind mistress, like a guardian angel, provides for them in health, tends them in sickness, and soothes their dying pillow. Wellington at Waterloo was a slave. He was bound to obey, or would, like admiral Bying, have been shot for gross misconduct, and might not, like a common laborer, quit his work at any moment. He had sold his liberty, and might not resign without the consent of his master, the king. The common laborer may quit his work at any moment, whatever his contract; declare that liberty is an inalienable right, and leave his employer to redress by a useless suit for damages. The highest and most honorable position on earth was that of the slave Wellington; the lowest, that of the free man who cleaned his boots and fed his hounds. The African cannibal, caught, christianized and enslaved, is as much elevated by slavery as was Wellington. The kind of slavery is adapted to the men enslaved. Wives and apprentices are slaves; not in theory only, but often in fact. Children are slaves to their parents, guardians and teachers. Imprisoned culprits are slaves. Lunatics and idiots are slaves also. Three-fourths of free society are slaves, no better treated, when their their wants and capacities are estimated, than negro slaves. The masters in free society, or slave society, if they perform properly their duties, have more cares and less liberty than the slaves themselves. "In the sweat of thy face shalt thou earn thy bread!" made all men slaves, and such all *good men* continue to be.

Negro slavery would be changed immediately to some form of peonage, serfdom or villienage, if the negroes were sufficiently intelligent and provident to manage a farm. No one would have the labor and trouble of management, if his negroes would pay in hires and rents one-half what free tenants pay in rent in Europe. Every negro in the South would be soon liberated, if he would take liberty on the terms that white tenants hold it. The fact that he cannot enjoy liberty on such terms, seems conclusive that he is only fit to be a slave.

But for the assaults of the abolitionists, much would have been done ere this to regulate and improve Southern slavery. Our negro mechanics do not work so hard, have many more privileges and holidays, and are better fed and clothed than field hands, and are yet more valuable to their masters. The slaves of the South are cheated of their rights by the purchase of Northern manufactures which they could produce. Besides, if we would employ our slaves in the coarser processes of the mechanic arts and manufactures, such as brick making, getting and hewing timber for ships and houses, iron mining and smelting, coal mining, grading railroads and plank roads, in the manufacture of cotton, tobacco, &c., we would find a vent in new employments for their increase, more humane and more profitable than the vent afforded by new states and territories. The nice and finishing processes of manufactures and mechanics should be reserved for the whites, who only are fitted for them, and thus, by diversifying pursuits and cutting off dependence on the North, we might benefit and advance the interests of our whole population. Exclusive agriculture has depressed and impoverished the South. We will not here dilate on this topic, because we intend to make it the subject of a separate essay. Free trade doctrines, not slavery, have made the South agricultural and dependent, given her a sparse and ignorant population, ruined her cities, and expelled her people.

Would the abolitionists approve of a system of society that set white children free, and remitted them at the age of fourteen, males and females, to all the rights, both as to person and property, which belong to adults? Would it be criminal or praiseworthy to do so? Criminal, of course. Now, are the average of negroes equal in information, in native intelligence, in prudence or providence,

to well-informed white children of fourteen? We who have lived with them for
forty years, think not. The competition of
the world would be too much for the children. They would be cheated out of their
property and debased in their morals. Yet
they would meet every where with sympa-
thizing friends of their own color, ready
to aid, advise and assist them. The negro
would be exposed to the same competition
and greater temptations, with no greater
ability to contend with them, with these
additional difficulties. He would be welcome nowhere; meet with thousands of
enemies and no friends. If he went North,
the white laborers would kick him and
cuff him, and drive him out of employment. If he went to Africa, the savages
would cook him and eat him. If he went
to the West Indies, they would not let him
in, or if they did, they would soon make
of him a savage and idolater.

We have a further question to ask. If it
be right and incumbent to subject children to the authority of parents and
guardians, and idots and lunatics to committees, would it not be equally right and
incumbent to give the free negroes masters,
until at least they arrive at years of discretion, which very few ever did or will
attain? What is the difference between the
authority of a parent and of a master?
Neither pay wages, and each is entitled to
the services of those subject to him. The
father may not sell his child forever, but
may hire him out till he is twenty-one.
The free negro's master may also be restrained from selling. Let him stand in
loco parentis, and call him papa instead
of master. Look closely into slavery, and
you will see nothing so hideous in it; or if
you do, you will find plenty of it at home
in its most hideous form.

The earliest civilization of which history gives account is that of Egypt. The
negro was always in contact with that
civilization. For four thousand years he
has had opportunities of becoming civilized. Like the wild horse, he must be
caught, tamed and domesticated. When

his subjugation ceases he again runs wild,
like the cattle on the Pampas of the South,
or the horses on the prairies of the West.
His condition in the West Indies proves
this.

It is a common remark, that the grand
and lasting architectural structures of
antiquity were the results of slavery. The
mighty and continued association of labor
requisite to their construction, when
mechanic art was so little advanced, and
labor-saving processes unknown, could
only have been brought about by a despotic authority, like that of the master
over his slaves. It is, however, very remarkable, that whilst in taste and artistic
skill the world seems to have been retrograding ever since the decay and abolition
of feudalism, in mechanical invention
and in great utilitarian operations requiring the wielding of immense capital
and much labor, its progress has been
unexampled. Is it because capital is more
despotic in its authority over free laborers
than Roman masters and feudal lords
were over their slaves and vassals?

Free society has continued long enough
to justify the attempt to generalize its
phenomena, and calculate its moral and
intellectual influences. It is obvious that,
in whatever is purely utilitarian and
material, it incites invention and stimu-
lates industry. Benjamin Franklin, as a
man and a philosopher, is the best exponent of the working of the system. His
sentiments and his philosophy are low,
selfish, atheistic and material. They tend
directly to make man a mere "featherless
biped," well-fed, well-clothed and comfortable, but regardless of his soul as
"the beasts that perish."

Since the Reformation the world has as
regularly been retrograding in whatever
belongs to the departments of genius,
taste and art, as it has been progressing
in physical science and its application to
mechanical construction. Medieval Italy
rivalled if it did not surpass ancient
Rome, in poetry, in sculpture, in painting, and many of the fine arts. Gothic

architecture reared its monuments of skill and genius throughout Europe, till the 15th century; but Gothic architecture died with the Reformation. The age of Elizabeth was the Augustan age of England. The men who lived then acquired their sentiments in a world not yet deadened and vulgarized by puritanical cant and levelling demagogism. Since then men have arisen who have been the fashion and the go for a season, but none have appeared whose names will descend to posterity. Liberty and equality made slower advances in France. The age of Louis XIV was the culminating point of French genius and art. It then shed but a flickering and lurid light. Frenchmen are servile copyists of Roman art, and Rome had no art of her own. She borrowed from Greece; distorted and deteriorated what she borrowed; and France imitates and falls below Roman distortions. The genius of Spain disappeared with Cervantes; and now the world seems to regard nothing as desirable except what will make money and what costs money. There is not a poet, an orator, a sculptor, or painter in the world. The tedious elaboration necessary to all the productions of high art would be ridiculed in this money-making, utilitarian, charlatan age. Nothing now but what is gaudy and costly excites admiration. The public taste is debased.

But far the worst feature of modern civilization, which is the civilization of free society, remains to be exposed. Whilst labor-saving processes have probably lessened by one half, in the last century, the amount of work needed for comfortable support, the free laborer is compelled by capital and competition to work more than he ever did before, and is less comfortable. The organization of society cheats him of his earnings, and those earnings go to swell the vulgar pomp and pageantry of the ignorant millionaires, who are the only great of the present day. These reflections might seem, at first view, to have little connexion with negro slavery; but it is well for us of the South

not to be deceived by the tinsel glare and glitter of free society, and to employ ourselves in doing our duty at home, and studying the past, rather than in insidious rivalry of the expensive pleasures and pursuits of men whose sentiments and whose aims are low, sensual and grovelling.

Human progress, consisting in moral and intellectual improvement, and there being no agreed and conventional standard weights or measures of moral or intellectual qualities and quantities, the question of progress can never be accurately decided. We maintain that man has not improved, because in all save the mechanic arts he reverts to the distant past for models to imitate, and he never imitates what he can excel.

We need never have white slaves in the South, because we have black ones. Our citizens, like those of Rome and Athens, are a privileged class. We should train and educate them to deserve the privileges and to perform the duties which society confers on them. Instead, by a low demagogism depressing their self-respect by discourses on the equality of man, we had better excite their pride by reminding them that they do not fulfil the menial offices which white men do in other countries. Society does not feel the burden of providing for the few helpless paupers in the South. And we should recollect that here we have but half the people to educate, for half are negroes; whilst at the North they profess to educate all. It is in our power to spike this last gun of the abolitionists. We should educate all the poor. The abolitionists say that it is one of the necessary consequences of slavery that the poor are neglected. It was not so in Athens, and in Rome, and should not be so in the South. If we had less trade with and less dependence on the North, all our poor might be profitably and honorably employed in trades, professions and manufactures. Then we should have a rich and denser population. Yet we but marshal her in the way that she was going. The South is already aware of the necessity of a new policy, and has begun to act on it. Every day more and more is done for education, the mechanic arts, manufactures and internal improvements. We will soon be independent of the North.

We deem this peculiar question of negro slavery of very little importance. The issue is made throughout the world on the general subject of slavery in the abstract. The argument has commenced. One set of ideas will govern and control after awhile the civilized world. Slavery will every where be abolished, or every where be re-instituted. We think the opponents of practical, existing slavery, are estopped by their own admission; nay, that unconsciously, as socialists, they are the defenders and propagandists of slavery, and have furnished the only sound arguments on which its defence and justification can be rested. We have introduced the subject of negro slavery to afford us a better opportunity to disclaim the purpose of reducing the white man any where to the condition of negro slaves here. It would be very unwise and unscientific to govern white men as you would negroes. Every shade and variety of slavery has existed in the world. In some cases there has been much of legal regulation, much restraint of the master's authority; in others, none at all. The character of slavery necessary to protect the whites in Europe should be much milder than negro slavery, for slavery is only needed to protect the white man, whilst it is more necessary for the government of the negro even than for his protection. But even negro slavery should not be outlawed. We might and should have laws in Virginia, as in Louisiana, to make the master subject to presentment by the grand jury and to punishment, for any inhuman or improper treatment or neglect of his slave.

We abhor the doctrine of the "Types of Mankind"; first, because it is at war with scripture, which teaches us that the whole human race is descended from a common parentage; and, secondly, because it encourages and incites brutal masters to treat negroes, not as weak, ignorant and dependent brethren, but as wicked beasts, without the pale of humanity. The Southerner is the negro's friend, his only friend. Let no inter-meddling abolitionist, no refined philosophy, dissolve this friendship.

We find slavery repeatedly instituted by God, or by men acting under his immediate care and direction, as in the instances of Moses and Joshua. Nowhere in the Old or New Testament do we find the institution condemned, but frequently recognized and enforced. In individual instances slavery may be treated as an evil, and no doubt it is often a very great one where its subject is fitted to take care of himself and would be happier and more useful as a freeman than as a slave. It was often imposed as a punishment for sin, but this affords no argument against its usefulness or its necessity. It is probably no cause of regret that men are so constituted as to require that many should be slaves. Slavery opens many sources of happiness and occasions and encourages the exercise of many virtues and affections which would be unknown without it. It begets friendly, kind and affectionate relations, just as equality engenders antagonism and hostility on all sides.

Select Bibliography for Problem 7

Boskin, Joseph. "Race Relations in Seventeenth Century America: The Problem of the Origins of Negro Slavery," *Sociology and Social Research,* 49 (July 1965), 446–455.

Comas, Juan. "Racial Myths," *The Race Question of Modern Science,* UNESCO (1956).

de Reuck, Anthony, and Julie Knight, eds. *Caste and Race: Comparative*

Approaches. Boston: Little, Brown and Company, 1967, pp. 1–27, 166–234, and 255–332.

Dodd, William E. "The Emergence of the First Social Order in the United States," *American Historical Review,* 40 (January 1935), 217–231.

Elkins, Stanley, and Eric McKitrick. "Institutions and the Law of Slavery: The Dynamics of Unopposed Capitalism," *American Quarterly,* 9 (Spring 1957), 3–21.

———. "Institutions and the Law of Slavery: Slavery in Capitalist and Non-Capitalist Cultures," *American Quarterly,* 9 (Summer 1957), 159–179.

Hamilton, Andrew. "Negro: How He's Different," *Science Digest,* 54 (October 1963), 6–11.

Handlin, Oscar and Mary. "Origins of the Southern Labor System," *William and Mary Quarterly,* 7 (April 1950), 199–222.

Hesseltine, William B. "Some New Aspects of the Pro-Slavery Argument," *Journal of Negro History,* 21 (January 1936), 1–14.

Isaacs, Harold R. "Group Identity and Political Change: The Role of Color and Physical Characteristics," *Daedalus,* 96 (Spring 1967), 353–375.

Jordan, Winthrop D. "Modern Tensions and the Origins of American Slavery," *Journal of Southern History,* 28 (February 1962), 18–30.

———, ed. *The Negro Versus Equality, 1762–1826.* The Berkeley Series in American History. Charles Sellers, ed. Skokie, Ill.: Rand McNally & Co., 1969.

Klien, Herbert S. "Anglicanism, Catholicism and the Negro Slave," *Comparative Studies in Society and History,* 8 (April 1966), 295–327.

McKitrick, Eric, ed. *Slavery Defended: The Years of the Old South.* Englewood Cliffs, N. J.: Prentice-Hall, Inc., 1963.

Moller, Herbert. "Sex Composition and Correlated Culture Patterns of Colonial America," *William and Mary Quarterly,* 2 (April 1945), 131–137.

Morrow, Ralph E. "Pro-Slavery Argument Revisited," *Mississippi Valley Historical Review,* 48 (June 1961), 79–94.

Myrdal, Gunnar. *An American Dilemma: The Negro Problem and Modern Democracy.* 2 vols. New York: Harper

Newby, I. A., ed. *The Development of Segregationist Thought.* Homewood, Ill.: Dorsey Press, 1968.

Osofsky, Gilbert, ed. *The Burden of Race: A Documentary History of Negro-White Relations in America.* New York: Harper & Row, Publishers, 1967, pp. 1–114.

Perkins, Howard C. "Defense of Slavery in the Northern Press on the Eve of the Civil War," *Journal of Southern History,* 9 (November 1943), 501–531.

Pressly, Thomas J. "Racial Attitudes, Scholarship, and Reconstruction: A Review Essay," *The Journal of Southern History,* 32 (February 1966), 88–93.

Ratner, Lorman. "Northern Concern for Social Order as Cause for Rejecting Anti-Slavery, 1831–1840," *Historian,* 28 (November 1965), 1–18.

Ruchames, Louis. "Sources of Racial Thought in Colonial America," *Journal of Negro History,* 52 (October 1967), 251–272.

Sio, Arnold A. "Interpretation of Slavery: The Slave Status in the Americas," *Comparative Studies in Society and History,* 7 (April 1965), 298–308.

Stampp, Kenneth M., ed. *The Causes of the Civil War*. Englewood Cliffs, N. J.: Prentice-Hall, Inc., 1965, pp. 108–152.

Tannenbaum, Frank. "Destiny of the Negro in the Western Hemisphere," *Political Science Quarterly*, 61 (March 1946), 1–41.

Thomas, John L., ed. *Slavery Attacked: The Abolitionist Crusade*. Englewood Cliffs, N. J.: Prentice-Hall, Inc., 1965.

Woodward, C. Vann. "Flight from History, the Heritage of the Negro," *Nation*, 201 (September 20, 1965), 142–146.

part 8

Reunion
and Reaction

chapter 23

Reconstruction

The Political Arena

ASSASSINATION OF LINCOLN

On April 4, 1865, Lincoln reaffirmed his belief in a conciliatory peace; but it was his last public statement. That night John Wilkes Booth, with derringer in hand, walked into the President's box at Ford's Theater in Washington and fired at point-blank range. Lincoln, mortally wounded, was carried across the street to the William Petersen house, where he died the next morning without ever regaining consciousness. Although the President was no friend to the Radical Republicans in Congress, his assassination provided them with another reason to punish the South.

LINCOLN'S PLAN OF RECONSTRUCTION

Thus, soon after Appomattox southerners began to experience the ordeal of a vanquished people. The pardoning remarks of Grant were soon forgotten, and the Lincoln plan of Reconstruction presented by Johnson was under attack from the Senate. Posturing his plan in a spirit of forgiveness, Lincoln offered a formula whereby all but a few of the higher ex-Confederate officers might be pardoned and a procedure whereby the southern states might be brought back into the Union. The latter procedure would be put into operation when the number taking the oath of allegiance amounted to 10 percent of the voting population of 1860; then the state might organize its government and apply for Union recognition.

RADICAL PLAN OF RECONSTRUCTION

Lincoln's plan was no sooner introduced than the Radical Republicans began drafting their own program of Reconstruction. Believing that Reconstruction belonged to the powers of Congress and that the ex-Confederate states should be dealt with more sternly, Benjamin F. Wade of Ohio and Henry W. Davis of Maryland introduced a formula that called for a census report and a loyalty oath of at least 50 percent of the adult white males in any state that requested readmission to the Union. The bill also demanded that slavery be abolished by the state constitutions and that all Confederate and state debts be renounced. As a prerequisite for voting, citizens would be required to take a second oath in which they would deny any voluntary support of the Confederacy. Lincoln was able to keep this "strong measure" out of the statutes by exercising a pocket veto.[1] Still another question arose over the right of the federal government to interfere with the internal

---

[1] This veto reportedly marked the first serious break between the President and Congress.

affairs of the states. Thus, when Andrew Johnson became President, neither Congress nor the President had established its area of jurisdiction with regard to the problem of rebuilding the South.

FREEDMAN'S BUREAU

Disturbed by the President's action in vetoing their bill, members of Congress were determined more than ever before to reconstruct the South. Accordingly, that body created the Freedman's Bureau, which was designed to provide relief for the Negroes and poor whites, and soon thereafter established a Joint Committee on Reconstruction, whose task was to investigate conditions in the South and recommend appropriate programs. This committee soon fell under the influence of Thaddeus Stevens, a Radical Republican from Pennsylvania.

JOHNSON'S PLAN OF RECONSTRUCTION

Knowing that the new President was of humble birth and sensitive to the needs of the downtrodden, a few Radical Republican elements in the Senate schemed to use Johnson to punish the South; but his allegiance was to the Union and not to politics, and his plan was not unlike that of Lincoln. In fact, his program appeared to be more generous in some areas. Johnson recognized the state governments that had already been formed under Lincoln's 10 percent plan, and he proclaimed a general amnesty to all citizens of the still unreconstructed states except ex-Confederate leaders, those whose wealth exceeded $20,000, and those who refused to swear allegiance to the Union. He was prepared, however, to bring those rebel states back into the Union that would repeal their secession ordinances, repudiate their Confederate war debts, abolish slavery and ratify the Thirteenth Amend-

ment.[2] By December, when Congress began to convene in order to take up the question of seating the representatives of the repatriated states, all except Texas had fulfilled these requirements and that state qualified by April 1866.

BLACK CODES

As the battle over Reconstruction raged in Washington, southern states began to reconstruct themselves. Passed partly to supply a stable labor force, the Black Codes[3] offered the southern legal definition of the "freedman." These codes not only encouraged separation of the races but prohibited the use of black jurors and black witnesses against whites, nor could the Negro vote or bear arms. Finally, the codes forced the black man into a kind of involuntary servitude by prohibiting vagrancy and by pressing those found guilty into labor camps that greatly benefited the large planters. On the positive side, the codes granted the freedman the right to make contracts, to take law suits to regular state courts, and to acquire and hold property.

Another weapon that the Radical Republicans used against the Johnson plan was their refusal to seat the newly repatriated congressmen from the South. Although this action carried dubious constitutionality, it gave the Radicals and their Joint Committee time to collect evidence for their own plan of reconstruction.

By February 1866 the Radical Republicans were ready to act. They accordingly passed a measure that enlarged the Freedman's Bureau by providing for agents, military protection for the freedman, and legal protection. The new bill also established schools for the blacks and provided for assistance in locating and

[2] This amendment went into effect on December 18, 1865.
[3] All of the ex-Confederate states except Tennessee adopted these codes.

leasing land. Once again, however, the President vetoed the bill, not only because it appeared unconstitutional, but because it provided no guarantees for trial by jury. Congress, nevertheless, managed to pass it over the veto.

CIVIL RIGHTS ACT

In April of 1866 a determined Congress passed the Civil Rights Act, which provided citizenship to "all persons born in the United States and not subject to any foreign power." President Johnson, feeling that the bill would permit an invasion of states' rights, exercised another veto but to no avail.

FOURTEENTH AMENDMENT

Determined to make this act a part of the more permanent Constitution, Congress wrote the bill into an amendment and submitted it to the several states for adoption. In addition to the provisions in the Civil Rights Act, it declared that "No State shall make or enforce any law which shall abridge the privileges or immunities of citizens of the United States; nor shall any State deprive any person of life, liberty, or property, without due process of law; nor deny to any person within its jurisdiction the equal protection of the laws." Also, "Representatives shall be apportioned among the several States according to their respective numbers, counting the whole number of persons in each state, excluding Indians not taxed."[4] It was further stated that if Negroes were not given the suffrage except as punishment for crime, they could not be counted in the representation of the state. Finally, this section denied federal and state office to those officials who supported the Confederacy. Moreover, only Congress could remove this political restriction.

Most of the South followed the lead of the President in rejecting the Fourteenth Amendment, but Congress, nevertheless, declared it ratified on July 28, 1868. Only one state, Tennessee, had ratified it—that is, after some coercion.

The Fourteenth Amendment set a new precedent in the powers of the federal government, particularly those of the Supreme Court, over the control of the citizenry. Before, the several states had exercised almost complete authority over their subjects; the new amendment, however, changed the spirit of the Constitution to permit the federal Supreme Court to abrogate a state law when such action was held to be in the interest of the citizens. It has been written that its passage was merely another significant milestone in fulfilling the promises of the war.

FIRST RECONSTRUCTION

By March 1867 Congress was ready to act on its first Reconstruction bill. Designed in part to enforce the Fourteenth Amendment, the First Reconstruction Act divided the former Confederacy into five military districts under martial law. In addition, the powers of commander in chief were taken from the President and given to General Grant, the commander of the army. It was the military's task to supervise and ensure justice at the several state constitutional conventions preparatory to readmission into the Union. When states refused to act on the convention or to extend suffrage to blacks, the military stepped in and initiated the necessary proceedings.

CARPETBAGGERS AND SCALAWAGS

Since hundreds of ex-Confederate officers and civic leaders had been barred from political office,[5] the vacuum was filled in

---

[4] This section repealed the three-fifths rule of voting.

[5] Thousands of southern whites refused to register for voting as a form of protest.

some cases by blacks[6] and in some instances by northern as well as southern opportunists and adventurers. Those radical whites from the North became known as "carpetbaggers" while those from the South, formerly Whigs turned Republicans, were called "scalawags." It should be observed, however, that there were men in both groups who had honorable intentions toward the South and the Negro.

KU KLUX KLAN

In some instances, the state governments established under these conditions were incompetent and corrupt. Consequently, the whites under these governments became even more embittered toward the North and, instead of cooperating with the uninvited system visited upon them, looked for ways to retaliate. Their answer to the problem was the formation of such organizations as the Ku Klux Klan and White Camelia. Founded in Tennessee in 1866, the Klan resorted to violence in a bid to restore white southern supremacy and until 1871 served that purpose very effectively. Its opponent was the Union League, a Radical Republican organization that sought to win the support of the blacks and enroll them as voters.

TENURE OF OFFICE ACT

The congressional elections of 1866 further strengthened the Radicals since they gave the Republicans a two-thirds majority in both houses. With this reassuring vote of confidence, they were ready to take even more severe measures against the harried President. In March 1867 Congress passed the Tenure of Office Act over Johnson's veto. The provisions of this bill directed the President to obtain the consent of the Senate before removing an appointee once he had been approved by that body of Congress. It has been

[6] Only in the legislatures of South Carolina and Louisiana did the Negroes ever manage to attain a majority.

observed that among other purposes the bill was designed to protect Secretary of War Edwin M. Stanton, a Lincoln appointee, who had become an obvious spy for the Radical Republican forces. Thus, under the new act should Johnson attempt to dismiss Stanton, he would be setting himself up for possible impeachment.

ATTEMPTED REMOVAL OF JOHNSON

Eager to test the constitutionality of such a "brazen act," Johnson fired Stanton in February 1868 and appointed General Grant in his place, but Grant soon resigned as the political war between the President and Congress neared a climax. The Radical Republicans again accepted the challenge by drawing up impeachment articles on the grounds that the President had violated the Tenure of Office Act and therefore was guilty of a "high misdemeanor." The lengthy trial dragged on for more than two months and finally, on May 16, produced a 35 to 19 vote in favor of conviction; the Senate failed by one vote to muster the two-thirds necessary for removal. It has been suggested by historians of the subject that this one crucial vote preserved the system of checks and balances between the executive and legislative branches in the federal government.

ELECTION OF 1868

As the election of 1868 approached, the Republicans met at Chicago and nominated the popular war hero General Ulysses S. Grant of Ohio for President and Schuyler Colfax of Indiana for Vice-President. Their platform praised Radical Reconstruction and pledged the party to support peace and equal suffrage for all loyal Americans. It condemned Johnson, on the other hand, and promised the payment of military bounties and pensions and recommended the gold standard for the ills of the economy.

In midsummer the Democrats met in

New York and selected Horatio Seymour of New York for President and Francis P. Blair, Jr., of Missouri for his running mate. Their platform attacked Radical Reconstruction, favored amnesty for all ex-Confederate political offenses, encouraged economy in office, and called for a return to greenbacks. Finally, they appealed to their fellow citizens to praise Johnson.

When the returns were all in and the electoral votes were cast, Grant had won by a landslide electoral vote of 214 to 80. He had captured twenty-six of the thirty-four states, six of which were located in the South, where the Radical Republicans controlled the political machinery.[7] Grant's popular vote, however, was less impressive—3,013,421 to 2,706,829—and it has been suggested that the margin of victory came from the southern Negro vote, where the elated Republicans made a new resolve to keep the black man enfranchised.

FIFTEENTH AMENDMENT

In March 1870 Congress took still another step in granting full rights to the Negro by ratifying the Fifteenth Amendment. It declared that "the right of citizens of the United States to vote shall not be denied or abridged by the United States or by any State on account of race, color, or previous condition of servitude." This amendment was deemed necessary since Negro suffrage was determined on the state level as prescribed by the Fourteenth Amendment.

FORCE ACTS

In the same year the first of a series of bills known as the Force Acts was approved by Congress. Its provisions guaranteed the enforcement of the Fourteenth and Fifteenth Amendments and in the process served as another deterrent to the Klan.

[7] Three southern states were not permitted to vote.

FAILURE OF RADICAL RECONSTRUCTION

In the final analysis, Radical Reconstruction failed mainly because its various state governments discredited themselves through extravagance and corruption. Moreover, the high cost of rebuilding the war-torn cities sent taxes upward and state indebtedness to new highs; the subsequent adverse reaction among the citizenry was often leveled at radical governments regardless of their records.

REDEMPTION OF THE SOUTH

Redemption, or the return of southern state governments to southern white leaders, began in 1870, and by the following year Democrats had captured the governments of Tennessee, Virginia, North Carolina, and Georgia. The last two southern states were repatriated in 1877, when President Rutherford B. Hayes withdrew the remainder of federal troops from South Carolina and Louisiana.[8]

Select Bibliography

Beale, Howard K. *The Critical Year, 1866: A Study of Andrew Johnson and Reconstruction.* New York: Frederick Ungar Publishing Co., Inc., 1958.

Bentley, George. *A History of the Freedmen's Bureau.* Philadelphia, Pa.: University of Pennsylvania Press, 1955.

Bowers, Claude. *The Tragic Era: The Revolution after Lincoln.* Boston: Houghton Mifflin Company, 1929.

Brock, W. R. *An American Crisis: Congress and Reconstruction, 1865–1867.*

[8] The presence of troops in these states should not suggest military rule. That form of government had ended in all southern states by 1870.

New York: St. Martin's Press, Inc., 1963.

Brodie, Fawn M. *Thaddeus Stevens: Scourge of the South.* New York: W. W. Norton & Co., Inc., 1959.

Buck, Paul H. *Road to Reunion, 1865–1900.* Boston: Little, Brown and Company, 1937.

Carter, Hodding. *The Angry Scar: The Story of Reconstruction, 1865–1890.* New York: Doubleday & Company, Inc., 1959.

Coleman, Charles H. *The Election of 1868.* New York: AMS Press, 1933.

Conway, Alan. *The Reconstruction of Georgia.* Minneapolis, Minn.: University of Minnesota Press, 1966.

Coulter, E. Merton. *The South during Reconstruction, 1865–1877.* Baton Rouge, La.: Louisiana State University Press, 1947.

Craven, Avery. *Reconstruction: The Ending of the Civil War.* New York: Holt, Rinehart and Winston, Inc., 1969.

DeWitt, David M. *The Impeachment and Trial of Andrew Johnson.* New York: Russell & Russell, Publishers, 1902.

Dorris, Jonathan. *Pardon and Amnesty under Lincoln and Johnson: The Restoration of the Confederates to Their Rights and Privileges, 1861–1898.* Chapel Hill, N.C.: University of North Carolina Press, 1953.

Du Bois, William E. B. *Black Reconstruction.* New York: Russell & Russell, Publishers, 1956.

Eaton, Clement. *The Waning of the Old South Civilization.* Berkeley, Calif.: University of California Press, 1969.

Franklin, John H. *From Slavery to Freedom.* New York: Alfred A. Knopf, 1956.

_____. *Reconstruction: After the Civil War.* Chicago: University of Chicago Press, 1961.

Gillette, William. *The Right to Vote: Politics and the Passage of the Fifteenth Amendment.* Baltimore, Md.: Johns Hopkins Press, 1969.

Graham, Howard J. *Everyman's Constitution: Historical Essays on the Fourteenth Amendment, the "Conspiracy Theory," and American Constitutionalism.* Madison, Wis.: Society Press, 1968.

Harris, William C. *Presidential Reconstruction in Mississippi.* Baton Rouge, La.: Louisiana State University Press, 1967.

Hesseltine, William B. *Lincoln's Plan of Reconstruction.* Gloucester, Mass.: Peter Smith, 1960.

Horn, Stanley. *The Invisible Empire: The Story of the Ku Klux Klan, 1866–1871.* New York: Haskell House Publishers, 1969.

Hyman, Harold, ed. *Heard Round the World: The Impact Abroad of the Civil War.* New York: Alfred A. Knopf, 1969.

James, Joseph B. *The Framing of the Fourteenth Amendment.* Gloucester, Mass.: Peter Smith, 1956.

Kutler, Stanley I. *Judicial Power and Reconstruction Politics.* Chicago: University of Chicago Press, 1968.

Lewinson, Paul. *Race, Class, and Party: A History of Negro Suffrage and White Politics in the South.* New York: Russell & Russell, Publishers, 1963.

Lomask, Milton. *Andrew Johnson: President on Trial.* New York: Farrar, Straus & Giroux, Inc., 1960.

McKitrick, Eric L. *Andrew Johnson and Reconstruction.* Chicago: University of Chicago Press, 1960.

Montgomery, David. *Beyond Equality: Labor and the Radical Republicans, 1862–1872.* New York: Alfred A. Knopf, 1967.

Patrick, Rembert W. *The Reconstruction of the Nation.* New York: Oxford University Press, 1967.

Singletary, Otis. *Negro Militia and Reconstruction.* New York: McGraw-Hill Book Company, 1957.

chapter 24

The Grant Happening

The Age of Scandal

Ulysses Simpson Grant was placed in the unenviable position whereby his accomplishments would necessarily be measured in the light of those of other soldier Presidents of the past—namely Washington, Jackson, and Taylor; but unlike his famous predecessors, Grant entered public office with little if any formal political knowledge. Thus, it is not surprising that he encountered problems early, in fact with his first cabinet appointments. Borrowing the spoils system, Grant tried to reward old army pals and loyal party workers for their moral and financial support and ended up with a cabinet marked by incompetency, Hamilton Fish being the one exception during his second administration.

BLACK FRIDAY

As political ethics bowed to military discipline, Grant soon became inadvertently embroiled in the Black Friday affair. The two men responsible were the notorious stock market manipulators Jim Fisk and Jay Gould, who conceived a plot in 1869 to corner all of the gold on the New York market. The success of their scheme, however, rested on their ability to persuade Secretary of the Treasury Boutwell to stop selling gold to redeem government bonds. By convincing the President that inflated gold prices would raise farm prices, 402

Gould and Fisk were able to bring about the suspension of the sale of gold; whereupon they began buying the precious metal in large quantities. As the price of gold climbed in late September, word got out that the President's family was involved in suspicious operations on Wall Street. On Friday, September 24, the soaring price of gold caused merchants and bankers to panic. The President, who at last realized what was happening, cut short a vacation in order to intervene and start the sale of government gold once again. A congressional committee subsequently investigated the scandal and cleared Grant.

In 1872 the country turned its attention to the presidential election. Grant's reputation had been tarnished somewhat by the scandal, but he was still number one as far as the Republican party was concerned.[1] Nevertheless, there were liberal elements within the Republican camp who felt that reconstruction had served its purpose and should therefore be ended and that civil service reform and honest government should be initiated. Forming their own party, the Liberals called a convention at Cincinnati and nominated Horace Greeley, editor of the *New York Tribune,* and the liberal governor of Missouri, B. Gratz Brown. Their platform also encouraged land grants for railroads, hard money, and a high tariff.

The Democratic convention, meeting at

[1] Henry Wilson of Massachusetts was nominated as Grant's Vice-President.

Baltimore, found itself short on outstanding candidates and decided to endorse the Liberal Republican ticket of Greeley and Brown.

With the loyal support of the Radical Republican machines in the South, the election went to Grant, who pulled 286 electoral votes. Greeley, who died soon after the election, received no electoral ballots.[2] It has been observed that Thomas Nast, professional caricaturist in good standing with the Grant administration, played a significant role in the defeat of Greeley by picturing the editor and his friends as morally contemptible men. On the other hand, the caricaturist of *Frank Leslie's Illustrated Newspaper* spared Grant little, but the general's features did not lend themselves to as effective caricature as did those of Greeley.

CRÉDIT MOBILIER

Graft and corruption continued unabated as Grant's second term got under way. In 1872 the charge was made that prominent officials, including Vice-President Colfax, had accepted bribes from an illegal railroad construction company. Operating under the name of Crédit Mobilier, the company was actually organized by the stockholders of the Union Pacific, who in turn hired themselves as builders of the railroad. Thus, they were able to charge excessive figures regardless of the actual cost. This sort of manipulating was not uncommon for the times, and the punishment was seldom severe. Although the public careers of some politicians were ruined by the scandal, the most prominent congressmen got off with a censure from the House.

WHISKEY RING

The books had hardly been closed on the Crédit Mobilier when the Whiskey Ring

was exposed in 1875. Again high officials were indicted, including General Orville E. Babcock, Grant's private secretary, who was reportedly saved from political disaster by the President. The investigation revealed that the Whiskey Ring had been formed for the purpose of defrauding the government in the collection of internal revenue taxes on distilled liquors. This time, however, the offenders were not to be absolved of their sins.

IMPEACHMENT OF THE SECRETARY OF WAR

The following year articles of impeachment were written against William W. Belknap, Secretary of War, for selling appointments to Indian trading posts. With conviction altogether likely, the secretary resigned from his office to escape impeachment. Nevertheless, the House proceeded with the impeachment, and the Senate went through the motions of the trial; Belknap was acquitted when the area of Senate jurisdiction over a private citizen was questioned.

TWEED RING

In the meantime municipal fraud was discovered in New York City. Headed by Boss William M. Tweed, the Tammany[3] gang not only won control of the city's

---

[2] Greeley's wife died during the election.

[3] Prior to the American Revolution, societies that sympathized with King George III bore such names as St. George, St. Andrew, and St. David. Soon, however, opposition societies emerged, the most famous of which was the Sons of St. Tammany (better known as the Sons of Liberty). The name honored the Delaware Indian Chief Tamanend, who was noted for his wisdom, love of freedom, and benevolence. "Saint" was thrown in as a form of ridicule. After the Revolution these organizations died out; but on May 12, 1898, the Society of Tammany was revived as a middle-class expression in opposition to the Society of Cincinnati, an aristocratic group with centralist and monarchial tendencies. By 1830 Tammany had lost much of its national influence and soon came to represent the executive committee of the Democratic party in New York County.

financial structure but also bribed legislators and newspaper editors, and controlled judges. Tweed's expertise lay in the art of padding bills, and the profits of such plunder were as high as $100 million. Ironically, it was neither the police nor another gang that broke Tweed but rather the cartoons of Thomas Nast. Unwilling to be bought off, the caricaturist hounded the gang until a citizens' council conducted a damaging investigation, and Tweed lost what remained of his empire in the elections of 1871. Two years later he was fined $12,000 and sentenced to twelve years in prison, where he died in 1876.

Such corruption in state and local governments was not uncommon across the United States. The Erie Ring of Jay Gould and Jim Fisk bribed legislators in New Jersey, while the railroad companies purchased key officials in almost every state and major city their lines touched.

Economic Crises

It has been written that Grant was not very knowledgeable in the area of finance, but the problems of the 1870s would have taxed the skills of the most learned economist. His main problem was to try to appease the farmer and satisfy business at the same time. Since the inflation of the currency through the issuance of greenbacks had raised commodity prices and eased credit even though it had devalued the dollar, the farmer and labor class in general favored inflation and naturally opposed the recall of greenbacks. Business interests on the other hand wanted fewer greenbacks on the market and warned that inflation would ruin business and damage the nation's credit rating. Moreover, business reminded the President that constant fluctuations in the value of greenbacks encouraged speculation and opened the door to such notorious stock gamblers as Gould and Fisk.

PANIC OF 1873

In 1873 a commercial panic, the worst to that date, gripped the country. The collapse of Jay Cooke and Company, financier of the Northern Pacific Railroad and reportedly the soundest banking house in the country, touched it off. Investments and enterprise in general came to a halt, and the depression grew worse as businesses failed by the thousands and unemployment figures reached new highs. The finger of blame was pointed at the wide circulation of paper money with no guarantee for specie payments, overspeculation in railroads, and overexpansion in industry and agriculture.

SPECIE RESUMPTION ACT

Grant favored a resumption of specie payments but opposed the permanent use of paper money and its expansion on the market. Responding to the President's wishes, Congress passed the Specie Resumption Act on January 14, 1875, which provided that greenbacks were to be redeemable in gold by January 1, 1879, and that the circulation of such paper money was to be limited to $300 million.

Tariff reform and income taxes were also opposed by the Grant administration. After slashing the protective tariff for reasons of political expediency in the election year of 1872, the President raised the duties once again in 1875. In the meantime, legislators repealed the last of the income taxes that had been on the books since the time of the Civil War.

ELECTION OF 1876

The victory-starved Democrats generated renewed hope as another presidential election approached in 1876. The Republican party was smarting from the numerous scandals and the Democratic party of the South was once again showing signs of life. Moreover, the depression was working for the Democrats.

Such was the picture in June as the Republicans assembled in Cincinnati to nominate Governor Rutherford B. Hayes, an Ohio veteran of the Civil War, and William A. Wheeler of New York on a platform of high tariffs, frugality in government, and civil service reform. The Democrats meanwhile met in St. Louis and selected Governor Samuel J. Tilden of New York, conqueror of the Tweed gang, and Thomas A. Hendricks of Indiana. Their platform was not greatly unlike the one of 1872.

COMPROMISE OF 1877

When all ballots had been counted, Tilden had captured the popular vote with 4,284,020 to 4,036,572 for his opponent; but he failed by one vote to win a majority in the electoral college. Confusion continued to mount as three southern states, Florida, Louisiana, and South Carolina, sent in two sets of conflicting electoral returns amid cries of fraud and corruption. Unable to untangle the votes, a joint committee of fifteen was organized to select the president with five members representing the House, five from the Senate, and five from the Supreme Court. The political party alignment within the committee was to be seven Democrats, seven Republicans, and one Independent; but when the one Independent on the Supreme Court suddenly resigned to take a seat in the Senate, the choice fell to Joseph P. Bradley, a Republican. Since the new composition of the committee was unacceptable to the Democrats, a compromise had to be arranged between the two political parties: Hayes was to become President in return for the removal of federal troops from Louisiana and South Carolina (the last two states still under martial law), the appointment of a southerner to the cabinet, and a promise of federal funds to help rebuild the war-devastated regions of the South and particularly the railroad system. Thus, with this compromise sectional differences were set aside after decades of strife, but then so were the problems of the black man.

Foreign Affairs

THE REMOVAL OF FRANCE FROM MEXICO

Johnson's two notable achievements in foreign affairs during his administration were his assistance in the removal of France from Mexico and the purchase of Alaska. The removal of France required only a stern demand from Secretary of State Seward in February of 1866, and the execution of Maximilian by the Mexicans in June 1867 removed the last foreign threat to that country's independence.

PURCHASE OF ALASKA

The purchase of Alaska, while momentarily unpopular across the United States, proved to be one of the great success stories in American diplomacy in later years. Exhausted of beaver pelts and in danger of falling under British dominion, Alaska appeared to be a diplomatic and economic liability to Russia by 1867. That country, therefore, offered the territory to the United States for the bargain price of $7,200,000, which was promptly accepted by Seward. Although Alaska was variously ridiculed as "Seward's Folly" and "Seward's Icebox," the treaty was ratified by the Senate and the transfer took place on October 18, 1867.

TREATY OF WASHINGTON

Relations between Great Britain and the United States had mellowed since the Civil War, and by 1869 there was reason to believe that the new prime minister might be inclined to settle the troublesome *Alabama* claims. Accordingly, representatives of the two nations met in that year and arranged for a ten-member joint commission to settle the affair. The commission met in Washington in the spring of 1871 and drafted a treaty, which provided that the British apologize for having let the *Alabama* and her sister raiders escape, and that the British pay damages the amount of which would be determined by a board of arbitration composed of representatives from the United States,[4] Great Britain, Italy, Brazil and Switzerland. Geneva agreed to host the board. The amount awarded to the United States was set at $15,500,000 in gold and covered all direct damages to American shipping, although the latter had made numerous claims for indirect damages as well.

The Treaty of Washington resolved another long-standing dispute over the north western boundary between Canada and the United States. The boundary had been fixed in 1846, but a clearer definition was required in order to identify the middle of the channel where the line separated Vancouvers Island from the continent. Accepting the role of arbiter in the controversy, the German emperor offered a ruling that favored the United States by awarding to her the San Juan Islands.

Finally, the treaty settled the ancient controversy over fishing rights in the North Atlantic. By its provisions the United States would be permitted to use Canadian coastal fisheries for a period of ten years, and American coastal waters north of the 39th parallel would be open to the Canadians. Duty-free Canadian fish would also be permitted to enter the United States.

Because the United States appeared to have won more than her share of concessions in the exchange and partly because British claims dating from the Civil War had never been resolved, the United States agreed to pay Britain $7,429,819.

[4] The United States was represented by Charles Francis Adams.

DOMINICAN REPUBLIC

Grant, like some of his predecessors, was not averse to adding new territory to the United States; and in 1870, when two American soldiers of fortune in the Dominican Republic suggested that the time for annexing that republic might be right, the President and his private secretary Babcock fell in with the scheme. Their treaty of annexation, however, was defeated in the Senate by Grant's old nemesis, Senator Charles Sumner.

CUBA

Cuba's struggle with Spain also found a sympathetic audience in the United States soon after the Civil War. Grant had offered to arbitrate for Spain and her colony in 1868, but the mother country rejected the offer. In 1873 the two powers moved to the brink of war when Spanish authorities captured a vessel, the *Virginius,* off the coast of Cuba. Illegally flying the American flag and sailing under questionable papers, the crew of mixed origins was accused of aiding the Cuban rebels and ordered executed. Fifty-three persons had been executed, when warnings from the British navy and protests from the United States forced the Spanish to release the remainder of the crew. It was mainly through the wise counsel and negotiations of Secretary of State Fish that war was averted. Spain subsequently paid an indemnity of $80,000 to American families of the executed.

Grant Reconsidered

The many scandals that shamed Grant's administrations have caused scholars to assign him a rather uncomplimentary rating as President, but all was not dark during his tenure of office. Under Grant's administrations the financial affairs of the national government were put on a sound basis, taxes were reduced, money was stabilized, and a law for the resumption of specie payments was passed. Under his auspices a theory of civil service employment was inaugurated, and a Universal Postal Union, which now covers the civilized world, was established. Moreover, as President during Reconstruction, Grant played a significant role in helping to reestablish normal relations of state and national authorities, which in turn restored a semblance of order in the South. Finally, in internal affairs one of his most satisfying achievements was providing the impetus for the completion of transcontinental railroads.

In foreign affairs, Grant established the principle of international arbitration through the Treaty of Washington and was responsible for the peaceful and successful adjudication of the *Alabama* claims.

Select Bibliography

Bowers, Claude. *The Tragic Era: The Revolution after Lincoln.* Boston: Houghton Mifflin Company, 1929.

Callow, Jr., Alexander B. *The Tweed Ring.* New York: Oxford University Press, 1966.

Chevigny, Hector. *Russian America: The Great Alaskan Venture, 1741–1867.* New York: The Viking Press, Inc., 1965.

Degler, Carl N. *Out of Our Past: The Forces That Shaped Modern America.* New York: Harper & Row, Publishers, 1969.

Dunning, William A. *Reconstruction, Political and Economic, 1865–1877.* New York: Harper & Row, Publishers, 1907.

Haworth, Paul L. *The Hayes-Tilden Disputed Presidential Election of 1876.* New York: Russell & Russell, Publishers, 1966.

Hesseltine, William B. *Ulysses S. Grant, Politician.* New York: Frederick Ungar Publishing Co., Inc., 1967.

Josephson, Matthew. *The Politicos, 1865–1896.* New York: Harcourt Brace Jovanovich, Inc., 1938.

Lynch, John R. *Facts of Reconstruction.* New York: Arno Press, 1968.

Nevins, Allan. *The Emergence of Modern America, 1865–1878.* New York: Crowell Collier and Macmillan, Inc., 1928.

————. *Hamilton Fish: Inner History of the Grant Administration.* 2 vols. New York: Frederick Ungar Publishing Co., Inc., 1957.

Nichols, Jeannette P. *Alaska: A History.* New York: Russell & Russell, Publishers, 1963.

Nugent, Walter T. K. *Money and American Society, 1865–1880.* New York: The Free Press, 1968.

Patrick, Rembert W. *The Reconstruction of the Nation.* New York: Oxford University Press, 1967.

Perkins, Dexter. *The Monroe Doctrine, 1867–1907.* Gloucester, Mass.: Peter Smith, 1937.

Riegel, Robert R. *The Story of the Western Railroads.* Lincoln, Nebr.: University of Nebraska Press, 1964.

Seitz, Don C. *The Dreadful Decade, 1869–1879.* Westport, Conn.: Greenwood Press, Inc., 1968.

Sharkey, Robert P. *Money, Class and Party: An Economic Study of Civil War and Reconstruction.* Baltimore, Md.: Johns Hopkins Press, 1959.

Stampp, Kenneth M. *The Era of Reconstruction, 1865–1877.* New York: Alfred A. Knopf, 1965.

Unger, I. F. *The Greenback: A Social and Political History of American*

Finance, 1865–1879. Princeton, N. J.: Princeton University Press, 1964.

Van Deusen, Glyndon G. *Horace Greeley: Nineteenth Century Crusader*. Philadelphia, Pa.: University of Pennsylvania Press, 1963.

White, Leonard D., and Jean Schneider. *Republican Era: 1869–1901: A Study in Administrative History*. New York: Crowell Collier and Macmillan, Inc., 1958.

Woodward, C. Vann. *The Origins of the New South, 1877–1913*. Baton Rouge, La.: Louisiana State University Press, 1951.

———. *Reunion and Reaction: The Compromise of 1877 and the End of Reconstruction*. Boston: Little Brown and Company, 1966.

Woolfork, George R. *The Cotton Regency: The Northern Merchants and Reconstruction, 1865–1880*. New York: Twayne Publishers, 1958.

problem 8

Reshaping the South: Reconstruction or Redestruction

Reconstruction, for the convenience of study, may be divided into two phases of development: the first was marked by a struggle over procedure between the Presidents and Congress, and the second was concerned with the implementation of the Reconstruction Acts of 1867. In this problem we will examine those great dramas.

One of the first and clearest statements of appraisal on Reconstruction was written in 1907 by William A. Dunning, who viewed the whole decade of Radical Republican rule in the South as one of tragedy. His treatise went virtually unchallenged until the 1930s, when historians like W. E. B. Du Bois began to question the faults ascribed to the freedman in southern legislatures. Others continued to reexamine the era during the 1940s and 1950s, and in 1965 Kenneth M. Stampp offered the belief that the radical governments ought to be placed and measured in the context of their times and to be recognized for what they tried to do for the freedman.

In recent years a third group of historians has held that Reconstruction failed not because it extended only "temporary" political reform to the freedman, but because it failed to reconstruct the economic system of the South in a way that would have offered the black man land and economic independence.

The following general and basic ques-

tions are offered for the student's consideration as he studies the problem.

General Questions for Reflection and Discussion

1. To what extent were the Radical Republicans justified in imposing their plan of Reconstruction on the South? What parts of their program might be considered radical?
2. How can we explain the fact that Radical Reconstruction started crumbling by 1876?
3. In what ways were political rights related to education and economic security?
4. How did Radical Reconstruction improve conditions for the freedman? Harm him?
5. To what extent was social change a considered part of presidential Reconstruction? Of Radical Reconstruction?
6. To what extent does the contemporary civil rights movement represent unfinished business of Reconstruction?

Basic Questions for Reflection and Discussion

1. How does Stevens define the powers of Congress with regard to Reconstruction?

409

2. Compare Stevens' interpretation of the Constitution with that of Raymond.

3. Why is Stevens opposed to court-martialing southern leaders?

4. Compare Stevens' views toward the status of the ex-Confederate states with those of Raymond.

5. Why does Stevens prefer "reconstruction" to "restoration"? What position on this subject did Raymond take?

6. Compare Dunning's treatment of the ability of the freedman with that of Stampp.

7. Compare Dunning's treatment of inefficiency and corruption in govern-ment with that of Stampp?

8. In what ways does Stampp's treatment with that of Stampp.
differ with that of Dunning?

9. According to Stampp, in what ways were education and economic programs actively pursued during Reconstruction?

10. To what extent did radical Reconstruction retard the economic recovery of the South?

11. To what extent is Dunning guilty of oversimplifying certain issues? Stampp?

12. What race attitudes and social movements do you suppose influenced Dunning in 1907? Stampp in 1965?

Thaddeus Stevens

Johnson's Plan
of Reconstruction Attacked

Fellow Citizens:

In compliance with your request I have come to give my views of the present condition of the rebel States; of the proper mode of reorganizing the Government, and the future prospects of the Republic. During the whole progress of the war I never for a moment felt doubt or despondency. I knew that the loyal North would conquer the rebel despots who

From John Anthony Scott, ed., *Living Documents in American History*, Vol. 2. Copyright © 1963 by John Anthony Scott. Reprinted by permission of Washington Square Press Division of Simon & Schuster, Inc.

sought to destroy freedom. But since that traitorous confederation has been sub-dued, and we have entered upon the work of "reconstruction" or "restoration," I cannot deny that my heart has become sad at the gloomy prospects before us.

Four years of bloody and expensive war waged against the United States by eleven States, under a government called the "Confederate States of America" to which they acknowledged allegiance, have over-thrown all governments within those States, which could be acknowledged as legitimate by the Union. The armies of the Confederate States having been con-quered and subdued, and their territories possessed by the United States, it becomes necessary to establish governments therein, which shall be republican in "form and principles, and form a more perfect union" with the parent government. It is desirable that such a course should be pursued as to exclude from those governments every vestige of human bondage and render the same forever impossible in this nation, and to take care that no principles of self-destruction shall be incorporated therein. In effecting this, it is to be hoped that no provision of the Constitution will be infringed, and no principle of the law of nations disregarded. Especially must we take care that in rebuking this unjust and treasonable war, the authorities of the Union shall indulge in no acts of usurpation which may tend to impair the stability and permanency of the nation within these limitations. We hold it to be the duty of the Government to inflict condign punishment on the rebel belligerents, and so weaken their hands that they can never again endanger the Union; and so reform their municipal institutions as to make them republican in spirit as well as in name.

We especially insist that the property of the chief rebels should be seized and appropriated to the payment of the national debt, caused by the unjust and wicked war which they instigated.

How can such punishments be inflicted and such forfeitures produced without doing violence to established principles? Two positions have been suggested.

1st To treat those States as never having been out of the Union, because the Constitution forbids secession, and, therefore, a fact forbidden by law could not exist.

2nd To accept the position in which they placed themselves as severed from the Union; an independent government *de facto*, and an alien enemy to be dealt with according to the laws of war.

It seems to me that while we do not aver that the United States are bound to treat them as an alien enemy, yet they have a right to elect so to do if it be for the interest of the nation; and that the "Confederate States" are estopped from denying that position.

South Carolina, the leader and embodiment of the rebellion, in the month of January, 1861, passed the following resolution by the unanimous vote of her Legislature.

> *Resolved,* That the separation of South Carolina from the Federal Union is *final,* and she has no further interests in the Constitution of the United States; and that the only appropriate negotiations between her and the Federal Government are as to their mutual relations as *foreign* States.

The convention that formed the government of the Confederate States and all the eleven States that composed it adopted the same declaration, and pledged their lives and fortunes to support it. That Government raised large armies, and by its formidable power, compelled the nations of the civilized world as well as our Government, to acknowledge them as an independent belligerent, entitled by the law of nations to be considered as engaged in a public war, and not merely in an insurrection. It is idle to deny that we treated them as a belligerent entitled to all the rights and subject to all the liabilities of an alien enemy. We blockaded their ports, which is an undoubted belligerent right; the extent of coast blockaded, marked the acknowledged extent of their territory—the territory criminally acquired but *de facto* theirs. We acknowledged their sea-rovers as privateers and not as pirates, by ordering their captive crews to be treated as prisoners of war. We acknowledged that a commission from the Confederate Government was sufficient to screen Semmes and his associates from the fate of lawless buccaneers. Who but an acknowledged government *de jure* or *de facto*, could have power to issue such a commission?

The invaders of the loyal States were not treated as outlaws, but as soldiers of war, because they were commanded by officers holding commissions from that government. The Confederate States were for four years what hey claimed to be—an alien enemy in all their rights and liabilities. To say that they were states under the protection of that Constitution which they were rending, and within the Union which they were assaulting with bloody defeats, simply because they became belligerents through crime, is making theory overrule fact to an absurd degree. It will I suppose at least be conceded that the United States, if not obliged so to do, has a right to treat them as an alien enemy now conquered, and subject to all the liabilities of a vanquished foe.

If we are also at liberty to treat them as never having been out of the Union, and that their declarations and acts were all void because they contravened the Constitution, and therefore they were never engaged in a public war but merely insurgents, let us inquire which position is best for the United States. If they have never been otherwise than States in the Union, and we desire to try certain of the leaders for treason, the Constitution requires that they should be indicted and tried *"by an impartial jury of the State and district wherein the crime shall have been committed, which district shall have been previously ascertained by law."*

The crime of treason can be committed only where the person is actually or potentially present. Jefferson Davis sitting in Richmond, counselling, or advising, or commanding an inroad into Pennsylvania, has committed no overt act in this State, and can be tried if anywhere only in the Richmond District. The doctrine of constructive presence, and constructive treason, will never I hope pollute our Statutes, or judicial decisions. Select an impartial jury from Virginia, and it is obvious that no conviction could ever be had. Possibly a jury might be packed to convict, but that would not be an "impartial" jury, it would be judicial murder, and would rank in infamy with the trial of Lord Russell, except only that the one was the murder of an innocent man, the other of a traitor. The same difficulties would exist in attempting forfeitures, which can only follow conviction in States protected by the Constitution; and then it is said only for the life of the male-factor. Congress can pass no "bill of attainder."

Nor under that theory, has Congress, much less the Executive, any power to interfere in remodeling those States upon reconstruction. What reconstruction is needed? Here are States which they say, have never been out of the Union and which are consequently now in it without asking leave of any one. They are competent to send Senators and Members to Congress. The state of war has broken no constitutional ligament, for it was only an insurrection of individuals, not a public war waged by States. Such is the reasoning notwithstanding every State acted in its municipal capacity; and the court in the Prize cases (2 Black 678) say: *"Hence in organizing this rebellion they have acted as States.* It is no loose unorganized rebellion, having no defined boundary or possessions. It has a boundary marked by lines of bayonets, and which can be crossed only by force—south of this line is *enemy's* territories, because it is claimed and held in possession by an organized, hostile, and belligerent power."

What right has any one to direct a convention to be held in a sovereign State of this Union, to amend its constitution and prescribe the qualifications of voters? The sovereign power of the nation is lodged in Congress. Yet where is the warrant in the Constitution for such sovereign power, much less the Executive, to intermeddle with the domestic institutions of a State, mould its laws, and regulate the elective franchise? It would be rank, dangerous, and deplorable usurpation.

In reconstruction, therefore, no reform can be effected in the Southern States if they have never left the Union. But reformation *must* be effected; the foundation of their institutions, both political, municipal, and social *must* be broken up and *relaid*, or all our blood and treasure have been spent in vain. This can only be done by treating and holding them as a conquered people. Then all things which we can desire to do follow with logical and legitimate authority. As conquered territory Congress would have full power to legislate for them; for the territories are not under the Constitution except so far as the express power to govern them is given to Congress. They would be held in a territorial condition until they are fit to form State Constitutions, republican in fact not in form only, and ask admission into the Union as new States. If Congress approve of their Constitutions, and think they have done works meet for repentance they would be admitted as new States. If their Constitutions are not approved of, they would be sent back, until they have become wise enough so to purge their old laws as to eradicate every despotic and revolutionary principle—until they shall have learned to venerate the Declaration of Independence.

I do not touch on the question of Negro suffrage. If in the Union, the States have long ago regulated that, and for the Central Government to interfere with it would be mischievous impertinence. If they are to be admitted as new States they must form their own Constitutions; and no enabling act could dictate its terms. Congress could prescribe the qualifications of voters, while a Territory, or when proceeding to call a convention to form a State government. That is the extent of the power of Congress over the elective franchise, whether in a territorial or state condition. The President has not even this or any other power to meddle in the subject, except by advice to Congress—and then on Territories. Congress, to be sure, has some sort of compulsory power by refusing the States admission until they shall have complied with its wishes over this subject. Whether those who have fought our battles shall all be allowed to vote, or only those of a paler hue, I leave to be discussed in the future when Congress can take legitimate cognizance of it.

If capital punishments of the most guilty are deemed essential as examples, we have seen that, on one theory, none of them can be convicted on fair trials—the complicity of the triers would defeat it. But, as a conquered enemy, they could not escape. Their trials would take place by court-martials. I do not think they could thus be tried for treason, but they could be tried as belligerents, who had forfeited their lives, according to the laws of war. By the strict rights of war, as anciently practiced, the victor held the lives, the liberty, and the property of the vanquished at his disposal. The taking of the life or reduction to bondage of the captives have long ceased to be practiced in case of ordinary wars; but the abstract right—the *summum jus*—is still recognized in exceptional cases where the cause of the war, or the character of the belligerent, or the safety of the victors justify its exercise. The same thing may be said of the seizure of property and land. Halleck ... says some modern writers—Hautefeuille, for example—contend for the ancient rule, "that private property on land may be subject to seizure. They are undoubtedly correct, with regard to the general abstract right, as deduced from the laws of nature and ancient of practice." Vattel says: "When, therefore, he has subdued a hostile nation, he undeniably may in the first place do himself justice, respecting the object which has given rise to the war and *indemnify himself for the expenses and damages* which he has sustained by it." ... "A conqueror, who has taken up arms not only against the sovereign, but against the nation herself, and whose intention it was to subdue a fierce and savage people, and once for all to reduce an obstinate enemy, such a conqueror may, with justice, lay burdens on the conquered nation, both as a compensation for the expenses of the war, and as a punishment."

I am happy to believe that the Government has come to this conclusion. I cannot otherwise see how Capt. Wirz can be tried by a Court-Martial at Washington for acts done by him at Andersonville. He was in no way connected with our military organization, nor did he as a citizen connect himself with our army so as to bring his case within any of the Acts of Congress. If he committed murder in Georgia, and Georgia was a State in the Union, then he should be tried according to her laws. The General Government has no jurisdiction over such crime, and the trial, and execution of this wretch by a United States Military Court would be illegal. But if he was an officer of a belligerent enemy, making war as an independent people, now. being conquered, it is competent holding them as a conquered foe to try him for doing acts contrary to the laws of war, and if found guilty to execute or otherwise punish him. As I am sure the loyal man at the head of the Government will not involve the nation in illegal acts and thus set a precedent injurious to our national character, I am glad to believe that hereafter we shall treat the enemy as conquered, and remit their condition and reconstruction to the sovereign power of the nation.

In short, all writers agree that the victor may inflict punishment upon the vanquished enemy even to the taking of his life, liberty, or the confiscation of all of his property; but that this extreme right is never exercised except upon a cruel, barbarous, obstinate, or dangerous foe who has waged an unjust war.

Upon the character of the belligerent, and of the justice of the war, and the manner of conducting it, depends our right to take the lives, liberty, and prop-erty of the belligerent. This war had its origin in treason without one spark of justice. It was prosecuted before notice of it, by robbing our forts and armories, and our navy-yards; by stealing our money from the mints and depositories, and by surrendering our forts and navies by perjurers who had sworn to support the Constitution. In its progress our prisoners, by the authority of their government, were slaughtered in cold blood. Ask Fort Pillow and Fort Wagner. Sixty thousand of our prisoners have been deliberately starved to death because they would not enlist in the rebel armies. The graves at Andersonville have each an accusing tongue. The purpose and avowed object of the enemy "to found an empire whose cornerstone should be slavery," render its perpetuity or revival dangerous to human liberty.

Surely, these things are sufficient to justify the exercise of the extreme rights of war—"to execute, to imprison, to confiscate." How many captive enemies it would be proper to execute, as an example to nations, I leave others to judge. I am not fond of sanguinary punishments, but surely some victims must propitiate the *manes* of our starved, murdered, slaughtered martyrs. A court-martial could do justice according to law.

But we propose to confiscate all the estate of every rebel belligerent whose estate was worth $10,000, or whose land exceeded two hundred acres in quantity. Policy if not justice would require that the poor, the ignorant, and the coerced should be forgiven. They followed the example and teachings of their wealthy and intelligent neighbors. The rebellion would never have originated with them. Fortunately those who would thus escape form a large majority of the people, though possessing but a small portion of the wealth. The proportion of those exempt compared with the punished would be I believe about nine-tenths.

There are about six millions of freemen in the South. The number of acres of land is 465,000,000. Of this those who own above two hundred acres each, number about 70,000 persons, holding in the aggregate (together with the States) about 394,000,000 acres . . . Divide this land into . . . farms. Give if you please forty acres to each adult male freedman. Suppose there are one million of them. That would require 40,000,000 of acres, which deducted from 394,000,000 leaves three hundred and fifty-four millions of acres for sale. Divide it into suitable farms and sell it to the highest bidders. I think it, including town property, would average at least ten dollars per acre. That would produce $3,540,000,000 — Three billions, five hundred and forty millions of dollars.

Let that be applied as follows to wit:

1.   Invest $300,000,000 in six percent government bonds, and add the interest semi-annually to the pensions of those who have become entitled by this villainous war.

2.   Appropriate $200,000,000 to pay the damages done to loyal men North and South by the rebellion.

3.   Pay the residue being $3,040,000,000 towards the payment of the National debt.

What loyal man can object to this? Look around you, and everywhere behold your neighbors, some with an arm, some with a leg, some with an eye carried away by rebel bullets. Others horribly mutilated in every form. And yet numerous others wearing the weeds which mark the death of those on whom they leaned for support. Contemplate these monuments of rebel perfidy, and of patriotic suffering, and then say if too much is asked for our valiant soldiers.

Look again, and see loyal men reduced to poverty by the confiscations by the Confederate States, and by the rebel States — see Union men robbed of their property, and their dwellings laid in ashes by rebel raiders, and say if too much is asked for them. But above all,

let us inquire whether imperative duty to the present generation and to posterity does not command us to compel the wicked enemy to pay the expenses of this unjust war. In ordinary transactions he who raises a false clamor and prosecutes an unfounded suit, is adjudged to pay the costs on his defeat. We have seen that, by the law of nations, the vanquished in an unjust war must pay the expense.

Our war debt is estimated from three to four billions of dollars. In my judgment, when all is funded and the pensions capitalized, it will reach more than four billions.

The interest at 6 percent only
(now much more) $240,000,000
The ordinary expenses of
our Government are   120,000,000
For some years the extra
ordinary expenses of our army
and navy will be   110,000,000
                             $470,000,000

Four hundred and seventy millions to be raised by taxation — our present heavy taxes will not in ordinary years, produce but little more than half that sum. Can our people bear double their present taxation? He who unnecessarily causes it will be accursed from generation to generation. It is fashionable to belittle our public debt, lest the people should become alarmed, and political parties should suffer. I have never found it wise to deceive the people. They can always be trusted with the truth. Capitalists will not be affected for they can not be deceived. Confide in the people, and you will avoid repudiation. Deceive them, and lead them into false measures, and you may produce it.

We pity the poor Englishmen whose national debt and burdensome taxation we have heard deplored from our childhood. The debt of Great Britain is just about as much as ours ($4,000,000,000) four billions. But in effect it is but half as large — it bears but three per cent interest. The current year the Chancellor of the Exchequer tells us the interest was $131,806,990; ours, when all shall be funded, will be nearly double.

The plan we have proposed would pay at least three-fourths of our debt. The balance could be managed with our present taxation. And yet to think that even that is to be perpetual is sickening. If it is to be doubled, as it must be, if "restoration" instead of "reconstruction" is to prevail, would to God the authors of it could see themselves as an execrating public and posterity will see them.

Our new Doctors of National law, who hold that the "Confederate States" were never out of the Union, but only insurgents and traitors, have become wiser than Grotius and Puffendorf and Rutherford and Vattel, and all modern publicists down to Halleck and Phillimore. They all agree that such a state of things as has existed here for four years is *public war* and constitutes the parties independent belligerents, subject to the same rules of war as the foreign nations engaged in open warfare.

The learned and able Professor of law in the Cambridge University, Theophilus Parsons, lately said in a public speech:

> As we are victorious in war we have a right to impose upon the defeated party any terms necessary for our security. This right is perfect. It is not only in itself obvious, but it is asserted in every book on this subject, and is illustrated by all the wars of history. The rebels forced a war upon us; it was a long and costly and bloody war; and now that we have conquered them, we have all the rights which victory confers.

The only argument of the Restorationists is, that the States could not and did not go out of the Union because the Constitution forbids it. By the same reasoning you could prove that no crime ever existed. No man ever committed murder for the law forbids it. He is a shallow reasoner who could make theory overrule fact!

I prefer to believe the ancient and modern publicists; and the learned Professors of legal science, to the extemporized doctrines of modern sciolists.

If "Restoration," as it is now properly christened, is to prevail over "Reconstruction," will some learned pundit of that school inform me in what condition slavery and the slave laws are? I assert that upon that theory not a Slave has been liberated; not a Slave law has been abrogated; but on the "Restoration" the whole Slave code is in legal force. Slavery was protected by our Constitution in every State in the Union where it existed. While they remained under that protection no power in the Federal Government could abolish Slavery. If, however, the Confederate States were admitted to be what they claimed—an independent belligerent *de facto*—then the war broke all treaties, compacts, and ties between the parties, and Slavery was left to its rights under the law of nations. These rights were none; for that law declares that "Man can hold no property in man." (Phillimore, page 316.) Then the laws of war enabled us to declare every bondman free, so long as we held them in military possession. And the conqueror, through Congress, may declare them forever emancipated. But if the States are "States in the Union," then when war ceases they resume their positions with all their privileges untouched. There can be no "mutilated" restoration. That would be the work of Congress, alone, and would be "Reconstruction."

While I hear it said everywhere that slavery is dead, I cannot learn who killed it. No thoughtful man has pretended that Lincoln's proclamation, so noble in sentiment, liberated a single slave. It expressly excluded from its operation all those within our lines. No slave within any part of the rebel States in our possession or in Tennessee, but only those beyond our limits and beyond our power were declared free. So Gen. Smith conquered Canada by a proclamation! The President did not pretend to abrogate the Slave Laws of any of the States. "Restoration," therefore will leave the "Union as it was,"—a heinous idea. I am aware that a very able and patriotic gentleman, and learned historian, Mr. Bancroft, has attempted to place their freedom on different grounds. He says what is undoubtedly true, that the proclamation of freedom did not free a slave. But he liberated them on feudal principles. Under the feudal system, when a king conquered his enemy, he parceled out his lands and conquered *subjects* among his chief retainers; the lands and serfs were held on condition of fealty and rendering military service when required. If the subordinate chief rebelled, he broke the condition on which he held them and the lands and serfs became forfeited to the Lord Paramount. But it did not free the serfs. They with the manors were bestowed on other favorites. But the analogy fails in another important respect. The American slave-holder does not hold by virtue of any grant from any Lord Paramount—least of all by a grant from General Government. Slavery exists by no law of the Union, but simply by local law, by the laws of the States. Rebellion against the National Authority is a breach of no condition of their tenure. It were more analogous to say that rebellion against a State under whose laws they held might work a forfeiture. But rebellion against neither government would *per se* have any such effect. On whom would the Lord Paramount again bestow the slaves? The theory is plausible, but has no solid foundation.

The President says to the rebel States "before you can participate in the government you must abolish Slavery and reform your election laws." *That* is the command of a Conqueror. *That* is Reconstruction not Restoration—Reconstruction too by assuming the powers of Congress. This theory will lead to melancholy re-sults. Nor can the constitutional amendment abolishing Slavery ever be ratified by three-fourths of the States, if *they* are States to be counted. Bogus Conventions of those States may vote for it. But no Convention honestly and fairly elected will ever do it. The frauds will not permanently avail. The cause of Liberty must rest on a firmer basis. Counterfeit governments like the Virginia, Louisiana, Tennessee, Mississippi, and Arkansas pretenses, will be disregarded by the sober sense of the people, by future law, and by the courts. "Restoration" is replanting the seeds of rebellion, which within the next quarter of a century will germinate and produce the same bloody strife which has just ended.

But, it is said, by those who have more sympathy with rebel wives and children than for the widows and orphans of loyal men, that this stripping the rebels of their estates and driving them to exile or to honest labor would be harsh and severe upon innocent women and children. It may be so; but that is the result of the necessary laws of war. But it is revolutionary, say they. This plan would, no doubt, work a radical reorganization in southern institutions, habits, and manners. It is intended to revolutionize their principles and feelings. This may startle feeble minds and shake weak nerves. So do all great improvements in the political and moral world. It requires a heavy impetus to drive forward a sluggish people. When it was first proposed to free the slaves, and arm the blacks, did not half the nation tremble? The prim conservatives, the snobs, and the male waiting-maids in Congress were in hysterics.

The whole fabric of southern society *must* be changed, and never can it be done if this opportunity is lost. Without this, this Government can never be, as it never has been, a true republic. Heretofore, it had more the features of aristocracy than of democracy. The Southern States have been despotisms, not governments of the people. It is impossible that any practical equality of rights can exist where a few thousand men monopolize the whole landed property. The larger the number of small proprietors the more safe and stable the government. As the landed interest must govern, the more it is subdivided and held by independent owners, the better. What would be the condition of the state of New York if it were not for her independent yeomanry? She would be overwhelmed and demoralized by the Jews, Milesians, and vagabonds of licentious cities. How can republican institutions, free schools, free churches, free social intercourse exist in a mingled community of nabobs and serfs; of the owners of twenty thousand acre manors with lordly palaces, and the occupants of narrow huts inhabited by "low white trash"? If the South is ever to be a safe republic let her lands be cultivated by the toil of the owners or the free labor of intelligent citizens. This must be done even though it drive her nobility into exile. If they go, all the better.

It will be hard to persuade the owner of ten thousand acres of land, who drives a coach and four, that he is not degraded by sitting at the same table, or in the same pew, with the embrowned and hard-handed farmer who has himself cultivated his own thriving homestead of 150 acres. This subdivision of the lands will yield ten bales of cotton to one that is made now, and he who produced it will own it and *feel himself a man.*

It is far easier and more beneficial to exile 70,000 proud, bloated, and defiant rebels, than to expatriate four millions of laborers, native to the soil and loyal to the Government. This latter scheme was a favorite plan of the Blairs with which they had for awhile inoculated our late sainted President. But, a single experiment made him discard it and its advisers. Since I have mentioned the Blairs, I may say a word more of those persistent apologists of the South. For, when the virus of Slavery has once entered the veins of the slave-holder, no subsequent effort seems capable of wholly eradicating it. They are a family of considerable power, some merit, of admirable audacity, and execrable selfishness; with impetuous alacrity they seize the White House, and hold possession of it, as in the late Administration, until shaken off by the overpowering force of public indignation. Their pernicious course had well nigh defeated the reelection of Abraham Lincoln; and if it should prevail with the present Administration, pure and patriotic as President Johnson is admitted to be, it will render him the most unpopular Executive—save one—that ever occupied the Presidential chair. But there is no fear of that. He will soon say, as Mr. Lincoln did: "YOUR TIME HAS COME!"

This remodeling the institutions, and reforming the rooted habits of a proud aristocracy, is undoubtedly a formidable task, requiring the broad mind of enlarged statesmanship, and the firm nerve of the hero. But will not this mighty occasion produce—will not the God of Liberty and order give us such men? Will not a Romulus, a Lycurgus, a Charlemagne, a Washington arise, whose expansive views will found a free empire, to endure till time shall be no more?

This doctrine of restoration shocks me. We have a duty to perform which our fathers were incapable of, which will be required at our hands by God and our Country. When our ancestors found a "more perfect Union" necessary, they found it impossible to agree upon a Constitution without tolerating, nay guaranteeing Slavery. They were obliged to acquiesce, trusting to time to work a speedy cure, in which they were disappointed. *They* had some excuse, some justification. But we can have none if we do not thoroughly eradicate Slavery and render it forever impossible in this republic. The Slave power made war upon the nation. They declared the "more perfect Union" dissolved. Solemnly declared themselves a foreign nation, alien to this republic; for four years were in fact what they claimed to be. We accepted the war which they tendered and treated them as a government capable of making war. We have conquered them, and as a conquered enemy we can give them laws; can abolish all their municipal institutions and form new ones. If we do not make those institutions fit to last through generations of free men, a heavy curse will be on us. Our glorious, but tainted republic has been born to new life through bloody, agonizing pains. But this frightful "Restoration" has thrown it into "cold obstruction, and to death." If the rebel states have never been out of the Union, any attempt to reform their State institutions either by Congress or the President, is rank usurpation.

Is then all lost? Is this great conquest to be in vain? That will depend upon the virtue and intelligence of the next Congress. To Congress alone belongs the power of Reconstruction—of giving law to the vanquished. This is expressly decided by the Supreme Court of the United States in the Dorr case (7 Howard 42). The Court say, "Under this article of the Constitution (the 4th) it rests with Congress to decide what government is the established one in a State, for the United States guarantees to each a republican form of government," et cetera. But we know how difficult it is for a majority of Congress to overcome preconceived opinions. Besides, before Congress meets, things will be so inaugurated—precipitated, it will still be more difficult to correct. If a majority of Congress can be found wise and firm enough to declare the Confederate States a conquered enemy,

Reconstruction will be easy and legitimate; and the friends of freedom will long rule in the Councils of the Nation. If Restoration prevails the prospect is gloomy, and new "Lords will make new laws." The Union party will be overwhelmed. The Copperhead party has become extinct with Secession. But with Secession [Restoration] it will revive. Under "Restoration" every rebel State will send rebels to Congress; and they, with their allies in the North, will control Congress, and occupy the White House. Then Restoration of Laws and ancient institutions will be sure to follow; our public debt will be repudiated or the rebel National debt will be added to ours, and the people be crushed beneath heavy burdens.

Let us forget all parties, and build on the broad platform of "reconstructing" the Government out of the conquered territory, converted into new and free States, and admitted into the Union by the sovereign power of Congress, with another plank—"THE PROPERTY OF THE REBELS SHALL PAY OUR NATIONAL DEBT, *and indemnify freedmen and loyal sufferers*" and that under no circumstances will we suffer the National debt to be repudiated, or the interest scaled below the contract rates; nor permit any part of the rebel debt to be assumed by the nation.

Let all who approve of these principles rally with us. Let all others go with Copperheads and rebels. Those will be the opposing parties. Young men, this duty devolves on you. Would to God, if only for that, that I were still in the prime of life, that I might aid you to fight through this last and greatest battle of freedom.

Henry J. Raymond

Johnson's Plan
of Reconstruction: A Defense

Mr. Raymond Mr. Chairman, I should be glad, if it meet the sense of those members who are present, to make some remarks upon the general question now before the House; but I do not wish to trespass at all upon their disposition in regard to this matter. I do not know, however, that there will be a better opportunity to say what little I have to say than is now offered; and if the House shall indicate no other wish, I will proceed to say it.

I need not say that I have been gratified to hear many things which have fallen from the lips of the gentleman from Ohio [Mr. Finck], who has just taken his seat. I have no party feeling, nor any other feeling, which would prevent me from rejoicing in the indications apparent on that side of the House of a purpose to concur with the loyal people of the country, and with the loyal administration of the Government, and with the loyal majorities in both Houses of Congress, in restoring peace and order to our common country. I cannot, perhaps, help wishing, sir, that these indications of an interest in the preservation of our Government had come somewhat sooner. I cannot help feeling that such expressions cannot now be of as much service to the country as they might once have been. If we could have

From John Anthony Scott, ed., *Living Documents in American History,* Vol. 2. Copyright © 1963 by John Anthony Scott. Reprinted by permission of Washington Square Press Division of Simon & Schuster, Inc.

had from that side of the House such indications of an interest in the preservation of the Union, such heartfelt sympathy with the efforts of the Government for the preservation of that Union, such hearty denunciation of those who were seeking its destruction, while the war was raging, I am sure we might have been spared some years of war, some millions of money, and rivers of blood and tears.

But, sir, I am not disposed to fight over again battles now happily ended. I feel, and I am rejoiced to find that members on the other side of the House feel, that the great problem now before us is to restore the Union to its old integrity, purified from everything that interfered with the full development of the spirit of liberty which it was made to enshrine. I trust that we shall have a general concurrence of the members of this House and of this Congress in such measures as may be deemed most fit and proper for the accomplishment of that result. I am glad to assume and to believe that there is not a member of this House, nor a man in this country, who does not wish, from the bottom of his heart, to see the day speedily come when we shall have this nation—the great American Republic—again united, more harmonious in its action than it has ever been, and forever one and indivisible. We in this Congress are to devise the means to restore its union and its harmony, to perfect its institutions, and to make it in all its parts and in all its action, through all time to come, too strong, too wise, and too free ever to invite or ever to permit the hand of rebellion again to be raised against it.

Now, sir, in devising those ways and means to accomplish that great result, the first thing we have to do is to know the point from which we start, to understand the nature of the material with which we have to work—the condition of the territory and the States with which we are concerned. I had supposed at the outset of this session that it was the purpose of this House to proceed to that work without discussion, and to commit it almost exclusively, if not entirely, to the joint committee raised by the two Houses for the consideration of that subject. But, sir, I must say that I was glad when I perceived the distinguished gentlemen from Pennsylvania [Mr. Stevens], himself the chairman on the part of this House of that great committee on reconstruction, lead off in a discussion of this general subject, and thus invite all the rest of us who choose to follow him in the debate. In the remarks which he made in this body a few days since, he laid down, with the clearness and the force which characterize everything he says and does, his point of departure in commencing this great work. I had hoped that the ground he would lay down would be such that we could all of us stand upon it and cooperate with him in our common object. I feel constrained to say, sir—and I do it without the slightest disposition to create or to exaggerate differences—that there were features in his exposition of the condition of the country with which I cannot concur. I cannot for myself start from precisely the point which he assumes.

In his remarks on that occasion he assumed that the States lately in rebellion were and are out of the Union. Throughout his speech—I will not trouble you with reading passages from it—I find him speaking of those States as "outside of the Union," as "dead States," as having forfeited all their rights and terminated their State existence. I find expressions still more definite and distinct; I find him stating that they "are and for four years have been out of the Union for all legal purposes"; as having been for four years a "separate power," and "a separate nation."

His position, therefore, is that these States, having been in rebellion, are now out of the Union, and are simply within the jurisdiction of the Constitution of the United States as so much territory to be dealt with precisely as the will of the conqueror, to use his own language, may dictate. Now, sir, if that position is correct, it prescribes for us one line of policy to be pursued very different from the one that will be proper if it is not correct. His belief is that what we have to do is to create new States out of this territory at the proper time—many years distant—retaining them meantime in a territorial condition, and subjecting them to precisely such a state of discipline and tutelage as Congress or the Government of the United States may see fit to prescribe. If I believed in the premises which he assumes, possibly, though I do not think probably, I might agree with the conclusion he has reached.

But, sir, I cannot believe that this is our condition. I cannot believe that these States have ever been out of the Union, or that they are now out of the Union. I cannot believe that they ever have been, or are now, in any sense a separate Power. If they were, sir, how and when did they become so? They were once States of this Union—that every one concedes; bound to the Union and made members of the Union by the Constitution of the United States. If they ever went out of the Union, it was at some specific time and by some specific act. I regret that the gentleman from Pennsylvania [Mr. Stevens] is not now in his seat. I should have been glad to ask him by what specific act, and at what precise time, any one of these States took itself out of the American Union. Was it by the ordinance of secession? I think we all agree that an ordinance of

422   *Reunion and Reaction*

secession passed by any State of this Union is simply a nullity, because it encounters in its practical operation the Constitution of the United States, which is the supreme law of the land. It could have no legal, actual force or validity. It could not operate to effect any actual change in the relations of the State adopting it to the national Government, still less to accomplish the removal of that State from the sovereign jurisdiction of the Constitution of the United States.

Well, sir, did the resolutions of these States, the declarations of their officials, the speeches of members of their Legislatures, or the utterances of their press accomplish the result? Certainly not. They could not possibly work any change whatever in the relations of these States to the General Government. All their ordinances and all their resolutions were simply declarations of a purpose to secede. Their secession, if it ever took place, certainly could not date from the time when their intention to secede was first announced. After declaring that intention, they proceeded to carry it into effect. How? By war. By sustaining their purpose by arms against the force which the United States brought to bear against it. Did they sustain it? Were their arms victorious? If they were, then their secession was an accomplished fact. If not, it was nothing more than an abortive attempt—a purpose unfulfilled. This, then, is simply a question of fact, and we all know what the fact is. They did not succeed. They failed to maintain their ground by force of arms —in other words, they failed to secede.

But the gentleman from Pennsylvania [Mr. Stevens] insists that they did secede, and that this fact is not in the least affected by the other fact that the Constitution forbids secession. He says that the law forbids murder, but that murders are nevertheless committed. But there is no analogy between the two cases. If secession had been accomplished, if these States had gone out, and overcome the armies that tried to prevent their going out, then the prohibition of the Constitution could not have altered the fact. In the case of murder the man is killed, and murder is thus committed in spite of the law. The fact of killing is essential to the committal of the crime; and the fact of going out is essential to secession. But in this case there was no such fact. I think I need not argue any further the position that the rebel States have never for one moment, by any ordinances of secession, or by any successful war, carried themselves beyond the rightful jurisdiction of the Constitution of the United States. They have interrupted for a time the practical enforcement and exercise of that jurisdiction; they rendered it impossible for a time for this Government to enforce obedience to its laws; but there has never been an hour when this Government, or this Congress, or this House, or the gentleman from Pennsylvania himself, ever conceded that those States were beyond the jurisdiction of the Constitution and laws of the United States.

During all these four years of war Congress has been making laws for the government of those very States, and the gentleman from Pennsylvania has voted for them, and voted to raise armies to enforce them. Why was this done if they were a separate nation? Why, if they were not part of the United States? Those laws were made for them as States. Members had voted for laws imposing upon them direct taxes, which are apportioned, according to the Constitution, only "among the several States" according to their population. In a variety of ways—to some of which the gentleman who preceded me has referred—this Congress has by its action assumed and asserted that they were still States in the Union, though in rebellion, and that it was with the rebellion that we were making war, and not with the States themselves as States, and still less as a separate, as a foreign, Power.

The gentleman from Pennsylvania

cited a variety of legal precedents and declarations of principle, nearly all of them, I believe, drawn from the celebrated decision of the Supreme Court pronounced by Justice Grier, in what are popularly known as the Prize Cases. His citations were all made for the purpose of proving that these States were in a condition of public war—that they were waging such a war as could only be waged by a separate and independent Power. But a careful scrutiny of that decision will show that it lends not the slightest countenance to such an inference. Gentlemen who hear me will doubtless recollect that the object of the trial in those cases was to decide whether certain vessels, captured in trying to break the blockade, were lawful prize of war or not; and the decision of this point turned on the question whether the war then raging was such a contest as justified a resort to the modes and usages of public war, of which blockade was one. Justice Grier decided that it was—that, so far as the purposes and weapons of war were concerned, the two parties were belligerents, and that the Government might blockade the ports and capture property within the lines of the district in rebellion, precisely as if that district were an independent nation engaged in a public war. But he said not one word which could assert or imply that it was an independent nation—that it had a separate existence, or had gone out of the sovereign jurisdiction of the United States. On the contrary, everything he said—the very passages quoted by the gentleman from Pennsylvania himself—imply and assert precisely the opposite. He speaks of them, not as sovereign, but as claiming to be sovereign; not as being separate, but as trying to be separate from the United States. In this paragraph quoted from that decision, for example—

Hence, in organizing this rebellion, they have acted as States *claiming* to be sovereign over all persons and property within

their respective limits, and *asserting* a right to absolve their citizens from their allegiance to the Federal Government. Several of these States have combined to form a new confederacy, *claiming* to be acknowledged by the world as a sovereign State. *Their right to do so is now being decided by wager of battle*—

the court asserts precisely the principle which I have already stated—that they were claiming independence, and that the validity of their claim would depend wholly and entirely upon the decision reached in the field of battle.

The same misconstruction is traceable in all the legal citations made by the gentleman from Pennsylvania. For example, he says:

Again, the court say, what I have been astonished that any one should doubt:

"The proclamation of blockade is itself official and conclusive evidence to the court that a state of war existed."

Now, what was the legal result of such a war?

"The conventions, the treaties, made with a nation, are broken or annulled by a war arising between the contracting parties."—Vattel, 372; Halleck, 371, section 23.

A blockade is evidence that a state of war exists; and a state of war annuls all treaties between the contending parties. But does this warrant the inference that the Constitution of the United States, which is not a treaty, was annulled, or its binding force in the least degree impaired, by the war of rebellion? But I will not go further in examining these citations. All they show is that the Government, as against the rebels, and in waging the war to suppress the rebellion, had the rights of belligerents, and that the rules and laws of war might and must be applied to this contest although it was not a war between separate and independent Powers. How, then, can this decision possibly be made to convey the idea that the parties to the war were separate and independent States? It proceeds throughout and in every part upon precisely the opposite idea.

The gentleman from Pennsylvania [Mr. Stevens] spoke of States forfeiting their State existence by the fact of rebellion. Well, I do not see how there can be any such forfeiture involved or implied. The individual citizens of those States went into the rebellion. They thereby incurred certain penalties under the laws and Constitution of the United States. What the States did was to endeavor to interpose their State authority between the individuals in rebellion and the Government of the United States, which assumed, and which would carry out the assumption, to declare those individuals traitors for their acts. The individuals in the States who were in rebellion, it seems to me, were the only parties who under the Constitution and laws of the United States could incur the penalties of treason. I know of no law, I know of nothing in the Constitution of the United States, I know of nothing in any recognized or established code of international law, which can punish a State as a State for any act it may perform. It is certain that our Constitution assumes nothing of the kind. It does not deal with States, except in one or two instances, such as elections of members of Congress, and the election of electors of President and Vice President.

Indeed, the main feature which distinguishes the Union under the Constitution from the old Confederation is this, that whereas the old Confederation did deal with States directly, making requisitions upon them for supplies and relying upon them for the execution of its laws, the Constitution of the United States, in order to form a more perfect Union, made its laws binding on the individual citizens of the several States, whether living in one State or in another. Congress, as the legislative branch of this Government, enacts a law which shall be operative upon every individual within its jurisdiction. It is binding upon each individual citizen, and if he resists it by force he is guilty of a crime and is punished accordingly, anything in the constitution or laws of his State to the contrary notwithstanding. But the States themselves are not touched by the laws of the United States or by the Constitution of the United States. A State cannot be indicted; a State cannot be tried; a State cannot be hung for treason. The individuals in a State may be so tried and hung, but the State as an organization, as an organic member of the Union, still exists, whether its individual citizens commit treason or not.

Mr. Kelley Will the gentleman from New York [Mr. Raymond] yield to me a moment for a question?

Mr. Raymond Certainly.

Mr. Kelley I desire to ask the gentleman this question: by virtue of what does a State exist? Is it by virtue of a constitution, and by virtue of its relation to the Union? That is, does a State of the Union exist, first by virtue of a constitution, and secondly by virtue of its practical relations to the Government of the United States? And further, I would ask whether those States, acting by conventions of the people, have not overthrown the constitution which made them parts of the Union, and thereby destroyed or suspended—phrase it as you will—the practical relations which made them parts of the Union?

Mr. Raymond I will say, in reply to the gentleman from Pennsylvania [Mr. Kelley], that it is not the practical relations of a State at any particular moment which make it a State or a part of the Union. What makes a State a part of the Union is the Constitution of the United States; and the rebel States have not yet destroyed that.

Mr. Kelley The question I propound is, whether a State does not exist by virtue of a constitution, its constitution, which is a thing which may be modified or overthrown?

Mr. Raymond Certainly.

Mr. Kelley And whether these rebellious constitutions or States have not been overthrown?

Mr. Raymond A State does not exist by virtue of any particular constitution. It always has a constitution, but it need not have a specific constitution at any specific time. A State has certain practical relations to the Government of the United States. But the fact of those relations being practically operative and in actual force at any moment does not constitute its relationship to the Government or its membership in the United States. Its practical operation is one thing. The fact of its existence as an organized community, one of the great national community of States, is quite another thing.

Mr. Kelley Let me interrupt the gentleman one moment longer. I will ask him whether, if the constitution be overthrown or destroyed and its practical relations cease, there be any State left?

Mr. Raymond Why, sir, if there be no constitution of any sort in a State, no law, nothing but chaos, then that State would no longer exist as an organization. But that has not been the case, it never is the case in great communities, for they always have constitutions and forms of government adapted to its relation to the Government of the United States; and that would be an evil to be remedied by the Government of the United States. That is what we have been trying to do for the last four years. The practical relations of the governments of those States with the Government of the United States were all wrong—were hostile to that Government. They denied our jurisdiction, and they denied that they were States of the Union, but their denial did not change the fact; and there was never any time when their organizations as States were destroyed. A dead State is a solecism, a contradiction in terms, an impossibility.

These are, I confess, rather metaphysical distinctions, but I did not raise them. Those who assert that a State is destroyed whenever its constitution is changed, or whenever its practical relations with this Government are changed, must be held responsible for whatever metaphysical niceties may be necessarily involved in the discussion.

I do not know, sir, that I have made my views on this point clear to the gentleman from Pennsylvania [Mr. Kelley], who has questioned me upon it, and I am still more doubtful whether, even if they are intelligible, he will concur with me as to their justice. But I regard these States as just as truly within the jurisdiction of the Constitution, and therefore just as really and truly States of the American Union now as they were before the war. Their practical relations to the Constitution of the United States have been disturbed, and we have been endeavoring, through four years of war, to restore them and make them what they were before the war. The victory in the field has given us the means of doing this; we can now reestablish the practical relations of those States to the Government. Our actual jurisdiction over them, which they vainly attempted to throw off, is already restored. The conquest we have achieved is a conquest over the rebellion, not a conquest over the States whose authority the rebellion had for a time subverted.

For these reasons I think the views submitted by the gentleman from Pennsylvania [Mr. Stevens] upon this point are unsound. Let me next cite some of the consequences which, it seems to me, must follow the acceptance of his position. If, as he asserts, we have been waging war with an independent Power, with a separate nation, I cannot see how we can talk of treason in connection with our recent conflict or demand the execution of Davis or anybody else as a traitor. Certainly if we were at war with any other foreign Power we should not talk of the treason of those who were opposed to us in the field. If we were engaged in a war with France and should take as prisoner the Emperor Napoleon, certainly we could not talk of him as a traitor or as liable to execution.

I think that by adopting any such assumption as that of the honorable gentleman, we surrender the whole idea of treason and the punishment of traitors. I think, moreover, that we accept, virtually and practically, the doctrine of State sovereignty, the right of a State to withdraw from the Union, and to break up the Union at its own will and pleasure. I do not see how upon those premises we can escape that conclusion. If the States that engaged in the late rebellion constituted themselves, by their ordinances of secession or by any of the acts with which they followed those ordinances, a separate and independent Power, I do not see how we can deny the principles on which they professed to act, or refuse assent to their practical results. I have heard no clearer, no stronger statement of the doctrine of State sovereignty as paramount to the sovereignty of the nation than would be involved in such a concession. Whether he intended it or not, the gentleman from Pennsylvania [Mr. Stevens] actually assents to the extreme doctrines of the advocates of secession.

Mr. Niblack   I beg leave to inquire of the gentleman [Mr. Raymond] whether the theory of the gentleman from Pennsylvania, which he is combating, would not also, if carried to its legitimate consequences, make those who resisted the confederacy in the insurrectionary States guilty of treason to the confederacy or to those States?

Mr. Raymond   I was just going to remark that another of the consequences of this doctrine, as it seems to me, would be our inability to talk of loyal men in the South. Loyal to what? Loyal to a foreign, independent Power, as the United States would become under those circumstances? Certainly not. Simply disloyal to their own Government, and deserters, or whatever you may choose to call them, from that to which they owe allegiance, to a foreign and independent State.

Now, there is another consequence of the doctrine which I shall not dwell upon, but simply suggest. If that confederacy was an independent Power, a separate nation, it had the right to contract debts; and we, having overthrown and conquered that independent Power, according to the theory of the gentleman from Pennsylvania, would become the successors, the inheritors, of its debts and assets, and we must pay them. Sir, that is not simply a theory or a claim thrown out in debate here; it is one advanced on behalf of the Government of Great Britain as against us. Every gentleman will remember the case in which cotton belonging to the southern confederacy was claimed in Liverpool, and the decision there was—

... Mr. Morrill   As the gentleman from New York [Mr. Raymond] evidently intended to reply to the gentleman from Pennsylvania [Mr. Stevens], I hope he will be allowed to go on unterruptedly.

Mr. Raymond   I am very much surprised to find myself involved in such a controversy. I did not rise to create or provoke controversy with any one upon this floor. I rose to express my own dissent from the views propounded here by the gentleman from Pennsylvania, and if in anything I said after that, embodying my own opinions, I gave proper warrant for, I will not say attacks upon me, for I do not believe any such thing was meant, but for the questions propounded as to my position on this subject, I am very much surprised, but not the less glad of this opportunity of stating and explaining what it is. I cannot assent to the intimations thrown out by the gentleman from Pennsylvania [Mr. Stevens], that the President concurred in views he had expressed, or that he had handed the whole subject of pacifying the States lately in rebellion, and of restoring the States to the practical exercise of their functions as members of the Union, to the hands of Congress. I can find no warrant in his message for believing that he designs thus to abandon duties which are evidently, in his judgment, devolved upon him as the Executive in the Government, and as Commander-in-Chief of the armies of the United States. On the contrary, I find him rehearsing, in clear and explicit language, the steps he has taken to restore the rightful energy of the General Government and the States. "To that end," he says,

> Provisional governors have been appointed for the States, conventions called, Governors elected, Legislatures assembled, and Senators and Representatives chosen to the Congress of the United States. At the same time the courts of the United States, as far as could be done, have been reopened, so that the laws of the United States may be enforced through their agency. The blockade has been removed and the customhouses reestablished in ports of entry, so that the revenue of the United States may be collected. The Post Office Department renews its ceaseless activity, and the General Government is thereby enabled to communicate promptly with its officers and agents. The courts bring security to persons and property; the opening of the ports invites the restoration of industry and commerce; the post office renews the facilities of social intercourse and of business.

He has exercised his power of pardon; he has invited the States lately in rebellion to participate in the ratification of the constitutional amendment securing the perpetual prohibition of slavery. "This done," he says,

> It will remain for the States, whose powers have been so long in abeyance, to resume their places in the two branches of the national Legislature, and thereby complete the work of restoration. *Here it is for you, fellow-citizens of the Senate, and for you, fellow-citizens of the House of Representatives, to judge, each of you for yourselves,* of the elections, returns, and qualifications of your own members.

All but this has been done in the exercise of his functions and in the performance of his duties, as President of the United States, and as Commander-in-Chief of their armies. The admission of members of Congress and the restoration of the judicial branch of the civil authority of the Government are necessarily referred to the deliberations and action of Congress.

Mr. Chairman, I am here to act with those who seek to complete the restoration of the Union, as I have acted with those through the last four years who have sought to maintain its integrity and prevent its destruction. I shall say no word and do no act and give no vote to recognize its division, or to postpone or disturb its rapidly-approaching harmony and peace. I have no right and no disposition to lay down rules by which others shall govern and guide their conduct; but for myself I shall endeavor to act upon this whole question in the broad and liberal temper which its importance demands. We are not conducting a controversy in a court of law. We are not seeking to enforce a remedy for private wrongs, nor to revenge or retaliate private griefs. We have great communities of men, permanent interests of great States, to deal with, and we are bound to deal with them in a large and liberal spirit. It may be for the welfare of this nation that we shall cherish toward the millions of our people lately in rebellion feelings of hatred and distrust; that we shall nurse the bitterness that their infamous treason has naturally and justly engendered, and make that the basis of our future dealings with them. Possibly we may best teach them the lessons of liberty, by visiting upon them the worst excesses of despotism. Possibly they may best learn to practice justice toward others, to admire and emulate our republican institutions, by suffering at our hands the absolute rule we denounce in others. It may be best for us and for them that we discard, in all our dealings with them, all the obligations and requirements of the Constitution, and assert as the only law for them the unrestrained will of conquerors and masters.

I confess I do not sympathize with the sentiments or the opinions which would dictate such a course. I would exact of them all needed and all just guarantees for their future loyalty to the Constitution and laws of the United States. I would exact from them, or impose upon them through the constitutional legislation of Congress, and by enlarging and extending, if necessary, the scope and powers of the Freedmen's Bureau, proper care and protection for the helpless and friendless freedmen, so lately their slaves. I would exercise a rigid scrutiny into the character and loyalty of the men whom they may send to Congress before I allowed them to participate in the high prerogative of legislating for the nation. But I would seek to allay rather than stimulate the animosities and hatred, however just they may be, to which the war has given rise. But for our own sake as well as for theirs I would not visit upon them a policy of confiscation which has been discarded in the policy and practical conduct of every civilized nation on the face of the globe.

I believe it important for us as well as for them that we should cultivate friendly relations with them, that we should seek the promotion of their interests as part and parcel of our own. We have been their enemies in war, in peace let us show ourselves their friends. Now that slavery has been destroyed—that prolific source of all our alienations, all our hatreds, and all our disasters—there is nothing longer to make us foes. They have the same interests, the same hopes, the same aspirations that we have. They are one with us; we must share their sufferings and they will share our advancing prosperity. They have been punished as no community was ever punished before for the treason they have committed. I trust, sir, the day will come ere long when all traces of this great conflict will be effaced, except those which mark the blessings that follow in its train.

I hope and believe we shall soon see the day when the people of the southern States will show us, by evidences that we cannot mistake, that they have returned, in all sincerity and good faith, to their allegiance to the Union; that they intend to join henceforth with us in promoting its prosperity, in defending the banner of its glory, and in fighting the battles of democratic freedom, not only here, but wherever the issue may be forced upon our acceptance. I rejoice with heartfelt satisfaction that we have in these seats of power—in the executive department and in these halls of Congress—men who will cooperate for the attainment of these great and beneficent ends. I trust they will act with wisdom; I know they will act from no other motives than those of patriotism and love of their fellowmen.

William Archibald Dunning

The Tragedy of Reconstruction

The disastrous collapse of the Liberal movement brought dismay and despair to the white people of the South; it seemed to postpone indefinitely the reversal of national policy which had been so sanguinely hoped for, and to forebode an increase of the rigor with which the enforcement acts were applied by the administration. Some mitigation of the burdens of which the southerners complained had, indeed, attended the progress of the Liberal movement. In 1871 the requirement of the iron-clad oath was repealed so far as ex-Confederates were concerned; the next year Congress, by a sweeping amnesty act, removed the disabilities from all but a small remnant, estimated at about seven hundred and fifty, of those whom the Fourteenth Amendment excluded from office; and an effort of the radicals to extend the term of the president's summary powers under the Ku-Klux act failed. Thus a host of southerners became again eligible to the political dignities to which their fellow-citizens might wish to raise them; and the suspension of the *habeas corpus* was no longer to be employed as it had been in South Carolina. But eligibility to office was of small practical consequence where election was impossible; and the enforcement acts permitted the

"Political and Social Demoralization in the South (1870–1873)" in *Reconstruction, Political and Economic 1865–1877*, Torchbook Edition by William Archibald Dunning. Copyright, 1907 by Harper & Brothers, Renewed, 1935 by Edward S. Cole. By permission of Harper & Row, Publishers, omitting footnotes except where necessary for understanding.

exercise of Federal power through Federal troops without reference to the provision concerning the *habeas corpus*. In the ordinary process of criminal justice, and at every election, the interposition of United States marshals accompanied by United States soldiers was a normal incident, and to that extent the sense of subjection was kept always active among the people. General Terry, commanding the Department of the South, reported in 1871 two hundred instances in which detachments of troops were sent out to aid civil officers, including state authorities as well as Federal.

This ever-present source of irritation came as an aggravation of the evils which by 1872 had in many places become intolerable, arising from the inefficiency, extravagance, and corruption of the radical southern state governments. That the practical working of these organizations was in all the states bad, and in some of them a mere travesty of civilized government, was made clear by the investigation of the joint committee of Congress, commonly known as the Ku-Klux committee; and it was not denied, though it was palliated, in the report of the Republican majority of that committee.

The most conspicuous feature of maladministration was that of the finances. To the ambitious northern whites, inexperienced southern whites, and unintelligent blacks who controlled the first reconstructed governments, the grand end of their induction into power was to put their states promptly abreast of those which led in the prosperity and progress at the North. Things must be done, they believed, on a larger, freer, nobler scale than under the debased régime of slavery. Accordingly, both by the new constitutions and by legislation, the expenses of the governments were largely increased: offices were multiplied in all departments; salaries were made more worthy of the now regenerated and progressive commonwealths; costly enterprises were undertaken for the promotion of the general welfare, especially where that welfare was primarily connected with the uplifting of the freedmen. The result of all this was promptly seen in an expansion of state debts and an increase of taxation that to the property-owning class were appalling and ruinous. And the fact which was of the first importance in the situation was that this class, which paid the taxes, was sharply divided politically from that which levied them, and was by the whole radical theory of the reconstruction to be indefinitely excluded from a determining voice in the government.

Of the objects of outlay which contributed to swell the annual deficit of the state treasuries, many were, of course, unexceptionable from any point of view. The rebuilding of roads, bridges, and levees, the renovation of public offices and other property, the restoration of town improvements that had suffered by the devastation of the war—all these works absorbed large sums and were unopposed by the conservatives, save where extravagance and corruption were manifest or suspected. In respect to the blacks, the governments had now to assume many responsibilities which in slavery either pertained to the masters or had no existence. Thus the administration of criminal justice for the newly enfranchised citizens and the regulation of their family and property relations made an important increase of public expenditure inevitable. One of the largest items in the budgets of reconstruction was the schools. Free public education

existed in only a rudimentary and sporadic form in the South before the war, but the new constitutions provided generally for complete systems on advanced northern models. The financial burden of these enterprises was very great, and the irritation thus caused was increased by the fact that the blacks were the chief beneficiaries of the new systems, while many of the white tax-payers considered the education of the negro, as carried on in the public schools, to be either useless or positively dangerous to society.

Perhaps the chief element in the vast expansion of state debts under the radical régime was that incidental to the construction of railroads. That many new lines and great improvements in the old were essential to the economic resurrection of the South, was recognized by conservatives and radicals alike, and almost all the new constitutions authorized the loan of the state's credit to railway enterprises. The North and West were at this time in the midst of the great railway-building era elsewhere described, and the spirit of these sections moved across Mason and Dixon's line and down to the Gulf. Projects of every degree of promise and of fatuity were laid before the southern legislatures for their authorization and endowment. Splendid pictures of economic rehabilitation were exhibited by the railway lobbyists, to follow the guarantee of specified bonds; and many a sable legislator whose financial experience before 1868 had been bounded by the modest limits of a bootblack's or a field hand's income was called upon to ponder the policy of enterprises whose cost to the state would run into the millions. The result was legislation of incredible recklessness executed with inconceivable corruption and fraud. On the debts to the extension of the government's regular expenses were piled great masses of actual or prospective liabilities incurred on behalf of the railways. A very conservative figure in 1872 put the increase of indebtedness of the eleven states since their reconstruction at $131,-717,777.81, of which more than two-thirds consisted of guarantees to various enterprises, chiefly railways. Much of this was well secured, so far as the terms of the law were concerned, by liens on the completed roads; but it happened in only too many instances that the issue of bonds preceded the completion of the work, with the result that great quantities of state-indorsed securities represented no property of ascertainable value. Moreover, in South Carolina, Georgia, and Alabama, railways that had been owned in whole or in part by the states were grossly mismanaged, and were exploited for the profit of politicians.

In the maladministration that brought ruin to the finances, inefficiency and corruption played about equal parts. The responsible higher officials were in many cases entirely honest, though pathetically stupid, in their schemes to promote the interests of their respective states. But the governments numbered in their *personnel,* on the other hand, a host of officers to whom place was merely an opportunity for plunder. The progressive depletion of the public treasuries was accompanied by great private prosperity among radical politicians of high and low degree. First to profit by their opportunity were generally the northerners who led in radical politics; but the "scalawag" southerners and the negroes were quick to catch the idea. Bribery became the indispensable adjunct of legislation, and fraud a common feature in the execution of the laws. The form and manner of this corruption, which has given so unsavory a connotation to the name "reconstruction," were no different from those which have appeared in many another time and place in democratic government. At the very time, indeed, when the administrations of Scott, in South Carolina, and Warmoth, in Louisiana, were establishing the southern high-water mark of rascality in public finance, the Tweed ring in New York

City was at the culmination of its closely parallel career. The really novel and peculiar element in the maladministration in the South was the social and race issue which underlay it, and which came to the surface at once when any attempt at reform was instituted.

In most of the reconstructed states the very first term of the radical administration developed a schism in the party in power. In a general way the line of this cleavage was that dividing the southern white from the northern white element — the scalawag from the carpet-bagger. Between these two elements there was a natural divergency of feeling and policy in respect to the blacks, who constituted the bulk of the party. As the negroes caught the spirit of politics and demanded more and more of the positions and essential power in their party, the southern whites could not bring themselves to the same amount of concession that the carpet-baggers made. The latter, therefore, became more and more decisively the controlling element of the party. Meanwhile the Democratic whites, constituting the main body of tax-payers, watched with deepest alarm the mounting debt and tax-rate in every state. They were carrying most of the burden which radical extravagance and corruption were creating, and they had small chance of success in any election against the compact mass of negroes. They welcomed, therefore, the chance to profit by the radical schisms, and accordingly we find in most of the states, by 1872, a coalition of reforming Republicans and Democrats, under the name conservatives, in opposition to the dominant radicals. The net outcome of this movement was a sharpening of race lines in party division — a loss to the radicals of a considerable fraction of the initially small white element which they possessed. The tendency towards purely race parties was promoted also by the return to the North of many of the better class of carpet-baggers, discouraged with the failure of their projects for making an honest fortune.

In the reshaping of parties the conservatives profited somewhat by the general amnesty act of Congress, which brought many influential men once more to the front. But the obstacles to a successful campaign against the radicals were appalling. Not only were the negroes impervious to arguments based on existing maladministration, but, where the whites were in the majority, the election laws of most of the states enabled the party in power to determine the result much at its will. In this matter the reconstructed constitutions and legislatures followed the example of the original acts of Congress, and conferred upon the governors much the same authority over the registration and elections as had been possessed by the district commanders during the military régime. Under cover of a purpose to insure protection to the negro voter, the control of the local electoral machinery was centralized at the state capitals, and extraordinary facilities for fraud were embodied in the laws regulating both the casting and the counting of the ballots. The capstone of the system was the "returning board," which in some of the states was so constituted and so endowed with power over the final canvass of the votes that the governor and his appointees could determine the result practically at their discretion, with but perfunctory reference to the earlier incidents of the election.

A final and terribly effective obstacle to political reformation by the conservatives was the power of the national administration. After the full committal of President Grant to the policy of the enforcement acts, the civil, judicial, and military service of the United States in the South became gradually a mere adjunct of the radical state governments. Energetically directed by the attorney-general at Washington, the district-attorneys and marshals, and in some flagrant instances the district judges themselves, gave indispensable support to the radical cause. Indictments under the Ku-Klux act, never brought to trial, were used as a moderating influence on conservative enthusiasts in close districts; and it became a leading function of United States soldiers to counteract by their presence any tendency of negro interest in politics to wane. Thus the useful service of the national power in restraining the rash and violent elements of southern white society that were active in the later phases of the Ku-Klux movement was gradually transformed into the support of a social and political system in which all the forces that made for civilization were dominated by a mass of barbarous freedmen.

With the dwindling of the white element in the radical party, it became increasingly apparent to reflecting men that the demoralization in the South was less political than social in its essence — that the antithesis and antipathy of race and color were crucial and ineradicable. Intelligence and political capacity were, indeed, almost exclusively in the one race; but this was not the key to the situation, for the relations of the higher class of whites with the blacks were notoriously far less hostile than those of the lower class. A map of the Ku-Klux operations which gave occasion for the enforcement acts does not touch the region of the great plantations and the black belts, where the aristocracy had their homes, but includes only the piedmont territory, where the poor whites lived. The negroes were disliked and feared almost in exact proportion to their manifestation of intelligence and capacity. What animated the whites was pride in their race as such and a dread, partly instinctive, partly rational, lest their institutions, traditions, and ideals were to be appropriated or submerged. Whether or not this feeling and spirit were abstractly preferable to those which animated the northern idealist who preached equality, the fact that such feeling and spirit were at work must be taken squarely into account by the historian.

The negro had no pride of race and no aspiration or ideals save to be like the whites. With civil rights and political power, not won, but almost forced upon him, he came gradually to understand and crave those more elusive privileges that constitute social equality. A more intimate association with the other race than that which business and politics involved was the end towards which the ambition of the blacks tended consciously or unconsciously to direct itself. The manifestations of this ambition were infinite in their diversity. It played a part in the demand for mixed schools, in the legislative prohibition of discrimination between the races in hotels and theatres, and even in the hideous crime against white womanhood which now assumed new meaning in the annals of outrage. But every form and suggestion of social equality was resented and resisted by the whites with the energy of despair. The dread of it justified in their eyes modes of lawlessness which were wholly subversive of civilization. Charles Sumner devoted the last years of his life to a determined effort to prohibit by Federal law any discrimination against the blacks in hotels, theatres, railways, steamboats, schools, churches, and cemeteries. His bill did not pass Congress till 1875, after his death, but his idea was taken up and enacted into law by most of the southern radical legislatures. The laws proved unenforceable and of small direct consequence, but the discussion of them furnished rich fuel to the flames of race animosity, and nerved many a hesitating white, as well as many an ambitious black, to violent deeds for the interest of his people.

The deeper springs of southern conditions were obscured to the northern masses by the cloud of partisan prejudice which hung over the subject. The radical claim that impenitent rebels were still responsible for all the troubles in the South, through their undying hatred of the negro and of the Republican party, served as a sufficient sedative for uneasiness, so long as economic prosperity in the North disposed the minds of the masses to optimism. Yet the situation in the reconstructed states in 1873, when the second administration of President Grant got fairly under headway, was full of justification for despair.

Four of the states—Tennessee, Virginia, Georgia, and North Carolina—had come under conservative control, and were gradually assuming the guise of settled and orderly communities. But of these Virginia and North Carolina were confessedly bankrupt; and in all the states still under radical control the finances were in the last stages of rottenness and chaos. The amount of the state debt was in some cases undiscoverable, because no record of bond issues had been preserved. Charges of fraud, bribery, and stealing constituted the burden of political discussion in every state. Three governors had been subjected to impeachment: Holden, of North Carolina, and Warmoth, of Louisiana, were convicted and deposed; Reed, of Florida, was aquitted, not, apparently, so much on the ground of innocence as for the purpose of preventing the succession of a conservative. Every election, state or national, was attended by charges on both sides of fraud, intimidation, and outrage. Disputes as to the results in 1872 were followed by the occupation of three state capitals—New Orleans, Montgomery, and Little Rock—by United States troops under the general direction of Attorney-General Williams. This officer's opinions on legal and political questions became practically a decisive factor in the result of every southern state election.

South Carolina and Louisiana were in 1873 the spectacular illustrations of the working of reconstruction. The former state was thoroughly Africanized. A native white man, Franklin J. Moses, Jr., of notoriously bad character, succeeded the carpet-bagger Scott as governor, but most of the other elected executive officers, two-thirds of the legislature, and four out of the five congressmen were negroes. The shameless caricature of government which had prevailed at Columbia since the blacks came to power was now known in its general features throughout the North. The disgust which it might have been expected to inspire was subdued, however, by the feeling that the original secessionists were meeting deserved retribution. Pathetic appeals of the small body of decent white men who were still striving to maintain their rights and their property against the flood of barbarism went unnoticed. President Grant, who found abundant ground for interfering in other states, met the prayer of a delegation from South Carolina with a *non possumus* in which the *nolumus* was unconcealed.

The situation in Louisiana was more dramatic than that in South Carolina. Henry C. Warmoth, the carpet-bagger who was elected governor in 1868, became involved during his term in a violent faction fight with adversaries in his own party headed by Packard, the United States marshal. In the election of 1872 Warmoth became a Liberal and supported the conservative state ticket against the radicals, who had the favor of President Grant. The result of the election depended chiefly on the returning board, and the legal composition of this body was in dispute. Warmoth, in an exceedingly bitter and unscrupulous conflict in the state courts, clearly outpointed his adversaries and secured a canvass of the returns by his own board, giving the presidential electors, the governorship, and the legislature to the conservatives. But Packard appealed to the United States district judge, Durell, who, in a grossly irregular way, prohibited the conserva-

tive legislature to meet, ordered Federal troops to occupy their hall and prevent their meeting, and directed a canvass of the returns of the election by a board which he said was the legal one. Warmoth took care that this board should not get possession of the actual returns, but a canvass was nevertheless made of affidavits, census reports, and politicians' guesses, and the radical electors, governor, and legislature were declared elected.

Thus double electoral returns were sent to Washington, and two governments were organized in New Orleans. The radical legislature went through the form of impeaching and deposing Warmoth, recognized the mulatto Pinchback as his temporary successor, and finally installed Kellogg, another carpet-bagger, as the duly elected governor. The conservative legislature recognized Warmoth till the end of his term, in January 1873, and then installed McEnery, their candidate, as governor. The president, urged by his brother-in-law, Casey, collector of the port at New Orleans, and by Packard, the United States marshal, recognized Pinchback and Kellogg, and directed the troops to protect them. Later he referred the matter to Congress, where it became a subject of hot factional conflict within the Republican majority. In counting the electoral votes in February, 1873, the two houses refused to accept either return from Louisiana. The Senate committee on elections, after making a careful investigation, denounced in unmeasured terms the proceeding of Judge Durell, but failed to find a basis for definitive recognition of either of the state governments, and advised that another election be held. No measure for this purpose could be passed, and Louisiana remained an anarchy. The city of New Orleans and the white population generally recognized the McEnery government; the blacks under their carpet-bagger chiefs recognized Kellogg. In the rural districts of the state serious collisions between the races were caused by the disputes about the offices. Most disastrous was the affair at Colfax, Grant Parish, in April, 1873, where in a pitched battle several white men and more than fifty negroes were killed. The troops of the United States were admittedly all that kept the whites from sweeping Kellogg and his black supporters into oblivion. Such was the situation which, even more glaringly than the conditions in South Carolina, displayed to the people of the North the *reductio ad absurdum* of reconstruction through negro suffrage and a régime of carpet-baggers.

Kenneth M. Stampp

Radical Governments Reconsidered

. . . When the radicals won control in the South, they did not displace a responsible political élite which had traditionally taken a large view of things; nor did they discharge a trained body of civil servants. This being the case, the change in leadership was far less disastrous than it has often been made to appear.

But the customary charges against the new southern leadership are extremely severe and need to be weighed carefully. It is essential, therefore, to examine in some detail each of the three elements in the radical coalition—the carpetbaggers, scalawags, and Negroes—to test the validity of the generalizations conservatives used to characterize them. The term "carpetbagger" was applied to recent northern settlers in the South who actively supported the radical Republicans.[1] Since the term has an invidious connotation, it is used here only for lack of another that is equally familiar but morally neutral. The so-called carpetbaggers were not all poor men who carried their meager possessions with them in carpetbags; they were not all ignorant; they were not all corrupt. Rather they were a heterogeneous lot who moved to the South for a variety of reasons.

Among the carpetbaggers were some who fitted the stereotype: disreputable opportunists and corruptionists who went south in search of political plunder or public office. Because these carpetbaggers were so conspicuous and gained such notoriety, conservative southern Democrats succeeded in portraying them as typical, though actually they constituted a small minority.

From *The Era of Reconstruction, 1865–1877* by Kenneth M. Stampp. Copyright © 1965 by Kenneth Stampp. Reprinted by permission of Alfred A. Knopf.

[1] Richard N. Current. "Carpetbaggers Reconsidered," *A Festschrift for Frederick B. Artz* (Durham, N.C.: Duke University Press, 1964), p. 144.

Few of the carpetbaggers came to the South originally for the purpose of entering politics; many of them arrived before 1867 when political careers were not even open to them. They migrated to the South in the same manner and for the same reasons that other Americans migrated to the West. They hoped to buy cotton lands or to enter legitimate business enterprises: to develop natural resources, build factories, promote railroads, represent insurance companies, or engage in trade. A large proportion of the carpetbaggers were veterans of the Union Army who were pleased with the southern climate and believed that they had discovered a land of opportunity. Others came as teachers, clergymen, officers of the Freedmen's Bureau, or agents of the various northern benevolent societies organized to give aid to the Negroes. These people went south to set up schools for Negroes and poor whites, to establish churches, and to distribute clothing and medical supplies. They were of all types— some well trained for their jobs, others not. Seldom, however, can they be dismissed as meddlesome fools, or can the genuineness of their humanitarian impulses be doubted. But whether honest or dishonest, northern settlers who became active in radical politics incurred the wrath of most white southern conservatives. For their supreme offense was not corruption but attempting to organize the Negroes for political action.

A scalawag is by definition a scamp, and white Southerners who collaborated with the radicals were thus stigmatized by the pejorative term that identified them. In southern society, according to one critic, scalawags constituted the "tory and deserter element, with a few from the obstructionists of the war time and malcontents of the present who wanted office"[2] But here, as in the case

of the carpetbaggers, the facts were more complex than this. All scalawags were not degraded poor whites, depraved corruptionists, or cynical opportunists who betrayed the South for the spoils of office.

The cases of three distinguished scalawags will illustrate the inadequacy of any simple generalization about the character or origin of this class of radicals. The first is that of Lieutenant General James A. Longstreet of the Confederate Army, a graduate of West Point and one of Lee's ablest corps commanders. After the war Longstreet moved to New Orleans and became a partner in a cotton factorage business and head of an insurance firm. In 1867, arguing that the vanquished must accept the terms of the victors, he joined the Republican party and endorsed radical reconstruction. In 1868 he supported Grant for President, and in subsequent years Republican administrations gave him a variety of offices in the federal civil service. The second case is that of James L. Orr of South Carolina, a secessionist who had sat in the Confederate Senate. After serving as the Johnsonian governor of his state, Orr switched to the radicals and in 1868 was rewarded with a circuit judgeship. In a private letter he explained why he now supported the Republicans: It is "important for our prominent men to identify themselves with the radicals for the purpose of controlling their action and preventing mischief to the state." The third case is that of R. W. Flournoy, a large slaveholder in ante-bellum Mississippi. Flournoy joined the radicals not for personal gain but because of a humanitarian interest in the welfare of the freedmen. In a letter to Stevens he once explained that he supported the Republicans as the party to whom the Negro "can alone look . . . for protection." Flournoy's support of radical equality made him one of the most hated scalawags in the state. None of these men fitted the scalawag sterotype.

---

[2] Walter L. Fleming. *Civil War and Reconstruction in Alabama* (New York: Columbia University Press, 1905), p. 402.

Others unfortunately did. Among those who gave the scalawags their reputation for corruption was Franklin J. Moses, Jr., of South Carolina. The son of a distinguished father, Moses entered politics before the war and was known as an ardent secessionist. In 1867, after a brief period as a Johnsonian, he joined the radicals. Both as a legislator and, from 1872 to 1874, as governor he looted the public treasury and repeatedly accepted bribes for using his influence to secure the passage of legislation. Other scalawags appeared to be pure opportunists who simply joined the winning side. Joseph E. Brown, Georgia's Civil War governor, provides a classic example. After the war, claiming that he had sense enough to know when he was defeated, Brown quit the Democrats and urged Southerners to accept the radicals' terms. During the years of reconstruction, in addition to his political activities, he found the time (and the opportunity) to become a wealthy capitalist: president of a railroad, a steamship company, a coal company, and an iron company. When the radicals were overthrown in Georgia, Brown, as always, landed on his feet and returned to the Democratic party. Now he helped to organize a powerful Democratic machine that dominated the state for many years and eventually sent him to the United States Senate.

Always a minority of the southern white population, more numerous in some states than in others,[3] the scalawags usually belonged to one or more of four distinct groups. The first and largest of these groups was the Unionists. Having been exposed to severe persecution from their Confederate neighbors during the

[3] In the presidential election of 1872, according to a recent estimate, approximately 150,000 white Southerners voted Republican; they constituted about 20 percent of the white voters. These scalawags were most numerous in Tennessee, North Carolina, Arkansas, Texas, and Virginia. Allen W. Trelease. "Who Were the Scalawags?" *Journal of Southern History,* 29 (1963), 458.

war, southern Unionists were often the most vindictive of the radicals; they were quite willing to support those who would now retaliate against the secessionists, and they hoped that congressional reconstruction would give them political control in their states. Early in 1866 a North Carolinian wrote Stevens that Union men were disillusioned with Johnson but still hoped "that traitors will be punished for the treatment that union men received at their hands."

However, a very large proportion of this Unionist-scalawag element had little enthusiasm for one aspect of the radical program: The granting of equal civil and political rights to the Negroes. They favored the disenfranchisement of the Confederates to enable them to dominate the new state governments, but they were reluctant to accept Negro suffrage. "There is some small amount of squirming about the privileges extended to the recent slaves," a Virginia Unionist informed Stevens, "but time will overcome all this as there is no union man who does not infinitely more fear and dread the domination of the recent Rebels than that of the recent slaves." In 1866, General Clinton B. Fisk, an officer of the Freedmen's Bureau, told the congressional Committee on Reconstruction that in Tennessee "among the bitterest oponents of the negro . . . are the intensely radical loyalists of the [eastern] mountain districts. . . . The great opposition to the measure in the Tennessee legislature, giving the negro the right to testify and an equality before the law, has come from that section, chiefly. In Middle Tennessee and in West Tennessee the largest and the wealthiest planters . . . have more cordially cooperated with me in my duties than the people of East Tennessee." The planters believed that they could control the Negro vote, and the scalawags feared that they would.

Insofar as there was any relationship between scalawags and the class structure of the South, it resulted from the fact that a minority of the poor whites and yeoman farmers were attracted to the radical cause.[4] There had always been, as we have seen, an undercurrent of tension between them and the planter class, and some of them deserted President Johnson when it appeared that his program would return the planters to power. Lower-class whites who joined the radicals sometimes hoped for a seizure of the planters' lands. In South Carolina, according to a Union officer, the idea of confiscation "was received with more favor by this caste than by the Negroes." He recalled numerous occasions when "dirty, ragged, stupid creatures slyly inquired of me, 'When is our folks a-gwine to git the lan'?'" But it was never easy for the yeomen or poor whites to become scalawags, for support of the radicals meant collaboration with Negroes, or at least acquiescence in Negro suffrage. As a result, this class of scalawags was most numerous in areas with a small Negro population. Elsewhere a few lower-class whites managed to submerge their race prejudice, but the great majority preferred the old conservative leadership to a party that seemed to preach equality of the races.

A third source of scalawag strength came from Southerners engaged in business enterprise and from those living in regions, such as East Tennessee, western Virginia and North Carolina, and northern Alabama, which were rich in natural resources and had an industrial potential. Among such men there was considerable support for the economic policies of the Republican party—for the national banking system, the protective tariff, and federal appropriations for internal improvements. In general, the radical governments invited northern capitalists to invest in the South, granted loans or subsidies to the railroads, and gave charters and franchises to new corporations. Some of the scalawags were thus identified with

the concept of a New South whose economy would be more diversified than that of the Old.

Finally, the radicals drew a little of their scalawag support and some of their leaders from upper-class Southerners who had been affiliated with the Whig party before the Civil War. The Whig party had been particularly attractive to the more affluent and socially secure members of southern society, and after the war many Whigs were reluctant to join their old foes, the Democrats. A few of them now looked upon the Republican party as the heir to the Whig tradition and wondered whether it might be possible not only to join but also to control its organization in the South. Upper-class Whig scalawags found it relatively easy to accept equal civil and political rights for Negroes, first, because among them race hatred was less often the prime motivating force of political action and, second, because they were optimistic about their chances of controlling the Negro vote. In Mississippi, for example, James L. Alcorn, elected governor on the Republican ticket in 1869, had been a prominent Whig planter before the war, as had been numerous other leading scalawags. Thus it would appear that the scalawags were in part an absurd coalition of class-conscious poor whites and yeoman farmers who hated the planters, and class-conscious Whig planters and businessmen who disliked the egalitarian Democrats. But politics has a logic of its own, and the history of American political parties is full of contradictions such as this.

Joining the carpetbaggers and scalawags in a radical coalition was the mass of southern Negroes, most of them illiterate, many easily intimidated. Because of their political inexperience and economic helplessness, they were sometimes misled and victimized not only by Republicans but also by southern white Democrats. But it would be far from the truth to say that their political behavior during reconstruction was altogether passive or irre-

---

[4] Most of the lower-class whites who became scalawags had been Unionists, but some had supported the Confederacy.

sponsible. This was untrue, if for no other reason, because the issues of reconstruction, so far as the Negroes were concerned, were relatively simple and clear-cut. Given their condition and the limited political choices open to them, most Negroes responded to the appeals of rival politicians in a manner that had an obvious logic to it.

To begin with, suffrage was not something thrust upon an indifferent mass of Negroes. Their leaders had demanded it from the start; and when the Johnson governments limited the ballot to the whites, many meetings of southern Negroes sent protests to Congress. In Tennessee, for example, Negroes first petitioned the legislature for the ballot, then asked Congress not to seat Tennesseeans until their petition was granted. On May 7, 1866, a meeting of freedmen in New Bern, North Carolina, resolved "That so long as the Federal Government refuses to grant us the right to protect ourselves by means of the ballot . . . we will hold it responsible before God for our protection."

Moreover, most Negroes fully appreciated the importance of achieving literacy, and they took advantage of the limited educational opportunities offered them with almost pathetic eagerness. They also understood that in the rural South land was the key to economic independence and that they needed government aid to get it. In 1865 they heard rumors that Congress would provide each of them with forty acres and a mule at Christmas time; the next year they heard the same rumors again; once more in 1867 they hoped to get land when the radicals formulated their reconstruction program. But each time the Negroes were disappointed, and by 1868 they knew that the Republicans in Congress were not going to assist them.

Nevertheless, an overwhelming majority of Negro voters continued to support the Republican party, and in 1868 they helped to elevate General Grant to the presidency. In the political campaigns of the reconstruction era, Democratic candidates occasionally tried to bid for the Negro vote, but the record of the Johnson governments and the commitment of the Democratic party to white supremacy caused the mass of Negroes to remain loyal Republicans. "The blacks know that many conservatives hope to reduce them again to some form of peonage," a Tennessee carpetbagger wrote Stevens. "Under the impulse of this fear they will roll up their whole strength . . . and will go entirely for the Republican candidate whoever he may be." As long as southern Democrats opposed Negro suffrage and insisted that white supremacy was the central political issue, this condition could hardly have changed. It was this that made it easy for the agents of the Republican Union League to mobilize and "control" the Negro vote. Yet white Democrats often cited this solid Negro support of the Republicans to illustrate the political irresponsibility of the freedmen. It was a curious argument, however, for the practical choice offered the Negro voters was between a party that gave them civil and political rights and a party whose stock-in-trade was racist demagoguery.

Perhaps the most important generalizations to be made about the role of the Negroes in reconstruction are the following. First, while they had influence in all of the southern radical governments —more in some than in others—they did not control any of them. They served in all of the state legislatures, but only in South Carolina, one of the two southern states in which they outnumbered the whites, were they in the majority.[5] In Mississippi, the other state in which the Negroes had a numerical majority, the carpetbaggers controlled politics; while in Tennessee, where the scalawags dom-

[5] South Carolina's first radical legislature contained 87 Negroes and 69 whites. The Negroes, however, had a majority only in the lower house. The upper house contained twice as many whites as Negroes.

inated the radical government, there were practically no Negro officeholders at all. Few Negroes were elected to higher offices; none became the governor of a state. At various times South Carolina had a Negro lieutenant governor, secretary of state, treasurer, speaker of the house, and associate justice of the state supreme court; Mississippi had a Negro lieutenant governor, secretary of state, superintendent of education, and speaker of the house; Louisiana had a Negro lieutenant governor, secretary of state, treasurer, and superintendent of public education; Florida had a Negro secretary of state, and superintendent of public instruction. Nearly all of them were men of ability and integrity. Fourteen Negroes were elected to the United States House of Representatives, six of them from South Carolina. Two Mississippi Negroes served in the United States Senate: Hiram R. Revels for a one-year unexpired term, and Blanche K. Bruce for a full term. (Revels and Bruce, incidentally, are the only Negroes who have ever been elected to the Senate from any state, North or South.) In general, however, white men dominated the higher offices of the southern radical governments. The Negroes, though filling many city and county offices, ordinarily were unable to advance beyond the state legislatures.

Second, the Negroes soon developed their own leadership and were not always the mere tools of white Republicans. In 1868 a Florida carpetbagger reported to Stevens that white radicals were having trouble getting the Negroes to support ratification of the new state constitution. "The colored preachers," he wrote, "are *the great power* in controlling and uniting the colored vote, and they are looked to, as political leaders, with more confidence . . . than to any other source of instruction and control." Some of the Negro leaders were corruptible, some incorruptible; some had great ability, some little. Most of them were conservatives on all issues except civil and political rights.

Finally, the Negroes were seldom vin-dictive in their use of political power or in their attitude toward native whites. To be sure, there were plenty of cases of friction between Negroes and whites, and Negro militiamen were sometimes inordinately aggressive. But in no southern state did any responsible Negro leader, or any substantial Negro group, attempt to get complete political control into the hands of the freedmen.[6] All they asked for was equal political rights and equality before the law. . . .

At the time that the new constitutions were ratified, elections were held for state officers and legislators. After the elections, when Congress approved of the constitutions, political power was transferred from the military to the new civil governments. Thus began the era of radical government in the South—an era which, according to tradition, produced some of the worst state administrations in American history. Some of the southern radical regimes earned their evil reputations, others did not; but viewed collectively, there was much in the record they made to justify severe criticism. To say that they were not always models of efficiency and integrity would be something of an understatement. "The great impediment of the Republican party in this state," wrote a Tennessee radical, "is the incompetence of its leaders. . . . After the war the loyal people in many counties had no competent men to be judges, lawyers or political leaders." Indeed, all of the radical governments suffered more or less from the incompetence of some, the dishonesty of a few, and above all the inexperience of most of the officeholders. Unquestionably the poorest records were made in South Carolina during the administrations of the carpetbagger Robert K. Scott and the scalawag Franklin J. Moses, Jr., and in Louisiana during the administrations of the carpetbaggers Henry C. Warmoth and William P. Kellogg.

The sins of various radical governments

[6] However, Negro leaders did protest when they thought that white radicals were trying to monopolize the offices.

included fraudulent bond issues; graft in land sales or purchases and in the letting of contracts for public works; and waste and extravagance in the use of state funds. Governor Warmoth was reputed to have pocketed $100,000 during his first year in office, though his salary was $8,000; another governor was accused of stealing and selling the supplies of the Freedmen's Bureau. A scalawag governor admitted taking bribes of more than $40,000; another fraudulently endorsed state bonds over to a group of railroad promoters. In Louisiana under both Warmoth and Kellogg there was corruption in the granting of charters and franchises, in the negotiation of construction contracts, in the use of school funds, in the collection of state taxes, and in the awarding of printing contracts. Some of the radical legislators, especially in South Carolina, apparently made bribery an integral part of the process of transacting legislative business. One South Carolina legislature issued bonds valued at $1,590,000 to redeem bank notes valued at $500,000; it voted a bonus of $1,000 to the speaker when he lost that amount in a bet on a horse race. For a time the legislators of this state enjoyed the services of a free restaurant and bar established for their private use; they billed the state for such "legislative supplies" as hams, ladies' bonnets, perfumes, champagne, and (for one unfortunate member) a coffin. The cost of state printing in South Carolina between 1868 and 1876 was greater than the cost had been from 1789 to 1868. On one occasion, as the legislature was about to adjourn, a Democratic newspaper in Charleston wrote the following epitaph: "In life it has been unlovely, and in death it has not belied its record. As it lived, it has died—an uncouth, malformed and abortive monstrosity, its birth a blunder, its life a crime, and its death a blessing."

Meanwhile, the credit of some of the southern states was impaired as public debts mounted. In Florida the state debt increased from $524,000 in 1868 to $5,621,000 in 1874. In South Carolina a legislative committee reported that between 1868 and 1871 the state debt had increased from $5,403,000 to $15,768,000, but another committee insisted that it had increased to $29,159,000. By 1872 the debts of the eleven states of the former Confederacy had increased by approximately $132,000,000. The burden on taxpayers grew apace. Between 1860 and 1870 South Carolina's tax rate more than doubled, while property values declined by more than fifty per cent. In Tennessee a radical reported that during the first three years after the war taxes had increased sevenfold, though property had declined in value by one third. Throughout the South the tax burden was four times as great in 1870 as it had been in 1860. Such rates, complained many southern landholders, were confiscatory; and, indeed, taxes and other adversities of the postwar years forced some of them to sell all or part of their lands. Sympathy for South Carolina's planter aristocracy caused a northern conservative to ask: "When before did mankind behold the spectacle of a rich, high-spirited, cultivated, self-governed people suddenly cast down, bereft of their possessions, and put under the feet of the slaves they had held in bondage for centuries?"

High taxes, mounting debts, corruption, extravagance, and waste, however, do not constitute the complete record of the radical regimes. Moreover, to stop with a mere description of their misdeeds would be to leave all the crucial questions unanswered—to distort the picture and to view it without perspective. For example, if some of these governments contained an uncommonly large number of inexperienced or incompetent office holders, if much of their support came from an untutored electorate, there was an obvious reason for this. Howard K. Beale, in a critique of various reconstruction legends, observed that the political rulers of the ante-bellum South "had fastened ignorance or inexperience on millions of whites as well as Negroes and that it was this ignorance and inexperience that caused trouble when Radicals were in power . . . . Wealthy Southerners . . . seldom recognized the need for general education of even the *white* masses."[7] Even in 1865 the men who won control of the Johnson governments showed little disposition to adopt the needed reforms. In South Carolina the Johnsonians did almost nothing to establish a system of public education, and at the time that the radicals came to power only one eighth of the white children of school age were attending school. The Negroes, of course, had been ignored entirely. It was probably no coincidence that the radicals made their poorest record in South Carolina, the state which had done the least for education and whose prewar government had been the least democratic.

As for the corruption of the radical governments, this phenomenon can be understood only when it is related to the times and to conditions throughout the country. One must remember that the administrations of President Grant set the moral tone for American government at all levels, national, state, and local. The best-remembered episodes of the Grant era are its numerous scandals—the Crédit Mobilier and the Whiskey Ring being the most spectacular of them—involving members of Congress as well as men in high administration circles. There were, moreover, singularly corrupt Republican machines in control of various northern states, including Massachusetts, New York, and Pennsylvania. But corruption was not a phenomenon peculiar to Republicans of the Gilded Age, as the incredible operations of the so-called Tweed Ring in New York City will testify. Indeed, the thefts of public funds by this organization of white Tammany Democrats surpassed the total thefts in all the southern states combined.

Clearly the presence of carpetbaggers, scalawags, and Negroes in the radical governments was not in itself a sufficient explanation for the appearance of corruption. The South was being affected by the same forces that were affecting the rest of the country. No doubt the most important of these forces were, first, the social disorganization that accompanied the Civil War and hit the defeated and demoralized South with particular severity; and, second, the frantic economic expansion of the postwar period, when the American economy was dominated by a group of extraordinarily talented but irresponsible and undisciplined business leaders. These entrepreneurs' rather flexible standards of public morality provided an unfortunate model for the politicians.

Whether southern Democrats would have been able to resist the corrupting forces of the postwar decade had they remained in power is by no means certain. Perhaps the old ruling class would have been somewhat less vulnerable to the temptations of the Gilded Age, but the record of the Johnson governments was spotty at best. In Louisiana the conservative government created by Lincoln and Johnson wasted a great deal of public money. In Mississippi the state treasurer of the Johnson government embezzled $62,000. (This, by the way, far surpassed the record of the only thief in the radical government, who embezzled $7,000.) E. Merton Coulter discovered that during the era of reconstruction some Democratic officeholders "partook of the same financial characteristics as Radicals" and "took advantage of openings" when they found them. He quotes a Georgia editor who claimed that the extravagance and corruption "benefitted about as many Democrats as Republicans"; and he notes that a Democratic administration in Alabama "in lack of honesty differed little from the administrations of the Radicals between whom it was sandwiched."[8]

In the 1870s, when the South's so-called

[7] Howard K. Beale. "On Rewriting Reconstruction History," *American Historical Review*, 45 (1940), 807–827.

[8] E. Merton Coulter, *The South during Reconstruction, 1865–1877* (Baton Rouge, La.: Louisiana State University Press, 1947), 152–153.

"natural leaders" returned to power, that troubled section did not always find itself governed by politicians distinguished for their selfless devotion to public service. In Mississippi the treasurer of the Democratic regime that overthrew the radicals in 1875 immediately embezzled $316,000, which broke all previous records! Elsewhere in the next decade eight other state treasurers were guilty of defalcations or embezzlements, including one in Louisiana who defrauded the state of more than a million dollars. Georgia was now ruled by a Democratic machine that was both ruthless and corrupt, a machine whose record was so offensive that by the end of the 1880s the white masses—some even willing to accept Negro support—rose in political rebellion against it. Reports about the Mississippi Democratic regime of the late nineteenth century are particularly colorful. One white editor charged that an "infamous ring" of "corrupt office-seekers . . . [had] debauched the ballot boxes . . . incurred useless and extravagant expenditures, raised the taxes, [and] plunged the State into debt." At the Mississippi constitutional convention of 1890, a white Democratic delegate gave the following description of politics in his state during the previous fifteen years: "Sir, it is no secret that there has not been a full vote and a fair count in Mississippi since 1875. . . . In other words we have been stuffing ballot boxes, committing perjury, and here and there in the state carrying the elections by fraud and violence . . . . No man can be in favor of perpetuating the election methods which have prevailed in Mississippi since 1875 who is not a moral idiot." Twelve years later an editor claimed that it would tax "the range and scope of the most fertile and versatile imagination to picture a condition of greater political rottenness" than existed in Mississippi at that time.

In the final analysis the crucial question about the extravagance and peculations of the radical governments is who the chief beneficiaries were. Only a few of the Negro and white radical leaders profited personally. The funds they stole, the money that prodigal legislators used for their own benefit, accounted for only a small fraction of the increased debts of the southern states. Nor did the total sums involved in bribery rise to a very impressive figure. And why was the tar brush applied exclusively to those who accepted the bribes and not to those who offered them? Under these circumstances is it really more blessed to give than to receive? For when the bribe-givers are identified we have located those who profited most from racial misdeeds. These men were the construction contractors, business speculators, and railroad promoters, or their agents, who hoped to persuade legislators to give them contracts, franchises, charters, subsidies, financial grants, or guarantees. They were the men who were also corrupting Congressmen and northern legislatures.

In Virginia much of the history of reconstruction concerns the rivalry of the Baltimore and Ohio Railroad and the Southside line for control of the Virginia and Tennessee Railroad. Both lines fought to control elections and legislators and backed whichever party promised to serve them, until, in 1870, the legislature ended the dispute by approving the consolidation plans of the Southside. Louisiana's reconstruction politics was enlivened by the attempt of a railroad and steamship corporation, headed by Charles Morgan of New York, to prevent the state from subsidizing a rival line between New Orleans and Houston, until Morgan forced the new line to take him in. In Alabama the North and South Railroad and the Alabama and Chattanooga Railroad battled for access to the ore deposits around Birmingham. In the process the competing groups corrupted both Johnson and radical legislatures, and in the latter both Republicans and Democrats.

Most of the debt increases in the southern states resulted not from the thefts and extravagance of radical legislators but from the grants and guarantees they gave to railroad promoters, among whom were always some native white Democrats. In Florida more than sixty per cent of the debt incurred by the radical regime was in the form of railroad guarantee bonds. In North Carolina the radical government, prodded by the carpetbagger Milton S. Littlefield, a skilled lobbyist, issued millions of dollars of railroad bonds. Among those who benefited were many of the state's "best citizens," including George W. Swepson, a local business promoter and Democrat. Most of Alabama's reconstruction debt—$18,000,-000 out of $20,500,000—was in the form of state bonds issued to subsidize railroad construction, for which the state obtained liens upon railroad property. When one measure for state aid was before the Alabama legislature, many Democrats were among the lobbyists working for its passage. Yet, complained a radical, the Democrats who expect to profit from the bill "will use the argument that the Republican party had a majority in the Legislature, and will falsely, but hopefully, charge it upon Republicans as a partisan crime against the state."

Indeed, all of the southern states, except Mississippi, used state credit to finance the rebuilding and expansion of their railroads, for private sources of credit were inadequate. This policy had been developed before the war; it was continued under the Johnsonians; and in some cases when the Democrats overthrew the radicals there was no decline in the state's generosity to the railroads. While the radicals controlled the southern legislatures, not only they but many members of the Democratic minority as well voted for railroad bond issues. According to an historian of reconstruction in Louisiana, "Such measures were supported by members of both parties, often introduced by Democrats, in every case supported by a large majority of Democrats in both

houses."[9] The subservience of many postwar southern legislatures to the demands of railroad and other business promoters is in some respects less shocking than pathetic. For it expressed a kind of blind faith shared by many Southerners of both parties that railroad building and industrialization would swiftly solve all of their section's problems. No price seemed too high for such a miracle.

In several states, for obviously partisan reasons, the actual increase in the size of the public debt was grossly exaggerated. In Mississippi, for example, there was a durable legend among white Democrats that the radicals had added $20,000,000 to the state debt, when, in fact, they added only $500,000. Mississippi radicals had guarded against extravagance by inserting a clause in the constitution of 1868 prohibiting the pledging of state funds to aid private corporations—a clause which the conservatives, incidentally, had opposed. In Alabama, apart from railroad bonds secured by railroad property, the radicals added only $2,500,000 to the state debt. They did not leave a debt of $30,000,000 as conservatives claimed. In most other states, when loans to the railroads are subtracted, the increases in state debts for which the radicals were responsible appear far less staggering.

As for taxes, one of the positive achievements of many of the radical governments was the adoption of more equitable tax systems which put a heavier burden upon the planters. Before the war the southern state governments had performed few public services and the tax burden of the landed class had been negligible; hence the vehement protests of the landholders were sometimes as much against radical tax policies as against the alleged waste of taxpayers' money. The restoration governments often brought with them a return to the old inequitable fiscal systems. In Mississippi the subsequent claim of the

[9] Elle Lonn. *Reconstruction in Louisiana after 1868* (New York, 1918) pp. 36–37.

conservatives that they had reduced the tax burden the radicals had placed upon property holders was quite misleading. The conservatives did lower the state property tax, but, as a consequence, they found it necessary to shift various services and administrative burdens from the state to the counties. This led to an increase in the cost of county government, an increase in the rate of county taxes, and a net increase in total taxes, state and county, that Mississippi property holders had to pay.

As a matter of fact, taxes, government expenditures, and public debts were bound to increase in the southern states during the postwar years no matter who controlled them. For there was no way to escape the staggering job of physical reconstruction—the repair of public buildings, bridges, and roads—and costs had started to go up under the Johnson governments before the radicals came to power. So far from the expenditures of the reconstruction era being totally lost in waste and fraud, much of this physical reconstruction was accomplished while the radicals were in office. They expanded the state railroad systems, increased public services, and provided public school systems—in some states for the first time. Since schools and other public services were now provided for Negroes as well as for whites, a considerable increase in the cost of state government could hardly have been avoided. In Florida between 1869 and 1873 the number of children enrolled in the public schools trebled; in South Carolina between 1868 and 1876 the number increased from 30,000 to 123,000. The economies achieved by some of the restoration governments came at the expense of the schools and various state institutions such as hospitals for the insane. The southern propertied classes had always been reluctant to tax themselves to support education or state hospitals, and in many cases the budget-cutting of the conservatives simply strangled them.

Thus radical rule, in spite of its shortcomings, was by no means synonymous with incompetence and corruption; far too many carpetbagger, scalawag, and Negro politicians made creditable records to warrant such a generalization. Moreover, conditions were improving in the final years of reconstruction. In South Carolina the last radical administration, that of the carpetbagger Governor Daniel H. Chamberlain, was dedicated to reform; in Florida "the financial steadiness of the state government increased toward the end of Republican rule."[10] In Mississippi the radicals made a remarkably good record. The first radical governor, James L. Alcorn, a scalawag, was a man of complete integrity; the second, Adelbert Ames, a carpetbagger, was honest, able, and sincerely devoted to protecting the rights of the Negroes. Mississippi radicals, according to Vernon L. Wharton, established a system of public education far better than any the state had known before; reorganized the state judiciary and adopted a new code of laws; renovated public buildings and constructed new ones, including state hospitals at Natchez and Vicksburg; and provided better state asylums for the blind, deaf, and dumb. The radicals, Wharton concludes, gave Mississippi "a government of greatly expanded functions at a cost that was low in comparison with that of almost any other state."[11] No major political scandal occurred in Mississippi during the years of radical rule—indeed, it was the best governed state in the postwar South. Yet white conservatives attacked the radical regime in Mississippi as violently as they did in South Carolina, which suggests that their basic grievance was not corruption but race policy.

[10] William W. Davis. *The Civil War and Reconstruction in Florida* (New York: Columbia University Press, 1913), pp. 672–673.

[11] Vernon L. Wharton. *The Negro in Mississippi* (Chapel Hill, N.C.: University of North Carolina Press, 1947), pp. 179–180.

Finally, granting all their mistakes, the radical governments were by far the most democratic the South had ever known. They were the only governments in southern history to extend to Negroes complete civil and political equality, and to try to protect them in the enjoyment of the rights they were granted. The overthrow of these governments was hardly a victory for political democracy, for the conservatives who "redeemed" the South tried to relegate poor men, Negro and white, once more to political obscurity. Near the end of the nineteenth century another battle for political democracy would have to be waged; but this time it would be, for the most part, a more limited version—for whites only. As for the Negroes, they would have to struggle for another century to regain what they had won—and then lost—in the years of radical reconstruction.

Select Bibliography for Problem 8

Alexander, Thomas B. "Persistent Whiggery in the Confederate South, 1860–1877," *Journal of Southern History,* 27 (August 1961), 305–329.

Anderson, George L. "The South and Post-Civil War Finance," *Journal of Southern History,* 9 (May 1943), 181–195.

Beale, Howard K. "On Rewriting Reconstruction History," *American Historical Review,* 45 (July 1940), 805–827.

Carpenter, John A. "Atrocities in the Reconstruction Period," *Journal of Negro History,* 47 (October 1962), 234–247.

Coben, Stanley. "Northeastern Business and Radical Reconstruction: A Re-Examination," *Mississippi Valley Historical Review,* 46 (June 1959), 67–90.

Cox, John H., and LaWanda. "General O. O. Howard and the 'Misrepresented Bureau,'" *Journal of Southern History,* 19 (November 1953), 427–456.

———. "Negro Suffrage and Republican Politics: The Problem of Motivation in Reconstruction Historiography," *Journal of Southern History,* 33 (August 1967), 303–330.

Current, Richard N., ed. *Reconstruction, 1865–1877.* Englewood Cliffs, N.J.: Prentice-Hall, Inc., 1965.

Donald, David. "The Scalawag in Mississippi Reconstruction," *Journal of Southern History,* 10 (November 1944), 447–460.

Dorris, Jonathan. "Pardoning the Leaders of the Confederacy," *Mississippi Valley Historical Review,* 15 (June 1928), 3–21.

Drake, Richard. "Freedmen's Aid Societies and Sectional Compromise," *Journal of Southern History,* 29 (May 1963), 175–186.

Du Bois, William E. B. "Reconstruction and Its Benefits," *American Historical Review,* 15 (July 1910), 781–799.

Graham, Howard J. "The 'Conspiracy Theory' of the Fourteenth Amendment," *Yale Law Journal,* 47 (January 1938), 371–403 and 48 (December 1938), 171–194.

Hesseltine, William B. "Economic Factors in the Abandonment of Reconstruction," *Mississippi Valley Historical Review,* 22 (September 1935), 191–210.

House, Albert V. "Northern Congressional Democrats as Defenders of the South during Reconstruction," *Journal of Southern History,* 6 (February 1940), 46–71.

James, Joseph B. "Southern Reaction to the Proposal of the Fourteenth Amendment," *Journal of Southern History,* 22 (November 1956), 477–497.

Johnson, Guion G. "Southern Paternalism toward Negroes after Emancipation," *Journal of Southern History*, 23 (November 1957), 483–509.

Kelley, Alfred H. "The Congressional Controversy over School Segregation, 1867–1875," *American Historical Review*, 44 (April 1959), 537–563.

Kolchin, Peter. "The Business Press and Reconstruction, 1865–1868," *Journal of Southern History*, 33 (May 1967), 183–196.

Kutler, Stanley I. "Reconstruction and the Supreme Court: The Numbers Game Reconsidered," *Journal of Southern History*, 32 (June 1966), 42–58.

Linden, Glenn. "Radicals and Economic Policies: The Senate, 1861–1873," *Journal of Southern History*, 32 (May 1966), 189-199.

Lomask, Milton. "When Congress Tried to Rule," *American Heritage*, 11 (December 1959), 60–61.

Lynd, Staughton, ed. *Reconstruction*. Interpretations of American History. John Higham and Bradford Perkins, eds. New York: Harper & Row, Publishers, 1967.

––––––. "Rethinking Slavery and Reconstruction," *Journal of Negro History*, 50 (July 1965), 198–209.

McPherson, James M. "Grant or Greeley? The Abolitionist Dilemma in the Election of 1872," *American Historical Review*, 71 (October 1965), 43–61.

McWhiney, Grady, ed. *Reconstruction and the Freedmen*. The Berkeley Series in American History. Charles Sellers, ed. Skokie, Ill.: Rand McNally & Co., 1963.

Moore, Albert B. "One Hundred Years of Reconstruction in the South," *Journal of Southern History*, 9 (May 1943), 153–180.

Niven, John, ed. *Years of Turmoil: Civil War and Reconstruction, Interpretative Articles and Documentary Sources.* American History in Focus. William H. Goetzmann, ed. Reading, Mass.: Addison-Wesley Publishing Company, 1969, pp. 165–241.

Riddleberger, Patrick W. "The Radicals' Abandonment of the Negro during Reconstruction," *Journal of Negro History*, 45 (April 1960), 88–102.

Rozwenc, Edwin C., ed. *Reconstruction in the South*. Problems in American Civilization. Boston: D. C. Heath

Russ, Jr., William A. "The Negro and White Disfranchisement during Radical Reconstruction," *Journal of Negro History*, 19 (April 1934), 171–193.

––––––. "Was There Danger of a Second Civil War during Reconstruction?" *Mississippi Valley Historical Review*, 25 (June 1938), 39–58.

Russell, James F. S. "The Railroads in the 'Conspiracy Theory' of the Fourteenth Amendment," *Mississippi Valley Historical Review*, 41 (March 1955), 602–622.

Scheiner, Seth M., ed. *Reconstruction: A Tragic Era?* American Problem Studies. Oscar Handlin, ed. New York: Holt, Rinehart and Winston, Inc., 1968.

Scroggs, Jack B. "Carpetbagger Constitutional Reform in the South Atlantic States, 1867–1868," *Journal of Southern History*, 27 (November 1961), 475–593.

––––––. "Southern Reconstruction: A Radical View," *Journal of Southern History*, 24 (November 1958), 407–429.

Shapiro, Herbert, "Ku Klux Klan during Reconstruction: The South Carolina Episode," *Journal of Negro History*, 49 (January 1964), 34–55.

Simkins, Francis. "New Viewpoints of Southern Reconstruction," *Journal of Southern History,* 5 (February 1939), 49–61.

Sproat, John G. "Blueprint for Radical Reconstruction," *Journal of Southern History,* 23 (February 1957), 25–44.

Stampp, Kenneth M. "Tragic Legend of Reconstruction," *Commentary,* 39 (January 1965), 44–50.

Swinney, Everette. "Enforcing the Fifteenth Amendment, 1870–1877," *Journal of Southern History,* 28 (May 1962), 202–218.

Unger, Irwin. "Business Men and Specie Resumption," *Political Science Quarterly,* 74 (March 1959), 67–90.

Weisberger, Bernard "The Dark and Bloody Ground of Reconstruction Historiography," *Journal of Southern History,* 25 (November 1959), 427–447.

Williams, T. Harry. "An Analysis of Some Reconstruction Attitudes," *Journal of Southern History,* 12 (November 1946), 469–486.

Williamson, Joel, ed. *The Origins of Segregation.* Problems in American Civilization. Boston: D. C. Heath & Company, 1968.

index

A